에듀윌과 함께 시작하면,
당신도 합격할 수 있습니다!

편입 합격 후 대학에 진학했으나 학과 전공이 맞지 않아
휴학 후 다시 편입을 결심하여 서강대에 합격한 3학년 대학생

직장생활을 하며 2년간 편입공부를 해
인서울 대학에 당당히 합격한 30대 직장인

대학진학을 포기하고 20살 때 학점은행제 독학사를 통해 전문학사를 취득하고
편입을 준비하여 합격한 21살 전문학사 수험생

군복무 중 취업에 대해 고민하다 공대계열 학과로 편입을 결심하여
1년 만에 한양대에 합격한 복학생

누구나 합격할 수 있습니다.
시작하겠다는 '다짐' 하나면 충분합니다.

마지막 페이지를 덮으면,

에듀윌과 함께
편입 합격이 시작됩니다.

에듀윌 편입 시리즈 전격 출간

3년 연속 100% 합격자 배출 교수진이 만든 교재로
합격의 차이를 직접 경험해 보세요.

* 본 교재 이미지는 변동될 수 있습니다.
* 여러분의 합격을 도와줄 편입 시리즈 정보는 에듀윌 홈페이지(www.eduwill.net)에서 확인하세요.

* 서성한반(P사) 교수진 전격입성 I 2019~2021년 서성한반(P사) 수강생 합격자 서울소재 20개 대학 기준 3년 연속 100% 합격자 배출
(서울소재 20개 대학: 연세, 고려, 서강, 성균관, 한양, 중앙, 이화, 한국외, 경희, 서울시립, 건국, 국민, 동국, 숭실, 홍익, 숙명, 세종, 명지, 광운, 서울여)

노베이스 수험생을 위한
쌩기초 풀-패키지 무료배포

클라쓰가 남다른 1타 교수진으로 새롭게 탄생!
한 달이면 기초 탈출! 신규회원이면 누구나 신청 가능!

1타 교수진의 쉽고 알찬 쌩기초 입문 강의

· 1타 교수진 노하우 총 집합
· 기초 지식부터 입문 이론까지
· 초단기 쌩 노베이스 완벽 탈출

24만원 상당

노베이스 토익커도 RC 단기졸업

가장 쉬운 토익 LC 왕초보 탈출

토익 베이직 RC/LC 강의

· 첫 토익부터 700+ 한 달이면 끝
· 편입 공인영어 성적 준비를 위한 토익 기초 지원
· 쉬운 토익 공식! 에듀윌 토익 강의

합격비법 가이드

· 대학별 최신 편입 전형 제공
· 최신 편입 관련 정보 모음
· 합격전략 및 합격자 수기 제공

기출어휘 체크북

· 편입생이 꼭 알아야 할 편입 어휘의 모든 것
· 최신 기출 어휘를 빈도순으로 구성
· 3,000개의 어휘를 한 권으로 압축

편입 합격!
에듀윌과 함께하면 현실이 됩니다.

쌩기초 풀패키지
무료 이벤트

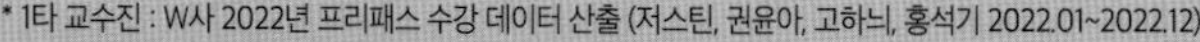
* 1타 교수진 : W사 2022년 프리패스 수강 데이터 산출 (저스틴, 권윤아, 고하늬, 홍석기 2022.01~2022.12)
* 본 혜택과 경로는 예고 없이 변경되거나 대체될 수 있습니다.

에듀윌 편입 솔루션

독해 BASIC

편저자 에듀윌 편입 LAB

READING BASIC

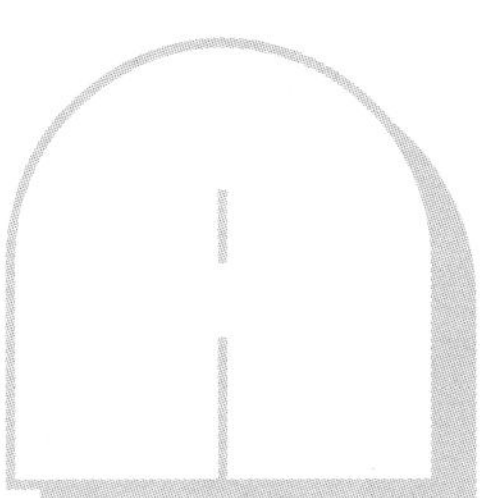

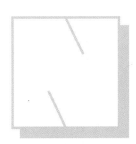

독해가 어려워?

이 책을 봐!

편입 최초
프리미엄 해설 수록

eduwill

Preface 이 책의 머리말

안녕하세요, 에듀윌 편입 LAB입니다.

에듀윌 편입 솔루션 독해 Basic은 대학 편입 시험에서 출제되는 독해 문항에 대비하기 위한 책입니다. 편입영어는 난이도 높은 입시영어이며 학교마다 다양한 형태의 영어 독해 문제들이 출제되기 때문에, 이 책에서는 이에 대비하여 다양한 실제 기출문제를 유형별로 제공해 드립니다.

에듀윌 편입 솔루션 독해 Basic은 학생들이 자신의 영어 독해 능력을 크게 개선할 수 있도록 편입영어 독해 문제의 패턴과 유형을 분석하여 엄선된 문제들로 구성하였습니다. 또한, 각 유형별로 문제를 풀이하는 데 도움이 되는 상세한 전략도 제공합니다.

에듀윌 편입 솔루션 독해 Basic의 가장 큰 장점은 체계적이고 자세한 프리미엄 해설입니다. 편입교재 중 최초로 문장별 구문 분석과 번역, 어휘 및 표현 정리, 보기 번역 및 오답 이유 분석을 포함하는 꼼꼼한 해설이 함께 제공됩니다.

에듀윌 편입 솔루션 독해 Basic으로 학습하여 편입 독해 문항의 고득점과 더불어 합격의 기쁨을 누리시길 기원합니다.

감사합니다.

Foreword 이 책의 구성

예제

예제의 풀이전략을 익히고 그 유형에 맞는 전략을 세우세요.

1강 제목

예제 한국외대 2020년

A big stereotype about the Gypsy way of life is that it's flashy, revealing, and attention grabbing. But we don't get a full picture of Gypsy culture. For example, Gypsy fashion for free-flowing clothes is guided by modesty, and strict cleanliness codes are common, developed through centuries of life on the road when hygiene was of utmost importance. If you search for "Gypsy" online, you'll find story after story that perpetuates the myth that the Gypsy community is ridden with crime, tax avoidance, and voluntary unemployment. Nothing could be further from the truth. Members of Gypsy communities are, in fact, statistically underrepresented in the mainstream prison population. Just like with any other community, you will find criminals, just as you will find teachers, nurses, police officers, artists, and entrepreneurs. Many Gypsies have made it through mainstream education to top universities, whilst at the same time retaining their identity.

Q. Which of the following is the best title for the passage?

① Myths About Gypsy Culture
② Dress Tastes in Gypsy Culture

연습문제

이 책은 최근 10년 동안의 편입 기출문제들로 구성되어 있습니다. 유형에 맞는 풀이전략을 세워 충분히 많은 지문들을 연습해 주세요.

Practice Answer p.2

01 **What is the best title for the passage?**

People in the majority can cause other group members to conform through normative influence. The conformity that occurs may be a case of public compliance without private acceptance. People in the minority can rarely influence others through normative means — the majority has little concern for how the minority views them. In fact, majority group members may be loath to agree publicly with the minority; they don't want anyone to think that they agree with those unusual, strange views of the minority. Minorities therefore exert their influence on the group via the other principal method, informational social influence. The minority introduces new and unexpected information to the group and causes the group to examine the issues more carefully. Such careful examination may cause the majority to realize that the minority view has merit, leading the group to adopt all or part of the minority's view. In short, minorities often achieve private acceptance because of informational social influence.

① How the Few Influence the Many
② When the Majority Becomes the Minority
③ The Abuse of Power Exercised by the Minority
④ How Normative Social Influence Differs from Informational Social Influence

정답과 해설

자신의 해석, 구문, 정답이 맞는지 꼼꼼하게 체크해 주세요.

LEVEL 1 중심 내용 파악하기

1강 제목

Practice

01	①	02	①	03	②	04	①	05	①	06	③	07	④	08	①	09	②	10	③
11	③	12	②	13	③	14	④	15	③	16	②	17	③	18	③	19	②	20	②
21	①	22	③	23	④	24	②	25	③	26	②	27	②	28	①	29	②	30	①

01 2019 가톨릭대 정답 ①

| 구문분석 | People (in the majority) can cause other group members to conform (through normative influence).
S V O O.C
대다수의 사람들은 규범적인 영향력을 통해 다른 집단 구성원들이 순응하도록 만들 수 있다.

The conformity (that occurs) may be a case (of public compliance without private acceptance).
S 관계대명사 V C
(이때) 발생하는 순응은 사적인 수용 없이 공적인 순응을 하는 경우일 수 있다.

People (in the minority) can rarely influence others (through normative means) — the majority has little concern (for how the minority views them).
S V O 대시: 부연설명 S V O
소수의 사람들은 규범적인 수단을 통해 다른 사람들에게 영향을 미치는 경우가 거의 없다—대다수는 소수가 그들을 어떻게 보는지에 대해 거의 관심

Guide 이 책의 수준별 학습방법과 활용법

초급자 **편입영어 독해가 처음인 초보자 수준**

해석과 구문 독해 위주의 학습

편입영어를 처음 공부한다면 영어 문장을 해석하고 이해하는 데 큰 어려움을 겪을 수 있습니다. 이 책은 실제 기출문제를 바탕으로 만들었기 때문에 기본기가 부족한 학생들은 각각의 문장을 하나씩 해석해 보고 해설지를 통해 자신이 한 해석이 맞는지 확인하면서 끊어읽기 연습, 구문의 이해, 영어 어휘 암기 위주로 학습해 보세요.

중급자 **영어 독해 문제 유형별 풀이를 원하는 학생**

독해 문제 유형별 연습

각 유형별로 다양한 학교의 문제를 풀면서 해당 유형에서 어떤 접근 방법과 전략을 사용해야 하는지 익혀 주세요. 각 문제 유형별로 중요하게 읽어야 하는 부분이 어디인지를 파악하고 문제를 풀면서 해설을 꼼꼼히 읽고 학습하며, 자신의 오답 이유가 무엇인지 스스로 분석해 보세요.

고급자 **편입영어의 고수가 되길 원하는 학생**

빠르고 정확하게 푸는 연습

편입 독해 문항에서 고득점을 받고자 하고, 자신의 독해 풀이 방법이 맞는지 확인해 보고 싶다면 자신의 풀이방법을 적용해 가며 최대한 빠르고 정확하게 풀어 보는 연습을 하세요. 자신의 풀이방법과 글 읽기에 부족한 점이 없는지 꼼꼼하게 체크해 가며 연습해 주세요.

Contents 이 책의 **차례**

LEVEL

1

에듀윌 편입

솔루션 독해 Basic

Reading

1강 제목

2강 주제 / 요지

3강 글의 목적 / 어조 / 태도

1강 제목

예제 2020 한국외대

A big stereotype about the Gypsy way of life is that it's flashy, revealing, and attention grabbing. But we don't get a full picture of Gypsy culture. For example, Gypsy fashion for free-flowing clothes is guided by modesty, and strict cleanliness codes are common, developed through centuries of life on the road when hygiene was of utmost importance. If you search for "Gypsy" online, you'll find story after story that perpetuates the myth that the Gypsy community is ridden with crime, tax avoidance, and voluntary unemployment. Nothing could be further from the truth. Members of Gypsy communities are, in fact, statistically underrepresented in the mainstream prison population. Just like with any other community, you will find criminals, just as you will find teachers, nurses, police officers, artists, and entrepreneurs. Many Gypsies have made it through mainstream education to top universities, whilst at the same time retaining their identity.

Q. Which of the following is the best title for the passage?

① Myths About Gypsy Culture
② Dress Tastes in Gypsy Culture
③ Changes in the Gypsy Community
④ The Strong Identity of the Gypsy Community

유형별 문제풀이 Point _ 제목

Point 1 중심소재 먼저 찾아보기

본문에서 포괄적으로 다루는 중심소재를 먼저 파악한다.
일반적으로 글의 도입부에서 구체적으로 다룰 소재를 제시하는 경우가 많다.

Point 2 중심소재를 전개하는 방향에 따라 주제문 찾아보기

글의 구조(두괄식, 미괄식, 양괄식, 중괄식)는 주제문의 위치를 알려 준다.
글의 전개방식과 연결표현에 주의하여 주제문을 찾는다.

Point 3 보기를 소거하면서 정답을 고르기

중심소재가 반영된 보기가 아니라면 먼저 소거한다.
중심소재가 같은 보기가 여러 개일 때는 주제문이 가장 잘 요약된 보기를 고른다.

정답 ①

분석 본문의 소재는 도입부에 제시된 '집시 공동체의 생활방식에 대한 고정관념'이며 역접 연결사를 사용하여 우리가 집시의 생활방식에 대한 이해가 부족하여 만들어 낸 잘못된 통념들을 언급하고 있다. 따라서 글의 제목으로 가장 적절한 것은 ① '집시 문화에 대한 잘못된 통념들'이다. 나머지 보기의 의미는 다음과 같다. ② 집시 문화의 의상에 대한 취향 ③ 집시 사회의 변화들 ④ 집시 사회의 강력한 정체성

어휘

stereotype ⓝ 고정관념
revealing ⓐ 노출이 심한
modesty ⓝ 겸손, 소박
utmost ⓐ 최고의, 극도의
myth ⓝ 근거 없는 통념
underrepresent ⓥ 실제의 수량이나 정도보다 적게 표시하다
prison population 교도소 수감자
flashy ⓐ 호화스러운, 화려하게 치장한
attention grabbing 관심을 사로잡는, 주목을 끄는
hygiene ⓝ 위생
perpetuate ⓥ 영구화하다, 영속시키다
tax avoidance ⓝ 조세 회피
identity ⓝ 신원, 독자성, (긴밀한) 유사성

해석 집시의 생활방식에 대한 큰 고정관념은 집시의 생활방식이 화려하고, 노출이 심하고, 관심을 사로잡는다는 것이다. 하지만 우리는 집시의 문화를 전체적으로 이해하지 못하고 있다. 예를 들어, 집시의 자유롭게 흐르는 의복 패션은 그들의 검소함에 의한 것이고 엄격한 청결 규칙은 위생이 가장 중요했던 수 세기 동안 걸친 도로 위에서 생활하며 형성된 일반적인 것이다. 인터넷에서 "집시"를 검색하면, 집시 공동체가 범죄, 세금 회피, 지발적인 실업으로 가득 차 있다는 통념을 영구화하는 이야기들을 차례로 찾을 수 있을 것이다. 이는 결코 사실이 아니다. 사실 집시 공동체의 구성원들은 주요 교도소 수감자 중에서 통계상으로 과소 대표된다(인구 비율 대비하여 수가 적다). 다른 공동체와 마찬가지로, 당신은 집시 사회에서도 교사, 간호사, 경찰관, 예술가와 기업가를 찾듯이, 범죄자도 발견할 것이다. 많은 집시들은 주류 교육을 통해 일류대학으로의 진학에 성공한 동시에 그들만의 정체성을 유지하고 있다.

Practice

정답과 해설 p.2

01 What is the best title for the passage?

People in the majority can cause other group members to conform through normative influence. The conformity that occurs may be a case of public compliance without private acceptance. People in the minority can rarely influence others through normative means — the majority has little concern for how the minority views them. In fact, majority group members may be loath to agree publicly with the minority; they don't want anyone to think that they agree with those unusual, strange views of the minority. Minorities therefore exert their influence on the group via the other principal method, informational social influence. The minority introduces new and unexpected information to the group and causes the group to examine the issues more carefully. Such careful examination may cause the majority to realize that the minority view has merit, leading the group to adopt all or part of the minority's view. In short, minorities often achieve private acceptance because of informational social influence.

① How the Few Influence the Many
② When the Majority Becomes the Minority
③ The Abuse of Power Exercised by the Minority
④ How Normative Social Influence Differs from Informational Social Influence

02 다음 글의 제목으로 가장 적절한 것은?

For most people, serious blows to the head don't occur often, but when they do, they can leave a legacy of damage. And despite sophisticated imaging techniques, brain-injury experts say such consequences, including sudden death, are difficult to predict. Clotting can occur in the aftermath of any head trauma, even after a concussion, when the brain is rattled inside the skull, causing delicate blood vessels to tear or stretch. Clots are notoriously unpredictable, however, and there aren't enough studies to say for certain how common they are after concussions. But doctors do know that a previous clot may increase the risk that additional ones will form.

① Unpredictable Consequences of Head Trauma
② Brain Injury and Imaging Techniques
③ Blood Vessels' Frailty
④ Brain's Physiological Traits

03 Which of the following would be the best title of the passage?

In modern developed societies, there is one variety of language that ranks above the others. This superposed variety is employed by the government and communications media, used and taught in educational institutions, and is the main or only written language. It is more fixed and resistant to change than any other variety in the community and is something of a yardstick against which other varieties are measured. It is to the written standard that prescriptivists, those who seek to regulate how others use language, usually appeal when they condemn some usage as incorrect, improper, or even barbarous.

① Language Varieties in Social Contexts
② The Status of the Standard Variety of a Language
③ Government Policies and Language Use
④ Influence of Government and Media on Language

04 What would be the best title for the above passage?

The idea of neurodiversity is really a paradigm shift in how we think about kids in special education. Instead of regarding these students as suffering from deficit, disease, or dysfunction, neurodiversity suggests that we speak about their strengths. Neruodiversity urges us to discuss brain diversity using the same kind of discourse that we employ when we talk about biodiversity and cultural diversity. We don't pathologize a colla lily by saying that it has a "petal deficit disorder." We simply appreciate its unique beauty. We don't diagnose individuals who have skin color that is different from our own as suffering from "pigmentation dysfunction." That would be racist. Similarly, we ought not to pathologize children who have different kinds of brains and different ways of thinking and learning.

① Neurodiversity and a paradigm shift
② Neurodiversity and its relationship with biodiversity
③ Neurodiversity as a way to diagnose personal characteristics
④ Neurodiversity to individualize children's strengths and value
⑤ Neurodiversity as a source for a clinical treatment

05 Which is the best title for the passage?

You may not always have access to a first aid kit in an emergency. Here are some suggestions for other everyday items you can use. If you don't have water to cool the burn, use juice, beer, or milk. In fact, use any cold, harmless liquid, until you have access to cold running water. The aim is to cool the area as quickly as possible, using whatever cold liquid is available. Remember: the burn should be cooled for at least ten minutes for the treatment to be effective. If you don't have cling film to cover the burn, use a clean plastic carrier bag, a freezer bag, or similar. These types of items will not stick to the burn and will create a barrier to stop infection. Plastic bags are particularly useful for covering a burned hand or foot.

① No First Aid Kit? No Problem
② Basic Ways to Prevent Burns!
③ Why Are We Learning First Aid?
④ Who to Treat First in Emergency
⑤ Alternative Medicine to Save People

06 What is the passage mainly about?

From the brain's complexity, it naturally follows that a genetic marker that predicts behavior will not necessarily be explanatory. In other words, it does not follow that linkage between a DNA marker and a psychiatric disease leads to an understanding of how the genetic variation alters behavior; or if the understanding of the intervening steps is achieved, comprehension may arrive years after the discovery and long after the genetic marker is used as a predictor. We may be able to predict whose brain works differently, but not be able to explain why. It's a little as if a policeman noticed that red cars are faster than blue cars. Perhaps the policeman begins to pay more attention to the red cars but what he hasn't figured out is that, for example, the red cars have a better engine than the blue cars. Although the brain's complexity is beginning to be unraveled, it is likely that the mechanism of action of a genetic variant predicting brain function will remain mysteriously long after we understand why some cars are faster than others.

① The complexity of the human DNA
② How to predict human behavior based on genetic variation
③ Difficulty of explaining associations between behavior and genetic markers
④ The possibility of using genetic information to predict violation of traffic rules

07 What is the passage mainly about?

As long as the term art is applied to a realm so vast and indefinite as to embrace literature, music and dance, theater and film, the visual and decorative arts, and other equally diverse activities, their classification — the way in which each is regarded as being either unique or like others — will remain a controversial but necessary undertaking. Classification is a useful approach to the organization of knowledge in any field: The classification of plants and animals in the 18th century led to the discovery of evolution in the 19th. In the arts, classification can be of immense help in understanding the interrelationships between arts and in drawing attention to characteristics of each that might otherwise go unnoticed.

① how we classify the wide range of arts
② the general classification procedure to follow
③ the main pitfalls we encounter in classifying arts
④ why classification is necessary in the field of arts

08 Which of the following is the best title for the passage?

Getting enough quality sleep can help protect your mental health, physical health, quality of life, and safety. We know all this very well, but the latest study indicates that it also keeps aging processes in check. For instance, scientists studied a group of 66 elderly volunteers, who had MRI brain scans and answered question about their sleep habit every two years. The study found that those who reported sleeping less on average showed swelling of a brain region indicating faster cognitive decline and thus aging in general. Other studies have suggested that adults need about seven hours of sleep a nigh to maintain proper brain function. Now that the role of sleeping in aging has been established, future research will investigate how sleep helps to preserve cognitive functions and hold off more rapid aging.

① Less Sleep Pushes Your Brain to Age Faster
② Science Reveals How Sleep Fights Rapid Aging
③ MRI: Breakthrough Imaging Technology in Sleep Research
④ Benefits and Disadvantages of Excessive Sleeping

09 Choose the best title for the following passage.

Numerous companies have embraced the open office and by most accounts, very few have moved back into traditional spaces with offices and doors. But research findings that we're 15% less productive, we have immense trouble concentrating and we're twice as likely to get sick in open working spaces, have contributed to a growing backlash against open offices. There's one big reason we'd all love a space with four walls and a door that shuts: focus. The truth is, we can't multitask, and small distractions can cause us to lose focus for upwards of 20 minutes. What's more, certain open spaces can negatively impact our memory. We retain more information when we sit in one spot without distractions. It's not so obvious to us each day, but we offload memories into our surroundings in the open spaces.

① The Pros and Cons of the Open Office
② The Myth of the Open Office Now Being Challenged
③ The Open Office: the Hub of Collaboration and Bond
④ The Rationale behind the Open Office

10 What is the best title for the passage?

The accuracy and speed of real-time automatic translation is undoubtedly going to improve dramatically in the near future, but it is going to take much longer before this medium becomes globally widespread and economically accessible to all. This poses a threat to the current availability and appeal of a global language. All the evidence suggests that the position of English as a global language is going to become stronger. By the time automatic translation matures as a popular communicative medium, that position will very likely have become impregnable. It will be very interesting to see what happens then — whether the presence of a global language will eliminate the demand for world translation services, or whether the economics of automatic translation will so undercut the cost of global language learning that the latter will become obsolete.

① What Are the Dangers of a Global Language?
② Why Computers Will Never Be a Smart Translator
③ The Battle Between Technology and Global Language
④ Automatic Translation and the End of Language Learning

11 Which is the best title for the passage?

If there is one requirement of architecture, it's that the structure must remain upright. Architects would be out of a job if their buildings continually failed to meet this one test. Yet some architects push the boundaries, seemingly daring with Newton's universal law of gravity, to design buildings that not only appear to defy the law, but are beautiful at that. From a cantilevered barn designed by the Dutch-based firm MVRD to an impressively stacked building in Hanover, Germany, by the Stuttgart-based firm Behnisch Architekten, these buildings seem impossible to conceive, let alone build. Of course, all of these structures passed strict zoning laws before they were erected. What is not guaranteed, however, is whether merely looking at them will cause you vertigo.

① Design Buildings on High Ground
② The Difficulty of Being an Architect
③ The Beautiful Buildings That Defy Gravity
④ Requirements and Laws of City Architecture
⑤ Be Daring If You Want to Achieve a Success

12 Which is the best title of the passage?

When I was 25, I attended a youth conference in the summer of 2008. I thought it would just be a refreshing weekend in the city. On the first day, I was a little nervous when the youth group went swimming. A burst appendix four years earlier had left me with a 12 cm scar on my abdomen and I couldn't stand people staring at me and wondering what had happened. This was made worse knowing that a guy I'd met might see it.

Little did I know that he was nervous about swimming too. When he was 17 he had a serious car accident and was left with a 15 cm scar on his abdomen. Talk about an icebreaker. Almost identical scars and so much in common, it was meant to be. We have just celebrated our sixth wedding anniversary.

① Stars Crossed
② Wonderful Coincidence
③ Our Wedding Anniversary
④ A Swimming Conference I Attended

13 Which is the best title for the passage?

Imperialism had long-lasting effects in the African and Asian colonies, even after the colonies gained their independence from Britain. Since the wealth went to the British rulers and a few native people who collaborated with them, the majority of people in these colonies were reduced to living in poverty. In some cases, the imperialists caused huge ecological damage, leaving the landscape scarred and barren. Imperialism denied the right of every country to govern itself: in the African and Asian colonies, native people, no matter how talented, were rarely allowed to serve in the colonial government. Finally, by sending out the degrading message that people of darker complexions were "inferior" to their lighter-skinned rulers, imperialists caused deep anger and resentment that persist to this day.

① The Poverty of the African and Asian Colonies
② The Colonies and Their Independence from British Rulers
③ The Impact of Imperialism on the African and Asian Colonies
④ The Positive Effect of Imperialism on the African and Asian Colonies

14 Which of the following is the best title for the passage?

For a story to be considered 'fantasy', it needs to contain some sort of magic system, in short, things that occur or exist in your story that cannot exist in the real world. These include elements of sorcery, witchcraft, and enchantment; fantastical creatures and the supernatural; or advanced abilities or powers. Basically, anything with no basis in real-world evidence or logic can be considered magic. This is where you can really set your story apart from others in the genre. If your magic system is unique and imaginative, your novel has a point of difference. An innovative, intriguing magic system is often the key to helping your novel stand out in the saturated fantasy market. Your magic system should play a key part in your story.

① The Similarity Between Magic and Science
② Various Reasons Readers Buy Books
③ A Fantasy World: Something Never Experienced
④ A Magic System: Fantasy's Essential Element

15 Which is the best title for the passage?

A behavioral theory asserts that consequences from the environment shape and maintain behaviors. Behaviors that are followed by positive reinforcement are most likely to continue or increase. Conversely, any behavior that is followed by negative consequences such as punishment, should theoretically decrease. However, research has not shown punishment to be an effective means of behavioral intervention. The main reason is that it simply works to stop misbehavior. In fact, it usually stops misbehavior only while the punisher is actually present.

A behavioral phenomenon called contingency-governed behavior may begin to develop at this time. Contingency-governed behavior means that an individual's behavior depends on the next consequence he perceives. This means that a person will try to get away with an inappropriate behavior if he thinks he will not get caught. Consequently, if the student believes the punisher will not see him or catch him in the misbehavior, he will try to get away with it. The problem behavior cycle escalates. If the student does not get caught, he feels successful, which is a form of positive reinforcement, so he continues the pattern of problem behavior.

① Behaviors Change over Time
② Effective Means of Punishment
③ Consequences Shape Behaviors
④ Controversy over Reinforcement

16 다음 글의 제목으로 가장 적절한 것은?

Those firms and industries that are not participating in the world market have to recognize that in today's trade environment isolation has become impossible. Willing or unwilling, more and more firms are becoming participants in global business affairs. Even if not by choice, most firms and individuals are affected directly or indirectly by economic and political developments that occur in the international marketplace. Those firms that refuse to participate are relegated to reacting to the global marketplace and therefore are unprepared for harsh competition from abroad.

Some industries have recognized the need for international adjustments. Farmers understand the need for high productivity in light of stiff international competition. Computer makers and firms in other technologically advanced industries have learned to forge global relationships to stay in the race. Firms in the steel, textile, and leather sectors have shifted production, and perhaps even adjusted their core business, in response to overwhelming onslaughts from abroad. Other industries in some countries have been caught unaware and have been unable to adjust. The result is the extinction of firms or entire industries, such as VCRs in the United States and coal mining and steel smelting in other countries.

① Road Not Taken: Entrepreneurship in the Future
② New Challenges Looming over the Global Market
③ Different Players, Different Rules in the Business World
④ Two Faces of Global Business: A Dilemma of Being "Global/Local"

17 다음 글의 제목으로 가장 적절한 것은?

The status of a character trait depends on the reference point. For instance, for an ape fingernails are considered primitive in relation to other primates because all other primates have fingernails. Thus, fingernails would not serve to distinguish apes from, for example, monkeys. Fingernails are a derived character for primates as a whole, however, because no other mammals have them. Thus, fingernails serve to distinguish primates from other mammals. The second character illustrated here — brow ridges — is found only in hominoids, not in other primates, and is therefore derived for hominoids. This character distinguishes apes from monkeys. In a chimpanzee, however, brow ridges would be considered to be primitive with respect to other hominoids; that is, the character would not distinguish a chimpanzee from, for example, a gorilla.

① Relative Status of Species
② Absolute Status of Species
③ Relative Status of Characters
④ Absolute Status of Characters

18 What is the passage mainly about?

Are there any benefits from drinking filtered water as opposed to municipal tap water? The short answer is yes. While the Environmental Protection Agency regulates municipal tap water and sets legal limits on certain contaminants, and most water utilities generally stay within these limits, some of the legal limits may be too lenient. And more than half of the chemicals found in municipal water are not regulated. Using the right water filter can help further reduce pollutants like lead from old water pipes, pesticide runoff in rural areas and byproducts of chemicals like chlorine that are used to treat drinking water. Radon, arsenic and nitrates are common pollutants in drinking water. Certain filters may help remove these impurities as well. But water contaminants and water quality vary from one local water utility to another, so you want to purchase a filter that is effective at capturing the right contaminants.

① environmental problems
② water shortage
③ safe water-drinking
④ water pollutions

19 다음 글의 제목으로 가장 적절한 것은?

In temperate regions, the leaves of many deciduous trees change color in the fall, transforming entire landscapes into a mosaic of reds and yellows. Red coloration is particularly intriguing because it is produced in the fall and is not merely a byproduct of the breakdown of green pigments (as is the case with yellows). Among the proposed explanations for fall's red coloration is the coevolutionary hypothesis, which posits that red leaves advertise something — for example, unpalatability or low nutritional quality — to herbivorous insects on their fall migration. Evidence for this hypothesis focuses on aphids and their potential winter host trees. For example, tree species with the strongest autumnal coloration tend to be those trees threatened by the greatest number of migrating aphids. There is reduced herbivory on red (versus green) leaves, and the peak of fall coloration coincides with the most active migratory period for aphids.

① A Paradox of Toxic Substances
② Coloration as Ecological Communication
③ The More Palatable, the More Protective
④ In Search of a Shared Protective Benefit
⑤ Migrating Insects, an Arsenal of Antipredator Adaptations

20 다음 글의 제목으로 가장 적절한 것은?

Professor Westbury has been doing important work, exploring the connections between language difficulties and brain function. As part of his inquiry, Westbury presents patients suffering from aphasia — whose comprehension of words and speech is often impaired — with a string of letters and asks whether or not it constitutes a real English word. One day, a graduate student pointed out something curious: certain nonsense words consistently made patients smile and sometimes even laugh out loud. "Particularly," Westbury says, "'snunkoople'." He started checking with friends and colleagues to see whether they had the same reaction, and the response was nearly unanimous. Snunkoople was funny. But why? Westbury presents what he believes could be the answer: the inherent funniness of a word, or at least of context-free non-words, can be quantified — and not all nonsense is created equal. According to Westbury, the less statistically likely it is for a certain collection of letters to form a real word in English, the funnier it is. The playwright Neil Simon seemed to grasp this implicitly in his 1972 work *The Sunshine Boys*, in which an old character tells his nephew, "If it doesn't have a 'k' in it, it's not funny!" — "k" being one of the least frequently used letters in the alphabet.

① Aphasia: The Way We Laugh
② Why Certain Words Are Funny
③ Humor as an Art of Equivocation
④ "Snunkoople," an Unusual Cluster of Letters

21 What is the passage mainly about?

The story goes that a Dublin theatre proprietor by the name of Richard Daly made a bet that he could, within forty-eight hours, make a nonsense word known throughout the city, and that the public would supply a meaning for it. After a performance one evening, he gave his staff cards with the word 'quiz' written on them, and told them to write the word on walls around the city. The next day the strange word was the talk of the town, and within a short time it had become part of the language. The most detailed account of this supposed exploit, in F. T. Porter's *Gleanings and Reminiscence* (1875), gives its date as 1791. The word, however, was already in use by then, meaning 'an eccentric person', and had been used in this sense by Fanny Burney in her diary entry for 24 June 1782.

① The history of the word 'quiz'
② Different forms of the word 'quiz'
③ Grammatical usages of the word 'quiz'
④ Changes in the meaning of the word 'quiz'

22 What would be the best title for the above passage?

This first decade of the twenty-first century, the world community is confronted with staggering problems. There are 6 billion people on our globe and forecasters project that the world population will reach 10 billion by 2050. Those people will need food, shelter, and an education that will allow them to lead fulfilled lives. The twentieth century saw great advances in many fields, but these advances did not come without costs. Acid rain, for example, polluted our vegetation, wild life, and the very bodies of millions of people. Together, the people of the world need to stop the systemic despoiling of our planet. Weaponry, such as nuclear devices and improvised explosive devices, daily threaten the world's peace and progress. Religious fanaticism, hunger, and poverty have bred a desperate terrorism in many corners of the world. It is no overstatement to say that we are in a race for global survival.

① Great Advances Made in the Twentieth Century
② Global Warming, Vegetation, and Wildlife
③ Great Advances Made with Significant Costs Paid
④ How to Lead Fulfilled Religious Lives
⑤ Desperate Terrorism and Global Survival

23 Choose the best title for the following passage.

In most paper and pencil tests, the test-taker is presented with all the items, usually in ascending order of difficulty, and is required to respond to as many of them as possible. This is not the most economical way of collecting information on someone's ability. There is no real need for strong candidates to attempt easy items, and no need for weak candidates to attempt difficult items. Computer adaptive testing offers a potentially more efficient way of collecting information on people's ability. All test-takers are presented initially with an item of average difficulty. The computer goes on to present individual candidates with items that are appropriate for their apparent level of ability as estimated by their performance on previous items, raising or lowering the level of difficulty until a dependable estimate at their ability is achieved.

① Rationale behind Test-takers' Preference for Computer Adaptive Testing
② How to Encourage Weak Candidates to Attempt Difficult Questions
③ The History of Sequencing Test Items Based on Item Difficulty
④ The Efficacy of Computer Adaptive Testing in Estimating Ability

24 Which is the best title of the passage?

Despite the increasing importance of leadership to business success, the on-the-job experiences of most people actually seem to undermine the development of the attributes needed for leadership. Nevertheless, some companies have consistently demonstrated an ability to develop people into outstanding leader-managers. Recruiting people with leadership potential is managing their career patterns. Individuals who are effective in large leadership roles often share a number of career experiences.

Perhaps the most typical and most important is significant challenge early in a career. Leaders almost always have had opportunities during their twenties and thirties to actually try to lead, to take a risk, and to learn from both triumphs and failures. Such learning seems essential in developing a wide range of leadership skills and perspectives. These opportunities also teach people something about both the difficulty of leadership and its potential for producing change.

① Competitive Leadership
② Developing Effective Leadership
③ Undermining Effective Leadership
④ Triumphs and Failure in Leadership

25 다음 글의 제목으로 가장 적절한 것은?

Why don't we run out of oxygen to breathe or water to drink? Many organisms produce oxygen during a process called photosynthesis, which constantly replenishes the oxygen consumed by all aerobic organisms. The physical materials on which life depends are limited to what is presently on earth. Water, for example, is naturally recycled from the atmosphere to the surface of Earth, through food webs and back to the atmosphere. Nitrogen, carbon and other essential substances are cycled in a similar manner. A natural resource that is replaced or recycled by natural processes is called a renewable resource. Other examples of renewable resources include plants, animals, food crops, sunlight and soil.

① Limits of Natural Processes
② Preservation or Consumption
③ Recycling Natural Resources
④ What if Oxygen is Run Out
⑤ Substances Essential for Life

26 Which of the following is the best title for the passage?

The best reason banana leaf is perfect for serving food is because of its size; you can serve a large variety of dishes in the leaf, from sweet to savory. We serve the small leaves for breakfast and dinner, and the large leaves are reserved for lunch, as lunch usually has a huge variety of dishes. It is very hygienic. Many hotels in India provide a banana leaf on top of the plate exactly cut to the plate's size, which I really like because we just have to sprinkle water and wipe, and the leaves are clean in a few seconds. It is eco-friendly to dispose of a banana leaf, whereas plastic plates worsen the environment. In a small way, if each of us starts using biodegradable natural materials, we will have a much cleaner environment. Banana leaves are full of antioxidants, and eating hot, freshly cooked food on them is one good way to get all the antioxidants easily.

① Cooking with Banana Leaves
② Banana Leaves for Serving Food
③ How to Pack Food with Banana Leaves
④ Ways to Protect Banana Plants

27 다음 글의 제목으로 가장 적절한 것은?

Rare earth elements are chemical elements that are composed of a group of seventeen metallic substances. These elements have been in high demand lately because they are needed to produce many modem-day electronics. This has unsurprisingly allowed China, where 95 percent of the world's supply exists, to control the export market. Recently, there have been concerns regarding the limited amount and expense of these elements, making it necessary to look for new sources in other countries. Until other deposits or equivalent substitutes can be found, electronics manufacturers will have to continue using rare earth metals in small amounts.

① The Response to China's Monopoly on Rare Earth Metals
② The Growing Demand and Restricted Supply of Rare Earth Elements
③ Alternatives to Rare Earth Elements in Electronics Devices
④ The Necessity of Finding Rare Earth Elements
⑤ The Influence of Rare Earth Elements on the Technological Market

28 다음 글의 제목으로 가장 적절한 것은?

The word jazz is related to jasm, a slang dating back to 1860 meaning "energy" in the U.S. In a 1912 article in the LA Times, a baseball pitcher described a pitch which he called a jazz ball "because it wobbles and you simply can't do anything with it." Its first documented use in a musical context was in a Times-Picayune article in 1916 about "jas bands." The musician Eubie Blake talked about his recollections of the original slang connotations of the term, "When Broadway picked it up, they called it 'JAZZ.' But it was spelled 'J-A-S-S.' That was dirty. If you knew what it was, you wouldn't say it in front of ladies."

① The Origin of the Word *Jazz*
② The History of Jazz in the U.S.
③ The Accord between Baseball and Jazz
④ The Slang Connotations of Jazz
⑤ The Dislike for Jazz by Ladies

29 What is the best title of the passage?

The ministry of education has decided to ban extra-curricular English classes for first and second graders in elementary school, and that is brewing major controversy. The ban is intended to prevent kids from studying English before third grade in elementary school, when English starts becoming part of the curriculum. However, despite the government's intention to curb the practice of studying ahead of the curriculum, voices are growing that the ban will make parents put their children into private English education instead.

① Banning Preschoolers from Studying English Confuses Teachers
② Ban on English Classes for First and Second Graders Stirs Dispute
③ Extra-curricular English Classes Are Not Welcomed among Parents
④ The Necessity of Private English Education for Preschoolers Is Not Evident

30 다음 글의 제목으로 가장 적절한 것은?

The fact that our communication abilities and behaviors are based partially on biology is obvious. Less obvious may be the fact that communication is *behavior* — precisely because it is biologically based. One of our daughters was asked in grade school what her father did at work. She responded that "... her father doesn't do anything. He just sits around and talks." Indeed, some people fail to recognize that talking is behaving, or performing some form of action. Communication is one of the most basic actions of all human behaviors. When people talk, they are doing something that is essential to their mental and physical well-being.

① Communication as Action
② Talking: Human Trait to Be Ignored
③ Communicative Abilities Learned from Society
④ Communicative Behavior Determined by Environment
⑤ Humans Uniquely Different from Animals in Communication

2강 주제 / 요지

예제 2020 건국대

Natural selection stresses survival in a hostile environment as fundamental to the prehistoric evolution of any adaptation. But if art is an adaptation, mere survival is a completely inadequate explanation for its existence. The reason is clear: artistic objects and performances are typically among the most ample, extravagant, and glittering creations of the human mind. The arts consume excessively brain power, physical effort, time, and precious resources. Natural selection, on the other hand, is economical: it weeds out inefficiency and waste. The origins and behaviors of animals are designed by natural selection to allow a species to survive and reproduce, making the most effective use of local resources. Evolution by natural selection is a severe accountant in the way it sorts out potential adaptation in terms of costs and benefits. How strange, therefore, to argue for a Darwinian genesis of the arts of man, which so often tend toward lavish excess, costly far beyond any obvious adaptive benefits for survival.

Q. 윗글의 요지로 가장 적절한 것은?

① 적대적 환경에서의 생존이 진화를 촉진한다.
② 자연 선택은 비용과 이익의 계산에 의해 결정된다.
③ 예술은 신체적 노력과 귀중한 자원을 과도하게 소비한다.
④ 예술은 인간의 가장 풍부하고 사치스러운 창작품에 속한다.
⑤ Darwin의 자연 선택 개념으로 예술을 설명하는 것은 부적절하다.

유형별 문제풀이 Point _ 주제 / 요지

Point ❶ **핵심 단어나 문장 파악하기**

글이 두괄식이라면 첫 문장이나 중요한 단어들을 찾아보고, 그것들이 연결되어 글 전체를 기술하는지 확인해 본다.
핵심 단어나 문장이 여러 번 반복되는 경우, 그것이 요지와 주제를 이루는 경우가 많다.

Point ❷ **글의 구조 파악하기**

글의 구조는 서론, 본론, 결론 등으로 이루어져 있으므로 각 부분이 어떤 내용을 다루고 있는지 파악하고, 어떤 부분에서 글의 핵심적 내용이 전달되는지 파악해 본다.

Point ❸ **저자의 의도 파악하기**

글을 쓴 작가가 어떤 의도를 가지고 글을 썼는지 파악하는 것이 요지를 찾는 핵심이다.
작가의 표현 방식, 연결사 사용 등을 살펴보면서, 작가가 전달하고자 하는 메시지가 무엇인지 생각해 본다.

정답 ⑤

분석 자연 선택은 가장 경제적이고 능률적으로 적응하는 반면에, 예술은 자원을 소비하는 방식으로 이루어진다고 언급하고 이에 따라 다윈의 자연 선택 개념으로 소비적인 예술을 설명하는 것은 적합하지 않다고 결론짓고 있으므로 이 글의 요지는 글의 결론인 ⑤가 적절하다.

어휘

natural selection 자연 선택[도태]
extravagant ⓐ 돈을 함부로 쓰는, 사치한
weed out (불필요하거나 부족한 대상 등을) 제거하다[뽑아 버리다]
sort out 선별하다, 분류하다
genesis ⓝ 발생, 기원
excess ⓝ 과다; 과잉
ample ⓐ 풍부한, 넉넉한, 다량의
glittering ⓐ 눈부신, 성공적인; 반짝이는
accountant ⓝ 회계사
lavish ⓐ 풍성한, 호화로운, 낭비하는 버릇이 있는

해석 자연 선택은 적대적인 환경에서의 생존을 선사시대에 있었던 모든 적응의 진화에 근본적인 것으로 강조한다. 그러나 만약 예술이 적응이라면 단순한 생존은 그것(예술)의 존재에 대한 완전히 불충분한 설명이다. 그 이유는 분명하다. 예술 작품과 예술 행위는 전형적으로 인간 정신의 가장 풍부하고, 사치스럽고, 화려한 창작물에 속한다. 예술은 두뇌력과 신체적 노력과 시간과 소중한 자원을 과도하게 소비한다. 반면에, 자연 선택은 경제적이다. 그것은 비효율과 낭비를 제거한다. 동물의 기원과 행동은 한 종(種)이 현지의 자원을 가장 효율적으로 사용하여 생존하고 번식할 수 있게 하도록 자연 선택에 의해 설계되어 있다. 자연 선택에 의한 진화는 가혹한 회계사처럼 비용과 혜택의 관점에서 잠재적인 적응을 선별해 낸다. 따라서 종종 지나치게 낭비적인 경향이 있으며 생존을 위한 그 어떤 확실한 적응의 혜택보다도 훨씬 더 많은 비용을 치르게 하는 인간의 예술에 대해 다윈식의 진화론적 기원을 주장하는 것은 얼마나 이상한 일인가.

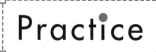

정답과 해설 p.37

01 What is the main idea of the passage?

Your doctor usually checks to see if you have healthy blood pressure in one arm, but a recent study from our research team suggests that taking readings in both arms may help better identify patients at higher risk of heart disease. When researchers analyzed data on nearly 3,400 patients over 13 years, they found that about 10 percent of participants showed higher systolic readings (the upper number) in one arm. Those with arm-to-arm discrepancies of ten points or more were 38 percent more likely to have a heart attack, stroke, or other coronary event. Such imbalances may indicate plaque in major arteries.

① Patients with high risk of heart disease seldom show uneven systolic readings for both arms.
② To find potential heart disease patients, we had better take readings in both arms.
③ Heart attacks or other coronary events may result from measuring blood pressure too often.
④ Arm-to-arm discrepancies of blood pressure could be signs of inefficient metabolism.

02 Which is the main idea of the passage?

It is unlikely that many of us will be famous, or even remembered. But no less important than the brilliant few that lead a nation or a literature to fresh achievements, are the unknown many whose patient efforts keep the world from running backward; who guard and maintain the ancient values, even if they do not conquer new; whose inconspicuous triumph it is to pass on what they inherited from their fathers, unimpaired and undiminished, to their sons.

Enough, for almost all of us, if we can hand on the torch and not let it down; content to win the affection, if possible, of a few who know us, and to be forgotten when they in their turn have vanished.

① We must learn from the experiences of other people.
② It is a few great men of genius that create civilization.
③ What the future world will be like is impossible to foresee.
④ Great men alone cannot keep up a high level of civilization.
⑤ One who wins the affection easily tends to be forgotten in that way.

03 다음 글의 주제로 가장 적절한 것은?

When your paper is returned to you, spend time examining the comments your teacher made. This is a good time to compare your classmates' responses to your teacher's, taken into account the changes you made between the original draft and the revised paper. Did you improve on the parts of your original paper that your classmates encouraged you to work on? Did your teacher comment on aspects of your paper that your classmates did not comment on? Share this information with the classmates you did peer-editing with. For each paper you looked at, compare the comments you made to the teacher's comments. Keep in mind the ideas you and your teacher had in common about each paper. Also notice comments that your teacher made that you missed. This is valuable information. You'll use it the next time you write and the next time you do peer-editing.

① Advantages and disadvantages of peer feedback
② Several tips for efficient drafting and proofreading
③ Importance of sharing ideas in peer-editing projects
④ Using wisely teacher's and peer's feedback in writing
⑤ Why we should consider others' feeling in peer-editing

04 Which best describes the main idea of the passage?

Attitudes to climate change seems to have been sharply polarized along political line at least in America. A large-scale survey in 2013 shows that 70% of Democratic voters saw evidence of man-made climate change in recent weather patterns, whereas only 19% of Republican voters did. It is not that conservatives are ignorant. Knowledge of science makes little difference to people's beliefs about climate change, except that it makes them more certain about what they believe. Republicans with a good knowledge of science are more skeptical about global warming than less knowledgeable Republicans.

The best explanation for the gap is that people's beliefs about climate change have become determined by feelings of identification with political groups. When people are asked for their views on climate change, they seem to translate this into a broader question: whose side are you on? The issue has become associated with Democrats, causing conservatives to dig in against it. The divide may not be resolved within a few years.

① Political conservatives are generally more optimistic.
② The progress of global warming is still under debate.
③ Scientific knowledge has nothing to do with people's beliefs.
④ People's views on climate change depend more on political orientation than on facts.

05 다음 글의 주제로 가장 적절한 것은?

In 1328, the Black Death took hold of Europe and did not let go for the next twenty years. As hundreds of millions succumbed to it and the medical community had no effective treatment, people began experimenting with odd techniques in a desperate attempt to stave off the pandemic. Some believed that pleasant odors could block the sickness, so they carried around sweet-smelling flowers or herbs.

But the only effect this had was to make a person smell nice for a time. A less enjoyable practice that a few opted for was to live in a sewer because it was thought that the air underground had not been contaminated by the disease. Naturally, it did nothing for the poor people who decided to go under; in fact, it only caused them to come down with more diseases due to the unsanitary conditions.

① The history and development of European medicine practices
② Why medical treatment for the Black Death did not work
③ Health-related myths believed by people in the 1300s
④ The unbelievable miracle of the Black Death
⑤ Unusual remedies used in attempting to cure the Black Death

06 What is the main point of the passage?

Art is much more than decoration, for it is laden with meaning, even if that content is sometimes shallow or obscure. Art enables us to communicate our understanding in ways that cannot be expressed otherwise. Truly a picture is worth a thousand words, not only in its descriptive value but also in its symbolic significance. In art, as in language, human being is above all an inventor of symbols to convey complex thoughts in new ways. We must think of art not in terms of everyday prose but as poetry, which is free to rearrange conventional vocabulary and syntax in order to convey new, often multiple meanings and moods. A painting likewise suggests much more than it states. Like a poem, the value of art lies equally in what it says and how it says it. It does so partly by implying meanings through allegory, pose, facial expression, and the like or by evoking them through the visual elements: line, form, color, and composition.

① The ultimate value of art is the beauty of description.
② Semantics takes a priority over syntax in art appreciation.
③ Artwork resembles a personal essay rather than a complex poem.
④ As in poetry, representation is as important as meaning in art.

07 Which is the main idea of the passage?

The white race divides itself upon economic grounds. The landowning whites look down on everyone else, mostly the working class Cajun whites. These poor whites serve the landowning whites by using violence to maintain the racial order. Despite their efforts, however, the landowning whites still detest and scorn them. In the black race, the Creole culture shuns all darker skin blacks. The Creoles are light skinned blacks who come from the original French colonists in Louisiana. When a Creole girl, Mary Agnes LeFarbre, goes to work on the Samson Plantation with common blacks, her family disowns her. Even though local whites consider the Creoles common blacks, the Creloes themselves refuse to mix with the general black population and act superior. The concept of racism within the black community itself suggests the ridiculousness in using skin color as a means of social division.

① The poor whites use violence for the rich whites.
② Class differences exist even inside the same race.
③ Humans erect boundaries to keep their fellows out.
④ Social frame of racial order constructs American identity.
⑤ People are bound to the traditional image of black and white.

08 What is the following passage mainly about?

There are many English surnames from place names, and a curious fact about them is that the places are often so obscure — mostly from places that few people have heard of. Why should there be so many more Middletons than Londons, so many more Worthingtons than Bristols? The main cities of medieval Britain — London, York, Norwich, Glasgow — are relatively uncommon as surnames even though many thousands of people lived there. To understand this seeming paradox you must remember that the purpose of surnames is to distinguish one person or family from the great mass of people. If a person called himself Peter of London, he would be just one of hundreds of such Peters and anyone searching for him would be at a loss. So as a rule, a person would become known as Peter of London only if he moved to a rural location, where London would be a clear identifying feature, but that did not happen often.

① the popular English surnames from place names
② the reason for the scarcity of big place names in English surnames
③ the untold myths about English surnames from place names
④ the source of confusion in English surnames from place names

09 Which of the following is the main idea of the passage?

Shakespeare killed off Hamlet, Macbeth and King Lear. How did the characters feel about it, and about him? Shakespeare's characters had their own viewpoints and still do, says playwright Naomi C. Wallace. In her play, *Madman William*, Hamlet, Macbeth and King Lear meet in a 20th-century London pub and discuss their resentment at having to die in every performance. In a dream scene, Shakespeare himself appears as well in the pub along with the three tragic figures and Mercutio, who is killed off early in *Romeo and Juliet*. The play gets its American premiere on Friday at the District of Columbia Arts Center and will continue at other sites in the Washington area through February. Last year it was produced in Edinburgh, Scotland; in Exeter and Shakespeare's hometown, Stratford-on-Avon, in England; and in Prague, Czech Republic.

① A witty play by Naomi C. Wallace made a huge success.
② Shakespeare enjoyed having his characters murdered at the end.
③ Shakespeare's tragic characters do not like being killed in their plays.
④ *Madman William* retells Shakespearean tragedies in the characters' perspectives.

10 다음 글의 주제로 가장 적절한 것은?

The trouble is with the assimilative nature of Italian immigrants. In a few years even the older immigrants are apt to pick up our language, and one by one to abandon their native customs and ways of thought. Even in the theater they spoke to each other mainly in English. In seeking amusement they fall prey to the flash and glare of our variety bill-posters. The new generation, who lack the traditions of the home country, and sometimes the knowledge of Italy to appreciate its drama, are almost certain to become Americanized in their tastes. An Italian theater could appeal only to new arrivals and to those of the past generation who have not forgotten their old life and the joy of true acting.

① Italian immigrants who cling in their old traditions and legends
② the power of the melting pot across ethnic and national boundaries
③ Italian immigrants' preference of American traditions to the traditions of their home country
④ a generational difference concerning cultural preferences between first-generation Italian immigrants and their offspring

11 Which is the main idea of the passage?

According to researchers, gossip has some benefits. Exchanging information can create a healthy connection. It can build rules for acceptable and unacceptable behavior. It can improve society. Similary, gossip is useful in the business world. Gossip researcher Professor Frank McAndrew says, "If people are talking about good things others do, we want to emulate that good behavior. It is a nice way of socially controlling people." When a company faces bad times, gossip about the future of the employees can reduce fear and uncertainty. It can also create a feeling of fellowship.

However, bad gossip, the negative talk about other people's lives, can be destructive. Disappointingly enough, the researchers spend little time on this form of malice. People engage in negative gossip for several reasons. They may do it to bond with another person. They may do it to pass the time or to deny problems. They may gossip to build themselves up through comparisons with others, or they may want to hurt others.

① People don't realize how destructive gossip can be.
② Gossip can be beneficial or negative for society and people's lives.
③ Gossip is needed because employees may be able to create a feeling of fellowship.
④ People may be involved in negative gossip for various reasons.

12 Which of the following is the main theme of the passage?

Professor Constantine Slobodchikoff and his colleagues have been decoding the communication system of prairie dogs, rodents not known for their smarts. And yet, Slobodchikoff's team has evidence that prairie dogs have a complex language, which they are starting to understand when prairie dogs see a predator, they warn one another using high-pitched chirps. To the untrained ear, these chirps may all sound the same, but they are not. Slobodchickoff thinks the alarm calls are a "Rosetta Stone" in decoding prairie-dog language, because they occur in a context people can understand, enabling interpretation. In his research, Slobodchikoff records the alarm calls and subsequent escape behaviors of prairie dogs in response to approaching predators. Then, when no predator is present, he plays back these recorded alarm class and films the prairie dogs' escape responses. If the escape responses to the playback match those when the predator was present, this suggests that meaningful information is encoded in the calls. And indeed, there seems to be. Slobodchikoff has discovered they have distinct calls pertaining to different predators. The calls even specify the color, size, and shape of the predator.

① Scientists began to understand the language of prairie dogs.
② Scientists observed prairie dogs' peculiar escape behavior.
③ Prairie dog language is structurally comparable to human language.
④ Prairie dogs have an elaborate system of conveying diverse emotions.

13 What is the main idea of the passage?

Natural selection is usually assumed to favor behaviors that promise survival, but almost no art theorist has ever proposed that art directly promotes survival. It costs too much time and energy and does too little. This problem was recognized very early in evolutionary theorizing about art. In his 1897 book *The Beginning of Art*, Ernst Grosse commented on art's wastefulness, claiming that natural selection would long ago have rejected those who wasted their efforts in so purposeless a way, in favor of others with practical talents; and art would not possibly have been developed so highly and richly as it has been. To Darwin, high cost, apparent uselessness and manifest beauty usually indicated that a behavior had a hidden courtship function. But to most art theorists, art's high cost and apparent uselessness has usually implied that a Darwinian approach is inappropriate — that art is uniquely exempt from natural selection's cost-cutting frugality.

① Art has no survival value, but displays a courtship function.
② Natural selection does not explain art in a plausible way.
③ Many art theorists appreciate art's evolutionary functions.
④ Biologists have found a way to explain art in Darwinian terms.

14 Which is the main idea of the passage?

A psychiatrist reported the case of a woman who claimed that she had stomach trouble because of a frog in her stomach. She "knew" she had swallowed a frog egg while on a picnic. Her physician ridiculed the idea but she was so insistent that he finally agreed to operate for the removal of the frog. Accordingly, he sent her to a hospital to be prepared for the operation and he, at the same time, hired a small boy to catch a frog for him. To give the woman the impression that she had really had an operation, an incision was made in her abdomen, and the doctor showed her the "frog" in a bottle of alcohol, which had presumably been removed from her stomach. The woman was delighted and at once recovered, but only temporarily. Three months after the pseudo-operation, she claimed that the first frog had laid some eggs and that she now had two frogs in her stomach.

① Ordinary logical thinking is useless in the consideration of the ailments which are psychiatrical rather than organic.
② Any form of invalidism can be cured by pseudo-operation.
③ Psychological problems should be treated by giving pseudo-medicine.
④ To satisfy a patient is very important in the psychiatrical treatment.

15 The theme of the above passage is ___________.

In 1979, when the party introduced the one-child policy, it believed that coercion was the only way to ensure that population growth did not become unsustainable. The party has since claimed that the policy has helped prevent 400 million births. In fact, there is little evidence to back this claim. China's birth rate had been falling rapidly since the early 1970s with the help of little more than education campaigns. The birth rate continued to fall under the new policy, but other countries have seen similar declines without resorting to cruelty and oppression. Their experience suggests that the more important factors behind China's lower birth rate were rising female participation in the workforce, improvements in education, later marriages and the rapidly increasing cost of education and housing. The main effect of the one-child policy was to foster egregious human-rights abuses against the minority who ignored it.

① female's role in China
② China's gender equality
③ censorship in China
④ China's lower death rate
⑤ family planning in China

16 다음 글의 요지로 가장 적절한 것은?

The nineteenth-century fetishism of facts was completed and justified by a fetishism of documents. The documents were the Ark of the Covenant in the temple of facts. The reverent historian approached them with bowed head and spoke of them in awed tones. If you find it in the documents, it is so. But when we get down to it, what do these documents — the decrees, the treaties, the rent-rolls, the blue books, the official correspondence, the private letters and diaries — tell us? No document can tell us more than what the author of the document thought, what he thought had happened, and what he thought ought to happen or would happen. None of this means anything until the historian has got to work on it and deciphered it. The facts, whether found in documents or not, have still to be processed by the historian before he can make any use of them.

* The Ark of the Covenant: (모세의 십계명을 새긴 돌을 넣은) 법궤

① Nineteenth-century historians were obsessive about facts and documents.
② All documents about the past are treated as historical facts by the historian.
③ The necessity of establishing historical facts rests on the quality of the facts themselves.
④ Knowledge of the past consists of elemental and impersonal atoms which nothing can alter.
⑤ The treatment of documents as a historical fact depends on the element of interpretation by historians.

17 What is the main idea of this passage?

A recent study in the journal *Lancet Planetary Health* found that airborne pollen counts have been increasing around the world as average temperatures climbed. The majority of the 17 sites studied showed an increase in the amount of pollen and longer pollen seasons over 20 years. And the faster the climate changes, the worse it gets. That's why residents of Alaska, which is warming twice as fast as the global average, now face especially high allergy risks.

Taken together over the long term, seasonal allergies present one of the most robust examples of how global warming is increasing risks to health. Allergies are already a major health burden, and they will become an even larger drain on the economy.

"It's very strong. In fact, I think there's irrefutable data," said Jeffrey Demain, director of the Allergy, Asthma, and Immunology Center of Alaska. "It's become the model of health impacts of climate change." And since so many are afflicted — some estimates say up to 50 million Americans have nasal allergies — scientists and health officials are now trying to tease out the climate factors driving these risks in the hopes of bringing some relief in the wake of growing pollen avalanches.

① Allergies are going to get controlled.
② Pollen is becoming impossible to avoid.
③ Alaska is too cold to suffer from pollen allergies.
④ Seasonal allergies play an important role in national economy.
⑤ Pollen allergy seasons get longer and more intense as temperatures rise.

18 Which is the main idea of the passage?

Greek mythology is largely made up of stories about gods and goddesses, but it must not be read as an account of the Greek religion. According to the most modern idea, a real myth has nothing to do with religion. It is an explanation of something in nature, how any and everything in nature came into existence: people, animals, trees or flowers, the stars, earthquakes, all that is and all that happens. Thunder and lightning, for instance, are caused when Zeus hurls his thunderbolt. Myths are early science, the result of people's first trying to explain what they saw around them.

① Mythology is often very closely associated with religion.
② The most modern idea emphasizes the value of Greek myths.
③ Greek myths frequently mention natural phenomena in detail.
④ Greek myths are explanations of nature rather than religion.
⑤ Science could be better understood by understanding myths.

19 What is the main idea of the passage?

Ecologists recognize that reducing the planet to a resource base for consumer use in an industrial society is already a spiritual and psychic degradation. Our main experience of the divine, the world of the sacred, has been diminished as money and utility values have taken precedence over spiritual, aesthetic, emotional, and religious values in our attitude toward the natural world. Any recovery of the natural world will require not only extensive financial funding but a conversion experience deep in the psychic structure of the human. Our present dilemma is the consequence of a disturbed psychic situation, a mental imbalance, an emotional insensitivity, none of which can be remedied by any quickly contrived adjustment. Nature has been severely, and in many cases irreversibly, damaged. Healing can occur and new life can sometimes be evoked, but only with the same intensity of concern and sustained vigor of action as that which brought about the damage in the first place. Yet, without this healing, the viability of the human is severely limited.

① It is now time to discard the misconception that environmental destruction is not happening.
② Humans need to compensate for the damage they have done to nature.
③ There is no means available for reversing the damage done to nature by humans.
④ Consumption must be curbed in order to replenish the earth's resources for a sustainable future.

20 다음 글의 요지로 가장 적절한 것은?

It is the duty of the man of wealth: first, to set an example of unostentatious living, shunning display or extravagance; to provide moderately for legitimate wants of those dependent upon him; and after doing so to consider all surplus revenues which come to him simply as trust funds, which he is called upon to administer, and strictly bound as matter of duty to administer in the manner which, in his judgment, is best calculated to produce the most beneficial results for the community — the man of wealth thus becoming the mere agent and trustee for his poorer brethren, bringing to their service his superior wisdom, experience, and ability to administer.

① Wisdom doesn't come with wealth.
② Wealthy men are not necessarily wise.
③ The wealthy need to step in to help the poor.
④ The tension between the wealthy and the poor is unavoidable.

3강 글의 목적 / 어조 / 태도

예제

2016 성균관대

In pointing out the absurdity of university students who demand protection from views with which they disagree, you exaggerated somewhat in stating that "Fifty years ago student radicals agitated for academic freedom and the right to engage in political activities on campus." At Berkeley in 1971 I remember a speaker who had the temerity to defend the ROTC on campus. He was shouted off the steps of Sproul Hall and prevented from talking. The Berkeley "Free Speech" movement did not stand for free speech, only for speech that agreed with the prevailing leftist orthodoxies of the time.

The only thing that appears to have changed is the justification for censorship. For years, many American faculty and student groups have demanded that "offensive" speech on college grounds be silenced, while reserving the right to designate which speech was offensive and which was not. Presented with the logical fallacy of such selective censorship, they now claim that their opponents' speech makes them feel "unsafe". What will come next? A claim that their opponents' speech causes physical illness?

Q. The mood of the passage is ____________.

① humorous
② gloomy
③ cynical
④ offensive
⑤ nostalgic

유형별 문제풀이 Point _ 글의 목적 / 어조 / 태도

Point 1 반복되는 표현 또는 어구에 주목하기

특정한 목적이나 어조 및 태도를 드러내기 위한 글의 경우 반복적으로 사용되는 표현이나 어구에 주목하여 글의 목적을 파악한다.

Point  주제문을 찾고 연결사와 강조표현에 주의하기

특정한 형식을 가지는 글(보도문, 기고문, 광고문)인지 주의하여 주제문을 찾는다. 특히 본문에 역접의 연결사나 강조표현이 있을 때는 필자가 글을 쓴 목적이나 어조가 연결사 이후나 강조표현에 제시되는 경우가 많아 주의가 필요하다.

Point  자주 등장하는 보기 어휘 학습하기

글의 목적이나 어조 및 작가의 태도를 묻는 문제에 자주 등장하는 보기들을 학습한다. 글에는 다양한 목적이 있으므로 요청, 축하, 설명, 주장, 경고 등 종류에 따라 빈출 보기들을 정리해 두면 문제풀이에 효과적이다.

정답 ③

분석 본문의 저자는 첫 단락에서는 반대자들의 연설을 막는 과거의 대학 풍토를 소개하고, 두 번째 단락에서도 현재까지 유지되고 있는 미국 교수들과 학생 단체들의 선택적인 검열의 논리를 첫 단락과 일관되게 냉소적인 태도로 비판하고 있다. 따라서 ③이 정답으로 가장 적절하다.

어휘

absurdity ⓝ 부조리, 불합리, 어리석음
radical ⓝ 급진주의자
temerity ⓝ 무모, 무모한 행위
leftist ⓝ 좌파(인 사람)
censorship ⓝ 검열 (계획), 검열 제도
silence ⓥ 침묵시키다
nostalgic ⓐ 향수의, 향수를 불러일으키는
exaggerate ⓥ 과장하다
agitate ⓥ 선동하다, 정치운동을 하다
stand for ~을 상징하다, ~을 대표하다
orthodoxy ⓝ 정설, 정통
faculty ⓝ 대학교수들
designate ⓥ 지시하다, 지정하다
fallacy ⓝ 오류

해석 동의하지 않는 견해들로부터의 보호를 요구하는 대학생들의 부조리함을 지적하면서, 당신은 "50년 전 학생 급진주의자들은 학문의 자유와 캠퍼스 내 정치 활동에 참여할 권리를 위해 선동했다."라고 다소 과장하며 말했다. 1971년 버클리에서 나는 대학 내의 ROTC를 옹호하는 대담함을 가졌던 한 연사를 기억한다. 그는 Sproul Hall의 계단에서 내려가라는 야유를 받았고 연설을 계속할 수 없었다. 버클리 대학의 "Free Speech" 운동은 언론의 자유를 지지하지 않았고 오직 당시의 지배적인 좌파 정통성에 동조하는 연설만을 지지했다.

바뀐 것으로 보이는 유일한 것이 있다면 그것은 검열 제도를 정당화하는 것이다. 수년 동안 많은 미국의 대학교수들과 학생 단체들은 어떤 연설이 불쾌하고 어떤 연설이 불쾌하지 않은지를 지정할 수 있는 권리를 유지하면서, 대학 내에서의 "공격적인" 연설을 침묵시킬 것을 요구해 왔다. 그러한 선택적인 검열의 논리적 오류를 가지고 있는 그들은, 이제 그들의 반대자들의 연설이 그들을 "불안하게" 만든다고 주장하고 있다. 다음은 무엇인가? 반대자들의 주장이 그들에게 신체적 질병을 일으킨다는 주장인가?

Practice

정답과 해설 p.61

01 Which best describes the tone of the passage?

Undoubtedly, the autobiography of Benjamin Franklin is riddled with faults. It is very muddled, particularly towards the end. It was not written in a continuous stretch, but rather pasted together out of separate fragments that were written years apart from one another: often, the author could not remember what he had even written in the previous sections. The work often takes an arrogant, condescending tone, yet it praises the virtue of humility. And perhaps most egregious of all, the part of Ben's life with the most historical significance — the American Revolution — is entirely omitted from the work. There is no real mention of events after 1760, 15 years before the outbreak of war. At that year the autobiography simply stops.

① critical ② praising
③ objective ④ indifferent
⑤ patronizing

02 What is the tone of the passage?

Those people who become perpetrators of evil deeds and those who become perpetrators of heroic deeds are basically alike in being just ordinary, average people. The banality of evil is matched by the banality of heroism. Neither is the consequence of dispositional tendencies; nor are they special inner attributes of pathology or goodness residing within the human psyche or the human genome. Both emerge in particular situations at particular times, when situational forces play a compelling role in moving individuals across the line from inaction to action. There is a decisive moment when the individual is caught up in a vector of forces emanating from the behavioral context. Those forces combine to increase the probability of acting to harm others or acting to help others. That decision may not be consciously planned or taken mindfully but impulsively driven by strong situational forces. Among them are group pressures, group identity, diffusion of responsibility, and a focus on the immediate moment without entertaining future cost or benefit. It is important for our society to foster the heroic imagination in our citizens by conveying the message that anyone is a hero-in-waiting who will be counted on to do the right thing when the time comes to make a heroic decision.

① earnest ② ambivalent
③ sardonic ④ haughty

03 다음 글의 목적으로 가장 적절한 것은?

Demarketing in a tourism context is the process of discouraging all or certain tourists from visiting a particular destination. General demarketing occurs when all visitors are temporarily discouraged from visiting a location, usually due to perceived carrying capacity problems. A notable example is Venice, where intensive summer crowding occasionally prompts local authorities to run ads depicting unpleasant scenes of litter, polluted water, dead pigeons and the like. The assumption is that the brand image of Venice is so strong that such imagery will not cause any permanent damage to the tourism industry. Most other destinations, however, do not have such a powerful brand and hence are generally reluctant to countermand brand-building efforts with demarketing.

① 역(逆) 마케팅의 개념을 소개하려고
② 베니스라는 브랜드 이미지의 형성 과정을 소개하려고
③ 특정 여행지를 방문하려는 관광객들에게 정보를 제공하려고
④ 관광산업에서 역(逆) 마케팅이 어떻게 활용되는지 설명하려고
⑤ 불쾌한 장면들을 묘사하는 광고를 만드는 방법을 소개하려고

04 Which of the following best describes the author's attitude?

College and university environments are places with a special purpose: student learning. Among the many methods employed to foster student learning and development, the use of the physical environment is perhaps the least understood and the most neglected. The physical environment, however, can contribute to college student learning and development in two important ways. First, the actual features of the physical environment can encourage or discourage the processes of learning and development. Second, the process of designing campus physical environments can also promote the acquisition of skills important to the process of learning and developing.

① inquisitive
② impassioned
③ sarcastic
④ explanatory

05 Which best identifies the tone of the author?

When someone feels better after using a product or procedure, it is natural to credit whatever was done. However, this is unwise. Most ailments are self-limiting, and even incurable conditions can have sufficient day-to-day variation to enable quack methods to gain large followings. Taking action often produces temporary relief of symptoms (a placebo effect). In addition, many products and services exert physical or psychological effects that users misinterpret as evidence that their problem is being cured. Scientific experimentation is almost always necessary to establish whether health methods are really effective.

① ironic
② skeptical
③ excited
④ humorous

06 The mood of the passage is very ________.

Like most patriotic Americans, my father was forever buying gizmos that proved to be disastrous — clothes steamers that failed to take the wrinkles out of suits but had wallpaper falling off the walls in whole sheets, an electric pencil sharpener that could consume an entire pencil in less than a second, a water pick that was so lively it required two people to hold and left the bathroom looking like the inside of a car wash, and much else.

But all of this was nothing compared with the situation today. We are now surrounded with items that do things for us to an almost absurd degree — automatic cat food dispensers, electric juicers and can openers, refrigerators that make their own ice cubes, automatic car windows, disposable toothbrushes that come with the toothpaste already loaded. People are so addicted to convenience that they have become trapped in a vicious circle: The more labor-saving appliances they acquire, the harder they need to work; the harder they work, the more labor-saving appliances they feel they need to acquire.

① agitating
② irritating
③ optimistic
④ cynical
⑤ gloomy

07 Which of the following best represents the author's tone in the passage?

Medical robots are, for the most part, tools to enhance a doctor's or a therapist's techniques — like orthotic devices, which help improve motor control and range of motion after a stroke or other trauma and can offer modified degrees of assistance as the patient recovers. Allison Okamura, a professor of mechanical engineering at Johns Hopkins in Baltimore, Maryland, is studying, along with a team of neuroscientists, the potential applications of a robotic external skeleton for patients who have suffered brain damage. Such patients have trouble controlling their limbs; the external skeleton robot would encase their arms and coordinate physical movements. The patient could use the robot until he recovered, or perhaps for the rest of his life if the debility persisted.

① truculent
② inspiring
③ sarcastic
④ expository

08 The author's tone on the digital currencies in the above passage can best be described as _____________.

Digital currencies, also known as virtual currencies or cash for the Internet, allow people to transfer value over the Internet, but are not legal tender. Because they don't require third-party intermediaries, merchants and consumers can avoid the fees associated with traditional payment systems. Advocates of virtual currencies also say that because personal information is not tied to transactions, digital currencies are less prone to identity theft. Many of the headlines generated by digital currencies have focused on problems with the system. In January, federal prosecutors charged the CEO of BitInstant, a major bitcoin exchange company, with laundering digital currency through the online drug marketplace. Although digital currencies are far from widespread, their growing popularity — and their potential for misuse — has prompted states to weigh in on the uncharted territory.

① adamant
② circumspect
③ imprudent
④ insouciant
⑤ passionate

09 What is the tone of the following passage?

The idea that the number of people per square mile is a key determinant of population pressure is as widespread as it is wrong. The key issue in judging overpopulation is not how many people can fit into any given space but whether the Earth can supply the population's long-term requirement for food, water, and other resources. Most of the empty land in the United States, for example, either grows the food essential to our well-being or supplies us with raw materials. Densely populated countries and cities can be crowded only because the rest of the world is not.

① wistful
② emphatic
③ dismayed
④ ambivalent

10 What is the general tone of the following passage?

Gee, let's tell all the children in the land to read teen magazines so they can become materialistic clones! Let's tell them that Britney Spears is "cool!" and that the Backstreet Boys are "totally dreamy!" And while we're at it, let's make the kids feel really bad about themselves if they don't look like they're made of plastic. With magazines like this, it's no wonder there are 12-YEAR-OLDS that want breast implants. Hey Kids! Just ask Mommy and Daddy to buy you an entire new body! If they really love you, they will.

① comic
② neutral
③ sarcastic
④ entertaining

11 광고에 대한 글쓴이의 태도로 가장 적절한 것은?

How often do we hear comments such as these: "I hate advertising," or "There's too much advertising in the world!" In the 21st century, it seems that advertising is everywhere we look. We see it along highways, in trains, buses, even in taxicabs, as ell as on the Internet and on TV. It's hard to escape advertising. But do we really want to? Actually, when you think about it, advertising provides us with quite a few benefits. First, advertising gives us information that we need. For instance, if you want to buy a new appliance or a new car, you can look for the best "deals" in ads that appear in newspapers, in magazines, on television, or even on the radio. Besides providing information, advertising also supports the entertainment industry, including television and radio. It may be annoying to sit through commercials during your favorite TV show, but the advertisers have paid for its production. This, in turn, pays the TV crew for their work.

① sardonic
② indifferent
③ defensive
④ opponent
⑤ skeptical

12 What is the PURPOSE of the passage?

American women should stop buying so-called women's magazines, because these publications lower their self-respect. First of all, publications like *Glamour* and *Cosmopolitan* appeal to women's insecurities in order to make millions. Topics like "Ten Days to Your More Slender Waist" and "How to Attract Mr. Right" lure women to buy seven million copies per month, reports Donna Kato in *The Miami Herald*, March 8, 2013. The message: women need to improve. Second, although many people — especially magazine publishers — claim these periodicals build self-esteem, they really do the opposite. One expert in readers' reactions, Deborah, says that almost all women, regardless of age or education, feel worse about themselves after reading one of these magazines. Alice, one of the women 1 spoke with, is a good example: "I flip through pictures of world-class beauties and six-foot-tall skinny women, and compare myself to them. In more ways than one, 1 come up short." Finally, if women spent the money and time these magazines cost to undertake more self-loving activities — studying new subjects, developing mental or physical fitness, setting goals and daring to achieve them — they would really build self-worth. Sisters, seek wisdom, create what you envision, and above all, know that you can!

① description
② definition
③ analysis
④ persuasion

13 다음 글의 목적으로 가장 적절한 것은?

Thousands of people will go into the bush this summer to cut the high cost of living. A man who gets his two weeks' salary while he is on vacation should be able to put those two weeks in fishing and camping and be able to save one week's salary clear. He ought to be able to sleep comfortably every night, to eat well every day and to return to the city rested and in good condition. But if he goes into the woods with a frying pan, an ignorance of black flies and mosquitoes, and a great and abiding lack of knowledge about cookery, the chances are that his return will be very different. He will come back with enough mosquito bites to make the back of his neck look like a relief map of the Caucasus. His digestion will be wrecked after a valiant battle to assimilate half-cooked or charred grub. And he won't have had a decent night's sleep while he has been gone. He will solemnly raise his right hand and inform you that he has joined the grand army of never-agains.

① To inform the benefits of comfortable camping out
② To prepare men before joining military camps
③ To advocate decent camping sites
④ To warn the dangers of unprepared camping out
⑤ To describe people's responses after camping out

14 What is the purpose of the passage?

When most people contemplate building a new home, they assume that the first order of business is to choose or design a plan to build. But, in fact, the first step is always to find the site that you want to build on. When you work with an architect, you'll find that the design for the house is as much influenced by the opportunities and constraints of the site as it is by your particular functional and aesthetic desires. This was eminently evident in one new house I saw a few years ago. The house was positioned on a hill, facing south overlooking a magnificent vista, but there was not a single window looking toward that extraordinary view. My guess is that the design had been picked out of a plan book long before the site had been chosen, and the original plan had been designed to be highly energy efficient with its blind face oriented to the north. This new house had the blind face oriented to the south just the direction one wants lots of glass in most climates.

① To explain the importance of aesthetic considerations in house construction
② To show the close connection between the design for a house and its site
③ To offer a step-by-step guide to the house building process
④ To illustrate how to build an energy-efficient house

15 What is the main purpose of the passage?

Experts say that if you feel drowsy during the day, even during boring activities, you haven't had enough sleep. If you routinely fall asleep within five minutes of lying down, you probably have severe sleep deprivation. The widespread practice of "burning the candle at both ends" in Western industrialized societies has created so much sleep deprivation that what is really abnormal sleepiness is now almost the norm.

Many studies make it clear that sleep deprivation is dangerous. Sleep-deprived people who are tested by using a driving simulator perform as badly as or worse than those who are intoxicated. Sleep deprivation also magnifies alcohol's effects on the body, so a fatigued person who drinks will become much more impaired than someone who is well rested. Since drowsiness is the brain's last step before falling asleep, driving while drowsy can lead to disaster. Caffeine and other stimulants cannot overcome the effects of severe sleep deprivation. The National Sleep Foundation says that if you have trouble keeping your eyes focused, if you can't stop yawning, or if you can't remember driving the last few miles, you are probably too drowsy to drive safely.

① To offer preventive measures for sleep deprivation
② To alert the signs and risks of not getting enough sleep
③ To discuss the effects of alcohol on a sleep-deprived person
④ To explain why sleeplessness is common in Western societies

16 What is the tone of this passage?

The role of second-hand smoke in causing disease has been under study for years. A mid-sized city in a western state unexpectedly added to our knowledge. Smoking in public and in workplaces was banned, and six months later the ban was lifted. During the time that smoking was prohibited in public places, the rate of hospital admissions for heart attacks was 24. During the typical six month period, the rate is 40 admissions. Researchers believe that this drop shows the negative effects of second-hand smoke. It adds to the body of evidence that second-hand smoke contributes to heart attacks by elevating the heart rate and decreasing the ability of blood vessels to dilate.

① elegiac
② repressive
③ challenging
④ informational

17 다음 글의 목적으로 가장 적절한 것은?

When you transport your goods internationally, several precautions must be taken to ensure proper shipment. Export shipments require greater handling than domestic transport and should be properly packaged and correctly documented so that they arrive safely and on time. You also need to make sure that breakable items are protected, and that other fragile goods will not be damaged by the stresses of air and ocean shipment, such as vibration and moisture.

You must first decide what mode of transport is best. When shipping within a continent, you may prefer land transportation. When shipping to another continent, the preferred method may be by sea or air. Although maritime shipping is generally less expensive than air, it can be much slower and thus less cost-effective. You should consider the additional costs of sea freight, such as surface transportation to and from the docks and port charges. Ocean freight can take longer than air freight and you may have to wait until the ship reaches its destination to receive payment.

① To inform freight forwarders about weight limitations
② To advise importers about insurance policies
③ To provide general information about shipping
④ To notify exporters about new safety measures
⑤ To help freight forwarders save money

18 The tone of the above passage can be described as ____________.

All science is subject to human bias. This is especially true for social scientists. Since human behavior is their area of study, they are actually part of the subject matter. Furthermore, human behavior patterns vary from one place to another and from one group to another. This is in contrast to the subject matter of the natural sciences. When a chemist studies hydrogen, he can assume that one hydrogen atom is very much like another, wherever it is found, and that the conditions surrounding it can be quite accurately controlled. The same is true when a physicist measures a metal bar; he can be quite sure that it will not stretch or shrink in length as long as natural conditions are the same. This is why Earl Babbie quotes economist Daniel Suits, who calls the natural sciences the “easy sciences” because of the predictable nature of their subject matter.

① critical
② objective
③ vindictive
④ cynical
⑤ ambivalent

19 What is the author's tone of the above passage?

A 19-year-old Detroit man was ordered Friday to stand trial in the non-fatal shooting of two city police officers who, according to his lawyer, the teen believed were burglars trying to break into his family's home. Judge Kenneth King said while he believes Juwan Plummer was "very much afraid" when he heard knocking on the door of his family's home in the late hours on April 16, the question is whether the teen had a "reasonable" belief that a break-in was underway. Citing Michigan case law, King said a trial judge will have to decide whether Plummer had a "reasonable" belief that he was in danger when he allegedly fired upon the officers after one of them approached the home in the 205 block of Lesure. The officers were responding to a report from someone in the home that a break-in was occurring at an unoccupied home across the street.

① impartial
② bigoted
③ impertinent
④ optimistic
⑤ wanton

20 다음 글의 목적으로 가장 적절한 것은?

Women have realized advances in the twentieth century. We have seen women involved politically, seeking — and obtaining — political office. In addition, women today are better educated than their sisters of the 19th century, a far greater number attending college. As a result, more and more women are entering the labor force. The relationship between men and women is undergoing profound changes as a result of the rise in women's status. A number of career women delayed marriage until they achieved professional success. Based on a recent study, these women have a greatly decreased chance of getting married after they reach thirty. Men are not willing to wait for women to finish their education and establish their careers. This is having a profound effect on the shape of modern marriage as well as the relationship between men and women. The change in women's status has made a drastic change in the way we live our lives today. While many of these changes are without doubt for the better of all, many feel a profound sense of loss, as the old realities give way to new truths.

① To illustrate the advantages of women's advancement in the twentieth century
② To argue that the rise in women's status has a negative influence on the relationship between men and women
③ To discuss the advantages and disadvantages of the change in women's status
④ To explain why women should actively participate in political office

LEVEL

2

에듀윌 편입

솔루션 독해 Basic

Reading

세부 내용 이해하기

4강 내용 일치 / 내용 추론

5강 내용 불일치 / 내용 비추론

6강 부분 이해 (지시어, 밑줄 추론)

7강 연결사 / 빈칸 추론

4강 내용 일치 / 내용 추론

예제 2020 한국외대

Never call back an unknown number because you could be opening the door to scammers. You might assume calling back is safe because a number is from your area code, but they are adept at faking phone numbers that come up on caller ID. Criminals purposely use familiar area codes to gain your trust. People are curious and thieves are counting on their victims to think they may have missed something important. At least, answering the phone or calling back increases your vulnerability to future scams because it confirms the number is attached to a real person willing to call back an unknown number. This tells scam artists they can use another ploy on another day. And at worst? Scammers could dupe you into giving out personal information. Even if they simply ask, "Can you hear me?" you should hang up. A recording of your answer, "Yes," can give them access to your bank, insurance, and other financial information. Just do not answer unknown numbers; remember that vital information will be left in your voicemail.

Q. According to the passage, which of the following is true?

① Criminals can record your answers to steal from you.
② The normal curiosity of people protects them from scammers.
③ People should make the effort to call back an unknown number.
④ Scammers cannot get your financial information if you answer briefly.

유형별 문제풀이 Point _ 내용 일치 / 내용 추론

Point 1 지문의 내용 파악하기

일치와 추론 문제의 가장 기본은 지문의 내용을 이해하고 파악하는 것이다. 따라서 지문을 읽고 지문의 전체적인 내용을 파악할 수 있는 어휘와, 구문 분석 능력이 필요하다.

Point  보기를 공략하기

각 보기를 비교하고 지문 내용과 가장 적합한 것을 고르는 것이 핵심이다.
보기의 내용을 정확히 파악하고 지문 내에서 각 보기가 언급된 곳을 찾아본다.

Point  글의 종류 파악하기

글이 주장하는 글이라면 일치와 추론의 보기는 글쓴이의 핵심 생각이 주로 들어가기 때문에 글의 주제를 파악해 보는 것이 중요하다.
글이 설명문이라면 글쓴이의 주장보다는 여러 가지 정보를 전달하기 때문에 보기들도 지문의 이곳저곳에 언급되어 있으므로 주의한다.

정답 

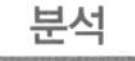

분석 마지막 부분에서 "제 목소리가 들립니까?"라는 질문에, 당신이 "네"라고 대답해 버리면 사기꾼들은 "네" 음성을 이용하여 당신의 은행, 보험, 금융 정보에 접근할 수 있게 한다고 했으므로 ①이 정답으로 적절하다.

어휘

scammer ⓝ 사기꾼, 난봉꾼 (= scam artist)
fake ⓥ 위조[날조/조작]하다
vulnerability ⓝ 약점이 있음, 취약성
dupe ... into ~ing …을 속여서 ~하게 하다
hang up 전화를 끊다
be adept at ~에 능숙하다
curious ⓐ 호기심 있는
ploy ⓝ 책략, 계획
give out 공개하다, 말해 버리다
access ⓝ 접근, 출입

해석 사기꾼에게 문을 열어 주는 일이 일어날 수 있으니 절대 모르는 전화번호로는 다시 전화하지 말라. 당신은 전화번호에 당신의 지역번호가 있어서 다시 전화를 거는 것이 문제가 안 된다고 생각할지도 모른다. 그러나 그들은 발신자 ID로 표시되는 전화번호를 인위적으로 조작하는 데 능숙하다. 범죄자들은 의도적으로 익숙한 지역번호를 사용하여 당신의 신뢰를 얻고자 한다. 사람들은 호기심이 많으며 도둑들의 입장에서는 피해자들이 중요한 것을 놓쳤을지도 모른다고 생각하기를 기대하고 있다. 적어도 전화를 받거나 전화를 다시 건다는 것은 자신에게 연결된 그 모르는 번호로 전화를 다시 걸려는 사람이 실제로 있다는 것을 확인시켜 주기 때문에 미래에 사기를 당할 취약함을 증가시킨다. 이것은 사기꾼들에게 그들이 또 다른 날에 다른 전략을 쓸 수 있다는 것을 말해 준다. 그리고 최악의 경우에는? 사기꾼들이 당신을 속여 당신의 개인 정보를 말해 버리게 할 수 있을 것이다. 사기꾼들이 단순히 "제 목소리가 들립니까?"라고 물어본다 해도 당신은 전화를 끊어야 한다. "네"라고 대답한 기록은 그들로 하여금 당신의 은행, 보험, 그리고 다른 금융 정보에 접근할 수 있게 만든다. 모르는 전화번호에 응답하지 말도록 하라. 당신이 보내는 음성 메시지에도 중요한 정보가 남겨질 것이라는 것을 기억하라.

정답과 해설 p.84

01 Which of the following is true of the passage?

A massive change occurred in the way that music was composed and played in the Romantic Period, from 1820 to 1910. Rather than being dependent on finance from patrons or employers, musicians were more independent. This gave them the opportunity to be more creative, so musical themes became more personal and emotional. Musicians also began experimenting with new techniques, developing more complex harmonies and rhythms in their compositions. Some even used new instruments like the clarinet and the piccolo to create totally new sounds.

① Patrons played an essential role in developing new musical themes in the Romantic Period.
② Employers in the Romantic Period encouraged musicians to be more independent and creative.
③ Music in the Romantic Period was characterized by the sophistication of ancient techniques.
④ Musicians in the Romantic Period had no scruples in experimenting with new instruments.

02 Which is true according to the passage?

I do not believe that genius is an entirely different thing from talent. I am not even sure that it depends on any great difference in the artist's natural gifts. For example, I do not think that Cervantes had an exceptional gift for writing; few people would deny him genius. Nor would it be easy in English literature to find a poet with a happier gift than Herrick and yet no one would claim that he had more than delightful talent. It seems to me that what makes genius is the combination of natural gifts for creation with an idiosyncrasy that enables its possessor to see the world personally in the highest degree and yet with such catholicity that his appeal is not to this type of man or to that type, but to all men. His private world is that of common men, but ampler and more pithy. He is supremely normal. By a happy accident of nature seeing life with immense vivacity, he sees it, with its infinite diversity, in the healthy way that mankind at large sees it. In other words, he sees life vigorously and sees it whole.

① Everyone believes Herrick is a genius with a charming talent for poetry.
② Most people agree that Cervantes is an unusually gifted writer, but not a genius.
③ A genius sees the world very personally but appeals to all kinds of men.
④ A genius does not need natural gifts but a strong, unique personality of the highest degree.

03 According to the passage, which is true?

If the democratic alternative to the totalitarian one-way broadcasts is a row of separate soapboxes, then I submit that the alternative is unworkable, is unreasonable, and is humanly unattractive. It is above all a false alternative. It is not true that liberty has developed among civilized men when anyone is free to set up a soapbox, is free to hire a hall where he may expound his opinions to those who are willing to listen. On the contrary, freedom of speech is established to achieve its essential purpose only when different opinions are expounded in the same hall to the same audience. For, while the right to talk may be the beginning of freedom, the necessity of listening is what makes the right important. What matters is not the utterance of opinions. What matters is the confrontation of opinions in debate. No man can care profoundly that every fool should say what he likes.

① There is no actual alternative to the totalitarian broadcasts.
② To get the freedom of speech, different opinions should be exposed in the same condition.
③ Separate soapboxes are the alternatives to totalitarianism.
④ To allow the freedom to speak one's own opinions is the most important thing.

04 Which of the following is true, according to the above passage?

Since our account of medieval architecture is mainly concerned with the development of style, we have until now confined our attention to religious structures, the most ambitious as well as the most representative efforts of the age. Secular building, indeed, reflects the same general trends, but these are often obscured by diversity of types, ranging from bridges to royal palaces, from barns to town halls. Moreover, social, economic, and practical factors play a more important part here than in church design, so that the useful life of the buildings is apt to be much briefer. As a consequence, our knowledge of secular structures of the pre-Gothic Middle Ages remains extremely fragmentary.

① Our account of religious structures is mainly concerned with their diverse types.
② Secular buildings are the most representative architecture in the medieval period.
③ The lifespan of secular buildings is much longer than that of religious ones.
④ Our knowledge about the secular structures of the Middle Ages is limited.

05 According to the passage, which of the following is true?

The Sears and Roebuck catalogue was a fixture in American society for many decades. Practically anything needed in the American home could be ordered through this comprehensive catalogue and delivered by mail. The catalogue made it easier for homeowners in urban areas to track down items they were trying to find; the catalogue was an absolute necessity for residents in out-of-the-way areas where many types of home supplies were not available for hundreds of miles.

In the early twentieth century, it was not just possible to buy home supplies from the Sears and Roebuck catalogue. It was actually possible to buy a mail-order house. If you ordered a house through the mail, you would receive all the necessary building materials as well as plans for constructing the house; all of this could be had for prices starting around $600.

① Items ordered through the catalogue had to be picked up at a Sears and Roebuck store.
② The average price of a mail-order house in the Sears and Roebuck catalogue was $600.
③ A mail-order house in the Sears and Roebuck catalogue needed to be assembled by the buyer.
④ Residents in remote areas could not afford most of the items in the Sears and Roebuck catalogue.

06 What can be inferred from the passage?

Dora was frustrated by a series of used cars she drove. It was she who commuted to work, but it was her husband, Hank, who chose the cars. Hank always went for cars that were "interesting", but in continual need of repair. After Dora was nearly killed when her brakes failed, they were in the market for yet another used car. Dora wanted to buy a late-model sedan from a friend. Hank fixed his sights on a 15-year-old sports car. She tried to persuade Hank that if made more sense to buy the boring but dependable car, but he would not be swayed.

Previously she would have acceded to his wishes. This time Dora bought the boring but dependable car and steeled herself for Hank's anger. To her amazement, he spoke not a word of remonstrance. When she later told him what she had expected, he scoffed at her fears and said she should have done what she wanted from the start if she felt that strongly about it.

① Dora is so pushy that Hank fears a confrontation with her.
② Dora used to avoid confrontation with Hank as to what car to buy.
③ Dora prefers walking to driving when going to work.
④ The couple are very close to Dora's friend whose car Dora wants to buy.

07 Which is true according to the passage?

Sigmund Freud never set out to be a psychologist. Much less did he see himself — until quite late in life — as contributing to the field of social psychology. He was simply a Viennese physician specializing in the treatment of nervous disorders. That this activity would lead him to fundamentally new ways of conceiving social behavior was little imagined by Freud when he took up this work.

In fact, Freud was already thirty years old before he began his private practice; and his reasons for doing so were originally more financial than scientific. After an engagement of four years, Freud married Martha Bernays in the fall of 1886. He needed to provide support for his parents as well as the new family he and his wife would be starting. It was at this time that Sigmund Freud, in search of improved financial security, embarked on his career as a private physician.

① In a way his financial situation forced Freud to be a private physician.
② Freud never saw himself as a contributor to the field of social psychology.
③ From the start Freud determined to be a pioneer in understanding human psyche.
④ Unfortunately Freud's marriage made him give up significant psychological researches.

08 Which of the following is true of the passage?

Languages spoken at high altitudes are more likely to contain a certain kind of sound using short bursts of air, according to a new study. "I had this hypothesis that certain sounds might be more common at high altitudes," said study author Everett. "When I actually looked at the data, the distribution was pretty overwhelming," he said. Using an online database that categorizes languages based on their features, Everett analyzed the locations of about 600 of the world's 7,000 languages. He found that 92 of the languages contained ejective consonants. Ejectives are sounds produced with an intensive burst of air and are not found in English. Moreover, most of the languages containing ejectives were spoken in, or near, five out of six high-altitude regions around the world. Ejectives are easier to produce at high altitudes because air pressure decreases with altitude, and it takes less effort to compress less-dense air. But there is one high-altitude region where the spoken languages did not contain ejectives: the Tibetan plateau. People there have a unique adaptation to high altitude that may account for this fact.

① Ejectives are easy to pronounce for native speakers of English.
② The decrease of air pressure can facilitate the pronunciation of ejectives.
③ There are no high elevation regions where ejectives are absent.
④ Ejectives are very common in languages around the world.

09 Which of the following can be inferred from the passage?

A holiday break is supposed to be just that — a break — and staying off your email and SNS can actually make you more productive when you come back. While unplugging feels great during your break, it can also make you feel in over your head when you get back to work. To avoid feeling frazzled on that first morning, get a head start while you are still on break. You should give yourself fifteen minutes to go through your messages the night before returning to alleviate a lot of anxiety on your first day back. Remember to limit yourself to that short chunk so you will not be concentrating on work when you are supposed to be relaxing. When you get into your office, you should not assume everyone else is rejuvenated. A week off work is supposed to be a stress-free time, but it does not always work out. You might be refreshed and ready to go, but your coworkers might still be burned out from hosting out-of-town relatives. Get a feel for what your colleagues' breaks were really like by specifically asking what they did for themselves over the holidays. And finally, take some time to transition from holiday mode to work mode. The night before the workweek starts again, lay out your office clothes and prepare for the next day. This prompts you to get ready for work.

① It is helpful to frequently check SNS for important messages.
② Asking about your colleagues' breaks is considered impolite.
③ It is a good idea to be mentally prepared to return to work after a holiday.
④ Hosting your relatives during the holidays reduces anxiety and stress.

10 What is inferred from the passage?

Phantom traffic jams, in which cars suddenly screech to a dead stop on highways for no apparent reason, have long annoyed drivers. Interestingly, MIT researchers have recently offered a solution to help alleviate this stop-and-go driving. The logic is rather simple: The problem is inherent in our way of driving a car. If one car suddenly brakes, the car behind it has to brake and the car behind it has to brake. The braking increases with distance until a car actually stops. Dr. Hornstein, professor at MIT's Computer Science and Artificial Intelligence Laboratory, proposes redesigning the cruise control feature on our car to consider the space in front and behind the vehicle. To be sure, there are advanced cruise control systems on the market today that will adapt to the speed of a lead vehicle in order to maintain a steady following distance. But the gap between the vehicle and a trailing car isn't considered. Keeping the same distance between the vehicle in front and the vehicle trailing a car would prevent traffic jams. The technical name proposed for the traffic-busting technology is bilateral control.

① Traffic jams could be solved by redesigned cruise control.
② Undesirable driving habits often cause highway traffic jams.
③ Research results show that highway traffic is beyond our control.
④ Traditional cruise control may increase vehicle crashes.

11 Which of the following is true of the passage?

Scientists are interested in how the brain grows and ages. Before a child is two years old, there is a surge in brain growth and development. During these early years, billions of new neurons are added to the body. Each one is connected to thousands of others, making trillions of connections. However, after the age of three, a new process begins. The connections that are used a lot remain strong and survive. Connections that are not used a lot become weak and are lost. For example, one child who is given books to read at an early age may learn to read by the age of four. On the other hand, a child who is not given any books to read at an early age may have trouble learning to read. This process continues, and our brains remain sensitive to stimulation and experience into old age. Older people who stay physically and mentally active can still make and keep neural connections.

① Aging can make neural connections stronger.
② An aged person cannot make new neural connections.
③ Brain development does not occur at a uniform rate.
④ Neural connections begin to form robustly after the age of three.

12 다음 글로부터 추론할 수 있는 것은?

Happiness is never more than partial. There are no pure states of mankind. What the Founding Fathers declared for us as an inherent right, we should do well to remember, was not happiness but the *pursuit* of happiness. What they might have underlined, could they have foreseen the happiness-market, is the cardinal fact that happiness is in the pursuit of itself, in the meaningful pursuit of what is life-engaging and life-revealing.

① There is such a thing as perfect happiness.
② People may be of the illusion that happiness can be bought.
③ According to the Founding Fathers, happiness is an inherent right.
④ Whatever else happiness may be, it is neither in having nor in being, but in becoming.

13 다음 글의 내용과 가장 부합하는 것은?

A word of encouragement for my working moms: You are actually more productive than your childless peers. Over the course of a 30-year career, mothers outperformed women without children at almost every stage of the game. In fact, mothers with at least two kids were the most productive of all. Here's how the researchers (all men, by the way) came up with those results: They wanted to understand the impact of having children on highly-skilled women, but their work is often difficult to quantify. How do you determine the productivity of a surgeon or a project manager? They decided to analyze the amount of research published by more than 10,000 academic economists as a proxy for performance. A job in the ivory tower of academia requires higher education by definition, and their work is easily searched, recorded, and ranked.

① The productivity of a project manager can be easily quantified and analyzed.
② Mothers of one child outperformed those with two or more children.
③ This study did not include mothers whose work was irrelevant to academia.
④ The research team that conducted this study was comprised mostly of women.
⑤ Mothers with children published a less amount of research than childless women.

14 Which of the following is true according to the passage?

The art of advertising contains many ambiguities. Some are charged with multiple shades of meaning. The demons may be taken to represent the problems and cares which one can presumably chase away through consumption of the advertised product. Or they can, just as easily, be taken as representations of the playful spirits which will be unleashed once the product has been consumed. The advertising creative director did not create the need to relax, or to get away from the stresses of daily life; he or she merely took advantage of these common human needs in developing a promotion strategy for the product.

① The advertisement should have a transparent point to show off.
② An image in advertisements can have different meanings according to the context.
③ The advertisement should lessen the stresses of consumers.
④ An image in advertisements should have a focus on which a consumer's need is fixed.

15 다음 글의 내용과 맞는 것은?

The 1930s had a devastating impact on American agriculture. The Great Depression coupled with a prolonged drought and dust storms in the nation's heartland spurred an exodus of displaced farmers to nearby cities or to the promised land of California. John Steinbeck's novel *The Grapes of Wrath* (1939) and a popular film based on the book captured their plight, tracing a dispossessed family's trek from Oklahoma to California. Before the book appeared, Steinbeck had written a series of newspaper articles based on interviews with local migrants, later gathered in a book, *The Harvest Gypsies*.

① *The Grapes of Wrath* was written prior to the newspaper articles.
② Displaced farmers migrated to urban areas solely because of the Great Depression.
③ The nation's heartland experienced a prolonged drought and dust storms in the 1930s.
④ *The Harvest Gypsies* was based on a dispossessed family's journey from Oklahoma to California.

16 What can be inferred from the passage?

An economist addressed the nature-nurture debate by taking a long-term quantitative look at the effects of parenting. He used three adoption studies, each of them containing in-depth data about the adopted children, their adoptive parents, and their biological parents. The researcher found that parents who adopt children are typically smarter, better educated, and more highly paid than the baby's biological parents. But the adoptive parents' advantages had little bearing on the child's school performance. Adopted children test relatively poorly in school; any influence the adoptive parents might exert is seemingly outweighed by the force of genetics. However, the researcher found the parents were not powerless forever. By the time the adopted children became adults, they had veered sharply from the destiny that IQ alone might have predicted. Compared to similar children who were not put up for adoption, the adoptees were far more likely to attend college and to have a well-paid job. It was the influence of the adoptive parents, the researcher concluded, that made the difference.

① The debate on nature versus nurture is outdated and unhelpful.
② Genetic factors may affect some children more strongly than others.
③ The influence of genes and environment may surface at different life stages.
④ Adopted children are not optimal subjects for examining environmental influence.

17 According to the passage, which of the following is true?

The Red Cross estimates that 6.8 million people donate blood in the U.S. every year, giving approximately 13.6 million units of blood. The earliest known human-to-human blood donation came in 1818, before humans even knew what blood types were, when obstetrician James Blundell transferred blood to a woman who had just given birth. Having watched many patients die in childbirth, Blundell wrote that his experimental procedure stemmed from being appalled at his own helplessness. For the rest of the century, scientists experimented with blood transfer. Not all of these ideas were successful — some advocated infusing humans with cow's milk, which was considered superior to actual blood. From 1873 through 1880, the milk-for-blood trend swept through the U.S. Thankfully, soon an Austrian biologist would make a discovery that would change everything. In 1901, Karl Landsteiner realized that foreign bodies were broken up in the human bloodstream by hemoglobin in human-to-human blood transfers. In 1909, when Landsteiner first classified human blood into types, his work really took off. These groups are what are known today as A, B, AB, and O.

① Nearly fourteen million Americans donate blood every year.
② Landsteiner took off work in 1909 in order to develop transfers.
③ Blundell felt aghast at his inability to prevent women from dying in childbirth.
④ Blood transfers currently disregard the groups that Landsteiner discovered.

18 다음 글의 내용과 일치하는 것은?

People from cultures on polychronic time live their lives quite differently than do those who move to the monochronic clock. The pace for P-time cultures is more leisurely than the one found in M-time cultures. One reason for this is that people and human relationships, not tasks, are at the center of polychronic cultures. These cultures are normally collective and deal with life in a holistic manner. For P-time cultures, time is less tangible; hence, feelings of wasted time are not as prevalent as in M-time cultures. Their members can interact with more than one person or do more than one thing at a time, while people from M-time cultures suppress spontaneity and tend to focus on one activity at a time. This explains why there are more interruptions in conversations carried on by people from Arabic, Asian, and Latin American cultures compared to the ones from Germany, Austria, Switzerland, and the U.S.

① Feelings of wasted time are more prevalent in P-time cultures.
② People in polychronic cultures can do multiple things simultaneously.
③ People in monochronic cultures think highly of relationships with others.
④ Arabic, Asian, and Latin American cultures are categorized as M-time cultures.

19 Select the statement most consistent with the passage.

Physiognomists study such features as the shape of the head, the length and thickness of the neck, the color and thickness of the hair, and the shape of the nose, mouth, eyes, and chin. They believe that round-faced people are self-confident. Prominent cheekbones show strength of character, while a pointed nose reveals curiosity. A related — though not as ancient — art is phrenology, the study of the bumps on the head. Phrenologists have identified 40 bumps of various shapes and sizes on the human head. They read these bumps to identify a person's talents and character. For example, a bump between the nose and forehead is said to be present in people who have natural elegance and a love of beauty. Phrenologists are not so much interested in health as they are in character and personality. They believe, for example, that a bulge in the center of the forehead is typical of people who have a good memory and a desire for knowledge.

① Phrenologists study people's appearances and how it affects their physical and mental health.
② Physiognomy differs from phrenology in that physiognomists predict people's future by reading their physical features.
③ It is not possible to understand a person's talents or personality without knowing all of the information about the body parts.
④ According to phrenology, there are forty different parts of the human head that show a person's talents and character.

20 What can be most likely inferred from the above passage?

Most obviously, cheaper energy prices will incrementally increase the temptation to fritter away precious power — to leave the car engine idling, or to fail to go upstairs to switch off that light. Little habits matter, because, with the clock ticking remorselessly down towards climate catastrophe, every little hurts. How much damage the great oil crash will do here depends on what happens next. In the past, the world has been stunned not only by the waning but also the waxing of the price. If what comes down soon goes back up, such direct effects may not prove so profound. What will matter more in the longer term is the dynamic effect on the energy infrastructure.

① Cheap oil will discourage investment in alternative energy.
② High energy prices will help to push inflation lower.
③ Manufacturers of electric cars will expand their production lines.
④ Oil-exporters will be the obvious winners from sliding oil prices.
⑤ The most exploitative schemes to extract fossil fuels will become more economic.

5강 내용 불일치 / 내용 비추론

예제

2020 건국대

Girls generally speak sooner, learn to read faster and have fewer learning disorders. The reason, according to Yale University professors of neurology, may be that they use neural regions on both sides of the brain when they read or engage in other verbal exercise. In contrast, males draw only on neural regions in the left hemisphere.

This approach may give women an advantage by allowing them to draw on the emotions and experiences of the right brain as well as the reasoning powers of the logical left brain. As adults, women tend to be more verbally adept than men: in timed tests, women think of more words that start with the same letter, list more synonyms and come up with names for colors or shapes more quickly than men. Women even memorize letters of the alphabet faster.

But the female brain's dual-hemisphere language processing provides far more significant benefit: It helps women who suffer stroke or brain injury recover more easily. "Because women activate a larger number of neurons than men when they speak or read, they're less vulnerable if part of the brain is damaged," says a neurologist. "In medicine, we've observed that women who have strokes tend to regain more of their verbal abilities than men do, and their use of neurons in both hemispheres may be why."

Q. 윗글의 내용과 일치하지 않는 것은?

① 언어활동을 할 때 여성들은 뇌의 양 측면을 사용한다.
② 여성들은 남성들보다 알파벳 글자들을 더 빨리 암기한다.
③ 여자아이들은 남자아이들보다 일반적으로 더 일찍 말을 시작한다.
④ 남성들은 말할 때 여성들보다 더 많은 수의 뉴런이 활성화된다.
⑤ 여성들은 뇌가 손상되더라도 남성들보다 회복이 용이하다.

유형별 문제풀이 Point _ 내용 불일치 / 내용 비추론

Point 1 보기를 공략하기

불일치, 비추론 문제는 보기 중 하나의 보기만이 잘못된 정보이기 때문에 나머지 보기는 지문의 내용과 맞는 보기이다. 따라서 보기를 먼저 읽어서 지문의 전반적 내용을 미리 파악해 본다.

Point  지문 내용 파악하기

지문을 읽어 가며 각각의 보기에 있는 내용이 지문의 어느 부분에 언급되어 있는지 찾아보고 지문과 불일치하는 보기를 찾아본다.

Point  자주 나오는 불일치, 비추론 보기 익히기

편입 독해의 불일치, 비추론 보기들이 어떤 식으로 많이 나오는지 학습해 본다.
일반화의 오류, 숫자, 날짜, 비교의 오류, 지나친 논리적 비약 등 불일치, 비추론 보기의 패턴을 파악한다.

정답 ④

분석 지문의 마지막 단락에서 한 신경학자는 "여성들이 말을 하거나 읽을 때 남성들보다 더 많은 수의 뉴런을 활성화시키기 때문에, 뇌의 일부가 손상된다 해도 그 손상에 덜 취약합니다."라고 언급했다. 따라서 보기 ④ '남성들은 말할 때 여성들보다 더 많은 수의 뉴런이 활성화된다.'는 지문의 내용과 일치하지 않는다.

어휘

neurology ⓝ 신경(병)학	neural ⓐ 신경(계)의
engage in ~에 관여[참여]하다	verbal ⓐ 언어[말]의
synonym ⓝ 동의어, 유의어	come up with ~을 떠올리다, ~을 생각해 내다
memorize ⓥ 기억하다, 암기하다	stroke ⓝ 뇌졸중
vulnerable ⓐ 취약한, 연약한	regain ⓥ 되찾다

해석 여자아이들이 일반적으로 말을 (남자아이들보다) 더 일찍 시작하며, 읽는 법을 더 빨리 배우고, 학습 장애는 더 적다. 예일대학교 신경과 교수들에 따르면, 그 이유는 여자아이들이 글을 읽거나 혹은 말하는 것과 관련된 다른 활동을 할 때 양쪽 뇌 모두의 신경 영역을 사용하기 때문일지도 모른다고 말한다. 그와 대조적으로 남자들은 오직 왼쪽 뇌의 신경 영역만을 사용한다.

이러한 접근법은 여성들로 하여금 논리적인 좌뇌의 추리력뿐만 아니라 우뇌의 감정과 경험도 이용을 허락함으로써 여성들에게 (남성보다) 더 유리한 이점을 제공할 것이다. 성인인 여성들은 남성들보다 언어에 더 능숙한 경향이 있다. 시간이 정해져 있는 테스트에서, 여성들은 남성들보다 같은 글자로 시작하는 단어들을 더 많이 생각해 내며, 더 많은 동의어를 나열하며, 색 또는 모양의 이름을 더 빨리 떠올린다. 여성들은 심지어 알파벳 글자를 더 빨리 외우기도 한다.

그러나 여성의 뇌의 이중반구(뇌 이용) 언어 처리는 훨씬 더 큰 이점을 제공하는데, 그것은 뇌졸중이나 뇌 손상을 입은 여성이 더 쉽게 회복될 수 있도록 돕는다. "여성들이 말을 하거나 읽을 때 남성들보다 더 많은 수의 뉴런을 활성화시키기 때문에 뇌의 일부가 손상된다 해도 그 손상에 덜 취약합니다. 의학계에서 우리는 뇌졸중을 앓고 있는 여성들이 남성들보다 언어 능력을 더 많이 회복하는 경향이 있다는 것을 관찰했는데 양쪽 뇌 모두의 뉴런을 사용하는 것이 그 이유일지도 모릅니다."라고 한 신경학자는 말한다.

정답과 해설 p.108

01 What CANNOT be inferred from the above passage?

In February of 1950, a US senator Joseph McCarthy publicly claimed that thousands of Americans were alleged to be communists; such accusations were frequently deemed valid even with unsubstantiated or questionable evidence. Scant members of the press dared challenge McCarthy, but Edward R. Murrow was an exception. On his TV show, he confronted the communist witch-hunt that was taking place. Murrow revealed to his public that the true threat to democracy was not the supposed Communists, but rather the way in which McCarthy had acted. Murrow articulated this in his tailpiece: "The line between investigating and persecuting is a very fine one. We must not confuse dissent with disloyalty."

① There were plenty of false accusations about the communist initiated by McCarthy.
② McCarthy was challenged by a considerable members of the press.
③ Murrow directly voiced condemnation of the Communist witch-hunt.
④ Murrow insisted on the necessity of proof before declaring guilt.

02 Which of the following is NOT true about snakes?

Unlike mammals and birds, snakes cannot generate body heat through the digestion of food. They must depend on external sources of heat, such as sunlight, to maintain body temperature. Temperature control is particularly important when snakes are digesting a meal, or in the case of females, reproducing. Many snakes increase the amount of time spent basking in the sun after they have eaten a large meal in order to speed up the digestive process. To conserve their heat, snakes coil up tightly, so that only a small portion of their skin is exposed to cooler air.

① They usually get heat by lying in sunlight.
② They coil their bodies in order to stay warm.
③ Food is an important source of their body heat.
④ Maintaining body temperature is important for digestion.

03 Which of the statements following the passage is NOT true?

The greatest problem for conservationists is that, while we can make laws to protect certain species, we are frequently incapable of controlling the environment in which they live and breed. In spite of taking action to prevent it, we may pollute rivers, making fish sterile. However good our intentions are in destroying insects that eat crops, at the same time, we deprive the birds that live on them. Man has not yet learned how to deal with the balance of nature, and whatever he does, he is bound to alter it without even knowing. But though it may not be possible to save all the endangered species, it may be possible to protect the majority by becoming aware of their serious condition before it is too late.

① We are not able to control the environment.
② We cannot protect our crops from insects without harming the birds.
③ Man has already learned how to deal with the balance of nature.
④ We cannot expect to rescue all of the endangered animals from dying out.

04 Which of the following is not true according to the passage?

For those of us who like to create controlled flame from time to time with the strike of a match, we can thank a British pharmacist and his dirty mixing stick. In 1826, John Walker noticed a dried lump on the end of a stick while he was stirring a mix of chemicals. When he tried to scrape it off, voila, sparks and flame. Jumping on the discovery, Walker marketed the first friction matches as "Friction Lights" and sold them at his pharmacy. The initial matches were made of cardboard but he soon replaced those with three-inch long hand-cut wooden splints. The matches came in a box equipped with a piece of sandpaper for striking. Although advised to patent his invention, he chose not to because he considered the product a benefit to mankind — which didn't stop others from ripping off the idea and taking over the market share, leading Walker to stop producing his version.

① Matches were invented by a British pharmacist.
② The invention of matches was by accident.
③ The first matches were made of wooden splints.
④ John Walker did not patent his invention.

05 According to the passage, which of the following is NOT true?

Numerous paintings of meals show what dining tables looked like before the seventeenth century. Forks were not included until about 1600, and very few spoons were shown. At least one knife was always depicted — an especially large one when it was the only one available for all the guests — but small individual knives were often at each place. Tin disks had already replaced the large wooden plates. This change in eating utensils typified the new table manners in Europe. In many other parts of the world, no utensils at all were used. In the Near East, for example, it was traditional to eat with the fingers of the right hand. Utensils were employed in part because of a change in the attitude toward meat. During the Middle Ages, whole sides of meat, or even an entire carcass, had been brought to the table and then carved in view of the diners. Beginning in the seventeenth century, at first in France but later elsewhere, the practice began to go out of fashion. One reason was that the family was decreasing in size and ceasing to be a production unit that did its own slaughtering; as that function was transferred to specialists outside the home, the family became essentially a consumption unit.

① Up to 1600 a meal scene was a frequent subject for painters.
② Forks were portrayed in paintings before knives and spoons.
③ The seventeenth century witnessed a change in the number of family members.
④ In the Middle Ages, a whole dead animal might have been served at the table.

06 Which statement CANNOT be inferred from each passage below?

In the last decades of the eighteenth century, and in the first half of the nineteenth century, a number of words came for the first time into common English use or acquired new and important meanings. There is a general pattern of change in these words, which can be used as a special kind of map by which to look at wider changes in life. Five words are the key points from which this map can be drawn. They are *industry*, *democracy*, *class*, *art*, and *culture*. The changes in their use, at this critical period, bear witness to a general shift in our characteristic ways of thinking about common life; about social, political, and economic institutions; and about the educational and artistic purposes which these institutions are designed to embody.

① Epistemic shifts in societies reverberate etymologically.
② Democracy was disparaged until the second half of the eighteenth century.
③ Semantic configurations transform diachronically within a culture.
④ The period from the late eighteenth to the early nineteenth century marks a watershed in English history.

07 Which statement CANNOT be inferred from each passage below?

In vitro fertilization does not contribute to developmental delays up to age 3, according to a new study. As many couples who use IVF to have children are older, for example, other factors can affect fetal development. The study showed that developmental delays were not more prevalent among children conceived through IVF. The new study also said children conceived through IVF were not at greater risk with full-blown developmental disabilities such as learning disabilities, speech or language disorders, or autism. The researchers found no significant difference between IVF and non-treatment groups of children with developmental delays — 13 percent of children conceived with IVF had a delay, while 18 percent of those not conceived with treatment had a delay.

① IVF is not one of the factors in neonatal developmental delays.
② The IVF industry has been disrupted by parental perturbations.
③ IVF is not more precarious than other factors for fetal development.
④ The age of parents can be germane to the health of their child.

08 다음 글의 내용과 일치하지 않는 것은?

We can observe that questions such as “Which language do you speak?” or “Which dialect do you speak?” may be answered quite differently by people who appear to speak in an identical manner. Many regions of the world provide plenty of evidence for a puzzling array of language and dialect divisions. Surely socio-cultural factors play a role in determining boundaries. Hindi and Urdu in India, Fanti and Twi in West Africa, Kechwa and Aimara in Peru, to name just a few, are recognized as discrete languages both popularly and in law, yet they are almost identical at the level of grammar. On the other hand, the literary and colloquial forms of Arabic used in Iraq, Morocco, and Egypt, or the Welsh of North and South Wales are grammatically quite separate, yet only one language is recognized in each case.

① Urdu는 인도에서 사용되는 언어 가운데 하나이다.
② 서아프리카 지역의 Fanti와 Twi는 문법이 거의 같다.
③ 이라크와 모로코의 아랍어는 회화체에서 매우 유사하다.
④ 웨일스 지방에서는 공식적으로 하나의 언어만이 존재한다.
⑤ 문법체계가 언어의 경계를 결정하는 유일한 요인은 아니다.

09 Which is NOT true according to the passage?

Capital is money that is invested in order to make more money. By extension the term capital is often used to refer to money that is available for investment or, indeed, any asset that can be readily turned into money for it. Thus, a person's house is often described as their capital, because they can turn it into capital either by selling it or by borrowing on the strength of it. Many small businesses are indeed set up in this way. It is, however, only possible to turn property into capital if its ownership is clearly established, its value can be measured, its title can be transferred, and a market exists for it. A characteristic feature of the development of capitalist societies is the emergence of institutions that enable the conversion of assets of all kinds into capital. Hernando de Soto has argued persuasively that it is the absence of these institutions, not to mention functioning systems of property law, that frustrates the emergence of local capitalisms in the Third World. He claims that an enormous amount of value that is located up in property cannot therefore be realized and put by entrepreneurs to productive use.

① Businesses, small or big, are always set up with bank loans.
② When money is used to gain more money, the money is capital.
③ In the Third Wold huge amount of value is locked up in property.
④ A capitalist society requires functioning systems of property law.

10 다음 글의 내용과 일치하는 않는 것은?

Plastic bags were found in the digestive systems of more than 400 leatherback turtles. The leatherback turtle is a critically endangered species. Jellyfish is their main diet. Mistaking the increased amounts of plastic bags drifting in the currents for drifting jellyfish is causing the leather backs harm. Plastic bags account for 12 percent of all marine debris, and plastic bottles and plastic caps and lids are also prevalent at six and eight percent respectively. Marine litter is one of the most pervasive and solvable pollution problems plaguing the world's oceans and waterways. A simple solution to the plastic bag issue is reusable shopping bags. An increased awareness of the effects of plastic bags has caused many states and countries to implement plastic bag related legislation. For example, when Ireland imposed a fee on each plastic bag used by consumers, single-use consumption dropped by 90 percent.

① 바다 장수거북의 소화기관에서 플라스틱이 발견되었다.
② 바다 장수거북은 멸종 위기종에 속한다.
③ 플라스틱병은 전체 해양 쓰레기의 6퍼센트를 차지한다.
④ 해양 오염은 해결이 거의 불가능하다.
⑤ 아일랜드에서는 플라스틱 봉투를 사용할 때 수수료를 내야 한다.

11 Which statement cannot be inferred from the passage?

Whereas beef and chicken appear in many New Mexican recipes, in Massachusetts, fish is very popular because of the nearby seacoast. New England is famous for its clam chowder, lobster, cod, scallops, and fish cakes. English herbs and spices are the seasonings used in New England dishes, which might taste rather bland to people accustomed to hot and spicy New Mexican food. Each region of the United States is unique. Louisiana has a French influence. Many Germans populate the Midwest. In traveling around America, a tourist has the opportunity not only to visit a variety of places and see diverse landscapes, but to taste a variety of foods as well.

① One may taste authentic German sausages and beers in the Midwest.
② Food in Massachusetts has been influenced by its geographical conditions.
③ It is uncommon to find top-quality beef dishes in New England.
④ Beef and chicken are frequently used in a traditional meal in New Mexico.

12 Which of the following is NOT stated about SPIN?

There are many ways technology simplifies life, but it also brings its own new complications. Many of our nifty devices need remote controllers, which end up cluttering our brains and our living rooms. Why do we need 50 buttons to control our environment? Do we really need five remotes to turn devices on and off?

The makers of the new SPIN Remote say the answer is "no," and they want to bring simplicity back into your life. SPIN is a universal remote in theory, but it is even more intuitive; you just turn it. The ultra-sensitive motion sensor in it, shaped like a knob, works when you rotate it, in the same way you would turn a doorknob or the key in your car's ignition. With a spin of the SPIN, you can control the volume of a movie, fast-forward or rewind a TV show, or turn your devices, such as stereos, on and off. You can even use it to dim or brighten smart lighting by simply pointing the remote at a lamp.

① It is a remote used for multiple devices.
② It can be used to adjust lamp brightness.
③ It is similar to a car key in appearance.
④ It has a sensor working by rotational motion.

13 다음 글의 내용과 가장 부합하지 않는 것은?

The Louvre Museum is one of the world's largest museums. Nearly 35,000 objects from prehistory to the 21st century are exhibited over an area of 652,300 square feet. The Louvre is the world's most visited museum, and received over 9.7 million visitors in 2014. The museum is housed in the Louvre Palace, originally built as a fortress in the 12th century. Remnants of the fortress are still visible in the basement of the museum. The building was extended many times to form the present Louvre Palace. The museum opened on August 10th, 1793 with an exhibition of 437 paintings, the majority of the works being confiscated church property. Because of structural problems, the museum was closed in 1796 until 1801. The collection was increased under Napoleon and the museum was renamed the Musee Napoleon, but after Napoleon's abdication, many works seized by his armies were returned to their original owners. The collection was increased during the Second Empire; the museum gained 25,000 pieces. Holdings have grown steadily through donations since the Third Republic.

① The Louvre has been extended to house more collections, and it is now a very large building in size.
② When the Louvre first opened, the exhibition was only composed of a few hundreds of paintings.
③ The Louvre Palace was built as a fortress, and its remnants are displayed in the museum's basement.
④ Napoleon's armies seized many collections, but they were later returned to their original owners.

14 Which is NOT true according to the passage?

Back in 1967, Scottish inventor John Shepherd-Barron thought getting cash should be as easy as getting a chocolate bar. He is credited with pioneering the first cash machine or ATM in a Barclays Bank in London, UK. But the difficulties lay in ensuring that you were who you said you were.

To prevent problems, Shepherd-Barron developed a special type of paper cheque that acted as a precursor to the debit cards we have today. Each cheque would cause his cash machine to request a personal identification number — or PIN — that only the account holder knew. Shepherd-Barron was going to make the machine require a six-digit PIN, but he was overruled ... by his wife. She believed that six digits were two too many to remember, and four became the standard.

① It was in the end Shepherd-Barron's wife who decided that PIN should be four digits.
② Shepherd-Barron thought earning money should be as easy as eating a chocolate bar.
③ Identification of the account holder was a main problem in introducing the cash machine.
④ A special type of paper cheque developed by Shepherd-Barron was a primitive type of the debit card.

15 Which of the following CANNOT be inferred from the above passage?

In medical usage, a "placebo" is a treatment that has no specific physical or chemical action on the condition being treated, but is given to affect symptoms by a psychologic mechanism, rather than a purely physical one. Ethicists believe that placebos necessarily involve a partial or complete deception by the doctor, since the patient is allowed to believe that the treatment has a specific effect. They seem unaware that placebos, far from being inert (except in the rigid pharmacological sense), are among the most powerful agents known to medicine. It can strengthen the weak or paralyze the strong, transform sleeping, feeding, or sexual patterns, remove or induce a vast array of symptoms, mimic or abolish the effect of very powerful drugs. It can even alter the functions of most organs.

① "Placebo" is a medical treatment based on the patient's psychology.
② Some people believe that "placebo" is wrong because it is a lie.
③ "Placebo" is actually an effective method to some patients.
④ "Placebo" has no effect on the patient's physical conditions.
⑤ The writer of the passage supports the use of "placebo."

16 Choose the statement that is not true according to each passage.

There's been a 33 percent jump in the number of medication-related poisonings in children ages 5 and younger since 2000, according to a recent study from Nationwide Children's Hospital in Ohio. This may be due to an increase in drugs in people's homes. Opioid painkillers, like Percocet, caused the most deaths and other severe outcomes, followed by over-the-counter cough and cold medications and pain relievers. "No bottle is childproof," says study author Henry Spiller. "Keep all drugs out of reach or locked up." If you think your child has ingested medication, call the National Poison Control hotline at 800–222–1222 immediately.

① Medication-related poisonings occurred to children at the age of 5 and under.
② One reason for medication-related poisonings in children lies in more drugs kept in homes.
③ Opioid painkillers cause medication-related poisonings.
④ It was over-the-counter cough drugs that resulted in the most deaths of children.
⑤ National Poison Control handles the problem with children's medication-related poisonings.

17 According to the passage, which of the following is NOT true?

Reggae is a music genre that originated in Jamaica in the late 1960s. A 1968 single "Do the Reggay" was the first popular song to use the word, effectively naming the genre and introducing it to a global audience. While sometimes used in a broad sense to refer to most types of popular Jamaican dance music, the term 'reggae' more properly denotes a particular music style that was strongly influenced by traditional *mento* as well as American jazz and R&B. Reggae is instantly recognizable from the counterpoint between the bass guitar and drum downbeat, and the offbeat rhythm section. It is common for reggae to be sung in Jamaican dialect and Jamaican English. Reggae has spread around the world, often incorporating local instruments and fusing with other genres. For instance, Caribbean music in the United Kingdom, including reggae, has been popular since the late 1960s, and has evolved into several subgenres and fusions. In Jamaica, authentic reggae is one of the biggest sources of income.

① Authentic reggae earns Jamaicans a lot of money.
② Reggae music has emerged without international influence.
③ Reggae lyrics are rarely written in American English.
④ There are many different types of reggae across the world.

18 Which of the following is NOT correct?

Writing is hard to see because it governs our thought, and hard to talk about because of the lack of consistent names for real categories. We know that writing is there to be read, but are not sure what we mean by "writing," so that it is fashionable in criticism to "read" works of art, to "read" Greek culture or manners of dress or almost anything, as if in understanding a work of art or a building or a social practice we are doing the same thing as when we read a text. Writing has been defined again and again, always in different ways, but let us say that writing is a system of markings with a conventional reference that communicates information, like the signs on this text. Where does such a definition take us?

Because writing is made up of markings it is material (not spiritual or emotional or mental). The meaning of such markings, their conventional reference, we might say their intellectual dimension, never comes from nature, nor from God (as many have believed), but from man. The elements of writing, the markings, are related in an organized way, in a conventional way, in order to tell the reader something, to communicate with the reader. Where there is writing there is a reader who understands the system of conventions, even if the reader is God or a god.

① Writing is a conventional way to communicate with the reader.
② Writing is spiritual and abstract in its nature.
③ Man, not God, creates writing.
④ There is always a reader who understands the system of writing.

19 다음 글의 내용과 일치하지 않는 것은?

Perhaps no musical innovation has generated as much puzzlement, dismay, and anger among its critics as rap music, which was popular in some urban African-American and Latino communities for years before becoming nationally visible beginning in the early 1980s. Unlike many earlier forms of black music that have attracted broad audiences, rap has relatively little melodic content. Indeed, many rap songs use almost identical musical and instrumental elements — sometimes even literally identical elements. Rap recordings often copy pieces of instrumental backgrounds from other recordings through a technique known as "sampling." Rap's most important element is its words. It is as much a form of language as a form of music.

① Rap caused anger among its singers.
② Rap recordings often borrow melodic content from other recordings.
③ Rap's words are more important than its melody.
④ Rap is one form of African-American music.
⑤ One of rap's common techniques is sampling.

20 Which is NOT true according to the passage?

Pizza is certainly one of the world's favorite foods. But where does pizza come from? And who made the first one?

In fact, people have been making pizza for a very long time. People in the Stone Age cooked grains on hot rocks to make dough — the basic ingredient of pizza. Over time, people used the dough as a plate, covering it with various other foods, herbs, and spices. They had developed the world's first pizza.

In the early 16th century, European explorers brought back the first tomatoes from the Americas. Tomatoes are a standard ingredient in many pizzas today. At first, however, most Europeans thought they were poisonous. For about 200 years, few people ate them. Slowly, people learned that tomatoes were safe to eat, as well as tasty. In the early 19th century, cooks in Naples, Italy, started the tradition of putting tomatoes on baking dough. The flat bread soon became popular with poor people all over Naples. In 1830, cooks in Naples took another bit step in pizza history — they opened the world's first pizza restaurant. Today, up to five billion pizzas are served every year around the world.

① Tomatoes had not existed in Europe until the early 16th century.
② In Europe, tomatoes became an ingredient in pizza in the early 19th century.
③ People in the Stone Age used hot rocks to make dough.
④ Cooks in Naples opened the world's first pizza restaurant.
⑤ The flat bread cost a lot, so only rich people in Naples ate it.

6강 부분 이해 (지시어, 밑줄 추론)

예제 2015 국민대

Like many other parts of the media industry, publishing is being radically reshaped by the growth of the internet. Online retailers are already among the biggest distributors of books. Now e-books threaten to boost sales of the old-fashioned kind. In response, publishers are trying to shore up their conventional business while preparing for a future in which e-books will represent a much bigger chunk of sales. Publishers fret that online shopping has conditioned consumers to expect lower prices for all kinds of books. And they worry that the downward spiral will further erode their already thin margins as well as bring further dismay to struggling brick-and-mortar booksellers. Unless things change, some in the industry predict that publishers will suffer a similar fate to that of music companies, whose fortunes faded when Apple turned the industry upside down by selling individual songs cheaply online.

Q. Which is closest in meaning to the underlined brick-and-mortar?

① factory
② wholesale
③ off-line
④ large-scaled

유형별 문제풀이 Point _ 부분 이해 (지시어, 밑줄 추론)

Point  **밑줄 추론으로 출제되었던 표현들을 정리하여 암기해 둔다.**

기출 표현이 다시 출제되는 경우가 많으니 정리하고 암기해 둔다. 표현들을 정리할 때는 한글 뜻뿐만 아니라 영영사전을 검색하여 자세한 뜻풀이를 통해 해당 표현을 완벽하게 이해할 수 있도록 하며 유사표현들을 함께 정리해 두는 것이 좋다.

Point 2 **모르는 표현일 때는 앞뒤 내용을 통해 의미를 유추한다.**

만일 밑줄 친 표현이 암기되어 있지 않다면 '빈칸'처럼 취급하여 앞뒤 내용을 통해 추론해야 한다. 편입영어는 객관식으로 출제되므로 앞뒤 내용을 고려했을 때 어색한 보기를 소거하면서 가장 적절한 보기를 정답으로 한다.

정답 ③

분석 밑줄 친 brick-and-mortar의 사전적 정의는 '소매의, 오프라인 거래의'이다. 이 표현을 암기하고 있었다면 의미를 추론하기 쉽다. 그러나 밑줄 친 표현을 모른다고 하더라도 문맥으로 유추하여 해결할 수 있으므로 밑줄 친 표현의 앞뒤 내용을 파악하여 정답을 추론해 보도록 하자. 본문에서는 인터넷의 성장으로 출판업계가 재편되고 있는 상황을 설명하는데 밑줄이 포함된 문장에서는 등위상관접속사인 'B as well as A(A뿐만 아니라 B도)'를 사용하여 출판업계의 어려운 상황을 언급했다. 전자책이 줄어든 서적의 판매수익을 더욱 잠식할 것이라는 내용과 자연스럽게 연결되도록 밑줄 친 표현을 추론해 본다면 어려움을 겪을 만한 판매업자에 가장 적절한 표현은 보기 ③일 것이다.

어휘

reshape ⓥ 모양[구조]을 고치다, 개조하다
conventional ⓐ 관습적인, 관례적인
chunk ⓝ 상당히 많은 양
fret ⓥ 조바심치다, 조마조마하다
condition ⓥ (특정 조건에 반응을 보이거나 익숙해지도록) 길들이다, 훈련시키다
downward spiral 하향곡선[추세]
margin ⓝ 여백, 이익
dismay ⓝ 실망, 경악

해석 미디어 산업의 다른 많은 분야들과 마찬가지로, 출판은 인터넷의 성장에 의해 급격하게 구조가 바뀌는 중이다. 온라인 소매업체들은 이미 가장 큰 서적 유통업체들에 속해 있다. 이제 전자책은 구식서적(종이책)의 매출이 증진되는 것을 위협한다. 이에 대응하여, 출판사들은 전자책이 훨씬 더 큰 매출의 부분을 차지하게 될 미래를 준비하면서 전통적인 사업을 유지하기 위해 노력하고 있다. 출판사들은 온라인 쇼핑이 소비자들로 하여금 모든 종류의 책들에 대해 더 낮은 가격을 기대하게 만들었다고 걱정한다. 그리고 그들은 하향곡선이 어려움을 겪고 있는 오프라인 소매서적 판매업자들에게 더 큰 실망을 가져다줄 뿐만 아니라 이미 줄어든 서적의 판매수익을 더욱 잠식할 것이라고 우려한다. 출판업계 일각에서는 만약 상황이 바뀌지 않는다면 출판사들이 음반사들과 비슷한 운명을 겪게 될 것이라고 예상하는데 음반사들은 Apple이 개별 곡들을 온라인에서 값싸게 팔아서 음반 시장을 뒤집었을 때 그 운명이 기울었다.

정답과 해설 p.132

01 Which of the following is closest in meaning to the underlined wringing of hands?

At the beginning of the 1960s, Andy Warhol began to produce flat, commodified, curiously exact paintings of household goods everyone in America knew and handled daily. Starting with a series of Coke bottles, he progressed rapidly to Campbell's soup cans, food stamps and dollar bills. He would soon be the most famous and charismatic proponent of Pop Art.

One talks about the shock of the new, but part of the reason Pop Art caused such a wringing of hands among artists, gallerists and critics alike, is that it looked on first glance like a category error, a painful collapse of the seemingly unquestionable boundary between high and low culture; good taste and bad. Warhol was painting things to which he was sentimentally attached, even loved; objects whose value derives not because they're rare or individual but because they are reliably the same. One dollar bill is not more attractive than another; drinking Coke puts the coal miner among the company of presidents and movie stars. It's the same democratic inclusive impulse that made Warhol want to call Pop Art Common Art.

① disturbance
② joy
③ apathy
④ applause

02 What does the underlined part mean?

You already know that making a good first impression can go a long way. But forget all the advice you've received about dressing to impress or putting on a cheesy smile. The true secret to building a lasting connection reaches much deeper than what you wear. According to Dr. Turner, who has researched first impressions for more than 10 years, everyone (consciously or subconsciously) asks two questions when meeting someone new: can I trust this person? And can I respect this person?

Both questions help you measure a person's warmth and competence, respectively. But, Dr. Turner says, you should put gaining your peers' trust over winning their respect, even in a workplace setting. "If someone you're trying to influence doesn't trust you, you're not going to get very far; in fact, you might even elicit suspicion because you come across as manipulative," Dr. Turner wrote in her article. "A warm, trustworthy person who is also strong elicits admiration, but only after you've established trust does your strength become a gift rather than a threat."

① you happen to meet somebody you can control easily
② you're considered as a competent and creative person
③ you're not confident but only suggestive in your discussion
④ you make an impression as being influential in a negative way

03 What does the underlined "This" mean?

Nobody reveals an accurate picture of their actual lives on social media. They omit the bickering, boring and unflattering aspects of their lives in favor of the fabulous moments. The downside of this "success theater" is that daily exposure to Facebook leaves people feeling inadequate. That constant barrage of other people's best moments creates the illusion that everyone else in the world is living these wonderful lives filled with success and joy and adventure while you're sitting there, well, looking at Facebook. This occurs on other sites like Instagram.

① The opposite illusion
② The boring aspect of others' lives
③ The more accurate picture
④ The same phenomenon

04 What does the underlined expression mean?

Do not wake up to the blue hue of your smartphone and immediately start working. Place it across the room, or better yet, in an adjacent one, and force yourself up and out of bed to turn off your alarm each morning. When the alarm does go off, get up and prepare for your day as you would for an office job: take a shower and get dressed. Business attire is (obviously) not required, but act as though you will be interacting with colleagues in person. After all, you never know when they may want to video chat, and you do not want to beg off because you are not wearing a shirt. This also sets the tempo for the day and discourages the sleepy notion that, perhaps, just maybe, you can crawl back into bed for a nap around lunch, although there is something to be said for workday naps.

① You need something for workday naps.
② Workday naps might be good for you.
③ No employers will allow workday naps.
④ Workday naps are something that you can talk about.

05 What is implied by the underlined sentence?

Machines won't bring about the economic robot apocalypse — but greedy humans will, according to physicist Stephen Hawking. In a recent seminar, the scientist predicted that economic inequality will skyrocket as more jobs become automated and the rich owners of machines refuse to share their fast-proliferating wealth. He said, "If machines produce everything we need, the outcome will depend on how things are distributed. Everyone can enjoy a life of luxurious leisure if the machine-produced wealth is shared, or most people can end up poor if the machine owners monopolize wealth. So far, the trend seems to be toward the second option, with technology driving ever-increasing inequality." Essentially, machine owners will become the bourgeoisie of a new era, in which the corporations they own won't provide jobs to actual human workers. As it is, the chasm between the super rich and the rest is growing. Capital — such as stocks or property — accrues value at a much faster rate than wages increase, and the working class can never even catch up. But if Hawking is right, the problem won't be about catching up. It'll be a struggle to even move past the starting line.

① It will be hard to start a business.
② It will be hard to benefit from robot automation.
③ It will be hard to tell who is rich and who is poor.
④ It will be hard to achieve a fast accumulation of capital.
⑤ It will be hard to get opportunities to overcome the inequality.

06 밑줄 친 this purchase의 내용은?

"In my view the acquisition of the South China Morning Post was driven completely by Jack Ma, whose hubris is his main motivating factor. One of Ma's top role models is the more cerebral Jeff Bezos, founder of Amazon, who made a similar purchase of the storied Washington Post in 2013. I haven't heard much about changes at the Washington Post since then. But I do think it was wise for Bezos to buy the newspaper personally rather than using Amazon funds, so that he won't be accused of burdening his company with such a problematic and also renowned asset. Ma appeared to be taking a similar approach, but changed course and decided to make this purchase through Alibaba. If that's the case, his motivation is probably a desire to find a place for the newspaper among his small but growing stable of related media assets like the Twitter of China. The company will need to use those resources and move quickly to revive the paper, but will also need to be careful of politically sensitive issues."

① Purchase of the South China Morning Post by Jack Ma
② Purchase of the Washington Post by Jeff Bezos
③ Purchase of Amazon by Jeff Bezos
④ Purchase of Alibaba by Jack Ma
⑤ Purchase of the Twitter of China by Alibaba

07 밑줄 친 부분의 의미를 가장 적절하게 표현한 것은?

In a society that worships at the altar of supermodels like Claudia, Christy and Kate, white teenagers are obsessed with staying thin. But there's growing evidence that black and white girls view their bodies in dramatically different ways. The latest findings come in a study to be published in the journal *Human Organization* this spring by a team of black and white researchers at the University of Arizona. While 90 percent of the white junior-high and high-school girls studied voiced dissatisfaction with their weight, 70 percent of African-American teens were satisfied with their bodies.

In fact, even significantly overweight black teens described themselves as happy. That confidence may not carry over to other areas of black teens' lives, but the study suggests that, at least here, it's a lifelong source of pride. Asked to describe women as they age, two thirds of the black teens said they get more beautiful, and many cited their mothers as examples. White girls responded that their mothers may have been beautiful — back in their youth. Says anthropologist Mimi Nichter, one of the study's coauthors, "In white culture, the window of beauty is so small."

① In general, black girls are slimmer than the whites.
② The white people are less interested in their appearance than the black people.
③ White teens have more strict standards for the beauty.
④ Most beautiful women are described as white girls.
⑤ The black girls are perceived to be more beautiful than the white.

08 The underlined expression "That's none of your business." ______________.

When I (Jane) was 12, my father decided the family should move to a nicer house 50 miles from his job. The move was an expensive one and Mom had to go to work. Dad bought a new car for commuting while Mom walked a mile to the bus stop. Dad spent his weekends at the track, playing the horses. If one of us was sick, that was Mom's responsibility. If the plumbing broke, it was our fault. My sister and I worked our way through college. Dad never gave us a dime.

Mom got cancer a few years after Dad retired, and everything that needed doing fell on me. He never lifted a finger. When Mom died, he found himself a girlfriend, bought a new car and had no time for our phone calls, The last time I called and asked, "What have you been doing lately?" He replied, "That's none of your business." This Christmas we won't worry that Dad is alone because he has a new car and a girlfriend and lots of stories to tell about how rotten his daughters are.

① demonstrates how chic Dad looks
② shows how poor Dad's sense of humor is
③ shows Dad's deep concern for Jane's waste of time
④ indicates that Dad gives Jane the cold shoulder

09 Which is NOT suitable for a paraphrase of the underlined mathematics is a collective activity?

Mathematics departments around the world regularly receive letters from amateur mathematicians who claim to have solved famous problems, and virtually without exception these 'solutions' are not merely wrong, but laughably so. Some, while not exactly mistaken, are so unlike a correct proof of anything that they are not really attempted solutions at all. Those that follow at least some of the normal conventions of mathematical presentation use very elementary arguments that would, had they been correct, have been discovered centuries ago. The people who write these letters have no conception of how difficult mathematical research is, of the years of effort needed to develop enough knowledge and expertise to do significant original work, or of the extent to which mathematics is a collective activity.

① Combined efforts of mathematicians usually lead the development of mathematics.
② Many mathematicians are simultaneously engaged in tackling mathematical questions.
③ A genius of mathematics is required to solve particularly difficult mathematical questions.
④ A lot of mathematicians contributed to the development of mathematics over a long period of time.

10 What does the underlined 'it' mean?

An argument often advanced for the encouragement of religion is that, to paraphrase St. Mathew's report of Jesus's words, it leads people to love their neighbors as themselves. That would be a powerful point were 'it' true. But is it? This was the question Jean Decety, a developmental neuroscientist at the University of Chicago, asked in a study just published in *Current Biology*.

Dr. Decety is not the first to wonder, in a scientific way, about the connection between religion and altruism. He is, though, one of the first to do it without recourse to that standard but peculiar laboratory animal beloved by psychologists, the undergraduate student. Instead, he collaborated with researchers in Canada, China, Jordan, South Africa and Turkey, as well as with fellow Americans, to look at children aged between 5 and 12 and their families.

① Most people are religious.
② The object of belief is not important.
③ Jesus emphasized the love of people.
④ Science and religion are not different.
⑤ Religion makes people help others.

11 The underlined expression means that drone pilots ____________.

Much of the ink spilt over drones concerns their targets. Some celebrate the ease with which America can now vaporize its foes. Others fret that innocents are too often caught in the blast zone. Less attention has been paid to the men and women who hold the joysticks. But now that the air force is training more drone pilots than fighter and bomber pilots combined, this is starting to change. "People assume these pilots have been desensitized, like they're playing a video game," says Nancy Cooke, a professor at Arizona State University. "The opposite is true." Being out of harm's way makes the job less fretful in some respects, but more so in others. Whereas fighter pilots drop a bomb and fly away, drone pilots may spend weeks monitoring a village or convoy, sussing out patterns and getting to know their enemies. This makes the act of killing more personal, particularly as these pilots are forced to witness the fallout. Afterwards, instead of bonding with fellow servicemen at a base, drone warriors go home, where they must keep their daily exploits a secret.

① are not affected by their mission
② might experience mental problems
③ are among the most highly educated
④ consider their work boring and worthless
⑤ can handle stress on their own

12 Which of the following is implied by the underlined a brave thing to do?

Barely a week goes by without a celebrity "opening up" about their "battle with depression." This, apparently, is a brave thing to do because, despite all efforts to get rid of prejudice against depression, it is still seen as some kind of mental and emotional weakness' But what if it was nothing of the sort? What if it was a physical illness that just happens to make people feel pretty lousy? Would that make it less of a big deal to admit to?

According to a growing number of scientists, this is exactly how we should be thinking about the condition. George Slavich, a clinical psychologist, has spent years studying depression, and has come to the conclusion that it has as much to do with the body as the mind. "I don't even talk about it as a psychiatric condition anymore," he says. "It does involve psychology, but it also involves equal parts of biology and physical health."

The basis of this new view is blindingly obvious once it is pointed out; everyone feels miserable when they are ill. That feeling of being too tired, bored, and fed up to move off the sofa and get on with life is known among psychologists as sickness behavior. It happens for a good reason, helping us avoid doing more damage or spreading an infection any further.

① Depression is a social stigma.
② Depression occurs to those who are afraid.
③ Depression is experienced by everybody.
④ Depression is like the heart catching a cold.

13 밑줄 친 "a nest egg"의 의미로 가장 알맞은 것은?

I set down choice experiences so that my own writings may inspire me, and at last I may make wholes of parts. Certainly, it is a distinct profession to rescue from oblivion and to fix the sentiments and thoughts which visit all men less generally, that the contemplation of the unfinished picture may suggest its harmonious completion. Associate reverently and as much as you can with your loftiest thoughts. Each thought that is welcomed and recorded is a nest egg, by the side of which more will be laid. Thoughts accidentally thrown together become a frame in which more may be developed and exhibited.

① surprise heretofore not discovered
② journal entry to be treasured and joined with other entries
③ a thought that will manifest itself as yet another thought
④ a memory that will stimulate thought and solicit a recording in a journal

14 Which of the following is different from the others in what they refer to?

The Chinese city of Chongqing has created a smartphone sidewalk lane. It's a path for those who are messaging and tweeting to watch where ⓐ they are going. The property manager says it's intended to remind people that it's dangerous to message or tweet while walking in the street. "There are a lot of elderly people and children in the street, and using cellphones on the go may cause unnecessary collisions here," said Nong Cheng who manages the area in the city's entertainment zone. It has a 165-foot stretch of pavement with two lanes; one that prohibits cellphone use is next to the other that allows pedestrians to use their cellphones at ⓑ their "own risk." Nong said the idea came from a similar stretch of pavement in Washington, which National Geographic Television created as part of a behavior experiment. She said, however, that pedestrians were not taking the new lanes seriously. Many were snapping pictures of the signs and sidewalks. "Those using ⓒ their cellphones have not heeded the markings on the pavement," she said. "They don't notice ⓓ them."

① ⓐ they
② ⓑ their
③ ⓒ their
④ ⓓ them

15 Which of the following best describes the main idea of This was especially so?

It happens that in England the State went somewhat further, and was compelled to make some attempt to control the movement of labour. So long as labour was provided within the manor by labourers who themselves had interests in the land of manor, the problem was one for the manor alone; but hired labour became more and more the practice as specialization developed, in ancillary trades as well as in agriculture itself, and labourers left their manors, with the result that the State interfered in the interests of public order and the needs of employers. This was especially so after the Black Death created a dearth of labour. Justices of labour were created to regulate labour, and were subsequently merged with the justices of the peace, who were originally concerned only with the apprehension of criminals.

① The intervention of the State was needed.
② The specialization of labour was emphasized.
③ The tradition of manor system should be kept.
④ The movement of labour need not to be controlled.

16 What does the underlined "them" refer to?

In the Middle Ages the inn was supplemented to some extent by the monastic houses, but these, as a rule, entertained only two classes, the very rich and the very poor. The first were received by the monks because they did not dare to refuse them, but many were their complaints regarding the excesses of their unwelcome guests. The monastery door, however, was always open to the poor man, who was never turned empty away.

The inns were used by the people between these two extremes, for they were too miserable for the nobility, and too expensive for the poor. They were frequented by the smaller gentry, merchants, packmen, and other traders. The entertainment was poor enough; a number of beds were spread out in one room on the floor, and each guest bought what food he required.

① the poor
② the inns
③ the nobility
④ the monastic houses

17 밑줄 친 "this country boy never lost touch with his roots"가 의미하는 것으로 가장 알맞은 것은?

In 1966, Eddie Arnold earned induction into the Country Music Hall of Fame. Ranked among the most popular country singers in U.S. history, Arnold used his smooth voice to escape from poverty. When his father died, the family farm was lost to creditors, and the Arnolds were forced to become sharecroppers. Even when achieving his lifelong dream of becoming a top-selling this country boy never lost touch with his roots. Even while gaining a rather sophisticated fan base with his succession of hits, he always referred to himself as the "Tennessee Plowboy." In his mind, his background as a hard-working farm hand prepared him for the demanding role of a successful singer. From the beginning, he cut a different figure from most of his contemporaries in the world of country singers. Unlike most of them who appeared either in jeans and plaid shirts or glittering sequins and spangles, Arnold always dressed in debonair attire. When he died in May 2008, the music world lost an immensely popular crooner of romantic ballads.

① Arnold remained connected to the family farm and continued to pursue agriculture.
② Arnold eschewed his humble beginnings and indulged in a more sophisticated lifestyle.
③ Arnold liked to be known as a farm hand and favored jeans and cowboy boots when he performed.
④ Arnold continued to identify himself with the attitudes and values of hardworking rural Americans.

18 Which is closest in meaning to the underlined People don't think anything of?

Individual guilt is triggered when we don't meet our own expectations. Psychologist Heidi Wiedemann describes this feeling as an internal struggle between what we presume our values to be and how we fail to live up to them. For many of us, she says, especially women, the impulse can be triggered by unrealistic social norms, whether they involve balancing family life and professional goals or maintaining fitness.

To overcome individual guilt, Wiedemann says we should try to be cognisant of any internalised unattainable expectations, then work on self-acceptance and letting go of judgement. We also need to remind ourselves of personal successes. "People don't think anything of speaking to themselves negatively," she says, "but when you tell them to start speaking to themselves with compassion, they look at you as though you're from another planet."

① People feel at a loss in
② People think it abnormal
③ People think too highly of
④ People do not care much about

19 Which is implied by the underlined part?

University of Pennsylvania researchers found that spouses who had major cardiac surgery had better functional recovery within two years than patients who were divorced, separated or widowed. That means they were more able to get dressed, bathe or go to the bathroom on their own. In fact, those who were no longer married were about 40% more likely to die or develop a new functional disability in the first two years postsurgery than those with a spouse at home. (There were not enough never-married people in the study to make an assessment on them.)

The researchers are not sure whether the results are because less-healthy people are more likely to be unmarried or because spouses make a big difference in rehabilitation. Either way, they say hospitals should consider marital status when helping people plan their post-heart-attack life.

① To make an assessment, we need enough married people.
② There were not enough people to marry before the surgery.
③ Never-married people were easy to assess.
④ The data to assess never-married people were not enough.

20 Which of the following is closest to what (A) refers to?

Have you ever heard of (A) a double Irish? It is not a drink but one of the controversial tax strategies that help some American companies keep profits abroad at lower rates. Such strategies are at the heart of the Aug. 30 ruling by the European Union demanding that Ireland claw back $14.5 billion in allegedly unpaid taxes from Apple, the world's most valuable tech company. The European regulators' investigation concluded that tax arrangements Ireland offered Apple in 1991 and 2007 were illegal, allowing the firm to pay annual tax rates of 0.005% to 1% on its European profits from 2003 to 2014. Those are much lower than Ireland's standard corporate rate, which is the second lowest in the E.U., at 12.5%. In an open letter, CEO Tim Cook disputed the decision and vowed to appeal, adding, "Apple follows the law, and we pay all the taxes we owe." Ireland's Finance Minister said the country would also fight the ruling.

① Apple's tax evasion in Ireland
② Ireland's two-tiered corporate tax rates
③ Doubled tax penalty for Ireland
④ The E.U.'s different standard for Ireland

7강 연결사 / 빈칸 추론

예제 2015 단국대

While comparing economic data, a group of sociologists concluded that, among all people at a certain income level, individuals in rural areas have greater purchasing power than those living in urban or suburban regions. The group factored in several data points, including the population density within a certain radius of city centers, the number of people per household, and the percentage of those households that included two working parents. Ultimately, ______________, the main premise was that the money spent by urban and suburban dwellers on their fundamental need for food and shelter could be spent by rural households on discretionary items.

Q. Which of the following is most appropriate for the blank?

① moreover
② for example
③ in fact
④ however

유형별 문제풀이 Point _ 연결사 / 빈칸 추론

Point 1 **다양한 연결사의 기능과 의미를 숙지한다.**

연결사들은 크게 순접 혹은 역접의 기능이 있다. 세부적으로는 순접의 경우 '예시, 첨가, 재진술, 인과관계, 요약' 등이 있고 역접의 경우에는 '정반대, 대조, 부정, 양보'와 같은 기능이 있다. 기능에 따라 연결사를 정리해 두면 문제 해결이 쉬워진다.

Point 2 **빈칸의 앞뒤 문장의 논리적 흐름을 파악한다.**

빈칸이 포함된 문장을 먼저 해석해 본 후 그 직전과 직후 문장(내용)의 논리적 흐름을 파악한다. 언제나 가장 중요한 단서는 빈칸 주변에 있으므로, 문제풀이를 할 때 빈칸 주변에 모르는 단어가 있다면 중요 단서로 다시 출제될 가능성이 있으므로 반드시 암기해 둔다. 마지막으로 빈칸이나 빈칸이 포함된 문장이 주제문일 가능성이 있으므로 '글 전체의 주제가 무엇인가'도 생각해 본다.

Point 3 **보기를 소거하거나 대입하며 정답을 찾는다.**

빈칸에 들어가기 어색한 보기는 먼저 소거하고 남은 보기들을 대입하여 정답을 찾는다. 특히 두 개의 연결사를 추론하는 문제풀이를 할 때는 둘 중 어색한 보기를 우선 소거하면 정답을 더 빠르게 고를 수 있다.

정답 ④

분석 빈칸에 알맞은 접속부사를 고르는 문제로 일단 접속부사가 포함된 문장과 직전 문장과의 관계를 파악하여 정답을 찾도록 하자. 빈칸의 직전 문장에서는 사회학자들이 활용한 데이터 포인트를 나열했으나 빈칸이 포함된 본문 마지막 문장에서는 연구의 주요 전제에 대해 설명하고 있다. 따라서 빈칸의 직전과 직후 문장은 '역접 관계'이며 보기 ④가 정답으로 가장 적절하다.

어휘

rural ⓐ 시골의, 지방의
urban ⓐ 도시의, 도회지의
suburban ⓐ 교외의; 평범한
data point ⓝ 도표에서 그래프가 지나는 각 점, 측정점
population density 인구 밀도
radius ⓝ 반지름, 반경
discretionary ⓐ 임의의, 자유 재량의

해석 경제자료들을 비교하는 동안, 한 그룹의 사회학자들은 일정한 소득 수준의 모든 사람들 중에서, 시골 지역에 거주하는 사람들이 도시나 교외 지역에 거주하는 사람들보다 더 큰 구매력을 가지고 있다고 결론지었다. 사회학자 그룹은 도시 중심부의 특정 반경 내 인구 밀도, 가구당 구성원의 수, 맞벌이 가구를 포함하는 가구들의 비율 등 몇몇 측정점들을 계산했다. 그러나 궁극적으로 이 연구의 주요 전제는 도시와 교외 거주자들이 필수적인 식료품과 주거에 쓰는 비용이 농촌 가구들의 경우 자유 재량적인 항목의 구입에 쓰일 수 있다는 것이었다.

Practice

정답과 해설 p.157

01 Which of the following is most appropriate for the blank?

The theory that skin color adapts to the level of ultraviolet radiation makes some sense. The ancestors of modern humans who lived predominantly near the equator in Africa had darker skin because it was more efficient at reflecting heat, helping the body cool down and preventing the skin from receiving harmful ultraviolet rays. ______________, less exposure to ultraviolet rays can lead to a deficiency in Vitamin D, also known as the "sunshine vitamin." This is the main reason why black people are at higher risk of contracting rheumatoid arthritis due to vitamin D deficiency.

① For instance
② Therefore
③ However
④ In conclusion

02 빈칸 [A], [B]에 들어갈 말로 가장 적절한 것은?

Many reports show that there are still very few women in high government positions. ______[A]______, only about 15% of the positions in government are held by women. In addition, more than half of the people who can't read and write are women. Being illiterate doesn't mean people are not intelligent. However, not being able to read and write does make it more difficult for people to change their lives. There are many programs to help people improve their farming skills. ______[B]______, for years, these programs provided money and training for men but not for women. Now this is changing. International organizations and programs are helping women, as well as men, improve their agricultural productions.

[A]		[B]
① In fact	–	However
② In fact	–	As a result
③ In other words	–	As a result
④ Therefore	–	However
⑤ Therefore	–	For example

03 Which of the following is most appropriate for the blank?

In the early 19th century, adventure stories gave Americans a taste for fast-paced, exciting tales of danger and heroism in distant places. At the same time, the growth of newspapers for the general public created a market for inexpensive publications aimed at a wide audience. These two conditions led to the advent of a new kind of literature: the "dime novel."

The dime novel was a short work of fiction, cheaply printed and often crudely written, about the adventures of a hero or heroine. Though dime novels were usually pure fantasy, they provided readers with an escape from the boredom of ______________ life, and helped create the popular image of outlaws and cowboys as romantic and even heroic figures.

① uncanny
② hallowed
③ humdrum
④ otherworldly

04 Choose the most appropriate one for the blank.

The growing importance of education contributed to the emergence of a separate youth culture. The idea of adolescence as a distinct period in the life of an individual was for the most part new to the twentieth century. In some measure it was a result of the influence of Freudian psychology. But it was a result, too, of society's recognition that a more extended period of training and preparation was necessary before a young person was ready to move into the workplace. Schools and colleges provided adolescents with a setting in which they could develop their own social patterns, their own hobbies, their own interests and activities. An increasing number of students saw school as a place not just for academic training but for organized athletics, other extracurricular activities, clubs, and fraternities and sororities — that is, as an institution that ______________.

① led young people to look for low-paying jobs
② specialized in teaching technical skills demanded in the modern economy
③ helped many men and women make more money to support their families
④ offered both instruction and services in traditional disciplines
⑤ allowed them to define themselves more in terms of their peer group

05 Which best fits in the blank?

The globe is losing valuable species day by day; 20% to 50% of the world's ______________ may be gone before the end of the next century, and the irony is that human beings will have contributed overwhelmingly to that loss. The human population is expected nearly to double within the next few decades. For third world agrarian economies especially, the competition for space and resources will grow during this "demographic winter," and the losers will be the wild animals.

① natural resources
② ozone layer
③ oil supply
④ biological diversity
⑤ financial institutions

06 Which is the most appropriate for the blanks [A] and [B]?

Although psychology was not recognized as its own field until the late nineteenth century, its early roots can be traced to the ancient Greeks. Plato and Aristotle, for instance, were philosophers concerned with the nature of the human mind. In the seventeenth century, René Descartes distinguished between the mind and body as aspects that interact to create human experience, thus paving the way for modern psychology. While philosophers relied on observation and logic to draw their conclusions, psychologists began to use scientific methods to study human thought and behavior. A German physiologist, Wilhelm Wundt, opened the world's first psychology laboratory at the University of Leipzig in 1879. He used experimental methods to study mental processes, such as reaction times. This research is regarded as marking the beginning of psychology as a separate field. The term psychiatry was first used by a German physician, Johann Reil, in 1808. ______[A]______, psychiatry as a field did not become popular until Sigmund Freud proposed a new theory of personality that focused on the role of the unconscious. ______[B]______, psychologists were concerned primarily with the conscious aspects of the mind, including perceptions, thoughts, memories, and fantasies of which a person is aware.

	[A]		[B]
①	For example	–	In the meantime
②	Otherwise	–	At the same time
③	As a result	–	After that time
④	However	–	Before that time

07 다음 글의 빈칸에 들어갈 말로 가장 적절한 것은?

Looking back over a twenty year career of playing, composing, and conducting different types of orchestra music, I often feel a sense of wonder — not at what I have accomplished, but how someone with my agrarian, rather workaday upbringing should have chosen such a path at all. It would have been easy for me to stay on the family farm as my parents wished, eventually to become part owner, as my brother did quite successfully. However, rewarding as this existence was, it was somehow unfulfilling; my youthful imagination, much to my parents' ______________, often cast about for other, greater pursuits to occupy it. Still, growing up as I did in a household where the radio dispensed milk prices instead of Mozart and hog futures instead of Handel, the thought of embarking on a career in classical music went beyond even my wildest imagination.

① delight
② approval
③ dismay
④ dejection

08 Which best fits in the blank?

The half of the world's people who now live in cities experience the most artificial environment ever created by humans. Large areas of countryside have been destroyed by the spread of houses, factories, roads and shopping centers across what were once fields, open spaces and woodland. In the 1990s alone over 800,000 hectares of European land was built on — if this rate continued through the rest of the twenty-first century it would result in a doubling of the current rural area. Cities also depend on very high energy use in building and sustaining them and in moving millions of people to and from work every day. Cities have many benefits — they are usually centers of cultural activity and have a much wider range of facilities than rural areas. However, although in some working-class areas strong, but informal, systems of community support developed, in general the flood of people into cities destroyed existing social bonds and institutions without creating new ones capable of helping and sustaining the inhabitants. Cities, as the nineteenth-century American writer Henry David Thoreau wrote, tend to be places characterized by '______________'.

① citizens helping and sustaining each other
② abundant opportunities of cultural activities
③ new facilities with large open spaces
④ the destruction of houses and factories
⑤ millions of people being lonely together

09 Which of the following best fits in thc blank?

From Ben Franklin to Horatio Alger to Oprah Winfrey, American heroes seem always to be the self-made men or women who strode into the world all on their own. It's almost a source of shame to follow in a parent's footsteps. But, actually, it's a great idea to study the example of your ancestors, as revealed in the stories of how they spent their lives. You may find clues to what to do based on shared talents, dispositions, or interests. There may be a compelling reason beyond good connections why so many medical school students have a parent who's a doctor or why farmers or firefighters run in some families. But you may find signs that are just as strong about ______________. If your mother despised sitting in an office all day, you might think twice about business school. On the other hand, if Uncle Louie wore out early as a construction worker, a desk job might not look too bad.

① what not to do
② what not to share
③ what you are good at
④ what you want to do

10 Which is the most appropriate for the blanks [A] and [B]?

The theory of constructivism was developed by Jean Piaget, the Swiss biologist and philosopher who became interested in the child's growing ability to think. ____[A]____, Piaget studied children as a way to understand the human mind and the origins of intelligence independent of culture. Piaget believed that many concepts that we heretofore had considered elementary, such as the concept of *hidden*, were actually extremely complicated and that we needed a new theory to explain how children younger than a year were able to learn such complicated notions. ____[B]____, the concepts learned at 2 years, 7 years, and 13 years were qualitatively more complex, necessitating a developmental theory that accounted for each stage of cognitive development.

	[A]		[B]
①	In fact	–	Nonetheless
②	In fact	–	Likewise
③	However	–	In contrast
④	However	–	In other words

11 Which of the following best fits into the blank?

Copyright initially was conceived as a way for government to restrict printing; the contemporary intent of copyright is to promote the creation of new works by giving authors right to control and profit from them. Copyrights are said to be ______________, which means that they do not extend beyond the scope of a specific state unless that state is a party to an international agreement. While many aspects of national copyright laws have been standardized through international copyright agreements, copyright laws of most countries have their own unique features.

① conservative
② territorial
③ international
④ comprehensive

12 Which of the following is most appropriate for the blank?

The most common treatment for post-traumatic stress disorder is known as exposure-based therapy. This asks those afflicted to imagine the sights and sounds that traumatized them, and helps them confront those memories. It often works. But not always. And it would undoubtedly be better if troops did not develop the condition in the first place. With this in mind, a team of engineers, computer scientists and psychologists led by Dr Skip Rizzo propose a form of psychological vaccination. By ______________, Dr Rizzo hopes to inure squaddies to anything they might witness on the field of battle. The idea of doing this developed from Dr Rizzo's work using virtual reality to help with exposure-based therapy. Such VR enables the sights, sounds, vibrations and even smells of the battlefield to be recreated in the safety of a clinic, and trials suggest it can help those who do not respond to standard exposure-based therapy. The success of such simulation led Dr Rizzo to wonder if a similar regime, experienced before actual battle, might prepare troops mentally in the way that traditional training prepares them physically. His preliminary results suggest it might.

① making soldiers relive the horrors of war as they come back
② presenting soldiers with the horrors of war before they go to fight
③ preparing soldiers more physically for battle
④ using a variety of stress-reduction tactics
⑤ speeding up the healing process with virtual training courses

13 Which of the following is the most appropriate for the blank?

The general notion is that the press can form, control or at least strongly influence public opinion. Can it really do any of these things? Hugh Cudlipp, editorial director of *The London Daily Mirror*, and a man who should know something about the effect of newspapers on public opinion, doesn't share this general notion about their power. He thinks newspapers can echo and stimulate a wave of popular feeling, but that's all. "A newspaper may successfully accelerate but never reverse the popular attitude that common sense has commended to the public." ____________, it can jump aboard the bandwagon once the bandwagon's under way, and exhort others to jump aboard too; but it can't start the bandwagon rolling, or change its direction after it's started.

① Conversely
② In addition
③ Nonetheless
④ In short

14 Read the passage and answer the questions.

Sugar contributes to premature ageing, just as cigarettes and UV rays do. When collagen and elastin — components that support the skin — break down from sun or other free-radical exposure, cells try to repair themselves. But this process slows down with age. And when sugar is present in the skin, it forms cross-links with amino acids that may have been damaged by free radicals. These cross-links jam the repair mechanism and, over time, leave you ______[A]______. Once cross-links form, they won't unhitch, so keep sugar intake ______[B]______. Avoid soft drinks and pastries, and swap sugar for cinnamon — it seems to slow down cross-linking, as do cloves, ginger and garlic.

*free radical: an atom or group of atoms having one or more unpaired electrons

• Which best fits into the blank [A]?

① with artificially sweetened cells
② with prematurely old-looking skin
③ with radically repaired mechanism
④ with a nutritionally balanced body

• Which best fits into the blank [B]?

① as low as you can
② as soon as possible
③ as long as you can
④ as much as possible

15 다음 글의 빈칸 [A], [B]에 들어갈 말로 가장 적절한 것은?

Between 1790 and 1861, approximately 400,000 Africans were imported into the United States. Yet by 1860, the black population had grown to more than 4 million — a tenfold increase in 160 years. These numbers suggest a tremendous rate of natural increase. Some planters continued to buy slaves brought into the country illegally after 1808. ______[A]______ most of the increase stemmed from births. The preferences of both slave owners and slaves account for this development. Southern planters encouraged black women to bear many children. ______[B]______, enslaved African Americans valued the family as a social unit; family ties provided support and solace for a people deprived of fundamental human rights. Even under harsh conditions, black people fell in love, married, had children, and reared families. Despite the lack of protection from local, state, and national authorities, the slave family proved a remarkably resilient institution.

	[A]		[B]
①	Thus	–	For example
②	Furthermore	–	Instead
③	But	–	At the same time
④	Thus	–	Meanwhile
⑤	But	–	In contrast

16 Which is the most appropriate for the blank?

For decades, feminists and feminism were almost exclusively evoked by newspapers, magazines and punditry as an ideological punching bag. Not so today, when those terms are breathlessly deployed by the likes of *CoverGirl*, Taylor Swift and Facebook's Sheryl Sandberg. Feminism, for better and for worse, has become trendy.

This kind of marketplace feminism is welcome because its optics are considered a media-friendly improvement on past feminist movements — more cleavage, less anger. But it also pulls focus from systemic issues and places it on individuals and personalities. It's easy to see Sandberg, ____________, urging women to lean in, and forget that leaning in puts the onus on women themselves — rather than on the corporate systems and values that oppress all workers regardless of gender.

① however
② nevertheless
③ for instance
④ in addition

17 다음 글의 빈칸에 들어갈 말로 가장 적절한 것은?

After simple animal skins, wool is probably the oldest material used for making clothing. We do not know exactly when people started to make woolen clothing, but it was probably quite early in human history. The wool was made from the hair of whatever kind of animal people had available. Most of the time these were sheep, but in some desert areas people made cloth from camel hair. In other areas, they used goat hair, and in the mountains of South America, they used the hair from llamas. All these kinds of wool ______________: They protect a person's body from outside changes in temperature. Woolen clothing keeps the body cool in summer and warm in winter.

① have one thing in common
② should be handled carefully
③ contain special chemical elements
④ are made from the same species of animal
⑤ originate from a specific region in the world

18 Which is most appropriate for the blank?

At first sight, East Coast Beach is ______________ for Singapore's open-water swimmers to gather. On any given day, dozens of ships lie at anchor off the shore, from tramp freighters to oil tankers, while others cruise the horizon. But the fast-moving currents that affect Singapore's isolated beaches are absent there, accounting for East Coast Beach's popularity.

True, visibility in the water isn't good — the sea gets clouded by sand churned up by all those sluicing hulls and whirling propellers — but the Singaporean government, which monitors the quality of water at all public beaches, deems these waters safe and clean enough for swimming. "Most swimmers are afraid of the dim visibility underwater," says Dad Lim, operator of local swimming school Yellowfish, "but there's no reason to be." And besides, it's best to keep your head above water, where you can look out for all the waterborne traffic.

① an unlikely place
② too far away
③ the best place
④ too crowded a place
⑤ an exciting place

19 다음 글의 빈칸에 들어갈 말로 가장 적절한 것은?

Farmers are shifting their spending priorities from fertilizers and pesticides to genetically altered seeds that do the same job. Eventually plants could be given desirable traits from animals. ______________, a gene from bacteria that kills insects can be put into a plant. Insects will then avoid it. Biotechnology researchers realized early on that if the genetic instructions for the manufacture of a desirable protein are inserted in a living cell's DNA, that cell not only manufactures the protein but also passes it on to future generations. To create an insect-repellent plant, the appropriate gene needs to be injected only into the parent plant, which subsequently hands down the characteristic to its offspring.

① Largely
② However
③ For example
④ On the other hand

20 Answer the questions after reading the passage below.

Originality is what distinguishes art from craft. We may say, therefore, that it is the ______[A]______ of artistic greatness or importance. Unfortunately, it is also very hard to define; the usual synonyms — uniqueness, novelty, freshness — do not help us very much, and the dictionaries tell us only that an original work must not be a copy, reproduction, imitation, or translation. What they fail to point out is that originality is always relative: There is no such thing as a completely original work of art. Thus, if we want to rate works of art on an "originality scale" our problem does not lie in deciding whether or not a given work is original but in ______[B]______.

• Which expression best fits [A]?

① yardstick
② creativity
③ pitfall
④ tradition
⑤ craftsmanship

• Which expression best completes [B]?

① achieving something original
② distinguishing art from non-art
③ establishing just exactly how original it is
④ assuming that there are timeless values in art
⑤ representing the lowest common denominator for popular taste

LEVEL

에듀윌 편입

솔루션 독해 Basic

3

Reading

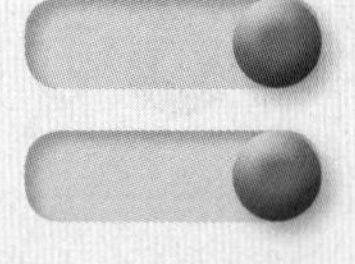

특수유형 익히기

8강 문장 배열

예제 2020 국민대

Several studies suggest that there are gender differences in language use in children as young as 3 years old. Preschool boys tend to be more assertive and demanding in their conversational style, whereas preschool girls tend to be more polite and cooperative.

[A] And, when conflict arises, boys handle it differently than girls do. Amy Sheldon (1990) videotaped same-sex triads of preschool girls and boys at a day care center.

[B] Given these gender differences in preschoolers' conversational style, perhaps it is not surprising that there are more disputes when preschool boys interact than when preschool girls interact.

[C] For example, it was found that boys tended to use simple imperatives in talking to their partner in pretend play. Girls in the same situation used fewer simple imperatives and instead used language that included the other child in planning.

She observed that when the boys had conflicts, they frequently issued directives and made threats. The girls, in contrast, tended more to try to negotiate a settlement.

Q. Which is the proper order of [A]–[C]?

① [A] – [B] – [C]
② [A] – [C] – [B]
③ [C] – [A] – [B]
④ [C] – [B] – [A]

유형별 문제풀이 Point _ 문장 배열

Point  다양한 연결어의 기능과 의미를 공략한다.

1. 문장을 배열할 때는 글의 전체적 흐름을 읽는 것이 중요하다.
2. 배열하는 문장들 속의 각종 순접, 역접의 연결어들을 파악하는 것이 중요하다.
3. 반전, 인과, 동시 상황 등 다양한 연결어의 기능을 익히는 것이 좋다.

Point  대명사, 관사에 주의한다.

대명사와 부정관사 a, 정관사 the는 문장 배열에서 핵심이 되는 경우가 많다. 각각의 대명사와 관사들의 쓰임새를 익히고 최대한 활용한다.

Point  글의 일반적인 법칙에 주의한다.

1. 글은 과거의 내용이나 진부한(old) 내용을 먼저 진술하고 새로운(new) 내용을 나중에 진술하는 것이 일반적이다.
2. 포괄적인 진술은 앞, 구체적 사례나 예시의 진술은 뒤로 가는 것이 일반적이다.
3. 시대순의 글은 시간의 순서대로 쓰는 것이 일반적이다.

정답 ④

분석 주어진 문장의 내용은 '남자아이와 여자아이의 대화 스타일에 차이가 존재한다'는 것인데 이 문장에 이어질 내용은 그것을 구체적으로 상술하는 [C]가 가장 적절하다. 그리고 [C]에 언급된 남녀 차이를 these gender differences로 받아 설명한 [B]가 그 뒤에 와야 하며, 그리고 [B]의 마지막에서 언급한 '논쟁 발생'에 대해 남아와 여아가 서로 다른 방식으로 해결한다는 내용의 [A]가 마지막으로 나와야 한다.

어휘

assertive ⓐ 단정적인, 독단적인	demanding ⓐ 요구가 많은
dispute ⓝ 논쟁, 분쟁	imperative ⓝ 명령
pretend play 가상놀이, 역할놀이	directive ⓝ 지시, 명령
negotiate ⓥ 협상하다	

해석 다양한 연구에 따르면 3세 아동들의 언어 사용에 성별 차이가 있다고 한다. 미취학 남자아이들은 대화 스타일이 더 단정적이고 요구가 많고, 반면에 미취학 여자아이들은 더 공손하고 협조적인 경향이 있다.

[C] 예를 들어, 남자아이들은 가상놀이에서 파트너와 대화할 때 단순 명령문을 사용하는 경향이 있음이 밝혀졌다. 여자아이들은 같은 상황에서 단순 명령문을 덜 사용했으며, 대신 다른 아이를 계획에 끌어들이는 언어를 사용했다.

[B] 미취학 아동들의 대화 스타일에서의 이러한 성별 차이를 고려할 때, 미취학 여자아이들이 또래 친구와 상호작용할 때보다 미취학 남자아이들이 상호작용할 때 더 많은 논쟁이 생긴다는 것은 놀라운 일이 아니다.

[A] 그리고 갈등이 발생하면 남자아이들은 여자아이들과 다르게 상황을 다룬다. 에이미 쉘던(Amy Sheldon) (1990)은 탁아소에서 남자아이들로만 그리고 여자아이들로만 이루어진 3인조들을 각각 비디오로 녹화했다.

그녀는 남자아이들이 갈등을 겪을 때 자주 지사를 내리고 위협을 가한다는 것을 관찰했다. 반대로 여아들은 협상으로 해결하려는 경향이 더 컸다.

Practice

정답과 해설 p.180

01 주어진 글 다음에 이어질 글의 순서로 가장 적절한 것은?

For the long centuries of the Middle Ages (500–1350 AD) the canon of scientific knowledge had experienced little change, and the Catholic Church had preserved acceptance of a system of beliefs based on the teachings of the ancient Greeks and Romans which it had incorporated into religious doctrine.

[A] However, during the Renaissance this doctrinal passivity began to change. The quest to understand the natural world led to the revival of botany and anatomy by thinkers such as Andreas Vesalius during the later sixteenth century.

[B] During this period there was little scientific inquiry and experimentation. Rather, students of the sciences simply read the works of the alleged authorities and accepted their word as truth.

[C] These scientific observers were surprised to find that their conclusions did not always match up with the accepted truths, and this finding inspired others to delve further into the study of the world around them.

① [A] – [B] – [C]
② [B] – [A] – [C]
③ [B] – [C] – [A]
④ [C] – [A] – [B]
⑤ [C] – [B] – [A]

02 주어진 글 다음에 이어질 글의 순서로 가장 적절한 것은?

Why does Dickens, so associated with the affairs of his own time, mean so much to the British nearly two centuries after his birth?

[A] His novel speaks as directly to us today as it did to its first readers 150 years ago.

[B] The other reason is his infectious confidence in the essential goodness of human nature.

[C] The first is that Dickens never dates.

[D] There are two reasons.

① [C] – [B] – [A] – [D]
② [C] – [A] – [B] – [D]
③ [D] – [C] – [B] – [A]
④ [D] – [C] – [A] – [B]

03 Which one is the right order?

For the past 30 years, computer-vision technologies have struggled to perform well, even in tasks as mundane as correctly recognizing faces in photographs. Recently, however, breakthroughs in deep learning have finally enabled computers to interpret several kinds of images better than people do.

[B] It excels because it is better able to learn, and draw inferences from subtle, revealing patterns in the images. [C] For instance, consider images of dogs and cats to understand its prowess. [D] Recent progress in a deep-learning approach known as a convolutional neural network (CNN) is essential to the latest strides. [E] Whereas humans can easily differentiate between them. CNNs allow machines to categorize specific breeds more successfully than people can.

① [D] – [B] – [E] – [C]
② [E] – [B] – [D] – [C]
③ [E] – [C] – [B] – [D]
④ [D] – [C] – [E] – [B]

04 주어진 글 다음에 이어질 글의 순서로 가장 적절한 것은?

> In recent decades, large numbers of Americans have led physically inactive lives.

[A] People shuffle out to their cars in the morning, sit or stand in one place most of the day, ride home, and settle into easy chairs.

[B] The exercise boom is a good example of how general social values and expectations affect health-related behaviors.

[C] Today, however, more and more people are jogging, swimming, bicycling, and engaging in other forms of aerobic exercise.

[D] In the process, people get little vigorous exercise.

① [A] – [B] – [D] – [C]
② [A] – [D] – [C] – [B]
③ [C] – [B] – [A] – [D]
④ [C] – [D] – [B] – [A]

05 전체 글의 의미가 통하도록 문장들 [A]~[C]의 순서를 알맞게 배열한 것은?

[A] Hundreds of millions of people have joined Facebook, KakaoTalk, and other sites so that they can communicate with those friends online.

[B] However, the meaning of the word "friend" seems to have changed.

[C] Social networking makes it very easy to have friends — lots and lots of friends.

> In the past, a friend was someone you had a close personal relationship with. Now, anyone in the world can be your friend online! Some people have thousands of friends, but what do you do if you don't want so many friends? Easy! You can dump an unwanted friend with just one press of your finger.

① [A] – [B] – [C] ② [A] – [C] – [B]
③ [C] – [B] – [A] ④ [C] – [A] – [B]

06 Which is the proper order of the four sentences [A]–[D]?

[A] The exact reason is unclear, but it may be related to the effect of carotenoid levels in the blood.

[B] A study conducted by the University of Queensland's School of Pharmacy involving more than 12,000 Australians revealed that the benefits of a fresh produce-rich diet extend beyond physical health.

[C] With every added daily portion of fruits or vegetables (up to eight), the subjects' happiness levels rose slightly.

[D] The researchers calculated that if someone were to switch from a diet free of fruit and vegetables to eight servings per day, he or she would theoretically gain as much life satisfaction as someone who transitioned from unemployment to a job.

① [A] – [C] – [B] – [D] ② [B] – [C] – [D] – [A]
③ [C] – [B] – [A] – [D] ④ [D] – [B] – [C] – [A]

07 전체 글의 의미가 통하도록 문장들 [A]~[C]의 순서를 알맞게 배열한 것은?

All cultures have collections of tales handed down from generation to generation that are collectively known as "folklore." Urban legends are simply contemporary examples of folklore. But what, exactly, are urban legends? For one thing, despite their name, they do not necessarily concern big cities. A better name for them might be contemporary legends.

[A] But in some ways the term urban legends is quite appropriate.

[B] Just as many medieval stories were set in forests, full of dangers and mysteries, many modern legends take place in big cities.

[C] The name urban legends — which was invented by folklorist Richard Dorson in the 1960s — was first used to distinguish them from legends of an earlier time, which primarily had rural settings.

Our cities sometimes seem as frightening as those dark forests did to our ancestors.

① [A] – [B] – [C]
② [B] – [A] – [C]
③ [B] – [C] – [A]
④ [C] – [A] – [B]

08 Reorder the following sentences in the best way to form a coherent passage for each question.

[A] Unique properties of TRPM8, a cold-sensing protein found in their systems, shield these rodents from harsh weather.

[B] This new research about TRPM8 brings scientists closer to understanding enigmas of hibernation.

[C] The uncanny ability to withstand prolonged cold results in part from an adaptation that thirteen-lined ground squirrels have developed in molecules they share with other mammals.

[D] It's really important because if they're too cold, they can't hibernate.

① [A] – [C] – [D] – [B]
② [B] – [C] – [D] – [A]
③ [C] – [B] – [A] – [D]
④ [C] – [A] – [D] – [B]

09 Choose the most logical order of the following sentences.

[A] This new social contract was underwritten by the expectation that the resources needed to support it would be forthcoming.

[B] Others were cultural resources for citizenship: information, knowledge, representation, and participation.

[C] With the granting of the vote to women, 'citizen' finally became a universally available identity in Britain.

[D] Some of these were material such as an adequate lifetime income, healthcare and personal safety.

[E] For the first time, every adult was promised the right to participate fully and equally in social and economic life and to help shape its future forms, together with a responsibility to contribute to building a sense of communality.

① [A] – [B] – [D] – [E] – [C]
② [C] – [A] – [E] – [B] – [D]
③ [C] – [E] – [A] – [D] – [B]
④ [E] – [A] – [C] – [B] – [D]
⑤ [E] – [B] – [D] – [C] – [A]

10 Reorder the following sentences in the best way to form a coherent passage for each question.

[A] Indeed, the evidence for fiber's benefits extends beyond any particular ailment.

[B] But while the benefits are clear, it's not so clear why fiber is so great.

[C] A diet of fiber-rich foods reduces the risk of developing diabetes, heart disease and arthritis.

[D] That's why experts are always saying how good dietary fiber is for us.

① [B] – [A] – [D] – [C]
② [C] – [B] – [A] – [D]
③ [C] – [A] – [D] – [B]
④ [B] – [D] – [A] – [C]

11 Which would be the correct order to make a logical paragraph of the above sentences?

[A] For one thing, this king had his own particular principle of carrying out justice and deciding cases of law.

[B] Here he was made to stand a special trial before the king himself.

[C] Instead, he was taken to a large arena.

[D] Many centuries ago, in a far-off country, there lived a king who had some rather strange ideas.

[E] When a person was accused of some crime, he was not taken before a judge or the usual court of law.

① [D] – [A] – [E] – [C] – [B]
② [D] – [E] – [B] – [C] – [A]
③ [A] – [E] – [D] – [C] – [B]
④ [E] – [C] – [B] – [D] – [A]

12 Choose the most logical order of the following sentences.

[A] People stop using a local language with few speakers and shift to one that has more speakers and is in general use over a larger area.

[B] All of these mean more contacts with people who do not belong to the local environment and do not speak the local language.

[C] Languages are vanishing in all parts of the world, and the course of events is similar everywhere.

[D] School education is expanding in almost all countries, and is usually offered only in big languages. Business and communications also become more important, which means a larger need for a language used by more people.

[E] The reasons are similar everywhere.

① [C] – [A] – [E] – [D] – [B]
② [D] – [A] – [B] – [E] – [C]
③ [A] – [D] – [E] – [B] – [C]
④ [A] – [E] – [D] – [C] – [B]
⑤ [C] – [D] – [E] – [B] – [A]

13 다음 [A]~[D]를 문맥에 맞게 배열한 것은?

Some sports heroes have overcome daunting obstacles to rise to the top of their sport. In 1957, for example, Jackie Robinson of the Brooklyn Dodgers became the first African-American to play in the modern major leagues.

[A] Although she wore a leg brace from the time she was 5 until she was 11, Rudolph still managed to play basketball and participate in track when she was 13. While still a high school sophomore, she competed in the 1956 Olympic Games.

[B] All these ailments left her with a bad leg that some said would prevent her even from walking.

[C] These days, Rudolph is remembered for her inspirational determination to overcome her physical challenges, and for her courage in rising above segregation and racism.

[D] Former Olympian Wilma Rudolph was born with polio and survived pneumonia and scarlet fever as a child.

① [A] – [B] – [D] – [C]
② [B] – [C] – [D] – [A]
③ [D] – [A] – [B] – [C]
④ [D] – [B] – [A] – [C]

14 다음 글의 밑줄 친 문장들을 바른 순서대로 나열한 것으로 가장 적합한 것은?

Because of the demands of measuring behavioral change across different ages, developmental researchers use several unique methods. The most frequently used cross-sectional research compares people of different ages at the same point in time. Cross-sectional studies provide information about differences in development between different age groups.

[A] A cohort is a group of people who grow up at similar times and places. In the case of IQ differences, any age differences we find in a cross-sectional study may reflect educational differences among the cohorts studied: people in the older age group may belong to a cohort that was less likely to attend college than were the people in the younger groups.

[B] Suppose, for instance, we were interested in the development of intellectual ability in adulthood. To carry out a cross-sectional study, we might compare a sample of 25-, 45-, and 65-year-olds who all take the same IQ test. We then can determine whether average IQ test scores differ in each age group.

[C] Cross-sectional research has limitations, however. For instance, we cannot be sure that the differences in IQ scores we might find in our example are due to age differences alone. Instead, the scores may reflect differences in the educational attainment of the cohorts represented.

① [C] – [B] – [A]
② [C] – [A] – [B]
③ [B] – [C] – [A]
④ [B] – [A] – [C]

15 다음 [A]~[D]를 문맥에 맞게 배열한 것은?

[A] Teens typically spend less time with their families and more with their friends. Privacy becomes very important to some, and they may start locking their bedroom door. Some become argumentative or rebellious, but that is just part of establishing autonomous values and principles.

[B] Adolescents are now responsible for their decisions, and they establish their own moral code based on introspection as opposed to abiding by the rules prescribed to them by their parents. All of these fascinating psycho-social changes result in additional changes in the behavior of adolescents.

[C] These are important skills when establishing identity, which involves getting a clear sense of one's values and beliefs, and determining one's goals and ambitions for the future. Through decision making, problem solving, and reasoning, adolescents become independent people, who make their own decisions and forge their own relationships.

[D] The development of an adult body is not the only change adolescents are experiencing. They are also developing adult thinking skills, which include reasoning and abstract thinking skills. By now, they are able to consider multiple variables and contemplate hypothetical situations.

① [A] – [D] – [C] – [B]
② [D] – [C] – [B] – [A]
③ [A] – [D] – [B] – [C]
④ [D] – [B] – [C] – [A]

16 Which is the proper order of the sentences [A]–[D]?

That genius is unusual goes without saying. [A] However another link, between savant syndrome and autism, is well established. [B] A link between artistic genius on the one hand and schizophrenia and manic-depression on the other is widely debated. [C] But is it so unusual that it requires the brains of those that possess it to be unusual in other ways, too? [D] It is, for example, the subject of films such as "Rain Man," in which the autistic brother shows an extraordinary talent of memorizing figures.

① [A] – [B] – [C] – [D]
② [A] – [D] – [C] – [B]
③ [C] – [B] – [D] – [A]
④ [C] – [B] – [A] – [D]

17 전체 글의 의미가 통하도록 문장들 [A]~[C]의 순서를 알맞게 배열한 것은?

Exercise can truly become addictive for women. The term "runner's high" does not simply refer to a psychological state of mind, because excessive running actually produces a morphine-like hormone known as beta-endorphin, which deadens pain, creating a certain stimulation.

[A] Just like drug addicts, they need their daily "fix" to function normally, and they don't realize that they are abandoning former friends and interests.

[B] I know two women, both lawyers, who have become so preoccupied with their fitness that not only must they begin and end their days with exercise, but they feel uncomfortable or irritable if someone or something prevents them from exercising.

[C] Fitness obsession reaches far beyond "runner's high" as it begins to affect other aspects of a woman's lifestyle, such as her job or personal relationships.

Exercise, like alcohol, can provide a means of escape so that a woman may never confront her fears or problems. The victim herself may never notice the problem unless she hits a distinct abyss.

① [A] – [B] – [C]　　② [A] – [C] – [B]

③ [C] – [B] – [A]　　④ [C] – [A] – [B]

18 Which of the following is the best order?

If we lived on a planet where nothing ever changed, there would be little to do. There would be nothing to figure out. [A] And if we lived in an unpredictable world, where things changed in random or very complex ways, we would not be able to figure things out. [B] Again, there would be no such thing as science. [C] But we live in an in-between universe, where things change, but according to patterns, rules, or, as we call them, laws of nature. [D] There would be no impetus for science. If I throw a stick up in the air, it always falls down. If the sun sets in the west, it always rises again the next morning in the east. And so it becomes possible to figure things out. We can do science, and with it we can improve our lives.

① [A] – [C] – [D] – [B]　　② [A] – [D] – [C] – [B]

③ [D] – [A] – [B] – [C]　　④ [D] – [C] – [A] – [B]

19 Reorder the following sentences in the best way to form a coherent passage for each question.

[A] Relatively few are looking at the way such people are taught in elementary school and high school and beyond.

[B] I happen to go to a professional meeting and hear papers presented, or afterwards, people talking in lobbies or corridors or restaurants–all those words, all those ideas, spoken by men and women who have no doubt about their importance, their achievements, and certainly, their ability to "communicate."

[C] Few are examining ever so closely the rhetoric of various business and professional people, nor the dreary, ponderous, smug, deadly words and phrases such people use.

[D] No one is proposing that jargon-filled scholars of one sort or another overcome their "cultural disadvantage."

① [B] – [D] – [C] – [A]
② [B] – [A] – [C] – [D]
③ [D] – [A] – [C] – [B]
④ [D] – [B] – [A] – [C]

20 Choose the most logical order of the following sentences.

[A] Endorsers include supermodel Kendall Jenner, who painted her living room in the bubblegum-like hue, and prison officials in Switzerland, where every fifth prison or police station has at least one pink cell. [B] No one could make the same claim today, eight decades on. [C] Take Baker-Miller pink, a shade some believe has a soothing effect. [D] Certain slivers of ROYGBIV — like Tiffany blue or T-Mobile magenta — have been copyrighted under federal law, while others have inspired scientific inquiry and even public policy interventions. [E] "I am convinced when I say that color has been a neglected art," Faber Birren declared in 1934.

– adapted from an article by Christopher Good

① [C] – [D] – [E] – [B] – [A]
② [E] – [B] – [D] – [C] – [A]
③ [D] – [C] – [B] – [E] – [A]
④ [D] – [A] – [C] – [B] – [E]
⑤ [E] – [D] – [A] – [B] – [C]

9강 문장 삽입

예제 2019 국민대(오후)

[A] Many supermarket chains discount food at regular intervals — for example, a certain ice cream might be half price once every four weeks. [B] Other staple foods that are discounted regularly include bread, juice, pasta sauce, coffee, biscuits, yoghurt and cereals. [C] Also, think about doing your shopping in the last hour before your local supermarket closes. [D] That's when you can find big discounts on perishable products such as bread, meat, fish and dairy products.

Q. Which is the best place for the following?

Once you're aware of the pattern, you need never buy these products at full price again.

① [A]
② [B]
③ [C]
④ [D]

유형별 문제풀이 Point _ 문장 삽입

Point 1 **주어진 문장에서 단서를 찾는다.**

문장 삽입 유형의 경우에는 주어진 문장의 구문분석과 정확한 번역이 우선된다. 일단 주어진 문장에 포함된 연결사(예시, 비교나 대조, 인과관계, 나열 등)와 지시어, 그리고 대명사 등에 표시하고 삽입할 위치를 찾아보자.

Point 2 **지문 속에서 단서를 찾고 주제를 생각해 본다.**

지문 안에서도 마찬가지로 삽입 가능한 위치마다 연결사(예시, 비교나 대조, 인과관계, 나열 등)와 지시어, 그리고 대명사 등에 표시를 하면서 읽는다. 지문을 읽으면서 주제가 무엇인지도 생각해 본다.

Point 3 **문장들 간의 논리적 흐름을 파악한다.**

문장들 간에 논리적 흐름이 끊기거나 연결사, 지시어, 대명사들을 고려했을 때 내용상 연결이 자연스럽지 않다고 생각되면 주어진 문장을 삽입해 본다.

정답 ③

분석 주어진 문장에서 'the pattern'과 'these products' 같은 단서가 문제풀이에 중요하다. 주어진 문장 앞에 특정 패턴이나 상품들에 대한 언급이 반드시 필요하므로 지문을 읽으며 찾아보도록 하자. 본문에서는 슈퍼마켓에서 식품 가격을 할인하는 패턴을 예를 들어 설명했으므로 첫 두 문장 다음인 [C]에 주어진 문장을 삽입하는 것이 가장 적절하다. 마지막 문장의 주어 'That'은 직전 문장의 'the last hour'를 지시하므로 내용상 자연스럽게 연결되기에 두 문장 사이에 주어진 문장을 삽입하는 것은 부자연스럽다.

어휘

discount ⓥ 할인하다, 할인해서 팔다
staple food 주요 식품
dairy product 유제품
at regular intervals 일정한 간격을 두고
perishable ⓐ (식품이) 잘 상하는, 썩는

해석 [A] 많은 슈퍼마켓 체인들은 정기적인 간격을 두고 식품 가격을 할인한다. 예를 들어, 어떤 아이스크림은 4주에 한 번 반값일 수 있다. [B] 정기적으로 할인되는 다른 주요 식품들은 빵, 주스, 파스타 소스, 커피, 비스킷, 요구르트 그리고 시리얼이 있다. [C] **〈일단 당신이 그 패턴을 알게 되면, 당신은 이 제품들을 다시 정가로 살 필요가 없다.〉** 또한 당신의 동네 슈퍼마켓이 문을 닫기 직전에 쇼핑하는 것도 한번 생각해 보라. [D] 그때 당신은 빵, 고기, 생선, 그리고 유제품과 같은 부패하기 쉬운 제품들을 대폭 할인받을 수 있다.

정답과 해설 p.199

01 글의 흐름으로 보아, 주어진 문장이 들어가기에 가장 적절한 곳은?

> Analysis of a newly discovered toothy, finned baleen fossil from North America promises to illuminate one part of this remarkable journey.

Archaeopteryx, a toothy, feathered fossil found in Germany in the 19th century, hinted at a crucial moment in the history of life — the point when dinosaurs took to the skies, and birds were thus born. [A] There are not many evolutionary journeys that can rival this, but that made by the descendants of some small, terrestrial mammals, which turned into the gigantic aquatic krill-eaters called baleen whales, is one such. [B] Baleen whales suck in large volumes of water and then force it out of their mouths through fibrous outgrowths known as baleen plates, to filter out small animals for consumption. [C] These plates sit where other mammals have teeth, but rather than robust dentine, the principal ingredient of teeth, they are composed of keratin, a flexible material that also makes up hair and fingernails. [D] Some researchers theorize that suction-filter feeding in whales began with teeth that could be gnashed together to form a simple sieve, and that only subsequently were these teeth replaced by baleen.

① [A] ② [B]
③ [C] ④ [D]

02 글의 흐름으로 보아, 주어진 문장이 들어가기에 가장 적절한 곳은?

> Yet other forms of literacy have become increasingly important in the twenty-first century.

[A] Since we have lived in a world in which the printed word was paramount, the chief burden of school has been to enable children to understand and produce with facility the written language of their society. [B] Much communication in our world takes place through graphic means — both static and dynamic. Web sites incorporate print, but they also feature cartoons, films, music, and the like. Representational redescriptions abound. [C] Moreover, the print on computer screens is often far less linear in form and argument than the print in a book. [D]

① [A] ② [B]
③ [C] ④ [D]

03 Which is the best place for the sentence given in the box?

The brain case, for example, is fully covered in bone.

Questions about whether snakes ever walked on legs have long intrigued scientists. But without any fossil evidence, there seemed no possibility of an answer. [A] That state of affairs changed dramatically, however, when what appear to be ancient fossils were discovered in an Israeli quarry. [B] To everyone's surprise, the fossil evidence indicates that some prehistoric snakes had hind legs, which could have been used for walking. [C] According to paleontologists Michael Caldwell and Michael Lee, the specimens found in Israel have hind legs along with characteristics that appear only in snakes. [D] In addition, the jaws are loosely connected, allowing for wide-mouthed flexibility — exactly the kind snakes need to swallow large prey. [E] Even the number and kind of vertebrae suggest that the fossils are those of ancient snakes. Finally, there may be just enough fossil evidence to prove that some snakes once walked on two legs.

① [A] ② [B]
③ [C] ④ [D]
⑤ [E]

04 Choose the best place in the passage for the sentence in the box.

Nevertheless, by the 1850s, the Irish had gained a measure of influence in America.

The Irish newcomers soon realized that their struggle against poverty, discrimination, and religious persecution would not end in the United States. [A] The large numbers of Irish immigrants who came to America in the 1830s threatened the jobs of native-born Protestants, who reacted with resentment and violence. [B] Employers posted signs outside their doors reading "No Irish Need Apply." [C] Despised for their Roman Catholicism and their supposed "clannishness," the Irish competed with African Americans for the low-paying jobs at the bottom of the economic ladder. [D] They filled many high positions in the Catholic Church and became active in the Democratic party. [E]

① [A] ② [B]
③ [C] ④ [D]
⑤ [E]

05 Which is the best place in the passage for the sentence in the box?

First the embalmers removed all the internal organs, leaving only the heart in place so that it could be judged.

The Egyptians believed that life continued after death. The dead were taken to the underworld where gods judged them by weighing their heart against the "feather of truth." Those who passed the test went to the Field of Reeds to live forever, while the heart of a person who failed the test was eaten by a creature called Ammut and the person was thus destroyed. [A] To allow people to enter the afterlife, Egyptians believed it necessary to preserve their bodies after death. [B] At first, they buried the dead in the desert sands, which soaked up the fluids and preserved the bodies naturally. [C] Later they developed a method of preserving bodies by embalming them, known as mummification. [D] Then they dried the body, coated it in resin and wrapped it in layers of linen strips. [E] Embalming was expensive and only the pharaoh and senior officials could afford the best treatment.

① [A]
② [B]
③ [C]
④ [D]
⑤ [E]

06 글의 흐름으로 보아, 주어진 문장이 들어가기에 가장 적절한 곳은?

Small fish feed upon the minute life forms in plankton, and they in turn are fed upon by large fish and other animals.

Sharks are no crueler than any other predator in the sea. [A] The marine environment is a harsh and pitiless world. [B] From the very start of life in the planktonic community, microscopic animal attacks and devours microscopic animal, in turn to be consumed by some larger form of life fighting the vicious and never-ending battle of survival. [C] And so on upward in size through the cycle to the sharks, the dominant predator of the oceans. [D] But the consumption of one living thing by another form of life is the order of survival, with nothing being wasted in nature. Only man is the indiscriminate killer.

① [A]
② [B]
③ [C]
④ [D]

07 글의 흐름으로 보아, 주어진 문장이 들어가기에 가장 적절한 곳은?

We now know that Jupiter, Uranus, and Neptune also have ring systems.

There are 140 known natural satellites, also called moons, in orbit around the various planets in our solar system, ranging from bodies larger than our own moon to small pieces of debris. [A] From 1610 to 1977, Saturn was thought to be the only planet with rings. [B] Particles in these ring systems range in size from dust to boulders to house-size. [C] And they may be rocky and/or icy. [D] Ancient astronomers believed that Earth was the center of the universe, and that the sun and all the other stars revolved around Earth. [E] Copernicus proved that Earth and the other planets in our solar system orbit our sun. Little by little, we are charting the universe.

① [A] ② [B]
③ [C] ④ [D]
⑤ [E]

08 글의 흐름으로 보아, 주어진 문장이 들어가기에 가장 적절한 곳은?

Generosity is not solely based on one's economic status.

Generosity is also defined as the habit of giving freely without expecting anything in return. It can involve offering time, assets or talents to aid someone in need. [A] Often equated with charity as a virtue, generosity is widely accepted in society as a desirable trait. [B] Generosity is a guiding principle for many registered charities, foundations and non-profit organizations. [C] Rather, it includes the individual's pure intentions of looking out for society's common good and giving from the heart. [D] Generosity should reflect the individual's passion to help others; in Buddhism, generosity is the antidote to the self-chosen poison called greed.

① [A] ② [B]
③ [C] ④ [D]

09 글의 흐름으로 보아, 주어진 문장이 들어가기에 가장 적절한 곳은?

When stated so starkly, this idea will appear problematical to many.

Theory is built upon an underlying assumption that specific events are not unique and do not have unique causes. Rather, we assume that most important events are single instances of broader patterns. [A] If we want to prevent wars, we must have some notion of what causes them. This requires a supposition that different wars have something in common. [B] For example, it might seem dubious to equate the causes of World War I with the causes of World War II. [C] However, if the lessons of the past are to be applied to the problems of today, we must assume that events in the future are somehow related to those in the past. There is a big difference between assuming that similar events have something in common and assuming that they are identical. [D] To develop a theory of wars, we only need assume that there are some causes in common.

① [A]
② [B]
③ [C]
④ [D]

10 Which is the best place for the sentence below?

Logic dictated that if ancient people were to be found at all, it would be on a large and long-populated landmass, not in the comparative fastness of an archipelago.

Just before Christmas 1887, a young Dutch doctor M. E. Dubois arrived in Sumatra, in the Dutch East Indies, with the intention of finding the earliest human remains on Earth. [A] Several things were extraordinary about this. [B] To begin with, no one had gone looking for ancient human bones before. Everything that had been found to this point had been found accidentally, and nothing in Dubois's background suggested that he was the ideal candidate to make the process intentional. He was an anatomist by training, with no background in paleontology. Nor was there any special reason to suppose that Sumatra would hold early human remains. [C] Dubois was driven to Sumatra on nothing stronger than a hunch and the knowledge that Sumatra was full of caves, the environment in which most of the important hominid fossils had so far been found. [D] What is most extraordinary in all this is that he found what he was looking for.

① [A]
② [B]
③ [C]
④ [D]

11 글의 흐름으로 보아, 주어진 문장이 들어가기에 가장 적절한 곳은?

Oddly enough, it has an apocalyptic sound today.

There has never been a period in medicine when the future has looked so bright. The scientists who do research on the cardiovascular system are entirely confident that they will soon be working close to the center of things, and they no longer regard the mechanisms of heart disease as impenetrable mysteries. The cancer scientists, for all their public disagreements about how best to organize their research, are in possession of insights into the intimate functioning of normal and neoplastic cells that were unimaginable a few years back. The neurobiologists can do all sorts of things in their investigation, and the brain is an organ different from what it seemed 25 years ago.

In short, I believe that the major diseases of human beings have become approachable biological puzzles, ultimately solvable. [A] It follows from this that it is now possible to begin thinking about a human society relatively free of disease. [B] This would surely have been an unthinkable notion a half century ago. [C] What will we do about dying, and about all that population, if such things were to come about? [D] What can we die of, if not disease?

① [A]　　② [B]
③ [C]　　④ [D]

12 Look at the four marked places, [A], [B], [C], and [D], which indicate where the following sentence could be inserted. Where would the sentence best fit?

In postindustrial societies, prestige is linked to occupational status, although income is also important.

[A] In the United States, the top-status occupations are the professions — physicians, lawyers, professors, and clergy — requiring many years of education and training. [B] At the other end of the hierarchy, the lowest prestige is associated with occupations requiring little formal education — for example, bus drivers, sanitation workers, and janitors. Prestige is linked to income, but there are exceptions, such as college professors, who have high prestige but relatively low salaries compared to physicians and lawyers. [C] Conversely, some low-prestige workers receive high union wages and benefits. [D] Criminals are often well rewarded with income and respect in their communities, while politicians — many of whom are wealthy — are frequently less respected than occupations such as secretary and bank teller.

① [A]　　② [B]
③ [C]　　④ [D]

13 글의 흐름으로 보아, 주어진 문장이 들어가기에 가장 적절한 곳은?

In short, both sides assume, one with euphoria and the other with fear, that global-scale business is the wave of the future.

Globalization, argues *New York Times* columnist Tom Friedman, is "making it possible for corporations to reach farther, faster, cheaper, and deeper around the world" and is fostering "a flowering of both wealth and technological innovation the likes of which the world has never before seen." To David Korten, a former Ford Foundation official and now a prominent globalization critic, it is "market tyranny extending its reach across the planet like a cancer, destroying livelihoods, and feeding on life in an insatiable quest for money." The careful listener to this by-now-familiar debate can actually discern a striking point of agreement. [A] Yet there's mounting evidence that multinational firms may be less capable of delivering competitive products than national or local firms. [B] Any first-year economics student learns that firms can lower average costs by expanding, but only up to a point. Beyond that point (according to the law of diminishing returns to scale), complexities, breakdowns, and inefficiencies begin to drive average costs back up. [C] The collapse of massive state-owned enterprises in the old Soviet Union and the bankruptcies of Chrysler and New York City are notable reminders of a lesson we should have absorbed from the dinosaur: Bigger is not always better. [D]

① [A] ② [B]
③ [C] ④ [D]

14 글의 흐름으로 보아, 주어진 문장이 들어가기에 가장 적절한 곳은?

> Unlike the endocrine system, which sends chemical signals through the bloodstream, the nervous system promptly transmits electrical signals via nerve cells. These rapid messages control split-second responses.

Animals rely on many kinds of chemical signals to regulate their body activities. The estrogens are one kind of signal, a hormone. [A] An animal hormone is a chemical signal that is carried by the circulatory system usually in the blood and that communicates regulatory messages throughout the body. [B] Hormones are made and secreted mainly by organs called endocrine glands. Collectively, all of an animal's hormone-secreting cells constitute its endocrine system, one of two bodily systems for communication and chemical regulation. The other system of internal communication and regulation is the nervous system. [C] The flick of a frog's tongue catching a fly and the jerk of your hand away from a flame result from high-speed nerve signals. The endocrine system coordinates slower but longer-lasting responses. [D] In some cases, the endocrine system takes hours or even days to act, partly because of the time it takes for hormones to be made and transported to all their target organs and partly because the cellular response may take time.

① [A] ② [B]
③ [C] ④ [D]

15 글의 흐름으로 보아, 주어진 문장이 들어가기에 가장 적절한 곳은?

These critics refuse to face the fact that competition is part of American society.

In 1993, about 7 percent of America's high schools had eliminated ranking their students by grade point average (GPA); thus, the schools also did away with honoring a valedictorian — the individual with the highest GPA — at graduation. [A] Since then, scrapping the valedictorian tradition has become a national trend. [B] Those who support the elimination of class rankings and valedictorians claim that ranking students makes the lower-performing students feel inadequate. [C] It's the desire to be the best that makes achievement a reality. [D] Maintaining the valedictorian tradition spurs student achievement; without it, our students have no incentive to excel.

① [A] ② [B]
③ [C] ④ [D]

16 글의 흐름으로 보아, 주어진 문장이 들어가기에 가장 적절한 곳은?

Weaknesses are not flaws, but rather negative traits that, through self-improvement, can be developed into more positive traits.

A best-selling book offers "Seven Ways to Become a Better Person." A radio ad promises you will feel great in 30 days or less just by taking some pills. If you buy our exercise equipment, a TV ad guarantees, you will have the body you have always wanted. In today's society, we are continually bombarded with the latest techniques of how to better ourselves, a focus which some feel is unhealthy. [A] A better approach would be to help people grow in character. [B] Building character involves taking a person's strengths and building on them. Such strengths as unselfishness can be developed into a lifelong habit of generosity, a positive spirit into an unfailing compassion for others. Everyone has strength in character and the ability to build on these strengths through self-improvement. [C] For example, impatience can be turned into determination to accomplish goals. Strong will turns into perseverance. [D] If a person can just find a way to capitalize on a weakness, it can be turned into a strength. Self improvement is the best way to do this.

① [A] ② [B]
③ [C] ④ [D]

17 글의 흐름으로 보아, 주어진 문장이 들어가기에 가장 적절한 곳은?

> But increasingly, demographers and other experts say that cities may actually be a critical means of limiting environmental damage.

Cities are where almost all remaining population growth will occur, demographers say. The roster of megacities, those with populations exceeding 10 million, is widely expected to climb, from 20 today to 36 by 2015. [A] These vast metropolises have been widely characterized as a nightmarish element of the new century, sprawling and chaotic and spawning waste and illness. [B] Most significantly, they say, family size drops sharply in urban areas. For the poor, access to health care, schools and other basic services is generally greater in the city than in the countryside. Energy is used more efficiently, and drinking and wastewater systems, although lacking now, can be built relatively easily. And for every person who moves to a city, that is one person fewer chopping firewood or poaching game. [C] Still, many cities face decisions now that may permanently alter the quality of human lives and the environment. The pivotal nature of these times is perfectly illustrated by Mexico City, which is just behind Tokyo atop the list of megacities. The sprawling megalopolis, where traffic is paralyzed, is about to choose in a referendum between double-decking its downtown highways or expanding its subway system. [D] One course could encourage sprawl and pollution; the other would conserve energy, experts say.

① [A] ② [B]
③ [C] ④ [D]

18 Which is the best place to fill the following sentence in?

The process of building defenses continues into the next phase.

All human beings, in their understanding of themselves, build sets of defenses to protect the ego. The newborn baby has no concept of its own self; gradually it learns to identify a self that is distinct from others. [A] In childhood, the growing degrees of awareness, responding, and valuing begin to create a system of affective traits that individuals identify with themselves. [B] In adolescence, the physical, emotional, and cognitive changes of the pre-teenager and teenager bring on mounting defensive inhibitions to protect a fragile ego, to ward off ideas, experiences, and feelings that threaten to dismantle the organization of values and beliefs on which appraisals of self-esteem have been founded. [C] Some persons — those with higher self-esteem and ego strength — are more able to withstand threats to their existence, and thus their defenses are lower. [D] Those with weaker self-esteem maintain walls of inhibition to protect what is self-perceived to be a weak or fragile ego, or a lack of self-confidence in a situation or task.

① [A] ② [B]
③ [C] ④ [D]

19 글의 흐름으로 보아, 주어진 문장이 들어가기에 가장 적절한 곳은?

This is a fatal assumption that will only result in confusion and frustration for your reader.

Mark Twain observed, "We are all ignorant, but about different things." [A] One mistake technical professionals mark when writing for non-technical readers is assuming their readers are as knowledgeable as they are about the subject. [B] Just because it's clear to you does not make it clear of your reader. [C] If you are an engineer or accountant writing to others in your field, then perhaps there will be less need to explain all aspects of your message. [D] If you're writing to the senior vice president of marketing, who is not familiar with software applications, then you will need to "walk" that reader through your message. [E] Remember that when it comes to technical knowledge, writers and readers are hardly equal.

① [A] ② [B]
③ [C] ④ [D]
⑤ [E]

20 글의 흐름으로 보아, 주어진 문장이 들어가기에 가장 적절한 곳은?

> He formulated the concept of regional parallelism, according to which vegetation responses to climate change were parallel in different parts of the world.

In 1916, Swedish geologist Lennart von Post showed that by identifying and counting pollen preserved at different depths in Swedish peat bogs he could infer changes in forest composition through time. Following his pioneering work, pollen analysis quickly became established as a key tool for understanding past vegetation, climate, and ecosystems. [A] Today, it is used widely to reconstruct past ecosystems and test hypotheses about drivers of ecosystem change. Using pollen analysis, von Post explored the temporal changes in postglacial forest composition at many sites in southern Sweden. [B] He then demonstrated the spatial patterns of change by mapping his pollen data at selected times. [C] He also developed pollen analysis as a relative-dating technique for resolving postglacial sea-level changes. [D] In the 1930s to 1950s, pollen-analytical studies around the world were performed to establish vegetation history, estimate pollen-accumulation rates, elucidate the relationship of modern pollen spectra to vegetation, and map pollen data through time.

① [A] ② [B]
③ [C] ④ [D]

10강 무관한 문장 / 단어 고르기

예제 2019 인하대

There are few problems more annoying than hiccups, which can last for hours or even days. [A] According to one doctor who has studied them, hiccups are usually caused by eating or drinking too quickly. [B] People do some pretty strange things to remedy this ridiculous problem. [C] Some common remedies include holding your breath, eating a teaspoon of sugar, and putting a paper bag over your head. [D] The best exercise for a healthy heart is walking. [E] Undoubtedly, that last one is the strangest one of all.

Q. Which of the following does not fit in the passage?

① [A]
② [B]
③ [C]
④ [D]
⑤ [E]

유형별 문제풀이 Point _ 무관한 문장 / 단어 고르기

Point 1 첫 보기 전까지의 내용을 확실히 파악한다.

도입 문장이 글 전체의 흐름을 결정하는 두괄식 구조의 지문이 자주 출제되므로 첫 보기 전까지의 내용을 완벽하게 이해하는 것이 중요하다. 지문을 읽으며 전개방식과 주제를 파악해 보도록 한다.

Point 2 글의 흐름에 방해가 되는 한 문장을 찾아본다.

주제를 파악했다면 보기가 포함된 문장들을 앞 문장과 계속 비교하면서 주제에서 벗어나는지를 확인해 본다. 이때 문장마다 지시어나 연결사 등의 단서를 적극적으로 활용하여 문장들의 연결성을 파악해 보자. 주제에서 벗어나는 문장을 골랐다면 그 문장을 제외한 앞뒤 문장이 서로 통일성이 있는지 확인해 보자.

Point 3 무관한 어휘를 고르는 문제의 경우

글의 흐름에 적절하지 않은 어휘를 고르는 유형의 경우에는 밑줄 친 어휘의 '사전적 정의'를 알아야 문제 해결이 가능하다. 밑줄 친 어휘가 글의 흐름에 부적절하다고 생각될 때 해당 어휘를 반의어로 바꿔 넣어 보거나 해당 어휘 앞에 'not'을 넣어 다시 읽어 보면 자연스러운 경우가 많으니 참고하자.

정답 ④

분석 본문은 '딸꾹질의 성가심과 사람들의 이상한 해결법'에 대해 설명했다. 첫 보기 전까지의 내용이 글의 흐름을 결정하므로 [A]부터 [E]까지 소재인 '딸꾹질'이나 '이상한 해결법'에 관한 내용이 언급되어야 한다. 그러나 [D]에서는 이와 무관한 '심장의 건강'이 언급되어 글의 흐름상 적절하지 않으므로 제거한다.

어휘

annoying ⓐ 성가신, 짜증스러운
ridiculous ⓐ 웃기는, 말도 안 되는, 터무니없는
undoubtedly ⓐⓓ 의심할 여지 없이, 확실히
hiccup ⓝ 딸꾹질
remedy ⓝ 처리방안, 해결책, 치료

해석 딸꾹질보다 더 성가신 문제는 거의 없는데 그것은 몇 시간 또는 심지어 며칠 동안 지속될 수도 있기 때문이다. [A] 딸꾹질을 연구한 한 의사에 따르면, 딸꾹질은 보통 너무 빨리 먹거나 마셔서 유발된다. [B] 사람들은 이 웃기는 문제를 해결하기 위해서 매우 이상한 행동을 한다. [C] 몇몇 흔한 치료법으로는 숨을 참는 것, 설탕을 한 찻숟가락 먹는 것, 종이봉지를 머리에 덮어씌우는 것 등이 있다. [D] **〈건강한 심장을 위한 최고의 운동은 걷는 것이다.〉** [E] 의심할 여지 없이, 마지막(마지막에 언급한 것)이 가장 이상하다.

Practice

정답과 해설 p.222

01 Which of the following does not fit in the passage?

Soon after an infant is born, many mothers hold their infants in such a way that they are face-to-face and gaze at them. [A] Mothers have been observed to address their infants, vocalize to them, ask questions, and greet them. [B] In other words, from birth on, the infant is treated as a social being and as an addressee in social interaction. [C] The infant's vocalizations, and physical movements and states are often interpreted as meaningful and are responded to verbally by the mother or other care-giver. [D] The cultural dispreference for saying what another might be thinking or feeling has important consequences for the organization of exchanges between care-giver and child. [E] In this way, protoconversations are established and sustained along a two-party, turn-taking model. Throughout this period and the subsequent language-acquiring years, care-givers treat very young children as communicative partners.

① [A] ② [B]
③ [C] ④ [D]
⑤ [E]

02 Which is LEAST consistent with the context?

The current academic system has fudged the distinctions between training and education. Administrations of most colleges and universities have responded to the economic and cultural uncertainties provoked by budget constraints and [A] a volatile job market by constructing their institutions on the model of the modern corporation. Consequently, many have thrust training to the fore and called it education. Lacking a unified national culture into which to socialize students and in any case lacking [B] an educational philosophy capable of steering an independent course, the academic system as a whole is caught in [C] a market logic that demands students be job-ready upon graduation. Under these imperatives colleges and universities are unable to implement an educational program that prepares students for [D] the competitive job market. Instead, academic leaders chant the mantra of "excellence," which means that all of the parts of the university "perform" and are judged according to how well they deliver knowledge and qualified labor to the corporate economy and how well the administration fulfills the recruitment and funding goals needed to maintain the institution.

① [A] ② [B]
③ [C] ④ [D]

03 Which of the following does NOT fit in the passage?

[A] Teotihuacan was one of the first true urban centers in the Western Hemisphere, covering nearly eight square miles at its heyday. [B] Precious artifacts recovered from the Pyramid of the Moon and other structures reveal that this was a wealthy trade metropolis with far-reaching connections. [C] Inexplicably, the city suffered sudden and violent collapse in about A.D. 600 and many people fled. [D] Assuming that some of the buildings were tombs, they called the boulevard Street of the Dead. [E] They left few written records, just the ruins of their city and intriguing clues about a once powerful culture.

① [A]
② [B]
③ [C]
④ [D]
⑤ [E]

04 다음 글에서 전체 흐름과 관계 없는 문장은?

The bright lights of the big city are getting a little bit duller. [A] Conservationism, rising energy costs and stricter building codes have conspired to transform Manhattan's nightscape into one with a gentler glow. [B] Manhattan currently boasts one of the best nightscapes in the world. [C] Instead of tower after tower shining at all hours, the skyline is becoming a patchwork of sparsely sparkling buildings decorated with lighted tops. [D] The tall towers with the illuminated floors on all night have become a thing of the past.

① [A]
② [B]
③ [C]
④ [D]

05 Which word is NOT appropriate in the context?

Darwin was quite familiar with the concept of [A] selective breeding. From his experience with livestock, he knew that over generations a breeder could eventually [B] maintain the appearance of an animal or plant. For example, the common rock pigeon is a relatively plain-looking bird. Native to southern Europe and northern Africa, it is now [C] common in parks and cities throughout the world. Humans first began keeping pigeons several thousand years ago. Breeders chose male and female birds with interesting [D] variations of feathers, colors, neck, beak shape, or flying behaviors and allowed them to breed. Over several generations, these traits became more [E] pronounced in their offspring until the features were well established in the birds. Thus, we now have different varieties of pigeons, such as the fan tail, archangel, and tumbler, each with its own distinct features.

① [A]
② [B]
③ [C]
④ [D]
⑤ [E]

06 Which of the following does not fit in the passage?

Before the Industrial Revolution, most goods were produced by hand in rural homes or urban workshops. [A] Merchants, known as entrepreneurs, distributed the raw materials to workers, collected the finished products, paid for the work, then sold them. [B] Growing demand for consumer products, together with a shortage of labour, placed pressure on entrepreneurs to find new, more efficient methods of production. [C] The great era of European exploration that began in the 15th century arose primarily out of a desire to seek out new trade routes and partners. [D] With the development of power-driven machines, it made economic sense to bring workers, materials and machines together in one place, giving rise to the first factories. [E] For added efficiency, the production process was broken down into basic individual tasks that a worker could specialize in, a system known as the division of labour.

① [A]
② [B]
③ [C]
④ [D]
⑤ [E]

07 다음 글에서 전체 흐름과 관계 없는 문장은?

Why don't we "think something different" more often? There are several main reasons. The first is that we don't need to be creative for most of what we do. [A] For example, we don't need to be creative when we're driving on the freeway, or riding in an elevator, or waiting in line at a grocery store. [B] We are creatures of habit when it comes to the business of living — from doing paperwork to tying our shoes. For most of our activities, these routines are indispensable. Without them, our lives would be in chaos, and we wouldn't get much accomplished. [C] If you got up this morning and started contemplating the bristles on your toothbrush or questioning the meaning of toast, you probably wouldn't make it to work. [D] These attitudes are necessary for most of what we do, but they can get in the way when we're trying to be creative. [E] Staying on routine thought paths enables us to do the many things we need to do without having to think about them.

① [A] ② [B]
③ [C] ④ [D]
⑤ [E]

08 다음 글에서 전체 흐름과 관계 없는 문장은?

Abraham Lincoln's election to the presidency in 1860 brought to a climax the long festering debate about the relative powers of the federal and the state government. [A] By the time of his inauguration, six Southern states had seceded from the Union and formed the Confederate States of America, soon to be followed by five more. [B] The war that followed between North and South put constitutional government to its severest test. [C] After four bloody years of war, the Union was preserved, four million African American slaves were freed, and an entire nation was released from the oppressive weight of slavery. [D] The war can be viewed in several different ways: as the final, violent phase in a conflict of two regional subcultures; as the breakdown of a democratic political system; as the climax of several decades of social reform; or as a pivotal chapter in American racial history. [E] As important as the war itself was the tangled problem of how to reconstruct the defeated South. However interpreted, the Civil War stands as a story of great heroism, sacrifice, triumph, and tragedy.

① [A] ② [B]
③ [C] ④ [D]
⑤ [E]

09 [A]~[E] 가운데, 문맥상 낱말의 쓰임이 적절하지 않은 것은?

Everyone knows what sharks look like. We also know that sharks can be dangerous. However, many people may not realize that sharks are one of the oldest species of animals on earth, as well as one of the most interesting. Sharks share some things in common with other fish, but they are somewhat [A] different. First of all, almost all sharks are carnivores, or meat eaters. They eat dolphins, seals, other sharks, and other fish. Like all fish, though, sharks are [B] cold-blooded animals — their bodies change temperature as the water temperature changes. Also, like other fish, the shark's body has gill slits, or openings that help the shark [C] breathe in the water. However, a shark's skeleton is unusual for a fish. Its bones are tough and [D] inflexible. In fact, shark bones feel like a human ear. In addition, a shark's skin is unusual for a fish. Its skin is like armor. It has many sharp spikes or nails to [E] protect it. Consequently, you can hurt yourself by just touching a shark's skin.

① [A]
② [B]
③ [C]
④ [D]
⑤ [E]

10 Which is NOT properly used in the context of the passage?

Humans are hardwired to hate uncertainty; we're constantly trying to find "sure things" to help us succeed. But ironically, Jamie Holmes argues in his new book, this aversion to ambiguity often hinders our ability to make the best decisions. In medicine, for instance, one study found that doctors who acknowledged that their patient had unclear symptoms would [A] nevertheless order a definitive test or prescription 77% of the time — often without asking follow-up questions. How can we [B] combat this impulsive desire for resolution? For starters, Holmes writes, we should be open to [C] second-guessing ourselves. This is especially true in schools, where teachers should encourage students to take the unfamiliar side of an argument or [D] ignore a problem riddled with errors — all in an attempt to hone their critical-thinking skills. After all, Holmes writes, "sometimes the illusion of knowing is more dangerous than not knowing at all."

① [A] nevertheless
② [B] combat
③ [C] second-guessing
④ [D] ignore

11 Which of the following does NOT fit in the context?

The most depressing response I encounter when I'm chatting someone up and I ask them if they ever go to the theatre is this: "I should go but I don't." [A] That emphatic "should" tells you all you need to know. [B] Imagine it in other contexts: "I should play Grand Theft Auto"; "I should watch Strictly Come Dancing." [C] Many critics still believe theatre has a quasi-educational/political role; that a play posits an argument that the playwright then proves or disproves. [D] That "should" tells you that people see theatre-going not as entertainment but as self-improvement, and the critical/academic establishment have to take some blame for that.

① [A] ② [B]
③ [C] ④ [D]

12 Which of the underlined words is NOT appropriate?

Sports facilities built in the late 1970s, 80s, and early 90s were routinely designed to enhance in-facility experiences but routinely ignored the potential for [A] harnessing associated economic activity that could take place on adjacent real estate. Facilities built during this time period were constructed with substantial public investments. The failure to [B] diminish property values and capitalize on the economic activity taking place within the venue generated substantial levels of discontent with the decision to support a team's effort to secure a new venue. As a result, all of the benefits from the building of venues [C] accrued to team owners and others linked to the sports industry. There was little if any financial return to the public sector partners. The situation was made worse when team owners were allowed to [D] retain most, if not all, of the revenue streams that were created in these new state-of-the-art facilities.

① [A] ② [B]
③ [C] ④ [D]

13 Which of the following does NOT fit in the context?

According to study experts, one tip for exam success is regular daily and weekly study. Another tip is to focus on, in your study sessions, ideas that the instructor has emphasized in class. [A] In addition, use the night before an exam for a careful review rather than a stressful cramming. [B] Then get up a bit early the next morning and review your notes one more time. [C] Study skills are tools and strategies used to make learning more efficient, organized, and successful. [D] Last, once the test begins, the advice of experts is to answer the easiest question first; then go back and tackle the hard ones.

① [A]　　② [B]
③ [C]　　④ [D]

14 Choose one that is unnecessary for the flow of the passage.

The natural surveillance provided by passers-by or by windows and balconies overlooking streets is enough to deter most crime and vandalism. [A] Well-designed neighborhoods promote this casual policing, which can work alongside more formal schemes for watching over one another's homes. [B] Homes should be flexible to adapt to a household's changing needs over time. [C] Thoughtfully sited car parking and bicycle storage, as well as well-integrated recycling bins, contribute not only to a sense of order but also to reducing litter, vandalism and theft. [D] To encourage these changes, police services award Secured by Design certificates to homes and developments whose design deters crime. It considers the materials and design of entry points such as doors and windows, the deployment of burglar alarms and video entry systems, and the natural surveillance offered by windows to open spaces.

① [A]　　② [B]
③ [C]　　④ [D]

15 다음 글에서 전체 흐름과 관계 없는 문장은?

Although scattered local airline companies began offering flights to passengers as early as 1913, scheduled domestic flights did not become widely available in the United States until the 1920s. [A] During the early years of commercial aviation, U.S. airline travel was limited to a small population of business travelers and wealthy individuals who could afford the high ticket prices. [B] The majority of travelers relied instead on more affordable train services for their intercity transportation needs. [C] Over ninety-five years later, the airlines have grown to be one of the most important and heavily used transportation options for American business and leisure travelers. [D] Following deregulation of the airline industry by the U.S. government in 1978, airline routes increased, ticket fares decreased, and discount carriers prospered, thus making airline travel accessible to a much broader segment of the U.S. population. [E] Plane tickets were generally prepared by hand using carbon paper and were given to passengers upon their arrival at the airports. In 2008 alone, 649.9 million passengers traveled on domestic flights on U.S. airlines.

① [A] ② [B]
③ [C] ④ [D]
⑤ [E]

16 다음 글에서 전체 흐름과 관계 없는 문장은?

Vigorous activity is usually a healthful pursuit but it can become maladaptive when carried to extremes. [A] There are runners and body builders, for instance, who use their obsessive workouts to avoid taking responsibility for other aspects of their lives, allowing little time for family, friends, or additional interests. [B] Rather than enjoying their fitness endeavors, they feel powerless to make any adjustments in their routines except to try to do more. [C] Pursuing pleasurable fitness endeavors can be a great coping strategy for lessening daily pressures. [D] Unfortunately, the exercise patterns of some adolescents and adults reflect deep-seated psychological problems. [E] They become dangerously fixated on trying to change their bodies by a combination of exhausting exercise and dieting, increasing their risk of serious health problems including substance abuse and eating disorders.

① [A] ② [B]
③ [C] ④ [D]
⑤ [E]

17 다음 글에서 전체 흐름과 관계 없는 문장은?

One phase of the business cycle is the expansion phase. This phase is a twofold one, including recovery and prosperity. [A] It is not prosperity itself but expectation of prosperity that triggers the expansion phase. During the recovery period there is ever-growing expansion of existing facilities, and new facilities for production are created. More businesses are created and older ones expanded. Improvements of various kinds are made. There is an ever-increasing optimism about the future of economic growth. Much capital is invested in machinery or heavy industry. More labor is employed. More materials are required. As one part of the economy develops, other parts are affected. [B] For example, a great expansion in automobiles results in an expansion of the steel, glass, and rubber industries. Roads are required; thus the cement and machinery industries are stimulated. [C] Demand for labor and materials results in greater prosperity for workers and suppliers of raw materials, including farmers. This increases purchasing power and the volume of goods bought and sold. Thus, prosperity is diffused among the various segments of the population. [D] This prosperity period may continue to rise and rise without an apparent end. However, a time comes when this phase reaches a peak and stops spiraling upwards. This is the end of the expansion phase.

① [A]　　② [B]
③ [C]　　④ [D]

18 다음 글에서 전체 흐름과 관계 없는 문장은?

Why do people choose to home educate their child? Some families make a carefully considered decision to home educate long before their child reaches "school age." [A] There may be philosophical, religious or various other reasons for their choice and ultimately they feel that in some way they can offer a more suitable education for their child at home.

[B] It is also a natural choice for parents who have enjoyed participating in their child's early learning and see no reason to give up this responsibility when the child reaches the age of five. [C] Other parents send their child into the school system, but later find that school does not work for their child. [D] In schools, students can get comparatively high marks by remembering what teachers have said. [E] School does not suit everyone. Sometimes children may find it hard to "fit in" so their parents may also decide to home educate.

① [A]　　② [B]
③ [C]　　④ [D]
⑤ [E]

19 다음 글에서 전체 흐름과 관계 없는 문장은?

In today's youth-obsessed culture, getting older is often seen as something to fear. [A] But a new study says at least one thing gets better with age: self-esteem. Age 60 seems to be best for self-esteem, according to Ulrich Orth, a professor of psychology at the University of Bern in Switzerland. Self-esteem first begins to rise between ages 4 and 11, as children develop socially and cognitively and gain some sense of independence. [B] Levels then seem to plateau — but not decline — as the teenage years begin from ages 11 to 15, the data show. That's somewhat surprising, given that many people assume that self-esteem takes a hit during the traditionally awkward early teenage years, "possibly because of pubertal changes and increased emphasis on social comparison at school," Orth says. "However, our findings show that this is not the case." [C] Instead, self-esteem appears to hold steady until mid-adolescence. After that lull, self-esteem seems to increase substantially until age 30, then more gradually throughout middle adulthood, before peaking around age 60 and remaining stable until age 70. [D] Old age frequently involves loss of social roles as a result of retirement and the empty nest, which lower self-esteem. [E] "Many people," Orth says, "are able to maintain a relatively high level of self-esteem even during old age."

① [A]
② [B]
③ [C]
④ [D]
⑤ [E]

20 다음 글에서 전체 흐름과 관계 없는 문장은?

The close relationship between language and religious belief pervades cultural history. Often, a divine being is said to have invented speech, or writing, and given it as a gift to mankind. One of the first things Adam has to do, according to the Book of Genesis, is to name the acts of creation. Many other cultures have a similar story. [A] In Egyptian mythology, the god Thoth is the creator of speech and writing. [B] It is Brahma who gives the knowledge of writing to the Hindu people. [C] Odin is the inventor of runic script, according to the Icelandic sagas. [D] Literacy is often introduced into a community by the spread of a religion. [E] A heaven-sent water turtle, with marks on its back, brings writing to the Chinese. All over the world, the supernatural provides a powerful set of beliefs about the origins of language.

① [A]
② [B]
③ [C]
④ [D]
⑤ [E]

MEMO

MEMO

MEMO

에듀윌 편입 솔루션 독해 Basic

발 행 일	2023년 7월 12일 초판
편 저 자	에듀윌 편입 LAB
펴 낸 이	김재환
펴 낸 곳	(주)에듀윌
등록번호	제25100-2002-000052호
주 소	08378 서울특별시 구로구 디지털로34길 55 코오롱싸이언스밸리 2차 3층

www.eduwill.net

대표전화 1600-6700

여러분의 작은 소리
에듀윌은 크게 듣겠습니다.

본 교재에 대한 여러분의 목소리를 들려주세요.
공부하시면서 어려웠던 점, 궁금한 점,
칭찬하고 싶은 점, 개선할 점, 어떤 것이라도 좋습니다.

에듀윌은 여러분께서 나누어 주신 의견을
통해 끊임없이 발전하고 있습니다.

에듀윌 도서몰 book.eduwill.net

- 부가학습자료 및 정오표: 에듀윌 도서몰 → 도서자료실
- 교재 문의: 에듀윌 도서몰 → 문의하기 → 교재(내용, 출간) / 주문 및 배송

에듀윌 편입의
독한 관리 시스템

전문 학습매니저의 독한 관리로
빠르게 합격할 수 있도록 관리해 드립니다.

독한 담임관리

- 진단고사를 통한 수준별 학습설계
- 일일 진도율부터 성적, 멘탈까지 관리
- 밴드, SNS를 통한 1:1 맞춤 상담 진행
- 담임 학습매니저가 합격할 때까지 독한 관리

독한 학습관리

- 학습진도 체크 & 학습자료 제공
- 데일리 어휘 테스트
- 모의고사 성적관리 & 약점 보완 제시
- 대학별 배치상담 진행

독한 생활관리

- 출석 관리
- 나의 학습량, 일일 진도율 관리
- 월별 총 학습시간 관리
- 슬럼프 물리치는 컨디션 관리
- 학원과 동일한 의무 자습 관리

에듀윌
편입 솔루션

독해 BASIC 정답과 해설

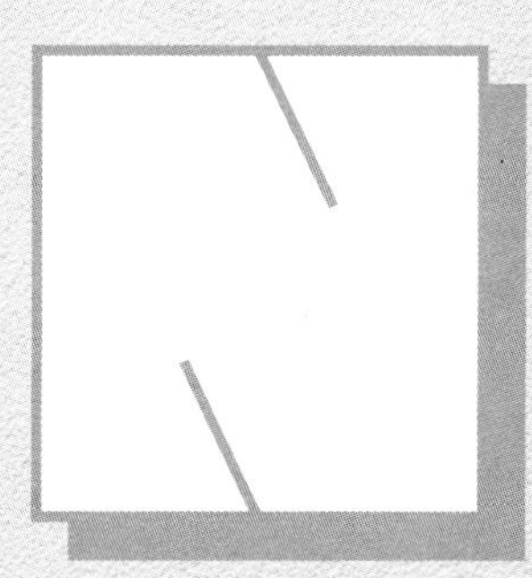

독해가 어려워?

이 책을 봐!

편입 최초
프리미엄 해설 수록

eduwill

에듀윌
편입 솔루션

독해 BASIC 정답과 해설

에듀윌 편입 솔루션

독해 BASIC 정답과 해설

READING BASIC

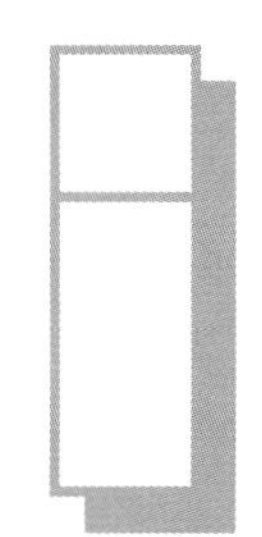

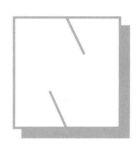

독해가 어려워?

이 책을 봐!

편입 최초
프리미엄 해설 수록

eduwill

LEVEL 1 중심 내용 파악하기

1강 제목

Practice

01	①	02	①	03	②	04	①	05	①	06	③	07	④	08	①	09	②	10	③
11	③	12	②	13	③	14	④	15	③	16	②	17	③	18	③	19	②	20	②
21	①	22	③	23	④	24	②	25	③	26	②	27	②	28	①	29	②	30	①

01 2019 가톨릭대

정답 ①

| 구문분석 | People (in the majority) can cause other group members to conform (through normative influence).
S V O O.C
대다수의 사람들은 규범적인 영향력을 통해 다른 집단 구성원들이 순응하도록 만들 수 있다.

The conformity (that occurs) may be a case (of public compliance without private acceptance).
S 관계대명사 V C
(이때) 발생하는 순응은 사적인 수용 없이 공적인 순응을 하는 경우일 수 있다.

대시: 부연설명
People (in the minority) can rarely influence others (through normative means) — the majority has little concern (for how the minority views them).
S V O S V O
소수의 사람들은 규범적인 수단을 통해 다른 사람들에게 영향을 미치는 경우가 거의 없다—대다수는 소수가 그들을 어떻게 보는지에 대해 거의 관심이 없다.

세미콜론: 부연설명
In fact, majority group members may be loath to agree publicly with the minority; they don't want anyone to think that they agree with those unusual, strange views of the minority.
접속부사 S V C S V O O.C 콤마: and
사실, 다수 집단의 구성원들은 공개적으로 소수 집단에 동의하는 것을 싫어한다. 그들은 그들이 소수 집단의 특이하고 이상한 견해에 동의한다고 생각하는 것을 원하지 않는다.

Minorities therefore exert their influence (on the group via the other principal method, informational social influence).
S 접속부사 V O =
따라서 소수자들은 다른 주요 방법인 정보에 의한 사회 영향력을 통해 집단에 영향력을 행사한다.

등위접속사
The minority introduces new and unexpected information (to the group) and causes the group to examine the issues more carefully.
S V_1 O V_2 O O.C
소수는 그룹에 새롭고 예상치 못한 정보를 소개하고 집단이 문제를 더 주의 깊게 검토하도록 한다.

Such careful examination may cause the majority to realize that the minority view has merit, (leading the group to adopt all or part of the minority's view).
S V O O.C 분사구문
그러한 신중한 검토는 다수가 소수의 관점이 가치를 가지고 있다는 것을 깨닫게 하여 집단이 소수의 관점의 전부 또는 일부를 채택하도록 이끌 수 있다.

In short, minorities often achieve private acceptance (because of informational social influence).
접속부사 S V O
요컨대, 소수자들은 종종 정보에 의한 사회적 영향력 때문에 사적인 수용을 달성한다.

| 어휘 | majority ⓝ (특정 집단 내에서) 가장 많은 수[다수] conform ⓥ 순응하다
normative ⓐ 규범적인 influence ⓝ 영향, 영향력
conformity ⓝ (규칙 · 관습 등에) 따름, 순응 compliance ⓝ (법 · 명령 등의) 준수
minority ⓝ (한 집단의 절반이 못 되는) 소수 loath ⓐ ~하기를 꺼리는
exert ⓥ (권력 · 영향력을) 가하다 principal ⓐ 주요한, 주된 method ⓝ 방법, 방식, 체계성
social influence (= social proof) 사회적 영향 introduce ⓥ 소개하다
merit ⓝ 가치, 훌륭함

| 전문해석 | 대다수의 사람들은 규범적인 영향력을 통해 다른 집단 구성원들이 순응하도록 만들 수 있다. (이때) 발생하는 순응은 사적인 수용 없이 공적인 순응을 하는 경우일 수 있다. 소수의 사람들은 규범적인 수단을 통해 다른 사람들에게 영향을 미치는 경우가 거의 없다—대다수는 소수가 그들을 어떻게 보는지에 대해 거의 관심이 없다. 사실, 다수 집단의 구성원들은 공개적으로 소수 집단에 동의하는 것을 싫어한다. 그들은 그들이 소수 집단의 특이하고 이상한 견해에 동의한다고 생각하는 것을 원하지 않는다. 따라서 소수자들은 다른 주요 방법인 정보적 사회 영향력을 통해 집단에 영향력을 행사한다. 소수는 그룹에 새롭고 예상치 못한 정보를 소개하고 집단이 문제를 더 주의 깊게 검토하도록 한다. 그러한 신중한 검토는 다수가 소수의 관점이 가치를 가지고 있다는 것을 깨닫게 하여 집단이 소수의 관점의 전부 또는 일부를 채택하도록 이끌 수 있다. 요컨대, 소수자들은 종종 정보적 사회적 영향력 때문에 사족인 수용을 달성한다.

| 보기분석 | ① How the Few Influence the Many
소수가 다수에 영향을 미치는 방법
② When the Majority Becomes the Minority 언급 안 한 정보
다수가 소수가 되는 때
③ The Abuse of Power Exercised by the Minority 언급 안 한 정보
소수가 행하는 권력 남용
④ How Normative Social Influence Differs from Informational Social Influence 언급 안 한 정보
규범에 의한 사회적 영향이 정보에 의한 사회적 영향과 어떻게 다른가

| 정답분석 | 본문에서 therefore와 in short 같은 연결표현을 사용하여 요약하는 내용을 참고하면 소수자들이 다수 집단에 어떻게 영향을 미치는지에 관한 내용을 주로 다루고 있으므로, 제목으로는 ①이 적절하다.

02 2013 경희대

정답 ①

| 구문분석 | (For most people), serious blows (to the head) don't occur often, but (when they do), they can leave a legacy (of damage).
(serious blows: S, don't occur: V, but: 등위접속사, when they do: 부사절: ~할 때, they: S, can leave: V, a legacy: O)

대부분의 사람들에게 있어 머리에 심각한 타격을 당하는 일은 흔히 발생하지는 않지만, 일단 발생하게 되면 뇌에 손상을 남기게 된다.

And (despite sophisticated imaging techniques), brain-injury experts say such consequences, (including sudden death), are difficult to predict.
(And: 등위접속사, brain-injury experts: S, say: V, such consequences: O)

그리고 정교한 영상기술에도 불구하고 뇌 손상 전문가들은 갑작스러운 죽음을 포함한 그러한 나쁜 결과들을 예측하기가 어렵다고 말한다.

Clotting can occur (in the aftermath of any head trauma), (even after a concussion), (when the brain is rattled (inside the skull), (causing delicate blood vessels to tear or stretch).
(Clotting: S, can occur: V, even after: 전치사, when: 부사절: ~할 때, causing: 분사구문)

뇌가 두개골 안에서 흔들려서 섬세한 혈관들이 찢어지거나 늘어나면 뇌진탕 이후에도 뇌 충격(뇌진탕)의 여파로 혈전이 발생할 수 있다.

Clots are notoriously unpredictable, however, and there aren't enough studies (to say for certain how common they are after concussions).
(Clots: S, are: V, unpredictable: C, however: 접속부사, and: 등위접속사, there: 유도부사, aren't: V, enough studies: S)

그러나 혈전은 예측할 수 없는 것으로 악명 높고 뇌진탕 이후에 얼마나 흔하게 발생하는지에 대해서 확신해서 말할 수 있는 충분한 연구가 없다.

등위접속사
But doctors do know that a previous clot may increase the risk (that additional ones will form).
S V O 관계대명사
하지만 의사들은 과거의 혈전이 추가적인 혈전을 발생시킬 위험성을 증가시킬 수 있다는 것을 알고 있다.

| 어휘 |

blow ⓝ 세게 때림, 강타	**occur** ⓥ 발생하다	**legacy** ⓝ 유산, 물려받은 것
damage ⓝ 손상, 피해	**sophisticated** ⓐ 정교한, 복잡한, 수준 높은	
imaging technique 영상기법	**predict** ⓥ 예측하다	**clotting** ⓝ 응고
aftermath ⓝ 여파, 후유증	**trauma** ⓝ 부상, 외상	**concussion** ⓝ 진동, 충격
rattle ⓥ 동요하다	**skull** ⓝ 두개골	**delicate** ⓐ 연약한, 허약한
tear ⓥ 찢다, 찢어지다	**clot** ⓝ 덩어리, (피가 엉긴) 혈전	**notoriously** ⓐ 이름난, 악명 높은

| 전문해석 | 대부분의 사람들에게 있어 머리에 심각한 타격을 당하는 일은 흔히 발생하지는 않지만, 일단 발생하게 되면 뇌에 손상을 남기게 된다. 그리고 정교한 영상기술에도 불구하고 뇌 손상 전문가들은 갑작스러운 죽음을 포함한 그러한 나쁜 결과들을 예측하기가 어렵다고 말한다. 뇌가 두개골 안에서 흔들려서 섬세한 혈관들이 찢어지거나 늘어나면 뇌진탕 이후에도 뇌 충격(뇌진탕)의 여파로 혈전이 발생할 수 있다. 그러나 혈전은 예측할 수 없는 것으로 악명 높고 뇌진탕 이후에 얼마나 흔하게 발생하는지에 대해서 확신해서 말할 수 있는 충분한 연구가 없다. 하지만 의사들은 과거의 혈전이 추가적인 혈전을 발생시킬 위험성을 증가시킬 수 있다는 것을 알고 있다.

| 보기분석 | ① Unpredictable Consequences of Head Trauma
뇌 외상의 예측할 수 없는 결과
② Brain Injury and Imaging Techniques 키워드 없음
뇌 손상 및 영상 기술
③ Blood Vessels' Frailty 언급 안 한 정보
혈관의 약점
④ Brain's Physiological Traits 언급 안 한 정보
뇌의 생리적 특징

| 정답분석 | 본문은 뇌의 충격으로 발생할 수 있는 혈전을 예측하기 어렵지만 추가적인 혈전이 발생할 위험성에 대해서도 설명하고 있다. 따라서 '뇌 외상의 결과'가 포함된 ①이 정답으로 가장 적절하다.

03 2012 서강대

정답 ②

| 구문분석 | (In modern developed societies), there is one variety of language (that ranks above the others).
유도부사 V S 관계대명사
현대 선진 사회에서는 다른 언어보다 상위에 위치하는 언어가 있다.

등위접속사
This superposed variety is employed (by the government and communications media), used and taught (in educational institutions), and is the main or only written language.
S V_1 V_2 V_3 등위접속사 V_4
이 (상위에 위치한) 언어는 정부와 통신 매체들에 의해 선택되고, 교육 기관들에서 사용되고 가르쳐지며, 주요한 혹은 유일한 문자언어이다.

등위접속사
It is more fixed and resistant (to change than any other variety in the community) and is something (of a yardstick (against which other varieties are measured).
S V_1 C_1 V_2 C_2 관계대명사
이 언어는 지역 사회의 다른 모든 언어들보다 고정되어 있고, 변화에 저항하며, 다른 모든 언어들을 평가하는 기준이다.

강조구문의 that
It is (to the written standard) that prescriptivists, those (who seek to regulate how others use language), usually appeal (when they condemn some usage as incorrect, improper, or even barbarous).
강조구문 S = 관계대명사 V 부사절: ~할 때
다른 사람들이 언어를 사용하는 방식을 규제하는 규범 문법학자들이 몇몇 언어들을 부정확하고, 부적절하고, 심지어는 야만적이라고 비난할 때, 이들은 이러한 문자 기준에 호소한다.

| 어휘 | **developed society** 선진 사회 **superpose** ⓥ (다른 것의) 위에 놓다, 겹쳐 놓다

employ ⓥ 고용하다, 이용하다 / educational institution 교육 기관 / written language 문어, 문자언어
resistant ⓐ 저항력 있는, ~에 잘 견디는 / yardstick ⓝ 기준
prescriptivist ⓝ 규범주의자, 규범문법학자[지지자]
seek ⓥ (필요한 것을 얻으려고) 구하다, 추구하다 / regulate ⓝ 규제, 통제 ⓥ 단속하다
appeal ⓥ 호소하다, 간청하다 / condemn ⓥ (도덕적인 이유로) 비난하다
barbarous ⓐ 잔혹한, 야만적인

| 전문해석 | 현대 선진 사회에서는 다른 언어보다 상위에 위치하는 언어가 있다. 이 상위에 위치한 언어는 정부와 통신 매체들에 의해 선택되고, 교육 기관들에서 사용되고 가르쳐지며, 주요한 혹은 유일한 문자언어이다. 이 언어는 지역 사회의 다른 모든 언어들보다 고정되어 있고, 변화에 저항하며, 다른 모든 언어들을 평가하는 기준이다. 다른 사람들이 언어를 사용하는 방식을 규제하는 규범 문법학자들이 몇몇 언어들을 부정확하고, 부적절하고, 심지어는 야만적이라고 비난할 때, 이들은 이러한 문자 기준에 호소한다.

| 보기분석 | ① Language Varieties in Social Contexts 언어의 다양성이 아닌 표준이 되는 상위언어에 관한 글임
사회적 맥락에서 언어의 다양성
② The Status of the Standard Variety of a Language
언어의 표준 다양성의 현황
③ Government Policies and Language Use 언급 안 한 정보
정부 정책 및 언어 사용
④ Influence of Government and Media on Language 언급 안 한 정보
정부와 미디어가 언어에 미치는 영향

| 정답분석 | 본문에서는 선진 사회에서 상위에 위치하는 언어는 다른 언어들을 평가하는 기준이라고 설명한다. 따라서 언어 사용의 표준이 되는 언어에 대해 언급한 ②가 정답으로 가장 적절하다.

04 2019 숙명여대

정답 ①

| 구문분석 | The idea (of neurodiversity) is really a paradigm shift (in how we think about kids in special education).
S V C
신경 다양성의 개념은 우리가 특수교육을 받는 아이들에 대해 생각하는 방식에 대한 인식 체계의 대전환이다.

(Instead of regarding these students as suffering from deficit, disease, or dysfunction), neurodiversity suggests that we speak about their strengths.
S V O
이런 학생들이 결핍, 질병 또는 기능장애로 고통받고 있다고 생각하는 대신, 신경 다양성은 우리가 그들의 장점들에 대해 말할 것을 제안한다.

Neruodiversity urges us to discuss brain diversity (using the same kind of discourse) (that we employ) (when we talk about biodiversity and cultural diversity).
S V O O.C 분사구문 관계대명사 부사절: ~할 때
신경 다양성은 생물 다양성과 문화적 다양성에 대해 이야기할 때 사용하는 것과 같은 종류의 담론을 사용하여 우리가 뇌의 다양성에 대해 논의하도록 권한다.

We don't pathologize a colla lily (by saying that it has a "petal deficit disorder.")
S V O
우리는 '꽃잎 결핍 장애(꽃잎이 많이 안 붙어 있음)'가 있다고 말함으로써 콜라 백합이 병을 앓고 있다고 하지 않는다.

We simply appreciate its unique beauty.
S V O
우리는 단지 그 꽃의 독특한 아름다움을 감상한다.

We don't diagnose individuals (who have skin color) (that is different from our own) (as suffering from "pigmentation dysfunction.")
S V O 관계대명사 관계대명사
우리는 우리와 다른 피부색을 가진 사람들을 '색소 기능장애'로 진단하지 않는다.

That would be racist.
S V O
그렇게 하는 것은 인종 차별주의적인 것이다.

Similarly, we ought not to pathologize children (who have different kinds of brains and different ways of thinking and learning).
S V O 관계대명사

마찬가지로 우리는 다른 종류의 두뇌를 가지고 다른 방법으로 생각하고 학습하는 아이들을 병적으로 다루어서는 안 된다.

| 어휘 | **neurodiversity** ⓝ 신경 다양성(다양한 신경질환을 정상의 범주에 포함시키는 운동)
paradigm shift 인식 체계[패러다임]의 대전환
special education 특수교육
deficit ⓝ 부족, 결함
dysfunction ⓝ 기능장애
strength ⓝ 강점, 장점
employ ⓥ 이용하다
biodiversity ⓝ (균형 잡힌 환경을 위한) 생물의 다양성
cultural diversity 문화적 다양성
pathologize ⓥ 병을 앓고 있다
lily ⓝ 백합
unique ⓐ 특별한, 고유의
diagnose ⓥ 진단하다
pigmentation ⓝ (피부 · 머리카락 · 나뭇잎 등의) 색소
racist ⓝ 인종 차별주의, 인종 차별행위

| 전문해석 | 신경 다양성의 개념은 우리가 특수교육을 받는 아이들에 대해 생각하는 방식에 대한 인식 체계의 대전환이다. 이런 학생들이 결핍, 질병 또는 기능장애로 고통받고 있다고 생각하는 대신, 신경 다양성은 우리가 그들의 장점들에 대해 말할 것을 제안한다. 신경 다양성은 생물 다양성과 문화적 다양성에 대해 이야기할 때 사용하는 것과 같은 종류의 담론을 사용하여 우리가 뇌의 다양성에 대해 논의하도록 권한다. 우리는 '꽃잎 결핍 장애(꽃잎이 많이 안 붙어 있음)'가 있다고 말함으로써 콜라 백합이 병을 앓고 있다고 하지 않는다. 우리는 단지 그 꽃의 독특한 아름다움을 감상한다. 우리는 우리와 다른 피부색을 가진 사람들을 '색소 기능장애'로 진단하지 않는다. 그렇게 하는 것은 인종 차별주의적인 것이다. 마찬가지로 우리는 다른 종류의 두뇌를 가지고 다른 방법으로 생각하고 학습하는 아이들을 병적으로 다루어서는 안 된다.

| 보기분석 | ✔① Neurodiversity and a paradigm shift
신경 다양성과 인식 체계의 전환
② Neurodiversity and its relationship with biodiversity 언급 안 한 정보
신경 다양성과 생물학적 다양성의 관계
③ Neurodiversity as a way to diagnose personal characteristics 언급 안 한 정보
개인의 성격을 진단하는 한 방법인 신경 다양성
④ Neurodiversity to individualize children's strengths and value 언급 안 한 정보
아동의 장점과 가치를 개별화하는 신경 다양성
⑤ Neurodiversity as a source for a clinical treatment 언급 안 한 정보
임상 치료의 근원인 신경 다양성

| 정답분석 | 본문은 서두에서 '신경 다양성' 개념을 소개하며 특수교육을 받는 아이들을 병적으로 간주하기보다는 '뇌의 다양성'에 대해 논의하는 것을 권장하고 있다. 그리고 콜라 백합이나 다른 피부색을 가진 사람들을 예를 들어 주제를 부연하고 있다. 따라서 ①이 제목으로 가장 적절하다.

05 2019 인하대

정답 ①

| 구문분석 | You may not always have access to a first aid kit (in an emergency).
S V O
응급상황이 발생했을 때 당신이 항상 구급상자를 사용할 수 있는 것은 아닐 수도 있다.

Here are some suggestions (for other everyday items you can use).
유도부사 V S
여기에 당신이 사용할 수 있는 다른 일상용품 몇 가지를 제안한다.

(If you don't have water to cool the burn), use juice, beer, or milk.
부사절: 만약 ~라면 V O
만약 당신이 화상 부위를 식힐 물이 없다면, 주스나 맥주 혹은 우유를 사용하라.

In fact, use any cold, harmless liquid, (until you have access to cold running water).
접속부사 V O 부사절: ~할 때까지
사실, 흐르는 찬물을 이용할 수 있을 때까지 차갑고 해가 없는 액체를 사용하라.

as ~ as possible: 가능한 한 ~한[하게]
The aim is to cool the area as quickly as possible, (using whatever cold liquid is available).
S V C 분사구문
목표는 사용 가능한 차가운 액체라면 무엇이나 사용하여 가능한 한 빨리 화상 부위를 식히는 것이다.

콜론: 부연설명
Remember: the burn should be cooled (for at least ten minutes) (for the treatment) (to be effective).
S V 의미상 주어 부사적용법: ~하기 위하여
명심하라: 화상 치료가 효과를 내기 위해서 화상 부위를 적어도 10분 동안 식혀야만 한다.

(If you don't have cling film to cover the burn), use a clean plastic carrier bag, a freezer bag, or similar.
부사절: 만일 ~라면 V O
화상 부위를 덮을 수 있는 (식품 포장용) 랩을 갖고 있지 않다면, 깨끗한 비닐 쇼핑백, 냉동용 봉지, 혹은 그 비슷한 것을 사용하라.

These types of items will not stick to the burn and will create a barrier (to stop infection).
S V_1 등위접속사 V_2 O
이런 종류의 물건들은 화상 부위에 들러붙지 않고 감염을 막는 보호막을 만들 것이다.

Plastic bags are particularly useful (for covering a burned hand or foot).
S V C
쇼핑용 비닐봉지는 화상을 입은 손이나 발을 덮는 데 특히 유용하다.

| 어휘 |

have access to ~에 접근[출입]할 수 있다		**first aid kit** ⓝ 구급상자
emergency ⓝ 비상상황	**suggestion** ⓝ 제안, 암시	**burn** ⓝ 화상
harmless ⓐ 해가 없는	**liquid** ⓝ 액체	**available** ⓐ 이용할 수 있는
cool ⓥ 식히다	**treatment** ⓝ 취급, 치료(법)	**effective** ⓐ 효과적인
cling film ⓝ (식품 포장용) 랩	**plastic carrier bag** ⓝ 비닐 쇼핑백	**freezer bag** ⓝ 냉동용 팩
stick ⓥ 들러붙다, 붙이다	**barrier** ⓝ 울타리, 장벽	**infection** ⓝ 전염, 감염

| 전문해석 | 응급상황이 발생했을 때 당신이 항상 구급상자를 사용할 수 있는 것은 아닐 수도 있다. 여기에 당신이 사용할 수 있는 다른 일상용품 몇 가지를 제안한다. 만약 당신이 화상 부위를 식힐 물이 없다면, 주스나 맥주 혹은 우유를 사용하라. 사실, 흐르는 찬물을 이용할 수 있을 때까지 차갑고 해가 없는 액체를 사용하라. 목표는 사용 가능한 차가운 액체라면 무엇이나 사용하여 가능한 한 빨리 화상 부위를 식히는 것이다. 명심하라: 화상 치료가 효과를 내기 위해서 화상 부위를 적어도 10분 동안 식혀야만 한다. 화상 부위를 덮을 수 있는 (식품 포장용) 랩을 갖고 있지 않다면, 깨끗한 비닐 쇼핑백, 냉동용 봉지, 혹은 그 비슷한 것을 사용하라. 이런 종류의 물건들은 화상 부위에 들러붙지 않고 감염을 막는 보호막을 만들 것이다. 쇼핑용 비닐봉지는 화상을 입은 손이나 발을 덮는 데 특히 유용하다.

| 보기분석 |
✓① No First Aid Kit? No Problem
구급상자가 없는가? 전혀 문제없다
② Basic Ways to Prevent Burns! 언급 안 한 정보
화상을 예방하기 위한 기본적인 방법들!
③ Why Are We Learning First Aid? 언급 안 한 정보
우리는 왜 응급처치를 배우고 있는가?
④ Who to Treat First in Emergency 언급 안 한 정보
응급상황에서 누구를 먼저 치료해야 하는가
⑤ Alternative Medicine to Save People 언급 안 한 정보
사람들을 구하는 대체 의학

| 정답분석 | 본문에서는 구급상자를 사용할 수 없는 상황에서 화상 사고가 발생했을 때 활용할 수 있는 일상용품들에 대해 설명하고 있다. 따라서 제목으로는 ①이 가장 적절하다.

06 2017 국민대 정답 ③

| 구문분석 | (From the brain's complexity), it naturally follows that a genetic marker (that predicts behavior) will not
가주어 V 진주어 that 관계대명사
necessarily be explanatory.
V C

두뇌의 복잡성으로 볼 때 행동을 예측하는 유전자 표지가 반드시 (행동의) 이유를 설명하지 못할 것이라는 결론은 당연하다.

In other words, it does not follow that linkage (between a DNA marker and a psychiatric disease) leads (to
접속부사 가주어 V 진주어 that
an understanding) (of how the genetic variation alters behavior); or (if the understanding (of the intervening
부사절: 비록 ~일지라도
steps) is achieved), comprehension may arrive years (after the discovery) and (long after the genetic marker
S V 등위접속사 부사절: ~한 오랜 후에도
is used as a predictor).

다시 말해, DNA 표지와 정신질환 간의 연관성이 유전자 변이가 어떻게 행동을 변화시키는지에 대한 이해로 이어지지는 않는다. 또는 만약 중간 단계들에 대한 이해가 달성된다 하더라도, 그 단계들을 발견하고 몇 년 후 유전자 표지가 예측자(예측 기준)로 사용되고 오랜 시간이 지난 뒤에야, 비로소 이해하게 될 것이다.

등위접속사
We may be able to predict whose brain works differently, but not be able to explain why.
S V_1 C_1 V_2 C_2

우리는 누구의 뇌가 다르게 작동하는지를 예측할 수는 있지만, 그 이유를 설명할 수는 없다.

It's a little (as if a policeman noticed that red cars are faster than blue cars).
S V 부사절: 마치 ~처럼

그것은 마치 경찰관이 빨간 차들이 파란 차들보다 더 빠르다는 것을 알아차리는 것과 같다.

Perhaps the policeman begins to pay more attention to the red cars but what he hasn't figured out is that,
S_1 V_1 O 등위접속사 S_2 V_2
for example, the red cars have a better engine than the blue cars.
접속부사 C

아마도 그 경찰관은 빨간 차들에 더 주의를 기울이기 시작할 것이지만, 그가 이해하지 못하는 것은, 예를 들어, 빨간 차들이 파란 차들보다 더 나은 엔진을 가지고 있다는 것이다.

부사절: 비록 ~일지라도 가주어
(Although the brain's complexity is beginning to be unraveled), it is likely that the mechanism (of action of a
V C 진주어 that
genetic variant) (predicting brain function) will remain mysteriously (long after we understand why some
부사절: ~한 오랜 후에도
cars are faster than others).

비록 뇌의 복잡성이 밝혀지고는 있지만, 뇌 기능을 예측하는 유전자 변이의 작용 메커니즘은 우리가 어떤 차들이 다른 차들보다 더 빠른 이유를 이해한 후에도 여전히 신비롭게 남아 있을 가능성이 있다.

| 어휘 |

genetic marker ⓝ 유전자 표지(유전적 해석에 지표가 되는 특정의 DNA 영역 또는 유전자)
predict ⓥ 예측하다
not necessarily 반드시 ~인 것은 아니다
explanatory ⓐ 이유를 밝히는, 설명하기 위한
it does not follow from ~ that ... ~라고 해서 반드시 …라고 말할 수는 없다
linkage ⓝ 연결, 결합
psychiatric ⓝ 정신 의학[질환]의
genetic variation ⓝ 유전 변이
intervene ⓥ 개입하다; 중재하다
predictor ⓝ 예측변수
pay attention to ~에 유의하다
figure out 이해하다
unravel ⓥ 해명하다
mechanism ⓝ 체계

| 전문해석 | 두뇌의 복잡성으로 볼 때 행동을 예측하는 유전자 표지가 반드시 (행동의) 이유를 설명하지 못할 것이라는 결론은 당연하다. 다시 말해, DNA 표지와 정신질환 간의 연관성이 유전자 변이가 어떻게 행동을 변화시키는지에 대한 이해로 이어지지는 않는다. 또는 만약 중간 단계들에 대한 이해가 달성된다 하더라도, 그 단계들을 발견하고 몇 년 후 유전자 표지가 예측자(예측 기준)로 사용되고 오랜 시간이 지난 뒤에야, 비로소 이해하게 될 것이다. 우리는 누구의 뇌가 다르게 작동하는지를 예측할 수는 있지만, 그 이유를 설명할 수는 없다. 그것은 마치 경찰관이 빨간 차들이 파란 차들보다 더 빠르다는 것을 알아차리는 것과 같다. 아마도 그 경찰관은 빨간 차들에 더 주의를 기울이기 시작할 것이지만, 그가 이해하지 못하는 것은, 예를 들어, 빨간 차들이 파란 차들보다 더 나은 엔진을 가지고 있다는 것이다. 비록 뇌의 복잡성이 밝혀지고는 있지만, 뇌 기능을

예측하는 유전자 변이의 작용 메커니즘은 우리가 어떤 차들이 다른 차들보다 더 빠른 이유를 이해한 후에도 여전히 신비롭게 남아 있을 가능성이 있다.

| 보기분석 | ① The complexity of the human DNA DNA의 복잡성이라기보다는 유전자 표지가 행동의 이유를 설명할 수 없음을 설명하는 글
인간 DNA의 복잡성
② How to predict human behavior based on genetic variation 언급 안 한 정보
유전적 변이를 기반으로 인간의 행동을 예측하는 방법
③ Difficulty of explaining associations between behavior and genetic markers
행동과 유전자 표지 사이의 연관성을 설명하는 것의 어려움
④ The possibility of using genetic information to predict violation of traffic rules 언급 안 한 정보
교통 규칙 위반 예측을 위해 유전자 정보를 사용할 가능성

| 정답분석 | 본문은 서두에서 행동을 예측하는 유전자 표지가 행동의 이유를 설명할 수 없으며 뇌의 다양한 작동에 대한 이유 또한 설명할 수 없다고 주장한다. 이어서 경찰관이 색이 다른 차들의 속도 차이에 대해 그 이유를 이해할 수 없다는 예시로 주장을 부연하고 있다. 따라서 ③이 제목으로 가장 적절하다.

07 2018 가톨릭대

정답 ④

| 구문분석 | [As long as the term art is applied to a realm (so vast and indefinite as to embrace literature, music and dance, theater and film, the visual and decorative arts, and other equally diverse activities)], their classification — the way (in which each is regarded as being either unique or like others) — will remain a controversial but necessary undertaking.

부사절: ~하는 한 / so ~ as to: …할 정도로 너무 ~한 / S / 대시: 동격 / 관계대명사 / V / C

'예술'이라는 용어가 너무나도 방대하고 무한한 영역에 적용되어 문학, 음악과 무용, 연극과 영화, 시각 및 장식 예술과 그리고 마찬가지로 다양한 활동들을 포함하는 한, 그 분류—각각이 독특하다거나 다른 것들과 비슷하다고 간주되는 방식—는 논란이 많지만 필요한 과제로 남아 있게 될 것이다.

Classification is a useful approach (to the organization of knowledge in any field): The classification (of plants and animals in the 18th century) led (to the discovery of evolution in the 19th).

S / V / C / 콜론: 재진술 / S / V

분류는 어느 분야에서든 지식을 구조화하는 유용한 접근방법이다: 18세기에 있었던 동식물의 분류는 19세기에 진화(론)의 발견을 이끌었다.

(In the arts), classification can be of immense help (in understanding the interrelationships between arts and in drawing attention to characteristics of each) (that might otherwise go unnoticed).

S / V / C / 관계대명사

예술에 있어서 분류는 예술 간의 상호관계들을 이해하는 데 있어서 그리고 그렇지 않으면 눈에 띄지 않을 수 있는 예술 각각의 특징에 주의를 기울이는 것에 있어서 엄청난 도움이 될 수 있다.

| 어휘 |

term ⓝ 용어; 기간	**apply** ⓥ 적용하다, 응용하다	**realm** ⓝ 범위, 영역
vast ⓐ 방대한, 거대한	**indefinite** ⓐ 불명확한	**embrace** ⓥ 수용하다, 받아들이다
literature ⓝ 문학	**visual** ⓐ 시각의; 눈에 보이는	**decorative** ⓐ 장식용의, 장식적인
diverse ⓐ 다양한, 가지각색의	**classification** ⓝ 분류	**unique** ⓐ 유일무이한, 독특한
controversial ⓐ 논란이 많은, 물의를 일으키는		**undertaking** ⓝ (중요한) 일, 약속
organization ⓝ 조직, 구성	**immense** ⓐ 막대한, 거대한	**interrelationship** ⓝ 상호관계
characteristic ⓝ 특질, 특성	**otherwise** ⓐⓓ (만약) 그렇지 않으면	
unnoticed ⓐ 주의를 끌지 않는, 남의 눈에 띄지 않는		

| 전문해석 | '예술'이라는 용어가 너무나도 방대하고 무한한 영역에 적용되어 문학, 음악과 무용, 연극과 영화, 시각 및 장식 예술과 그리고 마찬가지로 다양한 활동들을 포함하는 한, 그 분류—각각이 독특하다거나 다른 것들과 비슷하다고 간주되는 방식—는 논란이 많지만 필요한 과제로 남아 있게 될 것이다. 분류는 어느 분야에서든 지식을 구조화하는 유용한 접근방법이다: 18세기에 있었던 동식물의 분류는 19세기에 진화(론)의 발견을 이끌었다. 예술에 있어서 분류는 예술 간의 상호관계들을 이해

하는 데 있어서 그리고 그렇지 않으면 눈에 띄지 않을 수 있는 예술 각각의 특징에 주의를 기울이는 것에 있어서 엄청난 도움이 될 수 있다.

| 보기분석 | ① how we classify the wide range of arts 언급 안 한 정보
우리가 광범위한 예술을 분류하는 방법
② the general classification procedure to follow 언급 안 한 정보
따라야 할 일반적인 분류절차
③ the main pitfalls we encounter in classifying arts 언급 안 한 정보
우리가 예술을 분류할 때 마주치는 주요한 함정들
④ why classification is necessary in the field of arts
예술 분야에서 분류가 필요한 이유

| 정답분석 | 본문의 서두에서는 예술이라는 용어의 범위가 방대하고 무한한 영역에 적용되어 그 분류가 반드시 필요하다고 말한다. 또한 본문 마지막 문장에서는 예술 간의 상호관계를 이해하고 예술 하나하나의 특징에 주의를 기울이는 데에 분류가 엄청난 도움이 될 수 있음을 설명했다. 따라서 ④ '예술 분야에서 분류가 필요한 이유'가 글의 주제로 가장 적절하다.

08 2017 한국외대(학사 글로벌 일반)

정답 ①

| 구문분석 | Getting enough quality sleep (S) can help (V) (to) protect your mental health, physical health, quality of life, and safety (O).
충분한 수면을 취하는 것은 당신의 정신 건강, 신체 건강, 삶의 질과 안전을 보호하는 것에 도움을 줄 수 있다.

We (S_1) know (V_1) all this (O_1) very well, but (등위접속사) the latest study (S_2) indicates (V_2) that it also keeps aging processes in check (O_2).
우리는 이 모든 것을 매우 잘 알고 있지만, 최근의 연구 결과는 수면이 또한 노화 과정을 억제하기도 한다는 것을 나타낸다.

For instance (접속부사), scientists (S) studied (V) a group of 66 elderly volunteers (O), (who (관계대명사) had MRI brain scans and answered question about their sleep habit every two years).
예를 들어, 과학자들은 66명의 노인 지원자들 그룹을 연구했는데, 그들은 2년마다 MRI로 뇌 정밀검사를 받았고 그들의 수면 습관에 대한 질문에 답했다.

The study (S) found (V) that those (who (관계대명사) reported sleeping less on average) showed swelling of a brain region (indicating faster cognitive decline and (등위접속사) thus aging in general) (O).
그 연구는 평균적으로 수면이 부족하다고 보고한 사람들의 뇌 부위가 부풀어 올라 있었고 이것이 더 빠른 인지력 저하와 결과적으로 전반적인 노화가 진행되고 있음을 나타낸다는 것을 발견했다.

Other studies (S) have suggested (V) that adults need about seven hours of sleep a night to maintain proper brain function (O).
다른 연구들은 성인들이 적절한 뇌 기능을 유지하기 위해서는 하루 약 7시간의 수면이 필요하다고 제안했다.

(Now that (부사절: ~ 때문에) the role (of sleeping in aging) has been established), future research (S) will investigate (V) how sleep helps to preserve cognitive functions and hold off more rapid aging (O).
노화에 있어서 수면의 역할이 확립되었기 때문에, 미래의 연구는 어떻게 수면이 인지 기능을 유지하고 더 빠른 노화를 늦추는 데 도움을 주는지를 조사할 것이다.

| 어휘 |

quality sleep 질 높은 수면
protect ⓥ 보호하다, 지키다
mental health ⓝ 정신 건강
latest ⓐ (가장) 최근의
indicate ⓥ 나타내다, 보여 주다
elderly ⓐ 연세가 드신 (old보다 정중한 표현)
volunteer ⓝ 지원자
on average 평균적으로, 대체로
swelling ⓝ (몸의) 부어오름
cognitive decline 인지력 감퇴
aging ⓝ 노화
now that ~ 때문에
investigate ⓥ 조사하다, 연구하다
preserve ⓥ 유지하다
hold off 늦추다, 연기하다

| 전문해석 | 충분한 수면을 취하는 것은 당신의 정신 건강, 신체 건강, 삶의 질과 안전을 보호하는 것에 도움을 줄 수 있다. 우리는 이 모든 것을 매우 잘 알고 있지만, 최근의 연구 결과는 수면이 또한 노화 과정을 억제하기도 한다는 것을 나타낸다. 예를 들어, 과학자들은 66명의 노인 지원자들 그룹을 연구했는데, 그들은 2년마다 MRI로 뇌 정밀검사를 받았고 그들의 수면 습관에 대한 질문에 답했다. 그 연구는 평균적으로 수면이 부족하다고 보고한 사람들의 뇌 부위가 부풀어 올라 있었고 이것이 더 빠른 인지력 저하와 결과적으로 전반적인 노화가 진행되고 있음을 나타낸다는 것을 발견했다. 다른 연구들은 성인들이 적절한 뇌 기능을 유지하기 위해서는 하루 약 7시간의 수면이 필요하다고 제안했다. 노화에 있어서 수면의 역할이 확립되었기 때문에, 미래의 연구는 어떻게 수면이 인지 기능을 유지하고 더 빠른 노화를 늦추는 데 도움을 주는지를 조사할 것이다.

| 보기분석 | ① Less Sleep Pushes Your Brain to Age Faster
잠을 적게 자면 더 빨리 노화된다
② Science Reveals How Sleep Fights Rapid Aging 너무 포괄적
과학은 수면이 급속한 노화를 막는 방법을 밝힌다
③ MRI: Breakthrough Imaging Technology in Sleep Research 키워드 없음
MRI: 수면 연구에서 혁신적인 영상 기술
④ Benefits and Disadvantages of Excessive Sleeping 언급 안 한 정보
과도한 수면의 장점과 단점

| 정답분석 | 본문에서는 충분한 수면이 노화를 억제한다는 최근의 연구 결과를 소개한 후 연구 피험자들과 연구 결과에 대해 부연 설명했다. 미래의 연구도 어떻게 충분한 수면이 인지 기능을 유지시키고 노화를 늦추는지 조사할 것임을 추정하고 있다. 따라서 글의 제목으로 가장 적절한 것은 부족한 수면과 노화의 관계에 대해 서술한 ①이다.

09 2018 명지대

정답 ②

| 구문분석 | Numerous companies have embraced the open office and (by most accounts), very few have moved back (into traditional spaces with offices and doors).
S_1 / V_1 / O / 등위접속사 / S_2 / V_2

많은 기업들이 개방형 사무실을 수용했으며 대부분의 평가로 볼 때 사무실과 문이 있는 전통적인 공간으로 돌아간 기업은 거의 없다.

But research findings that we're 15% less productive, we have immense trouble concentrating and we're twice as likely to get sick (in open working spaces), have contributed (to a growing backlash against open offices).
등위접속사 / S / = / 동격 1 / 콤마: and / 동격 2 / 등위접속사 / 동격 3 / V

그러나 우리의 생산성이 15% 떨어지고 집중하는 데 엄청난 어려움을 겪고 있으며, 개방형 업무 공간에서 아플 가능성이 두 배로 높다는 연구 결과가 개방형 사무실에 대한 반발을 증가시키는 요인이 되었다.

There's one big reason (we'd all love a space) (with four walls and a door) (that shuts): focus.
유도부사 / V / S / why(관계부사) 생략 / 관계대명사 / 콜론: 동격

우리 모두가 4면이 벽으로 되어 있고 닫을 수 있는 문이 있는 공간을 좋아하는 한 가지 큰 이유가 있는데 그것은 바로 집중이다.

The truth is, we can't multitask, and small distractions can cause us to lose focus (for upwards of 20 minutes).
S / V / 등위접속사 / C

사실, 우리는 한꺼번에 여러 일을 처리할 수 없으며, 작은 산만함들로 인해 최대 20분이나 집중력을 잃을 수 있다.

What's more, certain open spaces can negatively impact our memory.
접속부사 / S / V / O

게다가, 어떤 개방형 사무실들은 우리의 기억력에 부정적인 영향을 미칠 수 있다.

We retain more information (when we sit in one spot without distractions).
S / V / O / 부사절: ~할 때

우리는 방해받지 않고 한자리에 앉아 있을 때 더 많은 정보를 기억한다.

It's not so obvious (to us each day), but we offload memories (into our surroundings in the open spaces).
S_1 V_1 / C / 등위접속사 / S_2 / V_2 / O_2

그것이 우리에게 그렇게 분명하게 매일 인지되는 것은 아니지만 우리는 개방형 사무실에서 우리의 기억을 주변 환경으로 옮긴다.

| 어휘 | numerous ⓐ 많은 embrace ⓥ 기꺼이 받아들이다[선택하다]
open office 개방형 사무실 account ⓝ 설명, 해석 traditional ⓐ 전통적인
finding ⓝ (조사 · 연구 등의) 결과 immense ⓐ 거대한 twice ⓐⓓ 두 번, 두 배로
backlash ⓝ (사회 변화 등에 대한 대중의) 반발
multitask ⓥ 다중 작업을 하다, 동시에 여러 가지 일을 하다 distraction ⓝ 집중을 방해하는 것
what's more 게다가 retain ⓥ 유지하다, 보유하다 spot ⓝ 장소, 자리
pros and cons 장단점 myth ⓝ (근거 없는) 믿음, 그릇된 통념 obvious ⓐ 분명한, 명백한
offload ⓥ (자기가 원치 않는 것을) 없애다

| 전문해석 | 많은 기업들이 개방형 사무실을 수용했으며 대부분의 평가로 볼 때 사무실과 문이 있는 전통적인 공간으로 돌아간 기업은 거의 없다. 그러나 우리의 생산성이 15% 떨어지고 집중하는 데 엄청난 어려움을 겪고 있으며, 개방형 업무 공간에서 아플 가능성이 두 배로 높다는 연구 결과가 개방형 사무실에 대한 반발을 증가시키는 요인이 되었다. 우리 모두가 4면이 벽으로 되어 있고 닫을 수 있는 문이 있는 공간을 좋아하는 한 가지 큰 이유가 있는데 그것은 바로 집중이다. 사실, 우리는 한꺼번에 여러 일을 처리할 수 없으며, 작은 산만함들로 인해 최대 20분이나 집중력을 잃을 수 있다. 게다가, 어떤 개방형 사무실들은 우리의 기억력에 부정적인 영향을 미칠 수 있다. 우리는 방해받지 않고 한자리에 앉아 있을 때 더 많은 정보를 기억한다. 그것이 우리에게 그렇게 분명하게 매일 인지되는 것은 아니지만 우리는 개방형 사무실에서 우리의 기억을 주변 환경으로 옮긴다.

| 보기분석 | ① The Pros and Cons of the Open Office 개방형 사무실의 장점은 언급되지 않음
개방형 사무실의 장단점
② The Myth of the Open Office Now Being Challenged
현재 도전받고 있는 개방형 사무실에 대한 근거 없는 믿음[통념]
③ The Open Office: the Hub of Collaboration and Bond 언급 안 한 정보
개방형 사무실: 협업과 유대의 중심지
④ The Rationale behind the Open Office 언급 안 한 정보
개방형 사무실의 이론적 근거

| 정답분석 | 본문 서두에서 소재인 '개방형 사무실'을 소개한 후 역접 표현인 'But'을 이용해서 개방형 사무실의 단점들(집중력 저하, 주의 산만, 기억력에 미치는 부정적 영향)을 다룬 연구를 언급했다. 따라서 ②와 같이 현재 많은 기업들이 수용하고 있는 '개방형 사무실'이 연구를 통해 밝혀진 단점들로 인해 효율성이 도전받고 있는 상황을 제목으로 설정하는 것이 바람직하다.

10 2017 가톨릭대 정답 ③

| 구문분석 | The accuracy and speed of real-time automatic translation (S) is undoubtedly going to improve (V) dramatically (in the near future), but (등위접속사) it (S) is going to take (V) much longer (before (부사절: ~ 전에) this medium becomes globally widespread and economically accessible to all).

실시간 자동 번역의 정확성과 속도는 틀림없이 가까운 미래에 급격하게 향상될 것이지만, 이 수단이 모든 사람들에게 전 세계적으로 확산되고 모두가 경제적으로 접근할 수 있게 되기까지는 훨씬 더 오랜 시간이 걸릴 것이다.

This (S) poses (V) a threat (O) (to the current availability and appeal of a global language).
이것(자동번역)은 세계 공용어의 현재 효용성과 매력에 위협이 된다.

All the evidence (S) suggests (V) that the position (of English as a global language) is going to become stronger (O).
모든 증거는 세계 공용어로서의 영어의 위치가 더 강해질 것을 암시한다.

(By the time (부사절: ~할 때까지는) automatic translation matures as a popular communicative medium), that position (S) will very likely have become (V) impregnable (C).
자동 번역이 대중적인 의사소통 수단으로 완성될 때면 이미, 영어의 위치가 난공불락이 되어 있을 가능성이 매우 높다.

가주어 / 대시: 부연설명

It will be very interesting to see what happens then — (whether the presence (of a global language) will eliminate the demand (for world translation services), or (whether the economics (of automatic translation) will so undercut the cost of global language learning that the latter will become obsolete).

(V: will be, C: very interesting, 진주어: to see ~, ~인지 아닌지: whether, 등위접속사: or, so ~ that: 너무 ~해서 그 결과 …하다)

세계 공용어의 존재가 세계 번역 서비스들에 대한 수요를 없앨 것인지 아니면 자동 번역의 경제적인 측면이 세계 공용어 학습비용을 크게 낮추어 그 결과 세계 공용어가 쓸모없게 될지 그다음에 어떤 일이 일어날지가 흥미롭다.

| 어휘 |

real-time ⓐ 실시간의, 리얼타임의
automatic translation ⓝ 자동 번역
undoubtedly ⓐⓓ 틀림없이, 확실히
dramatically ⓐⓓ 극적으로
medium ⓝ 매체, 수단
widespread ⓐ 널리 보급되어 있는
accessible ⓐ 접근하기 쉬운
pose a threat 위협이 되다
appeal ⓝ 호소, 매력
mature ⓥ 성숙하다, 성숙[발달]시키다
impregnable ⓐ 무적의, 공략하기 어려운
eliminate ⓥ 없애다, 제거하다
undercut ⓥ ~보다 저가로 팔다[공급하다]
obsolete ⓐ 더 이상 쓸모가 없는, 한물간

| 전문해석 | 실시간 자동 번역의 정확성과 속도는 틀림없이 가까운 미래에 급격하게 향상될 것이지만, 이 수단이 모든 사람들에게 전 세계적으로 확산되고 모두가 경제적으로 접근할 수 있게 되기까지는 훨씬 더 오랜 시간이 걸릴 것이다. 이것(자동 번역)은 세계 공용어의 현재 효용성과 매력에 위협이 된다. 모든 증거는 세계 공용어로서의 영어의 위치가 더 강해질 것을 암시한다. 자동 번역이 대중적인 의사소통 수단으로 완성될 때면 이미, 영어의 위치가 난공불락이 되어 있을 가능성이 매우 높다. 세계 공용어의 존재가 세계 번역 서비스들에 대한 수요를 없앨 것인지 아니면 자동 번역의 경제적인 측면이 세계 공용어 학습비용을 크게 낮추어 그 결과 세계 공용어가 쓸모없게 될지 그다음에 어떤 일이 일어날지가 흥미롭다.

| 보기분석 |

① What Are the Dangers of a Global Language? 언급 안 한 정보
무엇이 세계 공용어의 위험성인가?

② Why Computers Will Never Be a Smart Translator 언급 안 한 정보
컴퓨터가 똑똑한 번역가가 될 수 없는 이유

③ The Battle Between Technology and Global Language
기술과 세계 공용어 사이의 전쟁

④ Automatic Translation and the End of Language Learning 언급 안 한 정보
자동 번역과 언어 학습의 종료

| 정답분석 | 본문에서는 세계 공용어에 위협이 될 수 있는 자동 번역 기술을 소개하고 있다. 마지막 문장에서는 번역 기술이 향상되어 의사소통 수단으로 완성될 때가 되면 세계 공용어인 영어가 더 이상 쓸모가 없게 될지 아니면 그때 그 위치가 더욱 확고해진 세계 공용어의 존재로 인해 세계 번역 서비스들에 대한 수요가 없어질지에 대한 논쟁을 언급하고 있으므로 이 글의 제목으로는 ③이 적절하다.

11 2018 인하대

정답 ③

| 구문분석 |

(If there is one requirement of architecture), it's that the structure must remain upright.

부사절: 만약 ~라면 S V C

건축의 요건이 하나 있다면, 그것은 구조물은 반드시 똑바로 서 있어야 한다는 것이다.

Architects would be out of a job (if their buildings continually failed to meet this one test).

(S: Architects, V: would be, C: out of a job, 부사절: 만약 ~라면)

건축가들은 그들의 건물들이 이 시험을 충족하는 것에 계속해서 실패한다면 실직하게 될 것이다.

Yet some architects push the boundaries, (seemingly daring with Newton's universal law of gravity), to design buildings (that not only appear to defy the law, but are beautiful at that).

(접속부사: Yet, S: some architects, V: push, O: the boundaries, 분사구문: seemingly daring ~, 부사적용법: 그 결과, 관계대명사: that)

하지만 몇몇 건축가들은 뉴턴의 만유인력의 법칙에 도전하는 것처럼 한계를 뛰어넘어 그 법칙을 무시하는 것처럼 보일 뿐만 아니라 게다가 아름답기까지 한 건물들을 설계한다.

(From a cantilevered barn (designed by the Dutch-based firm MVRD) to an impressively stacked building (in Hanover, Germany, by the Stuttgart-based firm Behnisch Architekten), these buildings seem impossible to conceive, let alone build.

from A to B: A에서 B까지
S V C
let alone: ~은 말할 것도 없이

네덜란드에 본사를 둔 MVRD가 설계한 팔걸이식(한쪽 끝은 고정되고 다른 끝은 지면과 떨어져 있는 구조의) 헛간에서부터 슈투트가르트에 본사를 둔 Behnisch Architekten이 설계한 독일 하노버에 있는 인상적으로 쌓아 올린 건물에 이르기까지 이러한 건물들은 짓는 것은 말할 것도 없고 상상조차 불가능해 보인다.

Of course, all (of these structures) passed strict zoning laws (before they were erected).

S V O 부사절: ~ 전에

물론, 이 모든 건축물들은 세워지기 전에 엄격한 토지사용제한법을 통과했다.

What is not guaranteed, however, is whether merely looking at them will cause you vertigo.

S 접속부사 V C

그러나 그 건축물들을 보는 것만으로도 현기증이 날지는 장담할 수 없다.

| 어휘 |

requirement ⓝ 요건, 필요조건
architecture ⓝ 건축양식
structure ⓝ 구조물
upright ⓐ 똑바로 선
architect ⓝ 건축가
out of a job 실직해서
meet ⓥ (의무 · 조건 따위를) 충족시키다
test ⓝ (판단 · 평가의) 기준
boundary ⓝ 경계; 한계, 범위
dare ⓥ 감히[대담하게] ~하다
universal law of gravity 만유인력의 법칙
defy ⓝ 반항 ⓥ 저항하다
cantilevered ⓐ 캔틸레버형의(다리나 다른 구조물을 떠받치는 레버)
barn ⓝ 헛간
Dutch ⓐ 네덜란드식의
stacked ⓐ (무엇이) 잔뜩 쌓인
conceive ⓥ (감정 · 의견 따위를) 마음에 품다, (계획 등을) 착상하다
let alone ~은커녕, ~은 고사하고
zoning law 토지사용제한법
vertigo ⓝ 어지러움, 현기증

| 전문해석 | 건축의 요건이 하나 있다면, 그것은 구조물은 반드시 똑바로 서 있어야 한다는 것이다. 건축가들은 그들의 건물들이 이 시험을 충족하는 것에 계속해서 실패한다면 실직하게 될 것이다. 하지만 몇몇 건축가들은 뉴턴의 만유인력의 법칙에 도전하는 것처럼 한계를 뛰어넘어 그 법칙을 무시하는 것처럼 보일 뿐만 아니라 게다가 아름답기까지 한 건물들을 설계한다. 네덜란드에 본사를 둔 MVRD가 설계한 팔걸이식(한쪽 끝은 고정되고 다른 끝은 지면과 떨어져 있는 구조의) 헛간에서부터 슈투트가르트에 본사를 둔 Behnisch Architekten이 설계한 독일 하노버에 있는 인상적으로 쌓아 올린 건물에 이르기까지 이러한 건물들은 짓는 것은 말할 것도 없고 상상조차 불가능해 보인다. 물론, 이 모든 건축물들은 세워지기 전에 엄격한 토지사용제한법을 통과했다. 그러나 그 건축물들을 보는 것만으로도 현기증이 날지는 장담할 수 없다.

| 보기분석 |

① Design Buildings on High Ground 언급 안 한 정보
고지대 건축물 설계

② The Difficulty of Being an Architect 언급 안 한 정보
건축가가 되는 것의 어려움

③ The Beautiful Buildings That Defy Gravity
중력을 거스르는 아름다운 건물들

④ Requirements and Laws of City Architecture 언급 안 한 정보
도시 건축의 요구와 법칙

⑤ ~~Be Daring~~ If You Want to Achieve a Success 만유인력의 법칙을 어긴 건축물을 소개했으나 '대담하라'는 표현은 너무 포괄적
성공을 원한다면 대담하라

| 정답분석 | 본문 세 번째 문장에서 역접 표현인 'yet'을 활용하여 건축구조물은 똑바로 서 있어야 한다는 통념을 무시하면서도 아름다운 건물을 설계한 일부 건축가들을 소개했다. 본문에서 이러한 건물들에 대해 '만유인력의 법칙을 무시한다'라고 표현한 것을 참고하면, 제목으로는 ③이 가장 적절하다.

12 2017 국민대

정답 ②

| 구문분석 | (When I was 25), I attended a youth conference (in the summer of 2008).
부사절: ~할 때 S V O
내가 25살이던 2008년 여름, 나는 한 청년 회의에 참석했다.

(that)
I thought it would just be a refreshing weekend (in the city).
S V O
나는 그 청년 회의를 그저 도시에서 재미있는 주말을 보내는 것 정도로 생각했다.

On the first day, I was a little nervous (when the youth group went swimming).
S V C 부사절: ~할 때
첫째 날, 청년들이 수영을 하러 갔을 때 나는 약간 신경이 쓰였다.

등위접속사
A burst appendix four years earlier had left me (with a 12 cm scar on my abdomen) and I couldn't stand people (staring at me and wondering what had happened).
S_1 V_1 O_1 S_2 V_2 O_2
4년 전에 발생한 맹장 파열로 나는 배에 12cm의 흉터가 있었고, 나는 사람들이 내 배를 빤히 쳐다보며 어떻게 된 일인지 궁금해하는 것을 참을 수가 없었다.

This was made worse (knowing that a guy I'd met might see it).
S V O.C 분사구문
내가 거기서 만난 한 남자가 내 흉터를 보게 될지도 모른다는 것을 알고서 이런 감정은 더욱 심해졌다.

부정부사: 거의 ~ 않다
Little did I know that he was nervous (about swimming) too.
부정어 V S O
그 남자도 수영하는 것에 신경을 쓰고 있었다는 것을 나는 거의 알지 못하고 있었다.

등위접속사
(When he was 17) he had a serious car accident and was left (with a 15 cm scar on his abdomen).
부사절: ~할 때 S V_1 O V_2
17살 때 심각한 자동차 사고를 당해, 그의 배에도 15cm의 흉터가 있었던 것이다.

Talk (about an icebreaker).

어색함을 깨기에 더할 나위 없이 좋은 점이었다.

Almost identical scars and so much in common, it was meant to be.
C S V
거의 동일한 흉터에 너무나 많은 공통점이라니 그건 운명이었다.

We have just celebrated our sixth wedding anniversary.
S V O
이제 우리는 결혼 6주년을 맞이했다

| 어휘 |

attend ⓥ 참석하다
conference ⓝ 회의
refreshing ⓐ 신선한, 참신한
nervous ⓐ 불안해하는
burst appendix 맹장 파열
scar ⓝ 상처, 흉터
abdomen ⓝ 복부, 배
stare at ~을 빤히 쳐다보다
icebreaker ⓝ (사람들이 처음 만났을 때) 어색함을 누그러뜨리기 위한 말[행동]
celebrate ⓥ 기념하다, 축하하다
wedding anniversary ⓝ 결혼기념일

| 전문해석 | 내가 25살이던 2008년 여름, 나는 한 청년 회의에 참석했다. 나는 그 청년 회의를 그저 도시에서 재미있는 주말을 보내는 것 정도로 생각했다. 첫째 날, 청년들이 수영을 하러 갔을 때 나는 약간 신경이 쓰였다. 4년 전에 발생한 맹장 파열로 나는 배에 12cm의 흉터가 있었고, 나는 사람들이 내 배를 빤히 쳐다보며 어떻게 된 일인지 궁금해하는 것을 참을 수가 없었다. 내가 거기서 만난 한 남자가 내 흉터를 보게 될지도 모른다는 것을 알고서 이런 감정은 더욱 심해졌다.
그 남자도 수영하는 것에 신경을 쓰고 있었다는 것을 나는 거의 알지 못하고 있었다. 17살 때 심각한 자동차 사고를 당해, 그의 배에도 15cm의 흉터가 있었던 것이다. 어색함을 깨기에 더할 나위 없이 좋은 점이었다. 거의 동일한 흉터에 너무나 많은 공통점이라니 그건 운명이었다. 이제 우리는 결혼 6주년을 맞이했다.

| 보기분석 | ① Stars Crossed 언급 안 한 정보
불운한 운명

② Wonderful Coincidence
놀라운 우연의 일치
③ Our Wedding Anniversary 키워드 없음
우리의 결혼기념일
④ A Swimming Conference I Attended 키워드 없음
내가 참석한 수영회의

| 정답분석 | 이 글은 저자가 청년 회의에 참석했던 당시의 일화를 소개하는 글로, 배에 있는 흉터로 긴장하고 있던 저자가 동일한 흉터를 가진 남자를 운명같이 만나 결혼했다는 내용이므로, ②의 '놀라운 우연의 일치'가 글의 제목으로 가장 적절하다.

13 2017 단국대(자연계A)

정답 ③

| 구문분석 | Imperialism had long-lasting effects (in the African and Asian colonies), (even after the colonies gained their independence from Britain).
S V O / 부사절: 심지어 ~ 후에도

제국주의는 심지어 식민지들이 영국으로부터 독립한 이후에도 아프리카와 아시아 식민지들에서 오랫동안 영향을 미쳤다.

(Since the wealth went to the British rulers and a few native people (who collaborated with them), the majority (of people in these colonies) were reduced (to living in poverty).
부사절: ~ 때문에 / 관계대명사 / S V

그 부가 영국 통치자들과 그들에게 협력한 소수의 원주민들에게 돌아갔기 때문에, 이들 식민지에 살고 있던 사람들의 대부분은 궁핍한 생활을 할 수밖에 없었다.

(In some cases), the imperialists caused huge ecological damage, (leaving the landscape scarred and barren).
S V O / 분사구문 / 등위접속사

어떤 경우에는 제국주의자들은 생태계에 커다란 피해를 줬으며, 경관에 상흔을 남기고 불모의 땅으로 만들었다.

Imperialism denied the right (of every country) (to govern itself): (in the African and Asian colonies), native people, (no matter how talented), were rarely allowed to serve (in the colonial government).
S V O / 콜론: 부연설명 / S / 아무리 ~해도 / V / O.C

제국주의는 모든 나라가 스스로 통치할 수 있는 권리를 인정하지 않았다. 아프리카와 아시아 식민지들에 사는 원주민들은 그들이 아무리 재능이 뛰어나다 하더라도 식민 정부에서 일하는 것이 거의 허용되지 않았다.

Finally, (by sending out the degrading message) (that people of darker complexions were "inferior" to their lighter-skinned rulers), imperialists caused deep anger and resentment (that persist to this day).
관계대명사 / S V O / 관계대명사

마지막으로 피부가 검은 사람들이 피부가 하얀 통치자들보다 '열등하다는' 모멸적인 메시지를 전달함으로써, 제국주의자들은 오늘날까지 계속되고 있는 깊은 분노와 울분을 일으켰다.

| 어휘 |

imperialism ⓝ 제국주의	**long-lasting** ⓐ 오래 지속되는	**colony** ⓝ 식민지
independence ⓝ 독립, 자립	**wealth** ⓝ 많은 재산, 부유함	**collaborate** ⓥ 협력[협동]하다
reduce ⓥ (사람을 궁지 따위에) 밀어 넣다, 빠뜨리다		**ecological** ⓐ 생태계[학]의
scar ⓥ 상처를 남기다	**barren** ⓐ 척박한, 황량한	**govern** ⓥ (국가 · 국민을) 통치하다
talented ⓐ 타고난, 재능이 있는	**send out** (많은 사람들 · 장소로) ~을 보내다[발송하다]	
degrading ⓐ 비하하는, 모멸적인	**a dark complexion** 황인종[흑인종]의 얼굴색	

| 전문해석 | 제국주의는 심지어 식민지들이 영국으로부터 독립한 이후에도 아프리카와 아시아 식민지들에서 오랫동안 영향을 미쳤다. 그 부가 영국 통치자들과 그들에게 협력한 소수의 원주민들에게 돌아갔기 때문에, 이들 식민지에 살고 있던 사람들의 대부분은 궁핍한 생활을 할 수밖에 없었다. 어떤 경우에는 제국주의자들은 생태계에 커다란 피해를 줬으며, 경관에 상흔을 남기고 불모의 땅으로 만들었다. 제국주의는 모든 나라가 스스로 통치할 수 있는 권리를 인정하지 않았다. 아프리카와 아시아 식민지들에 사는 원주민들은 그들이 아무리 재능이 뛰어나다 하더라도 식민 정부에서 일하는 것이 거의 허용되지 않았다.

마지막으로 피부가 검은 사람들이 피부가 하얀 통치자들보다 '열등하다는' 모멸적인 메시지를 전달함으로써, 제국주의자들은 오늘날까지 계속되고 있는 깊은 분노와 울분을 일으켰다.

| 보기분석 | ① ~~The Poverty~~ of the African and Asian Colonies 제국주의의 여파로 빈곤뿐만 아니라 다른 영향들이 언급되므로 너무 지엽적
아프리카와 아시아 식민지의 빈곤
② The Colonies and Their Independence from British Rulers 언급 안 한 정보
식민지와 영국 통치자들로부터의 독립
③ The Impact of Imperialism on the African and Asian Colonies
제국주의가 아프리카와 아시아 식민지들에 미친 영향
④ The Positive Effect of Imperialism on the African and Asian Colonies 언급 안 한 정보
제국주의가 아프리카와 아시아 식민지들에 미치는 긍정적인 영향

| 정답분석 | '제국주의가 아프리카와 아시아 식민지에서 오랫동안 영향을 끼쳤는데, 이들 지역에 사는 대부분의 원주민들이 궁핍한 생활을 했으며, 제국주의자들은 식민지의 환경을 파괴하고, 식민지 주민이 스스로 통치할 권리를 인정하지 않았다'고 설명하고 있으므로, ③ '제국주의가 아프리카와 아시아 식민지들에 미친 영향'이 글의 제목으로 가장 적절하다.

14 2019 한국외대

정답 ④

| 구문분석 | (For a story) to be considered 'fantasy', it needs to contain some sort (of magic system), in short, things (that occur or exist in your story) (that cannot exist in the real world).
의미상 주어 / 부사적용법: ~하기 위하여 / it: S / needs: V / to contain some sort: O / in short: 접속부사 / that: 관계대명사 1 / that: 관계대명사 2
이야기(소설)가 '판타지(공상 소설)'로 간주되려면, 일종의 마법 체계를 담을 필요가 있는데, 요컨대, 현실 세계에서는 존재할 수 없지만 당신의 이야기 속에서는 일어나거나 존재하는 것들이다.

These include elements (of sorcery, witchcraft, and enchantment; fantastical creatures and the supernatural; or advanced abilities or powers).
These: S / include: V / elements: O / ; : 세미콜론: and 역할 / and: 등위접속사 / ; : 세미콜론: and 역할 / or: 등위접속사
이것들에는 마법, 마술, 요술의 요소들이나, 기이한 생물들과 초자연적인 존재나, 발달된 능력 또는 힘이 포함된다.

Basically, anything (with no basis in real-world evidence or logic) can be considered magic.
anything: S / can be considered: V / magic: O.C
기본적으로, 실제 세계의 증거 또는 논리에 근거하지 않는 것은 무엇이나 마법으로 여겨질 수 있다.

This is where you can really set your story apart from others in the genre.
This: S / is: V / where you can really set your story apart from others in the genre: C
이 부분에서 당신은 당신의 이야기를 그 장르의 다른 작품들과 차별화할 수 있다.

(If your magic system is unique and imaginative), your novel has a point (of difference).
부사절: 만약 ~라면 / your novel: S / has: V / a point (of difference): O
당신의 마법 체계가 독특하고 상상력이 풍부하다면, 당신의 소설은 차이점을 갖게 된다.

An innovative, intriguing magic system is often the key (to helping your novel stand out in the saturated fantasy market).
An innovative, intriguing magic system: S / is: V / the key: C
혁신적이고, 호기심을 자극하는 마법 체계는 종종 당신의 소설이 포화 상태의 판타지 소설 시장에서 돋보이도록 돕는 열쇠이다.

Your magic system should play a key part (in your story).
Your magic system: S / should play: V / a key part: C
당신의 마법 체계는 당신의 이야기에서 핵심적인 역할을 해야 한다.

| 어휘 |

fantasy ⓝ 공상, 상상, 〈문학〉 공상 소설 **sorcery** ⓝ 마법 **witchcraft** ⓝ 마술
enchantment ⓝ 마법, 마술 **supernatural** ⓐ 초자연적인 ⓝ 초자연적인 환상
basically ⓐⓓ 근본적으로 **set ~ apart from** ~을 …와 다르게[돋보이게] 만들다
real-world ⓐ 실세계의, 현실에 존재하는 **logic** ⓝ 논리
genre ⓝ (예술 작품의) 장르 **intriguing** ⓐ 아주 흥미로운 **stand out** 두드러지다

saturated ⓐ (시장이) 포화 상태인, 공급 과잉인

| 전문해석 | 이야기(소설)가 '판타지(공상 소설)'로 간주되려면, 일종의 마법 체계를 담을 필요가 있는데, 요컨대, 현실 세계에서는 존재할 수 없지만 당신의 이야기 속에서는 일어나거나 존재하는 것들이다. 이것들에는 마법, 마술, 요술의 요소들이나, 기이한 생물들과 초자연적인 존재나, 발달된 능력 또는 힘이 포함된다. 기본적으로, 실제 세계의 증거 또는 논리에 근거하지 않는 것은 무엇이나 마법으로 여겨질 수 있다. 이 부분에서 당신은 당신의 이야기를 그 장르의 다른 작품들과 차별화할 수 있다. 당신의 마법 체계가 독특하고 상상력이 풍부하다면, 당신의 소설은 차이점을 갖게 된다. 혁신적이고, 호기심을 자극하는 마법 체계는 종종 당신의 소설이 포화 상태의 판타지 소설 시장에서 돋보이도록 돕는 열쇠이다. 당신의 마법 체계는 당신의 이야기에서 핵심적인 역할을 해야 한다.

| 보기분석 | ① The Similarity Between Magic and Science 언급 안 한 정보
마술과 과학의 유사성
② Various Reasons Readers Buy Books 언급 안 한 정보
독자들이 책을 사는 다양한 이유
③ A Fantasy World: Something Never Experienced 키워드 없음
환상의 세계: 경험하지 못한 것
④ A Magic System: Fantasy's Essential Element
마법 체계: 판타지 소설의 필수 요소

| 정답분석 | 이 글은 이야기가 판타지 소설로 간주되기 위해 포함되어야 하는 필수 요소인 마법 체계(Magic System)를 주로 설명하고 있으므로, ④가 제목으로 적절하다.

15 2018 국민대

정답 ③

| 구문분석 | A behavioral theory asserts that consequences (from the environment) shape and maintain behaviors.
S V O
행동이론은 환경에서 비롯된 결과가 행동을 정하고 유지시킨다는 주장을 한다.

Behaviors (that are followed by positive reinforcement) are most likely to continue or increase.
S 관계대명사 V C
긍정적인 강화가 뒤따르는 행동은 지속되거나 늘어날 가능성이 매우 높다.

Conversely, any behavior (that is followed by negative consequences such as punishment), should theoretically decrease.
접속부사 S 관계대명사 V
이와는 반대로, 처벌과 같은 부정적인 결과가 뒤따르는 모든 행동은 이론적으로는 줄어들어야 한다.

However, research has not shown punishment to be an effective means (of behavioral intervention).
접속부사 S V O O.C
그러나 이제껏 처벌이 행동 개입의 효과적인 수단이라는 것을 보여 준 연구는 없었다.

The main reason is that it simply works to stop misbehavior.
S V C
그러한 주된 이유는 처벌이 단지 나쁜 행실을 멈추게 하는 데만 효과가 있기 때문이다.

In fact, it usually stops misbehavior (only while the punisher is actually present).
접속부사 S V O 부사절: ~하는 동안
사실, 처벌은 대개 처벌을 하는 사람이 실제로 있는 동안에만 나쁜 행실을 막을 수 있다.

A behavioral phenomenon (called contingency-governed behavior) may begin to develop (at this time).
S V O
이 시점에서 '유관 지배 행동(contingency-governed behavior)'이라 불리는 행동 현상이 생겨나기 시작할지도 모른다.

Contingency-governed behavior means that an individual's behavior depends on the next consequence he perceives.
S V O
유관 지배 행동이란 개인의 행동은 개인이 느끼는 다음번에 있을 결과에 좌우된다는 것을 의미한다.

부사절: 만약 ~라면

This means that a person will try to get away (with an inappropriate behavior) (if he thinks he will not get caught).
S V O

이는 만약 어떤 사람이 자신의 부적절한 행동이 발각되지 않을 거라 생각한다면, 그는 그 일을 저지르고 처벌을 받지 않고 무사히 빠져나가려 하는 경향이 있다는 것을 뜻한다.

Consequently, (if the student believes the punisher will not see him or catch him in the misbehavior), he will try to get away (with it).
접속부사 부사절: 만약 ~라면 S V O

결과적으로, 만약 나쁜 행실을 하는 자기를 처벌하는 사람이 보지 못하거나 발각하지 못할 거라 믿는다면, 그 학생은 그 행실을 저지르고 처벌을 받지 않고 무사히 빠져나가려 할 것이다.

The problem behavior cycle escalates.
S V

문제가 되는 행동은 반복되면서 더 심각해진다.

(If the student does not get caught), he feels successful, (which is a form of positive reinforcement, so he continues the pattern of problem behavior).
부사절: 만약 ~라면 S V C 관계대명사 등위접속사

그 학생이 발각되지 않는다면 그는 성공했다고 느끼는데, 이것은 일종의 긍정적인 강화여서 그는 문제 있는 행동 양식을 계속하게 된다.

| 어휘 |

behavioral ⓐ 행동의 **assert** ⓥ 단언하다, 주장하다 **consequence** ⓝ 결과
environment ⓝ (사회적 · 문화적인) 환경
shape ⓥ (어떤) 모양으로 만들다, (행동을) 형성하다 **maintain** ⓥ 지속하다, 유지하다
positive ⓐ 긍정적인 **reinforcement** ⓝ 강화 **conversely** ⓐⓓ 정반대로
punishment ⓝ 벌, 처벌 **theoretically** ⓐⓓ 이론적으로 **effective** ⓐ 효과적인, 유효한
intervention ⓝ 중재, 개입 **misbehavior** ⓝ 버릇없음, 품행 나쁨 **phenomenon** ⓝ 현상
contingency ⓝ 만일의 사태
contingency-governed behavior 유관 지배 행동(행동에 수반되어 일어나는 결과에 지배되는 행동)
perceive ⓥ 지각하다, 인식하다 **inappropriate** ⓐ 부적절한, 부적당한
get away with ~을 잘 해내다, (벌 따위를) 교묘히 모면하다 **escalate** ⓥ 확대되다

| 전문해석 |

행동이론은 환경에서 비롯된 결과가 행동을 정하고 유지시킨다는 주장을 한다. 긍정적인 강화가 뒤따르는 행동은 지속되거나 늘어날 가능성이 매우 높다. 이와는 반대로, 처벌과 같은 부정적인 결과가 뒤따르는 모든 행동은 이론적으로는 줄어들어야 한다. 그러나 이제껏 처벌이 행동 개입의 효과적인 수단이라는 것을 보여 준 연구는 없었다. 그러한 주된 이유는 처벌이 단지 나쁜 행실을 멈추게 하는 데만 효과가 있기 때문이다. 사실, 처벌은 대개 처벌을 하는 사람이 실제로 있는 동안에만 나쁜 행실을 막을 수 있다.

이 시점에서 '유관 지배 행동(contingency-governed behavior)'이라 불리는 행동 현상이 생겨나기 시작할지도 모른다. 유관 지배 행동이란 개인의 행동은 개인이 느끼는 다음번에 있을 결과에 좌우된다는 것을 의미한다. 이는 만약 어떤 사람이 자신의 부적절한 행동이 발각되지 않을 거라 생각한다면, 그는 그 일을 저지르고 처벌을 받지 않고 무사히 빠져나가려 하는 경향이 있다는 것을 뜻한다. 결과적으로, 만약 나쁜 행실을 하는 자기를 처벌하는 사람이 보지 못하거나 발각하지 못할 거라 믿는다면, 그 학생은 그 행실을 저지르고 처벌을 받지 않고 무사히 빠져나가려 할 것이다. 문제가 되는 행동은 반복되면서 더 심각해진다. 그 학생이 발각되지 않는다면 그는 성공했다고 느끼는데, 이것은 일종의 긍정적인 강화여서 그는 문제 있는 행동 양식을 계속하게 된다.

| 보기분석 |

① Behaviors Change over Time 언급 안 한 정보
행동은 시간이 흘러감에 따라 변한다

② Effective Means of Punishment 언급 안 한 정보
효과적인 처벌 방법

③ Consequences Shape Behaviors
결과가 행동을 결정한다

④ Controversy over Reinforcement 언급 안 한 정보
강화에 대한 논란

| 정답분석 | 본문에서는 개인의 행동이 환경에서 비롯되는 결과에 의해 좌우된다는 '행동이론'과 개인의 행동은 그 자신이 느끼는 다음 번에 있을 결과에 좌우된다는 것을 의미한다는 '유관 지배 행동'에 관하여 주로 이야기하고 있다. 그러므로 글의 제목으로는 ③이 적절하다.

16 2017 한양대

정답 ②

| 구문분석 | Those firms and industries (that are not participating in the world market) have to recognize that in today's trade environment isolation has become impossible.

S / 관계대명사 / V / O

세계 시장에 참여하고 있지 않은 기업들과 산업체들은 오늘날의 무역 환경에서는 고립이 불가능해졌다는 사실을 인식해야 한다.

(Willing or unwilling), more and more firms are becoming participants (in global business affairs).

분사구문 / S / V / C

좋든 싫든, 점점 더 많은 기업들이 글로벌 비즈니스에 참여하고 있는 중이다.

(Even if not by choice), most firms and individuals are affected (directly or indirectly) (by economic and political developments) (that occur in the international marketplace).

부사절: 비록 ~일지라도 / S / V / 관계대명사

비록 스스로 선택해서가 아니라 해도, 대다수의 기업들과 개인들은 직간접적으로 세계 시장에서 발생하는 경제적, 정치적 발전의 영향을 받고 있다.

Those firms (that refuse to participate) are relegated (to reacting to the global marketplace) and therefore are unprepared (for harsh competition from abroad).

S / 관계대명사 / V_1 / 등위접속사 / 접속부사 / V_2

(세계 시장에) 참여를 거부하는 기업들은 (미리 준비된 상황이 아닌) 세계 시장에 반동하는 처지가 되고 따라서 해외로부터의 강력한 경쟁에 대비가 되어 있지 않다.

Some industries have recognized the need (for international adjustments).

S / V / O

일부 산업체들은 세계 시장 적응의 필요성을 깨달았다.

Farmers understand the need (for high productivity in light of stiff international competition).

S / V / O

농민들은 극심한 국제 경쟁을 고려하면 생산성을 높여야 한다는 것을 이해하고 있다.

Computer makers and firms (in other technologically advanced industries) have learned to forge global relationships to stay in the race.

S / V / O

컴퓨터 제조업체와 기타 기술적으로 발전된 산업에 기반을 두고 있는 기업들은 경쟁에서 뒤처지지 않기 위해 국제적 관계를 형성하고 있는 중이다.

Firms (in the steel, textile, and leather sectors) have shifted production, and perhaps even adjusted their core business, (in response to overwhelming onslaughts from abroad).

S / V_1 / O / 등위접속사 / V_2 / O

철강, 직물, 피혁 분야의 기업들 역시 생산에 변화를 꾀했으며, 해외로부터의 강력한 공격에 대응하여 핵심 사업을 조정하기도 했을 것이다.

Other industries (in some countries) have been caught unaware and have been unable to adjust.

S / V_1 / V_2

일부 국가의 다른 사업체들은 이를 인식하지 못한 채 변화를 꾀하지 못하였다.

The result is the extinction (of firms or entire industries), (such as VCRs in the United States and coal mining and steel smelting in other countries).

S / V / C / 전치사: ~와 같은

그로 인한 결과는 미국의 VCR 사업이나 다른 국가의 탄광업이나 철강 제련업과 같이, 기업이나 전체 산업체가 종말을 맞게 되는 것이다.

| 어휘 |

relegate ⓥ 추방하다, 좌천시키다
harsh ⓐ 거친, 엄격한, 거슬리는
adjustment ⓝ 적응, 조절
in light of ~의 관점에서
stiff ⓐ 뻣뻣한, 경직된, 굳은; 완강한
forge ⓥ 만들다, 제조하다; 위조하다
in the race 경쟁하는
overwhelming ⓐ 압도적인
onslaught ⓝ 돌격, 공격, 습격

unaware ⓐ 인식하지 못한　　extinction ⓝ 사멸, 소멸　　smelt ⓥ 용해하다, 제련하다
loom ⓥ 나타나다, 출현하다

| 전문해석 | 세계 시장에 참여하고 있지 않은 기업들과 산업체들은 오늘날의 무역 환경에서는 고립이 불가능해졌다는 사실을 인식해야 한다. 좋든 싫든, 점점 더 많은 기업들이 글로벌 비즈니스에 참여하고 있는 중이다. 비록 스스로 선택해서가 아니라 해도, 대다수의 기업들과 개인들은 직간접적으로 세계 시장에서 발생하는 경제적, 정치적 발전의 영향을 받고 있다. (세계 시장에) 참여를 거부하는 기업들은 (미리 준비된 상황이 아닌) 세계 시장에 반동하는 처지가 되고 따라서 해외로부터의 강력한 경쟁에 대비가 되어 있지 않다.

일부 산업체들은 세계 시장 적응의 필요성을 깨달았다. 농민들은 극심한 국제 경쟁을 고려하면 생산성을 높여야 한다는 것을 이해하고 있다. 컴퓨터 제조업체와 기타 기술적으로 발전된 산업에 기반을 두고 있는 기업들은 경쟁에서 뒤처지지 않기 위해 국제적 관계를 형성하고 있는 중이다. 철강, 직물, 피혁 분야의 기업들 역시 생산에 변화를 꾀했으며, 해외로부터의 강력한 공격에 대응하여 핵심 사업을 조정하기도 했을 것이다. 일부 국가의 다른 사업체들은 이를 인식하지 못한 채 변화를 꾀하지 못하였다. 그로 인한 결과는 미국의 VCR 사업이나 다른 국가의 탄광업이나 철강 제련업과 같이, 기업이나 전체 산업체가 종말을 맞게 되는 것이다.

| 보기분석 | ① Road Not Taken: Entrepreneurship in the Future 언급 안 한 정보
가지 않은 길: 미래의 기업가 정신
② New Challenges Looming over the Global Market
세계 시장에서 떠오르고 있는 새로운 난제들
③ Different Players, Different Rules in the Business World 언급 안 한 정보
비즈니스 세계에서의 서로 다른 선수들과 서로 다른 규칙들
④ Two Faces of Global Business: A Dilemma of Being “Global/Local” 언급 안 한 정보
글로벌 비즈니스의 두 얼굴: '글로벌/로컬'의 딜레마

| 정답분석 | 오늘날의 무역 환경에서는 세계 시장에 참여하여 경쟁하는 것이 불가피하다는 점을 언급하면서 세계 시장이라는 무대에서 기업들이 인식해야 할 여러 가지 사항들을 다루고 있으므로, ②가 제목으로 가장 적절하다.

17 2017 한양대(에리카)　　정답 ③

| 구문분석 | The status of a character trait depends (on the reference point).
S　V
형질특성의 지위는 기준점에 달려 있다.

For instance, (for an ape) fingernails are considered primitive (in relation to other primates) (because all other primates have fingernails).
접속부사　S　V　O.C　부사절: 왜냐하면

예를 들어, 유인원의 손톱은 다른 모든 영장류 동물들이 손톱을 가지고 있기 때문에 다른 영장류 동물들에 비해 원시적인 것으로 간주된다.

Thus, fingernails would not serve to distinguish apes (from, for example, monkeys).
접속부사　S　V　O
따라서 손톱은 유인원을, 가령 원숭이와 구별하는 데 쓰이지 못할 것이다.

Fingernails are a derived character (for primates as a whole), however, (because no other mammals have them).
S　V　C　접속부사　부사절: 왜냐하면

그러나 다른 포유류 동물들은 손톱을 갖고 있지 않기 때문에 손톱은 전체 영장류 동물에게 파생 형질이다.

Thus, fingernails serve to distinguish primates (from other mammals).
접속부사　S　V　O
따라서 손톱은 영장류 동물을 다른 포유류 동물과 구별해 주는 역할을 한다.

The second character (illustrated here) — brow ridges — is found (only in hominoids, not in other primates), and is therefore derived (for hominoids).
S　└ 대시: 부연설명 ┘　V_1
등위접속사　접속부사　V_2
여기에서 설명하고 있는 두 번째 형질—눈두덩이—은 직립보행 영장류에서만 발견되며, 다른 영장류 동물에서는 발견되지 않기 때문에, 직립보행 영장류에 파생된 것이 된다.

This character distinguishes apes (from monkeys).
S V O
이러한 형질은 유인원과 원숭이를 구별해 준다.

(In a chimpanzee), however, brow ridges would be considered to be primitive (with respect to other hominoids); that is, the character would not distinguish a chimpanzee (from, for example, a gorilla).
세미콜론: 동격 접속부사 S V O.C 다시 말해 S V O
그러나 침팬지의 경우 눈두덩이가 다른 직립보행 영장류에 대해 본원적인 것으로 간주될 것이다. 다시 말해, 그 형질이 침팬지와, 가령 고릴라를 구별해 주지는 못할 것이다.

| 어휘 |

status ⓝ 상태, 지위, 중요도	**trait** ⓝ 특색, 특성	**reference point** (판단 · 비교용) 기준
ape ⓝ 원숭이, 유인원	**primitive** ⓐ 원시적인; 본원적인	**primate** ⓝ 영장류
distinguish ⓥ 구별하다, 분별하다	**derived character** 파생 형질	**mammal** ⓝ 포유동물
illustrate ⓥ 설명하다, 예증하다	**brow ridge** 눈두덩이	**hominoid** ⓝ 사람과 비슷한 동물

| 전문해석 | 형질특성의 지위는 기준점에 달려 있다. 예를 들어, 유인원의 손톱은 다른 모든 영장류 동물들이 손톱을 가지고 있기 때문에 다른 영장류 동물들에 비해 원시적인 것으로 간주된다. 따라서 손톱은 유인원을, 가령 원숭이와 구별하는 데 쓰이지 못할 것이다. 그러나 다른 포유류 동물들은 손톱을 갖고 있지 않기 때문에 손톱은 전체 영장류 동물에게 파생 형질이다. 따라서 손톱은 영장류 동물을 다른 포유류 동물과 구별해 주는 역할을 한다. 여기에서 설명하고 있는 두 번째 형질—눈두덩이—은 직립보행 영장류에서만 발견되며, 다른 영장류 동물에서는 발견되지 않기 때문에, 직립보행 영장류에 파생된 것이 된다. 이러한 형질은 유인원과 원숭이를 구별해 준다. 그러나 침팬지의 경우 눈두덩이가 다른 직립보행 영장류에 대해 본원적인 것으로 간주될 것이다. 다시 말해, 그 형질이 침팬지와, 가령 고릴라를 구별해 주지는 못할 것이다.

| 보기분석 |
① Relative Status of Species 키워드 없음
종의 상대적인 지위
② Absolute Status of Species 키워드 없음
종의 절대적인 지위
③ Relative Status of Characters
형질의 상대적인 지위
④ Absolute Status of Characters 절대적 지위가 아닌 상대적 지위에 관한 글임
형질의 절대적인 지위

| 정답분석 | 첫 번째 문장이 주제문이며, 나머지 전체는 주제문의 내용을 뒷받침하는 역할을 하고 있다. '형질특성의 지위는 기준점에 좌우된다.'는 것은 '형질특성의 지위가 상대적'이라는 것을 의미하므로 제목으로 ③이 적절하다.

18 2016 가톨릭대

정답 ③

| 구문분석 | Are there any benefits (from drinking filtered water) (as opposed to municipal tap water)? The short answer is yes.
V 유도부사 S
도시에서 운영하는 수돗물과 반대되는 위상을 가지고 있는 여과된 물을 마시는 경우 이점들이 있는 것일까? 이에 대한 짧은 답변은 '그렇다'이다.

(While the Environmental Protection Agency regulates municipal tap water and sets legal limits on certain contaminants, and most water utilities generally stay within these limits), some of the legal limits may be too lenient.
부사절: 반면에 S V_1 O V_2 O 등위접속사 S V_3 S V C
미국 환경보건국은 시에서 운영하는 수돗물을 규제하고 특정한 오염물질에 대해 법적인 제한을 정해 놓고 있고, 대부분의 상수도 시설들은 이러한 제한조치를 준수하고 있지만, 이들 법적 제한조치들 가운데 일부는 지나치게 관대하다.

And more than half of the chemicals (found in municipal water) are not regulated.
등위접속사 S V
그리고 시에서 운영하는 수돗물에서 발견되는 화학 물질들 중 절반 이상은 규제를 받고 있지 않는 것들이다.

Using the right water filter can help further (to) reduce pollutants (like lead from old water pipes, pesticide runoff in rural areas and byproducts of chemicals) (like chlorine (that are used to treat drinking water).

S: Using the right water filter / V: can help / O: reduce pollutants / that: 관계대명사

올바른 여과 필터를 사용하는 것을 통해서 우리는 낡은 수도관에서 납과 같은 오염물질, 시골 지역에서 발견되는 살충제 유출액체, 식수 처리에 사용되는 염소와 같은 화학 물질의 부산물들을 더 감소시키는 데 도움을 받을 수 있다.

Radon, arsenic and nitrates are common pollutants (in drinking water). Certain filters may help (to) remove these impurities as well.

S: Radon, arsenic and nitrates / V: are / O: common pollutants / S: Certain filters / V: may help / O: remove these impurities

라돈, 비소, 질산염 등은 식수에 흔히 들어 있는 오염물질이다. 어떤 필터들은 이들 불순물들을 제거하는 데 도움을 준다.

But water contaminants and water quality vary (from one local water utility to another), so you want to purchase a filter (that is effective at capturing the right contaminants).

S: water contaminants and water quality / V: vary / so: 등위접속사 / S: you / V: want / O: to purchase a filter / that: 관계대명사

그러나 수질 오염물질들과 수질은 각 지역의 상수도 시설마다 다르다. 그래서 여러분은 오염물질을 제대로 정확히 걸러 낼 수 있는 효과적인 필터를 구입하길 바랄 것이다.

| 어휘 |

municipal ⓐ 도시의, 자치권의; 자치제의
tap water 수돗물
contaminant ⓝ 오염물질
water utility 상수도 시설
lenient ⓐ 너그러운, 관대한
pesticide ⓝ 살충제
runoff ⓝ 땅 위를 흐르는 빗물, 유거수(流去水)
chlorine ⓝ 염소(냄새가 있는 화학 물질)
radon ⓝ 라돈(라듐의 방사성 붕괴로 생기는 방사성 희(希)가스 원소)
arsenic ⓝ 비소(독성 화학 물질)
nitrate ⓝ 질산염; 질산칼륨, 질산소다
impurity ⓝ 불결, 불순; 음란, 외설(obscenity)

| 전문해석 | 도시에서 운영하는 수돗물과 반대되는 위상을 가지고 있는 여과된 물을 마시는 경우 이점들이 있는 것일까? 이에 대한 짧은 답변은 '그렇다'이다. 미국 환경보건국은 시에서 운영하는 수돗물을 규제하고 특정한 오염물질에 대해 법적인 제한을 정해 놓고 있고, 대부분의 상수도 시설들은 이러한 제한조치를 준수하고 있지만, 이들 법적 제한조치들 가운데 일부는 지나치게 관대하다. 그리고 시에서 운영하는 수돗물에서 발견되는 화학 물질들 중 절반 이상은 규제를 받고 있지 않는 것들이다. 올바른 여과 필터를 사용하는 것을 통해서 우리는 낡은 수도관에서 납과 같은 오염물질, 시골 지역에서 발견되는 살충제 유출액체, 식수 처리에 사용되는 염소와 같은 화학 물질의 부산물들을 더 감소시키는 데 도움을 받을 수 있다. 라돈, 비소, 질산염 등은 식수에 흔히 들어 있는 오염물질이다. 어떤 필터들은 이들 불순물들을 제거하는 데 도움을 준다. 그러나 수질 오염물질들과 수질은 각 지역의 상수도 시설마다 다르다. 그래서 여러분은 오염물질을 제대로 정확히 걸러 낼 수 있는 효과적인 필터를 구입하길 바랄 것이다.

| 보기분석 |

① environmental problems 언급 안 한 정보 / 너무 포괄적
환경적 문제들

② water shortage 언급 안 한 정보
물 부족

③ safe water-drinking
안전한 물 섭취

④ water pollutions 주된 내용이 아닌 지엽적 내용
수질 오염물질들

| 정답분석 | 이 글은 안전한 식수를 확보할 수 있는 방법에 대해서 기술하고 있으므로 제목으로 ③이 적절하다.

19 한양대 2020

정답 ②

| 구문분석 | In temperate regions, the leaves of many deciduous trees change color in the fall, (transforming entire landscapes into a mosaic of reds and yellows).

S: the leaves of many deciduous trees / V: change / O: color / transforming ...: 분사구문

온대 지방에서는 가을이 되면 낙엽수들의 잎 색깔이 변하게 되고, 그것이 전체 풍경을 붉은색과 노란색의 모자이크로 만든다.

Red coloration is particularly intriguing (because it is produced in the fall and is not merely a byproduct of the breakdown of green pigments (as is the case with yellows)).
S V C 부사절: ~ 때문에

붉은색은 특히 흥미로운데, 그것이 가을에 만들어지고, 단지 녹색 색소가 분해되면서 생긴 부산물에 그치는 것이 아니기 때문이다(노랑의 경우에는 그러하다).

(Among the proposed explanations for fall's red coloration) is the coevolutionary hypothesis, which posits that red leaves advertise something (— for example, unpalatability or low nutritional quality —) (to herbivorous insects on their fall migration).
V S 관계대명사 V O 대시: 부연설명

가을의 붉은색을 설명하기 위해 제안된 설명들 중에는 공진화 가설이 있는데, 이것은 붉은 잎이 가을에 이주하는 초식성 곤충에게 무엇인가를, 예를 들어 맛없음이라거나 영양가가 낮음 등을 알린다는 것을 제시한다.

Evidence (for this hypothesis) focuses (on aphids and their potential winter host trees).
S V

이 가설에 대한 증거는 진딧물과 진딧물의 잠재적인 겨울 숙주 나무에 초점을 맞추고 있다.

For example, tree species (with the strongest autumnal coloration) tend to be those trees (threatened by the greatest number of migrating aphids).
접속부사 S V O

예를 들어, 가장 강렬한 가을 색을 갖는 나무종은 가장 많은 수의 이주하는 진딧물로부터 위협을 받는 나무인 경향이 있다.

There is (reduced) herbivory (on red (versus green) leaves), and the peak (of fall coloration) coincides (with the most active migratory period for aphids).
유도부사 V S 등위접속사 S V

붉은색 잎은 (푸른색과 반대로) 곤충들이 먹는 일이 줄어들게 되고, 가을 색이 절정을 이루는 시기가 진딧물이 가장 활발하게 이동하는 시기와 일치한다.

| 어휘 |

temperate ⓐ 온대의	deciduous ⓐ 낙엽성의	intriguing ⓐ 흥미를 일으키는
pigment ⓝ 색소	herbivorous ⓐ 초식의	posit ⓥ 가정하다
aphid ⓝ 진딧물	coincide ⓥ 일치하다	

| 전문해석 | 온대 지방에서는 가을이 되면 낙엽수들의 잎 색깔이 변하게 되고, 그것이 전체 풍경을 붉은색과 노란색의 모자이크로 만든다. 붉은색은 특히 흥미로운데, 그것이 가을에 만들어지고, 단지 녹색 색소가 분해되면서 생긴 부산물에 그치는 것이 아니기 때문이다(노랑의 경우에는 그러하다). 가을의 붉은색을 설명하기 위해 제안된 설명들 중에는 공진화 가설이 있는데, 이것은 붉은 잎이 가을에 이주하는 초식성 곤충에게 무엇인가를, 예를 들어 맛없음이라거나 영양가가 낮음 등을 알린다는 것을 제시한다. 이 가설에 대한 증거는 진딧물과 진딧물의 잠재적인 겨울 숙주 나무에 초점을 맞추고 있다. 예를 들어, 가장 강렬한 가을 색을 갖는 나무종은 가장 많은 수의 이주하는 진딧물로부터 위협을 받는 나무인 경향이 있다. 붉은색 잎은 (푸른색과 반대로) 곤충들이 먹는 일이 줄어들게 되고, 가을 색이 절정을 이루는 시기가 진딧물이 가장 활발하게 이동하는 시기와 일치한다.

| 보기분석 |
① A Paradox of Toxic Substances 언급 안 한 정보
독성 물질의 역설
② Coloration as Ecological Communication
생태적 의사소통으로서의 색채
③ The More Palatable, the More Protective 언급 안 한 정보
맛있을수록, 더 방어적이다
④ In Search of a Shared Protective Benefit 핵심 키워드인 색이 포함 ×
공유되는 방어적 이점을 찾아서
⑤ Migrating Insects, an Arsenal of Antipredator Adaptations 언급 안 한 정보
이주하는 곤충, 포식자 대항 적응의 무기

| 정답분석 | 이 글은 자신을 먹이로 삼는 곤충(진딧물)이 몰려들 때 나무는 스스로를 보호하려고 '맛없음', '영양가 낮음' 등을 알리기 위해 나뭇잎의 색깔을 붉은색으로 물들인다는 가설을 소개하는 글이다. 따라서 글의 제목으로는 ②가 가장 적절하다.

20 2017 한양대

정답 ②

| 구문분석 | Professor Westbury has been doing important work, (exploring the connections between language difficulties
S V O 분사구문
and brain function).

웨스트베리(Westbury) 교수는 언어장애와 뇌의 기능 사이의 연관성을 탐구하면서 중요한 연구를 수행해 오고 있다.

(As part of his inquiry), Westbury presents patients (suffering from aphasia) — whose comprehension of
S V1 O 대시: 부연설명
words and speech is often impaired — (with a string of letters) and asks whether or not it constitutes a real
등위접속사 V2 O
English word.

자신의 연구의 일환으로, 웨스트베리는 실어증 환자들—언어표현에 대한 이해력이 종종 손상된 사람들—에게 일련의 문자를 제시하고 그것이 진짜 영어 단어에 속하는 것인지 아닌지를 물어본다.

One day, a graduate student pointed out something curious: certain nonsense words consistently made
S V O 콜론: 재진술 S V
patients smile and sometimes even laugh out loud.
O O.C1 등위접속사 O.C2

어느 날, 한 대학원생이 어떤 무의미한 표현들이 지속적으로 환자들을 미소 짓게 하고 때로는 큰 소리로 웃게도 만든다는 기이한 점을 지적했다.

"Particularly," Westbury says, "'snunkoople'."
S V O

웨스트베리는 "특히 snunkoople이 그래요."라고 말한다.

He started checking (with friends and colleagues) (to see whether they had the same reaction), and the
S V O 부사적용법: ~하기 위하여 등위접속사
response was nearly unanimous. Snunkoople was funny. But why?
S V C

똑같은 반응을 보이는지 친구들과 동료들에게도 확인해 보았는데, 그 반응은 거의 일치했다. snunkoople이라는 표현은 우스꽝스럽다는 것이었다. 하지만 이유가 무엇일까?

Westbury presents what he believes could be the answer: the inherent funniness of a word, or at least of
S V O 콜론: 재진술
context-free non-words, can be quantified — and not all nonsense is created equal.
S V O.C

웨스트베리는 그에 대한 대답이라고 자신이 믿고 있는 것을 제시한다. 즉, 어떤 단어가 지니고 있는 고유의 우스꽝스러움 또는 적어도 문맥이 없는 무의미한 단어들의 고유한 우스꽝스러움은 정량화할 수 있고, 그래서 모든 무의미한 말이 평등한 상태로 탄생되는 것은 아니라는 것이다.

가주어
(According to Westbury), the less statistically likely it is (for a certain collection of letters) to form a real word
the 비교급 S V, the 비교급 S V: ~하면 할수록 더 …하다 V 진주어
in English, the funnier it is.
S V

웨스트베리에 따르면, 특정 조합의 문자들이 영어에서 실재하는 단어를 형성할 가능성이 통계적으로 더 적을수록 더 재미있게 된다.

The playwright Neil Simon seemed to grasp this implicitly (in his 1972 work *The Sunshine Boys*), (in which
S V C 관계대명사
an old character tells his nephew), "If it doesn't have a 'k' in it, it's not funny!" — "k" being one of the least
대시: 부연설명
frequently used letters in the alphabet.

1972년에, 극작가인 닐 사이먼(Neil Simon)은 그의 작품 *The Sunshine Boys*에서 이러한 함축적 의미를 파악한 것 같았는데, 그 작품에서는 한 나이 든 등장인물이 그의 조카에게 "만약에 알파벳에 'k'가—'k'는 알파벳에서 가장 적은 빈도로 사용되는 문자들 중 하나이다—없다면 그건 재미가 없을 거야!"라고 말하고 있다.

| 어휘 |

inquiry ⓝ 질문, 의문	**aphasia** ⓝ 실어증	**impair** ⓥ 손상시키다
laugh ⓥ 웃다; 비웃다	**unanimous** ⓐ 만장일치의	**implicity** ⓝ 암시, 내포, 함축

| 전문해석 | 웨스트베리(Westbury) 교수는 언어장애와 뇌의 기능 사이의 연관성을 탐구하면서 중요한 연구를 수행해 오고 있다. 자신의 연구의 일환으로, 웨스트베리는 실어증 환자들—언어표현에 대한 이해력이 종종 손상된 사람들—에게 일련의 문자를 제시하고 그것이 진짜 영어 단어에 속하는 것인지 아닌지를 물어본다. 어느 날, 한 대학원생이 어떤 무의미한 표현들이 지속적으로 환자들을 미소 짓게 하고 때로는 큰 소리로 웃게도 만든다는 기이한 점을 지적했다. 웨스트베리는 "특히

snunkoople이 그래요."라고 말한다. 똑같은 반응을 보이는지 친구들과 동료들에게도 확인해 보았는데, 그 반응은 거의 일치했다. snunkoople이라는 표현은 우스꽝스럽다는 것이었다. 하지만 이유가 무엇일까? 웨스트베리는 그에 대한 대답이라고 자신이 믿고 있는 것을 제시한다. 즉, 어떤 단어가 지니고 있는 고유의 우스꽝스러움 또는 적어도 문맥이 없는 무의미한 단어들의 고유한 우스꽝스러움은 정량화할 수 있고, 그래서 모든 무의미한 말이 평등한 상태로 탄생되는 것은 아니라는 것이다. 웨스트베리에 따르면, 특정 조합의 문자들이 영어에서 실재하는 단어를 형성할 가능성이 통계적으로 더 적을수록 더 재미있게 된다. 1972년에, 극작가인 닐 사이먼(Neil Simon)은 그의 작품 *The Sunshine Boys*에서 이러한 함축적 의미를 파악한 것 같았는데, 그 작품에서는 한 나이 든 등장인물이 그의 조카에게 "만약에 알파벳에 'k'가—'k'는 알파벳에서 가장 적은 빈도로 사용되는 문자들 중 하나이다—없다면 그건 재미가 없을 거야!"라고 말하고 있다.

| 보기분석 | ① ~~Aphasia~~: The Way We Laugh 실어증은 특정 단어들이 우스운 이유에 대한 부가적 설명으로 나왔으므로 이 글 전체를 담기에는 너무 지엽적
실어증: 우리가 웃는 방식

② Why Certain Words Are Funny
왜 특정 단어들은 우스꽝스러울까?

③ ~~Humor~~ as an Art of Equivocation 키워드 없음
한 가지 모호함의 기술로서의 유머

④ "~~Snunkoople~~," an Unusual Cluster of Letters 너무 지엽적
여러 문자들의 보기 드문 결합인 "Snunkoople"

| 정답분석 | 어떤 무의미한 표현들이 지속적으로 환자들을 미소 짓게 하고 때로는 큰 소리로 웃게도 만든다는 사실로부터 '왜 특정 단어는 우스꽝스러운가'에 대한 연구가 진행됐다는 것을 이야기하면서, 이에 대한 연구 결과를 설명하고 있는 내용이다. 따라서 제목으로는 ②가 적절하다.

21 2016 서울여대

정답 ①

| 구문분석 | The story(S) goes(V) that a Dublin theatre proprietor(S) (by the name of Richard Daly) made a bet(V) that(O₁) he could, within forty-eight hours, make a nonsense word known throughout the city, and(등위접속사) that(O₂) the public would supply a meaning for it.

Richard Daly라는 이름을 가진 더블린의 극장 소유자가 내기를 했다고 하는데, 그는 자신이 아무 의미 없는 단어를 48시간 이내에 도시 전역에 알릴 수 있으며, (그렇게 되면) 대중들이 그 단어에 의미를 부여할 것이라고 공언했다.

(After a performance one evening)(전치사), he(S) gave(V_1) his staff(I.O) cards(D.O) (with the word 'quiz' written on them), and(등위접속사) told(V_2) them(O) to write the word(O.C) (on walls around the city).

어느 날 저녁, 공연이 끝난 후, 그는 직원들에게 'quiz'라고 적혀 있는 카드를 나눠 주며, 도시 전역에 있는 벽에 그 단어를 쓰라고 지시했다.

The next day the strange word(S_1) was(V_1) the talk(C_1) (of the town), and(등위접속사) (within a short time) it(S_2) had become(V_2) part(C_2) (of the language).

다음날, 그 낯선 단어는 장안의 화제가 됐고, 더 나아가 눈 깜빡할 사이에, 언어의 일부가 되었다.

The most detailed account(S) (of this supposed exploit, in F. T. Porter's *Gleanings and Reminiscence* (1875)), gives(V) its date(O) (as 1791).

1875년에 출간된 F.T. Porter의 *Gleanings and Reminiscence*라는 책에 실린 이 영웅적 위업에 대한 매우 자세한 진술에서는 이 단어가 언어의 일부가 된 때가 1791년이라고 적혀 있다.

The word(S), however(접속부사), was(V_1) already (in use by then), (meaning 'an eccentric person')(분사구문), and(등위접속사) had been used(V_2) (in this sense) (by Fanny Burney in her diary entry for 24 June 1782).

그러나 이 단어는 그 당시에 이미 '별난 사람'이라는 의미로 사용되고 있었고, 1782년 6월 24일 Fanny Burney가 쓴 일기 속에도 이 단어는 이와 같은 의미로 기재되어 있었다.

| 어휘 | **proprietor** ⓝ 소유자, 소유주, 경영자 **make a bet** 내기를 하다 **talk of the town** 장안의 화제
exploit ⓝ 공훈, 업적, 위업 **gleaning** ⓝ 이삭줍기; (지식 등의) 수집; 수집물, 단편적 모음, 선집(選集)
reminiscence ⓝ 회상, 추억, 기억 **eccentric** ⓐ 별난, 특이한 **entry** ⓝ 입장; 표제어; 기재사항

| 전문해석 | Richard Daly라는 이름을 가진 더블린의 극장 소유자가 내기를 했다고 하는데, 그는 자신이 아무 의미 없는 단어를 48시간 이내에 도시 전역에 알릴 수 있으며, (그렇게 되면) 대중들이 그 단어에 의미를 부여할 것이라고 공언했다. 어느 날 저녁, 공연이 끝난 후, 그는 직원들에게 'quiz'라고 적혀 있는 카드를 나눠 주며, 도시 전역에 있는 벽에 그 단어를 쓰라고 지시했다. 다음날, 그 낯선 단어는 장안의 화제가 됐고, 더 나아가 눈 깜빡할 사이에, 언어의 일부가 되었다. 1875년에 출간된 F.T. Porter의 *Gleanings and Reminiscence*라는 책에 실린 이 영웅적 위업에 대한 매우 자세한 진술에서는 이 단어가 언어의 일부가 된 때가 1791년이라고 적혀 있다. 그러나 이 단어는 그 당시에 이미 '별난 사람'이라는 의미로 사용되고 있었고, 1782년 6월 24일 Fanny Burney가 쓴 일기 속에도 이 단어는 이와 같은 의미로 기재되어 있었다.

| 보기분석 | ✔ The history of the word 'quiz'
단어 'quiz'의 역사
② ~~Different forms~~ of the word 'quiz' 언급 안 한 정보
단어 'quiz'의 다른 형태들
③ ~~Grammatical usages~~ of the word 'quiz' 언급 안 한 정보
단어 'quiz'의 문법적 용법
④ ~~Changes in the meaning~~ of the word 'quiz' 의미의 변화를 주로 기술한 글이 아니므로 너무 지엽적
단어 'quiz'의 의미의 변화들

| 정답분석 | 이 글은 quiz라는 단어의 시작과 기원에 대하여 기술하고 있으므로 제목으로는 ①이 적절하다.

22 2019 숙명여대

정답 ③

| 구문분석 | This first decade of the twenty-first century, the world community(S) is confronted(V) (with staggering problems).
21세기에 들어서 첫 10년 동안, 세계 사회는 엄청난 문제에 직면해 있다.

There(유도부사) are(V) 6 billion people(S) (on our globe) and forecasters(S) project(V) that the world population will reach 10 billion by 2050(O).

지구상에는 60억 명의 인구가 있으며, 예측가들은 2050년이 되면 세계 인구가 100억 명이 될 것으로 보고 있다.

Those people(S) will need(V) food, shelter, and an education(O) (that(관계대명사) will allow them to lead fulfilled lives).
그 100억 명의 사람들은 그들로 하여금 만족한 삶을 영위하게 해 줄 음식, 주거지, 교육을 필요로 할 것이다.

The twentieth century(S) saw(V) great advances(O) (in many fields), but(등위접속사) these advances(S) did not come(V) (without costs).

20세기에는 여러 분야에서 큰 발전이 있었지만, 이런 발전이 대가 없이 이루어진 것은 아니었다.

Acid rain(S), for example(접속부사), polluted(V) our vegetation, wild life, and the very bodies(O) of millions of people.
예를 들면, 산성비는 우리의 식물과 야생 생물, 그리고 수많은 사람들의 몸을 오염시켰다.

Together, the people(S) (of the world) need(V) to stop the systemic despoiling of our planet(O).
전 세계 사람들은 협력하여 지구에 대한 체계적인 약탈(파괴)을 중단시킬 필요가 있다.

Weaponry(S), (such as(전치사) nuclear devices and improvised explosive devices), daily threaten(V) the world's peace and progress(O).

핵무기와 사제 폭발물과 같은 무기는 세계의 평화와 발전을 날마다 위협한다.

Religious fanaticism, hunger, and poverty have bred a desperate terrorism (in many corners of the world).
S V O
종교적 광신주의, 기아, 가난은 세계 곳곳에서 무모한 테러를 야기했다.

가주어
It is no overstatement to say that we are in a race for global survival.
V C 진주어
우리가 지금 전 인류의 생존을 위해 분투하고 있다고 말해도 과장된 표현이 아니다.

| 어휘 |

confront ⓥ 직면하다, 맞서다	**forecaster** ⓝ 예측자; (일기) 예보관	**project** ⓥ 예상[추정]하다
shelter ⓝ 주거지, 대피처	**acid rain** ⓝ 산성비	**pollute** ⓥ 오염시키다, 더럽히다
despoil ⓥ 약탈하다, 빼앗다	**improvised** ⓐ 즉흥[즉석]의, 임시변통의	
explosive device 폭파 장치	**desperate** ⓐ 필사적인, 무모한	**overstatement** ⓝ 과장한 말, 허풍

| 전문해석 | 21세기에 들어서 첫 10년 동안, 세계 사회는 엄청난 문제에 직면해 있다. 지구상에는 60억 명의 인구가 있으며, 예측가들은 2050년이 되면 세계 인구가 100억 명이 될 것으로 보고 있다. 그 100억 명의 사람들은 그들로 하여금 만족한 삶을 영위하게 해 줄 음식, 주거지, 교육을 필요로 할 것이다. 20세기에는 여러 분야에서 큰 발전이 있었지만, 이런 발전이 대가 없이 이루어진 것은 아니었다. 예를 들면, 산성비는 우리의 식물과 야생 생물, 그리고 수많은 사람들의 몸을 오염시켰다. 전 세계 사람들은 협력하여 지구에 대한 체계적인 약탈(파괴)을 중단시킬 필요가 있다. 핵무기와 사제 폭발물과 같은 무기는 세계의 평화와 발전을 날마다 위협한다. 종교적 광신주의, 기아, 가난은 세계 곳곳에서 무모한 테러를 야기했다. 우리가 지금 전 인류의 생존을 위해 분투하고 있다고 말해도 과장된 표현이 아니다.

| 보기분석 |
① Great Advances Made in the Twentieth Century 좋은 점만 기술한 글이 아님 / 너무 지엽적
20세기에 이룬 위대한 발전
② Global Warming, Vegetation, and Wildlife 언급 안 한 정보
지구 온난화, 초목, 그리고 야생 생물
③ Great Advances Made with Significant Costs Paid
상당한 희생을 치르고 이룬 큰 발전
④ How to Lead Fulfilled Religious Lives 키워드 없음
충만한 종교적인 삶을 사는 방법
⑤ Desperate Terrorism and Global Survival 너무 지엽적
무모한 테러와 전 세계의 생존

| 정답분석 | 엄청난 문제에 직면해 있는 지구의 상황을 설명하는 글로, 지난 20세기에 인간은 여러 분야에서 큰 발전을 이루었지만, 이런 발전이 대가 없이 이루어지지 않았다고 한 다음 이에 대한 예를 들고 있다. 따라서 ③이 글의 제목으로 적절하다.

23 2019 명지대

정답 ④

| 구문분석 | (In most paper and pencil tests), the test-taker is presented (with all the items), (usually in ascending order of difficulty), and is required to respond (to as many of them as possible).
S V_1 등위접속사 V_2 O.C
대부분의 지필시험에서는 보통 난이도가 쉬운 문제부터 어려운 문제 순으로 수험생에게 문항이 제시되며, 수험생은 가능한 많은 문항을 풀어야 한다.

This is not the most economical way (of collecting information on someone's ability).
S V C
이 지필시험은 수험생의 능력에 관한 정보를 수집하는 데 있어서 가장 경제적인 방식은 아니다.

There is no real need (for strong candidates) (to attempt easy items), and no need (for weak candidates) (to attempt difficult items).
유도부사 V S_1 to부정사의 의미상 주어 S_2 to부정사의 의미상 주어
실력이 뛰어난 수험생이 쉬운 문항을 풀 필요는 없으며, 실력이 떨어지는 수험생이 어려운 문항을 풀 필요도 없기 때문이다.

Computer adaptive testing offers a potentially more efficient way (of collecting information on people's ability).
S V O
컴퓨터 적응형 시험(CAT)은 아마도 수험생의 능력에 관한 정보를 수집하는 더 효율적인 방식일지도 모른다.

All test-takers are presented (initially with an item of average difficulty).
S V
모든 수험생들은 처음에 평균 난이도의 문항을 풀게 된다.

go on + toR: 계속해서 ~하다
The computer goes on to present individual candidates (with items) (that are appropriate for their apparent level of ability as estimated by their performance on previous items), (raising or lowering the level of difficulty) (until a dependable estimate at their ability is achieved).
S V O 관계대명사 분사구문 부사절: ~까지
컴퓨터는 직전에 풀었던 문항들의 성적에 의해 추정되는 수험생들의 외견상의 능력 수준에 알맞은 문항을 계속해서 개개의 수험생에게 제시하며, 계속 난이도를 조정하여 결국 수험생의 능력에 대한 믿을 만한 평가가 달성된다.

| 어휘 | **paper and pencil test** 지필시험(연필이나 펜으로 종이에 답을 쓰는 형식의 시험)
test-taker ⓝ 수험생 **be presented with** ~이 주어지다 **item** ⓝ 항목, 안건; 문항
in ascending order 오름차순으로 **candidate** ⓝ (자격 취득 시험의) 수험생
computer adaptive testing 컴퓨터 적응형 시험(응시자의 실력에 따라 난이도가 컴퓨터 내에서 조절되는 시험)
rationale ⓝ 논리적 근거 **sequence** ⓥ 차례로 배열하다 **efficacy** ⓝ 효능, 능률

| 전문해석 | 대부분의 지필시험에서는 보통 난이도가 쉬운 문제부터 어려운 문제 순으로 수험생에게 문항이 제시되며, 수험생은 가능한 많은 문항을 풀어야 한다. 이 지필시험은 수험생의 능력에 관한 정보를 수집하는 데 있어서 가장 경제적인 방식은 아니다. 실력이 뛰어난 수험생이 쉬운 문항을 풀 필요는 없으며, 실력이 떨어지는 수험생이 어려운 문항을 풀 필요도 없기 때문이다. (반면) 컴퓨터 적응형 시험(CAT)은 아마도 수험생의 능력에 관한 정보를 수집하는 더 효율적인 방식일지도 모른다. (컴퓨터 적응형 시험에서) 모든 수험생들은 처음에 평균 난이도의 문항을 풀게 된다. 컴퓨터는 직전에 풀었던 문항들의 성적에 의해 추정되는 수험생들의 외견상의 능력 수준에 알맞은 문항을 계속해서 개개의 수험생에게 제시하며, 계속 난이도를 조정하여 결국 수험생의 능력에 대한 믿을 만한 평가가 달성된다.

| 보기분석 | ① Rationale behind Test-takers' ~~Preference~~ for Computer Adaptive Testing 수험생의 선호도와 관련된 글이 아님
컴퓨터 적응형 시험에 대한 수험생의 선호도를 뒷받침하는 논리적 근거
② ~~How to Encourage~~ Weak Candidates to Attempt Difficult Questions 언급 안 한 정보
실력이 떨어지는 수험생들이 어려운 문제를 풀도록 용기를 북돋우는 방법
③ The ~~History~~ of Sequencing Test Items Based on Item Difficulty 언급 안 한 정보
문항 난이도에 근거해 시험문항을 차례로 배열하는 역사
✔④ The Efficacy of Computer Adaptive Testing in Estimating Ability
(수험생의) 능력을 평가하는 데 있어 컴퓨터 적응형 시험의 효율성

| 정답분석 | 지필시험과 컴퓨터 적응형 시험을 비교하면서, 컴퓨터 적응형 시험이 지필시험보다 수험생의 능력을 더 효율적으로 평가할 수 있음을 이야기하고 있다. 따라서 제목으로는 ④가 적절하다.

24 2017 국민대(인문 오전A형)

정답 ②

| 구문분석 | (Despite the increasing importance of leadership to business success), the on-the-job experiences (of most people) actually seem to undermine the development (of the attributes needed for leadership).
S V C
기업 성공에 리더십이 날로 더 중요해지고 있지만 대부분의 사람들의 경우에는 현장에서의 실무 경험이 리더십에 필요한 자질 계발을 실제로 방해하고 있는 것처럼 보인다.

Nevertheless, some companies have consistently demonstrated an ability (to develop people into outstanding leader-managers).
접속부사 S V O
그럼에도 불구하고 몇몇 기업에서는 사람들을 뛰어난 리더십을 가진 관리자로 양성하는 능력을 꾸준히 보여 주었다.

Recruiting people with leadership potential is managing their career patterns.
S V C
리더십을 보일 만한 잠재력을 가진 사람을 채용하는 것이 그들의 경력패턴을 관리하는 것이다.

Individuals (who are effective in large leadership roles) often share a number of career experiences.
S 관계대명사 V O
리더십이 필요한 큰 역할을 효과적으로 수행하는 사람들은 흔히 모두가 많은 실무 경험을 쌓은 사람들이다.

Perhaps the most typical and most important is significant challenge early in a career.
C V S
가장 전형적이고 중요한 것은 경력을 쌓기 시작한 초반에 경험하는 큰 도전(문제)일 것이다.

Leaders almost always have had opportunities (during their twenties and thirties) (to actually try to lead, to take a risk, and to learn from both triumphs and failures).
S V O
리더들은 사람들을 실제로 리드하고, 모험을 해 보고, 성공과 실패 모두로부터 배울 기회를 거의 항상 20대나 30대에 가져 본 적이 있다.

Such learning seems essential (in developing a wide range of leadership skills and perspectives).
S V C
이와 같은 배움은 광범위한 리더십 기술과 균형 잡힌 시야를 계발하는 데 필수적인 듯하다.

These opportunities also teach people something (about both the difficulty of leadership and its potential for producing change).
S V I.O D.O both A and B: A, B 둘 다
이러한 기회들은 또한 리더십의 어려움과 리더십의 변화 창출 잠재력, 두 가지 모두에 관해 사람들에게 가르침을 준다.

| 어휘 | **on-the-job** ⓐ 수습에서 익힌, 실습에서 익힌
undermine ⓥ (자신감 · 권위 등을) 약화시키다, 몰래 손상시키다; (건강 등을) 서서히 해치다
attribute ⓝ 속성, 특질, 특성 **consistently** ⓐⓓ 끊임없이, 일관되게
demonstrate ⓥ 증명[논증]하다; (감정 등을) 밖으로 나타내다, 드러내다
outstanding ⓐ 걸출한, 눈에 띄는, 현저한 **potential** ⓝ 잠재력, 가능성
typical ⓐ 전형적인, 모범적인 **significant** ⓐ 중요한, 의미 있는 **triumph** ⓝ 승리, 대성공
perspective ⓝ 전망, 시각, 견지; 원근법

| 전문해석 | 기업 성공에 리더십이 날로 더 중요해지고 있지만 대부분의 사람들의 경우에는 현장에서의 실무 경험이 리더십에 필요한 자질 계발을 실제로 방해하고 있는 것처럼 보인다. 그럼에도 불구하고 몇몇 기업에서는 사람들을 뛰어난 리더십을 가진 관리자로 양성하는 능력을 꾸준히 보여 주었다. 리더십을 보일 만한 잠재력을 가진 사람을 채용하는 것이 그들의 경력패턴을 관리하는 것이다. 리더십이 필요한 큰 역할을 효과적으로 수행하는 사람들은 흔히 모두가 많은 실무 경험을 쌓은 사람들이다. 가장 전형적이고 중요한 것은 경력을 쌓기 시작한 초반에 경험하는 큰 도전(문제)일 것이다. 리더들은 사람들을 실제로 리드하고, 모험을 해 보고, 성공과 실패 모두로부터 배울 기회를 거의 항상 20대나 30대에 가져 본 적이 있다. 이와 같은 배움은 광범위한 리더십 기술과 균형 잡힌 시야를 계발하는 데 필수적인 듯하다. 이러한 기회들은 또한 리더십의 어려움과 리더십의 변화 창출 잠재력, 두 가지 모두에 관해 사람들에게 가르침을 준다.

| 보기분석 | ① ~~Competitive~~ Leadership 언급 안 한 정보
경쟁적인 리더십
② Developing Effective Leadership
효과적인 리더십 계발하기
③ ~~Undermining~~ Effective Leadership 언급 안 한 정보
효과적인 리더십 약화시키기
④ ~~Triumphs and Failure~~ in Leadership 언급 안 한 정보
리더십의 성공과 실패

| 정답분석 | 본문은 기업 성공에 조직원의 리더십이 중요하다는 점을 지적하고 조직원들에게 리더십을 갖게 할 수 있는 방법을 소개하고 있는 내용이다. 따라서 제목으로는 ②가 적절하다.

25 2017 건국대(A형)

정답 ③

| 구문분석 | Why don't we run (out of oxygen) (to breathe or water to drink)?
의문사 S V
숨을 쉬기 위한 산소나 마실 물은 왜 고갈되지 않는 것일까?

Many organisms produce oxygen (during a process called photosynthesis), (which constantly replenishes the oxygen consumed by all aerobic organisms).
S V O 관계대명사
많은 유기체들은 광합성이라고 불리는 과정 중에 산소를 발생시킨다. 그것은 모든 호기성 유기체들에 의해 소비되는 산소를 지속적으로 다시 채운다.

The physical materials (on which life depends) are limited (to what is presently on earth).
S 관계대명사 V
생물이 의존하는 물질들은 현재 지구에 존재하는 것으로 한정돼 있다.

Water, for example, is naturally recycled (from the atmosphere to the surface of Earth), (through food webs and back to the atmosphere).
S 접속부사 V
예를 들어, 물은 대기에서 지면으로, 먹이 사슬을 통해 다시 대기로 자연스럽게 순환된다.

Nitrogen, carbon and other essential substances are cycled (in a similar manner).
S V
질소, 탄소 그리고 다른 중요한 물질들도 비슷한 방법으로 순환된다.

A natural resource (that is replaced or recycled by natural processes) is called a renewable resource.
S 관계대명사 V O.C
자연적인 과정에 의해 대체되거나 재순환되는 천연자원은 재생 가능 자원이라고 불린다.

Other examples (of renewable resources) include plants, animals, food crops, sunlight and soil.
S V O
재생 가능 자원의 다른 예들에는 식물, 동물, 식용 작물, 햇빛과 토양이 포함된다.

| 어휘 |

run out of ~을 다 써 버리다, ~이 없어지다
photosynthesis ⓝ 광합성
replenish ⓥ 다시 채우다; 새로 공급하다
aerobic ⓐ 호기성의; 산소의
nitrogen ⓝ 질소
carbon ⓝ 탄소
substance ⓝ 물질

| 전문해석 | 숨을 쉬기 위한 산소나 마실 물은 왜 고갈되지 않는 것일까? 많은 유기체들은 광합성이라고 불리는 과정 중에 산소를 발생시킨다. 그것은 모든 호기성 유기체들에 의해 소비되는 산소를 지속적으로 다시 채운다. 생물이 의존하는 물질들은 현재 지구에 존재하는 것으로 한정돼 있다. 예를 들어, 물은 대기에서 지면으로, 먹이 사슬을 통해 다시 대기로 자연스럽게 순환된다. 질소, 탄소 그리고 다른 중요한 물질들도 비슷한 방법으로 순환된다. 자연적인 과정에 의해 대체되거나 재순환되는 천연자원은 재생 가능 자원이라고 불린다. 재생 가능 자원의 다른 예들에는 식물, 동물, 식용 작물, 햇빛과 토양이 포함된다.

| 보기분석 |

① ~~Limits~~ of Natural Processes 한계와 문제점에 관한 글이 아님
자연 과정의 한계
② ~~Preservation or Consumption~~ 보존, 소비가 아닌 재순환에 관한 글임
보존 혹은 소비
③ Recycling Natural Resources
천연자원의 재순환
④ What if ~~Oxygen~~ is Run Out 키워드 없음
산소가 고갈되면 어떻게 될까
⑤ ~~Substances Essential~~ for Life 키워드 없음
생명에 중요한 물질

| 정답분석 | 산소나 물과 같이 생물이 의존하는 중요한 천연자원들이 고갈되지 않고 지속적으로 공급되는 것을 설명하고 있는 글이므로 ③이 글의 제목으로 적절하다.

26 2016 한국외대(C형) 정답 ②

| 구문분석 | The best reason (banana leaf is perfect for serving food) is (because of its size); you can serve a large variety (of dishes in the leaf, from sweet to savory).

(S: The best reason / (why) / V: is / 세미콜론: 부연설명 / S: you / V: can serve / O: a large variety)

바나나 잎이 음식을 차림에 있어서 완벽한 이유는 잎의 크기 때문이다. 당신은 달콤한 음식에서 짭짤한 음식에 이르기까지 매우 다양한 요리를 바나나 잎에 담아 내놓을 수 있다.

We serve the small leaves (for breakfast and dinner), and the large leaves are reserved (for lunch), (as lunch usually has a huge variety of dishes).

(S_1: We / V_1: serve / O_1: the small leaves / 등위접속사: and / S_2: the large leaves / V_2: are reserved / 부사절: 때문에)

우리는 아침 식사와 저녁 식사는 작은 잎으로 제공한다. 그리고 대개의 경우 점심 식사에는 다양한 요리가 나오기 때문에 점심 식사용으로 큰 잎이 준비된다.

It is very hygienic. Many hotels (in India) provide a banana leaf (on top of the plate) (exactly cut to the plate's size), which I really like (because we just have to sprinkle water and wipe, and the leaves are clean in a few seconds).

(S: Many hotels / V: provide / O: a banana leaf / 관계대명사: which / 부사절: 때문에)

바나나 잎은 아주 위생적이다. 인도에 있는 많은 호텔들은 접시 크기에 맞게 잘라 놓은 바나나 잎을 접시 위에 얹어 놓는다. 내가 바나나 잎을 정말로 좋아하는 이유는, 물을 뿌리고 난 뒤에 닦아 내면, 몇 초가 지나서 잎이 깨끗해지기 때문이다.

It is eco-friendly to dispose of a banana leaf, (whereas plastic plates worsen the environment).

(가주어: It / V: is / C: eco-friendly / 진주어: to dispose of / 부사절: 반면에)

바나나 잎을 버리는 것이 환경친화적인 반면, 플라스틱 그릇은 환경을 악화시킨다.

(In a small way), (if each of us starts using biodegradable natural materials), we will have a much cleaner environment.

(부사절: 만일 ~라면 / S: we / V: will have / O: a much cleaner environment)

작은 방식으로나마, 우리들 각자가 생물 분해성의 천연 재료를 사용한다면, 우리는 더 깨끗한 환경을 만들 수 있을 것이다.

Banana leaves are full (of antioxidants), and eating hot, freshly cooked food on them is one good way (to get all the antioxidants easily).

(S_1: Banana leaves / V: are / C: full / 등위접속사: and / S_2: eating hot, freshly cooked food on them / V: is / C: one good way)

바나나 잎은 항산화제로 가득 차 있어, 갓 요리한 음식을 바나나 잎 위에 놓고 뜨거운 상태로 먹는 것은, 항산화제를 쉽게 섭취할 수 있는 한 가지 좋은 방법이다.

| 어휘 | **serve food** 음식을 내놓다 **sweet** ⓝ 단 음식
savory ⓝ 구미를 돋우는 자극적인 요리 ⓐ 짭짤한 **hygienic** ⓐ 위생적인
plate ⓝ 접시; 요리 **dispose of** ~을 처리하다; ~을 치우다
biodegradable ⓐ 생물 분해성이 있는 **antioxidant** ⓝ 항산화제

| 전문해석 | 바나나 잎이 음식을 차림에 있어서 완벽한 이유는 잎의 크기 때문이다. 당신은 달콤한 음식에서 짭짤한 음식에 이르기까지 매우 다양한 요리를 바나나 잎에 담아 내놓을 수 있다. 우리는 아침 식사와 저녁 식사는 작은 잎으로 제공한다. 그리고 대개의 경우 점심 식사에는 다양한 요리가 나오기 때문에 점심 식사용으로 큰 잎이 준비된다. 바나나 잎은 아주 위생적이다. 인도에 있는 많은 호텔들은 접시 크기에 맞게 잘라 놓은 바나나 잎을 접시 위에 얹어 놓는다. 내가 바나나 잎을 정말로 좋아하는 이유는, 물을 뿌리고 난 뒤에 닦아 내면, 몇 초가 지나서 잎이 깨끗해지기 때문이다. 바나나 잎을 버리는 것이 환경친화적인 반면, 플라스틱 그릇은 환경을 악화시킨다. 작은 방식으로나마, 우리들 각자가 생물 분해성의 천연 재료를 사용한다면, 우리는 더 깨끗한 환경을 만들 수 있을 것이다. 바나나 잎은 항산화제로 가득 차 있어, 갓 요리한 음식을 바나나 잎 위에 놓고 뜨거운 상태로 먹는 것은, 항산화제를 쉽게 섭취할 수 있는 한 가지 좋은 방법이다.

| 보기분석 | ① ~~Cooking~~ with Banana Leaves 음식 제공이라는 말이 없음
바나나 잎으로 요리하기
✔② Banana Leaves for Serving Food
음식 제공을 위한 바나나 잎

③ How to Pack Food with Banana Leaves 음식 제공이라는 말이 없음
어떻게 바나나 잎으로 음식을 포장하는가
④ Ways to Protect Banana Plants 음식 제공이라는 말이 없음
바나나 식물들을 보호하는 방법들

| 정답분석 | 이 글은 상차림을 할 때 사용되는 바나나 잎의 장점에 대해서 기술하고 있으므로 ②가 제목으로 적절하다.

27 2018 상명대(인문 자연계)

정답 ②

| 구문분석 | Rare earth elements(S) are(V) chemical elements(O) (that(관계대명사) are composed of a group of seventeen metallic substances).
희토류 원소는 17개의 금속성 물질로 구성된 화학원소이다.

These elements(S) have been(V) (in high demand) lately (because(부사절: ~ 때문에) they are needed to produce many modem-day electronics).

이 원소들은 최근 들어 수요가 늘어났는데, 이는 현대의 많은 전자제품을 생산하는 데 이 원소들이 필요하기 때문이다.

This(S) has unsurprisingly allowed(V) China(O), (where(관계부사) 95 percent of the world's supply exists), to control the export market(O.C).

이로 인해 세계 공급량의 95%가 있는 중국이 수출시장을 지배할 수 있게 된 것은 놀라운 일이 아니었다.

Recently, there(유도부사) have been(V) concerns(S) (regarding the limited amount and expense of these elements), (making(분사구문) it(가목적어) necessary(O.C) to look(진목적어) for new sources in other countries).
최근 들어 희토류 원소의 한정된 양과 비용에 대해 우려하는 목소리가 있어 왔고, 이로 인해 다른 국가에서 새로운 공급원을 찾아야만 하게 되었다.

(Until(부사절: ~까지) other deposits or equivalent substitutes can be found), electronics manufacturers(S) will have to continue(V) using rare earth metals(O) (in small amounts).
또 다른 매장지나 이와 동등한 대체물이 발견될 수 있을 때까지, 전자제품 제조업체들은 적은 양의 희토류 원소를 계속 사용하는 수밖에 없을 것이다.

| 어휘 |

rare earth element 희토류 원소	**chemical** ⓐ 화학의, 화학적인	**be composed of** ~로 구성되어 있다
electronics ⓝ 전자제품	**supply** ⓝ 공급, 공급량	**limited** ⓐ 한정된, 유한의
expense ⓝ 지출, 비용	**deposit** ⓝ 침전물; (광석 · 석유 · 천연가스 등의) 매장물	
equivalent ⓐ 동등한, 같은, 대등한	**substitute** ⓝ 대체물, 대체품	**manufacturer** ⓝ 제조업자, 생산자

| 전문해석 | 희토류 원소는 17개의 금속성 물질로 구성된 화학원소이다. 이 원소들은 최근 들어 수요가 늘어났는데, 이는 현대의 많은 전자제품을 생산하는 데 이 원소들이 필요하기 때문이다. 이로 인해 세계 공급량의 95%가 있는 중국이 수출시장을 지배할 수 있게 된 것은 놀라운 일이 아니었다. 최근 들어 희토류 원소의 한정된 양과 비용에 대해 우려하는 목소리가 있어 왔고, 이로 인해 다른 국가에서 새로운 공급원을 찾아야만 하게 되었다. 또 다른 매장지나 이와 동등한 대체물이 발견될 수 있을 때까지, 전자제품 제조업체들은 적은 양의 희토류 원소를 계속 사용하는 수밖에 없을 것이다.

| 보기분석 | ① The Response to China's Monopoly on Rare Earth Metals 언급 안 한 정보
중국의 희토류 금속 독점에 대한 반응
② The Growing Demand and Restricted Supply of Rare Earth Elements
희토류 원소의 늘어나는 수요와 한정된 공급
③ Alternatives to Rare Earth Elements in Electronics Devices 언급 안 한 정보
전자기기에서의 희토류 원소에 대한 대안
④ The Necessity of Finding Rare Earth Elements 너무 지엽적
희토류 원소를 찾아야 할 필요성
⑤ The Influence of Rare Earth Elements on the Technological Market 너무 지엽적
희토류 원소가 과학기술 시장에 미치는 영향

| 정답분석 | 희토류 원소는 전자제품의 생산에 필요하기 때문에 최근 들어 그 수요가 증가했고, 이 원소의 한정된 양과 비용에 대한 우

려로 인해 최대 공급국가인 중국이 아닌 다른 나라에서 희토류 혹은 이것을 대체할 자원을 구해야 하는 상황이 되었다는 내용이다. 따라서 글의 제목으로는 ② '희토류 원소의 늘어나는 수요와 한정된 공급'이 적절하다.

28 2018 광운대(인문계A형)

정답 ①

| 구문분석 | The word jazz is related to jasm, a slang (dating back to 1860 meaning "energy" in the U.S.)
S V =

'jazz(재즈)'라는 단어는 '재즘(jasm)'과 관련이 있는데, 재즘은 1860년부터 사용된 속어로 미국에서 '에너지'를 의미한다.

(In a 1912 article in the LA Times), a baseball pitcher described a pitch (which he called a jazz ball ("because it wobbles and you simply can't do anything with it.")
S V O 관계대명사 부사절: ~ 때문에

1912년 LA 타임즈에 실린 기사에서 어떤 투수는 "흔들리면서 들어오기 때문에 전혀 손쓸 수 없다"는 이유로 자신이 재즈 볼이라고 부른 투구를 설명했다.

Its first documented use (in a musical context) was (in a Times-Picayune article in 1916 about "jas bands.")
S V

음악적 맥락에서 재즈라는 단어가 처음 사용된 기록은 1916년에 Times-Picayune에 실린 "재스(jas) 밴드"에 관한 기사에서였다.

The musician Eubie Blake talked (about his recollections of the original slang connotations of the term),
S V

("When Broadway picked it up), they called it 'JAZZ.'
부사절: ~ 때 S V O O.C

유비 블레이크(Eubie Blake)라는 뮤지션은 재즈라는 용어가 속어로 처음 사용되었을 때의 함축적 의미를 회상하면서 다음과 같이 이야기했다. "브로드웨이에서 이 단어를 쓰기 시작했을 때 그들은 그것을 '재즈(JAZZ)'라고 불렀다.

등위접속사
But it was spelled 'J-A-S-S.' That was dirty. (If you knew what it was), you wouldn't say it (in front of ladies)."
S V O.C S V C 부사절: 만일 ~라면 S V O

그러나 철자는 'J-A-S-S'로 썼다. 그것은 추잡한 말이었다. 만약 그게 무슨 의미인지 안다면(싸구려 창녀와 한번 즐기는 것), 숙녀 앞에서는 그것을 말하지 못할 것이다."

| 어휘 |
relate ⓥ 관계시키다, 관련시키다 **slang** ⓝ 속어, 은어 **date back to** ~로 거슬러 올라가다
article ⓝ 기사, 논설; 조항 **wobble** ⓥ 흔들리다, 동요하다, 떨리다
document ⓥ (상세한 내용을) 기록하다; 서류로 입증하다[뒷받침하다]
context ⓝ (글의) 전후 관계, 문맥; 배경; 상황 **connotation** ⓝ 함축, 함축된 의미

| 전문해석 | 'jazz(재즈)'라는 단어는 '재즘(jasm)'과 관련이 있는데, 재즘은 1860년부터 사용된 속어로 미국에서 '에너지'를 의미한다. 1912년 LA 타임즈에 실린 기사에서 어떤 투수는 "흔들리면서 들어오기 때문에 전혀 손쓸 수 없다"는 이유로 자신이 재즈 볼이라고 부른 투구를 설명했다. 음악적 맥락에서 재즈라는 단어가 처음 사용된 기록은 1916년에 Times-Picayune에 실린 "재스(jas) 밴드"에 관한 기사에서였다. 유비 블레이크(Eubie Blake)라는 뮤지션은 재즈라는 용어가 속어로 처음 사용되었을 때의 함축적 의미를 회상하면서 다음과 같이 이야기했다. "브로드웨이에서 이 단어를 쓰기 시작했을 때 그들은 그것을 '재즈(JAZZ)'라고 불렀다. 그러나 철자는 'J-A-S-S'로 썼다. 그것은 추잡한 말이었다. 만약 그게 무슨 의미인지 안다면(싸구려 창녀와 한번 즐기는 것), 숙녀 앞에서는 그것을 말하지 못할 것이다."

| 보기분석 |
① The Origin of the Word *Jazz*
'jazz(재즈)'라는 단어의 기원
② The History of Jazz in the U.S. 키워드가 다름
미국에서의 재즈의 역사
③ The Accord between Baseball and Jazz 너무 지엽적
야구와 재즈 사이의 조화
④ The Slang Connotations of Jazz 너무 지엽적
재즈가 가진 속어로서의 함축적 의미
⑤ The Dislike for Jazz by Ladies 언급 안 한 정보
재즈에 대한 숙녀들의 혐오감

| 정답분석 | 본문은 jazz라는 단어가 언제부터 사용되었고 어떤 과정을 통해 현재의 용례로 자리 잡게 되었는가를 설명하고 있는 내용이므로 제목으로는 ①이 적절하다.

29 2018 가톨릭대(인문계A형)

정답 ②

| 구문분석 | The ministry (of education) has decided to ban extra-curricular English classes for first and second graders in elementary school, and that is brewing major controversy.

S / V / O / 등위접속사

교육부는 초등학교 1학년과 2학년 아이들의 방과 후 영어 수업을 금지하기로 했는데, 그것이 큰 논란을 불러일으키고 있다.

The ban is intended (to prevent kids from studying English before third grade in elementary school), (when English starts becoming part of the curriculum).

S / V / 부사적용법: ~하기 위하여 / 부사절: ~ 때

교육부의 금지안은 영어가 교과 과정에 포함되기 시작하는 초등학교 3학년 이전에는 아이들이 영어를 공부하지 못하도록 하기 위한 것이다.

접속부사

However, (despite the government's intention to curb the practice of studying ahead of the curriculum), voices are growing [that the ban will make parents put their children into private English education instead].

S = / V

그러나 선행학습의 관행을 억제하겠다는 정부의 의도에도 불구하고, 교육부의 금지안은 그 대신 학부모들로 하여금 자녀를 영어 사교육으로 내몰게 할 것이라는 목소리가 커지고 있다.

| 어휘 |

ministry of education 교육부 **ban** ⓥ 금지하다 ⓝ 금지, 금지령

extra-curricular ⓐ 정규교과 외의, 과외의 **brew** ⓥ 양조하다; 꾸미다, 일으키다

controversy ⓝ 논쟁, 논의 **prevent** ⓥ 막다, 방해하다; 예방하다 **curriculum** ⓝ 커리큘럼

intention ⓝ 의도, 의향, 목적 **curb** ⓥ 억제하다, 구속하다

| 전문해석 | 교육부는 초등학교 1학년과 2학년 아이들의 방과 후 영어 수업을 금지하기로 했는데, 그것이 큰 논란을 불러일으키고 있다. 교육부의 금지안은 영어가 교과 과정에 포함되기 시작하는 초등학교 3학년 이전에는 아이들이 영어를 공부하지 못하도록 하기 위한 것이다. 그러나 선행학습의 관행을 억제하겠다는 정부의 의도에도 불구하고, 교육부의 금지안은 그 대신 학부모들로 하여금 자녀를 영어 사교육으로 내몰게 할 것이라는 목소리가 커지고 있다.

| 보기분석 |

① Banning Preschoolers from Studying English ~~Confuses Teachers~~ 언급 안 한 정보
취학 전의 아동들에게 영어 공부를 금지시키는 것이 선생님들에게 혼란을 준다

② Ban on English Classes for First and Second Graders Stirs Dispute
1, 2학년에 대한 영어 수업 금지가 논쟁을 일으킨다

③ Extra-curricular ~~English Classes~~ Are Not Welcomed among Parents 소재가 다름
방과 후 영어 수업은 부모들 사이에서 환영받지 못한다

④ The ~~Necessity~~ of Private English Education for Preschoolers Is Not Evident 언급 안 한 정보
미취학 아동을 위한 영어 사교육의 필요성은 불명확하다

| 정답분석 | 본문은 교육부가 초등학교 1학년과 2학년 아이들에 대한 방과 후 영어 수업을 금지하기로 한 결정과 그 배경, 그리고 그 결정에 대한 학부모들의 우려에 대한 내용이므로, 제목으로는 ②가 적절하다.

30 2016 인하대

정답 ①

| 구문분석 | The fact [that our communication abilities and behaviors are based partially on biology] is obvious.

S = / V / C

우리가 가지고 있는 의사소통 능력과 행동이 부분적으로나마 생물학에 기초하고 있다는 사실은 확실하다.

Less obvious may be the fact [that communication is *behavior*] — precisely (because it is biologically based).

C / V / S = / 대시: 부연설명 / 부사절: ~ 때문에

의사소통이 곧 '행동'이라는 사실은 덜 명확할 수도 있으며, 그 이유는 정확히 말해서 의사소통이라는 것이 생물학에 기반하고 있기 때문이다.

One (of our daughters) was asked (in grade school) what her father did at work.
S V D.O
나의 딸들 가운데 하나가 초등학교에서 자신의 아버지의 직업에 대한 질문을 받았다.

She responded that "... her father doesn't do anything. He just sits around and talks."
S V O S V_1 V_2
그 애는 "아버지는 아무 일도 안 해요. 아버지는 그냥 앉아서 이야기만 해요."라고 대답했다.

Indeed, some people fail to recognize that talking is behaving, or performing some form of action.
접속부사 S V O 등위접속사
실제로 어떤 사람들은 대화를 나누는 것을 행동하는 것 혹은 어떤 종류의 행동을 행하고 있는 것으로 인식하지 못한다.

Communication is one (of the most basic actions of all human behaviors).
S V C
의사소통은 인간이 행하는 모든 행동들 가운데서 가장 기본적인 행동들 중 하나이다.

(When people talk), they are doing something (that is essential to their mental and physical well-being).
부사절: ~ 때 S V O 관계대명사
대화를 나눌 때, 사람들은 그들의 정신적, 신체적 행복을 위해 무엇인가 중요한 일을 하고 있는 것이다.

| 어휘 | **communication** ⓝ 의사소통 **partially** ⓐⓓ 부분적으로 **grade school** 초등학교
well-being ⓝ 행복 **uniquely** ⓐⓓ 독특하게, 유일하게

| 전문해석 | 우리가 가지고 있는 의사소통 능력과 행동이 부분적으로나마 생물학에 기초하고 있다는 사실은 확실하다. 의사소통이 곧 '행동'이라는 사실은 덜 명확할 수도 있으며, 그 이유는 정확히 말해서 의사소통이라는 것이 생물학에 기반하고 있기 때문이다. 나의 딸들 가운데 하나가 초등학교에서 자신의 아버지의 직업에 대한 질문을 받았다. 그 애는 "… 아버지는 아무 일도 안 해요. 아버지는 그냥 앉아서 이야기만 해요."라고 대답했다. 실제로 어떤 사람들은 대화를 나누는 것을 행동하는 것 혹은 어떤 종류의 행동을 행하고 있는 것으로 인식하지 못한다. 의사소통은 인간이 행하는 모든 행동들 가운데서 가장 기본적인 행동들 중 하나이다. 대화를 나눌 때, 사람들은 그들의 정신적, 신체적 행복을 위해 무엇인가 중요한 일을 하고 있는 것이다.

| 보기분석 | ① Communication as Action
행동으로서의 의사소통
② ~~Talking~~: Human Trait to Be Ignored 키워드 없음
대화: 무시되고 있는 인간의 속성
③ ~~Communicative Abilities~~ Learned from Society 언급 안 한 정보
사회로부터 습득된 담화 능력
④ Communicative Behavior Determined ~~by Environment~~ 언급 안 한 정보
환경에 의해 결정된 담화적 행동
⑤ Humans Uniquely Different ~~from Animals~~ in Communication 언급 안 한 정보
의사소통에서 동물과는 특별히 다른 인간

| 정답분석 | 이 글을 통해서 글쓴이가 주장하고자 하는 것은 대화하기, 즉 의사소통도 행동이라는 것이므로 제목으로는 ①이 적절하다.

2강 주제 / 요지

Practice

01	②	02	④	03	④	04	④	05	⑤	06	④	07	②	08	②	09	④	10	④
11	②	12	①	13	②	14	①	15	⑤	16	⑤	17	⑤	18	④	19	②	20	③

01 2015 가톨릭대 정답 ②

| 구문분석 | Your doctor usually checks (to see if you have healthy blood pressure in one arm), but a recent study (from our research team) suggests that taking readings in both arms may help better identify patients at higher risk of heart disease.

(Your doctor: S / checks: V / to see: 부사적용법: ~하기 위하여 / but: 등위접속사 / a recent study: S / suggests: V / that taking ... disease: O)

의사는 당신의 혈압이 건강한지를 체크해 보기 위해서 대개 당신의 한 팔을 사용한다. 그러나 우리 연구팀이 행한 최근의 연구는 양쪽 팔의 혈압을 모두 측정하는 것이 심장병에 걸릴 확률이 높은 환자를 찾아내는 데 더 좋을지도 모른다는 점을 보여 주고 있다.

(When researchers analyzed data on nearly 3,400 patients over 13 years), they found that about 10 percent of participants showed higher systolic readings (the upper number) in one arm.

(When ~: 부사절: ~일 때 / they: S / found: V / that about ... arm: O)

13년 동안 거의 3400명에 달하는 환자들에 대한 데이터를 분석하는 것을 통해서 연구자들은 참여자들 가운데 10% 정도가 한쪽 팔에서 더 높은 심장 수축 수치를 보여 준다는 것을 발견했다.

Those (with arm-to-arm discrepancies of ten points or more) were 38 percent more likely to have a heart attack, stroke, or other coronary event.

(Those: S / were: V / 38 percent more likely: C / be likely toR: ~할 것 같다, ~할 가능성이 있다)

양쪽 팔에서 심장의 수축 수치가 10% 이상 차이가 나는 사람들은 심장마비, 뇌졸중 또는 그 외의 관상동맥 질환을 앓을 가능성이 38%나 더 높았다.

Such imbalances may indicate plaque (in major arteries).

(Such imbalances: S / may indicate: V / plaque: O)

이러한 불균형은 대동맥 안에 플라크가 있다는 것을 보여 주는 것인지도 모른다.

| 어휘 | **blood pressure** 혈압 **identify** ⓥ 식별하다, 동일시하다 **systolic** ⓐ 심장 수축의 **discrepancy** ⓝ 모순, 차이, 불일치 **coronary** ⓐ 관상의, 관상동맥의, 심장의

| 전문해석 | 의사는 당신의 혈압이 건강한지를 체크해 보기 위해서 대개 당신의 한 팔을 사용한다. 그러나 우리 연구팀이 행한 최근의 연구는 양쪽 팔의 혈압을 모두 측정하는 것이 심장병에 걸릴 확률이 높은 환자를 찾아내는 데 더 좋을지도 모른다는 점을 보여 주고 있다. 13년 동안 거의 3400명에 달하는 환자들에 대한 데이터를 분석하는 것을 통해서 연구자들은 참여자들 가운데 10% 정도가 한쪽 팔에서 더 높은 심장 수축 수치를 보여 준다는 것을 발견했다. 양쪽 팔에서 심장의 수축 수치가 10% 이상 차이가 나는 사람들은 심장마비, 뇌졸중 또는 그 외의 관상동맥 질환을 앓을 가능성이 38%나 더 높았다. 이러한 불균형은 대동맥 안에 플라크가 있다는 것을 보여 주는 것인지도 모른다.

| 보기분석 |
① Patients with high risk of heart disease seldom show uneven systolic readings for both arms. 지문 내용과 불일치
심장병 위험이 높은 환자들은 양팔의 불균형한 심장 수축 수치를 보여 주지 않는다.
② To find potential heart disease patients, we had better take readings in both arms.
잠재적인 심장병 환자를 찾기 위해서는 두 팔의 혈압을 모두 측정하는 것이 좋다.
③ Heart attacks or other coronary events may result from measuring blood pressure too often. 언급 안 한 정보
혈압을 너무 자주 측정하면 심장 발작이나 다른 심근 경색 같은 심장 질환을 일으킬 수 있다.
④ Arm-to-arm discrepancies of blood pressure could be signs of inefficient metabolism. 언급 안 한 정보
팔 간의 혈압 차이는 비효율적인 대사의 징후일 수 있다.

| 정답분석 | 양쪽 팔의 심장 수축 수치가 차이가 나므로 혈압을 잴 때 양쪽 팔을 모두 재야 한다는 것이 이 글의 주된 내용이므로 이 글의 요지는 ②가 적절하다.

02 2015 건국대

정답 ④

| 구문분석 | It is unlikely that many of us will be famous, or even remembered.

(가주어 / V / C / 진주어 that)

우리 가운데 많은 사람들이 유명해지거나 심지어 기억될 가능성은 그리 높지 않다.

A is no less B than C (is D): A가 B인 것은 C가 D인 것과 같다

But no less important than the brilliant few that lead a nation or a literature to fresh achievements, are the unknown many (whose patient efforts keep the world from running backward); (who guard and maintain the ancient values, even if they do not conquer new); (whose inconspicuous triumph it is to pass on what they inherited from their fathers, unimpaired and undiminished, to their sons).

(C / V / S / 관계대명사 1 / 세미콜론: and 역할 / 관계대명사 2 / 관계대명사 3)

그러나 국가나 문학계를 이끌어서 새로운 성과를 내는 뛰어난 소수 못지않게 중요한 것은 알려지지 않은 수많은 사람들인데, 그들은 끈기 있는 노력을 통해서 세계가 퇴보하는 것을 막아 냈고, 비록 새로운 가치를 만들어 내지는 못했지만 오래된 가치를 수호하고 보전했으며, 누구의 눈에도 쉽게 띄지 않는 그들이 거둔 승리는 자신들의 아버지로부터 물려받은 것들을 손상 없이 그리고 약화시키지 않고 그들의 후손에게 그대로 물려주는 것이다.

(It is) 가주어 Enough, (for almost all of us), (if we can hand on the torch and not let it down); (It is) 가주어 content to win the affection, (if possible), (of a few who know us), and to be forgotten (when they in their turn have vanished).

(부사절: 만약 ~라면 / 진주어 1 / 등위접속사 / 진주어 2 / 부사절: ~ 때)

우리 가운데 대다수는 만일 우리가 횃불을 내려놓지 않고 그 횃불을 후대에 전해 줄 수 있다면 그것으로 만족한다. 또 우리 가운데 대다수는 우리를 알고 있는 얼마 되지 않는 사람들의 호감을 얻어 내고(만일 그것이 가능하다면) 마침내 차례가 돼서 사라져 가고 잊히는 것에 대해서도 만족한다.

| 어휘 | **run backward** 퇴보하다 / **inconspicuous** ⓐ 눈에 띄지 않는, 주의를 끌지 않는, 뚜렷하지 않은

triumph ⓝ 승리 / **unimpaired** ⓐ 손상되지 않은, 해를 입지 않은, 완전한

undiminished ⓐ 줄어들지 않은, 약화되지 않은

hand on the torch 전통의 횃불을 후세에 전하다 / **vanish** ⓥ 사라지다, 없어지다

| 전문해석 | 우리 가운데 많은 사람들이 유명해지거나 심지어 기억될 가능성은 그리 높지 않다. 그러나 국가나 문학계를 이끌어서 새로운 성과를 내는 뛰어난 소수 못지않게 중요한 것은 알려지지 않은 수많은 사람들인데, 그들은 끈기 있는 노력을 통해서 세계가 퇴보하는 것을 막아 냈고, 비록 새로운 가치를 만들어 내지는 못했지만 오래된 가치를 수호하고 보전했으며, 누구의 눈에도 쉽게 띄지 않는 그들이 거둔 승리는 자신들의 아버지로부터 물려받은 것들을 손상 없이 그리고 약화시키지 않고 그들의 후손에게 그대로 물려주는 것이다.

우리 가운데 대다수는 만일 우리가 횃불을 내려놓지 않고 그 횃불을 후대에 전해 줄 수 있다면 그것으로 만족한다. 또 우리 가운데 대다수는 우리를 알고 있는 얼마 되지 않는 사람들의 호감을 얻고(만일 그것이 가능하다면) 마침내 차례가 돼서 사라져 가고 잊히는 것에 대해서도 만족한다.

| 보기분석 | ① We must learn from the experiences of ~~other people~~. 과거와 선조들로부터 물려받는다는 글이다.
우리는 다른 사람들의 경험에서 배워야 한다.

② It is a few great men of genius that create civilization. 지문 내용과 불일치
문명을 만드는 것은 몇몇 위대한 천재들이다.

③ What the future world will be like is impossible to foresee. 언급 안 한 정보
미래 세상이 어떻게 될지 예측하는 것은 불가능하다.

④ Great men alone cannot keep up a high level of civilization.
위대한 인물들만으로는 높은 수준의 문명을 유지할 수 없다.

⑤ One who wins the affection easily tends to be forgotten in that way. 언급 안 한 정보
쉽게 호감을 얻은 사람은 그런 방식으로 잊히기 쉽다.

| 정답분석 | 이 글은 인류문명을 창조함에 있어서 이름 없는 평범한 사람들이 가지고 있는 역할의 중요성에 대해서 진술하고 있으므로 이 글의 요지는 ④가 적절하다.

03 2017 건국대(A형)

정답 ④

| 구문분석 |

spend 시간 (in) ~ing: ~하는 데 시간을 들이다

(When your paper is returned to you), spend time examining the comments (your teacher made).
부사절: ~ 때 / 명령문 / 동명사 / (that)
과제를 다시 돌려받으면, 선생님이 적어 주신 코멘트를 검토하는 데 시간을 들이도록 하라.

This is a good time (to compare your classmates' responses to your teacher's), (taking into account the changes you made between the original draft and the revised paper).
S V O / 분사구문
지금이 당신이 초고와 수정된 원고 사이에 변경한 점들을 고려하면서 당신의 선생님이 해 주신 코멘트와 급우들의 반응을 비교해 보기에 좋은 때이다.

Did you improve (on the parts of your original paper) (that your classmates encouraged you to work on)?
S V / 관계대명사
Did your teacher comment (on aspects of your paper) (that your classmates did not comment on)?
S V / 관계대명사
당신의 초고 중에서 급우들이 당신에게 수정하도록 권한 부분을 바로잡아 고쳤는가? 당신의 과제 중에 급우들이 코멘트하지 않은 측면들에 대해 선생님이 코멘트를 해 주셨는가?

Share this information (with the classmates) (you did peer-editing with).
S O / (whom)
동료 간 상호 수정 작업을 함께 했던 급우들과 이런 정보를 공유해 보라.

compare A to B: A와 B를 비교하다, A를 B에 비유하다

(For each paper you looked at), compare the comments (you made) to the teacher's comments.
V O
당신이 살펴본 각각의 과제마다 당신이 해 주었던 코멘트를 선생님의 코멘트와 비교해 보도록 하라.

Keep (in mind) the ideas (you and your teacher had in common about each paper).
V O (that)
각각의 과제에 대해 당신과 선생님이 가지고 있던 공통된 생각에 유념하라.

(Also) notice comments (that your teacher made) (that you missed). This is valuable information.
V O / 관계대명사
또한 선생님은 해 주셨지만 당신은 놓친 코멘트에 주의하라. 이것은 귀중한 정보이다.

You'll use it the next time (you write) and the next time (you do peer-editing).
S V O / 관계부사 when 생략 / 관계부사 when 생략
다음에 글을 쓰고 동료 간 상호 수정 작업을 할 때 당신은 이 정보를 사용할 것이다.

| 어휘 |

take into account ~을 고려하다[참작하다]
draft ⓝ 초안, 초고
revised ⓐ 개정된, 수정된
peer ⓝ 동등한 사람, 동료
peer-editing ⓝ 동료 간 상호 수정(친구끼리 서로 바꿔 교정하기)
keep in mind 마음에 담아 두다, 명심하다
work on (해결 · 개선하기 위해) ~에 애쓰다[공들이다]

| 전문해석 |

과제를 다시 돌려받으면, 선생님이 적어 주신 코멘트를 검토하는 데 시간을 들이도록 하라. 지금이 당신이 초고와 수정된 원고 사이에 변경한 점들을 고려하면서 당신의 선생님이 해 주신 코멘트와 급우들의 반응을 비교해 보기에 좋은 때이다. 당신의 초고 중에서 급우들이 당신에게 수정하도록 권한 부분을 바로잡아 고쳤는가? 당신의 과제 중에 급우들이 코멘트하지 않은 측면들에 대해 선생님이 코멘트를 해 주셨는가? 동료 간 상호 수정 작업을 함께 했던 급우들과 이런 정보를 공유해 보라. 당신이 살펴본 각각의 과제마다 당신이 해 주었던 코멘트를 선생님의 코멘트와 비교해 보도록 하라. 각각의 과제에 대해 당신과 선생님이 가지고 있던 공통된 생각에 유념하라. 또한 선생님은 해 주셨지만 당신은 놓친 코멘트에 주의하라. 이것은 귀중한 정보이다. 다음에 글을 쓰고 동료 간 상호 수정 작업을 할 때 당신은 이 정보를 사용할 것이다.

| 보기분석 |

① Advantages and disadvantages of peer feedback 선생님 부분을 담을 수 없으므로 너무 지엽적
동료 피드백의 장단점
② Several tips for efficient drafting and proofreading 초안 작성을 다루는 글이 아님
효율적인 초안 작성과 교정을 위한 몇 가지 비결
③ Importance of sharing ideas in peer-editing projects 선생님 부분을 담을 수 없으므로 너무 지엽적
동료 간 상호 수정 프로젝트에서 의견을 공유하는 것의 중요성
④ Using wisely teacher's and peer's feedback in writing
글쓰기에서 선생님과 동료의 피드백을 현명하게 사용하는 것

⑤ Why we should consider others' feeling in peer-editing 감정과 관련하여 지문에 언급한 적이 없다.
동료 간 상호 수정에서 다른 사람들의 기분을 고려해야 하는 이유

| 정답분석 | '제출한 과제를 돌려받을 때 선생님이 해 주신 코멘트와 급우들의 반응을 비교해 볼 것, 급우가 교정한 것을 활용하고 선생님이 코멘트해 주신 내용을 놓치지 말고 잘 살필 것, 선생님은 해 주셨지만 당신은 놓친 코멘트에 주의할 것, 이 귀중한 정보를 당신이 다음에 글을 쓰고 동료 간 상호 수정을 할 때 사용할 것' 등을 이야기하고 있으므로, ④가 이 글의 주제로 가장 적절하다.

04 2016 국민대

정답 ④

| 구문분석 | Attitudes (to climate change) seems to have been sharply polarized (along political line at least in America).
S / V / C
적어도 미국에서는 기후 변화에 대한 태도가 정치적 노선을 따라 가파르게 다원화되어 왔던 것처럼 보인다.

A large-scale survey in 2013 shows that 70% of Democratic voters saw evidence of man-made climate change in recent weather patterns, (whereas only 19% of Republican voters did).
S / V / O
부사절: 반면에
2013년에 행해진 대규모의 여론조사는 민주당을 지지하는 유권자들의 70%가 최근의 기후 패턴에서 인간이 야기한 기후 변화의 증거를 보았던 반면, 공화당을 지지하는 유권자 가운데는 단지 19%만이 인간이 야기한 기후 변화의 증거를 인정했다.

It is not that conservatives are ignorant.
it is not that: ~ 때문이 아니다
이것은 보수주의자들이 무지하기 때문이 아니다.

Knowledge (of science) makes little difference (to people's beliefs about climate change), (except that it makes them more certain about what they believe).
S / V / O
~을 제외하고
과학적인 지식은, 과학적인 지식이 사람들로 하여금 그들이 믿고 있는 바를 더 확실하게 해 주는 것을 제외하고는, 기후 변화에 대해서 사람들이 가지고 있는 (기존의 고정된) 믿음을 달리 변화시키지 못하고 있다.

Republicans (with a good knowledge of science) are more skeptical (about global warming) than less knowledgeable Republicans.
S / V / C
비교급 than
상당히 많은 과학적 지식을 가지고 있는 공화당원들은 과학적 지식을 덜 가지고 있는 공화당원들에 비해 지구 온난화에 대해서 더 회의적이었다.

The best explanation (for the gap) is that people's beliefs about climate change have become determined (by feelings of identification with political groups).
S / V / C
이러한 차이에 대한 가장 좋은 설명은 기후 변화에 대한 사람들의 믿음이 정치집단으로서의 정체성에 의해서 결정되어 왔다는 것이다.

(When people are asked for their views on climate change), they seem to translate this (into a broader question): whose side are you on?
translate A into B: A를 B로 번역하다
부사절
S / V / C
콜론: 세부적으로 재진술
기후 변화에 대한 그들의 의견을 말해 달라고 요청받았을 때, 그들은 이 질문을 '이 질문을 던지는 당신은 누구 편인가.'라는 보다 더 범위가 큰 질문으로 번역하는 것처럼 보인다.

The issue has become associated (with Democrats), (causing conservatives to dig in against it). The divide may not be resolved (within a few years).
S / V / C
분사구문
S / V
기후 변화 이슈는 그동안 주로 민주당 지지자들과 관련을 맺어 왔는데, 바로 이런 이유 때문에 공화당 지지자들은 이에 반대했다. 이러한 분리는 수년 안에 해결될 것 같지 않다.

| 어휘 | **polarize** ⓥ 분열되다, 다양하게 되다 **conservative** ⓝ 보수주의자 **skeptical** ⓐ 회의적인
identification ⓝ 신분 증명, 정체성

| 전문해석 | 적어도 미국에서는 기후 변화에 대한 태도가 정치적 노선을 따라 가파르게 다원화되어 왔던 것처럼 보인다. 2013년에 행해

진 대규모의 여론조사는 민주당을 지지하는 유권자들의 70%가 최근의 기후 패턴에서 인간이 야기한 기후 변화의 증거를 보았던 반면, 공화당을 지지하는 유권자 가운데는 단지 19%만이 인간이 야기한 기후 변화의 증거를 인정했다. 이것은 보수주의자들이 무지하기 때문이 아니다. (사실) 과학적인 지식은, 과학적인 지식이 사람들로 하여금 그들이 믿고 있는 바를 더 확실하게 해 주는 것을 제외하고는, 기후 변화에 대해서 사람들이 가지고 있는 (기존의 고정된) 믿음을 별달리 변화시키지 못하고 있다. 상당히 많은 과학적 지식을 가지고 있는 공화당원들은 과학적 지식을 덜 가지고 있는 공화당원들에 비해 지구 온난화에 대해서 더 회의적이었다.

이러한 차이에 대한 가장 좋은 설명은 기후 변화에 대한 사람들의 믿음이 정치집단으로서의 정체성에 의해서 결정되어 왔다는 것이다. 기후 변화에 대한 그들의 의견을 말해 달라고 요청받았을 때, 그들은 이 질문을 '이 질문을 던지는 당신은 누구 편인가.'라는 보다 더 범위가 큰 질문으로 번역하는 것처럼 보인다. 기후 변화 이슈는 그동안 주로 민주당 지지자들과 관련을 맺어 왔는데, 바로 이런 이유 때문에 공화당 지지자들은 이에 반대했다. 이러한 분리는 수년 안에 해결될 것 같지 않다.

| 보기분석 | ① Political conservatives are generally more optimistic. 지문의 주된 내용이 아님
보수주의자들은 일반적으로 낙관적이다.
② The progress of global warming is still under debate. 기후 변화와 관련된 공화당과 민주당의 의견 차이가 논쟁의 여지가 있다는 글이다.
지구 온난화의 진행 상황은 아직 논란의 여지가 있다.
③ Scientific knowledge has nothing to do with people's beliefs. 지문 내용과 불일치
과학적 지식은 사람들의 신념과는 무관하다.
④ People's views on climate change depend more on political orientation than on facts.
기후 변화에 대한 사람들의 견해는 사실보다는 정치적 성향에 더 영향을 받는다.

| 정답분석 | 이 글은 기후 변화에 대한 사람들의 태도가 과학적 지식이 아니라 정치적 정체성에 영향을 받고 있다는 사실을 기술하고 있으므로 글의 요지로는 ④가 적절하다.

05 2018 상명대(인문 자연계)

정답 ⑤

| 구문분석 | In 1328, the Black Death (S) took hold (V_1) (of Europe) and (등위접속사) did not let go (V_2) (for the next twenty years).

1328년에 흑사병이 유럽을 장악해서 이후 20년 동안 놓아주지 않았다.

(As hundreds of millions succumbed to it and the medical community had no effective treatment) (부사절: 때문에), people (S) began (V) experimenting (O) (with odd techniques in a desperate attempt to stave off the pandemic).

수억 명의 사람들이 흑사병으로 목숨을 잃었고 의학계는 효과적인 치료법을 전혀 갖고 있지 않았기 때문에, 사람들은 그 전 세계적 유행병을 피하기 위한 절박한 시도로 기묘한 방법들을 시험해 보기 시작했다.

Some (S) believed (V) that pleasant odors could block the sickness (O), so (등위접속사) they (S) carried around (V) sweet-smelling flowers or herbs (O).

어떤 사람들은 좋은 냄새가 그 병을 막을 수 있다고 믿어서 달콤한 냄새가 나는 꽃이나 허브를 들고 다녔다.

But (등위접속사) the only effect (S) (this had) was (V) to make a person smell nice (C) (for a time).

그러나 이것이 가져다준 유일한 효과는 잠시 동안 사람에게서 좋은 냄새가 나게 하는 것뿐이었다.

A less enjoyable practice (S) (that (관계대명사) a few opted for) was (V) to live (C) (in a sewer) (because (부사절) it was thought that the air underground had not been contaminated by the disease).

소수의 사람들이 선택했던 보다 덜 유쾌한 방법은 하수도에서 사는 것이었는데, 지하의 공기가 그 질병에 오염되지 않았다고 생각했기 때문이었다.

Naturally, it (S) did (V) nothing (O) (for the poor people) (who (관계대명사) decided to go under); (세미콜론: and 역할) in fact, it (S) only caused (V) them (O) to come down with more diseases (O.C) (due to (전치사: ~ 때문에) the unsanitary conditions).

물론 이것은 지하로 가서 살기로 결정한 가련한 사람들에게 아무런 도움도 되지 못했다. 사실 이것은 비위생적인 환경으로 인해 그들로 하여금 더 많은 질병에 걸리도록 했을 뿐이었다.

| 어휘 | Black Death 흑사병 / take hold of ~을 장악하다, ~을 사로잡다
succumb ⓥ 굴복하다; 쓰러지다, 죽다 / effective ⓐ 효과적인 / treatment ⓝ 치료, 치료법
experiment ⓥ 실험하다, 시험하다 / odd ⓐ 이상한, 기묘한, 특이한 / desperate ⓐ 절박한, 필사적인
stave off 피하다, 간신히 모면하다 / pandemic ⓝ 전 세계적인 유행병 / odor ⓝ 냄새, 향기, 악취
herb ⓝ 풀, 약초 / sewer ⓝ 하수구, 하수도
contaminate ⓥ (접촉하여) 더럽히다, 오염시키다 / come down with (병에) 걸리다
unsanitary ⓐ 비위생적인

| 전문해석 | 1328년에 흑사병이 유럽을 장악해서 이후 20년 동안 놓아주지 않았다. 수억 명의 사람들이 흑사병으로 목숨을 잃었고 의학계는 효과적인 치료법을 전혀 갖고 있지 않았기 때문에, 사람들은 그 전 세계적 유행병을 피하기 위한 절박한 시도로 기묘한 방법들을 시험해 보기 시작했다. 어떤 사람들은 좋은 냄새가 그 병을 막을 수 있다고 믿어서 달콤한 냄새가 나는 꽃이나 허브를 들고 다녔다.

그러나 이것이 가져다준 유일한 효과는 잠시 동안 사람에게서 좋은 냄새가 나게 하는 것뿐이었다. 소수의 사람들이 선택했던 보다 덜 유쾌한 방법은 하수도에서 사는 것이었는데, 지하의 공기가 그 질병에 오염되지 않았다고 생각했기 때문이었다. 물론 이것은 지하로 가서 살기로 결정한 가련한 사람들에게 아무런 도움도 되지 못했다. 사실 이것은 비위생적인 환경으로 인해 그들로 하여금 더 많은 질병에 걸리도록 했을 뿐이었다.

| 보기분석 | ① The history and development of European medicine practices 중심소재 흑사병이 없음
유럽 의료 행위들의 역사와 발전
② Why medical treatment for the Black Death did not work 언급 안 한 정보
흑사병에 대한 치료법이 효과가 없는 이유
③ Health-related myths believed by people in the 1300s 중심소재 흑사병이 없음
1300년대에 사람들이 믿었던 건강과 관련된 미신
④ The unbelievable miracle of the Black Death 언급 안 한 정보
흑사병의 믿을 수 없는 기적
⑤ Unusual remedies used in attempting to cure the Black Death
흑사병을 치료하기 위해 사용된 특이한 치료법들

| 정답분석 | 흑사병에 대한 제대로 된 치료법이 존재하지 않던 상황에서 사람들이 이 질병의 치료를 위해 시도했던 기묘한 치료법들의 내용과 그 결과에 대해 이야기하고 있으므로, 글의 주제로는 ⑤가 적절하다.

06 2017 가톨릭대(A형)

정답 ④

| 구문분석 | Art(S) is(V) much more than decoration(C), for(등위접속사) it(S) is laden(V) (with meaning), (even if that content is sometimes shallow or obscure). [부사절: (비록) ~일지라도]

예술은 장식 이상의 것인데, 담겨 있는 내용이 때때로 피상적이거나 모호하더라도 예술에는 의미가 담겨 있기 때문이다.

Art(S) enables(V) us(O) to communicate our understanding(O.C) (in ways) (that[관계대명사] cannot be expressed otherwise).
예술은 우리가 이해하는 것을 달리 표현될 수 없는 (예술만의) 방식으로 전달할 수 있게 해 준다.

not only A but also B: A뿐 아니라 B도
Truly a picture(S) is worth a thousand words [be worth N: N의 가치가 있다], not only [등위상관접속사] (in its descriptive value) but also (in its symbolic significance).

정말이지 그림은 그 서술적인 가치뿐만 아니라 상징적인 중요성에서도 천 마디의 말만큼 가치 있다.

(In art, as in language), human being(S) is(V) (above all) an inventor(C) (of symbols) (to convey complex thoughts in new ways).

언어에서와 같이, 인간은 예술에서도 그 무엇보다도 복잡한 생각을 새로운 방식으로 전달하는 상징의 발명가이다.

We must think (of art) not (in terms of everyday prose) but (as poetry), (which is free to rearrange conventional vocabulary and syntax) (in order to convey new, often multiple meanings and moods).

S V / not A but B: A가 아니라 B / 관계대명사

우리는 예술을 일상적인 산문의 관점에서 생각하지 말고 시라고 생각해야 하는데, 시는 새롭고, 종종 다양한 의미와 분위기를 전달하기 위해 통상적인 어휘와 구문을 자유롭게 재배열할 수 있다.

A painting likewise suggests much more (than it states).

S 접속부사 V O

마찬가지로 그림도 그것이 말하는 것보다 훨씬 더 많은 것을 암시한다.

(Like a poem), the value of art lies equally (in what it says and how it says it).

S V

시처럼 예술의 가치도 그것이 말하는 내용과 그 내용을 말하는 방식에 똑같이 존재한다.

It does so (partly by implying meanings through allegory, pose, facial expression, and the like) or (by evoking them through the visual elements: line, form, color, and composition).

S V O / 등위접속사

예술은 부분적으로는 비유 이야기, 자세, 얼굴 표정 등을 통해 의미를 함축한다거나 선, 형태, 색 및 구성과 같은 시각적 요소를 통해 의미를 환기시키는 방법으로 그렇게 한다(실제 말하는 내용보다 훨씬 더 많은 것을 전달한다).

| 어휘 | **shallow** ⓐ 얕은, 피상적인 **obscure** ⓐ 분명치 않은, 모호한 **descriptive** ⓐ 서술하는
symbolic significance 상징적인 중요성[의미] **rearrange** ⓥ 재배열하다
conventional ⓐ 평범한, 인습적인 **syntax** ⓝ 통사론, 구문론 **allegory** ⓝ 우화, 풍자
pose ⓝ 자세, 포즈 **evoke** ⓥ 불러일으키다

| 전문해석 | 예술은 장식 이상의 것인데, 담겨 있는 내용이 때때로 피상적이거나 모호하더라도 예술에는 의미가 담겨 있기 때문이다. 예술은 우리가 이해하는 것을 달리 표현될 수 없는 (예술만의) 방식으로 전달할 수 있게 해 준다. 정말이지 그림은 그 서술적 가치뿐만 아니라 상징적인 중요성에서도 천 마디의 말만큼 가치 있다. 언어에서와 같이, 인간은 예술에서도 그 무엇보다도 복잡한 생각을 새로운 방식으로 전달하는 상징의 발명가이다. 우리는 예술을 일상적인 산문의 관점에서 생각하지 말고 시라고 생각해야 하는데, 시는 새롭고, 종종 다양한 의미와 분위기를 전달하기 위해 통상적인 어휘와 구문을 자유롭게 재배열할 수 있다. 마찬가지로 그림도 그것이 말하는 것보다 훨씬 더 많은 것을 암시한다. 시처럼 예술의 가치도 그것이 말하는 내용과 그 내용을 말하는 방식에 똑같이 존재한다. 예술은 부분적으로는 비유 이야기, 자세, 얼굴 표정 등을 통해 의미를 함축한다거나 선, 형태, 색 및 구성과 같은 시각적 요소를 통해 의미를 환기시키는 방법으로 그렇게 한다(실제 말하는 내용보다 훨씬 더 많은 것을 전달한다).

| 보기분석 | ① The ultimate value of art is the beauty of description. 표현만을 다루는 글이 아니므로 너무 지엽적
예술의 궁극적 가치는 표현의 아름다움이다.
② Semantics takes a priority over syntax in art appreciation. 구문에 대한 글이 아니므로 너무 지엽적
예술 감상에서 의미는 구문보다 우선한다.
③ Artwork resembles a personal essay rather than a complex poem. 지문의 내용과 불일치
예술 작품은 복잡한 시라기보다 개인적인 에세이와 유사하다.
④ As in poetry, representation is as important as meaning in art.
시에서처럼, 예술에서도 표현은 의미만큼 중요하다.

| 정답분석 | 예술을 시와 비교하면서 예술은 다양한 표현을 통해 그것이 전달하고자 하는 것보다 훨씬 많은 것을 전달한다고 했으며, 예술의 가치는 예술이 말하는 내용(의미)과 그 내용을 말하는 방식(표현)에 똑같이 존재한다고 했으므로, 이 글의 요지로는 ④가 적절하다.

07 2016 건국대

정답 ②

| 구문분석 | The white race divides itself (upon economic grounds).

S V O

백인종은 경제적 이유에 근거해서 나누어진다.

The landowning whites look down on everyone else, mostly the working class Cajun whites.
S V O =
토지를 소유하고 있는 백인들은 대부분이 노동계급인 케이준 백인들을 포함해서 다른 모든 사람들을 깔본다.

These poor whites serve the landowning whites (by using violence to maintain the racial order).
S V O
이들 가난한 백인들은 인종적인 질서를 유지하기 위해 폭력을 사용하는 것을 통해서 토지를 소유한 백인들에게 봉사한다.

(Despite their efforts), however, the landowning whites still detest and scorn them.
접속부사 S V O
그러나 이들의 노력에도 불구하고 토지를 소유한 백인들은 가난한 백인들을 혐오하고 경멸한다.

In the black race, the Creole culture shuns all darker skin blacks.
S V O
흑인종 중에서 크리올 문화는 피부색이 검은 흑인들과 접촉을 피한다.

The Creoles are light skinned blacks (who come from the original French colonists in Louisiana).
S V C 관계대명사
크리올들은 최초의 프랑스 식민지인 루이지애나 출신으로 피부색이 밝은 흑인이다.

(When a Creole girl, Mary Agnes LeFarbre, goes to work on the Samson Plantation with common blacks),
부사절: ~할 때
her family disowns her.
S V O
크리올 출신의 소녀인 Mary Agnes LeFarbre가 일반적인 흑인들과 함께 Samson Plantation(집단농장)에 일을 하기 위해 갈 때, 그녀의 가족들은 그녀와 의절한다.

(Even though local whites consider the Creoles common blacks), the Creoles themselves refuse to mix with
부사절: (비록) ~일지라도 S V O
the general black population and act superior.

비록 그 지역의 백인들은 크리올을 일반적인 흑인으로 여기지만 크리올들은 그들 자신이 일반적인 흑인 인구들과 뒤섞이는 것을 거절하고 그들보다 우월한 듯 행동한다.

The concept of racism (within the black community itself) suggests the ridiculousness (in using skin color
S V O
as a means of social division).

흑인 공동체 안에서의 인종주의 개념은 그 자체로, 사회적 분할의 수단으로서 피부색을 사용하는 것의 어리석음을 나타내 보여 준다.

| 어휘 | Cajun ⓝ 케이준(프랑스인 후손으로 프랑스어 고어의 한 형태인 케이준어를 사용하는 미국 루이지애나 사람)
shun ⓥ 피하다 Creole ⓝ 크리올 사람(특히 서인도 제도에 사는, 유럽인과 흑인의 혼혈인)
disown ⓥ 의절하다, 절연하다 erect ⓥ 세우다

| 전문해석 | 백인종은 경제적 이유에 근거해서 나누어진다. 토지를 소유하고 있는 백인들은 대부분이 노동계급인 케이준 백인들을 포함해서 다른 모든 사람들을 깔본다. 이들 가난한 백인들은 인종적인 질서를 유지하기 위해 폭력을 사용하는 것을 통해서 토지를 소유한 백인들에게 봉사한다. 그러나 이들의 노력에도 불구하고 토지를 소유한 백인들은 가난한 백인들을 혐오하고 경멸한다. 흑인종 중에서 크리올 문화는 피부색이 검은 흑인들과 접촉을 피한다. 크리올들은 최초의 프랑스 식민지인 루이지애나 출신으로 피부색이 밝은 흑인이다. 크리올 출신의 소녀인 Mary Agnes LeFarbre가 일반적인 흑인들과 함께 Samson Plantation(집단농장)에 일을 하기 위해 갈 때, 그녀의 가족들은 그녀와 의절한다. 비록 그 지역의 백인들은 크리올을 일반적인 흑인으로 여기지만 크리올들은 그들 자신이 일반적인 흑인 인구들과 뒤섞이는 것을 거절하고 그들보다 우월한 듯 행동한다. 흑인 공동체 안에서의 인종주의 개념은 그 자체로, 사회적 분할의 수단으로서 피부색을 사용하는 것의 어리석음을 나타내 보여 준다.

| 보기분석 | ① The poor whites use violence toward the rich whites. 백인만을 말하는 글이 아님
가난한 백인들은 부유한 백인들을 향해 폭력을 사용한다.
② Class differences exist even inside the same race.
같은 인종 내에서도 계급 간 차이가 존재한다.
③ Humans erect boundaries to keep their fellows out. 동료를 멀리한다는 것은 너무 극단적으로 지문에서 다룬 내용이 아님
인간은 자신들의 동료들을 멀리하기 위해 경계선을 만든다.
④ Social frame of racial order constructs American identity. 언급 안 한 정보
인종적 질서의 사회적 틀이 미국의 정체성을 형성한다.

⑤ People are bound to the traditional image of black and white. 언급 안 한 정보
사람들은 흑인과 백인의 전통적인 인식에 얽매여 있다.

| 정답분석 | 이 글은 인간이 같은 인종 사이에서도 경제력과 피부의 밝기에 따라 구분이 이루어진다는 글이므로 요지로는 ②가 적절하다.

08 2019 명지대

정답 ②

| 구문분석 | There are many English surnames (from place names), and a curious fact (about them) is that the places are often so obscure — mostly from places that few people have heard of.
(There: 유도부사, are: V, many English surnames: S, a curious fact: S, is: V, that the places are often so obscure: C, —: 대시: 부연설명)

영국에는 지명(地名)에서 유래한 성(姓)이 많은데, 이 성에 관해 흥미로운 사실은 이 지명들이 대부분 거의 들어 본 적 없는 잘 알려지지 않은 곳이라는 점이다.

Why should there be so many more Middletons than Londons, so many more Worthingtons than Bristols?
(Why: 의문사, should be: V, there: 유도부사, so many more Middletons: S_1, so many more Worthingtons: S_2)

왜 런던(London)보다 미들턴(Middleton)을 성으로 쓰는 사람들이 훨씬 더 많고, 브리스틀(Bristol)보다 워싱턴(Worthington)을 성으로 쓰는 사람들이 훨씬 더 많을까?

The main cities of medieval Britain (— London, York, Norwich, Glasgow —) are relatively uncommon (as surnames) (even though many thousands of people lived there).
(The main cities of medieval Britain: S, are: V, uncommon: C, even though: 부사절: (비록) ~일지라도)

중세 영국의 주요 도시인 런던, 요크(York), 노리치(Norwich), 글래스고(Glasgow)는 수많은 사람들이 그곳에 살았음에도 불구하고, 상대적으로 성으로는 드물게 쓰였다.

(To understand this seeming paradox) you must remember that the purpose of surnames is to distinguish one person or family from the great mass of people.
(To understand: 부사적용법: ~하기 위하여, you: S, must remember: V, that ~ people: O)

겉보기에 모순적인 이런 상황을 이해하기 위해서는, 성을 사용하는 목적이 한 사람 또는 한 가문을 수많은 대중과 구별하기 위한 것이라는 점을 기억해야 한다.

(If a person called himself Peter of London), he would be just one (of hundreds of such Peters) and anyone (searching for him) would be (at a loss).
(If ~: 부사절: 만일 ~라면, he: S, would be: V, just one: C, and: 등위접속사, anyone: S, would be: V)

만일 어떤 사람이 자신을 런던이라는 성을 가진 피터(Peter)라고 부른다면, 그는 그저 런던이라는 성을 가진 수백 명의 피터 중 한 명에 불과해 그를 찾고자 하는 사람이라면 누구나 어찌할 바를 모를 것이다.

So (as a rule), a person would become known (as Peter of London) only (if he moved to a rural location), (where London would be a clear identifying feature), but that did not happen often.
(So: 등위접속사: 따라서, a person: S, would become known: V, if: 부사절: 만일 ~라면, where: 관계부사, but: 등위접속사, that: S, did not happen: V)

따라서 대체적으로, 런던이라는 성을 가진 피터는 런던이라는 이름이 분명하게 일반 대중과 구별해 주는 특징이 될 시골지역으로 이사를 갔을 경우에만 런던이라는 성을 가진 피터로 알려지겠지만 그런 일은 자주 일어나지 않았다.

| 어휘 |

surname ⓝ 성(姓)	**place name** 지명(地名)	**obscure** ⓐ 잘 알려지지 않은
medieval ⓐ 중세의	**paradox** ⓝ 역설; 모순된[이치에 맞지 않는] 말	
distinguish ⓥ 구분하다, 구별하다	**be at a loss** 어쩔 줄을 모르다	**as a rule** 일반적으로
feature ⓝ 특징	**scarcity** ⓝ 부족, 결핍	**untold** ⓐ 알려지지 않은
myth ⓝ 신화; 지어낸 이야기		

| 전문해석 | 영국에는 지명(地名)에서 유래한 성(姓)이 많은데, 이 성에 관해 흥미로운 사실은 이 지명들이 대부분 거의 들어 본 적 없는 잘 알려지지 않은 곳이라는 점이다. 왜 런던(London)보다 미들턴(Middleton)을 성으로 쓰는 사람들이 훨씬 더 많고, 브리스틀(Bristol)보다 워싱턴(Worthington)을 성으로 쓰는 사람들이 훨씬 더 많을까? 중세 영국의 주요 도시인 런던, 요크(York), 노리치(Norwich), 글래스고(Glasgow)는 수많은 사람들이 그곳에 살았음에도 불구하고, 상대적으로 성으로는 드물게 쓰였다. 겉보기에 모순적인 이런 상황을 이해하기 위해서는, 성을 사용하는 목적이 한 사람 또는 한 가문을 수많은 대

중과 구별하기 위한 것이라는 점을 기억해야 한다. 만일 어떤 사람이 자신을 런던이라는 성을 가진 피터(Peter)라고 부른다면, 그는 그저 런던이라는 성을 가진 수백 명의 피터 중 한 명에 불과해 그를 찾고자 하는 사람이라면 누구나 어찌할 바를 모를 것이다. 따라서 대체적으로, 런던이라는 성을 가진 피터는 런던이라는 이름이 분명하게 일반 대중과 구별해 주는 특징이 될 시골지역으로 이사를 갔을 경우에만 런던이라는 성을 가진 피터로 알려지겠지만 그런 일은 자주 일어나지 않았다.

| 보기분석 | ① the popular English surnames from place names 글의 도입부로 이 글에서 주로 다루는 내용이 아님
지명(地名)에서 유래한 영국의 대중적인 성(姓)
② the reason for the scarcity of big place names in English surnames
영국의 성(姓)에 주요 도시 이름들이 부족한 이유
③ the untold myths about English surnames from place names 언급 안 한 정보
지명(地名)에서 유래한 영국의 성(姓)들에 관한 알려지지 않은 신화
④ the source of confusion in English surnames from place names 주요 내용이 되기에 너무 지엽적
지명(地名)에서 유래한 영국의 성(姓)이 혼동을 일으키는 원인

| 정답분석 | "영국의 성(姓)은 지명(地名)에서 유래한 것이 많은데, 그 지명이 중세 영국에서 사람들이 많이 거주했던 '주요 도시의 지명'이 아니라 '잘 알려지지 않은 지명'이며, 이렇게 잘 알려지지 않은 지명을 쓴 목적은 한 사람이나 한 가문을 일반 대중과 쉽게 구분하기 위한 것"이라는 내용이다. 따라서 이 글의 주요한 내용으로는 ②가 가장 적절하다.

09 2017 서울여대

정답 ④

| 구문분석 | Shakespeare(S) killed off(V) Hamlet, Macbeth and King Lear(O). How did the characters(S) feel(V) (about it, and about him)?

셰익스피어는 작품 속에서 햄릿, 맥베스, 리어왕을 죽게 만들었다. 그 등장인물들은 그것에 대해, 그리고 셰익스피어에 대해 어떻게 느꼈을까?

Shakespeare's characters had their own viewpoints and still do(O), says(V) playwright Naomi C. Wallace(S).

셰익스피어의 등장인물들은 그들 나름의 견해를 가지고 있었고, 지금도 여전히 그러하다고 극작가 나오미 월러스(Naomi C. Wallace)는 말한다.

(In her play, *Madman William*), Hamlet, Macbeth and King Lear(S) meet(V_1) (in a 20th-century London pub) and(등위접속사) discuss(V_2) their resentment(O) (at having to die in every performance).

그녀의 연극 *Madman William*에서, 햄릿, 맥베스, 리어왕은 20세기 런던의 술집에서 만나 매 공연 죽어야 하는 것에 대한 분개심을 이야기한다.

(In a dream scene), Shakespeare himself(S) appears(V) (as well)(부사: 또한) (in the pub) (along with the three tragic figures and Mercutio), (who(관계대명사) is killed off early in *Romeo and Juliet*).

꿈속의 한 장면에서, 셰익스피어 자신도 그 세 명의 비극적 인물, 그리고 '로미오와 줄리엣'에서 일찍 죽고 마는 머큐시오(Mercutio)와 함께 술집에 모습을 드러낸다.

The play(S) gets(V) its American premiere(O) (on Friday at the District of Columbia Arts Center) and(등위접속사) will continue(V) (at other sites in the Washington area through February).

이 연극은 금요일에 컬럼비아 특별구 아트센터에서 미국 내 첫 공연이 있을 예정이며, 워싱턴의 다른 지역에서도 2월 내내 공연이 열릴 것이다.

(Last year) it(S) was produced(V) (in Edinburgh, Scotland); (세미콜론: 등위접속사 기능) (in Exeter and Shakespeare's hometown, Stratford-on-Avon, in England); (세미콜론: 등위접속사 기능) and (in Prague, Czech Republic).

작년에는 이 연극이 스코틀랜드의 에든버러, 영국의 엑서터와 셰익스피어의 고향인 스트래트퍼드 온 에이븐, 체코의 프라하에서 공연되었다.

| 어휘 |
character ⓝ 특성; 성격; 인물; (소설의) 등장인물
viewpoint ⓝ 견해, 견지, 관점
playwright ⓝ 각본가; 극작가
pub ⓝ 술집
resentment ⓝ 원한, 분개
tragic ⓐ 비극의, 비극적인
figure ⓝ 모양, 형태; 인물
premiere ⓝ (영화의) 개봉; (연극의) 초연

| 전문해석 | 셰익스피어는 작품 속에서 햄릿, 맥베스, 리어왕을 죽게 만들었다. 그 등장인물들은 그것에 대해, 그리고 셰익스피어에 대해 어떻게 느꼈을까? 셰익스피어의 등장인물들은 그들 나름의 견해를 가지고 있었고, 지금도 여전히 그러하다고 극작가 나오미 월러스(Naomi C. Wallace)는 말한다. 그녀의 연극 *Madman William*에서, 햄릿, 맥베스, 리어왕은 20세기 런던의 술집에서 만나 매 공연 죽어야 하는 것에 대한 분개심을 이야기한다. 꿈속의 한 장면에서, 셰익스피어 자신도 그 세 명의 비극적 인물, 그리고 '로미오와 줄리엣'에서 일찍 죽고 마는 머큐시오(Mercutio)와 함께 술집에 모습을 드러낸다. 이 연극은 금요일에 컬럼비아 특별구 아트센터에서 미국 내 첫 공연이 있을 예정이며, 워싱턴의 다른 지역에서도 2월 내내 공연이 열릴 것이다. 작년에는 이 연극이 스코틀랜드의 에든버러, 영국의 엑서터와 셰익스피어의 고향인 스트래트퍼드 온 에이븐, 체코의 프라하에서 공연되었다.

| 보기분석 | ① A witty play by Naomi C. Wallace made a huge success. 글의 주요 내용이 아님
나오미 월러스의 위트 있는 연극이 대성공을 거두었다.
② Shakespeare enjoyed having his characters murdered at the end. 언급 안 한 정보
셰익스피어는 마지막에 그의 등장인물이 살해당하도록 하는 것을 즐겼다.
③ Shakespeare's tragic characters do not like being killed in their plays. 언급 안 한 정보
셰익스피어의 비극적 등장인물들은 자신들의 연극에서 죽는 것을 싫어한다.
④ *Madman William* retells Shakespearean tragedies in the characters' perspectives.
*Madman William*은 셰익스피어의 비극을 등장인물의 관점에서 재조명한다.

| 정답분석 | 이 글은 "햄릿, 맥베스, 리어왕과 같이 셰익스피어의 비극 작품 속에서 죽음을 맞는 등장인물들이 20세기에 다시 만나 매번 극 중에서 죽어야 하는 것에 대해 분개심을 호소하는 등, 자신들의 죽음과 셰익스피어에 대한 나름의 견해들을 서로 이야기 나눈다."는 내용을 담은 나오미 월러스의 연극 *Madman William*에 대해 이야기하고 있다. 그러므로 요지로는 ④가 적절하다.

10 2017 한양대

정답 ④

| 구문분석 | The trouble(S) is(V) (with the assimilative nature of Italian immigrants).
문제는 이탈리아 이민자들의 동화적 성격에 있다.

(In a few years) even the older immigrants(S) are(V) apt to pick up our language(C_1) [be apt to: ~하는 경향이 있다], and(등위접속사) (one by one) to abandon their native customs and ways of thought(C_2).

몇 년 사이에 고령의 이민자들조차도 우리의 언어(영어)를 습득하고는 하나씩 하나씩 그들의 고유한 관습과 사고방식을 버리는 경향이 있다.

(Even in the theater) they(S) spoke(V) (to each other mainly in English).
극장에서조차도 그들은 주로 영어로 서로 대화를 했다.

(In seeking amusement) they(S) fall prey to(V) the flash and glare of our variety bill-posters(O).
오락(즐거움)을 추구할 때, 그들은 우리의 다양한 광고 전단지의 화려함과 광채에 현혹당하고 만다.

The new generation(S), (who(관계대명사) lack the traditions of the home country, and sometimes the knowledge of Italy to appreciate its drama), are(V) almost certain(C) (to become Americanized in their tastes).
고국 이탈리아의 전통도 없고 때로는 이탈리아 연극을 감상하기 위한 이탈리아에 대한 지식도 없는 신세대들은 취향 면에서 미국화하게 될 것이 거의 틀림없다.

An Italian theater(S) could appeal(V) (only to new arrivals and to those of the past generation) (who(관계대명사) have not forgotten their old life and the joy of true acting).

이탈리아 극장은 이제 갓 미국에 당도한 (이탈리아) 이민자들에게나 자신들의 옛 삶과 진정한 연기의 즐거움을 잊지 못한 과거 세대 사람들에게만 호응을 얻을 수 있을 것이다.

| 어휘 | **assimilative** ⓐ 동화의, 동화하는 **apt** ⓐ ~하기 쉬운, ~하는 경향이 있는
fall prey to ~의 먹이가 되다 **flash** ⓝ 불빛 **bill-poster** ⓝ 벽보, (광고) 전단지

| 전문해석 | 문제는 이탈리아 이민자들의 동화적 성격에 있다. 몇 년 사이에 고령의 이민자들조차도 우리의 언어(영어)를 습득하고는 하나씩 하나씩 그들의 고유한 관습과 사고방식을 버리는 경향이 있다. 극장에서조차도 그들은 주로 영어로 서로 대화를 했다. 오락(즐거움)을 추구할 때, 그들은 우리의 다양한 광고 전단지의 화려함과 광채에 현혹당하고 만다. 고국 이탈리아의 전통도 없고 때로는 이탈리아 연극을 감상하기 위한 이탈리아에 대한 지식도 없는 신세대들은 취향 면에서 미국화하게 될 것이 거의 틀림없다. 이탈리아 극장은 이제 갓 미국에 당도한 (이탈리아) 이민자들에게나 자신들의 옛 삶과 진정한 연기의 즐거움을 잊지 못한 과거 세대 사람들에게만 호응을 얻을 수 있을 것이다.

| 보기분석 | ① Italian immigrants who cling in their old traditions and legends 지문의 내용과 불일치
그들의 옛 전통들과 전설들을 고수하는 이탈리아 이민자들

② the power of the melting pot across ethnic and national boundaries melting pot에 관한 글이 아님
모든 인종과 국적에 미치는 용광로(미국으로의 동화)의 위력

③ Italian immigrants' preference of American traditions to the traditions of their home country 세대 간의 차이를 설명하는 부분을 담지 못하며 일반화의 오류
고국의 전통보다 미국의 전통을 더 좋아하는 이탈리아 이민자들의 선호도

④ a generational difference concerning cultural preferences between first-generation Italian immigrants and their offspring
이탈리아 이민자 1세대와 그 후손들 사이의 문화적 선호도와 관련한 세대 차이

| 정답분석 | 이 글은 이탈리아 이민자들이 미국문화에 동화되어 가는 것에 관한 글인데, 동화란 곧 미국화하는 것이고 미국문화를 더 선호하는 것이라 할 수 있다. 이 글에서는 이탈리아 이민자들의 동화를 말하면서 그들의 미국문화 선호에 있어 세대 간에 정도의 차이가 있음을 드러내고 있다. 둘째 문장에서 '고령의 이민자들조차도'라고 한 것은 젊은 세대는 그런 경향이 더 심함을 의미하고, 마지막 두 문장은 신세대와 과거 세대를 대비시켜 이탈리아 연극은 이제는 일부 과거 세대에게나 어필할 수 있을 것이라고 하여 역시 세대 간에 차이가 있음을 나타낸다. 따라서 ④가 글의 주제로 적절하다.

11 2018 단국대

정답 ②

| 구문분석 | (According to researchers), gossip(S) has(V) some benefits(O). Exchanging information(S) can create(V) a healthy connection(O).

연구원들에 따르면, 잡담에는 몇 가지 이점이 있다고 한다. 정보를 교환하는 것은 건전한 관계를 형성할 수 있다.

It(S) can build(V) rules(O) (for acceptable and unacceptable behavior).

잡담은 받아들일 수 있는 행동과 받아들일 수 없는 행동에 대한 규칙을 만들 수 있다.

It(S) can improve(V) society(O). Similarly(접속부사), gossip(S) is(V) useful(C) (in the business world).

잡담은 사회를 개선시킬 수 있다. 마찬가지로, 잡담은 사업계에서도 유용하다.

(Gossip researcher Professor Frank McAndrew says)(삽입절), "(If people are talking about good things others do)(부사절: 만일 ~라면), we(S) want(V) to emulate that good behavior(O). It(S) is(V) a nice way(C) (of socially controlling people)."

잡담 연구가인 프랭크 맥앤드류(Frank McAndrew) 교수는 "만일 사람들이 다른 사람들이 하는 좋은 행동들에 대해 말을 하고 있으면, 우리는 그 좋은 행동을 모방하기를 원합니다. 이것은 사람들을 사회적으로 제어하는 좋은 방법입니다."라고 주장한다.

(When a company faces bad times)(부사절: ~할 때), gossip(S) (about the future of the employees) can reduce(V) fear and uncertainty(O). It(S) can also create(V) a feeling of fellowship(O).

회사가 힘든 시기를 겪을 때, 직원들의 앞날에 대한 잡담은 두려움과 불확실성을 줄일 수 있으며, 동료의식 또한 생기게 할 수 있다.

However(접속부사), bad gossip(S), (=) the negative talk about other people's lives, can be(V) destructive(C).

그러나 다른 사람들의 생활에 대한 부정적인 대화인 나쁜 잡담(험담)은 해로울 수 있다.

(Disappointingly enough), the researchers(S) spend(V) little time(O) (on this form of malice).

매우 실망스럽게도, 연구원들은 이런 형태의 악의(험담)에 대해서는 거의 시간을 들이지 않는다.

People engage (in negative gossip for several reasons). They may do it (to bond with another person). They may do it (to pass the time or to deny problems).
S V 등위접속사 S V O 부사적용법: ~하기 위하여 S V O 부사적용법: ~하기 위하여 부사적용법: ~하기 위하여

사람들은 몇 가지 이유로 부정적인 잡담을 한다. 사람들은 다른 사람과 친밀한 관계를 형성하기 위해 험담을 한다. 사람들은 시간을 때우기 위해서나 (당연한) 문제를 거부하기 위해 험담을 한다.

They may gossip (to build themselves up through comparisons with others), or they may want to hurt others.
S V 부사적용법: ~하기 위하여 등위접속사 S V O

사람들은 다른 사람과의 비교를 통해 자신을 치켜세우기 위해 또는 다른 사람들을 해할 목적으로 잡담을 할지도 모른다.

| 어휘 |

gossip ⓝ 소문, 잡담 emulate ⓥ 모방하다 fellowship ⓝ 동료의식, 우정
malice ⓝ 적개심, 원한 engage in ~에 관여하다 bond with ~와 친밀한 인연을 맺다
pass the time 빈 시간을 아무 생각 없이 보내다

| 전문해석 | 연구원들에 따르면, 잡담에는 몇 가지 이점이 있다고 한다. 정보를 교환하는 것은 건전한 관계를 형성할 수 있다. 잡담은 받아들일 수 있는 행동과 받아들일 수 없는 행동에 대한 규칙을 만들 수 있다. 잡담은 사회를 개선 시킬 수 있다. 마찬가지로, 잡담은 사업계에서도 유용하다. 잡담 연구가인 프랭크 맥앤드류(Frank McAndrew) 교수는 "만일 사람들이 다른 사람들이 하는 좋은 행동들에 대해 말을 하고 있으면, 우리는 그 좋은 행동을 모방하기를 원합니다. 이것은 사람들을 사회적으로 제어하는 좋은 방법입니다."라고 주장한다. 회사가 힘든 시기를 겪을 때, 직원들의 앞날에 대한 잡담은 두려움과 불확실성을 줄일 수 있으며, 동료의식 또한 생기게 할 수 있다.

그러나 다른 사람들의 생활에 대한 부정적인 대화인 나쁜 잡담(험담)은 해로울 수 있다. 매우 실망스럽게도, 연구원들은 이런 형태의 악의(험담)에 대해서는 거의 시간을 들이지 않는다. 사람들은 몇 가지 이유로 부정적인 잡담을 한다. 사람들은 다른 사람과 친밀한 관계를 형성하기 위해 험담을 한다. 사람들은 시간을 때우기 위해서나 (당연한) 문제를 거부하기 위해 험담을 한다. 사람들은 다른 사람과의 비교를 통해 자신을 치켜세우기 위해 또는 다른 사람들을 해할 목적으로 잡담을 할지도 모른다.

| 보기분석 |

① People don't realize how destructive gossip can be. 너무 지엽적
사람들은 잡담이 얼마나 유해한지를 깨닫지 못한다.

② Gossip can be beneficial or negative for society and people's lives.
잡담은 사회와 사람들의 인생에 이로울 수도 해로울 수도 있다.

③ Gossip is needed because employees may be able to create a feeling of fellowship. 너무 지엽적
직원들이 연대감을 형성할 수 있는 분위기를 조성할 수 있기 때문에 잡담은 필요하다.

④ People may be involved in negative gossip for various reasons. 너무 지엽적
사람들은 아마도 다양한 이유로 부정적인 잡담에 연루된다.

| 정답분석 | 이 글은 두 단락으로 나눠 잡담의 좋은 점과 나쁜 점에 대해 이야기하고 있으므로, ②의 '잡담은 사회와 사람들의 인생에 이로울 수도 해로울 수도 있다.'가 글의 요지로 적절하다.

12 2017 한국외대(C형 서울일반)

정답 ①

| 구문분석 | Professor Constantine Slobodchikoff and his colleagues have been decoding the communication system (of prairie dogs), rodents not known for their smarts.
S V O =

콘스탄틴 슬로보드치코프(Constantine Slobodchikoff)와 동료 교수들은 그 영리함에 대해 알려져 있지 않은 설치류인 프레리도그의 의사소통 체계를 해독해 왔다.

And yet, Slobodchikoff's team has evidence that prairie dogs have a complex language, (which they are starting to understand) (when prairie dogs see a predator), they warn one another (using high-pitched chirps).
등위접속사: 하지만 S V O = 관계대명사 부사절: ~할 때 S V O 분사구문

그러나 슬로보드치코프 교수팀은 프레리도그에게도 복잡한 언어가 있다는 증거를 갖고 있으며, 그들은 이 언어를 파악하는 일에 착수했다. 프레리도그는 약탈자를 보게 되면 그들은 서로 간에 고음의 찍찍 소리로 서로에게 경고한다.

(To the untrained ear), these chirps may all sound the same, but they are not.

훈련이 돼 있지 않은 사람들의 귀에는 이런 프레리도그 소리가 전부 같은 소리처럼 들릴 수도 있지만, 동일한 소리는 아니다.

Slobodchickoff thinks the alarm calls are a “Rosetta Stone” in decoding prairie-dog language, (because they occur in a context (people can understand), (enabling interpretation).

슬로보드치코프는 이런 경고음은 프레리도그 언어를 해독하는 데 있어 로제타스톤(Rosetta Stone)과 같은 것이라고 말하는데, 이런 경고음이 사람이 이해할 수 있는 상황 속에서 발생하여, 그 의미를 해석할 수가 있기 때문이다.

(In his research), Slobodchikoff records the alarm calls and subsequent escape behaviors (of prairie dogs in response to approaching predators).

그의 연구에서, 슬로보드치코프는 경고음과 포식동물의 접근에 따라 프레리도그들이 이로 인해 도망치는 행동을 기록한다.

Then, (when no predator is present), he plays back these recorded alarm class and films the prairie dogs' escape responses.

그러고는 근접한 포식동물이 없을 때에, 녹음한 그 경고음을 재생시켜서, 프레리도그들이 도망치는 반응을 영상으로 촬영한다.

(If the escape responses to the playback match those (when the predator was present), this suggests that meaningful information is encoded in the calls.

녹음한 경고음 소리에 따라 도망치는 반응이 포식동물이 있을 때의 반응과 일치한다면, 이것은 경고음 안에 의미 있는 정보가 암호화되어 있다는 것을 의미한다.

And indeed, there seems to be. Slobodchikoff has discovered they have distinct calls (pertaining to different predators).

그리고 실제로 의미 있는 정보가 내재되어 있는 것으로 보인다. 슬로보드치코프는 경고음에 포식동물들마다 관련된 서로 다른(독특한) 경고가 있다는 것을 밝혀냈다.

The calls even specify the color, size, and shape (of the predator).

이런 경고음은 심지어 포식동물의 색깔, 크기와 모양까지도 구체적으로 명시해 준다.

| 어휘 | **prairie dog** ⓝ 프레리도그(북미 대초원 지대에 사는 다람쥐과 동물), 개쥐 **decode** ⓥ 암호를 번역하다
high-pitched ⓐ 고음의 **chirp** ⓝ (새 · 벌레의) 찍찍 소리 **alarm call** ⓝ 경고음, 비상 신호
response ⓝ 응답, 반응 **comparable** ⓐ 유사한 **reflex** ⓝ 반사행동
encode ⓥ 암호화하다 **distinct** ⓐ 별개의; 명료한, 뚜렷한 **specify** ⓥ 열거하다, 지정하다

| 전문해석 | 콘스탄틴 슬로보드치코프(Constantine Slobodchikoff)와 동료 교수들은 그 영리함에 대해 알려져 있지 않은 설치류인 프레리도그의 의사소통 체계를 해독해 왔다. 그러나 슬로보드치코프 교수팀은 프레리도그에게도 복잡한 언어가 있다는 증거를 갖고 있으며, 그들은 이 언어를 파악하는 일에 착수했다. 프레리도그는 약탈자를 보게 되면 그들은 서로 간에 고음의 찍찍 소리로 서로에게 경고한다. 훈련이 돼 있지 않은 사람들의 귀에는 이런 프레리도그 소리가 전부 같은 소리처럼 들릴 수도 있지만, 동일한 소리는 아니다. 슬로보드치코프는 이런 경고음은 프레리도그 언어를 해독하는 데 있어 로제타스톤(Rosetta Stone)과 같은 것이라고 말하는데, 이런 경고음이 사람이 이해할 수 있는 상황 속에서 발생하여, 그 의미를 해석할 수가 있기 때문이다. 그의 연구에서, 슬로보드치코프는 경고음과 포식동물의 접근에 따라 프레리도그들이 이로 인해 도망치는 행동을 기록한다. 그러고는 근접한 포식동물이 없을 때에, 녹음한 그 경고음을 재생시켜서, 프레리도그들이 도망치는 반응을 영상으로 촬영한다. 녹음한 경고음 소리에 따라 도망치는 반응이 포식동물이 있을 때의 반응과 일치한다면, 이것은 경고음 안에 의미 있는 정보가 암호화되어 있다는 것을 의미한다. 그리고 실제로 의미 있는 정보가 내재되어 있는 것으로 보인다. 슬로보드치코프는 경고음에 포식동물들마다 관련된 서로 다른(독특한) 경고가 있다는 것을 밝혀냈다. 이런 경고음은 심지어 포식동물의 색깔, 크기와 모양까지도 구체적으로 명시해 준다.

| 보기분석 | ✓ Scientists began to understand the language of prairie dogs.
과학자가 프레리도그의 언어를 파악하기 시작했다.
② Scientists observed prairie dogs' peculiar escape behavior. 중심소재인 프레리도그 언어가 없음
과학자는 프레리도그의 특이한 탈출행동을 관찰했다.
③ Prairie dog language is structurally comparable to human language. 언급 안 한 정보
프레리도그의 언어는 구조적으로 인간의 언어에 비교될 수 있다.
④ Prairie dogs have an elaborate system of conveying diverse emotions. 감정 전달의 체계에 관한 글이 아님
프레리도그는 다양한 감정을 전달하는 정교한 체계가 있다.

| 정답분석 | 이 글은 과학자들이 프레리도그가 다양한 경고음을 통해 서로 의사소통한다는 것을 언급하며 프레리도그의 언어라고 할 수 있는 의사소통 시스템을 연구했다는 글이다. 따라서 ①이 주제로 적절하다.

13 2015 명지대

정답 ②

| 구문분석 | Natural selection(S) is usually assumed(V) to favor behaviors(O.C) (that(관계대명사) promise survival), but(등위접속사) almost no art theorist(S) has ever proposed(V) that art directly promotes survival(O).

자연 선택은 대개 생존을 약속하는 행동들을 선호하는 것으로 가정되지만, 거의 어떤 예술 이론가도 예술이 직접적으로 생존을 촉진시킨다고 제안하지는 않았다.

It(S) costs(V) too much time and energy(O) and(등위접속사) does(V) too little(O).

예술은 너무나 많은 시간과 에너지라는 비용을 지불하지만 실제로 (생존에 도움을 주는 어떤 것을) 행하는 경우는 거의 없다.

This problem(S) was recognized(V) (very early in evolutionary theorizing about art).

이러한 문제의식은 예술에 관한 진화론적인 이론이 생성되는 과정에서 매우 일찍 인식되었다.

(In his 1897 book *The Beginning of Art*), Ernst Grosse(S) commented(V) (on art's wastefulness), (claiming(분사구문) that natural selection would long ago have rejected those (who(관계대명사) wasted their efforts in so purposeless a way), (in favor of others with practical talents); and art would not possibly have been developed so highly and richly as it has been).

1897년 에른스트 그로스(Ernst Grosse)는, 그의 저서 *The Beginning of Art*에서, 예술의 헛된 낭비적인 면에 대해서 언급하면서, 자연 선택은 오랫동안 그와 같이 아무 목적도 없는 방식으로 자신들의 노력을 낭비하는 사람들을 거부해 오면서 쓸모 있는 재능을 가진 사람들을 선호해 왔다고 주장했다. 그리고 그는 예술이 지금까지 그래 왔던 것처럼 수준 높고 풍요롭게 발전하지 않았을 수도 있었다는 주장도 덧붙였다.

(To Darwin), high cost, apparent uselessness and manifest beauty(S) usually indicated(V) that a behavior had a hidden courtship function(O).

다윈에게 있어서, 높은 비용과 명백한 쓸모없음 그리고 분명한 아름다움은 대개 (이런 특징들을 포함하고 있는) 어떤 행동들이 숨겨진 구애의 기능을 가지고 있다는 것을 나타내는 지표였다.

But(등위접속사) (to most art theorists), art's high cost and apparent uselessness(S) has usually implied(V) that a Darwinian approach is inappropriate(O) — (대시: 부연설명) that art is uniquely exempt from natural selection's cost-cutting frugality.

그러나 대부분의 예술 이론가들에 있어서, 예술의 높은 비용과 명백한 쓸모없음은 대개 다윈주의적인 접근법이 적절하지 않고 예술이 자연 선택의 비용을 줄이고자 하는 절약지향성으로부터 벗어나 있는 독특한 예외라는 사실을 의미해 왔다.

| 어휘 |
natural selection 자연 선택, 자연 도태
assume ⓥ 가정하다
reject ⓥ 거부하다
manifest ⓐ 명백한, 분명한
courtship ⓝ 구혼 기간, 구애, 구혼
exempt ⓐ 면제된

| 전문해석 | 자연 선택은 대개 생존을 약속하는 행동들을 선호하는 것으로 가정되지만, 거의 어떤 예술 이론가도 예술이 직접적으로 생

존을 촉진시킨다고 제안하지는 않았다. 예술은 너무나 많은 시간과 에너지라는 비용을 지불하지만 실제로 (생존에 도움을 주는 어떤 것을) 행하는 경우는 거의 없다. 이러한 문제의식은 예술에 관한 진화론적인 이론이 생성되는 과정에서 매우 일찍 인식되었다. 1897년 에른스트 그로스(Ernst Grosse)는, 그의 저서 *The Beginning of Art*에서, 예술의 헛된 낭비적인 면에 대해서 언급하면서, 자연 선택은 오랫동안 그와 같이 아무 목적도 없는 방식으로 자신들의 노력을 낭비하는 사람들을 거부해 오면서 쓸모 있는 재능을 가진 사람들을 선호해 왔다고 주장했다. 그리고 그는 예술이 지금까지 그래 왔던 것처럼 수준 높고 풍요롭게 발전하지 않았을 수도 있었다는 주장도 덧붙였다. 다윈에게 있어서, 높은 비용과 명백한 쓸모없음 그리고 분명한 아름다움은 대개 (이런 특징들을 포함하고 있는) 어떤 행동들이 숨겨진 구애의 기능을 가지고 있다는 것을 나타내는 지표였다. 그러나 대부분의 예술 이론가들에 있어서, 예술의 높은 비용과 명백한 쓸모없음은 대개 다윈주의적인 접근법이 적절하지 않고 예술이 자연 선택의 비용을 줄이고자 하는 절약지향성으로부터 벗어나 있는 독특한 예외라는 사실을 의미해 왔다.

| 보기분석 | ① Art has no survival value, but displays a courtship function. 지문 내용과 불일치
예술은 생존 가치는 없다, 하지만 구애 기능을 나타낸다.
② Natural selection does not explain art in a plausible way.
자연 선택은 예술을 설득력 있는 방식으로 설명하지 못한다.
③ Many art theorists appreciate art's evolutionary functions. 언급 안 한 정보
많은 예술 이론가들은 예술의 진화적 기능을 높이 평가한다.
④ Biologists have found a way to explain art in Darwinian terms. 지문 내용과 불일치
생물학자들이 다윈주의적 용어로 예술을 설명하는 방법을 발견했다.

| 정답분석 | 이 글은 예술이 자연 선택의 일반 법칙에서 벗어나 있다는 내용을 주로 다루고 있다. 따라서 글의 요지로는 ②가 적절하다.

14 2018 단국대(자연계)

정답 ①

| 구문분석 | A psychiatrist(S) reported(V) the case(O) (of a woman) (who(관계대명사) claimed that she had stomach trouble because of a frog in her stomach).

한 정신과 의사가 자신의 위 속에 개구리가 있어 배탈이 났다고 주장하는 어느 여성의 사례를 보고했다.

She(S) "knew"(V) (that) she had swallowed a frog egg while on a picnic.(O)

그녀는 소풍 중에 자신이 개구리 알을 삼킨 것으로 '알고 있었다'.

Her physician(S) ridiculed(V) the idea(O) but(등위접속사) she(S) was(V) so insistent(C) that(so ~ that: 너무 ~해서 그 결과 …하다) he finally agreed to operate for the removal of the frog.

그녀의 주치의는 그런 그녀의 생각을 비웃었지만, 그녀가 너무 고집해서 그는 마침내 개구리 제거를 위한 수술을 하는 데 동의했다.

Accordingly, he(S) sent(V) her(O) (to a hospital to be prepared for the operation) and(등위접속사) he(S), at the same time, hired(V) a small boy(O) (to catch a frog for him).

그래서 그는 그녀를 병원에 보내 수술 준비를 하게 했고, 이와 동시에 그를 위해 개구리를 잡아 줄 어린 소년을 고용했다.

(To give(부사적용법: ~하기 위하여) the woman the impression that she had really had an operation), an incision(S) was made(V) (in her abdomen), and the doctor(S) showed(V) her(I.O) the "frog"(D.O) (in a bottle of alcohol), (which(관계대명사) had presumably been removed from her stomach).

그녀가 실제로 수술을 받았다는 느낌을 갖게 하려고 그녀의 복부를 절개했다. 그리고 그 의사는 그녀의 배에서 제거된 것으로 (가정)되어 있던 알코올 병 속의 개구리를 그녀에게 보여 주었다.

The woman(S) was delighted(V) and(등위접속사) (the woman was) (at once) recovered, but(등위접속사) only temporarily.

그녀는 매우 기뻐하며 곧 회복되었지만 일시적인 것에 불과했다.

(Three months after the pseudo-operation), she claimed that the first frog had laid some eggs and that she now had two frogs in her stomach.
S V O1 등위접속사 O2

가짜 수술을 받은 지 석 달 후에 그녀는 (그녀의 배 속에 있던) 첫 번째 개구리가 알을 낳았고 이제는 그녀의 배에 두 마리의 개구리가 있다고 주장했다.

| 어휘 |
psychiatrist ⓝ 정신과 의사
stomach ⓝ 위, 복부, 배
ridicule ⓥ 비웃다, 조롱하다, 조소하다, 놀리다
insistent ⓐ 강요하는, 주장하는
impression ⓝ 인상, 느낌
incision ⓝ (특히 외과 수술 중의) 절개
abdomen ⓝ 배, 복부
pseudo- pref 거짓의, 가짜의

| 전문해석 | 한 정신과 의사가 자신의 위 속에 개구리가 있어 배탈이 났다고 주장하는 어느 여성의 사례를 보고했다. 그녀는 소풍 중에 자신이 개구리 알을 삼킨 것으로 '알고 있었다'. 그녀의 주치의는 그런 그녀의 생각을 비웃었지만, 그녀가 너무 고집해서 그는 마침내 개구리 제거를 위한 수술을 하는 데 동의했다. 그래서 그는 그녀를 병원에 보내 수술 준비를 하게 했고, 이와 동시에 그를 위해 개구리를 잡아 줄 어린 소년을 고용했다. 그녀가 실제로 수술을 받았다는 느낌을 갖게 하려고 그녀의 복부를 절개했다. 그리고 그 의사는 그녀의 배에서 제거된 것으로 (가정)되어 있던 알코올 병 속의 개구리를 그녀에게 보여 주었다. 그녀는 매우 기뻐하며 곧 회복되었지만 일시적인 것에 불과했다. 가짜 수술을 받은 지 석 달 후에 그녀는 (그녀의 배 속에 있던) 첫 번째 개구리가 알을 낳았고 이제는 그녀의 배에 두 마리의 개구리가 있다고 주장했다.

| 보기분석 |
✔① Ordinary logical thinking is useless in the consideration of the ailments which are psychiatrical rather than organic.
신체의 병이 아닌 정신의 병을 고려할 때 평범한 논리적 사고는 무의미하다.
② Any form of invalidism can be cured by pseudo-operation. 지문의 내용과 불일치
어떤 형태의 병도 가짜 수술을 통해 치료될 수 있다.
③ Psychological problems should be treated by giving pseudo-medicine. 지문의 내용과 불일치
정신적인 문제는 가짜 약을 줌으로써 치료되어야 한다.
④ To satisfy a patient is very important in the psychiatrical treatment. 언급 안 한 정보
정신치료에서 환자를 만족시키는 것은 매우 중요하다.

| 정답분석 | '자신의 몸에 개구리가 있다고 믿는 사람에게 가짜 수술까지 해 가면서 개구리가 몸에 있지 않음을 확인시키려 했으나 얼마 가지 않아 다시 자신의 몸에 개구리가 있다고 생각하게 되었다'는 내용이다. 이는 정신병의 경우에는 일반적인 논리적 접근 방법이 그 치료에 아무 소용이 없다는 것을 보여 주는 것이므로 ①이 글의 요지로 적절하다.

15 2016 성균관대(A형)

정답 ⑤

| 구문분석 | (In 1979), (when the party introduced the one-child policy), it was believed that coercion was the only way to ensure that population growth did not become unsustainable.
부사절: ~할 때 / 가주어 / V / 진주어 that

1979년 (중국공산)당이 한 자녀 갖기 정책을 도입했을 때 공산당은 강압이 인구증가를 지속가능하지 않게 확실히 하는 유일한 방법이라고 믿었다.

The party has (since) claimed that the policy has helped (to) prevent 400 million births.
S / 부사: 그 이래로 / V / O

그 이후로 공산당은 한 자녀 갖기 정책이 4억 명의 아기들이 탄생하는 것을 막는 데 도움을 주었다고 주장했다.

In fact, there is little evidence (to back this claim).
접속부사 / 유도부사 / V / S

(하지만) 실제로는, 이러한 주장을 지지해 줄 수 있는 증거는 거의 없다.

China's birth rate had been falling (rapidly) (since the early 1970s with the help of little more than education campaigns).
S / V / ~에 지나지 않는

중국의 출산율은 1970년대 초 이후 교육 캠페인에 불과한 것의 도움을 받아 가며 급격하게 하락했다.

등위접속사
The birth rate continued to fall (under the new policy), but other countries have seen similar declines (without resorting to cruelty and oppression).
S V O S V O

새로운 정책(한 자녀 갖기 정책) 아래서 출산율은 지속적으로 떨어졌다. 그러나 다른 나라들은 (한 자녀 갖기 정책 같은) 잔인함과 억압에 의존하지 않고서도 유사한 출생률의 감소를 목격했다.

Their experience suggests [that the more important factors (behind China's lower birth rate) were rising female participation in the workforce, improvements in education, later marriages and the rapidly increasing cost of education and housing].
S V O C V S_1 S_2 S_3 S_4

그들의 경험은 중국의 낮은 출산율 뒤에 있는 중요한 요소들이, 일터에서의 여성 참여의 증가, 교육의 향상, 만혼, 그리고 빠르게 증가하는 교육비용과 주택비용 등이라는 사실을 나타내 보여 주고 있다.

The main effect (of the one-child policy) was to foster egregious human-rights abuses (against the minority (who ignored it).
S V C
관계대명사

한 자녀 갖기 정책의 주된 효과는 한 자녀 갖기 정책을 무시하는 소수의 인민들을 대상으로 한 악명 높은 인권 유린을 조장하는 것이었다.

| 어휘 | **coercion** ⓝ 강압, 강제 **unsustainable** ⓐ 지속할 수 없는 **back** ⓥ 지지하다
resort to ~에 의지하다

| 전문해석 | 1979년 (중국공산)당이 한 자녀 갖기 정책을 도입했을 때 공산당은 강압이 인구증가를 지속가능하지 않게 확실히 하는 유일한 방법이라고 믿었다. 그 이후로 공산당은 한 자녀 갖기 정책이 4억 명의 아기들이 탄생하는 것을 막는 데 도움을 주었다고 주장했다. (하지만) 실제로는, 이러한 주장을 지지해 줄 수 있는 증거는 거의 없다. 중국의 출산율은 1970년대 초 이후 교육 캠페인에 불과한 것의 도움을 받아 가며 급격하게 하락했다. 새로운 정책(한 자녀 갖기 정책) 아래서 출산율은 지속적으로 떨어졌다. 그러나 다른 나라들은 (한 자녀 갖기 정책 같은) 잔인함과 억압에 의존하지 않고서도 유사한 출생률의 감소를 목격했다. 그 나라들의 경험은 중국의 낮은 출산율 뒤에 있는 중요한 요소들이, 일터에서의 여성 참여의 증가, 교육의 향상, 만혼, 그리고 빠르게 증가하는 교육비용과 주택비용 등이라는 사실을 나타내 보여 주고 있다. 한 자녀 갖기 정책의 주된 효과는 한 자녀 갖기 정책을 무시하는 소수의 인민들을 대상으로 한 악명 높은 인권 유린을 조장하는 것이었다.

| 보기분석 |
① female's role in China 중심소재 없음
중국에서 여성의 역할
② China's gender equality 중심소재 없음
중국의 성평등
③ censorship in China 중심소재 없음
중국의 검열
④ China's lower death rate 중심소재 없음
중국의 낮은 사망률
⑤ family planning in China
중국의 가족계획 (정책)

| 정답분석 | 이 글은 중국의 강압적인 가족계획 정책인 한 자녀 갖기 정책의 부정적인 면을 부각시키고 있는 글이다. 보기에서 적절한 명사를 고르라는 것은 이 글 전체를 다루는 중심소재를 고르라는 것이므로 중국에서의 한 자녀 정책을 나타낼 수 있는 ⑤가 적절하다.

16 2019 한양대

정답 ⑤

| 구문분석 | The nineteenth-century fetishism of facts was completed and justified (by a fetishism of documents).
S V

19세기의 사실 숭배는 문서 숭배로 완성되고, 정당화되었다.

The documents were the Ark of the Covenant (in the temple of facts).
S V C

문서는 사실의 성전에 있는 법궤나 다름없었다.

등위접속사
The reverent historian approached them (with bowed head) and spoke of them in awed tones.
S V₁ O V₂
경건한 역사학자는 머리를 숙이고 문서로 다가가 경외감에 찬 어조로 문서에 관해 말하였다.

(If you find it in the documents), it is so.
부사절 S V C
만약 문서에 그렇게 나와 있다면, 그것은 그런 것이다.

등위접속사
But (when we get down to it), what do these documents (— the decrees, the treaties, the rent-rolls, the blue books, the official correspondence, the private letters and diaries —) tell us?
부사절: ~ 때 의문문 도치 S 대시: 동격 V O
그러나 우리가 이 점에 대해 진지하게 검토할 때, 이 문서들—법령들, 조약문들, 지대 장부, 정부 간행물, 공식 서간집, 개인적 편지들과 일기들—이 우리에게 무엇을 말해 주는가?

No document can tell us more than what the author of the document thought, what he thought had happened, and what he thought ought to happen or would happen.
S V I.O D.O₁ D.O₂ D.O₃
그 어떤 문서도 문서 저자가 생각한 것과, 저자가 일어났었다고 생각한 것과, 저자가 일어나야 한다거나 일어날 거라고 생각한 것 이상을 우리에게 말해 줄 수는 없다.

None (of this) means anything (until the historian has got to work on it and deciphered it).
S V O 부사절: ~까지
이것은 역사학자가 그것을 연구해서 해독해 내기까지는 아무 의미도 없는 것이다.

The facts, (whether found in documents or not), have still to be processed (by the historian) (before he can make any use of them).
S 부사절: ~이든지 아니든지 V 부사절: ~ 전에
문서에 있는 사실이든 문서에 없는 사실이든, 역사학자는 사실을 처리하고 난 후에야 사실을 어떻게라도 이용할 수 있는 것이다.

| 어휘 |
fetishism ⓝ 주물 숭배, 물신 숭배 **reverent** ⓐ 경건한 **awe** ⓥ 경외하다
get down to ~에 진지한 관심을 기울이다 **decree** ⓝ 법령, 포고, 명령
rent-roll ⓝ 지대[소작료/집세] 장부 **blue book** (의회나 정부의) 간행물, 보고서
correspondence ⓝ 서신집 **decipher** ⓥ 판독하다, 해독하다

| 전문해석 | 19세기의 사실 숭배는 문서 숭배로 완성되고, 정당화되었다. 문서는 사실의 성전에 있는 법궤나 다름없었다. 경건한 역사학자는 머리를 숙이고 문서로 다가가 경외감에 찬 어조로 문서에 관해 말하였다. 만약 문서에 그렇게 나와 있다면, 그것은 그런 것이다. 그러나 우리가 이 점에 대해 진지하게 검토할 때, 이 문서들—법령들, 조약문들, 지대 장부, 정부 간행물, 공식 서간집, 개인적 편지들과 일기들—이 우리에게 무엇을 말해 주는가? 모든 문서는 문서 저자가 생각한 것과, 저자가 일어났었다고 생각한 것과, 저자가 일어나야 한다거나 일어날 거라고 생각한 것 이상을 우리에게 말해 줄 수는 없다. 이것은 역사학자가 그것을 연구해서 해독해 내기까지는 아무 의미도 없는 것이다. 문서에 있는 사실이든 문서에 없는 사실이든, 역사학자는 사실을 처리하고 난 후에야 사실을 어떻게라도 이용할 수 있는 것이다.

| 보기분석 |
① Nineteenth-century historians were obsessive about facts and documents. 도입부를 말하며 글의 주된 내용이 아님
19세기 역사학자들은 사실과 문서에 대해 강박적으로 집착하였다.
② All documents about the past are treated as historical facts by the historian. 지문 내용과 불일치
과거에 관한 모든 문서들은 역사학자에 의해 역사적 사실로 다루어진다.
③ The necessity of establishing historical facts rests on the quality of the facts themselves. 지문 내용과 불일치
역사적 사실을 확정 지을 필요성은 사실의 속성 그 자체에 달려 있다.
④ Knowledge of the past consists of elemental and impersonal atoms which nothing can alter. 지문 내용과 불일치
과거에 관한 지식은 변경 불가능한 본질적이고 비인격적인 원자들로 이루어져 있다.
⑤ The treatment of documents as a historical fact depends on the element of interpretation by historians.
문서를 역사적 사실로 다루는 것은 역사학자에 의한 해석의 요소에 달려 있다.

| 정답분석 | 사실 및 문서에 대한 집착 그 자체가 역사적 사실을 의미 있게 하는 것이 아니라, 그러한 사실과 문서를 연구하고 해석하는 역사학자들의 작업으로 역사적 사실이 의미 있게 되는 것이라고 필자는 말하고 있다. 따라서 이 글의 요지로는 ⑤가 적절하다.

17 2020 인하대

정답 ⑤

| 구문분석 | A recent study (in the journal *Lancet Planetary Health*) found that airborne pollen counts have been increasing around the world (as average temperatures climbed).

S / V / O — as: 부사절: ~함에 따라

Lancet Planetary Health 저널에 실린 최근 한 연구에 의하면, 평균 기온이 상승함에 따라 전 세계에서 공기 중에 떠 있는 꽃가루의 수가 증가하고 있다고 한다.

The majority of the 17 sites (studied) showed an increase (in the amount of pollen and longer pollen seasons over 20 years).

S / V / O

연구 대상으로 삼은 17개 장소 중 대다수에서 20년 동안 꽃가루의 양이 늘어났고 꽃가루가 날리는 시기도 더 길어졌다.

the 비교급 + S V, the 비교급 + S V: ~하면 할수록, 더 …하다

And the faster the climate changes, the worse it gets.

S V / S V

그리고 기후 변화가 더 빠를수록 상황은 더 나빠진다.

관계대명사

That's why residents of Alaska, (which is warming twice as fast as the global average), now face especially high allergy risks.

S V / C

지구 평균보다 두 배나 빨리 따뜻해지고 있는 알래스카 주민들이 현재 특히 높은 알레르기의 위험에 직면해 있는 것도 이 때문이다.

(Taken together over the long term), seasonal allergies present one (of the most robust examples of how global warming is increasing risks to health).

분사구문 / S / V / O / 명사절

장기적으로 보면, 계절적 알레르기는 지구온난화가 어떻게 건강에 대한 위험을 증가시키고 있는지를 보여 주는 가장 강력한 사례 중 하나를 제시한다.

등위접속사

Allergies are already a major health burden, and they will become an even larger drain (on the economy).

S V C / S V C

알레르기는 이미 건강에 큰 부담을 주고 있으며, 경제를 고갈시키는 훨씬 더 큰 요인이 될 것이다.

"It's very strong. In fact, I think there's irrefutable data," said Jeffrey Demain, director of the Allergy, Asthma, and Immunology Center of Alaska. "It's become the model of health impacts of climate change."

O_1 / V / S = / O_2

"그것은 매우 강력합니다. 사실, 저는 반박할 수 없는 자료가 있다고 생각합니다. 그것은 기후 변화가 건강에 미치는 영향의 모델이 됐습니다."라고 알래스카의 알레르기, 천식, 면역학 센터의 소장인 제프리 디메인(Jeffrey Demain)이 말했다.

And (since so many are afflicted — some estimates say up to 50 million Americans have nasal allergies —) scientists and health officials are now trying to tease out the climate factors (driving these risks) (in the hopes of bringing some relief in the wake of growing pollen avalanches).

부사절: ~ 때문에 / 대시: 부연설명 / S / V / O

그리고 너무나도 많은 사람들이 고통을 받고 있기 때문에—일부 추정치에 따르면, 최대 5천만 명의 미국인들이 알레르기성 비염을 가지고 있다고 한다—꽃가루가 엄청나게 날리는 날이 늘어남에 따라 과학자들과 보건 당국자들은 이 상황을 조금이나마 완화시키려는 바람에서 이러한 위험을 유발하는 기후 요소를 파악하려고 현재 노력하고 있다.

| 어휘 |

pollen ⓝ 꽃가루
climate change 기후 변화
resident ⓝ 거주자, 거류민
robust ⓐ 튼튼한 강건한; 확고한
burden ⓝ 무거운 짐; 걱정, 부담
irrefutable ⓐ 반박할 수 없는, 논파할 수 없는
immunology ⓝ 면역학
impact ⓝ 충돌; 충격, 영향
afflict ⓥ 괴롭히다
estimate ⓝ 평가, 견적; 의견
nasal ⓐ 코의; 콧소리의
tease out (특히 복잡하거나 얻기 힘든 정보 · 의미를) 알아내려고 애쓰다
factor ⓝ 요인, 요소
relief ⓝ (고통 · 곤란 따위의) 경감 제거; 구제
avalanche ⓝ 눈사태; (질문 등의) 쇄도

| 전문해석 | *Lancet Planetary Health* 저널에 실린 최근 한 연구에 의하면, 평균 기온이 상승함에 따라 전 세계에서 공기 중에 떠 있는 꽃가루의 수가 증가하고 있다고 한다. 연구 대상으로 삼은 17개 장소 중 대다수에서 20년 동안 꽃가루의 양이 늘어났고 꽃

가루가 날리는 시기도 더 길어졌다. 그리고 기후 변화가 더 빠를수록 상황은 더 나빠진다. 지구 평균보다 두 배나 빨리 따뜻해지고 있는 알래스카 주민들이 현재 특히 높은 알레르기의 위험에 직면해 있는 것도 이 때문이다.

장기적으로 보면, 계절적 알레르기는 지구온난화가 어떻게 건강에 대한 위험을 증가시키고 있는지를 보여 주는 가장 강력한 사례 중 하나를 제시한다. 알레르기는 이미 건강에 큰 부담을 주고 있으며, 경제를 고갈시키는 훨씬 더 큰 요인이 될 것이다.

"그것은 매우 강력합니다. 사실, 저는 반박할 수 없는 자료가 있다고 생각합니다. 그것은 기후 변화가 건강에 미치는 영향의 모델이 됐습니다."라고 알래스카의 알레르기, 천식, 면역학 센터의 소장인 제프리 디메인(Jeffrey Demain)이 말했다. 그리고 너무나도 많은 사람들이 고통을 받고 있기 때문에—일부 추정치에 따르면, 최대 5천만 명의 미국인들이 알레르기성 비염을 가지고 있다고 한다—꽃가루가 엄청나게 날리는 날이 늘어남에 따라 과학자들과 보건 당국자들은 이 상황을 조금이나마 완화시키려는 바람에서 이러한 위험을 유발하는 기후 요소를 파악하려고 현재 노력하고 있다.

| 보기분석 | ① Allergies are going to get controlled. 언급 안 한 정보
알레르기는 통제될 것이다.
② Pollen is becoming impossible to avoid. 지문의 주요한 내용이 아님
꽃가루는 피하는 것이 불가능해지고 있다.
③ Alaska is too cold to suffer from pollen allergies. 지문 내용과 불일치
알래스카는 너무 추워서 꽃가루 알레르기로 고통받지 않는다.
④ Seasonal allergies play an important role in national economy. 너무 지엽적
계절성 알레르기는 국가 경제에 중요한 역할을 한다.
⑤ Pollen allergy seasons get longer and more intense as temperatures rise.
온도가 상승함에 따라 꽃가루 알레르기의 시즌은 더 길어지고 더 심해진다.

| 정답분석 | 이 글은 '지구온난화로 인해 공기 중에 떠 있는 꽃가루의 양이 늘어나고 꽃가루가 날리는 시기도 더 길어지고 있으며, 그로 인해 건강 문제가 초래되고 있음'을 이야기하고 있다. 따라서 글의 요지로는 ⑤가 적절하다.

18 2016 건국대

정답 ④

| 구문분석 | Greek mythology(S) is largely made up(V) (of stories about gods and goddesses), but(등위접속사) it(S) must not be read(V) (as an account of the Greek religion).

그리스 신화는 주로 남신들과 여신들에 관한 이야기로 구성되어 있다. 그러나 그리스 신화는 그리스 종교의 이야기로 읽혀서는 안 된다.

(According to the most modern idea), a real myth(S) has(V) nothing(O) (to do with religion). [have nothing to do with: ~와 관련 없다]

가장 현대적인 사상에 따르면, 진정한 신화는 종교와 아무런 관련성도 가지고 있지 않다.

It(S) is(V) an explanation(C) (of something in nature, how any and everything in nature came into existence): people, animals, trees or flowers, the stars, earthquakes, all (that is) and all (that happens). [콜론: (세부적) 재진술] [that: 관계대명사]

신화는 자연 속에 있는 어떤 것에 대한 설명이자 자연 속에 있는 어떤 것과 모든 것들이 어떻게 존재하게 되었는가에 대한 설명이다. 사람들, 동물들, 나무들 혹은 꽃들, 별들, 지진들 등 존재하는 모든 것과 생겨난 모든 것에 대한 설명이다.

Thunder and lightning(S), for instance, are caused(V) (when Zeus hurls his thunderbolt)(부사절).

예를 들어 천둥과 번개는 제우스가 벼락을 던질 때 발생한다.

Myths(S) are(V) early science(C), = the result of people's first trying to explain what they saw around them.

신화는 초기 과학이고 그들의 주변에서 본 것들을 설명하고자 하는 사람들의 최초 시도가 야기한 결과이다.

| 어휘 |

mythology ⓝ 신화	**account** ⓝ 진술, 설명; 계좌; 중요성; 고려할 만한 사항
come into existence 존재하게 되다	**thunderbolt** ⓝ 벼락, 번개

| 전문해석 | 그리스 신화는 주로 남신들과 여신들에 관한 이야기로 구성되어 있다. 그러나 그리스 신화는 그리스 종교의 이야기로 읽혀서는 안 된다. 가장 현대적인 사상에 따르면, 진정한 신화는 종교와 아무런 관련성도 가지고 있지 않다. 신화는 자연 속에 있는 어떤 것에 대한 설명이자 자연 속에 있는 어떤 것과 모든 것들이 어떻게 존재하게 되었는가에 대한 설명이다. 사람들,

동물들, 나무들 혹은 꽃들, 별들, 지진들 등 존재하는 모든 것과 생겨난 모든 것에 대한 설명이다. 예를 들어 천둥과 번개는 제우스가 벼락을 던질 때 발생한다. 신화는 초기 과학이고 그들의 주변에서 본 것들을 설명하고자 하는 사람들의 최초 시도가 야기한 결과이다.

| 보기분석 | ① Mythology is often very closely associated with religion. 지문 내용과 불일치
신화는 종종 종교와 매우 밀접한 관련이 있다.
② The most modern idea emphasizes the value of Greek myths. 지문 내용과 불일치
가장 현대적인 아이디어는 그리스 신화의 가치를 강조한다.
③ Greek myths frequently mention natural phenomena in detail. 지문의 주요 내용이 아님
그리스 신화는 자연 현상을 자세히 언급하는 경우가 많다.
④ Greek myths are explanations of nature rather than religion.
그리스 신화는 종교보다는 자연을 설명하는 것이다.
⑤ Science could be better understood by understanding myths. 언급 안 한 정보
과학은 신화를 이해함으로써 더 잘 이해될 수 있다.

| 정답분석 | 이 글은 주로 신화가 종교와 관련이 있는 것이 아니라 과학과 관련이 있다는 것을 다루고 있으므로 글의 요지로는 ④가 적절하다.

19 2012 고려대

정답 ②

| 구문분석 | Ecologists recognize [that reducing the planet to a resource base for consumer use in an industrial society is already a spiritual and psychic degradation].
(Ecologists: S / recognize: V / [that ...]: O / reducing the planet: S / is: V / a spiritual and psychic degradation: C)

생태학자들의 인식에 의하면, 지구를 산업사회 소비자가 이용할 수 있는 자원기지로 환원시키는 것은 이미 정신적, 심리적 타락이다.

Our main experience (of the divine, the world of the sacred), has been diminished (as money and utility values have taken precedence over spiritual, aesthetic, emotional, and religious values in our attitude toward the natural world).
(Our main experience: S / has been diminished: V / as: 부사절 / money and utility values: S / have taken: V / precedence: O)

자연계에 대한 인간의 태도에서 돈과 실용가치가 영적, 미적, 정서적, 종교적 가치보다 우선시되면서 신성한 것, 신성함의 세계에 대한 중요한 경험이 줄어들어 왔다.

not only A but (also) B: A뿐만 아니라 B도

Any recovery (of the natural world) will require not only extensive financial funding but a conversion experience (deep in the psychic structure of the human).
(Any recovery: S / will require: V / extensive financial funding: A / a conversion experience: B)

자연계를 회복하려면 광범위한 재정조달뿐만 아니라 인간 심리 구조 깊숙한 곳의 정신개조가 일어나야 한다.

Our present dilemma is the consequence (of a disturbed psychic situation, a mental imbalance, an emotional insensitivity), none of which can be remedied (by any quickly contrived adjustment).
(Our present dilemma: S / is: V / the consequence: C / none of which: S 부정대명사 of 관계대명사 / can be remedied: V)

현재 우리가 봉착한 난제는 심리적 동요, 정신적 불균형, 정서적 둔감함이 초래한 결과로서, 이들 중 그 무엇도 대응책을 급조함으로써 치유할 수는 없다.

Nature has been (severely, and in many cases irreversibly), damaged.
(Nature: S / has been: V / damaged: C)

이미 자연은 심각하게, 그리고 많은 경우 돌이킬 수 없을 만큼 손상을 입었다.

the same A as B: B와 똑같은 A

Healing can occur and new life can sometimes be evoked, but (only with the same intensity of concern and sustained vigor of action as that (which brought about the damage in the first place).
(Healing: S / can occur: V / and: 등위접속사 / new life: S / can sometimes be evoked: V / but: 등위접속사 / intensity of concern and sustained vigor of action: A / that: B / which: 관계대명사)

치유도 가능하고 새로운 삶을 일으킬 수도 있지만 그러려면 애초에 자연계의 손상을 초래했던 것과 동일한 정도로 상당한 집중적 관심과 지속적 활동이 반드시 필요하다.

Yet, (without this healing), the viability (of the human) is severely limited.
(Yet: 접속부사 / the viability: S / is severely limited: V)

그러나 막상 손상된 자연을 이렇게 치유하지 않는다면 인간의 생존가능성은 심각할 만큼 한계에 봉착하게 된다.

| 어휘 |

ecologist ⓝ 생태학자	**reduce A to B** A를 B로 환원시키다	**resource base** 자원기지
spiritual ⓐ 영적인	**degradation** ⓝ 퇴락, 타락	**sacred** ⓐ 신성한
diminish ⓥ 줄이다, 감소시키다	**funding** ⓝ 재정조달	**financial** ⓐ 재정의, 금융의, 돈의
conversion ⓝ 개조, 개심	**conversion experience** 인간의 믿음이나 신념을 바꾸는 경험	
psychic ⓐ 심리의, 심리적인	**dilemma** ⓝ 난제, 딜레마	**consequence** ⓝ 결과
disturb ⓥ 괴롭히다, 교란시키다	**insensitivity** ⓝ 둔감함	**irreversibly** ⓐⓓ 회복할 수 없을 만큼
intensity ⓝ 강도, 집중도	**vigor** ⓝ 활기	**in the first place** 애초부터
viability ⓝ 생존가능성	**limit** ⓥ 제한하다	

| 전문해석 | 생태학자들의 인식에 의하면, 지구를 산업사회 소비자가 이용할 수 있는 자원기지로 환원시키는 것은 이미 정신적, 심리적 타락이다. 자연계에 대한 인간의 태도에서 돈과 실용가치가 영적, 미적, 정서적, 종교적 가치보다 우선시되면서 신성한 것, 신성함의 세계에 대한 중요한 경험이 줄어들어 왔다. 자연계를 회복하려면 광범위한 재정조달뿐만 아니라 인간 심리 구조 깊숙한 곳의 정신, 신념의 개조가 일어나야 한다. 현재 우리가 봉착한 난제는 심리적 동요, 정신적 불균형, 정서적 둔감함이 초래한 결과로서, 이들 중 그 무엇도 대응책을 급조함으로써 치유할 수는 없다. 이미 자연은 심각하게, 그리고 많은 경우 돌이킬 수 없을 만큼 손상을 입었다. 치유도 가능하고 새로운 삶을 일으킬 수도 있지만 그러려면 애초에 자연계의 손상을 초래했던 것과 동일한 정도로 상당한 집중적 관심과 지속적 활동이 반드시 필요하다. 그러나 막상 손상된 자연을 이렇게 치유하지 않는다면 인간의 생존가능성은 심각할 만큼 한계에 봉착하게 된다.

| 보기분석 | ① It is now time to discard the misconception that environmental destruction is not happening. 언급 안 한 정보
이제는 환경 파괴가 일어나지 않고 있다는 오해를 버려야 한다.
② Humans need to compensate for the damage they have done to nature.
인간은 자연에 가한 피해를 보상해야 한다.
③ There is no means available for reversing the damage done to nature by humans. 지문 내용과 불일치
인간이 자연에 가한 피해를 되돌릴 방법은 없다.
④ Consumption must be curbed in order to replenish the earth's resources for a sustainable future. 너무 지엽적
올바른 지속 가능한 미래를 위해 지구의 자원을 보충하기 위해 소비를 제한해야 한다.

| 정답분석 | 이 글은 자연환경을 소비재로 전락시키는 타락이라는 문제점을 이야기하고 이를 해결할 필요가 있다고 주장하는 글이므로 요지로는 ②가 적절하다. ④의 경우도 주장이지만 소비를 제한해야 한다는 주장은 글에서 주장하는 전반적인 환경 피해 복구 노력에 비해 규모가 작은 답이므로 전체를 포괄하는 요지가 되기에는 부적합하다. ③은 글에서는 인간의 노력 여하에 따라 환경 피해를 복구할 수 있다고 했으므로 정답이 아니다.

20 2013 한양대

정답 ③

| 구문분석 | It(가주어) is(V) the duty(C) (of the man of wealth): first, to set(콜론: 부연설명, 진주어 1) an example of unostentatious living, (shunning(분사구문) display or extravagance); to provide(세미콜론: and 역할, 진주어 2) moderately for legitimate wants of those dependent upon him; and (after doing so) to consider(진주어 3) all surplus revenues which come to him simply as trust funds, (which(관계대명사) he is called upon to administer, and strictly bound as matter of duty to administer in the manner) (which(관계대명사), in his judgment, is best calculated to produce the most beneficial results for the community) — (대시: 부연설명) the man of wealth thus becoming the mere agent and trustee for his poorer brethren, bringing to their service his superior wisdom, experience, and ability to administer.

부자들의 의무는 다음과 같다: 첫 번째, 사치스러운 행위를 보여 주는 것을 멀리하면서 검소한 생활의 예시가 되는 것이며, (둘째로) 그에게 의존하고 있는 사람들의 정당한 요구에 대해 적당한 정도를 제공해야 한다. 그러고 난 다음에는, 그에게 신탁 자금으로 맡겨진 모든 남은 수익에 대해 생각해야 한다. 신탁 기금은 그가 관리하도록 요구받은 것이며, 그가 판단하건대 사회를 위해 최고로 유리한 결과를 생산하도록 계산된 방식으로 의무적으로 관리해야 한다. 따라서 부자들은 그의 가난한 형제들을 위한 행위자이자 수탁자에 불과한 사람으로, 그들을 위해서 자신의 뛰어난 지혜와 경험과 관리 능력을 사용해야 한다.

| 어휘 | unostentatious ⓐ 검소한, 수수한 / shun ⓥ 피하다 / extravagance ⓝ 사치, 방종 / moderate ⓐ 적당한 / legitimate ⓐ 정당한 / surplus ⓐ 나머지의, 과잉의 / revenue ⓝ 소득, 수익 / trust fund 신탁 자금 / in the manner ~하는 방식으로 / trustee ⓝ 수탁자 / brethren ⓝ 형제

| 전문해석 | 부자들의 의무는 다음과 같다. 첫 번째, 사치스러운 행위를 보여 주는 것을 멀리하면서 검소한 생활의 예시가 되는 것이며, (둘째로) 그에게 의존하고 있는 사람들의 정당한 요구에 대해 적당한 정도를 제공한다. 그러고 난 다음에는, 그에게 신탁 자금으로 맡겨진 모든 남은 수익에 대해 생각한다. 신탁 기금은 그가 관리하도록 요구받은 것이며, 그가 판단하건대 사회를 위해 최고로 유리한 결과를 생산하도록 계산된 방식으로 의무적으로 관리해야 한다. 따라서 부자들은 그의 가난한 형제들을 위한 행위자이자 수탁자에 불과한 사람으로, 그들을 위해서 자신의 뛰어난 지혜와 경험과 관리 능력을 사용해야 한다.

| 보기분석 | ① Wisdom doesn't come with wealth. 지문 내용과 불일치
부가 있어도 지혜는 오지 않는다.
② Wealthy men are not necessarily wise. 지문 내용과 불일치
부자가 반드시 지혜로울 필요는 없다.
③ The wealthy need to step in to help the poor.
부유한 사람들은 가난한 사람들을 돕기 위해 나설 필요가 있다.
④ The tension between the wealthy and the poor is unavoidable. 지문 내용과 불일치
부자와 가난한 사람들 사이의 긴장은 불가피하다.

| 정답분석 | 이 글은 부자들의 의무에 관한 글인데, 부자들은 자신의 돈을 사회가 자신에게 맡긴 신탁 자금으로 생각하고, 사회를 위해, 가난한 형제를 위해 최대한 이용하고 관리해야 한다는 내용이므로 이 글의 요지는 ③이 적절하다.

3강 글의 목적 / 어조 / 태도

Practice

01	①	02	①	03	④	04	④	05	②	06	④	07	④	08	②	09	②	10	③
11	③	12	④	13	④	14	②	15	②	16	④	17	③	18	②	19	①	20	③

01 2016 건국대

정답 ①

| 구문분석 | Undoubtedly, the autobiography (of Benjamin Franklin) is riddled (with faults).
S / V
의심할 여지 없이, 벤저민 프랭클린(Benjamin Franklin)의 자서전은 결점투성이다.

It is very muddled, (particularly towards the end).
S / V
특히 자서전의 후반부는 뒤죽박죽이다.

not A but B: A가 아니라 B
It was not written (in a continuous stretch), but rather pasted together (out of separate fragments) (that were written years apart from one another): often, the author could not remember what he had even written (in the previous sections).
S / V_1 / V_2 / 관계대명사 / 콜론: 재진술 / S / V / O
자서전은 연속적으로 쓰인 것이 아니라 서로 몇 년씩 떨어진 시기에 쓰인 별개의 조각 글들을 이어 붙인 것이다: 종종, 저자는 그가 이전 장에서 썼던 것이 무엇인지를 기억해 내지 못했다.

등위접속사
The work often takes an arrogant, condescending tone, yet it praises the virtue of humility.
S_1 / V_1 / O_1 / S_2 / V_2 / O_2
그 작품은 종종 거만하고 생색을 내는 어조를 취하지만 겸손의 미덕을 칭찬한다.

And perhaps most egregious of all, the part of Ben's life (with the most historical significance — the American Revolution —) is entirely omitted (from the work).
등위접속사 / S / 대시: 부연설명 / V
그리고 아마도 가장 악명 높은 점은, 벤저민 프랭클린의 삶에 있어서 그 역사적인 중요성이 가장 큰 시기인 미국 독립전쟁 시절이 자서전 속에서 전부 생략되어 있다는 것이다.

There is no real mention (of events after 1760), 15 years before the outbreak of war.
유도부사 V / S / =
전쟁이 발발하기 15년 전인 1760년 이후의 사건에 대한 실제 언급은 없다.

(At that year) the autobiography simply stops.
S / V
바로 그해에 자서전은 바로 멈춘다.

| 어휘 |
autobiography ⓝ 자서전 **be riddled with** ~ 투성이다 **muddle** ⓥ 혼란시키다
stretch ⓝ 연속 **paste** ⓥ 풀로 바르다[붙이다] **arrogant** ⓐ 거만한
condescending tone 아랫사람 다루듯 하는 말투, 잘난 척하는 말투 **humility** ⓝ 겸손
egregious ⓐ 지독한, 엄청난 **omit** ⓥ 빠뜨리다, 제외시키다

| 전문해석 | 의심할 여지 없이 벤저민 프랭클린(Benjamin Franklin)의 자서전은 결점투성이다. 특히 자서전의 후반부는 뒤죽박죽이다. 자서전은 연속적으로 쓰인 것이 아니라 서로 몇 년씩 떨어진 시기에 쓰인 별개의 조각 글들을 이어 붙인 것이다: 종종, 저자는 그가 이전 장에서 썼던 것이 무엇인지를 기억해 내지 못했다. 그 작품은 종종 거만하고 생색을 내는 어조를 취하지만 겸손의 미덕을 칭찬한다. 그리고 아마도 가장 악명 높은 점은, 벤저민 프랭클린의 삶에 있어서 그 역사적인 중요성이 가장 큰 시기인 미국 독립전쟁 시절이 자서전 속에서 전부 생략되어 있다는 것이다. 전쟁이 발발하기 15년 전인 1760년 이후의 사건에 대한 실제 언급은 없다. 바로 그해에 자서전은 바로 멈춘다.

| 보기분석 | ① critical 비판적인
② praising 칭찬하는, 찬양하는
③ objective 객관적인
④ indifferent 무관심한
⑤ patronizing 생색을 내는

| 정답분석 | 이 글은 주로 Benjamin Franklin 자서전의 결점에 대해서 증거를 나열하여 설명하고 있으므로 정답은 ①이 가장 적절하다.

02 2013 고려대

정답 ①

| 구문분석 | Those people (who become perpetrators of evil deeds) and those (who become perpetrators of heroic deeds) are basically alike (in being just ordinary, average people).

(Those people: S_1, who: 관계대명사, and: 등위접속사, those: S_2, who: 관계대명사, are: V, alike: C)

악행을 저지르는 사람이나 영웅적인 행동을 저지르는 사람이나 보통의, 평범한 사람에 지나지 않는다는 점에서 기본적으로 비슷하다.

The banality of evil is matched (by the banality of heroism).

(The banality of evil: S, is matched: V)

악의 진부함은 영웅주의의 진부함과 일치한다.

Neither is the consequence of dispositional tendencies; nor are they special inner attributes (of pathology) or goodness (residing within the human psyche or the human genome).

(Neither: 등위상관접속사, neither A nor B: A, B 둘 다 아닌, is: V, the consequence of dispositional tendencies: S, are: V, they: S, special inner attributes: C_1, goodness: C_2)

둘 중 어느 것도 기질적 경향의 결과가 아니며, 어떤 특별한 병적인 내적 성향 혹은 선한 내적 성향이 인간 정신이나 인간 유전자 속에 내재되어 있는 것도 아니다.

Both emerge (in particular situations at particular times), (when situational forces play a compelling role (in moving individuals across the line from inaction to action).

(Both: S, emerge: V, when: 부사절: ~할 때, situational forces: S, play: V, a compelling role: O)

악행이나 영웅주의는 모두 특정한 시간의 특정한 상황에서 나타난다. 상황적 힘이 개인을 비행위의 선을 넘어 행위를 하게 만들 때 강력한 역할을 한다.

There is a decisive moment (when the individual is caught up (in a vector of forces) (emanating from the behavioral context).

(is: V, a decisive moment: S, when: 부사절: ~할 때)

개인들이 행동의 맥락에서 나타나는 힘의 영향에 사로잡히게 되는 결정적인 순간이 있다.

Those forces combine (to increase the probability (of acting to harm others or acting to help others).

(Those forces: S, combine: V, to increase: 부사적용법: ~하기 위하여)

그러한 힘들은 다른 사람들에게 해를 끼치거나 다른 사람들을 돕기 위해 행동할 확률을 높이기 위해 결합한다.

That decision may not be consciously planned or taken mindfully but impulsively driven (by strong situational forces).

(That decision: S, may not be consciously planned: V_1, or: 등위접속사, taken: V_2, but: 등위접속사, driven: V_3)

그러한 결정은 의식적으로 계획되거나 마음을 먹고 하는 것이 아니라 강력한 상황적 힘에 의해 충동적으로 강제되었을 수 있다.

(Among them) are group pressures, group identity, diffusion of responsibility, and a focus (on the immediate moment) (without entertaining future cost or benefit).

(are: V, group pressures: S_1, group identity: S_2, diffusion of responsibility: S_3, and: 등위접속사, a focus: S_4)

이러한 힘들에는 집단의 압박, 집단 정체성, 책임의 확산, 미래의 비용이나 이익을 고려하지 않은 당장의 순간에 대한 몰입 등이 있다.

It is important (for our society) to foster the heroic imagination (in our citizens) (by conveying the message) (that anyone is a hero-in-waiting (who will be counted on to do the right thing (when the time comes to make a heroic decision).

(It: 가주어, is: V, important: C, for our society: 의미상 주어, to foster ...: 진주어, the message = that ..., who: 관계대명사, to do: 부사적용법: ~하기 위하여, when: 부사절: ~할 때)

우리 사회는 모든 사람은 영웅적인 결정을 해야 할 때가 오면 그런 올바른 일을 할 수 있으리라고 믿어도 좋은, 그런 영웅이 될 수 있는 사람이라는 메시지를 시민들에게 전달함으로써 시민들에게 영웅적 상상력을 불러일으키는 것이 중요한 일이다.

| 어휘 |

perpetrator ⓝ 범죄자	evil deed 악행	heroic deed 용맹한 행위
banality ⓝ 진부함	heroism ⓝ 영웅적 행위	dispositional ⓐ 성향의
attribute ⓝ 자질, 속성, 성향	pathology ⓝ 병리학	inaction ⓝ 행동을 안 하는 행실
vector ⓝ 충동, 영향, 매개체	emanate ⓥ 나오다, 방사하다	mindful ⓐ 주의 깊은
diffusion ⓝ 전파, 확산	entertain ⓥ 마음에 품다, 생각하다	count on ~을 믿다, ~을 의지하다

| 전문해석 | 악행을 저지르는 사람이나 영웅적인 행동을 저지르는 사람이나 보통의, 평범한 사람에 지나지 않는다는 점에서 기본적으로 비슷하다. 악의 진부함은 영웅주의의 진부함과 일치한다. 둘 중 어느 것도 기질적 경향의 결과가 아니며, 어떤 특별한 병적인 내적 성향 혹은 선한 내적 성향이 인간 정신이나 인간 유전자 속에 내재되어 있는 것도 아니다. 악행이나 영웅주의는 모두 특정한 시간의 특정한 상황에서 나타난다. 상황적 힘이 개인을 비행위의 선을 넘어 행위를 하게 만들 때 강력한 역할을 한다. 개인들이 행동의 맥락에서 나타나는 힘의 영향에 사로잡히게 되는 결정적인 순간이 있다. 그러한 힘들은 다른 사람들에게 해를 끼치거나 다른 사람들을 돕기 위해 행동할 확률을 높이기 위해 결합한다. 그러한 결정은 의식적으로 계획되거나 마음을 먹고 하는 것이 아니라 강력한 상황적 힘에 의해 충동적으로 강제되었을 수 있다. 이러한 힘들에는 집단의 압박, 집단 정체성, 책임의 확산, 미래의 비용이나 이익을 고려하지 않은 당장의 순간에 대한 몰입 등이 있다. 우리 사회는 모든 사람은 영웅적인 결정을 해야 할 때가 오면 그런 올바른 일을 할 수 있으리라고 믿어도 좋은, 그런 영웅이 될 수 있는 사람이라는 메시지를 시민들에게 전달함으로써 시민들에게 영웅적 상상력을 불러일으키는 것이 중요한 일이다.

| 보기분석 |

① earnest 진지한
② ambivalent 반대 감정이 양립하는
③ sardonic 냉소적인
④ haughty 거만한, 오만한

| 정답분석 | 본문에서는 악행이나 영웅주의는 기질적 결과가 아니며 특정한 상황에 따라 나타난다고 진지하게 주장하고 있다. 따라서 정답은 ①이 가장 적절하다.

03 2018 건국대

정답 ④

| 구문분석 |

Demarketing (S) (in a tourism context) is (V) the process of discouraging all or certain tourists (C) (from visiting a particular destination).

관광업에서 역 마케팅은 모든 또는 특정 관광객들이 특정 여행지를 방문하려는 의욕을 꺾는 과정이다.

General demarketing (S) occurs (V) (when all visitors are temporarily discouraged from visiting a location) [부사절: ~할 때], usually due to perceived carrying capacity problems.

일반적인 역 마케팅은 어떤 지역을 방문하고자 하는 모든 방문객들을 대개 수용력에 있어서의 인지된 문제로 인해 일시적으로 어떤 장소를 방문하지 못하도록 할 때 일어난다.

A notable example (S) is (V) Venice (C), (where [관계부사] intensive summer crowding occasionally prompts local authorities to run ads (depicting unpleasant scenes of litter, polluted water, dead pigeons and the like).

주목할 만한 예는 베니스인데 이곳은 여름철의 집중적인 인파로 인해 때때로 지방자치 단체들이 쓰레기, 오염된 물, 죽은 비둘기 등의 불쾌한 장면을 묘사하는 광고를 게재하도록 촉구한다.

The assumption (S) is (V) that the brand image of Venice is so strong that such imagery will not cause any permanent damage to the tourism industry (C). [so ~ that: 너무 ~해서 그 결과 …하다]

베니스의 브랜드 이미지가 너무 강해서 그러한 불쾌한 장면들이 관광산업에 영구적인 피해를 주지 않을 것이라는 생각이 깔려 있다.

Most other destinations, however, do not have such a powerful brand and hence are generally reluctant to countermand brand-building efforts (with demarketing).
S / 접속부사 / V_1 / O / V_2 / C

하지만 대부분의 다른 관광지들은 그런 강력한 브랜드를 갖고 있지 않기 때문에 일반적으로 브랜드를 구축하는 노력을 역 마케팅으로 철회하기를 주저한다.

| 어휘 |
demarketing ⓝ 역(逆) 마케팅(수요 억제를 위한 활동)
discourage ⓥ (무엇을 어렵게 만들거나 반대하여) 막다
carrying capacity 적재량, 수용력
notable ⓐ 주목할 만한, 유명한
intensive ⓐ 집중적인
litter ⓝ 쓰레기
reluctant ⓐ 꺼리는, 주저하는
countermand ⓥ (특히 다른 주문을 함으로써 앞의 주문을) 철회하다, 취소하다

| 전문해석 | 관광업에서 역 마케팅은 모든 또는 특정 관광객들이 특정 여행지를 방문하려는 의욕을 꺾는 과정이다. 일반적인 역 마케팅은 어떤 지역을 방문하고자 하는 모든 방문객들을 대개 수용력에 있어서의 인지된 문제로 인해 일시적으로 어떤 장소를 방문하지 못하도록 할 때 일어난다. 주목할 만한 예는 베니스인데 이곳은 여름철의 집중적인 인파로 인해 때때로 지방자치 단체들이 쓰레기, 오염된 물, 죽은 비둘기 등의 불쾌한 장면을 묘사하는 광고를 게재하도록 촉구한다. 베니스의 브랜드 이미지가 너무 강해서 그러한 불쾌한 장면들이 관광산업에 영구적인 피해를 주지 않을 것이라는 생각이 깔려 있다. 하지만 대부분의 다른 관광지들은 그런 강력한 브랜드를 갖고 있지 않기 때문에 일반적으로 브랜드를 구축하는 노력을 역 마케팅으로 철회하기를 주저한다.

| 보기분석 |
① 역(逆) 마케팅의 개념을 소개하려고 너무 포괄적. 본문에서는 관광산업에서의 역 마케팅 개념만 설명함
② 베니스라는 브랜드 이미지의 형성 과정을 소개하려고
③ 특정 여행지를 방문하려는 관광객들에게 정보를 제공하려고
④ 관광산업에서 역(逆) 마케팅이 어떻게 활용되는지 설명하려고
⑤ 불쾌한 장면들을 묘사하는 광고를 만드는 방법을 소개하려고

| 정답분석 | 본문에서는 관광업에서 관광객의 수요를 억제하기 위해 역 마케팅이 어떻게 활용되는지 예를 들어 설명하고 있다. 따라서 ④가 글의 목적으로 가장 적절하다.

04 2017 가천대

정답 ④

| 구문분석 | College and university environments are places (with a special purpose: student learning).
S / V / C / 콜론: 재진술

대학 환경은 특별한 목적을 가진 장소다: (그것은) 학생 학습이다.

(Among the many methods) (employed to foster student learning and development), the use of the physical environment is perhaps the least understood and the most neglected.
등위접속사 / S / V / C

학생들의 학습과 발전을 촉진하기 위해 사용되는 많은 방법들 중에서, 물리적 환경의 사용은 아마도 가장 덜 알려지고 무시되어 온 방법일 것이다.

The physical environment, however, can contribute (to college student learning and development) (in two important ways).
S / 접속부사 / V

그러나, 물리적 환경은 두 가지 중요한 방식으로 대학에서 학생들의 학습과 발달에 도움을 줄 수 있다.

First, the actual features of the physical environment can encourage or discourage the processes of learning and development.
S / V / O

첫 번째는 물리적 환경의 실제 특징은 학습과 발달 과정을 자극할 수도 있고 방해할 수도 있다는 점이다.

Second, the process of designing campus physical environments can also promote the acquisition of skills (important to the process of learning and developing).
S V O
형용사의 후치수식
두 번째는 캠퍼스의 물리적 환경을 설계하는 과정도 또한 학습과 발달 과정에 있어 중요한 기술의 습득을 촉진시킬 수 있다는 점이다.

| 어휘 | employ ⓥ 고용하다; (물건 · 수단을) 쓰다, 이용하다 foster ⓥ 조성하다, 발전시키다
contribute ⓥ 기부하다, 기여하다 feature ⓝ 특징 encourage ⓥ 장려하다
discourage ⓥ 실망시키다; 단념시키다 acquisition ⓝ 습득, 획득

| 전문해석 | 대학 환경은 특별한 목적을 가진 장소다: (그것은) 학생 학습이다. 학생들의 학습과 발전을 촉진하기 위해 사용되는 많은 방법들 중에서, 물리적 환경의 사용은 아마도 가장 덜 알려지고 무시되어 온 방법일 것이다. 그러나, 물리적 환경은 두 가지 중요한 방식으로 대학에서 학생들의 학습과 발달에 도움을 줄 수 있다. 첫 번째는 물리적 환경의 실제 특징은 학습과 발달 과정을 자극할 수도 있고 방해할 수도 있다는 점이다. 두 번째는 캠퍼스의 물리적 환경을 설계하는 과정도 또한 학습과 발달 과정에 있어 중요한 기술의 습득을 촉진시킬 수 있다는 점이다.

| 보기분석 | ① inquisitive 호기심이 많은 ② impassioned 열정적인, 간절한
③ sarcastic 빈정대는, 비꼬는 ④ explanatory 설명하기 위한

| 정답분석 | 본문에서는 '대학에서 학생들의 학습과 발달을 증진시키기 위해 물리적 환경을 활용하는 방법'에 대해 설명하고 있다. 따라서 ④가 정답으로 가장 적절하다.

05 2015 인하대(인문 예체능) 정답 ②

| 구문분석 | (When someone feels better after using a product or procedure), it is natural to credit whatever was done.
부사절: ~할 때 가주어 V C 진주어
어떤 사람이 어떤 제품이나 어떤 방법을 사용한 후, 기분이 나아졌다고 느낄 때, 무엇이 행해졌든, 행해진 그 무엇을 믿는 것은 당연하다.

However, this is unwise.
접속부사 S V C
하지만 이것은 현명한 것이 아니다.

Most ailments are self-limiting, and even incurable conditions can have sufficient day-to-day variation (to enable quack methods to gain large followings).
S_1 V_1 C 등위접속사 S_2 V_2 O
대부분의 질병은 자가 제한적이며, 심지어 불치병도 사이비 치료 방법들이 많은 추종자를 거느리기에 충분할 만큼 날마다 변화를 보인다.

Taking action often produces temporary relief of symptoms (a placebo effect).
S V O
어떤 조치가 취해져도 그 조치는 종종 일시적인 증상 완화를 만들어 낸다(플라세보 효과).

In addition, many products and services exert physical or psychological effects (that users misinterpret as evidence (that their problem is being cured).
접속부사 S V O 관계대명사 =
게다가, 많은 제품과 서비스들은, 사용자들이 자신들이 가지고 있는 문제들이 치유됐다는 증거로 잘못 해석하는 신체적 또는 심리적 효과를 발휘한다.

Scientific experimentation is almost always necessary (to establish whether health methods are really effective).
S V C 부사적용법: ~하기 위하여
과학적 실험은 건강을 증진시키는 방법들이 정말로 효과가 있는지를 확인함에 있어서 거의 항상 필요하다.

| 어휘 | credit ⓥ 믿다, 신뢰하다 ailment ⓝ 질병
self-limiting ⓐ 스스로 제한하는, 자기 제어 방식의 incurable ⓐ 불치의
variation ⓝ 변화 quack ⓐ 가짜 의사의, 엉터리의 symptom ⓝ 증상

placebo effect 플라세보 효과(위약 투여에 의한 심리 효과 등으로 실제로 증상이 호전되는 효과)
exert ⓥ (영향력을) 가하다, 행사하다 **misinterpret** ⓥ 오해하다

| 전문해석 | 어떤 사람이 어떤 제품이나 어떤 방법을 사용한 후, 기분이 나아졌다고 느낄 때, 무엇이 행해졌든, 행해진 그 무엇을 믿는 것은 당연하다. 하지만 이것은 현명한 것이 아니다. 대부분의 질병은 자가 제한적이며, 심지어 불치병도 사이비 치료 방법들이 많은 추종자를 거느리기에 충분할 만큼 날마다 변화를 보인다. 어떤 조치가 취해져도 그 조치는 종종 일시적인 증상 완화를 만들어 낸다(플라세보 효과). 게다가, 많은 제품과 서비스들은, 사용자들이 자신들이 가지고 있는 문제들이 치유됐다는 증거로 잘못 해석하는 신체적 또는 심리적 효과를 발휘한다. 과학적 실험은 건강을 증진시키는 방법들이 정말로 효과가 있는지를 확인함에 있어서 거의 항상 필요하다.

| 보기분석 | ① ironic 반어의 ② skeptical 회의적인, 의심 많은
③ excited 흥분한 ④ humorous 익살스러운

| 정답분석 | 본문에서는 과학적으로 검증되지 않는 치료법들에 대해서 회의적인 태도로 설명하고 있다. 따라서 ②가 정답으로 가장 적절하다.

06 2018 성균관대(인문계 A형)

정답 ④

| 구문분석 | (Like most patriotic Americans), my father was forever buying gizmos (that proved to be disastrous — clothes steamers (that failed to take the wrinkles out of suits but had wallpaper falling off the walls in whole sheets, an electric pencil sharpener (that could consume an entire pencil (in less than a second), a water pick (that was so lively it required two people to hold and left the bathroom looking like the inside of a car wash), and much else.

(Like: 전치사 / my father: S / was forever buying: V / gizmos: O / that: 관계대명사 / —: 대시: 부연설명 / that: 관계대명사, failed: V_1, had: V_2 / that: 관계대명사, and: 등위접속사 / that: 관계대명사, was: V_1, left: V_2)

대부분의 애국적인 미국인들처럼, 나의 아버지는 형편없는 것으로 판명된 장치들을 계속해서 구매해 왔다. 양복의 주름을 없애는 데는 실패했지만 벽지를 벽에서 몽땅 떨어지게 하는 다리미, 1초도 안 되는 시간에 연필 전체를 다 깎아 버릴 수 있는 전기 연필깎이, 너무 수압이 강해서 두 사람이 잡고 있어야 하고, 욕실을 세차장의 내부처럼 보이게 만드는 구강 세척기 등이 있었다.

But all of this was nothing (compared with the situation today).

(But: 등위접속사 / all of this: S / was: V / nothing: C)

그러나 이런 모든 장치들은 오늘날의 상황에 비하면 아무것도 아니다.

We are now surrounded (with items) (that do things (for us) (to an almost absurd degree — automatic cat food dispensers, electric juicers and can openers, refrigerators (that make their own ice cubes), automatic car windows, disposable toothbrushes (that come with the toothpaste already loaded).

(We: S / are now surrounded: V / that: 관계대명사 / —: 대시: 부연설명 / that: 관계대명사 / that: 관계대명사)

우리는 이제 거의 터무니없는 수준으로 우리를 위해 일을 하는 물건들로 둘러싸여 있다. 자동 고양이 사료 분배기, 전기 주스기와 캔 오프너, 얼음을 직접 만드는 냉장고, 자동 자동차 창문, 치약이 이미 장전된 상태로 제공되는 일회용 칫솔 등이다.

People are so addicted (to convenience) that they have become trapped in a vicious circle: The more labor-saving appliances they acquire, the harder they need to work; the harder they work, the more labor-saving appliances they feel they need to acquire.

(People: S / are: V / so ~ that: 너무 ~해서 그 결과 …하다 / :: 콜론: 재진술 / ;: 세미콜론: and 역할 / the 비교급 S V, the 비교급 S V: ~하면 할수록 더 …하다)

사람들이 편리함에 너무 중독되어 악순환에 빠져 있다: 사람들이 노동을 덜어 주는 기기를 많이 구입할수록, 더 열심히 일해야 하고, 더 열심히 일할수록, 더 많은 노동력을 절약하는 가전제품을 구입해야 한다고 느끼게 된다.

| 어휘 | **patriotic** ⓐ 애국적인 **gizmo** ⓝ 간단한 장치 **disastrous** ⓐ 처참한, 형편없는
wallpaper ⓝ 벽지 **pencil sharpener** ⓝ 연필깎이 **surround** ⓥ 에워싸다, 둘러싸다

absurd ⓐ 터무니없는　　to a degree 대단히, 매우

dispenser ⓝ 디스펜서(손잡이나 단추 등을 눌러 안에 든 것을 바로 뽑아 쓰는 장치)

load ⓥ (재료를) 넣다, (사람이나 짐을) 태우다　　addicted ⓐ 중독된

trap ⓥ 덫을 놓다　　labor-saving ⓐ 노동력 절약형의　　appliance ⓝ 가전제품, 기기

| 전문해석 | 대부분의 애국적인 미국인들처럼, 나의 아버지는 형편없는 것으로 판명된 장치들을 계속해서 구매해 왔다. 양복의 주름을 없애는 데는 실패했지만 벽지를 벽에서 몽땅 떨어지게 하는 다리미, 1초도 안 되는 시간에 연필 전체를 다 깎아 버릴 수 있는 전기 연필깎이, 너무 수압이 강해서 두 사람이 잡고 있어야 하고, 욕실을 세차장의 내부처럼 보이게 만드는 구강 세척기 등이 있었다. 그러나 이런 모든 장치들은 오늘날의 상황에 비하면 아무것도 아니다. 우리는 이제 거의 터무니없는 수준으로 우리를 위해 일을 하는 물건들로 둘러싸여 있다. 자동 고양이 사료 분배기, 전기 주스기와 캔 오프너, 얼음을 직접 만드는 냉장고, 자동 자동차 창문, 치약이 이미 장전된 상태로 제공되는 일회용 칫솔 등이다. 사람들이 편리함에 너무 중독되어 악순환에 빠져 있다: 사람들이 노동을 덜어 주는 기기를 많이 구입할수록, 더 열심히 일해야 하고, 더 열심히 일할수록, 더 많은 노동력을 절약하는 가전제품을 구입해야 한다고 느끼게 된다.

| 보기분석 |
① agitating 선동하는, 동요하게 하는
② irritating 신경 쓰이게 하는
③ optimistic 낙관적인, 낙천적인
④ cynical 냉소적인, 비꼬는
⑤ gloomy 울적한, 침울한

| 정답분석 | 본문에서 저자는 현대인들이 터무니없는 여러 가지 물건들에 둘러싸여 편리함만을 추구하고 이에 중독되는 악순환에 빠져 있다며 냉소적인 태도로 서술하고 있다. 따라서 이 글의 어조로 적절한 것은 ④이다.

07 2012 서강대　　정답 ④

| 구문분석 | Medical robots(S) are(V), (for the most part), tools(C) (to enhance a doctor's or a therapist's techniques — like(전치사) orthotic devices, (which(관계대명사) help(V_1) improve motor control and range of motion (after a stroke or other trauma) and(등위접속사) can offer(V_2) modified degrees of assistance(O) (as the patient recovers)(부사절: ~함에 따라서).

(대시: 부연설명)

의료용 로봇은 대체로 의사나 치료사들의 기술을 향상시키는 도구들—뇌졸중이나 기타 외상 후 운동 제어 및 운동의 범위를 향상시키는 데 도움을 주는 교정 장치 같은 것들—이고 의료용 로봇은 환자가 회복함에 따라 다양한 정도의 도움을 제공할 수도 있다.

Allison Okamura(S), (=) a professor of mechanical engineering at Johns Hopkins in Baltimore, Maryland, is studying(V), (along with a team of neuroscientists), the potential applications of a robotic external skeleton(O) (for patients) (who(관계대명사) have suffered brain damage).

메릴랜드주 볼티모어에 있는 존스 홉킨스 대학 기계공학과 교수 앨리슨 오카무라(Allison Okamura)는 신경 과학자팀과 함께 뇌 손상을 입은 환자들을 위한 로봇 외부 골격의 잠재적 적용 가능성에 대해 연구하고 있다.

Such patients(S_1) have(V_1) trouble(O_1) (controlling their limbs); (세미콜론: 부연설명) the external skeleton robot(S_2) would encase(V_2) their arms(O_2) and(등위접속사) coordinate(V_3) physical movements(O_3).

이러한 환자들은 자신의 손발을 잘 통제하는 데 어려움을 겪는다; 외부 골격 로봇은 그들의 팔을 감싸고 신체의 움직임을 조정한다.

The patient(S) could use(V) the robot(O) (until he recovered(부사절: ~할 때까지), or(등위접속사) perhaps for the rest of his life) (if the debility persisted)(부사절: 만약 ~라면).

환자는 회복될 때까지 이 로봇을 이용할 수 있고 또는 만일 그의 장애가 지속된다면, 평생 로봇을 이용할 수도 있다.

| 어휘 |
therapist ⓝ 치료 전문가, 치료사　　orthotic device 교정 장치　　motor control 운동 제어

stroke ⓝ 발작, 뇌졸중　　trauma ⓝ 외상(성 증상)　　neuroscientist ⓝ 신경 과학자

external skeleton 외골격　　have trouble ~ing ~하는 데 어려움을 겪다
limb ⓝ 손발, 사지　　encase ⓥ (특히 보호하기 위해) 감싸다, 둘러싸다
coordinate ⓥ 조정하다, 조화시키다　　demise ⓝ 서거, 사망　　debility ⓝ (육체적인) 약함

| 전문해석 | 의료용 로봇은 대체로 의사나 치료사들의 기술을 향상시키는 도구들—뇌졸중이나 기타 외상 후 운동 제어 및 운동의 범위를 향상시키는 데 도움을 주는 교정 장치 같은 것들—이고 의료용 로봇은 환자가 회복함에 따라 다양한 정도의 도움을 제공할 수도 있다. 메릴랜드주 볼티모어에 있는 존스 홉킨스 대학 기계공학과 교수 앨리슨 오카무라(Allison Okamura)는 신경 과학자팀과 함께 뇌 손상을 입은 환자들을 위한 로봇 외부 골격의 잠재적 적용 가능성에 대해 연구하고 있다. 이러한 환자들은 자신의 손발을 잘 통제하는 데 어려움을 겪는다; 외부 골격 로봇은 그들의 팔을 감싸고 신체의 움직임을 조정한다. 환자는 회복될 때까지 이 로봇을 이용할 수 있고 또는 만일 그의 장애가 지속된다면, 평생 로봇을 이용할 수도 있다.

| 보기분석 | ① truculent 공격적인, 반항적인　　② inspiring 용기를 주는, 고무하는
③ sarcastic 빈정거리는, 비꼬는　　④ expository 설명하는

| 정답분석 | 본문에서는 의료용 로봇의 여러 가지 기능과 활용 목적에 대해 설명하고 있다. 따라서 정답으로는 ④가 가장 적절하다.

08 2015 숙명여대

정답 ②

| 구문분석 | Digital currencies(S), (also known(분사구문) as virtual currencies or cash for the Internet), allow(V_1) people(O) to transfer value over the Internet(O.C), but(등위접속사) are(V_2) not legal tender(C).

가상화폐 또는 디지털 현금이라고 알려져 있는 전자화폐는, 사람들로 하여금 인터넷을 통해 가치를 전달할 수 있게 해 주지만, 법정 화폐인 것은 아니다.

(Because(부사절: ~ 때문에) they don't require third-party intermediaries), merchants and consumers(S) can avoid(V) the fees(O) (associated with traditional payment systems).

전자화폐는 중개인 역할을 하는 제삼자를 요구하지 않기 때문에, 상인들과 소비자들은 기존 결제시스템과 관련된 수수료를 피할 수 있다.

Advocates of virtual currencies(S) also say(V) that (because(부사절: ~ 때문에) personal information is not tied to transactions), digital currencies are less prone to identity theft(O).

가상화폐 옹호자들은 또한 개인 정보가 거래와 관련이 없기 때문에 디지털 화폐는 신분 도용의 가능성이 낮다고 말한다.

Many of the headlines(S) (generated by digital currencies) have focused(V) (on problems with the system).

전자화폐가 만들어 낸 신문기사의 헤드라인들 가운데 상당수는 전자화폐 체계가 가지고 있는 문제점들에 초점을 맞춰 왔다.

(In January), federal prosecutors(S) charged(V) the CEO of BitInstant(O), a major bitcoin exchange company(=), (with laundering digital currency) (through the online drug marketplace).

지난 1월, 연방 검사들은 대형 비트코인 거래소들 가운데 하나인 BitInsant의 최고경영자를 온라인 마약시장을 통해 전자화폐를 세탁한 혐의로 기소했다.

(Although(부사절: 비록 ~일지라도) digital currencies are far from widespread), their growing popularity(S) — and their potential for misuse —(대시: 부연설명) has prompted(V) states(O) to weigh in on the uncharted territory(O.C).

비록 전자화폐는 널리 쓰이고 있지는 않지만, 전자화폐의 증가하는 인기—그리고 전자화폐의 오용 가능성—는 주 정부들로 하여금 아직까지 미지의 영역인 전자화폐 분야를 고려하게 만들었다.

| 어휘 | digital currency ⓝ 디지털 통화, 전자화폐　　virtual ⓐ 가상의
legal tender 법정 통화　　intermediary ⓝ 매개, 중재자, 조정자　　fee ⓝ 요금, 수수료

transaction ⓝ 처리, 거래
identity theft 신원 도용(개인의 금융정보를 이용하여 사기를 치려는 신용도용 범죄)
prosecutor ⓝ 검찰관, 기소검사 **launder** ⓥ (부정한 돈을) 돈세탁하다
weigh in on ~에 대한 의견을 내다, 끼어들다 **uncharted territory** 미지의 영역

| 전문해석 | 가상화폐 또는 디지털 현금이라고 알려져 있는 전자화폐는, 사람들로 하여금 인터넷을 통해 가치를 전달할 수 있게 해 주지만, 법정 화폐인 것은 아니다. 전자화폐는 중개인 역할을 하는 제삼자를 요구하지 않기 때문에, 상인들과 소비자들은 기존 결제시스템과 관련된 수수료를 피할 수 있다. 가상화폐 옹호자들은 또한 개인 정보가 거래와 관련이 없기 때문에 디지털 화폐는 신분 도용의 가능성이 낮다고 말한다. 전자화폐가 만들어 낸 신문기사의 헤드라인들 가운데 상당수는 전자화폐 체계가 가지고 있는 문제점들에 초점을 맞춰 왔다. 지난 1월, 연방 검사들은 대형 비트코인 거래소들 가운데 하나인 BitInsant의 최고경영자를 온라인 마약시장을 통해 전자화폐를 세탁한 혐의로 기소했다. 비록 전자화폐는 널리 쓰이고 있지는 않지만, 전자화폐의 증가하는 인기—그리고 전자화폐의 오용 가능성—는 주 정부들로 하여금 아직까지 미지의 영역인 전자화폐 분야를 고려하게 만들었다.

| 보기분석 | ① adamant 요지부동의, 단호한
② circumspect 신중한
③ imprudent 경솔한
④ insouciant 무관심한
⑤ passionate 열정적인

| 정답분석 | 본문에서 전자화폐의 장점과 문제점들을 이어서 설명한다. 저자는 증가하는 인기와 오용 가능성을 동시에 가지고 있는 전자화폐에 대해 마지막까지 신중한 태도를 취하므로 정답으로는 ②가 가장 적절하다.

09 2011 한양대

정답 ②

| 구문분석 | The idea (that the number of people per square mile is a key determinant of population pressure) is as widespread as it is wrong.
(The idea: S, that: =, is: V, widespread: C / as ~ as ...: …만큼 ~한)

1평방마일당 사람들의 수가 인구 과잉의 중요한 결정 요소가 된다는 생각은 그것이 잘못된 만큼이나 널리 퍼져 있다.

The key issue (in judging overpopulation) is not how many people can fit into any given space but whether the Earth can supply the population's long-term requirement for food, water, and other resources.
(The key issue: S, is: V, how many ... space: C_1, whether ... resources: C_2 / not A but B: A가 아닌 B / whether: ~인지 아닌지)

인구 과잉을 판단하는 데 중요한 쟁점은 얼마나 많은 사람들이 주어진 공간에 들어갈 수 있느냐가 아니라 지구가 식량, 식수 그리고 다른 자원에 대한 사람들의 장기적인 필요량을 공급할 수 있느냐의 문제이다.

Most of the empty land (in the United States), for example, either grows the food (essential to our well-being) or supplies us with raw materials.
(Most of the empty land: S, for example: 접속부사, grows: V_1, the food: O, essential ...: 형용사의 후치수식, supplies: V_2 / either A or B: A이거나 B인)

예를 들어, 사람들이 살지 않는 미국의 땅 대부분은 우리들의 번영에 필수적인 식량 혹은 원자재를 우리에게 공급한다.

Densely populated countries and cities can be crowded only (because the rest of the world is not).
(Densely populated countries and cities: S, can be crowded: V / because ...: 부사절: ~ 때문에)

인구 밀도가 높은 나라들과 도시들은 세계의 나머지 지역들이 그렇지 않기 때문에 붐빌 수 있다.

| 어휘 | **determinant** ⓝ 결정 요소, 결정 인자 **population pressure** 인구 과잉 **widespread** ⓐ 널리 보급된, 만연한
overpopulation ⓝ 인구 과잉

| 전문해석 | 1평방마일당 사람들의 수가 인구 과잉의 중요한 결정 요소가 된다는 생각은 그것이 잘못된 만큼이나 널리 퍼져 있다. 인구 과잉을 판단하는 데 중요한 쟁점은 얼마나 많은 사람들이 주어진 공간에 들어갈 수 있느냐가 아니라 지구가 식량, 식수 그리고 다른 자원에 대한 사람들의 장기적인 필요량을 공급할 수 있느냐의 문제이다. 예를 들어, 사람들이 살지 않는 미국의

땅 대부분은 우리들의 번영에 필수적인 식량 혹은 원자재를 우리에게 공급한다. 인구 밀도가 높은 나라들과 도시들은 세계의 나머지 지역들이 그렇지 않기 때문에 붐빌 수 있다. (미국의 경우 미국의 대부분의 빈 땅은 사람들의 생활과 생존에 필요한 식량과 자원을 제공하기 때문에 인구 과잉이라고 볼 수 없는 반면, 미국이 아닌 인구 밀도가 높은 다른 국가들은 그들의 땅이 사람들의 생존에 필요한 식량과 자원을 충분히 공급하지 않기 때문에 인구 과잉 상태라는 의미이다.)

| 보기분석 | ① wistful 아쉬워하는 ② emphatic 명확한, 단호한 ③ dismayed 실망한 ④ ambivalent 반대감정이 양립하는

| 정답분석 | 본문에서 저자는 '인구 과잉에 대해 사람들의 잘못된 생각이 널리 퍼져 있다'고 말하며 인구 과잉을 판단하기 위한 중요 쟁점에 대해 강한 어조로 설명하고 있다. 따라서 정답으로는 ②가 가장 적절하다.

10 2010 한양대

정답 ③

| 구문분석 | Gee, let's tell all the children (in the land) to read teen magazines so they can become materialistic clones!
(let's tell: V_1, all the children: O_1, to read teen magazines: O.C, so: 등위접속사, they: S_2, can become: V_2, materialistic clones: C)
세상에, 이 땅의 모든 아이들에게 십 대 잡지를 읽어서 그들이 물질주의적 복제품이 되어 보라고 이야기하자!

Let's tell them that Britney Spears is "cool!" and that the Backstreet Boys are "totally dreamy!"
(Let's tell: V, them: I.O, that Britney Spears is "cool!": $D.O_1$, and: 등위접속사, that the Backstreet Boys are "totally dreamy!": $D.O_2$)
그들에게 브리트니 스피어스는 '근사하고', 백스트리트 보이즈는 '매우 멋지다'라고 말하자.

And (while we're at it), let's make the kids feel really bad (about themselves) (if they don't look like they're made of plastic).
(And: 등위접속사, while we're at it: 부사절: ~하는 동안, let's make: V, the kids: O, feel really bad: O.C, if ~: 부사절: 만약 ~라면)

그리고 우리가 이런 일을 하는 동안 만약에 그들이 플라스틱으로 만들어진 것처럼 보이지 않는다면 아이들이 스스로에게 좋지 않은 감정을 갖게끔 하자.

With magazines like this, it's no wonder there are 12-YEAR-OLDS (that want breast implants).
(it: 가주어, 's: V, no wonder: C, (that) 진주어 that 생략, that: 관계대명사)
이와 같은 잡지가 있으니 12살짜리 아이들이 가슴성형 수술을 하고 싶은 것도 당연하다.

Hey Kids! Just ask Mommy and Daddy to buy you an entire new body!
(ask: V, Mommy and Daddy: O, to buy you an entire new body: O.C)
얘들아! 엄마, 아빠에게 완전히 새로운 몸뚱이를 사 달라고 해라!

(If they really love you), they will.
(If ~: 부사절: 만약 ~라면)
부모님께서 진정으로 너희를 사랑한다면, 그렇게 해 주실 것이다.

| 어휘 | **materialistic** ⓐ 물질만능주의적인 **clone** ⓝ 복제품
implant ⓝ (수술을 통해 인체에) 주입하는 물질

| 전문해석 | 세상에, 이 땅의 모든 아이들에게 십 대 잡지를 읽어서 그들이 물질주의적 복제품이 되어 보라고 이야기하자! 그들에게 브리트니 스피어스는 '근사하고', 백스트리트 보이즈는 '매우 멋지다'라고 말하자. 그리고 우리가 이런 일을 하는 동안 만약에 그들이 플라스틱으로 만들어진 것처럼 보이지 않는다면 아이들이 스스로에게 좋지 않은 감정을 갖게끔 하자. 이와 같은 잡지가 있으니 12살짜리 아이들이 가슴성형 수술을 하고 싶은 것도 당연하다. 얘들아! 엄마, 아빠에게 완전히 새로운 몸뚱이를 사 달라고 해라! 부모님께서 진정으로 너희를 사랑한다면, 그렇게 해 주실 것이다.

| 보기분석 | ① comic 익살스러운, 우스운 ② neutral 중립적인 ③ sarcastic 빈정대는, 비꼬는 ④ entertaining 재미있는, 즐거움을 주는

| 정답분석 | 본문에서 작가는 십 대 잡지에 나오는 내용이 아이들을 물질주의적 복제품으로 만들고 부적절한 성형을 원하도록 만든다고 비꼬고 있다. 따라서 정답으로는 ③이 가장 적절하다.

11 2017 건국대(A형)

정답 ③

| 구문분석 | How often do(V) we(S) hear comments(O) such as(전치사: ~와 같은) these:(콜론: 재진술) "I hate advertising," or "There's too much advertising in the world!"

우리는 얼마나 자주 이런 말을 듣는가: "나는 광고를 싫어한다" 또는 "세상에는 광고가 너무 많다!"

(In the 21st century), it(가주어) seems(V) that(진주어 that) advertising is everywhere we look. We(S) see(V) it(O) (along highways, in trains, buses, even in taxicabs, as well as(as well as: ~뿐만 아니라) on the Internet and on TV).

21세기에는 광고가 우리가 보는 모든 곳에 있는 것처럼 보인다. 우리는 고속도로, 기차, 버스, 심지어 택시, 인터넷과 TV에서도 그것을 볼 수 있다.

It(가주어)'s(V) hard(C) to escape advertising(진주어).

광고에서 벗어나는 것은 어렵다.

But(등위접속사) do(V) we(S) really want to?

그러나 우리는 정말 광고를 피하기를 원하는가?

Actually, (when you think about it)(부사절: ~할 때), advertising(S) provides(V) us(O) (with quite a few benefits).

사실, 당신이 그것에 대해 생각해 볼 때, 광고는 우리에게 꽤 많은 이점을 제공한다.

First, advertising(S) gives(V) us(O) information(O) (that(관계대명사) we need).

첫째, 광고는 우리가 필요로 하는 정보를 제공한다.

For instance(접속부사), (if you want to buy a new appliance or a new car)(부사절: 만약 ~라면), you(S) can look(V) for the best "deals" in ads (that(관계대명사) appear in newspapers, in magazines, on television, or even on the radio).

예를 들어, 당신이 새로운 가전제품이나 새 자동차를 사고 싶다면, 당신은 신문, 잡지, 텔레비전 또는 심지어 라디오에 나오는 광고에서 최상의 '거래'를 찾아볼 수 있다.

(Besides providing information), advertising(S) also supports(V) the entertainment industry, including television and radio(O).

광고는 정보를 제공하는 것 이외에도 텔레비전과 라디오를 비롯한 엔터테인먼트 사업을 지원한다.

It(가주어) may be(V) annoying(C) to sit through commercials(진주어) (during your favorite TV show), but(등위접속사) the advertisers(S) have paid(V) for its production.

당신이 좋아하는 TV쇼를 보는 동안 광고를 보는 것은 귀찮을 수도 있지만, 광고주들은 그것의 제작비를 지불해 왔다.

This(S), in turn(접속부사), pays(V) the TV crew(O) (for their work).

이것은, 차례로, TV 제작진에게 그들의 일에 대한 보수로 지불되는 것이다.

| 어휘 | **annoying** ⓐ 짜증스러운 **sit through** 끝까지 자리를 지키다 **crew** ⓝ 승무원, 무리, 일당

| 전문해석 | 우리는 얼마나 자주 이런 말을 듣는가: "나는 광고를 싫어한다" 또는 "세상에는 광고가 너무 많다!" 21세기에는 광고가 우리가 보는 모든 곳에 있는 것처럼 보인다. 우리는 고속도로, 기차, 버스, 심지어 택시, 인터넷과 TV에서도 그것을 볼 수 있다. 광고에서 벗어나는 것은 어렵다. 그러나 우리는 정말 광고를 피하기를 원하는가? 사실, 당신이 그것에 대해 생각해 볼 때, 광고는 우리에게 꽤 많은 이점을 제공한다. 첫째, 광고는 우리가 필요로 하는 정보를 제공한다. 예를 들어, 당신이 새로운 가전제품이나 새 자동차를 사고 싶다면, 당신은 신문, 잡지, 텔레비전 또는 심지어 라디오에 나오는 광고에서 최상의 '거래'를 찾아볼 수 있다. 광고는 정보를 제공하는 것 이외에도 텔레비전과 라디오를 비롯한 엔터테인먼트 사업을 지원한다. 당신이 좋아하는 TV쇼를 보는 동안 광고를 보는 것은 귀찮을 수도 있지만, 광고주들은 그것의 제작비를 지불해 왔다. 이것은, 차례로, TV 제작진에게 그들의 일에 대한 보수로 지불되는 것이다.

| 보기분석 | ① sardonic 냉소적인
③ defensive 옹호하는
⑤ skeptical 회의적인
② indifferent 무관심한
④ opponent 반대하는

| 정답분석 | 본문의 다섯 번째 문장부터 내용이 역접되면서 광고가 제공하는 이점들을 설명한다. 따라서 저자는 광고를 옹호하고 있으며 정답으로는 ③이 가장 적절하다.

12 2018 강남대(인문계A형)

정답 ④

| 구문분석 | American women (S) should stop (V) buying so-called women's magazines (O), (because (부사절: ~ 때문에) these publications lower their self-respect).

미국 여성들은 소위 여성잡지를 사는 것을 중단해야 한다. 왜냐하면 이러한 잡지들은 여성의 자존감을 낮추기 때문이다.

First of all, publications (S) (like *Glamour* and *Cosmopolitan*) appeal (V) to women's insecurities (in order to make millions).

무엇보다도, 글래머(Glamour)와 코스모폴리탄(Cosmopolitan)과 같은 출판물들은 수백만 달러의 수익을 올리기 위해 여성들의 불안감에 호소한다.

Topics (like (전치사) "Ten Days to Your More Slender Waist" and "How to Attract Mr. Right") lure women to buy seven million copies per month (O), reports (V) Donna Kato (S) (in *The Miami Herald*, March 8, 2013).

2013년 3월 8일 *The Miami Herald*에서 도나 카토(Donna Kato)는 "10일 만에 더 날씬한 허리를 가지는 방법" 그리고 "이상적인 남자를 유혹하는 방법"과 같은 주제들이 여성들로 하여금 매달 7백만 부를 구매하도록 유혹한다고 보도한다.

The message: (콜론: 재진술) women (S) need (V) to improve (O).

그 보도의 메시지: 여성들이 개선할 필요가 있다는 것이다.

Second, (although (부사절: 비록 ~일지라도) many people — (대시: 부연설명) especially magazine publishers — claim these periodicals build self-esteem), they (S) really do (V) the opposite (O).

둘째로, 비록 많은 사람들, 특히 잡지 출판업자들이 이러한 정기 간행물들이 자존감을 형성한다고 주장하지만, 그것들은 정말로 그 반대이다.

One expert (S) (in readers' reactions), Deborah, says (V) that almost all women, (regardless of age or education), feel worse about themselves after reading one of these magazines (O).

독자들의 반응을 연구한 한 전문가 드보라(Deborah)는 나이와 학력에 상관없이 거의 모든 여성들이 이런 잡지들 중 하나를 읽고 나서 자신에 대해 더 나쁘게 느낀다고 말한다.

Alice (S), (=) one of the women I spoke with, is (V) a good example (C): (콜론: 재진술) "I (S) flip through (V_1) pictures of world-class beauties and six-foot-tall skinny women, and (등위접속사) compare (V_2) myself to them.

나와 이야기를 나눴던 여성 중 한 명인 앨리스(Alice)가 좋은 예이다. 그녀는 "저는 세계적인 미인들과 키가 6피트인 마른 여성들의 사진들을 훑어보고는 그들과 저를 비교합니다.

In more ways than one, I (S) come up short (V)."

여러 면에서 저는 부족합니다."라고 말한다.

Finally, (if women spent the money and time these magazines cost to undertake more self-loving
부사절: 만약 ~라면
activities — studying new subjects, developing mental or physical fitness, setting goals and daring to
대시: 부연설명
achieve them —) they would really build self-worth.
S V O
마지막으로, 만약 여성들이 이런 잡지에 드는 돈과 시간을 더 많은 자기애적인 활동들—새로운 주제를 공부하고 정신 또는 신체를 단련하고, 목표를 세우고 그것을 달성하려고 대담하게 도전하는 등—을 하는 데 쓴다면, 그들은 진정으로 자부심을 키우게 될 것이다.

Sisters, seek wisdom, create what you envision, and above all, know that you can!
S V_1 O_1 V_2 O_2 등위접속사 V_3 O_3
여성들이여, 지혜를 추구하고 여러분이 마음에 그리는 것을 창조하고, 무엇보다도 여러분이 할 수 있다는 것을 알자!

| 어휘 |
so-called ⓐ 소위, 이른바
self-respect ⓝ 자기 존중, 자존심
insecurity ⓝ 불안, 불안감
slender ⓐ 날씬한, 호리호리한
Mr. Right 이상형
periodical ⓝ 정기 간행물
flip through ~을 훑어보다, ~을 휙휙 넘기다
skinny ⓐ 깡마른
come up short 기대에 미치지 못하다
undertake ⓥ (책임을 맡아서) 착수하다, 시작하다
self-loving ⓐ 자기애의
fitness ⓝ 건강
self-worth ⓝ 자부심
envision ⓥ 그리다, 상상하다

| 전문해석 | 미국 여성들은 소위 여성잡지를 사는 것을 중단해야 한다. 왜냐하면 이러한 잡지들은 여성의 자존감을 낮추기 때문이다. 무엇보다도, 글래머(Glamour)와 코스모폴리탄(Cosmopolitan)과 같은 출판물들은 수백만 달러의 수익을 올리기 위해 여성들의 불안감에 호소한다. 2013년 3월 8일 *The Miami Herald*에서 도나 카토(Donna Kato)는 "10일 만에 더 날씬한 허리를 가지는 방법" 그리고 "이상적인 남자를 유혹하는 방법"과 같은 주제들이 여성들로 하여금 매달 7백만 부를 구매하도록 유혹한다고 보도한다. 그 보도의 메시지: 여성들이 개선할 필요가 있다는 것이다. 둘째로, 비록 많은 사람들, 특히 잡지 출판업자들이 이러한 정기 간행물들이 자존감을 형성한다고 주장하지만, 그것들은 정말로 그 반대이다. 독자들의 반응을 연구한 한 전문가 드보라(Deborah)는 나이와 학력에 상관없이 거의 모든 여성들이 이런 잡지들 중 하나를 읽고 나서 자신에 대해 더 나쁘게 느낀다고 말한다. 나와 이야기를 나눴던 여성 중 한 명인 앨리스(Alice)가 좋은 예이다. 그녀는 "저는 세계적인 미인들과 키가 6피트인 마른 여성들의 사진들을 훑어보고는 그들과 저를 비교합니다. 여러 면에서 저는 부족합니다."라고 말한다. 마지막으로, 만약 여성들이 이런 잡지에 드는 돈과 시간을 더 많은 자기애적인 활동들—새로운 주제를 공부하고 정신 또는 신체를 단련하고, 목표를 세우고 그것을 달성하려고 대담하게 도전하는 등—을 하는 데 쓴다면, 그들은 진정으로 자부심을 키우게 될 것이다. 여성들이여, 지혜를 추구하고 여러분이 마음에 그리는 것을 창조하고, 무엇보다도 여러분이 할 수 있다는 것을 알자!

| 보기분석 |
① description 본문에 포함되어 있으나 궁극적 목적과는 거리가 멀다.
묘사, 서술
② definition 본문에 포함되어 있으나 궁극적 목적과는 거리가 멀다.
정의
③ analysis
분석
④ persuasion
설득

| 정답분석 | 본문에서 작가는 여성의 자존감을 낮추는 여성 잡지를 구매하는 대신에 자부심을 키울 수 있는 활동을 하도록 촉구하고 있다. 따라서 정답으로는 ④가 가장 적절하다.

13 2019 상명대

정답 ④

| 구문분석 | Thousands of people will go into the bush this summer (to cut the high cost of living).
S V 부사적용법: ~하기 위하여
수천 명의 사람들이 이번 여름에 높은 생활비를 줄이기 위해 숲으로 들어갈 것이다.

A man (who gets his two weeks' salary) (while he is on vacation) should be able to put those two weeks in
S 관계대명사 부사절: ~하는 동안 V_1 C_1
fishing and camping and be able to save one week's salary clear.
등위접속사 V_2 C_2
휴가 중에 2주 치의 월급을 받는 사람은 그 2주 동안 낚시와 캠핑을 할 수 있을 것이고 1주 치의 월급을 확실하게 절약할 수 있을 것이다.

He ought to be able to sleep comfortably every night, to eat well every day and to return to the city rested and in good condition.

S V C_1 C_2 등위접속사 C_3

그는 매일 밤 편안하게 잠을 자고, 매일 잘 먹고, 휴식을 취하고 컨디션이 좋은 상태로 도시로 돌아올 수 있을 것이다.

등위접속사
But (if he goes into the woods with a frying pan), an ignorance (of black flies and mosquitoes), and a great and abiding lack (of knowledge about cookery), the chances are that his return will be very different.

부사절: 만약 ~라면 / 등위접속사 / S V C

하지만 만약 그가 프라이팬을 들고 숲으로 들어간다면, 흑파리와 모기에 대한 무지, 요리에 대한 크고 지속적인 지식 부족으로 그의 복귀는 매우 다를 것이다.

He will come back (with enough mosquito bites) (to make the back of his neck look like a relief map of the Caucasus).

S V

그는 목 뒤에 코카서스의 입체모형 지도처럼 보이는 모기 물린 상처를 가지고 돌아올 것이다.

His digestion will be wrecked (after a valiant battle (to assimilate half-cooked or charred grub).

S V 부사적용법: ~하기 위하여

그의 소화 기능은 반쯤 익었거나 검게 탄 음식을 소화하기 위해 용맹한 전투를 벌인 끝에 파괴될 것이다.

And he won't have had a decent night's sleep (while he has been gone).

S V O 부사절: ~하는 동안

그리고 그는 숲에서 지내는 동안 하룻밤도 제대로 잠을 자지 못할 것이다.

등위접속사
He will solemnly raise his right hand and inform you that he has joined the grand army of never-agains.

S V_1 O V_2 I.O D.O

그는 다시는 가고 싶지 않은 휴가의 대열에 자신이 동참했음을 엄숙하게 오른손을 들고 당신에게 알려 줄 것이다.

| 어휘 |

bush ⓝ 숲	**salary** ⓝ 급여, 월급	**rested** ⓐ 피로가 풀린
ignorance ⓝ 무지, 무식	**abiding** ⓐ 지속적인, 영속적인	**cookery** ⓝ 요리, 요리법
relief map 입체모형 지도	**digestion** ⓝ 소화; 소화력	**wreck** ⓥ 파괴하다, 망가뜨리다
valiant ⓐ 용감한	**assimilate** ⓥ (음식물을) 소화[흡수]하다	
half-cooked ⓐ 설익은	**charred** ⓐ 새까맣게 탄	**solemnly** ⓐⓓ 엄숙하게, 진지하게

| 전문해석 | 수천 명의 사람들이 이번 여름에 높은 생활비를 줄이기 위해 숲으로 들어갈 것이다. 휴가 중에 2주 치의 월급을 받는 사람은 그 2주 동안 낚시와 캠핑을 할 수 있을 것이고 1주 치의 월급을 확실하게 절약할 수 있을 것이다. 그는 매일 밤 편안하게 잠을 자고, 매일 잘 먹고, 휴식을 취하고 컨디션이 좋은 상태로 도시로 돌아올 수 있을 것이다. 하지만 만약 그가 프라이팬을 들고 숲으로 들어간다면, 흑파리와 모기에 대한 무지, 요리에 대한 크고 지속적인 지식 부족으로 그의 복귀는 매우 다를 것이다. 그는 목 뒤에 코카서스의 입체모형 지도처럼 보이는 모기 물린 상처를 가지고 돌아올 것이다. 그의 소화 기능은 반쯤 익었거나 검게 탄 음식을 소화하기 위해 용맹한 전투를 벌인 끝에 파괴될 것이다. 그리고 그는 숲에서 지내는 동안 하룻밤도 제대로 잠을 자지 못할 것이다. 그는 다시는 가고 싶지 않은 휴가의 대열에 자신이 동참했음을 엄숙하게 오른손을 들고 당신에게 알려 줄 것이다.

| 보기분석 |

① To inform the benefits of comfortable camping out
편안한 캠핑의 이점을 알려 주기 위해

② To prepare men before joining military camps 언급 안 한 정보
군사 캠프에 참가하기 전에 사람들을 준비시키기 위해

③ To advocate decent camping sites
괜찮은 캠핑 장소를 지지하기 위해

④ To warn the dangers of unprepared camping out
준비가 안 된 캠핑의 위험성을 경고하기 위해

⑤ To describe people's responses after camping out 언급 안 한 정보
캠핑 후에 사람들의 반응을 설명하기 위해

| 정답분석 | 본문에서 저자는 준비가 안 된 상태에서 숲으로 캠핑을 간다면 모기에 물릴 수 있으며 설익거나 탄 음식을 먹어 소화 기능에 장애가 생길 수 있으며 수면에 문제가 생길 수 있다고 경고했다. 따라서 ④가 글의 목적으로 가장 적절하다.

14 2018 경기대 정답 ②

| 구문분석 | (When most people contemplate building a new home), they assume that the first order of business is to choose or design a plan to build.
부사절: ~할 때 / S / V / O

대부분의 사람들이 새로운 집을 짓는 것을 고려할 때, 그들은 사업의 첫 번째 순서는 건축할 계획을 선택하거나 설계하는 것이라고 가정한다.

But, in fact, the first step is always to find the site (that you want to build on).
등위접속사 / 접속부사 / S / V / C / 관계대명사

하지만 실제로, 첫 번째 단계는 항상 집을 짓기 원하는 부지를 찾는 일이다.

(When you work with an architect), you'll find that the design for the house is as much influenced (by the opportunities and constraints of the site) as it is (by your particular functional and aesthetic desires).
부사절: ~할 때 / S / V / O / as ~ as ...: …만큼 ~한

당신이 건축가와 함께 일을 할 때, 당신은 주택의 설계가 특정한 기능적, 미적인 욕망에 의해 영향을 받는 만큼 그 부지가 주는 기회와 제약에도 많은 영향을 받는다는 것을 알게 될 것이다.

This was eminently evident (in one new house I saw a few years ago).
S / V / C

이러한 점은 내가 몇 년 전에 보았던 한 새집에서 두드러지게 드러났다.

The house was positioned (on a hill), (facing south overlooking a magnificent vista), but there was not a single window (looking toward that extraordinary view).
S / V / 분사구문 / 등위접속사 / 유도부사 / V / S

그 집은 웅장한 경치가 내려다보이는 남쪽을 향한 언덕 위에 위치해 있었지만, 그 멋진 전망을 바라보는 창문은 하나도 없었다.

My guess is that the design had been picked out of a plan book (long before the site had been chosen), and the original plan had been designed to be highly energy efficient (with its blind face) (oriented to the north).
S / V / C / 부사절: ~하기 오래전에 / 등위접속사

내 생각에 그 집의 설계는 부지가 선택되기 훨씬 전에 건축도면 책자에서 선택된 것으로 보이며 원래 도면은 창문이 없는 면이 북쪽을 향해 있어서 에너지 효율이 매우 좋도록 설계되어 있었을 것이다.

This new house had the blind face (oriented to the south) just the direction (one wants lots of glass in most climates).
S / V / O / = / the south = just the direction

이 새집은 창문이 없는 면이 남쪽을 향해 있었는데, 대부분의 기후에서는 남쪽으로 많은 창문을 내길 원한다.

| 어휘 |

contemplate ⓥ 심사숙고하다	**site** ⓝ 현장, 부지	**architect** ⓝ 건축가
constraint ⓝ 강제, 구속	**aesthetic** ⓐ 심미적인	**eminently** ⓐⓓ 대단히, 탁월하게
evident ⓐ 분명한, 명백한	**overlook** ⓥ 바라보다, 내려다보다	**magnificent** ⓐ 장엄한, 훌륭한
vista ⓝ 전망, 경치	**extraordinary** ⓐ 대단한, 비범한	**efficient** ⓐ 능률적인, 효과적인
blind ⓐ 앞이 안 보이는		

| 전문해석 | 대부분의 사람들이 새로운 집을 짓는 것을 고려할 때, 그들은 사업의 첫 번째 순서는 건축할 계획을 선택하거나 설계하는 것이라고 가정한다. 하지만 실제로, 첫 번째 단계는 항상 집을 짓기 원하는 부지를 찾는 일이다. 당신이 건축가와 함께 일을 할 때, 당신은 주택의 설계가 특정한 기능적, 미적인 욕망에 의해 영향을 받는 만큼 그 부지가 주는 기회와 제약에도 많은 영향을 받는다는 것을 알게 될 것이다. 이러한 점은 내가 몇 년 전에 보았던 한 새집에서 두드러지게 드러났다. 그 집은 웅장한 경치가 내려다보이는 남쪽을 향한 언덕 위에 위치해 있었지만, 그 멋진 전망을 바라보는 창문은 하나도 없었다. 내 생각에 그 집의 설계는 부지가 선택되기 훨씬 전에 건축도면 책자에서 선택된 것으로 보이며 원래 도면은 창문이 없는 면이 북쪽을 향해 있어서 에너지 효율이 매우 좋도록 설계되어 있었을 것이다. 이 새집은 창문이 없는 면이 남쪽을 향해 있었는데, 대부분의 기후에서는 남쪽으로 많은 창문을 내길 원한다.

| 보기분석 | ① To explain the importance of aesthetic considerations in house construction 언급 안 한 정보
주택 건설의 미적 고려 사항의 중요성을 설명하기 위해
② To show the close connection between the design for a house and its site
집의 설계와 부지 사이에 밀접한 연관이 있음을 보여 주기 위해

③ To offer a step-by-step guide to the house building process 언급 안 한 정보. 본문에서는 건축의 첫 단계인 '부지 찾기'만 언급함.
주택 건축 과정에 대한 단계별 지침을 제공하기 위해
④ To illustrate how to build an energy-efficient house
에너지 효율이 뛰어난 집을 짓는 법을 설명하기 위해

| 정답분석 | 본문에서 저자는 주택의 건축할 계획은 '부지'를 찾는 일부터 시작하며 '부지가 주는 기회와 제약에 많은 영향을 받는다'고 주장한다. 이 주장을 자신이 목격한 사례를 들면서 부연하고 있으므로 글의 목적으로는 ②가 가장 적절하다.

15 2018 한양대, 2015 단국대

정답 ②

| 구문분석 | Experts say that (if you feel drowsy during the day, even during boring activities), you haven't had enough sleep.
S V O / 부사절: 만약 ~라면

전문가들은 만약 여러분이 낮 동안, 심지어 지루한 활동 중에도 졸린다면, 여러분은 충분한 수면을 취하지 못했다고 말한다.

(If you routinely fall asleep within five minutes of lying down), you probably have severe sleep deprivation.
부사절: 만약 ~라면 / S V O
만약 여러분이 누워서 5분 이내에 일상적으로 잠이 든다면, 여러분은 아마도 심각한 수면 부족 상태일 것이다.

The widespread practice (of "burning the candle at both ends" in Western industrialized societies) has created so much sleep deprivation that what is really abnormal sleepiness is now almost the norm.
S V O / so ~ that: 너무 ~해서 그 결과 …다
서구의 산업화된 사회에서 널리 퍼져 있는 관행인 "양쪽 끝의 촛불을 태우는 것(아침부터 밤까지 지나치게 일만 하여 녹초가 되는 것)"은 너무나도 심각한 수면 부족을 만들어 냈기 때문에 정말로 비정상적인 졸림이 이제는 거의 일반적이다.

Many studies make it clear that sleep deprivation is dangerous.
S V 가목적어 O.C 진목적어
많은 연구들은 수면 부족이 위험하다는 것을 분명히 하고 있다.

Sleep-deprived people (who are tested (by using a driving simulator) perform as badly as or worse than those (who are intoxicated).
S 관계대명사 V as ~ as ...: …만큼 ~한 / 관계대명사
운전 시뮬레이터를 사용하여 테스트를 받은 수면 부족자들은 술에 취한 사람들만큼 또는 더 나쁜 결과를 보인다.

Sleep deprivation also magnifies alcohol's effects (on the body), so a fatigued person (who drinks) will become much more impaired than someone (who is well rested).
S_1 V O 등위접속사 S_2 관계대명사 / V C 관계대명사
수면 부족은 또한 알코올이 신체에 미치는 영향을 확대하기 때문에, 술을 마시는 피곤한 사람은 잘 쉬는 사람보다 훨씬 더 손상될 것이다.

(Since drowsiness is the brain's last step before falling asleep), driving (while drowsy) can lead to disaster.
부사절: ~ 때문에 / S V
졸음은 잠들기 전 뇌의 마지막 단계이기 때문에 졸음운전은 재앙으로 이어질 수 있다.

Caffeine and other stimulants cannot overcome the effects (of severe sleep deprivation).
S V O
카페인과 다른 여러 각성제들을 통해 심각한 수면 부족이 미치는 영향을 극복할 수 없다.

The National Sleep Foundation says that (if you have trouble keeping your eyes focused, if you can't stop yawning, or if you can't remember driving the last few miles), you are probably too drowsy to drive safely.
S V 부사절 1: 만약 ~라면 콤마: and 부사절 2 / 등위접속사 부사절 3 O too ~ to ...: …하기에는 너무 ~한
국립수면재단은 만약 여러분이 눈의 초점을 유지하는 데 어려움을 겪거나, 하품을 멈출 수 없거나, 마지막 몇 마일을 운전한 것을 기억할 수 없다면, 여러분은 아마도 너무 졸려서 안전하게 운전할 수 없을 것이라고 말한다.

| 어휘 |

drowsy ⓐ 졸리는, 나른하게 만드는 **sleep deprivation** 수면 박탈, 수면 부족
norm ⓝ 기준, 규범, 모범 **sleep-deprived** ⓐ 수면이 박탈된, 잠이 부족한

simulator ⓝ 모의실험 장치 intoxicated ⓐ (술 · 마약에) 취한 magnify ⓥ 확대하다
fatigued ⓐ 피로해진, 지친 impaired ⓐ 건강이 나빠진 stimulant ⓝ 흥분제, 각성제
yawn ⓥ 하품하다

| 전문해석 | 전문가들은 만약 여러분이 낮 동안, 심지어 지루한 활동 중에도 졸린다면, 여러분은 충분한 수면을 취하지 못했다고 말한다. 만약 여러분이 누워서 5분 이내에 일상적으로 잠이 든다면, 여러분은 아마도 심각한 수면 부족 상태일 것이다. 서구의 산업화된 사회에서 널리 퍼져 있는 관행인 "양쪽 끝의 촛불을 태우는 것(아침부터 밤까지 지나치게 일만 하여 녹초가 되는 것)"은 너무나도 심각한 수면 부족을 만들어 냈기 때문에 정말로 비정상적인 졸림이 이제는 거의 일반적이다.

많은 연구들은 수면 부족이 위험하다는 것을 분명히 하고 있다. 운전 시뮬레이터를 사용하여 테스트를 받은 수면 부족자들은 술에 취한 사람들만큼 또는 더 나쁜 결과를 보인다. 수면 부족은 또한 알코올이 신체에 미치는 영향을 확대하기 때문에, 술을 마시는 피곤한 사람은 잘 쉬는 사람보다 훨씬 더 손상될 것이다. 졸음은 잠들기 전 뇌의 마지막 단계이기 때문에 졸음운전은 재앙으로 이어질 수 있다. 카페인과 다른 여러 각성제들을 통해 심각한 수면 부족이 미치는 영향을 극복할 수 없다. 국립수면재단은 만약 여러분이 눈의 초점을 유지하는 데 어려움을 겪거나, 하품을 멈출 수 없거나, 마지막 몇 마일을 운전한 것을 기억할 수 없다면, 여러분은 아마도 너무 졸려서 안전하게 운전할 수 없을 것이라고 말한다.

| 보기분석 | ① To offer preventive measures for sleep deprivation 언급 안 한 정보
수면 부족에 대한 예방책들을 제공하기 위해서
② To alert the signs and risks of not getting enough sleep
수면 부족의 징후와 위험을 경고하기 위해서
③ To discuss the effects of alcohol on a sleep-deprived person 언급 안 한 정보
술이 수면이 부족한 사람에게 미치는 영향을 논의하기 위해서
④ To explain why sleeplessness is common in Western societies 언급 안 한 정보
서구사회에서 왜 불면증이 흔한지를 설명하기 위해서

| 정답분석 | 본문에서 작가는 어떤 사람이 수면 부족[박탈]에 해당되는지와 수면이 부족한 사람들에게는 어떤 위험이 발생할 수 있는지에 대한 연구 결과를 이어서 소개하고 있다. 따라서 글의 목적으로는 ②가 가장 적절하다.

16 2011 한양대

정답 ④

| 구문분석 | The role of second-hand smoke (in causing disease) has been under study for years.
(S: The role of second-hand smoke / V: has been / C: under study for years)
질병을 일으키는 간접흡연의 역할은 수년간 연구가 진행되어 왔다.

A mid-sized city (in a western state) unexpectedly added to our knowledge.
(S: A mid-sized city / V: added to / O: our knowledge)
서부 주에 있는 한 중소도시가 예상치 못하게 우리의 (간접흡연에 대한) 지식을 더해 주었다.

Smoking (in public and in workplaces) was banned, and six months later the ban was lifted.
(S_1: Smoking / V_1: was banned / 등위접속사: and / S_2: the ban / V_2: was lifted)
공공장소와 직장에서의 흡연은 금지되었다가 6개월 후에 그 금지가 해제되었다.

(During the time that smoking was prohibited in public places), the rate of hospital admissions (for heart attacks) was 24.
(전치사: During / S: the rate of hospital admissions / V: was / C: 24)
공공장소에서 흡연이 금지된 기간 동안, 심장마비로 인한 병원 입원율은 1,000명당 24명이었다.

(During the typical six month period), the rate is 40 admissions.
(전치사: During / S: the rate / V: is / C: 40 admissions)
전형적인 6개월의 경우, 입원율은 1,000명당 40명 수준이다.

Researchers believe that this drop shows the negative effects of second-hand smoke.
(S: Researchers / V: believe / O: that this drop shows the negative effects of second-hand smoke)
연구자들은 이러한 입원율의 감소가 간접흡연의 부정적 영향을 보여 준다고 믿는다.

It adds to the body of evidence that second-hand smoke contributes to heart attacks (by elevating the heart rate and decreasing the ability of blood vessels to dilate).
S V O = 등위접속사
그것은 간접흡연이 심장 박동수를 높이고 혈관이 확장되는 능력을 감소시킴으로써 심장마비에 기여한다는 근거를 더한다.

| 어휘 | second-hand smoke 간접흡연 ban ⓝ 금지, 금지령
lift ⓥ 들어 올리다, 향상시키다, (규제 등을) 해제하다
hospital admission rate 병원 입원 비율 dilate ⓥ 팽창시키다, 넓히다

| 전문해석 | 질병을 일으키는 간접흡연의 역할은 수년간 연구가 진행되어 왔다. 서부 주에 있는 한 중소도시가 예상치 못하게 우리의 (간접흡연에 대한) 지식을 더해 주었다. 공공장소와 직장에서의 흡연은 금지되었다가 6개월 후에 그 금지가 해제되었다. 공공장소에서 흡연이 금지된 기간 동안, 심장마비로 인한 병원 입원율은 1,000명당 24명이었다. 전형적인 6개월의 경우, 입원율은 1,000명당 40명 수준이다. 연구자들은 이러한 입원율의 감소가 간접흡연의 부정적 영향을 보여 준다고 믿는다. 그것은 간접흡연이 심장 박동수를 높이고 혈관이 확장되는 능력을 감소시킴으로써 심장마비에 기여한다는 근거를 더한다.

| 보기분석 | ① elegiac 구슬픈, 우울한
② repressive 억압적인, 탄압하는
③ challenging 도전적인, 도발적인
④ informational 정보를 담은

| 정답분석 | 본문에서는 서부의 한 중소도시의 사례를 통해 간접흡연과 질병과의 관계에 대해 설명하고 있다. 따라서 정답으로는 ④가 가장 적절하다.

17 2017 상명대

정답 ③

| 구문분석 | (When you transport your goods internationally), several precautions must be taken to ensure proper shipment.
부사절: ~할 때 S V

당신의 물건을 국제 운송으로 보낼 때, 적절한 운송을 보장하기 위해 고려해야 할 몇 가지 주의사항이 있다.

Export shipments require greater handling than domestic transport and should be properly packaged and correctly documented (so that they arrive safely and on time).
S V_1 O 등위접속사 V_2 등위접속사 V_3 부사절: ~하기 위하여
수출 화물은 국내 운송보다 더 많은 취급 주의가 필요하며, 물건이 안전하게 제시간에 도착할 수 있도록 적절하게 포장되고 정확하게 문서화되어야 한다.

You also need to make sure that breakable items are protected, and that other fragile goods will not be damaged by the stresses of air and ocean shipment, (such as vibration and moisture).
S V O_1 등위접속사 O_2 전치사: ~와 같은
당신은 또한 파손될 수 있는 물품들이 보호되고, 다른 파손되기 쉬운 물건들이 진동과 습기와 같은 항공운송과 해상운송의 충격에서 손상되지 않도록 조치할 필요가 있다.

You must first decide what mode of transport is best.
S V O
당신은 우선 어떤 운송 수단이 가장 좋은지 결정해야 한다.

(When shipping within a continent), you may prefer land transportation.
부사절: ~할 때 S V O
대륙 내에서 운송될 때, 당신은 육상 교통수단을 선호할지도 모른다.

(When shipping to another continent), the preferred method may be by sea or air.
부사절: ~할 때 S V
다른 대륙으로 운송될 때, 선호되는 방법은 해상 또는 항공운송이 될 수 있다.

(Although maritime shipping is generally less expensive than air), it can be much slower and thus less cost-effective.
부사절: 비록 ~일지라도 / it: S / can be: V / much slower and thus less cost-effective: C / and: 등위접속사

비록 해상운송이 일반적으로 항공운송보다 덜 비싸지만, 훨씬 느릴 수 있고 따라서 비용 효율적이지 않다.

You should consider the additional costs of sea freight, such as surface transportation to and from the docks and port charges.
You: S / should consider: V / the additional costs of sea freight: O / such as: 전치사: ~와 같은

당신은 부두까지 오고 가는 육상 교통비와 항만요금과 같은 해양 화물 운송의 추가 비용을 고려해야 한다.

Ocean freight can take longer than air freight and you may have to wait (until the ship reaches its destination to receive payment).
Ocean freight: S_1 / can take: V_1 / and: 등위접속사 / you: S_2 / may have to wait: V_2 / until: 부사절: ~할 때까지

해상운송은 항공운송보다 더 오래 걸릴 수 있으며, 선박이 목적지에 도착할 때까지 기다려야 대금을 받을 수 있다.

| 어휘 |

transport ⓥ 수송하다, 운반하다 **precaution** ⓝ 조심, 예방책 **ensure** ⓥ 보장하다
fragile ⓐ 부서지기[손상되기] 쉬운 **vibration** ⓝ 떨림[흔들림], 진동 **moisture** ⓝ 습기, 수분
cost-effective ⓐ 비용 효율이 높은 **freight** ⓝ 화물, 화물 운송 **surface transportation** 육상 교통
port charge 항만료

| 전문해석 | 당신의 물건을 국제 운송으로 보낼 때, 적절한 운송을 보장하기 위해 고려해야 할 몇 가지 주의사항이 있다. 수출 화물은 국내 운송보다 더 많은 취급 주의가 필요하며, 물건이 안전하게 제시간에 도착할 수 있도록 적절하게 포장되고 정확하게 문서화되어야 한다. 당신은 또한 파손될 수 있는 물품들이 보호되고, 다른 파손되기 쉬운 물건들이 진동과 습기와 같은 항공운송과 해상운송의 충격에서 손상되지 않도록 조치할 필요가 있다.

당신은 우선 어떤 운송 수단이 가장 좋은지 결정해야 한다. 대륙 내에서 운송될 때, 당신은 육상 교통수단을 선호할지도 모른다. 다른 대륙으로 운송될 때, 선호되는 방법은 해상 또는 항공운송이 될 수 있다. 비록 해상운송이 일반적으로 항공운송보다 덜 비싸지만, 훨씬 느릴 수 있고 따라서 비용 효율적이지 않다. 당신은 부두까지 오고 가는 육상 교통비와 항만요금과 같은 해양 화물 운송의 추가 비용을 고려해야 한다. 해상운송은 항공운송보다 더 오래 걸릴 수 있으며, 선박이 목적지에 도착할 때까지 기다려야 대금을 받을 수 있다.

| 보기분석 |

① To inform freight forwarders about weight limitations 언급 안 한 정보
허용 중량을 화물 운송업자에게 알려 주기 위해서
② To advise importers about insurance policies 언급 안 한 정보
보험 증권에 대해 수입업자에게 조언하기 위해서
③ To provide general information about shipping
운송에 대한 일반적인 정보를 제공하기 위해서
④ To notify exporters about new safety measures 언급 안 한 정보
새로운 안전 조치를 수출업자들에게 통지하기 위해서
⑤ To help freight forwarders save money 너무 지엽적. 운송 비용에 관한 정보는 일부 언급되나 궁극적 목적이라 보기 어려움.
화물 운송업자들이 돈을 절약할 수 있도록 돕기 위해서

| 정답분석 | 본문에서는 적절한 운송을 보장하기 위해 고려할 주의사항들과 육상, 해상, 항공 운송 시 고려해야 할 정보를 제공하고 있다. 따라서 이 글의 목적으로 가장 적절한 것은 ③이다.

18 2015 숙명여대(일반)

정답 ②

| 구문분석 |

All science is subject to human bias.
All science: S / is: V / subject to human bias: C

모든 과학은 인간의 편견의 대상이다.

This is especially true (for social scientists).
This: S / is: V / true: C

이것은 특히 사회과학자들에게 해당된다.

(Since human behavior is their area of study), they are actually part of the subject matter.
부사절: ~ 때문에 S V C
인간의 행동이 사회과학자들의 연구영역이기 때문에, 사회과학자들은 실제로 그 자신이 연구 대상의 일부이다.

Furthermore, human behavior patterns vary (from one place to another and from one group to another).
접속부사 S V 등위접속사
게다가, 인간의 행동 양식은 장소마다 그리고 집단에 따라서도 다양하다.

This is in contrast to the subject matter (of the natural sciences).
S V C
이러한 점은 자연과학의 연구 대상과 대조를 이룬다.

(When a chemist studies hydrogen), he can assume that one hydrogen atom is very much like another, wherever it is found, and that the conditions surrounding it can be quite accurately controlled.
부사절: ~할 때 S V O_1 등위접속사 O_2
어떤 화학자가 수소에 대해서 연구할 때, 그는, 하나의 수소 원자가 어디에서 발견된 것이든 상관없이 다른 것과 매우 유사한 것이고, 수소 원자를 둘러싸고 있는 조건들이 꽤 정확하게 통제될 수 있다고 가정할 수 있다.

세미콜론: and 역할
The same is true (when a physicist measures a metal bar); he can be quite sure that it will not stretch or shrink in length (as long as natural conditions are the same).
S V C 부사절: ~할 때 S V C 부사절: ~하는 한
물리학자가 금속 막대를 측정할 때도 마찬가지이다; 물리학자는, 자연적인 조건이 변하지 않는 한 금속 막대가 늘어나거나 줄어들지 않을 것이라고 꽤 확신할 수 있다.

관계대명사
This is why Earl Babbie quotes economist Daniel Suits, (who calls the natural sciences the "easy sciences" (because of the predictable nature of their subject matter).
S V C

Earl Babbie가 경제학자 Daniel Suits의 말을 인용하는 이유도 이와 같은데, Suits는 자연과학의 연구 대상의 예측 가능한 특성 때문에 자연과학을 '쉬운 과학'이라고 부른다.

| 어휘 |

bias ⓝ 편견	**in contrast to** ~와 대조를 이루어	**hydrogen** ⓝ 수소
atom ⓝ 원자	**assume** ⓥ (사실일 것으로) 가정하다	**stretch** ⓥ 뻗다
shrink ⓥ 오그라들다, 줄어들다	**quote** ⓥ 인용하다	

| 전문해석 | 모든 과학은 인간의 편견의 대상이다. 이것은 특히 사회과학자들에게 해당된다. 인간의 행동이 사회과학자들의 연구영역이기 때문에, 사회과학자들은 실제로 그 자신이 연구 대상의 일부이다. 게다가, 인간의 행동 양식은 장소마다 그리고 집단에 따라서도 다양하다. 이러한 점은 자연과학의 연구 대상과 대조를 이룬다. 어떤 화학자가 수소에 대해서 연구할 때, 그는, 하나의 수소 원자가 어디에서 발견된 것이든 상관없이 다른 것과 매우 유사한 것이고, 수소 원자를 둘러싸고 있는 조건들이 꽤 정확하게 통제될 수 있다고 가정할 수 있다. 물리학자가 금속 막대를 측정할 때도 마찬가지이다; 물리학자는, 자연적인 조건이 변하지 않는 한 금속 막대가 늘어나거나 줄어들지 않을 것이라고 꽤 확신할 수 있다. Earl Babbie가 경제학자 Daniel Suits의 말을 인용하는 이유도 이와 같은데, Suits는 자연과학의 연구 대상의 예측 가능한 특성 때문에 자연과학을 '쉬운 과학'이라고 부른다.

| 보기분석 |
① critical
비판적인
② objective
객관적인
③ vindictive
원한을 품은
④ cynical
냉소적인, 비꼬는
⑤ ambivalent
반대감정이 양립하는

| 정답분석 | 본문은 편견에 영향을 잘 받는 사회과학의 연구 대상과 이와는 대조적으로 자연과학의 예측 가능한 연구 대상의 차이를 객관적으로 설명한다. 따라서 정답으로는 ②가 가장 적절하다.

19 2018 숙명여대(인문 자연계)

정답 ①

| 구문분석 | A 19-year-old Detroit man was ordered Friday to stand trial (in the non-fatal shooting of two city police officers) (who, according to his lawyer, the teen believed were burglars trying to break into his family's home).

S: A 19-year-old Detroit man / V: was ordered / O.C: to stand trial / who: 관계대명사

19세의 디트로이트 남성이, 그의 변호사에 따르면, 그의 가족의 집에 침입하려고 시도하는 강도라고 믿었던 두 명의 시 경찰관에게 치명적이지 않은 총격을 가한 데 대해 금요일에 재판을 받으라는 명령을 받았다.

Judge Kenneth King said (that) (while he believes Juwan Plummer was "very much afraid") (when he heard knocking on the door of his family's home in the late hours on April 16), the question is whether the teen had a "reasonable" belief that a break-in was underway.

S: Judge Kenneth King / V: said / while: 부사절: ~하는 반면에 / when: 부사절: ~할 때 / O: the question is whether the teen had a "reasonable" belief that a break-in was underway

케네스 킹(Kenneth King) 판사는 주완 플러머(Juwan Plummer)가 4월 16일 밤 늦은 시간에 누군가가 가족의 집 문을 두드리는 소리를 들었을 때 "매우 두려워했다"고 생각하지만, 문제는 그가 침입이 이루어지고 있다는 "합리적인" 믿음을 가지고 있었는지 여부라고 말했다.

(Citing Michigan case law), King said (that) a trial judge will have to decide whether Plummer had a "reasonable" belief that he was in danger (when he allegedly fired upon the officers) (after one of them approached the home (in the 205 block of Lesure).

Citing Michigan case law: 분사구문 / S: King / V: said / O: a trial judge will have to decide whether Plummer had a "reasonable" belief that he was in danger / when: 부사절: ~할 때 / after: 부사절: ~한 후에

킹은 미시간주 판례법을 인용해 플러머가 경찰관들 중 한 명이 레수어 205블록의 그 집에 접근한 후 그들에게 총을 쐈다고 주장했을 때 그가 위험에 처해 있다는 "합리적인" 믿음을 가지고 있었는지 여부를 공판 판사가 결정해야 할 것이라고 말했다.

The officers were responding (to a report (from someone in the home) that a break-in was occurring at an unoccupied home across the street).

S: The officers / V: were responding / a report = that a break-in was occurring at an unoccupied home across the street

그 경찰관들은 길 건너 빈집에 침입이 발생하고 있다는 신고를 그 집에 있는 누군가로부터 받고 대응하고 있던 중이었다.

| 어휘 |

stand trial 재판을 받다	**burglar** ⓝ 강도	**break into** 몰래 잠입하다
reasonable ⓐ 합리적인, 온당한, 적당한		**allegedly** ⓐⓓ 주장하는 바에 의하면
fire ⓥ 사격하다, 발사하다	**break-in** ⓝ (보통 절도를 위한) 침입	**underway** ⓐ 진행 중인
unoccupied ⓐ (사람이 살거나 이용하지 않고) 비어 있는		

| 전문해석 | 19세의 디트로이트 남성이, 그의 변호사에 따르면, 그의 가족의 집에 침입하려고 시도하는 강도라고 믿었던 두 명의 시 경찰관에게 치명적이지 않은 총격을 가한 데 대해 금요일에 재판을 받으라는 명령을 받았다. 케네스 킹(Kenneth King) 판사는 주완 플러머(Juwan Plummer)가 4월 16일 밤 늦은 시간에 누군가가 가족의 집 문을 두드리는 소리를 들었을 때 "매우 두려워했다"고 생각하지만, 문제는 그가 침입이 이루어지고 있다는 "합리적인" 믿음을 가지고 있었는지 여부라고 말했다. 킹은 미시간주 판례법을 인용해 플러머가 경찰관들 중 한 명이 레수어 205블록의 그 집에 접근한 후 그들에게 총을 쐈다고 주장했을 때 그가 위험에 처해 있다는 "합리적인" 믿음을 가지고 있었는지 여부를 공판 판사가 결정해야 할 것이라고 말했다. 그 경찰관들은 길 건너 빈집에 침입이 발생하고 있다는 신고를 그 집에 있는 누군가로부터 받고 대응하고 있던 중이었다.

| 보기분석 |

✓① impartial 편견 없는
② bigoted 편협한
③ impertinent 버릇없는
④ optimistic 낙관적인
⑤ wanton 터무니없는

| 정답분석 | 본문에서 저자는 경찰관 총격 사건에 대해 객관적으로 설명하고 있다. 따라서 글의 어조로는 ①이 적절하다.

20 2012 가톨릭대(일반학사B형)

정답 ③

| 구문분석 | Women have realized advances (in the twentieth century).
S V O

여성들은 20세기에 진보를 실현했다.

대시: 부연설명

We have seen women involved politically, seeking — and obtaining — political office.
S V O O.C

우리는 여성들이 공직을 추구하고 획득하며 정치적으로 참여하는 것을 보아 왔다.

In addition, women today are better educated than their sisters of the 19th century, (a far greater number attending college).
접속부사 S V C
분사구문

게다가, 오늘날 여성들은 19세기 여성들보다 더 나은 교육을 받고 있으며 훨씬 더 많은 수가 대학에 다니고 있다.

As a result, more and more women are entering the labor force.
접속부사 S V O

결과적으로, 점점 더 많은 여성들이 노동력에 진입하고 있다.

The relationship between men and women is undergoing profound changes (as a result of the rise in women's status).
S V O

남녀관계는 여성의 지위 상승의 결과로 근본적인 변화를 겪고 있다.

A number of career women delayed marriage (until they achieved professional success).
S V O 부사절: ~할 때까지

수많은 직업을 가진 여성들이 직업적 성공을 거둘 때까지 결혼을 미루었다.

(Based on a recent study), these women have a greatly decreased chance of getting married (after they reach thirty).
분사구문 S V O 부사절: ~한 후에

최근의 연구에 의하면 이들은 30세 이후에 결혼할 확률이 크게 감소했다.

Men are not willing to wait (for women) (to finish their education and establish their careers).
S V 의미상 주어

남성들은 여성이 교육을 마치고 안정된 경력을 쌓을 때까지 기꺼이 기다리지 않는다.

This is having a profound effect (on the shape of modern marriage as well as the relationship (between men and women).
S V O as well as: ~뿐만 아니라

이는 남녀관계뿐만 아니라 현대 결혼의 양상에도 지대한 영향을 미치고 있다.

The change (in women's status) has made a drastic change (in the way we live our lives today).
S V O

여성의 지위 변화는 오늘날 우리의 삶의 방식에 급격한 변화를 가져왔다.

(While many of these changes are (without doubt for the better of all), many feel a profound sense of loss, (as the old realities give way to new truths).
부사절: ~이긴 하지만 S V C
부사절: ~ 때문에

이러한 변화의 대부분은 의심할 여지 없이 모두에게 좋지만 많은 사람들은 오래된 현실이 새로운 진실에 자리를 내주기 때문에 깊은 상실감을 느끼고 있다.

| 어휘 |

realize ⓥ (소망 · 계획 등을) 실현하다
political office 공직
attend ⓥ ~에 다니다
labor force 노동력, 노동 인구
status ⓝ 상태, 지위
drastic ⓐ 과감한, 강렬한
without doubt 의심의 여지 없이, 확실히
sense of loss 상실감
give way to ~에게 양보하다

| 전문해석 | 여성들은 20세기에 진보를 실현했다. 우리는 여성들이 공직을 추구하고 획득하며 정치적으로 참여하는 것을 보아 왔다. 게다가, 오늘날 여성들은 19세기 여성들보다 더 나은 교육을 받고 있으며 훨씬 더 많은 수가 대학에 다니고 있다. 결과적으로,

점점 더 많은 여성들이 노동력에 진입하고 있다. 남녀관계는 여성의 지위 상승의 결과로 근본적인 변화를 겪고 있다. 수많은 직업을 가진 여성들이 직업적 성공을 거둘 때까지 결혼을 미루었다. 최근의 연구에 의하면 이들은 30세 이후에 결혼할 확률이 크게 감소했다. 남성들은 여성이 교육을 마치고 안정된 경력을 쌓을 때까지 기꺼이 기다리지 않는다. 이는 남녀관계뿐만 아니라 현대 결혼의 양상에도 지대한 영향을 미치고 있다. 여성의 지위 변화는 오늘날 우리의 삶의 방식에 급격한 변화를 가져왔다. 이러한 변화의 대부분은 의심할 여지 없이 모두에게 좋지만 많은 사람들은 오래된 현실이 새로운 진실에 자리를 내주기 때문에 깊은 상실감을 느끼고 있다.

| 보기분석 | ① To illustrate the advantages of women's advancement in the twentieth century 지엽적. 본문에서는 여성 지위 향상의 장단점을 모두 논의함.
20세기 여성의 진보의 이점들을 설명하기 위해

② To argue that the rise in women's status has a negative influence on the relationship between men and women
여성의 지위 상승이 남녀관계에 부정적인 영향을 미친다고 주장하기 위해

③ To discuss the advantages and disadvantages of the change in women's status
여성의 지위 변화의 장단점을 논의하기 위해

④ To explain why women should actively participate in political office 언급 안 한 정보
여성이 정치적인 일에 적극적으로 참여해야 하는 이유를 설명하기 위해

| 정답분석 | 본문에서 저자는 여성의 지위 변화로 인한 긍정적인 영향과 부정적인 영향을 설명하고 있는 글이다. 따라서 글의 목적으로는 ③이 가장 적절하다.

LEVEL 2 세부 내용 이해하기

4강 내용 일치 / 내용 추론

Practice

01	④	02	③	03	②	04	④	05	③	06	②	07	①	08	②	09	③	10	①
11	③	12	④	13	③	14	②	15	③	16	③	17	③	18	②	19	④	20	①

01 2018 가천대 정답 ④

| 구문분석 | A massive change(S) occurred(V) (in the way) (that(관계부사) music was composed and played in the Romantic Period, from 1820 to 1910).

1820년부터 1910년까지 낭만주의 시대에 음악을 작곡하고 연주하는 방식에 엄청난 변화가 일어났다.

(Rather than being dependent on finance from patrons or employers), musicians(S) were(V) more independent(C).

음악가들은 후원자들이나 고용주들의 자금에 의존하는 대신, 보다 더 독립적이었다.

This(S) gave(V) them(I.O) the opportunity(D.O) (to be more creative), so(등위접속사: 따라서) musical themes(S) became(V) more personal and emotional(C).

이것이 그들에게 보다 창조적이 될 수 있는 기회를 주었고, 따라서 음악의 주제는 더 개인적이고 감정적이 되었다.

Musicians(S) also began(V) experimenting(O) (with new techniques), (developing(분사구문) more complex harmonies and rhythms (in their compositions).

음악가들은 또한 새로운 기법을 실험하기 시작했으며, 그들의 음악 작품들에서 보다 더 복잡한 화성과 리듬을 발전시켰다.

Some(S) even used(V) new instruments(O) (like the clarinet and the piccolo) (to create(부사적용법: 결과) totally new sounds).

일부 음악가들은 심지어 클라리넷이나 피콜로와 같은 새로운 악기를 사용해서 완전히 새로운 소리를 만들어 냈다.

| 어휘 |
compose ⓥ 구성하다; 작곡하다
dependent ⓐ 의존하는, 의지하고 있는
finance ⓝ 재원, 자금; 재정, 재무
patron ⓝ 후원자; 단골, 고객, 손님
independent ⓐ 독립한; 독자적인
composition ⓝ (음악 · 미술 · 시 등의) 작품; 작곡(법)
instrument ⓝ 기계, 기구; 악기; 수단
sophistication ⓝ 지적 교양, 세련; (기계 등의) 복잡[정교]화
scruple ⓝ 양심의 가책; 망설임, 거리낌

| 전문해석 | 1820년부터 1910년까지 낭만주의 시대에 음악을 작곡하고 연주하는 방식에 엄청난 변화가 일어났다. 음악가들은 후원자들이나 고용주들의 자금에 의존하는 대신, 보다 더 독립적이었다. 이것이 그들에게 보다 창조적이 될 수 있는 기회를 주었고, 따라서 음악의 주제는 더 개인적이고 감정적이 되었다. 음악가들은 또한 새로운 기법을 실험하기 시작했으며, 그들의 음악 작품들에서 보다 더 복잡한 화성과 리듬을 발전시켰다. 일부 음악가들은 심지어 클라리넷이나 피콜로와 같은 새로운 악기를 사용해서 완전히 새로운 소리를 만들어 냈다. 보기 ④ 근거

| 보기분석 |
① Patrons played an ~~essential role~~ in developing new musical themes in the Romantic Period. 지문 내용과 불일치
낭만주의 시대에 후원자들은 새로운 음악적 주제를 발전시키는 데 중요한 역할을 했다.
② Employers in the Romantic ~~Period encouraged~~ musicians to be more independent and creative. 지문 내용과 불일치
낭만주의 시대에 고용주들은 음악가들에게 더 독립적이고 창조적이 되도록 장려했다.

③ Music in the Romantic Period was characterized by the sophistication of ancient techniques. 오래된 기법이 아니라 새로운 기법을 사용함
낭만주의 시대에 음악은 오래된 기법들의 정교화를 특징으로 하고 있었다.
④ Musicians in the Romantic Period had no scruples in experimenting with new instruments.
낭만주의 시대에 음악들은 새로운 악기로 실험하는 데 있어 망설임이 없었다.

| 정답분석 | 마지막 문장에서 "일부 음악가들은 클라리넷이나 피콜로와 같은 새로운 악기를 사용해서 완전히 새로운 소리를 만들어 냈다."고 했으므로, ④가 본문의 내용과 일치한다. 한편 ①, ② 낭만주의 시대에 음악가들은 후원자들이나 고용주들에 의존하기보다 더 독립적이고 창조적이었으며, 이를 통해 새로운 음악적인 주제를 전개시킬 수 있었다고 했다. 따라서 낭만주의 시대에 후원자들이나 고용주들이 음악의 발전에 중요한 역할을 했다는 것은 적절하지 않다.

02 2018 국민대

정답 ③

| 구문분석 | I do not believe that genius is an entirely different thing from talent.
(I: S / do not believe: V / that genius is an entirely different thing from talent: O)
나는 천재성이 재능과 전혀 다른 것이라고는 생각하지 않는다.

be sure that: ~을 확신하다
I am not even sure that it depends on any great difference in the artist's natural gifts.
(I: S / am not even sure: V / that it depends on any great difference in the artist's natural gifts: O)
더욱이 천재성이 예술가의 타고난 재능에 있어서의 어떤 큰 차이에 좌우된다고 확신하지도 못한다.

For example, I do not think that Cervantes had an exceptional gift for writing; few people would deny him genius.
(For example: 접속부사 / I: S / do not think: V / that Cervantes had an exceptional gift for writing: O / ;: 세미콜론: but 역할 / few people: S / would deny: V / him: I.O / genius: D.O)
예를 들어, 나는 세르반테스(Cervantes)가 글 쓰는 특별한 재능을 가졌다고 생각하지 않는다. 그렇더라도 세르반테스의 천재성을 부인할 사람은 거의 없을 것이다.

등위접속사: 또한 아니다 (Nor) / and yet = yet = but
Nor would it be easy (in English literature) to find a poet (with a happier gift than Herrick) and yet no one would claim that he had more than delightful talent.
(it: 가주어 / to find a poet: 진주어 / no one: S / would claim: V / that he had more than delightful talent: O)
그리고 또한 영문학에서 헤릭(Herrick)만큼 훌륭한 재능을 지니고 있던 시인을 찾아보는 것은 쉽지 않은데, 하지만 그를 두고 유쾌한 재능 이상의 것을 가지고 있었다고 주장할 사람은 아무도 없을 것이다.

It seems (to me) that what makes genius is the combination (of natural gifts for creation with an idiosyncrasy) (that enables its possessor to see the world personally in the highest degree and yet with such catholicity that his appeal is not to this type of man or to that type, but to all men).
(It: 가주어 / seems: V / that ~: 진주어 that / what makes genius: S / is: V / the combination: C / that: 관계대명사 / such ~ that: 너무 ~해서 …하다, …할 정도로 ~하다)
내가 보기에 천재를 만드는 것은 타고난 창작 재능과 개인적 특이성의 결합인 것 같은데 개인적 특이성은 그 특이성의 소유자로 하여금 세계를 지극히 개성적인 눈으로, 그러나 그를 이런저런 유형의 사람에게가 아니라 모든 사람에게 매력적이게 만들 정도로 보편적인 눈으로 볼 수 있게 해 주는 것이다.

His private world is that of common men, but (his private world is) ampler and more pithy. He is supremely normal.
(His private world: S / is: V / that: C / He: S / is: V / normal: C)
그의 사적인 세계는 보통 사람의 세계와 다르지 않지만 보다 더 넓고(풍부하고) 보다 더 깊이가 있다(함축적이다). 그는 지극히 정상적이다.

(By a happy accident of nature seeing life with immense vivacity), he sees it, (with its infinite diversity, in the healthy way) (that mankind at large sees it).
(he: S / sees: V / it: O / that: 관계부사)
우연히 운 좋게도 인생을 쾌활하게 보는 찬성이다 보니, 그는 인생을 무한히 다양한 모습으로, 대부분의 사람들과 마찬가지로 건강한 방식으로 바라본다.

In other words, he sees life vigorously and sees it whole.
(In other words: 접속부사 / he: S / sees: V_1 / life: O_1 / and: 등위접속사 / sees: V_2 / it: O_2)
다시 말하면, 그는 인생을 활기차게 보고 인생을 전체로 본다는 것이다.

| 어휘 | **genius** ⓝ 천재; 천재성 **gift** ⓝ 재능, 적성

exceptional ⓐ 예외적; 특별히 빼어난, 비범한
idiosyncrasy ⓝ (어느 개인의) 특이성, 특이한 성격[경향]
enable ⓥ ~에게 힘[능력]을 주다, ~에게 가능성을 주다
degree ⓝ 정도, 등급
appeal ⓝ 호소; 간청; 매력
ample ⓐ 광대한, 넓은; 충분한
pithy ⓐ 속[골수]이 있는; (표현 따위가) 힘찬, 함축적인, 간결한
immense ⓐ 막대한, 무한한
vivacity ⓝ 생기, 활기, 활발
infinite ⓐ 무한한; 막대한
diversity ⓝ 차이, 변화, 다양성
vigorously ⓐⓓ 원기왕성하게, 활발하게

| 전문해석 | 나는 천재성이 재능과 전혀 다른 것이라고는 생각하지 않는다. 더욱이 천재성이 예술가의 타고난 재능에 있어서의 어떤 큰 차이에 좌우된다고 확신하지도 못한다. 예를 들어, 나는 세르반테스(Cervantes)가 글 쓰는 특별한 재능을 가졌다고 생각하지 않는다. 그렇더라도 세르반테스의 천재성을 부인할 사람은 거의 없을 것이다. 그리고 또한 영문학에서 헤릭(Herrick)만큼 훌륭한 재능을 지니고 있던 시인을 찾아보는 것은 쉽지 않은데, 하지만 그를 두고 유쾌한 재능 이상의 것을 가지고 있었다고 주장할 사람은 아무도 없을 것이다. 내가 보기에 천재를 만드는 것은 타고난 창작 재능과 개인적 특이성의 결합인 것 같은데 개인적 특이성은 그 특이성의 소유자로 하여금 세계를 지극히 개성적인 눈으로, 그러나 그를 이런저런 유형의 사람에게가 아니라 모든 사람에게 매력적이게 만들 정도로 보편적인 눈으로 볼 수 있게 해 주는 것이다.(보기 ③ 근거) 그의 사적인 세계는 보통 사람의 세계와 다르지 않지만 보다 더 넓고(풍부하고) 보다 더 깊이가 있다(함축적이다). 그는 지극히 정상적이다. 우연히 운 좋게도 인생을 쾌활하게 보는 찬성이다 보니, 그는 인생을 무한히 다양한 모습으로, 대부분의 사람들과 마찬가지로 건강한 방식으로 바라본다. 다시 말하면, 그는 인생을 활기차게 보고 인생을 전체로 본다는 것이다.

| 보기분석 | ① Everyone believes Herrick is ~~a genius~~ with a charming talent for poetry. 지문 내용과 다름: 지문은 헤릭은 훌륭한 재능은 있지만, 천재는 아니라고 했다.
모든 사람들은 헤릭이 시에 대해 훌륭한 재능을 가진 천재라고 믿고 있다.
② Most people agree that Cervantes is an unusually gifted writer, but ~~not a genius~~. 지문 내용과 다름: 지문은 세르반테스는 재능은 없지만, 천재라고 언급했다.
대부분의 사람들은 세르반테스가 매우 재능 있는 작가이지만 천재는 아니라는 데 동의한다.
③ A genius sees the world very personally but appeals to all kinds of men.
천재는 세상을 매우 개인적으로 바라보지만 모든 이들에게 매력적이다.
④ A genius does ~~not need~~ natural gifts but a strong, unique personality of the highest degree. 지문 내용과 다름
천재는 타고난 재능이 아니라, 고도의 굳세고 독특한 성격을 필요로 한다.

| 정답분석 | 지문에서 "천재는 지극히 개성적인 눈으로 세계를 보면서도, 보편성을 갖추고 있기에 모든 이들에게 매력적이다"라고 언급하였다. 따라서 ③이 정답으로 적절하다.

03 2018 단국대

정답 ②

| 구문분석 | (If the democratic alternative to the totalitarian one-way broadcasts is a row of separate soapboxes), then I submit that the alternative is unworkable, is unreasonable, and is humanly unattractive.
(부사절: 만일 ~라면 / I: S / submit: V / that ~ unattractive: O)
전체주의적인 일방통행식 방송에 대한 민주적인 대안이 만일 서로 별개인 연단들의 연속이라면, 나는 그 대안이 실행 불가능하고, 불합리하며, 인간적으로 매력이 없다고 말하는 바이다.

It is (above all) a false alternative.
(It: S / is: V / a false alternative: C)
그 대안은 무엇보다도 잘못된 대안이다.

It is not true that liberty has developed among civilized men (when anyone is free to set up a soapbox, is free to hire a hall [where he may expound his opinions to those (who are willing to listen)]).
(It: 가주어 / that: 진주어 that / when ~: 부사절: ~할 때 / anyone: S / is: V_1 / is: V_2 / where: 관계부사 / who: 관계대명사)
누구든지 연단을 자유롭게 설치하고, 누구든지 듣고자 하는 사람들에게 자신의 의견을 말할 수 있는 강당을 자유롭게 빌릴 수 있을 때 자유가 문명인들 사이에 발달하게 된 것이 아니다.

On the contrary, freedom of speech is established to achieve its essential purpose (only when different opinions are expounded in the same hall to the same audience).
(On the contrary: 접속부사 / freedom of speech: S / is established: V / to achieve: 부사적용법: 결과 / only when ~: 부사절: 오로지 ~할 때)

그와는 반대로, 다양한 의견들이 똑같은 강당에서 똑같은 청중에게 전달될 때 비로소 언론의 자유는 자리를 잡아 본연의 목적을 달성하게 된다.

부사절: ~이긴 하지만
For, (while the right to talk may be the beginning of freedom), the necessity of listening is what makes the right important.
등위접속사: 왜냐하면 S V O

왜냐하면 말할 권리가 자유의 시작일지 모르지만, 반드시 들어야 할 필요성이 말할 권리를 중요하게 만들기 때문이다.

What matters is not the utterance of opinions. What matters is the confrontation (of opinions in debate).
S V C S V C

중요한 것은 (각자) 의견을 말하는 것이 아니다. 중요한 것은 토론에서의 여러 의견들의 대립이다.

No man can care profoundly that every fool should say what he likes.
S V C

모든 바보가 자기 하고 싶은 말을 한다고 해서 크게 관심 가질 사람은 없다.

| 어휘 | **alternative** ⓝ 대안 **totalitarian** ⓐ 전체주의의(개인의 모든 활동은 민족 · 국가와 같은 전체의 존립과 발전을 위해서만 존재한다는 이념 아래 개인의 자유를 억압하는 사상의) **one-way** ⓐ 일방적인, 일방통행의 **soapbox** ⓝ (가두연설대 등으로 쓰는) 비누상자; 임시[가두] 연단 **submit that** ~라고 말하다[진술하다] **unworkable** ⓐ 실행[실시] 불가능한 **unreasonable** ⓐ 불합리한; 무분별한 **civilized** ⓐ 문명화된 **be free to *do*** 마음대로 ~하다 **expound** ⓥ 자세히 설명하다 **matter** ⓥ 중요하다 **utterance** ⓝ 입 밖에 내기, 발언 **profoundly** ⓐⓓ 깊이

| 전문해석 | 전체주의적인 일방통행식 방송에 대한 민주적인 대안이 만일 서로 별개인 연단들의 연속이라면, 나는 그 대안이 실행 불가능하고, 불합리하며, 인간적으로 매력이 없다고 말하는 바이다. 그 대안은 무엇보다도 잘못된 대안이다. 누구든지 연단을 자유롭게 설치하고, 누구든지 듣고자 하는 사람들에게 자신의 의견을 말할 수 있는 강당을 자유롭게 빌릴 수 있을 때 자유가 문명인들 사이에 발달하게 된 것이 아니다. 그와는 반대로, 다양한 의견들이 똑같은 강당에서 똑같은 청중에게 전달될 때 비로소 언론의 자유는 자리를 잡아 본연의 목적을 달성하게 된다.(보기 ② 근거) 왜냐하면 말할 권리가 자유의 시작일지 모르지만, 반드시 들어야 할 필요성이 말할 권리를 중요하게 만들기 때문이다. 중요한 것은 (각자) 의견을 말하는 것이 아니다. 중요한 것은 토론에서의 여러 의견들의 대립이다. 모든 바보가 자기 하고 싶은 말을 한다고 해서 크게 관심 가질 사람은 없다.

| 보기분석 | ① There is no actual alternative to the totalitarian broadcasts. 지문 내용과 다름
전체주의적 방송에 대한 대안은 실제로 존재하지 않는다.
② To get the freedom of speech, different opinions should be exposed in the same condition.
언론의 자유를 얻기 위해서는, 다양한 의견들이 동일한 조건에서 노출되어야 한다.
③ Separate soapboxes are the alternatives to totalitarianism. 지문 내용과 다름
서로 떨어진 연단이 전체주의의 대안이다.
④ To allow the freedom to speak one's own opinions is the most important thing. 지문 내용과 다름
자신의 의견을 말할 수 있는 자유가 가장 중요한 것이다.

| 정답분석 | 지문에서 잘못된 대안이 존재하고 있는 상황이라고 했으므로, ① 실제 아무런 대안이 존재하지 않는다는 말은 불일치이다. 또한, 서로 떨어진 연단은 전체주의의 잘못된 대안이라 했으므로 ③도 틀린 보기이다. 마지막으로, 지문에서 '중요한 것은 각자가 자신의 의견을 말하는 것이 아니다'라고 했기 때문에 ④도 지문과 일치하지 않는다. 반면, 다양한 의견들이 똑같은 강당에서 똑같은 청중에게 전달될 때 비로소 언론의 자유는 자리 잡게 된다고 했으므로, ② '언론의 자유를 얻기 위해서는, 다양한 의견들이 동일한 조건에서 노출되어야 한다.'가 지문과 일치가 될 수 있다.

04 2016 가톨릭대

정답 ④

| 구문분석 | (Since our account of medieval architecture is mainly concerned with the development of style), we have (until now) confined our attention (to religious structures), the most ambitious as well as the most representative efforts of the age.
부사절: ~ 때문에 B as well as A: A뿐만 아니라 B도 S V O = B A

중세 건축에 대한 우리의 설명은 주로 양식의 발전과 관련이 있기 때문에, 우리는 지금까지 중세시대를 가장 잘 대표할 뿐 아니라 가장 야심 찬 노력인 종교 건축물에 우리의 관심을 한정시켜 왔다.

등위접속사
Secular building, indeed, reflects the same general trends, but these are often obscured (by diversity of types), (ranging from bridges to royal palaces, from barns to town halls).
S V O S V
분사구문

실제로는 세속적인 건물들도 이런 동일하고 일반적인 경향들을 반영하고 있지만, 그러나 이러한 일반적인 경향들은 다리에서부터 왕궁에 이르고, 헛간에서부터 시청에 이르는 그 형태의 다양성에 의해서 종종 흐릿해지곤 한다.

Moreover, social, economic, and practical factors play a more important part (here) (than in church design), (so that the useful life of the buildings is apt to be much briefer).
접속부사 S V O
부사절: 그 결과

더욱이, 이들 세속 건축물들은 교회의 건축물에 비해서 사회적, 경제적, 그리고 실용적인 요인들이 더 중요한 역할을 하기 때문에, 건물이 유용하게 사용되는 기간이 (종교 건축물에 비해) 훨씬 더 짧은 경향이 있다.

(As a consequence), our knowledge (of secular structures of the pre-Gothic Middle Ages) remains extremely fragmentary.
S V C

그 결과, 고딕 이전 중세의 세속적인 건축물들에 관한 우리의 지식은 여전히 매우 단편적이다.

| 어휘 |
account ⓝ 설명, 진술 **style** ⓝ 건축에 있어서의 양식 **confine** ⓥ 한정하다, 제한하다; 가두다
representative ⓐ 대표적인 **secular** ⓐ 세속적인
obscure ⓥ 불명료하게 하다; 눈에 띄지 않게 하다; 희미하게 하다 **barn** ⓝ 헛간, 광; 헛간 같은 건물
be apt to *do* ~하는 경향이 있다 **fragmentary** ⓐ 파편의; 단편으로 이루어진, 단편적인

| 전문해석 | 중세 건축에 대한 우리의 설명은 주로 양식의 발전과 관련이 있기 때문에, 우리는 지금까지 중세시대를 가장 잘 대표할 뿐 아니라 가장 야심 찬 노력인 종교 건축물에 우리의 관심을 한정시켜 왔다. 실제로는 세속적인 건물들도 이런 동일하고 일반적인 경향들을 반영하고 있지만, 그러나 이러한 일반적인 경향들은 다리에서부터 왕궁에 이르고, 헛간에서부터 시청에 이르는 그 형태의 다양성에 의해서 종종 흐릿해지곤 한다. 더욱이, 이들 세속 건축물들은 교회의 건축물에 비해서 사회적, 경제적, 그리고 실용적인 요인들이 더 중요한 역할을 하기 때문에, 건물이 유용하게 사용되는 기간이 (종교 건축물에 비해) 훨씬 더 짧은 경향이 있다. 그 결과, 고딕 이전 중세의 세속적인 건축물들에 관한 우리의 지식은 여전히 매우 단편적이다. 보기 ④ 근거

| 보기분석 |
① Our account of ~~religious structures~~ is mainly concerned with their diverse types. 세속적 건물이 다양성과 관련 있다.
종교적 건축물들에 대한 우리의 설명은 주로 건축물의 다양한 종류와 관련 있다.
② ~~Secular buildings~~ are the most representative architecture in the medieval period. 중세를 대표하는 건물은 세속이 아니라 종교적 건물이다.
세속적 건물들은 중세시대의 가장 대표적인 건물이다.
③ The lifespan of secular buildings is ~~much longer~~ than that of religious ones. 세속적 건물의 수명은 종교적 건물보다 짧다.
세속적 건물들의 수명은 종교적 건물들의 수명보다 훨씬 더 길다.
④ Our knowledge about the secular structures of the Middle Ages is limited.
중세시대 세속적 건물에 관한 우리의 지식은 제한되어 있다.

| 정답분석 | 지문의 마지막 문장에서 고딕 이전 중세의 세속적인 건축물들에 관한 우리의 지식은 여전히 매우 단편적이라고 언급했으므로 ④가 정답으로 적절하다.

05 2018 서울여대

정답 ③

| 구문분석 | The Sears and Roebuck catalogue was a fixture (in American society for many decades).
S V C

시어스 앤 로벅(the Sears and Roebuck) 카탈로그는 수십 년 동안 미국 사회에서 하나의 고정 비품이었다.

S
Practically anything (needed in the American home) could be ordered (through this comprehensive catalogue) and (could be) delivered (by mail).
V_1
등위접속사 V_2

미국 가정에서 필요로 하는 사실상 모든 것들을 이 포괄적인 카탈로그를 통해서 주문하여 우편을 통해 배달시킬 수 있었다.

The catalogue made it easier (for homeowners in urban areas) to track down items they were trying to find; the catalogue was an absolute necessity (for residents in out-of-the-way areas) (where many types of home supplies were not available for hundreds of miles).

(가목적어 / S / V / O.C / to부정사의 의미상 주어 / 진목적어 / 세미콜론: and 역할 / S / V / C / 관계부사)

그 카탈로그는 도시 지역 집주인들이 그들이 찾고 있는 물품을 쉽게 찾을 수 있게 해 주었다. 수백 마일을 가도 다양한 종류의 가정용품을 구할 수 없는 외딴 지역 주민들에게는 그 카탈로그가 절대적 필수품이었다.

(In the early twentieth century), it was not just possible to buy home supplies from the Sears and Roebuck catalogue.

(가주어 / V / C / 진주어)

20세기 초에는, 시어스 앤 로벅 카탈로그를 통해 가정용품만 구입할 수 있는 것이 아니었다.

It was actually possible to buy a mail-order house.

(가주어 / V / C / 진주어)

우편 주문으로 주택을 구입하는 것도 실제로 가능했다.

(If you ordered a house through the mail), you would receive all the necessary building materials as well as plans for constructing the house; all of this could be had for prices starting around $600.

(부사절: 만일 ~라면 / S / V / B / A / B as well as A: A뿐만 아니라 B도)

만약 우편을 통해 주택을 주문하면, 그 주택을 건설하기 위한 설계도뿐 아니라 필요한 모든 건축 재료도 받을 것이다. 이 모든 것들을 약 600달러부터 시작하는 가격으로 가질 수 있었다.

| 어휘 | **fixture** ⓝ 정착물, 비품, 설비 **decade** ⓝ 10년간
comprehensive ⓐ 포괄적인, 범위가 넓은 **track down** ~의 뒤를 쫓다, 추적하다
necessity ⓝ 필요, 필요성 **resident** ⓝ 거주자, 거류민
out-of-the-way ⓐ 벽지의, 외딴곳에 있는 **supply** ⓝ 공급; 공급[보급]량; 공급품
construct ⓥ 조립하다, 세우다, 건설[건조]하다

| 전문해석 | 시어스 앤 로벅(the Sears and Roebuck) 카탈로그는 수십 년 동안 미국 사회에서 하나의 고정 비품이었다. 미국 가정에서 필요로 하는 사실상 모든 것들을 이 포괄적인 카탈로그를 통해서 주문하여 우편을 통해 배달시킬 수 있었다. 그 카탈로그는 도시 지역 집주인들이 그들이 찾고 있는 물품을 쉽게 찾을 수 있게 해 주었다. 수백 마일을 가도 다양한 종류의 가정용품을 구할 수 없는 외딴 지역 주민들에게는 그 카탈로그가 절대적 필수품이었다.
20세기 초에는, 시어스 앤 로벅 카탈로그를 통해 가정용품만 구입할 수 있는 것이 아니었다. 우편 주문으로 주택을 구입하는 것도 실제로 가능했다. 만약 우편을 통해 주택을 주문하면, 그 주택을 건설하기 위한 설계도뿐 아니라 필요한 모든 건축 재료도 받을 것이다. (보기 ③ 근거) 이 모든 것들을 약 600달러부터 시작하는 가격으로 가질 수 있었다.

| 보기분석 | ① Items ordered through the catalogue had to be picked up at a Sears and Roebuck store. 카탈로그로 주문한 물건은 우편으로 배송된다.
카탈로그로 주문한 물건은 시어스 앤 로벅 매장에서 수령해야만 했다.
② The average price of a mail-order house in the Sears and Roebuck catalogue was $600. 평균 가격이 아니라 대략 600달러에서 시작한다.
시어스 앤 로벅 카탈로그에서 주문한 주택의 평균 가격은 600달러였다.
③ A mail-order house in the Sears and Roebuck catalogue needed to be assembled by the buyer.
시어스 앤 로벅 카탈로그에서 주문한 주택은 구매자가 조립할 필요가 있었다.
④ Residents in remote areas could not afford most of the items in the Sears and Roebuck catalogue.
외딴 지역의 주민들은 시어스 앤 로벅 카탈로그의 대부분 상품을 구매할 여유가 없었다. 외딴 지역 사람들에게 카탈로그는 필수라고 했다.

| 정답분석 | 지문에서 '주택을 주문하는 경우 설계도와 건축 재료를 보내줬다'고 언급하였는데, 이것은 구매자가 직접 그 주택을 조립해야 했다는 것을 의미하므로 ③이 정답으로 적절하다.

06 2016 경기대

정답 ②

| 구문분석 | Dora was frustrated (by a series of used cars (she drove).

(S / V)

도라(Dora)는 운전했던 여러 개의 중고차에 실망했다.

등위접속사
It was she who commuted to work, but it was her husband, Hank, who chose the cars.
it is ~ that[who] 강조구문 it is ~ that[who] 강조구문
중고차를 몰고 회사에 출퇴근하는 사람은 도라였지만, 지금까지 도라가 운전했던 차를 선택한 사람은 도라의 남편 행크(Hank)였다.

Hank always went (for cars) (that were "interesting", but in continual need of repair).
S V 관계대명사
행크는 항상 '흥미롭기는' 하지만 계속해서 수리를 필요로 하는 차를 좋아했다.

(After Dora was nearly killed when her brakes failed), they were (in the market for yet another used car).
부사절: ~ 이후 부사절: 때 S V
브레이크가 제대로 작동하지 않아서 도라가 거의 죽을 뻔했던 일이 있고 난 후, 두 사람은 또 다른 중고차를 보기 위해 중고차 매장에 갔다.

Dora wanted to buy a late-model sedan (from a friend).
S V O
도라는 친구로부터 최신형 승용차를 사고 싶어 했다.

Hank fixed his sights (on a 15-year-old sports car).
S V O
행크는 15년 된 스포츠카를 향해 눈을 고정했다.

등위접속사
She tried [to persuade Hank that if made more sense to buy the boring but dependable car], but he would not be swayed.
S V O a_1 a_2 S V
도라는 보기에 좀 심심해 보여도 믿을 수 있는 차를 사는 것이 더 합리적이라고 행크를 설득했으나, 행크는 자신의 마음을 바꾸려고 하지 않았다.

Previously she would have acceded (to his wishes).
S V
예전 같았으면 도라는 행크가 원하는 대로 했을 것이다.

steel oneself: 마음을 단단히 먹다
(This time) Dora bought the boring but dependable car and steeled herself (for Hank's anger).
S V_1 O_1 등위접속사 V_2 O_2
이번의 경우는 도라는 좀 지루해 보이지만 믿을 만한 차를 구입했고 더 나아가 행크가 화를 낼 것에 대해서도 마음을 단단히 먹었다.

to one's 감정명사: ~하게도
(To her amazement), he spoke not a word (of remonstrance).
S V O
놀랍게도, 행크는 불평의 말을 한마디도 내뱉지 않았다.

should have p.p.: ~했었어야 했다(실제론 하지 않았다)
(When she later told him what she had expected), he scoffed (at her fears) and said (that) she should have done what she wanted from the start (if she felt that strongly about it).
부사절: 때 S V_1 V_2 S V O
나중에, 도라가 행크에게 그가 화를 낼 줄 알았다고 말하자, 그는 그녀가 느꼈을 두려움을 놀렸고, 중고차를 사는 일에 대해서 그녀가 그렇게나 강한 자기 의견을 가지고 있었다면, 처음부터 그녀가 원하는 차를 샀어야 했다고 말했다.

| 어휘 |

frustrated ⓐ 실망한, 좌절한
commute ⓥ 통근하다; 바꾸다, 전환하다
go for 좋아하다; 찬성하다
continual ⓐ 자주 일어나는; 잇따른, 계속되는
persuade ⓥ 설득하다, 납득시키다
dependable ⓐ 의존할 수 있는, 믿을 수 있는
sway ⓥ 흔들리다, 동요하다
accede ⓥ 동의하다; 취임하다, 가입하다
steel oneself 마음을 단단히 먹다
remonstrance ⓝ 항의, 불평
scoff ⓥ 비웃다, 조롱하다
confrontation ⓝ 직면, 대응, 갈등
amazement ⓝ 놀람, 경악
pushy ⓐ 강압적인, 억지가 센

| 전문해석 | 도라(Dora)는 운전했던 여러개의 중고차에 실망했다. 중고차를 몰고 회사에 출퇴근하는 사람은 도라였지만, 지금까지 도라가 운전했던 차를 선택한 사람은 도라의 남편 행크(Hank)였다. (보기 ② 근거 1) 행크는 항상 '흥미롭기는' 하지만 계속해서 수리를 필요로 하는 차를 좋아했다. 브레이크가 제대로 작동하지 않아서 도라가 거의 죽을 뻔했던 일이 있고 난 후, 두 사람은 또 다른 중고차를 보기 위해 중고차 매장에 갔다. 도라는 친구로부터 최신형 승용차를 사고 싶어 했다. (그러나) 행크는 15년 된 스포츠카를 향해 눈을 고정했다. 도라는 보기에 좀 심심해 보여도 믿을 수 있는 차를 사는 것이 더 합리적이라고 행크를 설득했으나, 행크는 자신의 마음을 바꾸려고 하지 않았다.
예전 같았으면 도라는 행크가 원하는 대로 했을 것이다. (보기 ② 근거 2) 그러나 이번의 경우 도라는 좀 심심해 보이지만 믿을 만한 차를 구입했고 더 나아가 행크가 화를 낼 것에 대해서도 마음을 단단히 먹었다. 놀랍게도, 행크는 불평의 말을 한마디도 내뱉지 않

았다. 나중에, 도라가 행크에게 그가 화를 낼 줄 알았다고 말하자, 그는 그녀가 느꼈을 두려움을 놀렸고, 중고차를 사는 일에 대해서 그녀가 그렇게나 강한 자기 의견을 가지고 있었다면, 처음부터 그녀가 원하는 차를 샀어야 했다고 말했다.

| 보기분석 | ① Dora is so pushy that Hank fears a confrontation with her. 지문 내용과 불일치
도라는 너무 강압적이어서, 행크는 그녀와의 대립을 두려워한다.
② Dora used to avoid confrontation with Hank as to what car to buy.
도라는 이전에는, 어떤 차를 사야 할지에 대한 행크와의 마찰을 피했었다.
③ Dora prefers walking to driving when going to work. 언급한 적이 없으므로 알 수 없음
도라는 일하러 갈 때, 운전하는 것보다 걷는 것을 더 선호한다.
④ The couple are very close to Dora's friend whose car Dora wants to buy. 언급한 적이 없으므로 알 수 없음
(도라와 행크) 부부는 도라가 사길 원하는 차를 가진 친구와 매우 가깝다.

| 정답분석 | 지문에서 '지금까지 도라가 운전했던 중고차를 고른 것은 도라의 남편 행크(Hank)였다'라는 진술로부터 그동안은 도라가 중고차를 선택할 때 행크에게 양보했음을 알 수 있다. 따라서 ②가 정답으로 적절하다.

07 2016 국민대

정답 ①

| 구문분석 | Sigmund Freud (S) never set out (V) to be a psychologist (O).
set out toR: ~을 시작하다, 착수하다
지그문트 프로이트(Sigmund Freud)는 심리학자가 되고자 하지 않았다.

Much less did he (S) see (V) himself (O) (— until quite late in life —) as contributing to the field of social psychology (O.C).
부정어 문두 도치 / see A as B: A를 B라고 여기다
그는 노년에 이르기까지 그 자신이 사회 심리학 분야에 별달리 큰 기여를 했다고 여기지도 않았다.

He (S) was (V) simply a Viennese physician (C) (specializing in the treatment of nervous disorders).
그는 단지 신경증 치료를 전문으로 하는 비엔나의 내과의사였다.

명사절
That this activity would lead him to fundamentally new ways of conceiving social behavior (S) was little imagined (V) (by Freud) (when he took up this work).
부사절: ~할 때
이러한 활동이 그로 하여금 인간의 사회적 행동을 인지하는 근본적으로 새로운 방식으로 그를 이끌었다는 사실은 그가 그 일을 행하고 있었을 때에는 프로이트 자신도 거의 상상하지 못했던 일이다.

In fact (접속부사), Freud (S_1) was (V_1) already thirty years old (C) (before he began his private practice); and (등위접속사) his reasons (S_2) (for doing so) were (V_2) originally more financial (C) (than scientific).
사실, 프로이트가 사적인 진료(정신분석적인 진료)를 시작했을 때 프로이트의 나이는 이미 서른이었다. 그리고 그가 이러한 진료를 시작한 이유는 애초부터 과학적인 이유 때문이 아니라 금전적인 이유 때문이었다.

(After an engagement of four years) (전치사: ~ 이후), Freud (S) married (V) Martha Bernays (O) (in the fall of 1886).
4년 동안 약혼 상태를 지속하고 나서 프로이트는 1886년 가을 Martha Bernays와 결혼했다.

He (S) needed (V) to provide support (O) (for his parents (B)) as well as the new family (A) ((that) he and his wife would be starting).
B as well as A: A뿐만 아니라 B도
그는, 그와 그의 아내가 시작하고자 하는 새로운 가족은 물론이고 부모에 대한 부양도 제공할 필요가 있었다.

It was at this time that (it is ~ that 강조구문) Sigmund Freud (S), (in search of improved financial security), embarked (V) (on his career as a private physician).

지그문트 프로이트는, 향상된 금전적인 안전 상태를 추구하는 과정 속에서, 개인의사로서의 그의 경력을 시작했다.

| 어휘 | **physician** ⓝ 내과의사 **nervous disorder** 신경장애 **engagement** ⓝ 약혼
embark ⓥ 시작하다, 승선하다

| 전문해석 | 지그문트 프로이트(Sigmund Freud)는 심리학자가 되고자 하지 않았다. 그는 노년에 이르기까지 그 자신이 사회 심리학 분야에 별달리 큰 기여를 했다고 여기지도 않았다. 그는 단지 신경증 치료를 전문으로 하는 비엔나의 내과의사였다. 이러한

활동이 그로 하여금 인간의 사회적 행동을 인지하는 근본적으로 새로운 방식으로 그를 이끌었다는 사실은 그가 그 일을 행하고 있었을 때에는 프로이트 자신도 거의 상상하지 못했던 일이다.

사실, 프로이트가 사적인 진료(정신분석적인 진료)를 시작했을 때 프로이트의 나이는 이미 서른이었다. 그리고 그가 이러한 진료를 시작한 이유는 애초부터 과학적인 이유 때문이 아니라 금전적인 이유 때문이었다. 보기 ① 근거 4년 동안 약혼 상태를 지속하고 나서 프로이트는 1886년 가을 Martha Bernays와 결혼했다. 그는, 그와 그의 아내가 시작하고자 하는 새로운 가족은 물론이고 부모에 대한 부양도 제공할 필요가 있었다. 지그문트 프로이트는, 향상된 금전적인 안전 상태를 추구하는 과정 속에서, 개인의사로서의 그의 경력을 시작했다.

| 보기분석 | ✓ In a way his financial situation forced Freud to be a private physician.
어떤 면에서는, 재정적 상황이 프로이트로 하여금 개인의사가 되도록 만들었다.

② Freud never saw himself as a contributor to the field of social psychology. 지문에서 노년까지는 기여자라고 생각하지 않았다는 것은 노년 이후에는 생각했다는 것이다.
프로이트는 결코 자기 자신이 사회 심리학 분야에 기여한 사람이라고 생각하지 않는다.

③ From the start Freud determined to be a pioneer in understanding human psyche. 첫 줄에서 처음에는 그럴 의도가 없다고 했다.
처음부터 프로이트는 인간의 심리를 이해하는 데 있어서 선구자가 되기로 결심했다.

④ Unfortunately Freud's marriage made him give up significant psychological researches. 지문 내용과 불일치
불행하게도, 프로이트의 결혼은 그를 중요한 심리학 연구를 포기하게 만들었다.

| 정답분석 | 지문에서 프로이트가 개인의사 일을 시작한 것은 과학적 이유가 아니라 금전적인 이유 때문이라고 언급했으므로 ①이 정답으로 적절하다.

08 2014 한국외대

정답 ②

| 구문분석 | Languages (spoken at high altitudes) are more likely to contain a certain kind of sound (using short bursts of air), (according to a new study).
S V O

한 새로운 연구에 따르면, 고위도 지역에서 발음하는 언어들은 공기의 짧은 방출을 이용하는 특정한 소리를 포함할 가능성이 있다고 한다.

"I had this hypothesis [that certain sounds might be more common at high altitudes]," said study author Everett.
S V O =

"나는 어떤 소리들은 고위도에서 더 흔할 것이라는 이 가설을 세웠습니다."라고 이 연구의 저자 Everett은 말한다.

"(When I actually looked at the data), the distribution was (pretty) overwhelming," he said.
S V ⓐ 상당히 C

"내가 데이터를 실제로 살펴보니 분포가 상당히 놀랍습니다."라고 그는 말했다.

(Using an online database that categorizes languages based on their features), Everett analyzed the locations (of about 600 of the world's 7,000 languages).
분사구문 S V O

언어들을 그들이 갖고 있는 특징에 따라 분류하는 온라인 데이터베이스를 사용하여, Everett은 세계 7,000개의 언어 중 약 600개의 언어의 지역을 분석하였다.

He found that 92 of the languages contained ejective consonants.
S V O

그는 92개의 언어에 방출음이 있음을 발견했다.

Ejectives are sounds (produced with an intensive burst of air and are not found in English).
S V C

방출음은 강력한 공기 파열과 함께 만들어지는 소리이며 영어에서는 찾아볼 수 없는 소리이다.

Moreover, most of the languages (containing ejectives) were spoken (in, or near, five out of six high-altitude regions around the world).
접속부사 S V

더 나아가, 방출음이 있는 대부분의 언어들은, 세계의 고위도 지역 6곳 중 5곳에서 또는 그곳과 가까이에서 사용된다.

Ejectives are easier (to produce at high altitudes) (because air pressure decreases with altitude), and it takes less effort to compress less-dense air.
S V C 등위접속사
it takes 시간, 돈, 노력 toR: toR 하는 데 시간, 돈, 노력이 들다
고도가 높아짐에 따라 기압은 낮아지고, 밀도가 낮은 공기를 압축하는 것은 힘이 덜 들기 때문에 방출음은 고위도에서 발음하기가 더 쉽다.

But (there) is one high-altitude region (where the spoken languages did not contain ejectives): the Tibetan plateau.
V S 관계부사

그러나 고위도 지역인데도 그곳의 언어에 방출음이 없는 한 지역이 있다. 그리고 그것은 티베트고원이다.

People (there) have a unique adaptation (to high altitude) (that may account for this fact).
S V O 관계대명사
그곳에 사는 사람들은 이러한 사실을 아마도 설명해 줄 고위도에 적응하는 특별한 적응력을 갖고 있다.

| 어휘 |

altitude ⓝ 위도	**burst** ⓝ 파열, 폭발 ⓥ 터뜨리다	**hypothesis** ⓝ 가설
distribution ⓝ 분포, 분배	**ejective consonant** 방출음	**intensive** ⓐ 강한, 집중적인
compress ⓥ 압축하다	**plateau** ⓝ 고원	**facilitate** ⓥ 용이하게 하다, 촉진하다

| 전문해석 | 한 새로운 연구에 따르면, 고위도 지역에서 발음하는 언어들은 공기의 짧은 방출을 이용하는 특정한 소리를 포함할 가능성이 있다고 한다. "나는 어떤 소리들은 고위도에서 더 흔할 것이라는 이 가설을 세웠습니다."라고 이 연구의 저자 Everett은 말한다. "내가 데이터를 실제로 살펴보니 분포가 상당히 놀랍습니다."라고 그는 말했다. 언어들을 그들이 갖고 있는 특징에 따라 분류하는 온라인 데이터베이스를 사용하여, Everett은 세계 7,000개의 언어 중 약 600개의 언어의 지역을 분석하였다. 그는 92개의 언어에 방출음이 있음을 발견했다. 방출음은 강력한 공기 파열과 함께 만들어지는 소리이며 영어에서는 찾아볼 수 없는 소리이다. 더 나아가, 방출음이 있는 대부분의 언어들은, 세계의 고위도 지역 6곳 중 5곳에서 또는 그곳과 가까이에서 사용된다. 고도가 높아짐에 따라 기압은 낮아지고, 밀도가 낮은 공기를 압축하는 것은 힘이 덜 들기 때문에 방출음은 고위도에서 발음하기가 더 쉽다.(보기 ② 근거) 그러나 고위도 지역인데도 그곳의 언어에 방출음이 없는 한 지역이 있다. 그리고 그것은 티베트고원이다. 그곳에 사는 사람들은 이러한 사실을 아마도 설명해 줄 고위도에 적응하는 특별한 적응력을 갖고 있다.

| 보기분석 | ① Ejectives are easy to pronounce for native speakers of English. 영어에는 방출음이 없다고 했음
방출음은 영어가 모국어인 사람들에게 발음하기 쉽다.
② The decrease of air pressure can facilitate the pronunciation of ejectives.
공기 압력의 감소는 방출음의 발음을 용이하게 할 수 있다.
③ There are no high elevation regions where ejectives are absent. 고산지대임에도 방출음이 있는 지역이 한 군데 있다고 했음
고산지대에서 방출음이 없는 지역은 없다.
④ Ejectives are very common in languages around the world. 600개의 언어 중 92개에 방출음이 있으므로 흔하지 않음
방출음은 전 세계 언어에서 매우 흔하다.

| 정답분석 | 본문에 따르면 고도가 높아짐에 따라 기압은 낮아지고, 밀도가 낮은 공기를 압축하는 것은 힘이 덜 들기 때문에 방출음은 고위도에서 발음하기가 더 쉽다고 언급하였는데 이는 보기 ② '공기 압력의 감소는 방출음의 발음을 용이하게 할 수 있다.'와 일치한다. 따라서 ②가 정답으로 적절하다.

09 2018 한국외대

정답 ③

| 구문분석 | A holiday break is supposed to be just that (— a break —) and staying off your email and SNS can actually make you more productive (when you come back).
be supposed toR: ~하기로 되어 있다 / 등위접속사
S_1 V_1 O.C S_2 V_2 O O.C
휴가 기간에는 다름 아닌 바로 휴식을 취해야 하며 이메일과 SNS를 멀리하는 것이 휴가에서 복귀할 때 실제로 당신을 더욱 생산적이게 만들어 줄 수 있다.

(While unplugging feels great during your break), it can also make you feel (in over your head) (when you get back to work).
부사절: ~이긴 하지만 S V O O.C

휴가 기간 동안 플러그를 뽑아 놓는 것(이메일, SNS 등을 하지 않는 것)에 기분 좋은 느낌이 들지만, 그것은 당신이 업무에 복귀할 때 업무가 버거운 감이 들게 만들 수도 있다.

(To avoid feeling frazzled on that first morning), get a head start (while you are still on break).
부사적용법: ~하기 위하여 V O
휴가에서 복귀한 첫날 아침에 지친 느낌이 들지 않도록, 휴가 중인 동안에 업무를 미리 앞당겨 시작하라.

You should give yourself fifteen minutes (to go through your messages) (the night before returning to alleviate a lot of anxiety on your first day back).
S V I.O D.O 부사절: 전날 밤에

회사에 복귀한 첫날의 많은 불안감을 덜기 위해서 돌아오기 전날 밤에 15분 정도 시간을 내어 메시지를 살펴보라.

Remember to limit yourself to that short chunk (so you will not be concentrating on work) (when you are supposed to be relaxing).
V O so (that) 부사절: ~하기 위하여

느긋하게 휴식을 취해야 하는 때(휴가 기간)에 일에 몰두하게 되지 않으려면 (메시지를 살펴보는 시간을) 짧은 시간(15분)으로만 한정해야 한다는 것을 기억하라.

(When you get into your office), you should not assume (that) everyone else is rejuvenated.
부사절: ~할 때 S V
당신이 휴가 후에 출근할 때, 다른 모든 사람이 피로에서 회복하고 왔다고 생각해서는 안 된다.

A week off work is supposed to be a stress-free time, but it does not always work out.
S V O.C 등위접속사 S V
일주일간의 휴가는 스트레스가 없는 시간이어야 하지만, 항상 그렇게 되는 것은 아니다.

You might be refreshed and ready (to go), but your coworkers might still be burned out (from hosting out-of-town relatives).
S V C_1 C_2 등위접속사 S V

당신은 상쾌한 기분으로 일을 할 준비가 되어 있을지 모르지만, 동료들은 다른 지역에 사는 친척들을 접대한 일로 인해 여전히 지쳐 있을지도 모른다.

Get a feel (for what your colleagues' breaks were really like) (by specifically asking what they did for themselves over the holidays).
V O what S be like: S는 어떠한가

휴가 중에 (회사를 떠나) 개인적으로 무엇을 했는지 동료들에게 구체적으로 물어봄으로써 그들의 휴가가 어떠했는지 느껴 보도록 하라.

And finally, take some time (to transition) (from holiday mode to work mode).
V O
그리고 마지막으로 휴가 모드에서 업무 모드로 전환하는 시간을 가지도록 하라.

(The night before the workweek starts again), lay out your office clothes and prepare (for the next day).
부사절: 전날 밤에 V_1 O V_2
한 주의 근무가 다시 시작되기 전날 밤에, 근무복을 꺼내 놓고 다음 날을 준비하도록 하라.

This prompts you to get ready (for work).
S V O O.C
이것은 당신이 일할 준비를 하도록 자극한다.

| 어휘 |

stay off 삼가다, 멀리하다
unplug ⓥ ~에서 마개를 뽑다; ~에서 막힌 것[장애물]을 제거하다
in over one's head 힘에 벅차서; 자신이 감당할 수 있는 양을 상회하여 버거운
frazzled ⓐ 신경이 곤두선
head start 징조가 좋은 시작, 기선
go through ~을 살펴보다[조사하다]
chunk ⓝ 상당한 양, 대량
rejuvenate ⓥ 활기를 되찾게 하다
stress-free ⓐ 스트레스 없는
work out (일이) 잘 풀리다
burn out 에너지를 소진하다[소진하게 만들다]
transition ⓝ 변천, 이행
workweek ⓝ 근무 주 (*cf.* workday 근무일)
lay out (보기 쉽게, 사용할 수 있도록) ~을 펼치다, ~을 꺼내 놓다

| 전문해석 | 휴가 기간에는 다름 아닌 바로 휴식을 취해야 하며 이메일과 SNS를 멀리하는 것이 휴가에서 복귀할 때 실제로 당신을 더욱 생산적이게 만들어 줄 수 있다. 휴가 기간 동안 플러그를 뽑아 놓는 것(이메일, SNS 등을 하지 않는 것)에 기분 좋은 느낌이 들지만, 그것은 당신이 업무에 복귀할 때 업무가 버거운 감이 들게 만들 수도 있다. 휴가에서 복귀한 첫날 아침에 지친 느낌이 들지 않도록, 휴가 중인 동안에 업무를 미리 앞당겨 시작하라. 회사에 복귀한 첫날의 많은 불안감을 덜기 위해서 돌아오기 전날 밤에 15분 정도 시간을 내어 메시지를 살펴보라. 느긋하게 휴식을 취해야 하는 때(휴가 기간)에 일에 몰두하게
보기 ③ 근거

되지 않으려면 (메시지를 살펴보는 시간을) 짧은 시간(15분)으로만 한정해야 한다는 것을 기억하라. 당신이 휴가 후에 출근할 때, 다른 모든 사람이 피로에서 회복하고 왔다고 생각해서는 안 된다. 일주일간의 휴가는 스트레스가 없는 시간이어야 하지만, 항상 그렇게 되는 것은 아니다. 당신은 상쾌한 기분으로 일을 할 준비가 되어 있을지 모르지만, 동료들은 다른 지역에 사는 친척들을 접대한 일로 인해 여전히 지쳐 있을지도 모른다. 휴가 중에 (회사를 떠나) 개인적으로 무엇을 했는지 동료들에게 구체적으로 물어봄으로써 그들의 휴가가 어떠했는지 느껴 보도록 하라. 그리고 마지막으로 휴가 모드에서 업무 모드로 전환하는 시간을 가지도록 하라. 한 주의 근무가 다시 시작되기 전날 밤에, 근무복을 꺼내 놓고 다음 날을 준비하도록 하라. 이것은 당신이 일할 준비를 하도록 자극한다.

| 보기분석 | ① It is helpful to ~~frequently check~~ SNS for important messages. 지문 내용과 불일치
중요한 메시지를 확인하기 위해 SNS를 자주 확인하는 것은 유용하다.
② Asking about your colleagues' breaks is considered ~~impolite~~. 지문 내용과 불일치
동료들의 휴가에 관해 묻는 것은 예의 없는 것으로 여겨진다.
③ It is a good idea to be mentally prepared to return to work after a holiday.
휴가 후에 다시 일에 집중할 수 있도록 정신적으로 준비하는 것이 좋은 생각이다.
④ Hosting your relatives during the holidays ~~reduces~~ anxiety and stress. 지문 내용과 불일치
휴일 동안 친척을 접대하는 것은 불안과 스트레스를 감소시킨다.

| 정답분석 | 휴가 기간에 이메일, SNS를 멀리하라고 하였지만, 휴가에서 복귀하는 데 앞서 중요한 메시지를 짧게 살펴보고, 근무복을 꺼내 놓고 다음 날을 준비하도록 하라고 했으므로 이는 업무에 복귀하기 전에 마음의 준비를 하는 것에 해당한다. 따라서 ③이 정답으로 적절하다.

10 2018 가톨릭대

정답 ①

| 구문분석 | Phantom traffic jams (S), (in which cars suddenly screech to a dead stop on highways for no apparent reason) (관계대명사), have long annoyed (V) drivers (O).
뚜렷한 이유 없이 자동차가 고속도로에서 갑자기 서면서 꽉 막히는 유령 정체는 오랫동안 운전자들을 괴롭혀 왔다.

Interestingly, MIT researchers (S) have recently offered (V) a solution (O) (to help alleviate this stop-and-go driving).
흥미롭게도, 최근에 MIT의 연구원들은 이와 같이 가다 서다 운전을 완화하는 데 도움을 줄 수 있는 해결책을 제시했다.

The logic (S) is (V) rather simple (C): (콜론: 세부사항 재진술) The problem (S) is (V) inherent (C) (in our way of driving a car).
논리는 꽤 단순하다. 문제는 우리가 운전을 하는 방식에 내재해 있다는 것이다.

(If one car suddenly brakes) (부사절: 만약 ~라면), the car (S_1) (behind it) has to brake (V_1) and (등위접속사) the car (S_2) (behind it) has to brake (V_2).
만약 어떤 차가 급브레이크를 밟으면, 그 차의 뒤에 있는 차도 브레이크를 밟아야 하고, 그 뒤에 있는 차도 브레이크를 밟아야 한다.

The braking (S) increases (V) (with distance) (until a car actually stops) (부사절: ~까지).
차가 실제로 멈출 때까지 거리에 비례해서 브레이크를 밟는 차는 늘어난다.

Dr. Hornstein (S), (=) professor at MIT's Computer Science and Artificial Intelligence Laboratory, proposes (V) redesigning the cruise control feature (O) (on our car) (to consider the space in front and behind the vehicle) (부사적용법: ~하기 위하여).
MIT의 컴퓨터과학 및 인공지능 연구실의 교수인 혼스타인(Hornstein) 박사는 우리의 자동차에 달려 있는 크루즈 컨트롤 기능을 차량 앞뒤의 공간을 고려하도록 재설계할 것을 제안한다.

(To be sure), there (유도부사) are (V) advanced cruise control systems (S) (on the market today) (that will adapt to the speed of a lead vehicle in order to maintain a steady following distance) (관계대명사).

확실히, 뒤따라가는 거리를 일정하게 안정적으로 유지하기 위해 앞서가는 차량의 속도에 맞추는 첨단 크루즈 컨트롤 시스템이 현재 출시되어 있긴 하다.

등위접속사
But the gap (between the vehicle and a trailing car) isn't considered.
S V
그러나 차량과 뒤따라오는 차량 사이의 간격은 고려되지 않고 있다.

Keeping the same distance (between the vehicle in front and the vehicle trailing a car) would prevent traffic jams.
S V O

앞쪽의 차량과 뒤쪽의 차량 간에 똑같은 거리를 유지하는 것은 교통 정체를 막아 줄 것이다.

The technical name (proposed for the traffic-busting technology) is bilateral control.
S V C
교통 정체를 해결하는 그 기술에 대해 제안된 전문 용어는 양방향 컨트롤이다.

| 어휘 | **phantom** ⓝ 환영, 유령; 환각 **screech** ⓥ 날카로운[새된] 소리를 내다; (자동차 따위가) 갑자기 서다
apparent ⓐ (눈에) 또렷한, 보이는; 명백한 **solution** ⓝ 해답, 해법; 용액
alleviate ⓥ 경감하다, 완화하다 **inherent** ⓐ 본래부터 가지고 있는, 본래의, 고유의
feature ⓝ 특징, 특색 **adapt** ⓥ 적합하게 하다, 적응시키다
vehicle ⓝ (사람 · 물건의) 수송 수단, (자동차 등의) 탈것; 매개물
trail ⓥ 질질 끌다; ~의 뒤에서 따라가다 **prevent** ⓥ 막다, 예방하다
bilateral ⓐ 양측의; 쌍무적인

| 전문해석 | 뚜렷한 이유 없이 자동차가 고속도로에서 갑자기 서면서 꽉 막히는 유령 정체는 오랫동안 운전자들을 괴롭혀 왔다. 흥미롭게도, 최근에 MIT의 연구원들은 이와 같이 가다 서다 운전을 완화하는 데 도움을 줄 수 있는 해결책을 제시했다. 논리는 꽤 단순하다. 문제는 우리가 운전을 하는 방식에 내재해 있다는 것이다. 어떤 차가 급브레이크를 밟으면, 그 차의 뒤에 있는 차도 브레이크를 밟아야 하고, 그 뒤에 있는 차도 브레이크를 밟아야 한다. 차가 실제로 멈출 때까지 거리에 비례해서 브레이크를 밟는 차는 늘어난다. MIT의 컴퓨터과학 및 인공지능 연구실의 교수인 혼스타인(Hornstein) 박사는 우리의 자동차에 달려 있는 크루즈 컨트롤 기능을 차량 앞뒤의 공간을 고려하도록 재설계할 것을 제안한다. 보기 ① 근거 1 확실히, 뒤따라가는 거리를 일정하게 안정적으로 유지하기 위해 앞서가는 차량의 속도에 맞추는 첨단 크루즈 컨트롤 시스템이 현재 출시되어 있긴 하다. 그러나 차량과 뒤따라오는 차량 사이의 간격은 고려되지 않고 있다. 앞쪽의 차량과 뒤쪽의 차량 간에 똑같은 거리를 유지하는 것이 교통 정체를 막아 줄 것이다. 교통 정체를 해결하는 그 기술에 대해 제안된 전문 용어는 양방향 컨트롤이다. 보기 ① 근거 2

| 보기분석 | ① Traffic jams could be solved by redesigned cruise control.
교통 체증은 재설계된 크루즈 컨트롤로 해결될 수 있다.
② Undesirable driving habits often cause highway traffic jams. 앞차가 브레이크를 밟으면 뒤차도 브레이크를 밟는 운전자들의 행동이 교통 체증의 원인인데, 브레이크를 밟는 것이 바람직하지 않은 운전 습관은 아님
바람직하지 않은 운전 습관들이 종종 고속도로 교통 체증의 원인이다.
③ Research results show that highway traffic is beyond our control. 통제가 가능한 해결책을 제안하는 글임
연구 결과들은 고속도로 교통이 우리의 통제를 벗어난다는 것을 보여 준다.
④ Traditional cruise control may increase vehicle crashes. 언급한 적이 없으므로 알 수 없음
전통적인 크루즈 컨트롤이 아마도 차량 충돌을 증가시킨다.

| 정답분석 | 이 지문은 현재의 크루즈 컨트롤 기능은 앞차와의 간격만을 유지하게 하는데, 그것만으로는 한계가 있으므로 새로운 해결책으로서 뒤차와의 간격도 앞차와의 간격만큼 유지하게 하도록 하면 '유령 정체' 문제를 해결할 수 있다는 내용이다. 따라서 ①이 정답으로 적절하다.

11 2013 한국외대

정답 ③

| 구문분석 | Scientists are interested (in how the brain grows and ages).
S V C
과학자들은 뇌가 어떻게 성장하고 늙어 가는지에 관심을 갖고 있다.

(Before a child is two years old), (there) is a surge (in brain growth and development).
V S
아이가 두 살이 되기 전에는 뇌의 성장과 발전에 있어서 큰 상승이 존재한다.

(During these early years), billions of new neurons are added (to the body).
S V
이러한 첫 몇 년 동안 수십억 개의 새로운 뉴런이 더해진다.

Each one is connected (to thousands of others), (making trillions of connections).
S V 분사구문
각각의 뉴런은 수천 개의 다른 뉴런과 연결되어, 수백억 개의 연결이 이루어진다.

However, (after the age of three), a new process begins. The connections (that are used a lot) remain strong and survive).
접속부사: 그러나 S V S 관계대명사 V_1 C V_2
하지만 세 살이 지나면 새로운 과정이 시작된다. 많이 사용되던 연결은 튼튼한 상태로 살아남는다.

(connections)
Connections (that are not used a lot) become weak and are lost.
S 관계대명사 V_1 C 등위접속사 V_2
많이 사용되지 않았던 연결들은 약해져서 사라지게 된다.

For example, one child (who is given books to read at an early age) may learn to read (by the age of four).
접속부사 S V O
예를 들어, 한 살 때 책을 접해 본 아이는 네 살 정도쯤에는 읽는 법을 배울 수도 있다.

have trouble ~ing : ~하는 데 어려움을 겪다
On the other hand, a child (who is not given any books to read at an early age) may have trouble (learning to read).
접속부사 S V O

반면에 유아기에 책을 전혀 접해 보지 않은 아이는 글 읽는 법을 배울 때 어려움을 겪을 수도 있다.

등위접속사
This process continues, and our brains remain sensitive (to stimulation and experience into old age).
S_1 V_1 S_2 V_2 C
이런 과정은 계속되고 나이가 들어서까지 우리의 뇌는 자극과 경험에 예민한 상태로 유지된다.

Older people (who stay physically and mentally active) can still make and keep neural connections.
S 관계대명사 V O
신체적으로도 정신적으로도 활동적인 노년층은 나이가 들어서도 뉴런의 연결을 만들고 유지한다.

| 어휘 | **surge** ⓝ 급상승 **neuron** ⓝ 뉴런 **sensitive** ⓐ 민감한

| 전문해석 | 과학자들은 뇌가 어떻게 성장하고 늙어 가는지에 관심을 갖고 있다. 아이가 두 살이 되기 전에는 뇌의 성장과 발전에 있어서 큰 상승이 존재한다. 이러한 첫 몇 년 동안 수십억 개의 새로운 뉴런이 더해진다. 각각의 뉴런은 수천 개의 다른 뉴런과 연결되어, 수백억 개의 연결이 이루어진다. 하지만 세 살이 지나면 새로운 과정이 시작된다. 많이 사용되던 연결은 튼튼한 상태로 살아남는다. 많이 사용되지 않았던 연결들은 약해져서 사라지게 된다. 예를 들어, 한 살 때 책을 접해 본 아이는 네 살 정도쯤에는 읽는 법을 배울 수도 있다. 반면에 유아기에 책을 전혀 접해 보지 않은 아이는 글 읽는 법을 배울 때 어려움을 겪을 수도 있다. 이런 과정은 계속되고 나이가 들어서까지 우리의 뇌는 자극과 경험에 예민한 상태로 유지된다. 신체적으로도 정신적으로도 활동적인 노년층은 나이가 들어서도 뉴런의 연결을 만들고 유지한다.
(보기 ③ 근거 1, 보기 ③ 근거 2)

| 보기분석 |
① ~~Aging~~ can make neural connections stronger. 노화가 아니라 사용 여부가 신경 연결을 강하게 만듦
노화는 신경 연결을 더 강하게 만들 수 있다.
② An aged person ~~cannot make~~ new neural connections. 지문 내용과 불일치
나이 든 사람은 새로운 신경 연결을 형성할 수 없다.
③ Brain development does not occur at a uniform rate.
뇌 발달은 획일적인 속도로 일어나지 않는다.
④ Neural connections begin to form robustly ~~after~~ the age of three. 신경 연결은 3세 전에 강하게 형성됨
신경 연결은 3세 이후로 강하게 형성되기 시작한다.

| 정답분석 | 지문에서 두 살까지 뇌는 급속히 성장하고 그 이후에는 사용 여부에 따라 발전하기도 하고 퇴화하기도 한다고 했으므로 '뇌 발달은 획일적인 속도로 일어나지 않는다.'는 ③이 정답으로 적절하다.

12 2013 한양대

정답 ④

| 구문분석 | Happiness is never more than partial.
S V C

행복은 불완전한 것 이상이 결코 아니다.

There are no pure states of mankind.
유도부사 V S

인간에게 순수한 완전한 상태란 것은 없다.

not A but B: A가 아니라 B

What the Founding Fathers declared (for us as an inherent right), (we should do well to remember), was not happiness but the *pursuit* of happiness.
S V A B

우리가 기억해야 하는 것은, 우리의 선조들이 우리의 타고난 권리라고 선언한 것은 행복이 아니라, 행복의 '추구'라는 점이다.

if절에서 if를 생략하면 S와 V를 도치한다. If they could have foreseen ~ = could they have foreseen ~

What they might have underlined, (could they have foreseen the happiness-market), is the cardinal fact [that happiness is in the pursuit of itself, in the meaningful pursuit of what is life-engaging and life-revealing].
S if 생략 도치 V C =

그들이 행복 시장을 예언했더라면 그들이 아마도 강조했었을 것은 행복은 행복 자체를 추구하는 데 있다는 것, 다시 말해 삶을 매력적으로 만들어 주고, 삶을 흥미롭게 해 주는 것을 의미 있게 추구하는 데 있다는 중요한 사실일 것이다.

| 어휘 |

partial ⓐ 불완전한
Founding Fathers 미국 헌법 제정자들
inherent ⓐ 선천적인
inherent right 생득권
do well to *do* ~하는 편이 낫다
underline ⓥ 강조하다
cardinal ⓐ 주요한, 기본적인
engaging ⓐ 매력적인
revealing ⓐ 흥미로운 사실을 드러내는[보여 주는]

| 전문해석 | 행복은 불완전한 것 이상이 결코 아니다. 인간에게 순수한 완전한 상태란 것은 없다. 우리가 기억해야 하는 것은, 우리의 선조들이 우리의 타고난 권리라고 선언한 것은 행복이 아니라, 행복의 '추구'라는 점이다. 그들이 행복 시장을 예언했더라면 그들이 아마도 강조했었을 것은 행복은 행복 자체를 추구하는 데 있다는 것, 다시 말해 삶을 매력적으로 만들어 주고, 삶을 흥미롭게 해 주는 것을 의미 있게 추구하는 데 있다는 중요한 사실일 것이다.
보기 ④ 근거 / 보기 ④ 근거 / 보기 ④ 근거

| 보기분석 |

① There is such a thing as perfect happiness. 지문에서 완벽한 행복은 없다고 했음
완벽한 행복과 같은 그런 것이 존재한다.

② People may be of the illusion that happiness can be bought. 언급한 적이 없으므로 알 수 없음
사람들은 아마도 행복을 돈으로 살 수 있다는 착각을 한다.

③ According to the Founding Fathers, happiness is an inherent right. 지문에서 타고난 권리는 행복이 아니라 행복의 추구라고 했음
미국 건국 선조들에 따르면, 행복은 타고난 권리이다.

④ Whatever else happiness may be, it is neither in having nor in being, but in becoming.
행복이 무엇이든지, (행복을) 소유하든지 (현재 이미) 행복한 것이 아니라, 행복하게 되어 가는 것에 있다.

| 정답분석 | 이 글은 행복이란 완전하고, 완성된 게 아니며 행복은 추구하는 것에 있다는 글이다. 한편 become의 의미는 '~이 되다'라는 변화의 의미를 내포하고 있는데 따라서 '추구'와 같은 의미를 가질 수 있다. 그러므로 ④가 이 글을 통해 추론 가능한 가장 적절한 답이다.

13 2015 광운대

정답 ③

| 구문분석 | A word of encouragement (for my working moms): You are actually more productive than your childless peers.
S 콜론: 재진술

워킹맘들을 위한 격려의 말이 있다. 당신들은 실제로 아이가 없는 또래의 동료들보다 더 생산적이다.

(Over the course of a 30-year career), mothers outperformed women (without children at almost every stage of the game).
S V O

30년에 걸친 직장생활 동안, 어머니들은 거의 모든 단계에서 아이가 없는 여성들보다 더 나은 수행능력을 보여 주었다.

In fact, mothers (with at least two kids) were the most productive (of all).
접속부사 S V C
사실, 최소한 두 명의 아이가 있는 어머니들이 가장 생산성이 높았다.

= Here is 콜론: 재진술
Here's how the researchers (all men, by the way) came up with those results: They wanted to understand the impact (of having children on highly-skilled women), but their work is often difficult (to quantify).
유도부사 V S S_1 V_1 O 등위접속사 S_2 V_2 C
어떻게 연구원들(그런데 연구원들은 모두 남자였다)이 그와 같은 결과를 내놓았는지는 여기에 있다. 그들은 아이를 가지는 것이 고숙련 여성들에게 미치는 영향을 알기를 원했다. 그러나 그들의 작업은 종종 수량화하기가 쉽지 않다.

How do you determine the productivity (of a surgeon or a project manager)?
의문문 도치 S V O
외과 의사나 프로젝트 매니저의 생산성을 어떻게 결정할 수 있겠는가?

They decided to analyze the amount (of research) (published by more than 10,000 academic economists as a proxy for performance).
S V O
그들은 10,000명 이상의 (여성) 경제학자들이 발표한 연구의 양을 업무 수행을 위한 대체물로서 분석하기로 결정했다.

A job (in the ivory tower of academia) requires higher education (by definition), and their work is easily searched, recorded, and ranked.
S_1 V_1 O 등위접속사 S_2 V_2
학계의 상아탑 속에서의 일은 당연히 고등교육이 필요하고, 그들(경제학자)의 일[업적]은 찾아지고, 기록되고, 평가하기 쉽다.

| 어휘 |

outperform ⓥ 능가하다 come up with 제시하다 quantify ⓥ 수량화하다
proxy ⓝ 대리, 대용물, 대체물 ivory tower ⓝ 상아탑(실사회에서 동떨어진 사색의 세계, 특히 대학)
academia ⓝ 학계 by definition 정의상으로, 당연하게

| 전문해석 |

워킹맘들을 위한 격려의 말이 있다. 당신들은 실제로 아이가 없는 또래의 동료들보다 더 생산적이다. 30년에 걸친 직장생활 동안, 어머니들은 거의 모든 단계에서 아이가 없는 여성들보다 더 나은 수행능력을 보여 주었다. 사실, 최소한 두 명의 아이가 있는 어머니들이 가장 생산성이 높았다. 어떻게 연구원들(그런데 연구원들은 모두 남자였다)이 그와 같은 결과를 내놓았는지는 여기에 있다. 그들은 아이를 가지는 것이 고숙련 여성들에게 미치는 영향을 알기를 원했다. 그러나 그들의 작업은 종종 수량화하기가 쉽지 않다. 외과 의사나 프로젝트 매니저의 생산성을 어떻게 결정할 수 있겠는가? 연구원들은 10,000명 이상의 (여성) 경제학자들이 발표한 연구의 양을 업무 수행을 위한 대체물로서 분석하기로 결정했다. 학계의 상아탑 속에서의 일은 당연히 고등교육이 필요하고, 그들(경제학자)의 일[업적]은 찾아지고, 기록되고, 평가하기 쉽다.
보기 ③ 근거

| 보기분석 |

① The productivity of a project manager can be easily quantified and analyzed. 프로젝트 매니저의 생산성은 측정, 분석이 쉽지 않음
프로젝트 매니저의 생산성은 쉽게 양적으로 측정하고 분석할 수 있다.
② Mothers of one child outperformed those with two or more children. 최소한 두 명의 아이가 있는 어머니들이 생산성이 제일 높았음
한 명의 자녀를 둔 어머니들이 둘 이상의 자녀를 둔 어머니들보다 성과가 더 좋았다.
③ This study did not include mothers whose work was irrelevant to academia.
이 연구는 학문과 관련이 없는 일을 하는 어머니들은 포함되지 않았다.
④ The research team that conducted this study was comprised mostly of women. 연구진들은 모두 남자라고 언급함
이 연구를 수행한 연구팀은 주로 여성으로 구성되어 있다.
⑤ Mothers with children published a less amount of research than childless women. 아이가 있는 어머니들이 생산성이 높다고 했으므로 더 많은 연구를 게재했을 것임
아이가 있는 어머니들은 아이가 없는 여성들보다 더 적은 연구를 게재했다.

| 정답분석 |

지문에서 고숙련 여성들의 생산성을 측정하는 것이 어려워서, 10,000명에 달하는 (여성) 경제학자들이 발표한 연구의 양을 분석하기로 했다고 언급했다. 결국 연구에는 경제학과 관련된 어머니들만 포함되었으므로 ③은 지문 내용을 통해 알 수 있으며, 따라서 정답으로 적절하다.

14 2015 단국대

정답 ②

| 구문분석 |

The art of advertising contains many ambiguities.
S V O
광고기법은 많은 애매모호한 표현들을 포함하고 있다.

be charged with: ~로 가득 차다
Some are charged (with multiple shades of meaning).
S V
어떤 광고들은 다양하고 미묘한 차이와 의미로 가득 차 있다.

The demons may be taken (to represent the problems and cares) (which one can presumably chase away through consumption of the advertised product).
S V 관계대명사

악마들은 광고되는 상품의 소비를 통해서 누군가가 쫓아버릴 수 있다고 가정된 문제들과 걱정들을 나타내는 것으로 여겨질 수 있다.

Or they can, just as easily, be taken (as representations of the playful spirits) (which will be unleashed (once the product has been consumed).
S V 관계대명사 부사절: 일단 ~하면

혹은 악마들은 상품이 소비되고 나면 풀려날 수 있는 장난기 많은 귀신을 표현한 것으로 여겨질 수도 있다.

The advertising creative director did not create the need (to relax), or (to get away from the stresses of daily life); he or she merely took advantage (of these common human needs) (in developing a promotion strategy for the product).
S V O 1 2
세미콜론: and 역할
S V O
take advantage of: ~을 이용하다

광고를 창조적으로 제작하는 감독은 휴식을 취하려는 욕구나 일상의 스트레스로부터 벗어나고자 하는 욕구를 창조하고자 하지 않는다. 그 혹은 그녀(감독)는 단지 상품의 판매를 촉진하는 전략을 개발하는 데 이들 보편적인 인간의 욕구를 이용할 뿐이다.

| 어휘 | **ambiguity** ⓝ 애매모호함, 명확하지 않음
be charged with 가득 차 있다, 책임 맡고 있다, 혐의를 받다 **shade** ⓝ 그늘, 색조의 미묘한 차이
demon ⓝ 악마 **presumably** ⓐⓓ 추측건대 **unleash** ⓥ 포박을 풀다, 해방되다
promotion ⓝ 승진, 진급, 조장, 장려, 판촉

| 전문해석 | 광고기법은 많은 애매모호한 표현들을 포함하고 있다. 어떤 광고들은 다양하고 미묘한 차이와 의미로 가득 차 있다. 악마들은 광고되는 상품의 소비를 통해서 누군가가 쫓아버릴 수 있다고 가정된 문제들과 걱정들을 나타내는 것으로 여겨질 수 있다. 혹은 악마들은 상품이 소비되고 나면 풀려날 수 있는 장난기 많은 귀신을 표현한 것으로 여겨질 수도 있다. 광고를 창조적으로 제작하는 감독은 휴식을 취하려는 욕구나 일상의 스트레스로부터 벗어나고자 하는 욕구를 창조하고자 하지 않는다. 그 혹은 그녀(감독)는 단지 상품의 판매를 촉진하는 전략을 개발하는 데 이들 보편적인 인간의 욕구를 이용할 뿐이다.
보기 ② 근거

| 보기분석 | ① The advertisement should have a ~~transparent point~~ to show off. 광고는 판매를 촉진하는 데만 신경 쓴다고 했으므로 솔직한 관점과는 상관없음
광고는 과시(광고)를 위해 분명하고 솔직한 관점을 가져야 한다.
② An image in advertisements can have different meanings according to the context.
광고에서의 어떤 이미지는 상황에 따라 다른 의미를 가질 수 있다.
③ The advertisement ~~should lessen~~ the stresses of consumers. 광고 감독이 판매 촉진을 목적으로 소비자의 스트레스를 줄이거나 휴식을 취하려는 욕구를 이용한다고만 언급했지, 줄여야 하는 것은 아님
광고는 소비자들의 스트레스를 줄여야 한다.
④ An image in advertisements should ~~have a focus~~ on which a consumer's need is fixed. 소비자의 욕구에 맞추는 것이 아니라 판매 촉진을 위해 소비자의 욕구를 이용하는 것임
광고 이미지는 소비자의 필요에 고정된[맞춘] 초점을 가져야 한다.

| 정답분석 | 지문에서 '광고기법은 많은 애매모호한 표현들을 포함하고 있다.'라고 했는데 결국 광고는 받아들이는 사람에 따라 의미가 달라지는 '상대적인' 것일 수 있다는 것이다. 따라서 ②가 정답으로 적절하다.

15 2015 한양대(에리카)

정답 ③

have an impact on: ~에 영향을 주다
| 구문분석 | The 1930s had a devastating impact (on American agriculture).
S V O
1930년대는 미국의 농업에 파괴적인 충격을 가했다.

The Great Depression (coupled with a prolonged drought and dust storms) (in the nation's heartland) spurred an exodus (of displaced farmers to nearby cities or to the promised land of California).
S V
O
미국의 심장부에서 벌어진 대공황과 장기간 이어진 가뭄, 그리고 먼지 폭풍은 농민들이 부근의 도시나 약속의 땅 캘리포니아를 향해 집단적으로 이주하는 것을 부추겼다.

John Steinbeck's novel *The Grapes of Wrath* (1939) and a popular film (based on the book) captured their plight, (tracing a dispossessed family's trek from Oklahoma to California).
S V O
분사구문

존 스타인벡(John Steinbeck)의 소설 '분노의 포도(*The Grapes of Wrath*)(1939)'와 그 책을 원작으로 하여 인기를 끈 영화는 전 재산을 잃은 한 가정이 오클라호마에서부터 캘리포니아까지 가는 여정을 따라가면서, 그들의 비참한 곤경을 정확하게 담아냈다.

(Before the book appeared), Steinbeck had written a series of newspaper articles (based on interviews with local migrants), later (gathered in a book, *The Harvest Gypsies*).
부사절: ~ 전에 S V O =

그 책이 등장하기 전, 스타인벡은 지역 이주민들과의 인터뷰를 바탕으로 한 연재 신문 기사를 쓴 적이 있었는데, 나중에, 스타인벡은 그 기사들을 한데 모아서 '추수하는 집시들(*The Harvest Gypsies*)'이라는 책을 냈다.

| 어휘 |

devastating ⓐ 황폐시키는, 파괴적인
impact ⓝ 충돌, 충격
the Great Depression 대공황
dust storm 모래 폭풍, 황사
heartland ⓝ 심장부, 중심지역
spur ⓥ 박차를 가하다
exodus ⓝ 집단적 대이동
displace ⓥ 쫓아내다, 추방하다
capture ⓥ 포착하다, 표현하다
plight ⓝ 곤경, 궁지
dispossessed ⓐ 쫓겨난, 재산을 빼앗긴
article ⓝ 기사, 논설

| 전문해석 | 1930년대는 미국의 농업에 파괴적인 충격을 가했다. 미국의 심장부에서 벌어진 대공황과 장기간 이어진 가뭄, 그리고 먼지 폭풍은 농민들이 부근의 도시나 약속의 땅 캘리포니아를 향해 집단적으로 탈출하는 것을 부추겼다. 존 스타인벡(John Steinbeck)의 소설 '분노의 포도(*The Grapes of Wrath*)(1939)'와 그 책을 원작으로 하여 인기를 끈 영화는 전 재산을 잃은 한 가정이 오클라호마에서부터 캘리포니아까지 가는 여정을 따라가면서, 그들의 비참한 곤경을 정확하게 담아냈다. 그 책이 등장하기 전, 스타인벡은 지역 이주민들과의 인터뷰를 바탕으로 한 연재 신문 기사를 쓴 적이 있었는데, 나중에, 스타인벡은 그 기사들을 한데 모아서 '추수하는 집시들(*The Harvest Gypsies*)'이라는 책을 냈다.
보기 ③ 근거

| 보기분석 |
① *The Grapes of Wrath* was written ~~prior to~~ the newspaper articles. '분노의 포도' 전에 기사를 쓴 적이 있다고 함
신문 기사보다 이전에 '분노의 포도(*The Grapes of Wrath*)'가 쓰였다.
② Displaced farmers migrated to urban areas ~~solely~~ because of the Great Depression. 경제뿐 아니라 가뭄과 같은 자연재해도 이유임
쫓겨난 농부들이 도시로 이주한 것은 오로지 경제 대공황 때문이다.
③ The nation's heartland experienced a prolonged drought and dust storms in the 1930s.
1930년대 미국 중심지역은 장기간의 가뭄과 먼지 폭풍을 겪었다.
④ *The ~~Harvest Gypsies~~* was based on a dispossessed family's journey from Oklahoma to California.
'추수하는 집시들(*The Harvest Gypsies*)'은 쫓겨난 가족의 오클라호마에서 캘리포니아로의 여정을 기반으로 한다. 쫓겨난 가족의 여정은 '추수하는 집시들'이 아니라 '분노의 포도'임

| 정답분석 | 지문에 따르면, 1930년대 미국의 심장부는 가뭄과 먼지 폭풍으로 고통받았다고 언급했다. 따라서 ③이 정답으로 적절하다.

16 2017 가톨릭대

정답 ③

| 구문분석 | An economist addressed the nature-nurture debate (by taking a long-term quantitative look) (at the effects of parenting).
S V O

한 경제학자는 양육의 영향에 대한 장기적인 정량적 관찰을 통해 본성(선천) 대 양육(후천)에 대한 논쟁을 다루었다.

He used three adoption studies, each of them (containing in-depth data) (about the adopted children, their adoptive parents, and their biological parents).
S V O =

그는 세 가지 입양 연구를 사용했는데, 이 각각의 연구에는 입양아와 그들의 양부모, 그리고 친부모에 대한 상세한 데이터가 담겨 있었다.

The researcher found [that parents (who adopt children) are typically smarter, better educated, and more highly paid than the baby's biological parents].
S V O 관계대명사

그 연구자는 아이를 입양한 부모들이 친부모보다 일반적으로 더 똑똑하고, 더 많은 교육을 받았으며, 고액의 연봉을 받는다는 것을 확인했다.

have bearing on: ~와 관련 있다

But the adoptive parents' advantages had little bearing (on the child's school performance).
S V O

그러나 양부모의 이러한 장점들이 입양된 아이의 학업 성적과는 관련이 없었다.

세미콜론: and 역할 (that)

Adopted children test (relatively poorly in school); any influence (the adoptive parents might exert) is seemingly outweighed (by the force of genetics).
S_1 V_1 S_2 V_2

입양아들은 학교에서 상대적으로 시험성적이 좋지 못하며, 양부모가 미칠지도 모르는 영향력이 유전적인 힘보다 중요하지 않아 보인다.

(that)

However, the researcher found the parents were not powerless forever.
접속부사 S V O

그러나 그 연구가는 양부모가 언제나 무력하지는 않다는 것을 확인했다.

(By the time the adopted children became adults), they had veered (sharply from the destiny) (that IQ alone might have predicted).
부사절: ~할 때쯤 S V 관계대명사

입양아들이 성인이 되었을 때, 그들은 IQ(지능지수)만을 통해 예측되었던 운명에서 상당히 달라져 있었다.

be likely to: ~일 가능성이 있다
likely ⓐ 그럴듯한, 가능성이 있는

(Compared to similar children who were not put up for adoption), the adoptees were far more likely (to attend college and to have a well-paid job).
분사구문 S V C

입양이 되지 않은 비슷한 아이들과 비교해서 입양아들은 대학에 입학하고 보수가 좋은 직장에 다닐 확률이 훨씬 높았다.

It was the influence of the adoptive parents, the researcher concluded, that made the difference.
강조구문의 it 강조구문의 that

연구자는 양부모의 영향이 그 차이를 만들어 냈다고 결론을 내렸다.

| 어휘 |

quantitative ⓐ 양적인	**in-depth** ⓐ 철저한, 면밀한	**adopted child** 양자
adoptive parents 양부모	**have a bearing on** ~와 관계가 있다	**exert** ⓥ 발휘하다, 행사하다
seemingly ⓐⓓ 외견상으로, 겉보기에는	**outweigh** ⓥ ~보다 더 크다[대단하다]	**genetics** ⓝ 유전학
powerless ⓐ 힘없는, 무력한	**veer** ⓥ 바뀌다, 전향하다	

| 전문해석 | 한 경제학자는 양육의 영향에 대한 장기적인 정량적 관찰을 통해 본성(선천) 대 양육(후천)에 대한 논쟁을 다루었다. 그는 세 가지 입양 연구를 사용했는데, 이 각각의 연구에는 입양아와 그들의 양부모, 그리고 친부모에 대한 상세한 데이터가 담겨 있었다. 그 연구자는 아이를 입양한 부모들이 친부모보다 일반적으로 더 똑똑하고, 더 많은 교육을 받았으며, 고액의 연봉을 받는다는 것을 확인했다. 그러나 양부모의 이러한 장점들이 입양된 아이의 학업 성적과는 관련이 없었다. 입양아들은 학교에서 상대적으로 시험성적이 좋지 못하며, 양부모가 미칠지도 모르는 영향력이 유전적인 힘보다 중요하지 않아 보인다. 그러나 그 연구가는 양부모가 언제나 무력하지는 않다는 것을 확인했다. 입양아들이 성인이 되었을 때, 그들은 IQ(지능지수)만을 통해 예측되었던 운명에서 상당히 달라져 있었다. 입양이 되지 않은 비슷한 아이들과 비교해서 입양아들은 대학에 입학하고 보수가 좋은 직장에 다닐 확률이 훨씬 높았다. 연구자는 양부모의 영향이 그 차이를 만들어 냈다고 결론을 내렸다.
보기 ③ 근거 1
보기 ③ 근거 2

| 보기분석 |

① The debate on nature versus nurture is ~~outdated~~ and unhelpful. 지문 내용과 불일치
본성 대 양육에 대한 논쟁은 시대에 뒤떨어졌으며 도움이 되지 않는다.

② Genetic factors may affect some children ~~more strongly~~ than others. 어릴 적에는 유전적 영향이 나타나고, 다 큰 뒤에는 환경의 영향이 나타난다는 글이므로 둘 다 아이들에게 영향을 준다.
유전적인 요인들이 다른 요인들보다 아이들에게 더 강하게 영향을 미칠지도 모른다.

③ The influence of genes and environment may surface at different life stages.
유전과 환경의 영향은 삶의 다른 단계에서 아마도 나타날지도 모른다.

④ Adopted children are ~~not~~ optimal subjects for examining environmental influence. 입양된 아이는 후천(환경)적 영향을 조사하는 데 적합한 대상이다.
입양된 아이들은 환경적 영향을 조사하는 데 최적의 대상이 아니다.

| 정답분석 | 지문에서 "본성 대 양육에 대한 연구에서, 입양아가 어렸을 때는 양부모의 영향력이 입양아의 학업 성적에 큰 영향력을 주지 못하며, 유전적인 요인이 양부모가 미치는 영향보다 크다고 했지만, 아이가 성인이 되어서는 대학에 입학하고 보수가 좋은 직장에 다닐 확률이 높았다."고 했으므로, ③ '유전과 환경의 영향은 삶의 다른 단계에서 아마도 나타날지도 모른다.'가 정답으로 적절하다.

17 2019 한국외대

정답 ③

| 구문분석 | The Red Cross(S) estimates(V) that 6.8 million people donate blood in the U.S. every year(O), (giving approximately 13.6 million units of blood)(분사구문).

적십자는 매년 미국에서 680만 명의 사람들이 헌혈을 해서, 약 1,360만 통의 혈액을 제공하고 있는 것으로 추정하고 있다.

The earliest known human-to-human blood donation(S) came(V) (in 1818), (before humans even knew what blood types were)(부사절: ~ 전에), (when obstetrician James Blundell transferred blood to a woman who had just given birth)(관계부사: 1818년을 수식).

인간이 혈액형이 무엇인지 알기도 전인 1818년에, 최초로 알려져 있는 인간에게서 인간으로의 헌혈이 이루어졌는데, 당시 산부인과 의사인 제임스 브룬델(James Blundell)은 막 출산한 여성에게 수혈을 했다.

(Having watched many patients die in childbirth)(분사구문), Blundell(S) wrote(V) that his experimental procedure stemmed from being appalled at his own helplessness(O).

많은 환자들이 출산 중에 죽는 것을 목격한 브룬델은 그의 실험적인 수술이 자신의 무력함에 충격을 받은 데서 비롯되었다고 기록했다.

(For the rest of the century), scientists(S) experimented(V) (with blood transfer).

남은 19세기 기간 동안, 과학자들은 수혈을 실험했다.

Not all of these ideas(S) were(V) successful(C) (— some advocated infusing humans with cow's milk), (which(관계대명사) was considered superior to actual blood).

이런 과학자들의 생각들이 모두 성공적이었던 것은 아니었다. 예를 들어, 우유가 실제 인간의 혈액보다 우수한 것으로 생각해서 일부 과학자들은 인간에게 우유를 주입할 것을 주장했다.

(From 1873 through 1880), the milk-for-blood trend(S) swept(V) (through the U.S).

1873년부터 1880년까지 수혈을 우유로 하는 추세는 미국 전역을 휩쓸었다.

Thankfully, soon an Austrian biologist(S) would make(V) a discovery(O) (that(관계대명사) would change everything).

다행스럽게도, 얼마 지나지 않아 오스트리아의 한 생물학자가 모든 것을 바꿔 놓는 발견을 했다.

(In 1901), Karl Landsteiner(S) realized(V) that foreign bodies were broken up in the human bloodstream by hemoglobin in human-to-human blood transfers(O).

1901년, 카를 란트슈타이너(Karl Landsteiner)는 인간 간의 수혈에서 이물질(다른 사람의 혈액)이 헤모글로빈에 의해 인체의 혈류에서 파괴된다는 것을 깨달았다.

(In 1909), (when(관계부사) Landsteiner first classified human blood into types), his work(S) really took off(V).

1909년에 란트슈타이너는 처음으로 인간의 피를 여러 혈액형으로 분류했고, 그의 연구가 실제로 시작되었다.

These groups(S) are(V) what are known today as A, B, AB, and O(C).

이들 혈액형은 현재 A, B, AB, O형으로 알려져 있는 것들이다.

| 어휘 |
blood type ⓝ 혈액형
obstetrician ⓝ 산부인과 의사
procedure ⓝ 절차, 방법; 수술
appall ⓥ 오싹하게[질겁하게] 하다, 질리게 하다
stem from ~에서 생겨나다, 기인하다
helplessness ⓝ 무력함
infuse ⓥ (정맥에 서서히) 주입하다
sweep through ~을 휩쓸다
bloodstream ⓝ (인체의) 혈류

| 전문해석 | 적십자는 매년 미국에서 680만 명의 사람들이 헌혈을 해서, 약 1,360만 통의 혈액을 제공하고 있는 것으로 추정하고 있다. 인간이 혈액형이 무엇인지 알기도 전인 1818년에, 최초로 알려져 있는 인간에게서 인간으로의 헌혈이 이루어졌는데, 당시 산부인과 의사인 제임스 브룬델(James Blundell)은 막 출산한 여성에게 수혈을 했다. 많은 환자들이 출산 중에 죽는 것을

목격한 브룬델은 그의 실험적인 수술이 자신의 무력함에 충격을 받은 데서 비롯되었다고 기록했다. 남은 19세기 기간 동안, 과학자들은 수혈을 실험했다. 이런 과학자들의 생각들이 모두 성공적이었던 것은 아니었다. 예를 들어, 우유가 실제 인간의 혈액보다 우수한 것으로 생각해서 일부 과학자들은 인간에게 우유를 주입할 것을 주장했다. 1873년부터 1880년까지 수혈을 우유로 하는 추세는 미국 전역을 휩쓸었다. 다행스럽게도, 얼마 지나지 않아 오스트리아의 한 생물학자가 모든 것을 바꿔 놓는 발견을 했다. 1901년, 카를 란트슈타이너(Karl Landsteiner)는 인간 간의 수혈에서 이물질(다른 사람의 혈액)이 헤모글로빈에 의해 인체의 혈류에서 파괴된다는 것을 깨달았다. 1909년에 란트슈타이너는 처음으로 인간의 피를 여러 혈액형으로 분류했고, 그의 연구가 실제로 시작되었다. 이들 혈액형은 현재 A, B, AB, O형으로 알려져 있는 것들이다.

보기 ③ 근거

| 보기분석 |

① Nearly fourteen million Americans donate blood every year. 헌혈하는 미국인은 680만 명임
매년 거의 1,400만 명의 미국인들이 헌혈을 한다.

② Landsteiner took off work in 1909 in order to develop transfers. 란트슈타이너는 인간의 피를 여러 혈액형으로 분류하고자 실험을 시작했다.
란트슈타이너는 수혈을 발전시키기 위해 1909년에 연구를 시작했다.

③ Blundell felt aghast at his inability to prevent women from dying in childbirth.
브룬델은 여성들이 출산 중에 죽는 것을 막지 못한 자신의 무능함에 대해 아연실색했다.

④ Blood transfers currently disregard the groups that Landsteiner discovered. 언급한 적이 없으므로 알 수 없음
혈액 수혈은 현재 란트슈타이너가 발견한 혈액형의 분류를 무시한다.

| 정답분석 | 지문에서 브룬델은 출산 중에 죽어 가는 많은 여성들을 보고 자신의 무력함에 충격을 받고 실험적인 수술(수혈)을 하게 되었다고 했으므로, ③이 정답으로 적절하다.

18 2017 한양대

정답 ②

| 구문분석 |

People (from cultures on polychronic time) live their lives (quite differently) (than do those who move to the monochronic clock).
S V O

다중시간(P-time) 문화 출신의 사람들은 단일시간(M-time)에 따라 움직이는 사람들과 다르게 삶을 살고 있다.

The pace for P-time cultures is more leisurely (than the one found in M-time cultures).
S V C

P-time 문화들의 속도는 M-time 문화들에서 발견된 것보다 더 여유롭고 느긋하다.

One reason (for this) is that people and human relationships, not tasks, are at the center of polychronic cultures.
S V C

이에 대한 한 가지 이유는 업무가 아니라 사람들과 인간관계가 P-time 문화의 중심에 있다는 것이다.

등위접속사

These cultures are normally collective and deal (with life in a holistic manner).
S V_1 C V_2

이러한 문화들은 보통은 집단적이고 삶을 전체적인 방식으로 다룬다.

as ~ as 원급 구문에서 앞의 as는 부사이며 뒤의 as는 부사절을 이끄는 접속사이다.

(For P-time cultures), time is less tangible; hence, feelings of wasted time are not (as) prevalent (as in M-time cultures).
S V C 접속부사 S V C

P-time 문화에서는 시간은 덜 유형적이고 따라서 시간 낭비라는 느낌은 M-time 문화에서만큼 만연되어 있지는 않다.

등위접속사

Their members can interact (with more than one person) or do more than one thing (at a time), (while people from M-time cultures suppress spontaneity and tend to focus on one activity at a time).
S V_1 V_2 O 부사절: 반면에

그들 구성원들은 한 사람 이상과 교류할 수 있거나 한 번에 한 가지 이상의 일을 할 수 있는 데 반해, M-time 문화의 사람들은 자발성을 억제하고 한 번에 한 가지 활동에 초점을 둔다.

This explains why there are more interruptions (in conversations) (carried on by people from Arabic, Asian, and Latin American cultures compared to the ones from Germany, Austria, Switzerland, and the U.S.)
S V C

이것은 독일, 오스트리아, 스위스 그리고 미국 문화권 사람들에 비해 아랍, 아시아, 그리고 라틴 아메리카 문화권 사람들이 하는 대화가 더 중단되는 일이 잦은 이유를 설명해 준다.

| 어휘 | **polychronic** ⓐ 다중시간형의 **monochronic** ⓐ 단일시간형의 **holistic** ⓐ 전체적인, 전체론의 **tangible** ⓐ 만져서 알 수 있는; 명백한 **prevalent** ⓐ 널리 보급된, 만연한 **spontaneity** ⓝ 자발성, 자발적 행동

| 전문해석 | 다중시간(P-time) 문화 출신의 사람들은 단일시간(M-time)에 따라 움직이는 사람들과 다르게 삶을 살고 있다. P-time 문화들의 속도는 M-time 문화들에서 발견된 것보다 더 여유롭고 느긋하다. 이에 대한 한 가지 이유는 업무가 아니라 사람들과 인간관계가 P-time 문화의 중심에 있다는 것이다. 이러한 문화들은 보통은 집단적이고 삶을 전체적인 방식으로 다룬다. P-time 문화에서는 시간이 덜 유형적이고 따라서 시간 낭비라는 느낌은 M-time 문화에서만큼 만연되어 있지는 않다. 그들 구성원들은 한 사람 이상과 교류할 수 있거나 한 번에 한 가지 이상의 일을 할 수 있는 데 반해, M-time 문화의 사람들은 자발성을 억제하고 한 번에 한 가지 활동에 초점을 둔다. 이것은 독일, 오스트리아, 스위스 그리고 미국 문화권 사람들에 비해 아랍, 아시아, 그리고 라틴 아메리카 문화권 사람들이 하는 대화가 더 중단되는 일이 잦은 이유를 설명해 준다.
보기 ② 근거

| 보기분석 | ① Feelings of wasted time are more prevalent in P-time cultures. 지문 내용과 불일치
시간 낭비라는 느낌은 P-time 문화에서 더 만연되어 있다.
② People in polychronic cultures can do multiple things simultaneously.
P-time 문화의 사랑들은 동시에 여러 가지 일을 할 수 있다.
③ People in monochronic cultures think highly of relationships with others. 지문 내용과 불일치
M-time 문화의 사람들은 다른 이들과의 관계를 몹시 중시한다.
④ Arabic, Asian, and Latin American cultures are categorized as M-time cultures. 지문 내용과 불일치
아랍, 아시아, 그리고 라틴 아메리카 문화들은 M-time 문화로 분류된다.

| 정답분석 | 지문에서 'P-time 문화의 구성원들은 한 번에 한 가지 이상의 일을 할 수 있다'고 했으므로, 정답으로 ②가 적절하다.

19 2013 서강대

정답 ④

| 구문분석 | such N as = N such as: ~와 같은
Physiognomists(S) study(V) such features(O) (as the shape of the head, the length and thickness of the neck, the color and thickness of the hair, and the shape of the nose, mouth, eyes, and chin).

인상학자들은 머리의 형태, 목의 길이 및 굵기, 머리카락의 색과 두께, 코, 입, 눈, 빰의 형태와 같은 특징들에 관한 연구한다.

They(S) believe(V) that round-faced people are self-confident(O).
이들은 둥근 얼굴을 한 사람들은 자신감이 있는 사람이라고 믿는다.

Prominent cheekbones(S) show(V) strength(O) of character, (while a pointed nose reveals curiosity).
부사절: ~ 반면에
광대뼈가 두드러진 사람은 성격이 강한 사람이고, 코가 뾰족한 사람은 호기심이 많은 사람이다.

A related (— though not as ancient —) art(S) is(V) phrenology(C), the study (of the bumps on the head).
인상학만큼은 오래되지 않았지만, 그와 비슷한 기술로서 골상학이 있는데, 골상학은 머리에 있는 융기에 관한 연구이다.

Phrenologists(S) have identified(V) 40 bumps(O) (of various shapes and sizes on the human head).
골상학자들은 인간의 머리에서 다양한 형태와 크기의 40개의 튀어나온 부분을 확인하였다.

They(S) read(V) these bumps(O) (to identify a person's talents and character).
부사적용법: ~하기 위하여 or 그 결과
이들은 이러한 튀어나온 부분들을 읽어 사람의 재능과 성격을 확인하였다.

For example, a bump(S) (between the nose and forehead) is said(V) (to be present) (in people) (who have natural elegance and a love of beauty).
관계대명사

예를 들어 코와 이마 사이에 튀어나온 부분이 있으면, 그 사람은 타고나길 우아한 사람이며, 아름다움을 사랑하는 사람이다.

not so much A as B = not A but B
Phrenologists(S) are(V) not so much interested in health(A) as they are (interested) in character and personality(B).
골상학자들은 건강보다는 성격이나 개성에 더 관심이 있었다.

They believe, for example, that a bulge in the center of the forehead is typical of people (who have a good memory and a desire for knowledge).
S V O 관계대명사

예를 들어 이들은 이마 한가운데에 융기가 있으면 그 사람은 기억이 좋고 지식에 대한 욕망이 충만한 사람이라고 생각했다.

| 어휘 | **physionomist** ⓝ 인상학자 **feature** ⓝ 특징 **phrenology** ⓝ 골상학
bump ⓝ 융기 **forehead** ⓝ 이마 **not so much A as B** A보다는 B이다
bulge ⓝ 부풀어 오름

| 전문해석 | 인상학자들은 머리의 형태, 목의 길이 및 굵기, 머리카락의 색과 두께, 코, 입, 눈, 뺨의 형태와 같은 특징들에 관한 연구한다. 이들은 둥근 얼굴을 한 사람들은 자신감이 있는 사람이라고 믿는다. 광대뼈가 두드러진 사람은 성격이 강한 사람이고, 코가 뾰족한 사람은 호기심이 많은 사람이다. 인상학만큼은 오래되지 않았지만, 그와 비슷한 기술로서 골상학이 있다는데, 골상학은 머리에 있는 융기에 관한 연구이다. 골상학자들은 인간의 머리에서 다양한 형태와 크기의 40개의 튀어나온 부분을 확인하였다. 이들은 이러한 튀어나온 부분들을 읽어 사람의 재능과 성격을 확인하였다. 예를 들어 코와 이마 사이에 튀어나온 부분이 있으면, 그 사람은 타고나길 우아한 사람이며, 아름다움을 사랑하는 사람이다. 골상학자들은 건강보다는 성격이나 개성에 더 관심이 있었다. 예를 들어 이들은 이마 한가운데 융기가 있으면 그 사람은 기억이 좋고 지식에 대한 욕망이 충만한 사람이라고 생각했다.
보기 ④ 근거

| 보기분석 | ① Phrenologists study people's appearances and how it affects their ~~physical and mental health~~. 지문 내용과 불일치
골상학자들은 인간의 외모를 연구하고 그것이 신체적, 정신적 건강에 어떤 영향을 미치는지를 연구한다.
② Physiognomy differs from phrenology in that physiognomists predict ~~people's future~~ by reading their physical features. 지문 내용과 불일치
인상학자들은 인간의 신체적인 특징을 읽어 사람들의 미래를 예측한다는 점에서 인상학과 골상학은 다르다.
③ It ~~is not possible~~ to understand a person's talents or personality without knowing ~~all~~ of the information about the body parts. 지문 내용과 불일치
신체의 여러 기관들과 관련된 모든 정보를 알지 못하고는 한 사람의 재능이나, 성격을 이해하는 것은 가능하지 않다.
④ According to phrenology, there are forty different parts of the human head that show a person's talents and character.
골상학에 따르면 인간의 머리에는 인간의 재능과 성격을 보여 주는 40가지의 별개의 부분이 있다.

| 정답분석 | 지문에서 '골상학자들은 인간의 머리에서 다양한 형태와 크기의 40개의 튀어나온 부분을 확인하고, 이러한 튀어나온 부분들을 읽어 사람의 재능과 성격을 확인하였다.'고 언급했으므로 ④가 정답으로 적절하다.

20 2015 숙명여대

정답 ①

| 구문분석 | Most obviously, cheaper energy prices will incrementally increase the temptation (to fritter away precious power) — (to leave the car engine idling, or to fail to go upstairs to switch off that light).
S V O
대시: 부연설명

분명한 점은, 더 값싸진 에너지 가격이, 귀중한 에너지원을 조금씩 낭비하게 하는 유혹을 점진적으로 증가시킨다는 것이다—자동차 엔진을 공회전하도록 내버려 두고, 전등을 끄기 위해 위층으로 올라가지 않게 된다.

Little habits matter, (because, with the clock ticking remorselessly down towards climate catastrophe, every little hurts).
S V 부사절: ~ 때문에

작은 습관들이 중요하다. 그 이유는 기후적 대재앙을 향해 시간이 무자비하게 시시각각 흘러가는 와중에서는 사소한 모든 것들이 해를 입힐 수 있기 때문이다.

How much damage the great oil crash will do here depends (on what happens next).
S V

유가의 폭락이 얼마나 많은 해를 입힐 것인가는, 다음에 일어나는 일에 달려 있다.

not only A but also B: A뿐 아니라 B도
In the past, the world has been stunned not only by the waning but also the waxing of the price.
S V A B

과거에, 세계는 유가의 하락은 물론이고 유가의 상승에 의해서도 큰 타격을 받았다.

(If what comes down soon goes back up), such direct effects may not prove so profound.
부사절: 만일 ~라면 S V C
만일 떨어지고 있는 에너지 가격이 다시 반등한다면, 그와 같은 직접적인 영향은 그렇게 심각하지는 않을 것이다.

What will matter more in the longer term is the dynamic effect (on the energy infrastructure).
S V C
장기적인 관점에서 보았을 때 더 중요한 것은 에너지 하부구조에 대한 역동적인 영향이다.

| 어휘 |

incrementally ⓐⓓ 점진적으로
temptation ⓝ 유혹
fritter away 조금씩 허비하다, 낭비하다
idle ⓥ 공회전하다
remorselessly ⓐⓓ 냉혹하게, 무자비하게
catastrophe ⓝ 파국, 대재앙
stun ⓥ 기절시킬 정도로 놀라게 하다
wane ⓥ 작아지다, 약해지다
wax ⓥ 커지다
profound ⓐ (충격 등이) 큰, 심각한
infrastructure ⓝ (조직 · 제도 따위의) 하부구조, 토대

| 전문해석 | 분명한 점은, 더 값싸진 에너지 가격이, 귀중한 에너지원을 조금씩 낭비하게 하는 유혹을 점진적으로 증가시킨다는 것이다 (보기 ① 근거) —자동차 엔진을 공회전하도록 내버려 두고, 전등을 끄기 위해 위층으로 올라가지 않게 된다. 작은 습관들이 중요하다, 그 이유는 기후적 대재앙을 향해 시간이 무자비하게 시시각각 흘러가는 와중에서는 사소한 모든 것들이 해를 입힐 수 있기 때문이다. 유가의 폭락이 얼마나 많은 해를 입힐 것인가는, 다음에 일어나는 일에 달려 있다. 과거에, 세계는 유가의 하락은 물론이고 유가의 상승에 의해서도 큰 타격을 받았다. 만일 떨어지고 있는 에너지 가격이 다시 반등한다면, 그와 같은 직접적인 영향은 그렇게 심각하지는 않을 것이다. 장기적인 관점에서 보았을 때 더 중요한 것은 에너지 하부구조에 대한 역동적인 영향이다.

| 보기분석 |

① Cheap oil will discourage investment in alternative energy.
싼 유가는 대체에너지에 대한 투자를 저하시킬 것이다.

② High energy prices will help to push inflation lower. 인플레이션(물가상승)은 언급한 적이 없음
높은 에너지 가격은 인플레이션을 낮추는 데 도움이 될 것이다.

③ Manufacturers of electric cars will expand their production lines. 전기차 제조업체들에 대해 언급한 적이 없음
전기 자동차 제조업체들은 생산 라인을 확장할 것이다.

④ Oil-exporters will be the obvious winners from sliding oil prices. 원유 수출국에 대해 지문을 통해 알 수 없음
원유 수출국들은 원유 가격 하락에서 명백한 승자가 될 것이다.

⑤ The most exploitative schemes to extract fossil fuels will become more economic. 기름도 화석 연료에 속하는데 그것이 미래에 더 경제적인지는 지문을 통해 알 수 없음
화석 연료를 추출하는 가장 착취적 계획들이 더 경제적인 것이 될 것이다.

| 정답분석 | 지문 내용을 근거로 해 보면 에너지 가격이 높다면 값싼 대체에너지를 찾으려 할 것인데, 에너지 가격이 낮으면 계속해서 그 에너지를 사용하기 때문에, 대체에너지의 필요성을 생각하지 못할 것이다. 따라서 ① '싼 유가는 대체에너지에 대한 투자를 저하시킬 것이다.'가 정답으로 적절하다.

5강 내용 불일치 / 내용 비추론

Practice

01	②	02	③	03	③	04	③	05	②	06	②	07	②	08	③	09	①	10	④
11	③	12	③	13	①	14	②	15	④	16	④	17	②	18	②	19	①	20	⑤

01 2018 가천대

정답 ②

| 구문분석 |

(In February of 1950), a US senator Joseph McCarthy publicly claimed that thousands of Americans were alleged to be communists; such accusations were frequently deemed valid (even with unsubstantiated or questionable evidence).
(S: a US senator Joseph McCarthy / V: claimed / O: that thousands of Americans were alleged to be communists; 세미콜론: and 역할; S: such accusations / V: were frequently deemed / O.C: valid)

1950년 2월, 미국의 상원의원인 조셉 매카시(Joseph McCarthy)는 수천 명의 미국인들이 공산주의자라고 공개적으로 주장했다. 그러한 비난은 심지어 근거 없던지 의심스러운 증거로도 종종 타당한 것으로 여겨졌다.

Scant members of the press dared challenge McCarthy, but Edward R. Murrow was an exception.
(S: Scant members of the press / V: dared challenge / O: McCarthy; dare (to)R: 과감히 ~하다; but: 등위접속사; S: Edward R. Murrow / V: was / C: an exception)

얼마 안 되는 기자들만이 과감히 매카시에게 이의를 제기했지만, 에드워드 머로(Edward R. Murrow)는 예외였다.

(On his TV show), he confronted the communist witch-hunt (that was taking place).
(S: he / V: confronted / O: the communist witch-hunt; that: 관계대명사)

그의 TV쇼에서 그는 (그 당시에) 발생 중이던 공산주의자 마녀사냥에 정면으로 맞섰다.

Murrow revealed (to his public) [that the true threat to democracy was not the supposed Communists, but rather the way (in which McCarthy had acted)].
(S: Murrow / V: revealed / O: [that ...]; in which: 관계대명사)

민주주의의 진짜 위기는 공산주의자로 추정되는 이들이 아니라 오히려 매카시가 그동안 취해 왔던 방식이라고 머로는 대중들에게 말했다.

Murrow articulated this (in his tailpiece): "The line (between investigating and persecuting) is a very fine one.
(S: Murrow / V: articulated / O: this; 콜론: 동격; S: The line / V: is / C: a very fine one)

머로는 그의 TV쇼가 끝날 무렵 다음과 같이 말했다. "조사와 박해를 구분하는 선은 매우 미세한 선입니다.

We must not confuse dissent (with disloyalty)."
(S: We / V: must not confuse / O: dissent; confuse A with B: A와 B를 혼동하다)

우리는 반대와 불충을 혼동해서는 안 됩니다."

| 어휘 |

- **senator** ⓝ 상원의원
- **allege** ⓥ 단언하다
- **accusation** ⓝ 비난
- **deem** ⓥ 생각하다, 여기다
- **unsubstantiated** ⓐ 근거 없는
- **scant** ⓐ 얼마 안 되는, 불충분한, 부족한
- **exception** ⓝ 예외
- **confront** ⓥ (문제나 곤란한 상황에) 맞서다
- **witch-hunt** ⓝ 마녀사냥
- **articulate** ⓥ (생각을) 표현하다
- **tailpiece** ⓝ (글 끝의) 추가 부분
- **persecute** ⓥ 박해하다, 학대하다
- **dissent** ⓝ 이의, 반대의견
- **disloyalty** ⓝ 불충, 불성실
- **initiate** ⓥ 시작하다
- **considerable** ⓐ 상당한, 많은
- **condemnation** ⓝ 심한 비난, 책망
- **declare** ⓥ 선언하다
- **guilt** ⓝ 유죄

| 전문해석 |

1950년 2월, 미국의 상원의원인 조셉 매카시(Joseph McCarthy)는 수천 명의 미국인들이 공산주의자라고 공개적으로 주장했다. 그러한 비난은 심지어 근거 없던지 의심스러운 증거로도 종종(보기 ① 근거) 타당한 것으로 여겨졌다. 얼마 안 되는 기자들만이 과감히 매카시에게 이의를 제기했지만, 에드워드 머로(Edward R. Murrow)는 예외였다. 그의 TV쇼에서 그는 (그 당시에)

발생 중이던 공산주의자 마녀사냥에 정면으로 맞섰다. 민주주의의 진짜 위기는 공산주의자로 추정되는 이들이 아니라 오히려 매카시가 그동안 취해 왔던 방식이라고 머로는 대중들에게 말했다. 머로는 그의 TV쇼가 끝날 무렵 다음과 같이 말했다. "조사와 박해를 구분하는 선은 매우 미세한 선입니다. 우리는 반대와 불충을 혼동해서는 안 됩니다."

보기 ③ 근거 / 보기 ④ 근거

| 보기분석 | ① There were plenty of false accusations about the communist initiated by McCarthy.
매카시가 시작한 공산주의자에 대한 거짓된 비난이 많았다.

② McCarthy was challenged by a ~~considerable~~ members of the press. 지문 내용과 불일치
매카시는 상당한 언론인들에게 도전받았다.

③ Murrow directly voiced condemnation of the Communist witch-hunt.
머로는 공산주의자 마녀사냥에 대한 비난을 직접적으로 표명했다.

④ Murrow insisted on the necessity of proof before declaring guilt.
머로는 유죄 판결 전에 증거의 필요성을 주장했다.

| 정답분석 | 지문에서 얼마 안 되는 기자들만이 매카시의 의견에 이의를 제기했다고 했는데 보기 ②에서는 '상당한 언론인들'에게 도전받았다고 했으므로 ②가 정답으로 적절하다.

02 2018 가톨릭대

정답 ③

| 구문분석 | (Unlike mammals and birds), snakes(S) cannot generate(V) body heat(O) (through the digestion of food).
포유류나 새와 달리, 뱀은 음식의 소화를 통해 체열을 발생시키지 못한다.

They(S) must depend(V) (on external sources of heat, such as sunlight), (to maintain body temperature).
부사적용법: ~하기 위하여
뱀은 체온을 유지하기 위해 햇빛과 같은 외부의 열원에 의지한다.

Temperature control(S) is(V) particularly important(C) (when snakes are digesting a meal, or in the case of females, reproducing).
등위접속사
체온 조절은 뱀이 먹은 것을 소화하고 있거나 혹은 암컷의 경우에는 번식을 하고 있는 때에 특히 중요하다.

Many snakes(S) increase(V) the amount of time(O) (spent basking in the sun) (after they have eaten a large meal in order to speed up the digestive process).
부사절: ~ 이후에
(in order) toR: ~하기 위하여
많은 뱀은 많은 양의 음식을 먹은 후에는 소화 과정을 더 빠르게 하고자 햇볕을 쬐는 데 쓰는 시간의 양을 늘린다.

(To conserve their heat), snakes(S) coil up(V) tightly, so that only a small portion of their skin is exposed to cooler air.
부사적용법: ~하기 위하여 / 부사절: 결과
열을 보존하기 위해, 뱀은 몸을 단단히 감고 그 결과 피부의 극히 일부만 차가운 공기에 노출되도록 한다.

| 어휘 |
mammal ⓝ 포유류, 포유동물
generate ⓥ 산출하다, 생기게 하다; 발생시키다, 일으키다
digestion ⓝ 소화, 소화력
external ⓐ 외부의, 밖의
source ⓝ 원천; 근원
maintain ⓥ 지속하다, 유지하다; 주장하다
temperature ⓝ 기온, 체온
reproduce ⓥ 생식하다, 번식하다
bask ⓥ 몸을 녹이다, 햇볕을 쬐다
coil ⓥ (고리 모양으로) 감다, 휘감다
conserver ⓥ 보존하다, 보호하다
expose ⓥ 노출시키다, (몸을) 드러내다

| 전문해석 | 포유류나 새와 달리, 뱀은 음식의 소화를 통해 체열을 발생시키지 못한다. 뱀은 체온을 유지하기 위해 햇빛과 같은 외부의 열원에 의지한다. 체온 조절은 뱀이 먹은 것을 소화하고 있거나 혹은 암컷의 경우에는 번식을 하고 있는 때에 특히 중요하다. 많은 뱀은 많은 양의 음식을 먹은 후에는 소화 과정을 더 빠르게 하고자 햇볕을 쬐는 데 쓰는 시간의 양을 늘린다. 열을 보존하기 위해, 뱀은 몸을 단단히 감고 그 결과 피부의 극히 일부만 차가운 공기에 노출되도록 한다.

보기 ① 근거 / 보기 ④ 근거 / 보기 ② 근거

| 보기분석 | ① They usually get heat by lying in sunlight.
그들은 일반적으로 태양 빛에 누워 열을 얻는다.

② They coil their bodies in order to stay warm.
그들은 체온을 따뜻하게 유지하기 위해 몸을 둥글게 감는다.

③ Food is an ~~important~~ source of their body heat. 지문 내용과 불일치
음식은 그들 몸의 열의 중요한 원천이다.
④ Maintaining body temperature is important for digestion.
체온 유지는 소화에 중요하다.

| 정답분석 | 첫 번째 문장에서 '포유류나 새와 달리, 뱀은 음식의 소화를 통해 체열을 발생시키지 못한다.'고 했으므로, ③이 뱀에 대해 옳지 않은 진술이다.

03 2018 강남대

정답 ③

| 구문분석 | The greatest problem(S) for conservationists is(V) [that(C), (while we can make laws to protect certain species), we are frequently incapable of controlling the environment in which they live and breed].

자연보호론자들에게 있어 가장 큰 문제는 우리가 특정 종(種)을 보호하는 법을 만들 수는 있지만, 그 종들이 서식하고 새끼를 낳는 환경은 종종 통제할 수 없다는 점이다.

(In spite of taking action to prevent it), we(S) may pollute(V) rivers(O), (making fish sterile)(분사구문).

그것을 막기 위한 조치를 취함에도 불구하고 우리는 강을 오염시켜 물고기를 불임으로 만들지도 모른다.

부사절: 아무리 ~한다 해도
(However good our intentions are in destroying insects that eat crops), (at the same time), we(S) deprive(V) the birds (that(관계대명사) live on them).
live on: ~을 먹고 살다

농작물을 먹는 해충을 박멸하려는 우리의 의도가 아무리 좋다 하더라도 이와 동시에, 우리는 해충을 먹고 사는 새들에게서 먹이를 빼앗는 것이다.

be bound toR: 반드시 ~하다
Man(S) has not yet learned(V) how to deal with the balance of nature(O), and (whatever he does)(부사절 : 어떤 것이든, 무엇이든), he(S) is bound(V) (to alter it) (without even knowing).

인간은 아직 자연의 균형을 다루는 법을 배우지 못했으며 무슨 일을 해도 인간은 자신도 모르는 가운데 반드시 환경을 바꾸어 놓게 된다.

부사절: 비록 ~일지라도
But (though it(가주어) may not be possible to save(진주어) all the endangered species), it(가주어) may be possible to protect(진주어) the majority (by becoming aware of their serious condition before it is too late).

그러나 모든 멸종 위기에 처한 종들을 보호하는 것은 불가능할지 모르지만, 너무 늦기 전에 이들 종들의 심각한 상황을 알게 됨으로써 대다수의 종을 보호할 수는 있을지도 모른다.

| 어휘 |

conservationist ⓝ 자연보호론자	**breed** ⓥ 새끼를 낳다	**take action** 조치를 취하다
pollute ⓥ 오염시키다	**sterile** ⓐ 불임의	**deprive** ⓥ 빼앗다, 탈취하다
be bound to *do* 반드시 ~하다	**alter** ⓥ 변하다, 바꾸다, 고치다	**become aware of** ~을 알게 되다

| 전문해석 | 자연보호론자들에게 있어 가장 큰 문제는 우리가 특정 종(種)을 보호하는 법을 만들 수는 있지만, 그 종들이 서식하고 새끼를 낳는 환경은 종종 통제할 수 없다는 점이다. 그것을 막기 위한 조치를 취함에도 불구하고 우리는 강을 오염시켜 물고기를 불임으로 만들지도 모른다. 농작물을 먹는 해충을 박멸하려는 우리의 의도가 아무리 좋다 하더라도 이와 동시에, 우리는 해충을 먹고 사는 새들에게서 먹이를 빼앗는 것이다.(보기 ② 근거) 인간은 아직 자연의 균형을 다루는 법을 배우지 못했으며 무슨 일을 해도 인간은 자신도 모르는 가운데 반드시 환경을 바꾸어 놓게 된다. 그러나 모든 멸종 위기에 처한 종들을 보호하는 것은 불가능할지 모르지만, 너무 늦기 전에 이들 종들의 심각한 상황을 알게 됨으로써 대다수의 종을 보호할 수는 있을지도 모른다.

| 보기분석 | ① We are not able to control the environment.
우리는 환경을 통제할 수 없다.
② We cannot protect our crops from insects without harming the birds.
새를 해치지 않으면서는 작물을 벌레로부터 보호할 수 없다.
③ Man has ~~already learned~~ how to deal with the balance of nature. 지문 내용과 불일치
인간은 이미 자연의 균형을 다루는 방법을 배웠다.
④ We cannot expect to rescue all of the endangered animals from dying out.
우리는 멸종 위기에 처한 모든 동물들을 구조할 것을 기대할 수는 없다.

| 정답분석 | 지문에서 "인간은 아직 자연의 균형을 다루는 법을 배우지 못했다."라고 했으므로 ③이 지문과 불일치한다.

04 2018 명지대

정답 ③

| 구문분석 | (For those of us) (who like to create controlled flame from time to time with the strike of a match), we can thank a British pharmacist and his dirty mixing stick.

관계대명사 / we: S / can thank: V / a British pharmacist: O_1 / his dirty mixing stick: O_2

우리 중에 때때로 성냥을 그어 제어된 불꽃을 만들고 싶어 하는 사람은 영국의 어떤 약제사와 그의 더러운 혼합용 막대기에 감사할 일이다.

In 1826, John Walker noticed a dried lump (on the end of a stick) (while he was stirring a mix of chemicals).

John Walker: S / noticed: V / a dried lump: O / while: 부사절: ~ 동안에

1826년, 존 워커(John Walker)는 화학물질 혼합액을 (막대기로) 젓고 있다가 막대기 끝에 말라붙은 덩어리를 발견했다.

(When he tried to scrape it off), (voila), sparks and flame.

sparks and flame: V

그가 그 말라붙은 덩어리를 긁어 떼어 내려고 했을 때 보란 듯이 불꽃이 일더니 점화가 되었다.

(Jumping on the discovery), Walker marketed the first friction matches (as "Friction Lights") and sold them (at his pharmacy).

분사구문 / Walker: S / marketed: V_1 / the first friction matches: O / sold: V_2 / them: O

이 발견에 힘입어, 존 워커는 최초의 마찰 성냥을 "Friction Lights"라고 하며 시판에 나서 그가 운영하던 약국에서 팔았다.

The initial matches were made (of cardboard) but he soon replaced those (with three-inch long hand-cut wooden splints).

The initial matches: S / were made: V / but: 등위접속사 / he: S / replaced: V (replace A with B: A를 B로 대체하다) / those: O

최초의 성냥은 판지로 만들어져 있었으나, 그는 곧 그것을 손으로 만든 3인치 길이의 나무 성냥개비로 교체했다.

The matches came (in a box) (equipped with a piece of sandpaper for striking).

The matches: S / came: V

그 성냥은 성냥을 긋는 용도의 사포 조각이 붙어 있는 상자에 넣어져 출시되었다.

(Although advised to patent his invention), he chose not to (because he considered the product a benefit to mankind) (— which didn't stop others from ripping off the idea and taking over the market share, (leading Walker to stop producing his version).

Although: 부사절: 비록 ~일지라도 / he: S / chose: V / not to: O / because: 부사절: 때문에 / leading: 분사구문

비록 그의 발명품에 특허를 받으라는 조언을 받았지만, 존 워커는 자신이 만든 마찰 성냥이 인류 모두에게 이익이 되는 제품이라 여겨서 특허를 받지 않기로 했는데, 그로 인해 다른 사람들이 그의 생각을 훔쳐 가서 시장점유율을 차지하는 것을 막지 못했고, 결국 존 워커는 자신이 생산하던 성냥의 생산을 중지하게 되었다.

| 어휘 |

flame ⓝ 불꽃	**from time to time** 때때로	**strike** ⓥ (성냥을) 긋다
match ⓝ 성냥	**pharmacist** ⓝ 약사, 약제사	**lump** ⓝ (일정한 형태가 없는) 덩어리
stir ⓥ (저어 가며) 섞다	**scrape** ⓥ (무엇을 떼어 내기 위해) 긁다, 긁어내다	
voila int 자 봐, 보란 말이야, 어때	**pharmacy** ⓝ 약국	**cardboard** ⓝ 판지
splint ⓝ (성냥 따위의) 개비	**sandpaper** ⓝ 사포	**patent** ⓥ 특허를 받다
rip something off ~을 훔치다	**take over** (~을) 탈취[장악]하다	

| 전문해석 | 우리 중에 때때로 성냥을 그어 제어된 불꽃을 만들고 싶어 하는 사람은 영국의 어떤 약제사와 그의 더러운 혼합용 막대기에 감사할 일이다. 1826년, 존 워커(John Walker)는 화학물질 혼합액을 (막대기로) 젓고 있다가 막대기 끝에 말라붙은 덩어리를 발견했다. 그가 그 말라붙은 덩어리를 긁어 떼어 내려고 했을 때 보란 듯이 불꽃이 일더니 점화가 되었다. 이 발견에 힘입어, 존 워커는 최초의 마찰 성냥을 "Friction Lights"라고 하며 시판에 나서 그가 운영하던 약국에서 팔았다. 최초의 성냥은 판지로 만들어져 있었으나, 그는 곧 그것을 손으로 만든 3인치 길이의 나무 성냥개비로 교체했다. 그 성냥은 성냥을 긋는 용도의 사포 조각이 붙어 있는 상자에 넣어져 출시되었다. 비록 그의 발명품에 특허를 받으라는 조언을 받았지만, 존 워커는 자신이 만든 마찰 성냥이 인류 모두에게 이익이 되는 제품이라 여겨서 특허를 받지 않기로 했는데(보기 ④ 근거), 그로 인해 다른 사

람들이 그의 생각을 훔쳐 가서 시장점유율을 차지하는 것을 막지 못했고, 결국 존 워커는 자신이 생산하던 성냥의 생산을 중지하게 되었다.

| 보기분석 | ① Matches were invented by a British pharmacist.
성냥은 영국의 약제사에 의해 발명되었다.
② The invention of matches was by accident.
성냥은 우연히 발명되었다.
③ The first matches were made of ~~wooden splints~~. 지문 내용과 불일치
최초의 성냥은 나뭇개비로 만들어졌다.
④ John Walker did not patent his invention.
존 워커는 그의 발명품에 대해 특허를 받지 않았다.

| 정답분석 | 지문에서 최초의 성냥은 판지로 만들어져 있었으나, 그는 곧 그것을 손으로 만든 3인치 길이의 나무 성냥개비로 교체했다고 했으므로, ③이 지문과 불일치한다.

05 2018 한국외대

정답 ②

| 구문분석 | Numerous paintings of meals(S) show(V) what dining tables looked like(O) (before the seventeenth century).
what S be like: S가 어떠한가
식사가 그려진 다양한 그림들은 17세기 이전에 식탁의 모습이 어떠했는지를 보여 준다.

Forks(S) were not included(V) (until about 1600), and very few spoons(S) were shown(V).
대략 1600년까지 포크는 그림에 없었으며, 숟가락도 거의 보이지 않았다.

At least one knife(S) was always depicted(V) (— an especially large one when it was the only one available for all the guests —) but small individual knives(S) were(V) (often at each place).
적어도 한 개의 나이프—모든 손님들이 이용할 수 있는 하나밖에 없는 나이프이면 특별히 큰 나이프—는 항상 묘사되었지만 작은 개인용 나이프들이 각 사람의 자리에 있는 경우도 종종 있었다.

Tin disks(S) had already replaced(V) the large wooden plates(O).
주석 원반 접시가 이미 큰 나무 접시를 대체했다.

This change in eating utensils(S) typified(V) the new table manners(O) (in Europe).
식기류의 이런 변화는 유럽에서 새로운 식사 예절의 특징이 되는 것이었다.

(In many other parts of the world), no utensils(S) at all were used(V).
세계의 다른 많은 지역에서는 식기류가 전혀 사용되지 않았다.

(In the Near East), for example(접속부사), it(가주어) was traditional to eat(진주어) with the fingers of the right hand.
예를 들면, 근동(아라비아, 북동아프리카, 동남아시아, 발칸 등을 포함하는 지역)에서는 오른손으로 식사를 하는 것이 전통이었다.

Utensils(S) were employed(V) (in part) (because of a change in the attitude toward meat).
식기류가 사용된 이유의 일부는 고기에 대한 태도의 변화에 있었다.

(During the Middle Ages), whole sides of meat(S), (or even an entire carcass), had been brought(V_1) to the table and(등위접속사) then carved(V_2) in view of the diners.
중세시대 동안에는, 고기 전체 부위나 심지어 고기 몸통 전체가 식대에 올려졌으며, 식사하는 사람들이 보는 앞에서 고기를 베어 나누었다.

(Beginning(분사구문) in the seventeenth century), (at first in France but later elsewhere), the practice(S) began(V) to go out of fashion(O).

17세기 때부터, 프랑스에서 처음으로 그러나 그 이후에 다른 지역에서, 그런 관습은 시들기 시작했다.

One reason was that the family was decreasing in size and ceasing to be a production unit that did its own slaughtering; (as that function was transferred to specialists outside the home), the family became essentially a consumption unit.

S V C 부사절: ~함에 따라 S V C

그 이유 중 하나는 가족의 규모가 점점 줄어들고 있었으며, 가족이 더 이상 가축을 자체적으로 도살하는 생산단위가 되는 것을 멈췄다는 것이다. 그러한 기능이 집 밖의 전문가들에게로 넘어감에 따라 가족은 본질적으로 소비 단위가 되었다.

| 어휘 |

depict ⓥ (그림 · 조각으로) 그리다 **tin** ⓝ 주석, 주석 그릇 **utensil** ⓝ 가정용품, 부엌 용품
employ ⓥ 쓰다, 이용하다 **in part** 부분적으로는; 어느 정도는
carcass ⓝ 시체, (도살하여 내장을 제거한) 짐승 몸통
carve ⓥ (고기를) 베다, 저미다; 베어 나누다 **slaughtering** ⓝ 도살
cease ⓥ 그만두다, 멈추다 **consumption** ⓝ 소비, 소모 **typify** ⓥ 전형적[대표적]이다, 특징이다

| 전문해석 | 식사가 그려진 다양한 그림들은 17세기 이전에 식탁의 모습이 어떠했는지를 보여 준다. 대략 1600년까지 포크는 그림에 없었으며, 숟가락도 거의 보이지 않았다.(보기 ① 근거) 적어도 한 개의 나이프—모든 손님들이 이용할 수 있는 하나밖에 없는 나이프이면 특별히 큰 나이프—는 항상 묘사되었지만 작은 개인용 나이프들이 각 사람의 자리에 있는 경우도 종종 있었다. 주석 원반 접시가 이미 큰 나무 접시를 대체했다. 식기류의 이런 변화는 유럽에서 새로운 식사 예절의 특징이 되는 것이었다. 세계의 다른 많은 지역에서는 식기류가 전혀 사용되지 않았다. 예를 들면, 근동(아라비아, 북동아프리카, 동남아시아, 발칸 등을 포함하는 지역)에서는 오른손으로 식사를 하는 것이 전통이었다. 식기류가 사용된 이유의 일부는 고기에 대한 태도의 변화에 있었다. 중세시대 동안에는, 고기 전체 부위나 심지어 고기 몸통 전체가 식대에 올려졌으며,(보기 ④ 근거) 식사하는 사람들이 보는 앞에서 고기를 베어 나누었다. 17세기 때부터, 프랑스에서 처음으로 그러나 그 이후에 다른 지역에서, 그런 관습은 시들기 시작했다. 그 이유 중 하나는 가족의 규모가 점점 줄어들고 있었으며,(보기 ③ 근거) 가족이 가축을 자체적으로 도살하는 생산단위가 되는 것을 멈췄다는 것이다. 그러한 기능이 집 밖의 전문가들에게로 넘어감에 따라 가족은 본질적으로 소비 단위가 되었다.

| 보기분석 |
① Up to 1600 a meal scene was a frequent subject for painters.
1600년까지 식사 장면은 화가들이 자주 그리는 주제였다.
② Forks were portrayed in paintings ~~before~~ knives and spoons. 지문 내용과 불일치
나이프와 숟가락에 앞서 그림에는 포크가 먼저 묘사되었다.
③ The seventeenth century witnessed a change in the number of family members.
17세기는 가족 구성원 수의 변화를 목격했다.
④ In the Middle Ages, a whole dead animal might have been served at the table.
중세시대에는 아마도 전체 죽은 동물이 통째로 식탁에 올려졌을 것이다.

| 정답분석 | 두 번째 문장에서 "1600년까지 포크는 그림에 없었으며, 숟가락도 거의 보이지 않았다. 적어도 한 개의 나이프는 항상 (그림에) 묘사되었다."라고 했으므로, 포크보다 앞서 그림에서 묘사된 것은 나이프와 숟가락이었다. 따라서 ②가 본문의 내용과 일치하지 않는다.

06 2016 서강대

정답 ②

| 구문분석 | (In the last decades of the eighteenth century, and in the first half of the nineteenth century), a number of words came (for the first time) (into common English use) or acquired new and important meanings.

S V_1 V_2 O

18세기의 마지막 몇십 년과 19세기의 전반기 동안, 많은 단어들이 처음으로 영어의 일상적인 용례 속으로 들어왔든지 아니면 새롭고 중요한 의미를 얻어 냈다.

There is a general pattern of change (in these words), (which can be used as a special kind of map by which to look at wider changes in life).

유도부사 V S 관계대명사

이들 단어들에는 일반적인 변화의 패턴이 존재하는데, 이러한 패턴은 삶에서 일어나는 보다 폭넓은 변화를 바라볼 수 있는 특별한 지도로 사용될 수 있다.

Five words are the key points (from which this map can be drawn).
S V C 관계대명사
이 지도로부터 이끌어 낼 수 있는 다섯 가지의 핵심 단어가 있다.

They are *industry*, *democracy*, *class*, *art*, and *culture*.
S V C
그것들(그 단어들)은 '산업', '민주주의', '계급', '예술', 그리고 '문화'이다.

The changes (in their use, at this critical period), bear witness (to a general shift) (in our characteristic ways of thinking) (about common life); about social, political, and economic institutions; and about the educational and artistic purposes (which these institutions are designed to embody).
S 세미콜론: and 역할 V O 세미콜론: and 역할 관계대명사
이 중요한 시기에, 이 단어들의 사용에서 나타난 변화는 (당대의) 일반적인 삶과 (당대의) 사회적, 정치적 그리고 경제적인 제도, 그리고 이 제도들이 구현하고자 하는 교육적 및 예술적 목적에 대한 우리의 특징적인 사유방식 속에서 발생한 일반적인 변화에 대해 증언하고 있다.

| 어휘 | **institution** ⓝ 설립, 제도, 학회; 관습; 규정
embody ⓥ 구체화하다; 형체를 주다; 통합하다, 포함하다
epistemic shifts 당대의 지배적인 시대정신의 변화
reverberate ⓥ 반향시키다, 울려 퍼지다; 굴절하다
disparage ⓥ 얕보다; 헐뜯다, 비난하다
configuration ⓝ 배치, 배열, 구성; 환경설정
diachronically ⓐⓓ 〈언어〉 통시적[역사적]으로 (*opp.* synchronically 공시적으로)
watershed ⓝ 분기점, 중대한 시기; 위기
etymologically ⓐⓓ 어원학적으로
semantic ⓐ 의미의, 의미론의

| 전문해석 | 18세기의 마지막 몇십 년과 19세기의 전반기 동안, 많은 단어들이 처음으로 영어의 일상적인 용례 속으로 들어왔든지 아니면 새롭고 중요한 의미를 얻어 냈다. 이들 단어들에는 일반적인 변화의 패턴이 존재하는데, 이러한 패턴은 삶에서 일어나는 보다 폭넓은 변화를 바라볼 수 있는 특별한 지도로 사용될 수 있다. 이 지도로부터 이끌어 낼 수 있는 다섯 가지의 핵심 단어가 있다. 그것들(그 단어들)은 '산업', '민주주의', '계급', '예술', 그리고 '문화'이다. 이 중요한 시기에, 이 단어들의 사용에서 나타난 변화는 (당대의) 일반적인 삶과 (당대의) 사회적, 정치적 그리고 경제적인 제도, 그리고 이 제도들이 구현하고자 하는 교육적 및 예술적 목적에 대한 우리의 특징적인 사유방식 속에서 발생한 일반적인 변화에 대해 증언하고 있다.
(보기 ④ 근거, 보기 ③ 근거, 보기 ① 근거)

| 보기분석 | ① Epistemic shifts in societies reverberate etymologically. 사회 속의 변화가 언어에 영향을 준다는 의미
사회에서 인식(생각) 변화는 어원적으로 반향(영향)을 일으킨다.
② Democracy was disparaged until the second half of the eighteenth century. 지문에서 언급하지 않은 내용
민주주의는 18세기 후반까지 폄하되었다.
③ Semantic configurations transform diachronically within a culture. 한 문화 안에서 단어의 의미가 시대에 따라 변화한다는 의미
의미적 구성들은 문화 내에서 통시적으로 변화한다. diachronic(통시적인): 한 대상의 변천 과정을 시간의 흐름으로 보는 것
④ The period from the late eighteenth to the early nineteenth century marks a watershed in English history.
18세기 후반부터 19세기 초반까지의 시기는 영국 역사에서 중요한 변화의 지점이다.

| 정답분석 | 이 지문에서는 민주주의가 폄하되었다는 말은 언급되지 않았다. 따라서 ②는 지문을 통해 알 수 없는 내용이다.

07 2016 서강대

정답 ②

| 구문분석 | In vitro fertilization does not contribute (to developmental delays) (up to age 3), (according to a new study).
S V
새로운 연구에 따르면 체외수정은 3세까지의 발육지연의 원인이 아니라고 한다.

(As many couples who use IVF to have children are older, for example), other factors can affect fetal development.
부사절: ~ 때문에 S V O

예를 들어, 체외수정을 통해 아이를 갖는 부부들은 나이가 많은 편이기 때문에, (체외수정이 아닌) 다른 요인들이 태아의 발육에 영향을 줄 수 있다.

The study showed that developmental delays were not more prevalent among children conceived through IVF.
S V O

연구는 발육지연이 인공수정을 통해 임신된 아이들 사이에서 더 널리 퍼져 있지 않다는 것을 보여 주었다.

The new study also said (that) children conceived through IVF were not at greater risk with full-blown developmental disabilities (such as learning disabilities, speech or language disorders, or autism).
S V O

새로운 연구 또한 체외수정을 통해 임신된 아이들이 학습장애, 언어장애, 그리고 자폐증 등과 같은 상당히 진행된 발달장애에 걸릴 위험이 더 크지 않다고 말했다.

The researchers found no significant difference (between IVF and non-treatment groups of children) (with developmental delays) (— 13 percent of children conceived with IVF had a delay, while 18 percent of those not conceived with treatment had a delay).
S V O
between A and B: A와 B 사이에

연구자들은 발육지연에 관한 한, 체외수정을 통해 태어난 아이들과 그러한 시술을 받지 않고 태어난 아이들 사이에 별다른 차이가 없다는 것을 발견했는데, 체외수정을 통해 태어난 아이들의 13%가 발육지연 증상을 보인 반면, 체외수정 시술 없이 태어난 아이들 가운데는 18%가 발육지연 증상을 보였다.

| 어휘 | **in vitro fertilization** 체외수정 **developmental delay** 발육지연 **autism** ⓝ 자폐
fetal ⓐ 태아의 **prevalent** ⓐ 일반적으로 행해지는, 유행하는
conceive ⓥ 임신하다; 상상하다, 생각[이해]하다 **full-blown** ⓐ 만개한, 활짝 핀
neonatal ⓐ 신생아의 **perturbation** ⓝ (심리적인) 동요, 불안의 원인, 혼란 상태
precarious ⓐ 위험한; 불안정한; 불분명한; 근거가 빈약한
germane ⓐ (~와) 밀접한 관계가 있는, 적절한(pertinent)

| 전문해석 | 새로운 연구에 따르면 체외수정은 3세까지의 발육지연의 원인이 아니라고 한다. 예를 들어, 체외수정을 통해 아이를 갖는 부부들은 나이가 많은 편이기 때문에, (체외수정이 아닌) 다른 요인들이 태아의 발육에 영향을 줄 수 있다. 연구는 발육지연이 인공수정을 통해 임신된 아이들 사이에서 더 널리 퍼져 있지 않다는 것을 보여 주었다. 새로운 연구 또한 체외수정을 통해 임신된 아이들이 학습장애, 언어장애, 그리고 자폐증 등과 같은 상당히 진행된 발달장애에 걸릴 위험이 더 크지 않다고 말했다. 연구자들은 발육지연에 관한 한, 체외수정을 통해 태어난 아이들과 그러한 시술을 받지 않고 태어난 아이들 사이에 별다른 차이가 없다는 것을 발견했다—체외수정을 통해 태어난 아이들의 13%가 발육지연 증상을 보인 반면, 체외수정 시술 없이 태어난 아이들 가운데는 18%가 발육지연 증상을 보였다.
보기 ④ 근거

| 보기분석 | ① IVF is not one of the factors in neonatal developmental delays.
IVF(체외수정)는 신생아 발달 지연의 요인 중 하나가 아니다.
② The IVF industry has been disrupted by parental perturbations. 지문에서 언급하지 않은 내용
IVF 산업은 부모들의 동요로 인해 저지받았다.
③ IVF is not more precarious than other factors for fetal development.
IVF가 태아 발달에 있어서 다른 요인들보다 더 위험한 것은 아니다.
④ The age of parents can be germane to the health of their child.
부모의 나이는 자녀의 건강과 관련이 있을 수 있다.

| 정답분석 | 이 지문의 주요한 내용은 체외수정을 통해 태어난 아이들이 그렇지 않은 아이들과 별반 다르지 않다는 것인데 보기 ②는 지문의 주요 내용에서 벗어나 지문을 통해 알 수 없는 내용이다.

08 2016 건국대

정답 ③

| 구문분석 | We can observe [that questions (such as "Which language do you speak?" or "Which dialect do you speak?") may be answered (quite differently) (by people) (who appear to speak in an identical manner)].
S V S V 관계대명사

우리는 "어떤 언어를 사용하십니까?"나 "어떤 방언을 사용하십니까?"와 같은 질문들이 동일한 방식으로 말을 하는 것처럼 보이는 사람들에 의해서 매우 다르게 답변되는 것을 관찰할 수 있다.

Many regions of the world provide plenty of evidence (for a puzzling array of language and dialect divisions).
S V O
이 세계의 많은 지역들은 곤혹스러울 정도로 많은 언어와 방언의 구분을 위한 상당한 증거를 제공한다.

play a role: 역할을 하다
Surely socio-cultural factors play a role (in determining boundaries).
S V O
확실히 사회문화적 요인들은 경계들을 결정함에 있어서 역할을 수행하고 있다.

to name a few: 몇 가지의 예를 들면
Hindi and Urdu in India, Fanti and Twi in West Africa, Kechwa and Aimara in Peru, (to name just a few), are recognized (as discrete languages) (both popularly and in law), yet they are almost identical at the level of grammar.
S_1 S_2 S_3 V 등위접속사: 하지만 S V C

인도의 Hindi어와 Urdu어, 서아프리카의 Fanti어와 Twi어, 페루의 Kechwa어와 Aimara어 등과 같은 몇 가지 예들은 일반적으로나 법적으로 개별적인 언어라고 여겨지지만 이들 언어들은 문법적인 차원에서 거의 동일하다.

On the other hand, the literary and colloquial forms (of Arabic used in Iraq, Morocco, and Egypt, or the Welsh of North and South Wales) are grammatically quite separate, yet only one language is recognized in each case.
접속부사 S V C 등위접속사: 하지만 S V

반면에 이라크, 모로코, 그리고 이집트 등에서 사용되는 문학적이고 구어적인 형태의 아랍어 혹은 웨일스 남부와 북부에서 사용되는 웨일스 말은 문법적으로는 심하게 분리되어 있다. 그러나 각각의 경우, 이들 언어들은 단 하나의 언어로 인정된다.

| 어휘 | **puzzling** ⓐ 곤혹하게 하는, 헷갈리게 하는, 영문 모를 **discrete** ⓐ 개별의, 별개의
popularly ⓐⓓ 일반적으로 **colloquial** ⓐ 구어적인

| 전문해석 | 우리는 "어떤 언어를 사용하십니까?"나 "어떤 방언을 사용하십니까?"와 같은 질문들이 동일한 방식으로 말을 하는 것처럼 보이는 사람들에 의해서 매우 다르게 답변되는 것을 관찰할 수 있다. 이 세계의 많은 지역들은 곤혹스러울 정도로 많은 언어와 방언의 구분을 위한 상당한 증거를 제공한다. 확실히 사회문화적 요인들은 경계들을 결정함에 있어서 역할을 수행하고 있다. 인도의 Hindi어와 Urdu어, 서아프리카의 Fanti어와 Twi어, 페루의 Kechwa어와 Aimara어 등과 같은 몇 가지 예들은 일반적으로나 법적으로 개별적인 언어라고 여겨지지만 이들 언어들은 문법적인 차원에서 거의 동일하다. 반면에 이라크, 모로코, 그리고 이집트 등에서 사용되는 문학적이고 구어적인 형태의 아랍어 혹은 웨일스 남부와 북부에서 사용되는 웨일스 말은 문법적으로는 심하게 분리되어 있다. 그러나 각각의 경우, 이들 언어들은 단 하나의 언어로 인정된다.

| 보기분석 | ① Urdu는 인도에서 사용되는 언어 가운데 하나이다.
② 서아프리카 지역의 Fanti와 Twi는 문법이 거의 같다.
③ 이라크와 모로코의 아랍어는 회화체에서 매우 유사하다. 지문 내용과 불일치
④ 웨일스 지방에서는 공식적으로 하나의 언어만이 존재한다.
⑤ 문법체계가 언어의 경계를 결정하는 유일한 요인은 아니다.

| 정답분석 | 지문에서 "이라크, 모로코, 그리고 이집트 등에서 사용되는 문학적이고 구어적인 형태의 아랍어 혹은 웨일스 남부와 북부에서 사용되는 웨일스 말은 문법적으로는 심하게 분리되어 있다."고 언급했으므로 ③은 지문과 불일치한다.

09 2016 국민대

정답 ①

| 구문분석 | Capital is money (that is invested in order to make more money).
S V C 관계대명사
자본은 돈을 벌기 위해서 투자되는 돈이다.

(By extension) the term capital is often used (to refer to money) (that is available for investment or, indeed, any asset that can be readily turned into money for it).
S V 부사적용법: ~하기 위하여 관계대명사

더 확장해 보면, 자본이라는 용어는 투자를 위해 이용 가능한 돈이나 투자를 위한 돈으로 전환될 수 있는 자산을 언급할 때도 자주 사용된다.

Thus, a person's house is often described (as their capital), (because they can turn it into capital) (either by selling it or by borrowing on the strength of it).

접속부사 S V 부사절: 때문에 either A or B: A 혹은 B 둘 중 하나 A B

따라서, 누군가가 소유하고 있는 주택은 종종 그들의 자본으로 여겨지는데, 그 이유는 그들이 그 주택을 팔거나 담보대출을 받는 것을 통해 그 주택을 자본으로 전환시킬 수 있기 때문이다.

Many small businesses are indeed set up (in this way).

S V

많은 소규모의 사업들은 실제로도 이러한 방식으로 이루어진다.

가주어 turn A into B: A를 B로 바꾸다

It is, however, only possible to turn property into capital (if its ownership is clearly established, its value can be measured, its title can be transferred, and a market exists for it).

접속부사 진주어 부사절: 만일 ~라면

그러나 주택과 같은 자산은, 주택의 소유 관계가 명확하게 확립되어 있고, 주택이 가지고 있는 가치를 측정할 수 있고, 주택의 명의를 바꿀 수 있고, 주택을 위한 시장이 존재하는 경우에만 자본으로 전환될 수 있다.

A characteristic feature (of the development of capitalist societies) is the emergence (of institutions) (that enable the conversion of assets of all kinds into capital).

S V C 관계대명사

자본주의 사회의 발전에 있어서 한 가지 특징은 이러한 모든 종류의 자산들을 자본으로 전환시킬 수 있는 제도들의 등장이다.

Hernando de Soto has argued persuasively [that it is the absence of these institutions, not to mention functioning systems of property law, that frustrates the emergence of local capitalisms in the Third World].

S V O 강조구문 it not to mention: ~은 말할 것도 없이 강조구문 that

에르난도 데 소토(Hernando de Soto)는, 제3세계 지역 자본주의의 좌절은 자산법 체계의 작동은 말할 것도 없고, 제도 자체의 부재 때문이라는 사실을 설득력 있게 주장해 왔다.

He claims [that an enormous amount of value (that is located up in property) cannot therefore be realized and put by entrepreneurs to productive use].

S V S 관계대명사 V_1 V_2

그는, 그러한 이유 때문에, (제3세계의 경우) 자산에 들어 있는 거대한 양의 가치가 기업가들이 생산적으로 사용할 수 있는 자본으로 실현될 수 없다고 주장한다.

| 어휘 | **capital** ⓝ 자본; 수도 **asset** ⓝ 자산, 재산 **property** ⓝ 재산, 자산, 소유물 **institution** ⓝ 시설, 제도, 설립 **entrepreneur** ⓝ 기업가

| 전문해석 | 자본은 돈을 벌기 위해서 투자되는 돈이다. 더 확장해 보면 자본이라는 용어는 투자를 위해 이용 가능한 돈이나 투자를 위한 돈으로 전환될 수 있는 자산을 언급할 때도 자주 사용된다. 따라서, 누군가가 소유하고 있는 주택은 종종 그들의 자본으로 여겨지는데, 그 이유는 그들이 그 주택을 팔거나 담보대출을 받는 것을 통해 그 주택을 자본으로 전환시킬 수 있기 때문이다. 많은 소규모의 사업들은 실제로도 이러한 방식으로 이루어진다. 그러나 주택과 같은 자산은, 주택의 소유 관계가 명확하게 확립되어 있고, 주택이 가지고 있는 가치를 측정할 수 있고, 주택의 명의를 바꿀 수 있고, 주택을 위한 시장이 존재하는 경우에만 자본으로 전환될 수 있다. 자본주의 사회의 발전에 있어서 한 가지 특징은 이러한 모든 종류의 자산들을 자본으로 전환시킬 수 있는 제도들의 등장이다. 에르난도 데 소토(Hernando de Soto)는, 제3세계 지역 자본주의의 좌절은 자산법 체계의 작동은 말할 것도 없고, 제도 자체의 부재 때문이라는 사실을 설득력 있게 주장해 왔다. 그는, 그러한 이유 때문에, (제3세계의 경우) 자산에 들어 있는 거대한 양의 가치가 기업가들이 생산적으로 사용할 수 있는 자본으로 실현될 수 없다고 주장한다.

보기 ④ 근거 보기 ③ 근거

| 보기분석 |

① Businesses, small or big, are always set up with bank loans. 일반화의 오류
작은 규모건 큰 규모건 모든 비즈니스는 항상 은행 대출로 시작된다.

② When money is used to gain more money, the money is capital.
돈이 더 많은 돈을 벌기 위해 사용되었을 때, 그 돈은 자본이다.

③ In the Third Wold huge amount of value is locked up in property.
제3세계에서는 막대한 가치가 자산에 갇혀 있다.

④ A capitalist society requires functioning systems of property law.
자본주의 사회는 재산법 체계의 작동을 요구한다.

| 정답분석 | 지문에서 많은 소규모 사업체들이 담보대출을 통해서 사업을 한다고 언급하였는데 그렇다고 해서 사업체들이 언제나 대출을 받아서 설립되는 것은 아니기 때문에 보기 ①은 일반화의 오류라고 할 수 있다.

10 2019 건국대

정답 ④

| 구문분석 | Plastic bags(S) were found(V) (in the digestive systems of more than 400 leatherback turtles).

플라스틱 봉투(비닐봉지)가 400마리 이상의 바다 장수거북의 소화기관에서 발견되었다.

The leatherback turtle(S) is(V) a critically endangered species(C). Jellyfish(S) is(V) their main diet(C).

바다 장수거북은 매우 심각한 멸종 위기에 처해 있는 종이다. 해파리가 그들의 주식이다.

mistake A for B: A를 B라고 오인하다

Mistaking the increased amounts of plastic bags(S) (drifting in the currents) (for drifting jellyfish) is causing(V) the leather backs(I.O) harm(D.O).

해류에 떠다니는 많은 양의 플라스틱 봉투를 떠다니는 해파리로 오인하는 것이 바다 장수거북에게 해를 끼치고 있다.

Plastic bags(S) account(V) (for 12 percent of all marine debris), and(등위접속사) plastic bottles and plastic caps and lids(S) are(V) also prevalent(C) at six and eight percent respectively.

플라스틱 봉투는 모든 해양 쓰레기의 12%를 차지한다. 그리고 플라스틱병과 플라스틱 마개와 뚜껑들 또한 각각 6%와 8%로 널리 퍼져 있는 상태이다.

Marine litter(S) is(V) one of the most pervasive and solvable pollution problems(C) (plaguing(분사구문) the world's oceans and waterways).

해양 쓰레기는 전 세계의 바다와 수로를 망치는 가장 만연해 있으면서도 해결이 가능한 오염 문제 중 하나이다.

A simple solution(S) (to the plastic bag issue) is(V) reusable shopping bags(C).

플라스틱 봉투 문제에 대한 가장 간단한 해결책은 재활용이 가능한 쇼핑백이다.

An increased awareness(S) (of the effects of plastic bags) has caused(V) many states and countries(O) to implement(O.C) plastic bag related legislation.

플라스틱 봉투의 영향에 대한 인식 증가는 많은 주와 국가들이 플라스틱 봉투와 관련된 법을 시행하게 만들었다.

For example(접속부사), (when(부사절: 때) Ireland imposed a fee on each plastic bag used by consumers), single-use consumption(S) dropped(V) (by 90 percent).

예를 들면, 아일랜드가 소비자들이 사용하는 각각의 플라스틱 봉투에 대해 수수료를 부과했을 때, 일회용 플라스틱 봉투의 소비가 90% 감소했다.

| 어휘 |

digestive ⓐ 소화의; 소화를 돕는	**leather turtle** ⓝ 장수거북(= leatherback)	
jellyfish ⓝ 해파리	**mistake A for B** A를 B라고 오인[혼동]하다	
current ⓝ 기류; 해류	**debris** ⓝ 잔해, 쓰레기	**lid** ⓝ 뚜껑
respectively ⓐⓓ 각자, 각각	**litter** ⓝ 쓰레기	**solvable** ⓐ 풀 수 있는, 해결할 수 있는
plague ⓥ 괴롭히다	**impose** ⓥ 도입하다; 부과하다	

| 전문해석 | 플라스틱 봉투(비닐봉지)가 400마리 이상의 바다 장수거북의 소화기관에서 발견되었다. 바다 장수거북은 매우 심각한 멸종 위기에 처해 있는 종(種)이다. 해파리가 그들의 주식이다. 해류에 떠다니는 많은 양의 플라스틱 봉투를 떠다니는 해파리로 오인하는 것이 바다 장수거북에게 해를 끼치고 있다. 플라스틱 봉투는 모든 해양 쓰레기의 12%를 차지한다. 그리고 플라스틱병과 플라스틱 마개와 뚜껑들 또한 각각 6%와 8%로 널리 퍼져 있는 상태이다. 해양 쓰레기는 전 세계의 바다와 수로를 망치는 가장 만연해 있으면서도 해결이 가능한 오염 문제 중 하나이다. 플라스틱 봉투 문제에 대한 가장 간단한 해결책은 재활용이 가능한 쇼핑백이다. 플라스틱 봉투의 영향에 대한 인식 증가는 많은 주와 국가들이 플라스틱 봉투와 관련된 법을

시행하게 만들었다. 예를 들면, 아일랜드가 소비자들이 사용하는 각각의 플라스틱 봉투에 대해 수수료를 부과했을 때, 일회용 플라스틱 봉투의 소비가 90% 감소했다.

| 보기분석 | ① 바다 장수거북의 소화기관에서 플라스틱이 발견되었다.
② 바다 장수거북은 멸종 위기종에 속한다.
③ 플라스틱병은 전체 해양 쓰레기의 6퍼센트를 차지한다.
④ 해양 오염은 해결이 거의 불가능하다. 지문 내용과 불일치
⑤ 아일랜드에서는 플라스틱 봉투를 사용할 때 수수료를 내야 한다.

| 정답분석 | "해양 쓰레기는 전 세계의 바다와 수로를 망치는 가장 만연하고도 해결 가능한 오염 문제 중 하나이다."라고 했으며, 플라스틱 봉투 문제에 대한 가장 간단한 해결책인 재활용이 가능한 쇼핑백을 언급하고 있다. 따라서 해양 오염은 해결이 가능한 것이므로, ④가 이 글의 내용과 일치하지 않는다.

11 2013 서강대

정답 ③

| 구문분석 | (Whereas beef and chicken appear in many New Mexican recipes, in Massachusetts), fish is very popular (because of the nearby seacoast).
접속사: 반면에 / fish: S, is: V, very popular: C

소고기와 닭고기가 많은 뉴멕시코 지역의 요리법에 등장하지만, 매사추세츠는 바다에서 가깝기 때문에 생선이 아주 흔하다.

New England is famous (for its clam chowder, lobster, cod, scallops, and fish cakes).
New England: S, is: V, famous: C

뉴잉글랜드는 클램차우더, 랍스터, 대구, 가리비, 생선튀김으로 유명하다.

English herbs and spices are the seasonings (used in New England dishes), (which might taste rather bland to people accustomed to hot and spicy New Mexican food).
English herbs and spices: S, are: V, the seasonings: C, which: 관계대명사

영국의 허브와 양념이 뉴잉글랜드 지역에서 양념으로 사용된다. 따라서 이 지역의 음식은 맵고 자극적인 뉴멕시코 지역 음식에 익숙한 사람들에게는 다소 밍밍하게 느껴질 수 있다.

Each region of the United States is unique. Louisiana has a French influence. Many Germans populate the Midwest.
Each region of the United States: S, is: V, unique: C / Louisiana: S, has: V, a French influence: O / Many Germans: S, populate: V, the Midwest: O

미국의 각 지역들은 특이하다. 루이지애나는 프랑스의 영향을 받았다. 많은 독일인들이 중서부 지방에 모여 살고 있다.

not only A but also B = not only A but B as well: A뿐만 아니라 B도

(In traveling around America), a tourist has the opportunity not only to visit a variety of places and see diverse landscapes, but to taste a variety of foods (as well).
a tourist: S, has: V, the opportunity: O, to visit a variety of places and see diverse landscapes: A, to taste a variety of foods: B

미국을 이리저리 여행하다 보면 여행객들은 다양한 장소를 보고 다양한 풍경을 볼 수 있는 기회는 물론 다양한 음식도 맛볼 수 있는 기회를 가질 수 있다.

| 어휘 |

recipe ⓝ 요리	**cod** ⓝ 대구	**scallop** ⓝ 가리비
fish cake 생선튀김	**spice** ⓝ 양념	**seasoning** ⓝ 조미료
bland ⓐ 부드러운, 밍밍한		

| 전문해석 | 소고기와 닭고기가 많은 뉴멕시코 지역의 요리법에 등장하지만, 매사추세츠는 바다에서 가깝기 때문에 생선이 아주 흔하다. (보기 ② 근거) 뉴잉글랜드는 클램차우더, 랍스터, 대구, 가리비, 생선튀김으로 유명하다. 영국의 허브와 양념이 뉴잉글랜드 지역에서 양념으로 사용된다. 따라서 이 지역의 음식은 맵고 자극적인 뉴멕시코 지역 음식에 익숙한 사람들에게는 다소 밍밍하게 느껴질 수 있다. 미국의 각 지역들은 특이하다. 루이지애나는 프랑스의 영향을 받았다. 많은 독일인들이 중서부 지방에 모여 살고 있다. 미국을 이리저리 여행하다 보면 여행객들은 다양한 장소를 보고 다양한 풍경을 볼 수 있는 기회는 물론 다양한 음식도 맛볼 수 있는 기회를 가질 수 있다. (보기 ① 근거)

| 보기분석 | ① One may taste authentic German sausages and beers in the Midwest. 독일인이 모여 있는 중서부 지역에서는 아마도 독일 음식을 맛볼 수 있을 것이다.
중서부 지역에서는 아마도 진정한 독일 소시지와 맥주를 맛볼 수 있다.
② Food in Massachusetts has been influenced by its geographical conditions.
매사추세츠의 음식은 지리적 조건에 영향을 받았다.
③ It is uncommon to find top-quality beef dishes in New England. 지문을 통해 알 수 없음
뉴잉글랜드에서 고품질의 소고기 요리를 찾는 것은 흔하지 않다.
④ Beef and chicken are frequently used in a traditional meal in New Mexico.
뉴멕시코에서 전통적인 식사에는 소고기와 닭고기가 자주 사용된다.

| 정답분석 | 지문은 미국에는 다양한 민족이 사는 만큼, 다양한 음식을 맛볼 수 있다는 글인데, 뉴잉글랜드는 클램차우더, 랍스터, 대구, 가리비, 생선튀김으로 유명하다고 언급했다고 해서 그 지역에서 고품질의 소고기 요리를 찾기 어렵다는 것을 알 수는 없으므로 ③이 지문을 통해 추론할 수 없는 내용이다.

12 2015 한국외대

정답 ③

| 구문분석 | There are many ways (technology simplifies life), but it also brings its own new complications.
(유도부사 There / V are / S many ways / (how) / 등위접속사 but / S it / V brings / O its own new complications)
기술이 삶을 단순화시키는 방법은 많이 있다. 그러나 기술은 기술 자체가 가지고 있는 복잡함을 가지고 온다.

Many of our nifty devices need remote controllers, (which end up cluttering our brains and our living rooms).
(S Many of our nifty devices / V need / O remote controllers / 관계대명사 which / end up ~ing: 결국 ~하다)
우리의 멋들어진 많은 장비들은 리모트 컨트롤러들을 필요로 하는데, 이 리모트 컨트롤러들은 우리의 뇌와 우리의 거실을 혼란스럽게 만든다.

Why do we need 50 buttons (to control our environment)? Do we really need five remotes (to turn devices on and off)?
(의문문 도치 Why do / S we / V need / O 50 buttons; 의문문 도치 Do / S we / V need / O five remotes)
우리의 환경을 통제하기 위해 우리는 왜 50개나 되는 버튼을 필요로 하는가? 우리는 장비들을 켜고 끄기 위해 정말로 다섯 개의 리모트 컨트롤러가 필요한 것인가?

The makers (of the new SPIN Remote) say the answer is "no," and they want to bring simplicity back into your life.
(S The makers / V say / (that) / O the answer is "no," / 등위접속사 and / S they / V want / O to bring simplicity back into your life)
새로운 SPIN 리모트 컨트롤러의 제조사들은 이 질문에 대해 "no"라고 대답한다. 그리고 그들은 당신의 삶에 단순함을 되돌려주겠다고 공언한다.

SPIN is a universal remote in theory, but it is even more intuitive; you just turn it.
(S SPIN / V is / C a universal remote / 등위접속사 but / S it / V is / C even more intuitive / 세미콜론: and 역할 / S you / V turn / O it)
SPIN은 이론상 모든 것에 다 통하는 만능 리모트 컨트롤러인데 심지어는 직관적이기조차하다. 당신은 단지 SPIN을 돌리기만 하면 된다.

The ultra-sensitive motion sensor in it, (shaped like a knob), works (when you rotate it), (in the same way you would turn a doorknob or the key in your car's ignition).
(S The ultra-sensitive motion sensor in it / V works / 부사절: ~할 때)
둥근 손잡이 형태를 가진 SPIN 안에 장착된 극도로 민감한 동작 센서는, 문손잡이나 자동차 키를 돌리는 것과 같은 방식으로 당신이 SPIN을 돌리면 작동한다.

(With a spin of the SPIN), you can control the volume of a movie, fast-forward or rewind a TV show, or turn your devices, (such as stereos), on and off.
(S you / V_1 can control / O the volume / V_2 fast-forward / V_3 rewind a TV show / V_4 turn / turn ~ on/off: 어떤 장치를 켜다/끄다)
SPIN의 회전을 통해서 당신은 영화의 볼륨, TV쇼의 빠른 건너뛰기와 되감기, 스테레오 같은 장비를 켜고 끄는 것 등을 통제할 수 있다.

You can even use it (to dim or brighten smart lighting) (by simply pointing the remote at a lamp).
(S You / V can even use / O it)
당신은 심지어 SPIN 리모트 컨트롤러를 램프 쪽으로 향하게 함으로써 스마트 조명기기들을 어둡게 하거나 밝게 할 수도 있다.

| 어휘 | **nifty** ⓐ 익살맞은, 재치 있는, 멋들어진 **clutter** ⓥ 어지르다, 혼란스럽게 하다 **intuitive** ⓐ 직관적인
knob ⓝ 혹; 둥근 손잡이; 작은 덩어리 **ignition** ⓝ (차량의) 점화 장치[스위치]

| 전문해석 | 기술이 삶을 단순화시키는 방법은 많이 있다. 그러나 기술은 기술 자체가 가지고 있는 복잡함을 가지고 온다. 우리의 멋들어진 많은 장비들은 리모트 컨트롤러들을 필요로 하는데, 이 리모트 컨트롤러들은 우리의 뇌와 우리의 거실을 혼란스럽게

만든다. 우리의 환경을 통제하기 위해 우리는 왜 50개나 되는 버튼을 필요로 하는가? 우리는 장비들을 켜고 끄기 위해 정말로 다섯 개의 리모트 컨트롤러가 필요한 것인가?

새로운 SPIN 리모트 컨트롤러의 제조사들은 이 질문에 대해 "no"라고 대답한다. 그들은 당신의 삶에 단순함을 되돌려주겠다고 공언한다. SPIN은 이론상 모든 것에 다 통하는 만능 리모트 컨트롤러인데 심지어는 직관적이기조차하다. 당신은 단지 SPIN을 돌리기만 하면 된다. 둥근 손잡이 형태를 가진 SPIN 안에 장착된 극도로 민감한 동작 센서는, 문손잡이나 자동차 키를 돌리는 것과 같은 방식으로 당신이 SPIN을 돌리면 작동한다. SPIN의 회전을 통해서 당신은 영화의 볼륨, TV쇼의 빠른 건너뛰기와 되감기, 스테레오 같은 장비를 켜고 끄는 것 등을 통제할 수 있다. 당신은 심지어 SPIN 리모트 컨트롤러를 램프 쪽으로 향하게 함으로써 스마트 조명기기들을 어둡게 하거나 밝게 할 수도 있다.

| 보기분석 | ① It is a remote used for multiple devices.
그것은 여러 기기에 사용할 수 있는 리모컨이다.

② It can be used to adjust lamp brightness.
그것은 램프의 밝기를 조절하는 데 사용할 수 있다.

③ It is similar to a car ~~key in appearance~~. 지문 내용과 불일치
그것은 자동차 열쇠와 생김새가 비슷하다.

④ It has a sensor working by rotational motion.
그것은 회전 운동으로 작동하는 센서가 있다.

| 정답분석 | 지문에서 SPIN 리모트 컨트롤러는 자동차 열쇠처럼 돌릴 수 있다고 했고 생김새는 둥근 문손잡이와 닮은꼴이라고 했기 때문에 생김새가 자동차 열쇠와 비슷한 것은 아니다. 따라서 ③이 정답으로 적절하다.

13 2015 광운대

정답 ①

| 구문분석 | The Louvre Museum(S) is(V) one(C) (of the world's largest museums).
루브르 박물관은 세계에서 가장 규모가 큰 박물관들 가운데 하나이다.

Nearly 35,000 objects(S) (from prehistory to the 21st century) are exhibited(V) (over an area of 652,300 square feet).
역사 이전 시대부터 21세기에 이르는, 거의 35,000점의 작품들이 652,300평방피트의 공간에 전시되어 있다.

The Louvre(S) is(V_1) the world's most visited museum(C), and received(V_2) over 9.7 million visitors(O) in 2014.
루브르 박물관은 세계에서 찾는 사람들이 가장 많은 박물관이고, 2014년의 경우에는 970만 명 이상의 방문객을 맞이했다.

The museum(S) is housed(V) (in the Louvre Palace), (originally built as a fortress in the 12th century).
박물관은 12세기에 요새로 지어진 루브르궁전에 자리 잡고 있다.

Remnants(S) (of the fortress) are(V) still visible(C) (in the basement of the museum).
요새의 흔적들은 아직도 박물관의 지하에서 볼 수 있다.

The building(S) was extended(V) many times (to form the present Louvre Palace)(부사적용법: 결과).
루브르궁전 건물은 여러 차례의 증축을 통해서 현재의 루브르궁전이 되었다.

The museum(S) opened(V) (on August 10th, 1793 with an exhibition of 437 paintings), (the majority of the works being confiscated church property)(분사구문).
루브르 박물관은 1793년 8월 10일, 437점의 회화 작품을 전시하며 처음 문을 열었는데, 이때 전시된 작품들의 대부분은 교회로부터 압수한 것이었다.

(Because of structural problems), the museum(S) was closed(V) in 1796 until 1801.
구조적인 문제들 때문에, 루브르 박물관은 1796년에서부터 1801년까지 문을 닫았다.

The collection was increased (under Napoleon) and the museum was renamed the Musee Napoleon, but
S V S V O.C
(after Napoleon's abdication), many works (seized by his armies) were returned (to their original owners).
S V
나폴레옹 치하에서 소장품들은 증가했고, 박물관의 이름이 나폴레옹 박물관으로 바뀌기도 했다. 그러나 나폴레옹이 퇴위한 다음, 군대에 의해서 압류되었던 많은 작품들은 애초의 소유자들에게 돌아갔다.

세미콜론: and 역할
The collection was increased (during the Second Empire); the museum gained 25,000 pieces.
S V S V O
제2제정 시대에 소장품은 다시 늘어나기 시작했다; 루브르 박물관은 25,000여 점의 작품을 획득했다.

Holdings have grown steadily (through donations since the Third Republic).
S V
제3공화정 시대 이래, 소장품들은 기증을 통해서 지속적으로 증가해 왔다.

| 어휘 | **house** ⓥ 보관하다, 소장하다 **fortress** ⓝ 요새
remnant ⓝ 잔존물, 유물, 자취(relic), 나머지 **confiscate** ⓥ 몰수하다, 압수하다
collection ⓝ 수집품, 소장품 **abdication** ⓝ 퇴위, (고관의) 사직, (권력의) 포기, 기권

| 전문해석 | 루브르 박물관은 세계에서 가장 규모가 큰 박물관들 가운데 하나이다. 역사 이전시대부터 21세기에 이르는, 거의 35,000점의 작품들이 652,300평방피트의 공간에 전시되어 있다. 루브르 박물관은 세계에서 찾는 사람들이 가장 많은 박물관이고, 2014년의 경우에는 970만 명 이상의 방문객을 맞이했다. 박물관은 12세기에 요새로 지어진 루브르궁전에 자리 잡고 있다. 요새의 흔적들은 아직도 박물관의 지하에서 볼 수 있다. 루브르궁전 건물은 여러 차례의 증축을 통해서 현재의 루브르궁전이 되었다. 루브르 박물관은 1793년 8월 10일, 437점의 회화 작품을 전시하며 처음 문을 열었는데, 이때 전시된 작품들의 대부분은 교회로부터 압수한 것이었다. 구조적인 문제들 때문에, 루브르 박물관은 1796년에서부터 1801년까지 문을 닫았다. 나폴레옹 치하에서 소장품들은 증가했고, 박물관의 이름이 나폴레옹 박물관으로 바뀌기도 했다. 그러나 나폴레옹이 퇴위한 다음, 군대에 의해서 압류되었던 많은 작품들은 애초의 소유자들에게 돌아갔다. 제2제정 시대에 소장품은 다시 늘어나기 시작했다; 루브르 박물관은 25,000여 점의 작품을 획득했다. 제3공화정 시대 이래, 소장품들은 기증을 통해서 지속적으로 증가해 왔다.
(보기 ③ 근거 / 보기 ② 근거 / 보기 ④ 근거)

| 보기분석 | ① The Louvre has been extended to house more collections, and it is now a very large building in size.
루브르 박물관은 더 많은 전시품을 수용하기 위해 확장되었으며, 지금은 매우 큰 건물이다. 지문 내용과 불일치
② When the Louvre first opened, the exhibition was only composed of a few hundreds of paintings.
루브르 박물관이 처음 문을 열었을 때 전시는 몇백 점의 그림으로만 구성되어 있었다.
③ The Louvre Palace was built as a fortress, and its remnants are displayed in the museum's basement.
루브르궁전은 요새로 건설되었으며, 그 유적들이 박물관 지하에 전시되어 있다.
④ Napoleon's armies seized many collections, but they were later returned to their original owners.
나폴레옹의 군대가 많은 소장품을 압수했지만, 이후에 그것들은 원래 소유자에게 반환되었다.

| 정답분석 | 지문에서 루브르는 박물관으로서가 아니라 궁전으로서 증축되었다고 나와 있으므로 ①은 지문과 불일치한다.

14 2015 국민대

정답 ②

| 구문분석 | Back in 1967, Scottish inventor John Shepherd-Barron thought (that) getting cash should be as easy as getting a chocolate bar.
S V O

지난 1967년, 스코틀랜드의 발명가인 존 쉐퍼드 배런(John Shepherd-Barron)은 현금을 얻게 되는 것[인출하는 것]이 초콜릿 바를 얻는 것만큼이나 쉬운 일이 되어야 한다고 생각했다.

be credited with: ~의 공을 인정받다
He is credited (with pioneering the first cash machine or ATM in a Barclays Bank in London, UK).
S V
그는 영국 런던의 바클레이스 은행에 ATM 또는 현금인출기를 최초로 설치한 공로가 있는 것으로 인정받고 있다.

But the difficulties lay (in ensuring that you were who you said you were).
S V
그런데 그 당시에는 현금인출기를 사용할 때 사용자의 신원을 확실히 하는 데 어려움이 있었다.

(To prevent problems), Shepherd-Barron developed a special type of paper cheque (that acted as a precursor to the debit cards we have today).
S V C 관계대명사

쉐퍼드 배런은 그 문제를 방지하기 위해서 특별한 종류의 종이 수표를 개발했는데 이것은 오늘날 우리가 사용하고 있는 직불카드의 선구자 역할을 했다.

Each cheque would cause his cash machine to request a personal identification number — or PIN — (that only the account holder knew).
S V O O.C 관계대명사

각각의 수표에 대해서 현금인출기는 오직 예금주만이 알고 있는 개인 식별 번호(혹은 PIN)를 요구했다.

등위접속사
Shepherd-Barron was going to make the machine require a six-digit PIN, but he was overruled ... (by his wife).
S V O O.C S V

쉐퍼드 배런은 애초에 여섯 자리 숫자의 개인 식별 번호를 요구하는 현금인출기를 만들고자 했다. 그러나 그의 아내가 그 일을 가로막고 나섰다.

too ~ toR: 너무 ~해서 toR 할 수 없다
She believed that six digits were two too many to remember, and four became the standard.
S V O S V C

그의 아내는 여섯 자리 숫자는 기억하기에 너무 길다고 믿었고 그 결과 네 자리 숫자가 비밀번호의 표준이 되었다.

| 어휘 | **be credited with** 공로를 인정받다 **cheque** ⓝ 수표(check) **precursor** ⓝ 선구자
identification ⓝ 신원 확인, 동일시 **account** ⓝ 은행 계좌
overrule ⓥ 반대를 기각하다, 반대하여 결정하다, 무효로 하다 **digit** ⓝ 숫자

| 전문해석 | 지난 1967년, 스코틀랜드의 발명가인 존 쉐퍼드 배런(John Shepherd-Barron)은 현금을 얻게 되는 것[인출하는 것]이 초콜릿 바를 얻는 것만큼이나 쉬운 일이 되어야 한다고 생각했다. 그는 영국 런던의 바클레이스 은행에 ATM 또는 현금인출기를 최초로 설치한 공로가 있는 것으로 인정받고 있다. 그런데 그 당시에는 현금인출기를 사용할 때 사용자의 신원을 확실히 하는 데 어려움이 있었다.
쉐퍼드 배런은 그 문제를 방지하기 위해서 특별한 종류의 종이 수표를 개발했는데 이것은 오늘날 우리가 사용하고 있는 직불카드의 선구자 역할을 했다. 각각의 수표에 대해서 현금인출기는 오직 예금주만이 알고 있는 개인 식별 번호(혹은 PIN)를 요구했다. 쉐퍼드 배런은 애초에 여섯 자리 숫자의 개인 식별 번호를 요구하는 현금인출기를 만들고자 했다. 그러나 그의 아내가 그 일을 가로막고 나섰다. 그의 아내는 여섯 자리 숫자는 기억하기에 너무 길다고 믿었고 그 결과 네 자리 숫자가 비밀번호의 표준이 되었다.
(보기 ④ 근거)

| 보기분석 | ① It was in the end Shepherd-Barron's wife who decided that PIN should be four digits.
결국 쉐퍼드 배런의 아내가 PIN을 네 자리로 해야 한다고 결정했다.
② Shepherd-Barron thought earning money should be as easy as eating a chocolate bar. 지문 내용과 불일치
쉐퍼드 배런은 돈을 버는 것이 초콜릿 바를 먹는 것만큼 쉬워야 한다고 생각했다.
③ Identification of the account holder was a main problem in introducing the cash machine.
현금인출기를 도입하는 데에는 계좌 소유자의 신원 확인이 주요 문제였다.
④ A special type of paper cheque developed by Shepherd-Barron was a primitive type of the debit card.
쉐퍼드 배런이 개발한 특별한 종류의 수표는 직불카드의 원시적인 형태였다.

| 정답분석 | 지문에서 쉐퍼드 배런은 돈을 인출하는 것이 초콜릿 바를 얻는 것만큼이나 쉬운 일이 되어야 한다고 언급했는데, 보기 ②는 돈을 버는 것이 초콜릿 바를 먹는 것만큼 쉬워야 한다고 진술되어 있으므로 지문과 일치하지 않는다.

15 2017 숙명여대

정답 ④

| 구문분석 | (In medical usage), a "placebo" is a treatment (that has no specific physical or chemical action on the condition being treated, but is given to affect symptoms by a psychologic mechanism, rather than a purely physical one).
S V C 관계대명사

의학적인 용도로 사용되는 '위약'은 치료하고 있는 질환에 대해 그 어떤 특정한 물리적 혹은 화학적인 작용도 하지 않지만, 순전히 물리적인 메커니즘이 아니라 심리적인 메커니즘으로 증상에 영향을 주기 위해 주어지는 치료법이다.

Ethicists believe that placebos necessarily involve a partial or complete deception by the doctor, (since the patient is allowed to believe that the treatment has a specific effect).
S V O 부사절: 때문에

윤리학자들은 위약에는 필연적으로 의사에 의한 부분적 또는 완전한 속임수가 포함되어 있다고 생각하는데, 그 치료법에 특정한 효과가 (없는데도) 있다고 환자가 믿게 만들기 때문이다.

be unaware that: ~을 모르다
They seem unaware [that placebos, far from being inert (except in the rigid pharmacological sense), are among the most powerful agents known to medicine].
S V C S V

그들은 위약이 (엄격하게 약리학적인 의미에서가 아니면) 무활동적이기는커녕 의학계에 알려진 가장 강력한 치료제 중 하나라는 것을 모르는 것 같다.

It can strengthen the weak or paralyze the strong, transform sleeping, feeding, or sexual patterns, remove or induce a vast array of symptoms, mimic or abolish the effect of very powerful drugs.
S V_1 V_2 V_3 V_4 V_5

위약은 약한 부분을 강화시키고 강한 것은 무력화시킬 수 있으며 수면, 식사, 성생활을 변화시킬 수 있고, 일련의 광범위한 증상들을 없애거나 유발할 수 있으며, 매우 강력한 약물의 효과를 똑같이 내게 하거나 없앨 수 있다.

It can even alter the functions (of most organs).
S V O
그것은 심지어 대부분의 신체기관의 기능을 바꿀 수도 있다.

| 어휘 | usage ⓝ (단어의) 용법[어법]; 사용 placebo ⓝ 위약(환자를 안심시키기 위해 주는 약)
psychologic ⓐ 심리적인 mechanism ⓝ 구성, 장치 purely ⓐⓓ 순전히, 아주
ethicist ⓝ 윤리학자, 도학자, 도덕가 inert ⓐ 자력으로 행동할 수 없는, (물질이) 불활성의
pharmacological ⓐ 약리학의, 약학적인 strengthen ⓥ 강하게 하다, 강화하다
paralyze ⓥ 무력하게 만들다, 쓸모없게 만들다 induce ⓥ 일으키다, 촉진하다
mimic ⓥ 흉내 내다 abolish ⓥ (법률 등을) 폐지하다, 없애다
alter ⓥ 변경하다, 바꾸다

| 전문해석 | 의학적인 용도로 사용되는 '위약'은 치료하고 있는 질환에 대해 그 어떤 특정한 물리적 혹은 화학적인 작용도 하지 않지만, 순전히 물리적인 메커니즘이 아니라 심리적인 메커니즘으로 증상에 영향을 주기 위해 주어지는 치료법이다. 보기 ① 근거 윤리학자들은 위약에는 필연적으로 의사에 의한 부분적 또는 완전한 속임수가 포함되어 있다고 생각하는데, 그 치료법에 특정한 효과가 (없는데도) 있다고 환자가 믿게 만들기 때문이다. 그들은 위약이 (엄격하게 약리학적인 의미에서가 아니면) 무활동적이기는커녕 의학계에 알려진 가장 강력한 치료제 중 하나라는 것을 모르는 것 같다. 보기 ③, ⑤ 근거 위약은 약한 부분을 강화시키고 강한 것은 무력화시킬 수 있으며 수면, 식사, 성생활을 변화시킬 수 있고, 일련의 광범위한 증상들을 없애거나 유발할 수 있으며, 매우 강력한 약물의 효과를 똑같이 내게 하거나 없앨 수 있다. 그것은 심지어 대부분의 신체기관의 기능을 바꿀 수도 있다.

| 보기분석 | ① "Placebo" is a medical treatment based on the patient's psychology.
'위약'은 환자의 심리에 기초한 치료제이다.
② Some people believe that "placebo" is wrong because it is a lie.
일부 사람들은 '위약'이 거짓이기 때문에 옳지 않다고 생각한다.
③ "Placebo" is actually an effective method to some patients.
'위약'은 실제로 어떤 환자들에게는 효과적인 방법이다.
④ "Placebo" has no effect on the patient's physical conditions. 이 글의 주제와 반대되는 내용
'위약'은 환자의 신체 상태에 어떠한 영향도 주지 않는다.
⑤ The writer of the passage supports the use of "placebo."
이 글의 저자는 '위약'의 사용을 지지한다.

| 정답분석 | '위약'은 질환에 대해 어떠한 물리적인 작용도 하지 않지만, 심리적인 방법으로 증상에 영향을 줄 수 있는 치료법이라고 소개하고 있으므로, '위약'이 환자의 신체 상태에 영향을 줄 수 있다고 볼 수 있다. 따라서 ④가 추론할 수 없는 내용이다.

16 2017 인하대

정답 ④

| 구문분석 | There's been a 33 percent jump (in the number of medication-related poisonings in children ages 5 and younger since 2000, according to a recent study from Nationwide Children's Hospital in Ohio).
유도부사 V S

오하이오주 네이션와이드 아동병원에서 발표한 최근 연구 결과에 의하면, 5세 이하 어린이들의 약품 관련 중독 사고 건수가 2000년 이후로 33% 늘어났다.

be due to: ~ 때문이다
This may be due (to an increase in drugs in people's homes).
S V C

이것은 가정에다 두는 약품의 수가 늘어난 데 따른 것일 수도 있다.

Opioid painkillers, (like Percocet), caused the most deaths and other severe outcomes, (followed by over-the-counter cough and cold medications and pain relievers).
S V O

퍼코셋(Percocet)과 같은 마약성 진통제로 인한 사망 사고와 기타 심각한 사고가 가장 많았으며, 처방전 없이 살 수 있는 기침감기약과 진통제가 그 뒤를 이었다.

"No bottle is childproof," says study author Henry Spiller. "Keep all drugs (out of reach or locked up)."
O_1 V S O_2

"아이들이 열 수 없는 약병은 없습니다. 모든 약을 아이들의 손이 닿지 않는 곳에 두거나 자물쇠로 잠글 수 있는 안전한 곳에 넣어 둬야 합니다."라고 연구저자 헨리 스필러(Henry Spiller)는 말한다.

(If you think your child has ingested medication), call the National Poison Control hotline at 800–222–1222 immediately.
부사절: 만일 ~라면 V O

아이가 약품을 삼켰다는 생각이 들면, 국립 독극물 방제소 비상 전화번호 800–222–1222로 즉시 전화하십시오.

| 어휘 |
medication ⓝ 약물, 약물치료, 투약 **medication-related** ⓐ 약물과 관련된 **poisoning** ⓝ 중독; 독살
opioid ⓝ 합성마약, 오피오이드(아편과 비슷한 작용을 하는 합성 진통 · 마취제) **painkiller** ⓝ 진통제
outcome ⓝ 결과, 과정, 성과 **over-the-counter** ⓐ 처방전 없이 살 수 있는
cough ⓝ 기침, 헛기침 **pain reliever** 진통제
childproof ⓐ 아이들이 열 수 없게 만든; 아이들에게 안전한
ingest ⓥ (음식 · 약 등을) 섭취하다; (정보 등을) 수집하다

| 전문해석 | 오하이오주 네이션와이드 아동병원에서 발표한 최근 연구 결과에 의하면, 5세 이하 어린이들의 약품 관련 중독 사고 건수가 2000년 이후로 33% 늘어났다. 이것은 가정에다 두는 약품의 수가 늘어난 데 따른 것일 수도 있다.(보기 ② 근거) 퍼코셋(Percocet)과 같은 마약성 진통제로 인한 사망 사고와 기타 심각한 사고가 가장 많았으며, 처방전 없이 살 수 있는 기침감기약과 진통제가 그 뒤를 이었다. "아이들이 열 수 없는 약병은 없습니다. 모든 약을 아이들의 손이 닿지 않는 곳에 두거나 자물쇠로 잠글 수 있는 안전한 곳에 넣어 둬야 합니다."라고 연구저자 헨리 스필러(Henry Spiller)는 말한다. 아이가 약품을 삼켰다는 생각이 들면, 국립 독극물 방제소 비상 전화번호 800–222–1222로 즉시 전화하십시오.

| 보기분석 |
① Medication-related poisonings occurred to children at the age of 5 and under.
약품 관련 중독 사고는 5세 이하의 아이들에게 일어났다.
② One reason for medication-related poisonings in children lies in more drugs kept in homes.
약품 관련 중독 사고가 발생하는 이유 가운데 하나는 집에서 보관하는 약이 더 많아졌다는 것이다.
③ Opioid painkillers cause medication-related poisonings.
마약성 진통제가 약품 관련 중독 사고를 초래한다.
④ It was ~~over-the-counter cough drugs~~ that resulted in the most deaths of children. 지문 내용과 불일치
아이들의 사망 사고를 가장 많이 초래한 것은 처방전 없이 살 수 있는 감기약이었다.
⑤ National Poison Control handles the problem with children's medication-related poisonings.
국립 독극물 방제소에서 아이들의 약물 관련 중독에 따른 문제들을 처리하고 있다.

| 정답분석 | 지문에서 "5세 이하 아이들의 약품 관련 사고 가운데 마약성 진통제로 인한 사망 사고와 기타 심각한 사고가 가장 많았으며, 처방전 없이 살 수 있는 기침감기약과 진통제가 그 뒤를 이었다."라고 했으므로 ④가 지문과 불일치한다.

17 2017 한국외대

정답 ②

| 구문분석 | Reggae is a music genre (that originated in Jamaica in the late 1960s).
S V C 관계대명사

레게는 1960년대 후반에 자메이카에서 유래한 음악 장르이다.

A 1968 single "Do the Reggay" was the first popular song (to use the word), (effectively naming the genre and introducing it to a global audience).
S V C 분사구문 분사구문

1968년에 발표된 싱글곡인 "Do the Reggay"는 그 단어(레게)를 사용한 최초의 대중가요였으며, (노래 제목으로 인해) 그 장르의 이름을 효과적으로 정하고 전 세계 관객에게 그 장르를 효과적으로 소개하게 되었다.

(While sometimes used in a broad sense to refer to most types of popular Jamaican dance music), the term 'reggae' more properly denotes a particular music style (that was strongly influenced by traditional *mento* as well as American jazz and R&B).
부사절: 반면에 S V O 관계대명사

'레게'라는 용어는 때때로 넓은 의미로 대부분의 대중적인 자메이카 댄스 음악 양식을 지칭하는 것으로 사용되기도 하지만, 더 정확하게는 미국 재즈와 리듬 앤드 블루스뿐만 아니라 전통적인 '멘토(칼립소와 유사한 자메이카의 민속음악)'의 영향을 강하게 받은 특정한 음악 양식을 의미한다.

Reggae is instantly recognizable (from the counterpoint between the bass guitar and drum downbeat, and the offbeat rhythm section).
S V C

레게는 베이스 기타와 드럼의 다운비트 사이에서 대위법으로 연주되는 선율과 오프비트(강세를 붙이지 않는 박자) 리듬 악기부로 인해 바로 식별할 수 있다.

It is common (for reggae) to be sung in Jamaican dialect and Jamaican English.
가주어 의미상 주어 진주어

레게를 자메이카 방언과 자메이카식 영어로 부르는 것은 흔한 일이다.

Reggae has spread (around the world), (often incorporating local instruments and fusing with other genres).
S V 분사구문

레게는 전 세계에 널리 퍼졌으며 종종 현지 악기들과 혼합되고 다른 장르들과 융합되었다.

For instance, Caribbean music (in the United Kingdom, including reggae), has been popular (since the late 1960s), and has evolved into several subgenres and fusions.
접속부사 S V_1 C 등위접속사 V_2

예를 들면, 레게가 포함된 영국의 카리브해 음악은 1960년대 후반 이후로 인기를 끌어 왔으며, 여러 하위 장르와 퓨전 음악으로 진화했다.

In Jamaica, authentic reggae is one of the biggest sources of income.
S V C

자메이카에서 정통 레게음악은 국가의 가장 큰 수입원 중 하나이다.

| 어휘 |
originate ⓥ 비롯되다, 유래하다 **name** ⓥ 이름을 붙이다 **denote** ⓥ 나타내다, 의미하다
counterpoint ⓝ 대위법으로 연주되는 선율 **downbeat** ⓝ 〈음악〉 강박, 하박
offbeat ⓝ 〈음악〉 오프비트, 약한 박자
rhythm section 리듬 악기부(보통 드럼과 베이스로 이뤄지고 가끔은 피아노도 쓰임)
fuse with ~와 융합하다 **evolve** ⓥ 진화하다, 발전하다

| 전문해석 | 레게는 1960년대 후반에 자메이카에서 유래한 음악 장르이다. 1968년에 발표된 싱글곡인 "Do the Reggay"는 그 단어(레게)를 사용한 최초의 대중가요였으며, (노래 제목으로 인해) 그 장르의 이름을 효과적으로 정하고 전 세계 관객에게 그 장르를 효과적으로 소개하게 되었다. '레게'라는 용어는 때때로 넓은 의미로 대부분의 대중적인 자메이카 댄스 음악 양식을 지칭하는 것으로 사용되기도 하지만, 더 정확하게는 미국 재즈와 리듬 앤드 블루스뿐만 아니라 전통적인 '멘토(칼립소와 유사한 자메이카의 민속음악)'의 영향을 강하게 받은 특정한 음악 양식을 의미한다. 레게는 베이스 기타와 드럼의 다운비트 사이에서 대위법으로 연주되는 선율과 오프비트(강세를 붙이지 않는 박자) 리듬 악기부로 인해 바로 식별할 수 있다. 레게를 자메이카 방언과 자메이카식 영어로 부르는 것은 흔한 일이다. (보기 ③ 근거) 레게는 전 세계에 널리 퍼졌으며 종종 현지 악기들과 혼합되고

다른 장르들과 융합되었다. 예를 들면, 레게가 포함된 영국의 카리브해 음악은 1960년대 후반 이후로 인기를 끌어 왔으며, 여러 하위 장르와 퓨전 음악으로 진화했다. 자메이카에서 정통 레게음악은 국가의 가장 큰 수입원 중 하나이다. 보기 ① 근거

| 보기분석 | ① Authentic reggae earns Jamaicans a lot of money.
정통 레게음악은 자메이카 사람들이 많은 돈을 벌게 해 준다.
② Reggae music has emerged ~~without~~ international influence. 지문 내용과 불일치
레게음악은 국제적인 영향을 받지 않고 생겨났다.
③ Reggae lyrics are rarely written in American English.
레게 가사는 거의 미국식 영어로 쓰여 있지 않다.
④ There are many different types of reggae across the world.
전 세계에는 다양한 종류의 레게음악이 있다.

| 정답분석 | 지문에서 레게음악은 '미국 재즈와 리듬 앤드 블루스뿐만 아니라 자메이카 전통 음악인 멘토의 영향을 받은 독특한 음악 형식'이라고 했으므로, 레게음악이 국제적인 영향을 받지 않고 생겨났다고 볼 수 없다. 따라서 ②가 정답이다.

18 2015 숭실대

정답 ②

| 구문분석 | Writing(S) is(V) hard(C1) (to see) (because it governs our thought)(부사절: ~ 때문에), and hard(C2) (to talk about) (because of the lack of consistent names for real categories).

글쓰기가 이해하기 어려운 이유는 그것이 우리의 생각을 지배하기 때문이고, 글쓰기에 대해서 이야기하는 것이 힘든 이유는 진정한 범주들에 대한 일관되고 지속적인 이름들이 없기 때문이다.

We(S) know(V) that writing is there to be read, but are not sure what we mean by "writing,"(O) (so that(부사절: 결과) it(가주어) is fashionable in criticism to "read" works of art(진주어 1), to "read" Greek culture or manners of dress or almost anything(진주어 2)), (as if(부사절: 마치 ~처럼) in understanding a work of art or a building or a social practice we are doing the same thing as when we read a text).

우리는 글쓰기가 읽히기 위해 존재하고 있음을 알고 있지만, 우리가 '글쓰기'가 의미하는 바가 무엇인지를 확신하지 못하고 있다. 그래서 비평에 있어서 예술작품을 읽고, 그리고 문화나 옷을 입는 방식이나 혹은 그 외의 거의 모든 것을 읽어 낸다고 하는 것이 유행인데, 이는 마치 우리가 예술작품이나 건축물이나 사회적 관행 등을 이해하고자 할 때 텍스트를 읽을 때와 같은 방식을 취하는 것이다.

Writing(S) has been defined(V) (again and again, always in different ways), but(등위접속사) let us say(= let's say) that writing(S) is(V) a system of markings(C) (with a conventional reference) (that(관계대명사) communicates information, like the signs on this text). Where does such a definition take us?(의문문 도치)

글쓰기는 항상 여러 가지 다른 방식으로 반복해서 정의 내려져 왔지만, 글쓰기란 것이, 이 텍스트에 쓰인 기호들과 같이, 정보를 전달하는 관습적인 지시 관계를 가진 표식들의 체계라고 편의상 정의해 두기로 하자. 이와 같은 정의는 우리를 어디로 이끌고 가는가?

(Because writing is made up of markings)(부사절: ~ 때문에) it(S) is(V) material(C) (not spiritual or emotional or mental).

글쓰기는 표식들로 이루어져 있기 때문에, 글쓰기란 (영적이거나 감정적이거나 정신적이지 않고) 물질적이다.

The meaning of such markings(S1), their conventional reference(S2), (we might say) their intellectual dimension(S3), never comes(V) from nature, nor(등위접속사: 또한 아니다) from God (as many have believed), but from man. (not[never] A but B: A가 아니라 B)

그러한 표식들이 가진 의미, 관습적인 지시 관계, 지적인 차원은 결코 자연으로부터 오는 것이 아니고, (많은 사람들이 믿어 왔던 것처럼) 신(神)으로부터 오는 것도 아니고, 인간으로부터 오는 것이라 말할 수 있을 것이다.

The elements of writing(S), (=) the markings, are related(V) (in an organized way), (in a conventional way), (in order to tell the reader something, to communicate with the reader).

글쓰기의 구성요소들인 표식들은 조직화된 방식과 관습적인 방식으로 서로 관계되어 있는데, 이는 독자에게 무언가를 말하고, 독자와 의사소통하기 위해서이다.

(Where there is writing) there is a reader (who understands the system of conventions), (even if the reader is God or a god).
부사절: ~한 장소에 V S 부사절: 비록 ~일지라도

글쓰기가 있는 곳에는 글쓰기라는 관행의 체계를 이해하는 독자가 있기 마련이다. 심지어 그 독자는 하느님이나 신이 될 수도 있다.

| 어휘 | **fashionable** ⓐ 유행의, 우아한; 받아들여진, 관례적인
conventional ⓐ 전통적인, 인습적인, 틀에 박힌 **definition** ⓝ (어떤 개념의) 정의
reference ⓝ (서적 따위의) 참고, 언급; 관련, 인용문, 관계, 지시 **dimension** ⓝ 크기, 치수; 차원

| 전문해석 | 글쓰기가 이해하기 어려운 이유는 그것이 우리의 생각을 지배하기 때문이고, 글쓰기에 대해서 이야기하는 것이 힘든 이유는 진정한 범주들에 대한 일관되고 지속적인 이름들이 없기 때문이다. 우리는 글쓰기가 읽히기 위해 존재하고 있음을 알고 있지만, 우리가 '글쓰기'가 의미하는 바가 무엇인지를 확신하지 못하고 있다. 그래서 비평에 있어서 예술작품을 읽고, 그리고 문화나 옷을 입는 방식이나 혹은 그 외의 거의 모든 것을 읽어 낸다고 하는 것이 유행인데, 이는 마치 우리가 예술작품이나 건축물이나 사회적 관행 등을 이해하고자 할 때 텍스트를 읽을 때와 같은 방식을 취하는 것이다. 글쓰기는 항상 여러 가지 다른 방식으로 반복해서 정의 내려져 왔지만, 글쓰기란 것이, 이 텍스트에 쓰인 기호들과 같이, 정보를 전달하는 관습적인 지시 관계를 가진 표식들의 체계라고 편의상 정의해 두기로 하자. 이와 같은 정의는 우리를 어디로 이끌고 가는가?
글쓰기는 표식들로 이루어져 있기 때문에, 글쓰기란 (영적이거나 감정적이거나 정신적이지 않고) 물질적이다. 그러한 표식들이 가진 의미, 관습적인 지시 관계, 지적인 차원은 결코 자연으로부터 오는 것이 아니고, (많은 사람들이 믿어 왔던 것처럼) 신(神)으로부터 오는 것도 아니고, 인간으로부터 오는 것이라 말할 수 있을 것이다. 글쓰기의 구성요소들인 표식들은 조직화된 방식과 관습적인 방식으로 서로 관계되어 있는데, 이는 독자에게 무언가를 말하고, 독자와 의사소통하기 위해서이다. 글쓰기가 있는 곳에는 글쓰기라는 관행의 체계를 이해하는 독자가 있기 마련이다. 심지어 그 독자는 하느님이나 신이 될 수도 있다.
보기 ③ 근거 / 보기 ④ 근거

| 보기분석 | ① Writing is a conventional way to communicate with the reader.
글쓰기는 독자와 의사소통하기 위한 전통적인 방법이다.
② Writing is spiritual and abstract in its nature. 지문 내용과 불일치
글쓰기는 본질적으로 영적이고 추상적인 것이다.
③ Man, not God, creates writing.
신이 아닌 인간이 글쓰기를 창조했다.
④ There is always a reader who understands the system of writing.
언제나 글쓰기 체계를 이해하는 독자가 존재한다.

| 정답분석 | 지문에서 글쓰기는 물질적인 것이라고 언급했으므로 그와 반대되는 영적이고 추상적인 것은 지문과 일치하지 않는다. 따라서 ②가 정답으로 적절하다.

19 2015 상명대

정답 ①

as ~ as 원급 구문에서 앞의 as는 부사이며 뒤의 as는 부사절을 이끄는 접속사이다.

| 구문분석 | Perhaps no musical innovation has generated as much puzzlement, dismay, and anger (among its critics) (as rap music), which was popular in some urban African-American and Latino communities for years before becoming nationally visible beginning in the early 1980s.
S V as ~ as 구문 O_1 O_2 O_3 관계대명사

아마도 랩 음악만큼이나 비평가들 사이에서 당황, 실망, 그리고 분노를 일으킨 음악적 혁신은 없었을 것이다. 1980년대 초반부터 전국적으로 눈에 띄기 전에는, 랩 음악은 오랫동안 일부 도시 지역 흑인 공동체와 라틴계 공동체에서 인기를 끌었다.

(Unlike many earlier forms of black music) (that have attracted broad audiences), rap has relatively little melodic content.
관계대명사 S V O

광범위한 청중을 끌어들였던 이전의 다른 많은 형태의 흑인 음악과는 달리, 랩 음악은 상대적으로 멜로디적인 요소가 거의 없다.

Indeed, many rap songs use almost identical musical and instrumental elements (— sometimes even literally identical elements).
접속부사 S V O

실제로, 많은 랩 노래들은 거의 동일한 음악적 요소들과 악기의 요소들을 사용한다—때때로, 심지어는 문자 그대로 똑같은 요소들을 사용한다.

Rap recordings often copy pieces of instrumental backgrounds (from other recordings through a technique known as "sampling.")
S V O

랩 음반은 '샘플링'으로 알려진 테크닉을 통해서 다른 음반에서 악기로 연주되는 배경음악의 일부를 종종 복사해서 사용한다.

as ~ as 원급 구문에서 앞의 as는 부사이며 뒤의 as는 부사절을 이끄는 접속사이다.

Rap's most important element is its words. It is as much a form of language (as a form of music).
S V C S V C

랩에서 가장 중요한 요소는 가사다. 랩은 음악의 형식인 만큼 언어의 형식이기도 하다.

| 어휘 |

innovation ⓝ 혁신 | puzzlement ⓝ 당혹스러움, 곤혹 | dismay ⓝ 실망, 낙담, 실망
instrumental ⓐ 악기의; 도구의 | literally ⓐⓓ 문자 그대로 | sampling ⓝ 샘플링
lyric ⓝ 가사

| 전문해석 | 아마도 랩 음악만큼이나 비평가들 사이에서 당황, 실망, 그리고 분노를 일으킨 음악적 혁신은 없었을 것이다. 1980년대 초반부터 전국적으로 눈에 띄기 전에는, 랩 음악은 오랫동안 일부 도시 지역 흑인 공동체와 라틴계 공동체에서 인기를 끌었다. (보기 ④ 근거) 광범위한 청중을 끌어들였던 이전의 다른 많은 형태의 흑인 음악과는 달리, 랩 음악은 상대적으로 멜로디적인 요소가 거의 없다. 실제로, 많은 랩 노래들은 거의 동일한 음악적 요소들과 악기의 요소들을 사용한다—때때로, 심지어는 문자 그대로 똑같은 요소들을 사용한다. 랩 음반은 '샘플링'으로 알려진 테크닉을 통해서 다른 음반에서 악기로 연주되는 배경음악의 일부를 종종 복사해서 사용한다. (보기 ② 근거) 랩에서 가장 중요한 요소는 가사다. 랩은 음악의 형식인 만큼 언어의 형식이기도 하다.

| 보기분석 |

① Rap caused anger among its singers. 지문 내용과 불일치
랩은 가수들 사이에서 분노를 일으켰다.
② Rap recordings often borrow melodic content from other recordings.
랩 음반은 종종 다른 음반에서 멜로디 콘텐츠를 가져온다.
③ Rap's words are more important than its melody.
랩의 가사는 멜로디보다 더 중요하다.
④ Rap is one form of African-American music.
랩은 흑인 미국인 음악 중 하나이다.
⑤ One of rap's common techniques is sampling.
랩의 일반적인 기술 중 하나는 샘플링이다.

| 정답분석 | 지문의 첫 문장에서 랩 음악에 분노한 사람들은 가수들이 아니라 평론가들이었다고 언급했으므로 ①은 지문과 일치하지 않는다.

20 2015 건국대

정답 ⑤

| 구문분석 | Pizza is certainly one of the world's favorite foods. But where does pizza come from? And who made the first one?
S V C 등위접속사 등위접속사

피자는 틀림없이 전 세계 사람들이 가장 좋아하는 음식들 가운데 하나이다. 그런데 피자는 어디에서 유래된 것일까? 그리고 피자를 처음 만든 사람은 누구였을까?

In fact, people have been making pizza (for a very long time).
접속부사 S V O

사실상 사람들은 아주 오랫동안 피자를 만들어 왔다.

People (in the Stone Age) cooked grains (on hot rocks) (to make dough) (— the basic ingredient of pizza).
S V O 부사적용법: ~하기 위하여

석기시대의 사람들은 피자의 가장 기본적인 식재료인 밀가루 반죽을 만들기 위해 뜨겁게 달군 바위 위에 곡물을 놓고 요리했다.

Over time, people used the dough (as a plate), (covering it with various other foods, herbs, and spices).
S V O 분사구문
시간이 지남에 따라 사람들은 밀가루 반죽을 (일종의 접시 같은) 판으로 사용했고 그 밀가루 반죽 위를 다양한 종류의 음식, 약초, 향신료 등으로 뒤덮었다.

They had developed the world's first pizza.
S V O
세계 최초로 피자를 만든 사람들은 바로 그들이었다.

In the early 16th century, European explorers brought back the first tomatoes (from the Americas).
S V O
16세기 초에 유럽의 탐험가들은 아메리카 대륙으로부터 처음 토마토를 가져왔다.

Tomatoes are a standard ingredient in many pizzas today.
S V C
토마토는 오늘날 많은 피자에서 사용되는 기본적인 식재료이다.

At first, however, most Europeans thought (that) they were poisonous.
접속부사 S V O
그러나 토마토가 처음 소개되었을 때 많은 유럽 사람들은 토마토에 독이 들어 있다고 생각했다.

B as well as A: A뿐만 아니라 B도

For about 200 years, few people ate them. Slowly, people learned that tomatoes were safe to eat, as well as tasty.
S V O S V O
대략 200년 동안 극소수의 사람들만이 토마토를 먹었다. 천천히 유럽 사람들은 토마토가 맛도 있고 안전한 먹을거리라는 것을 알게 되었다.

(In the early 19th century), cooks (in Naples, Italy), started the tradition (of putting tomatoes on baking dough).
S V O
19세기 초, 이탈리아 나폴리의 요리사들은 구운 밀가루 반죽 위에 토마토를 올려놓는 전통을 시작했다.

The flat bread soon became popular (with poor people all over Naples).
S V C
납작한 빵은 곧 나폴리 전역에 있는 가난한 사람들 사이에서 인기를 얻게 되었다.

In 1830, cooks (in Naples) took another bit step (in pizza history) (— they opened the world's first pizza restaurant).
S V O 대시: 세부 내용 재진술
1830년, 나폴리의 요리사들은 세계 최초로 피자 레스토랑을 오픈하는 것을 통해 피자의 역사에서 한발 더 나아간 진전을 이루어 냈다.

Today, up to five billion pizzas are served (every year around the world).
S V
오늘날 세계 전역에서 해마다 50억 판이 넘는 피자가 만들어져 서빙되고 있다.

| 어휘 | **grain** ⓝ 곡물 **dough** ⓝ 밀가루 반죽 **ingredient** ⓝ (요리 등의) 재료, 성분 **serve** ⓥ 음식을 서빙하다

| 전문해석 | 피자는 틀림없이 전 세계 사람들이 가장 좋아하는 음식들 가운데 하나이다. 그런데 피자는 어디에서 유래된 것일까? 그리고 피자를 처음 만든 사람은 누구였을까?

사실상 사람들은 아주 오랫동안 피자를 만들어 왔다. 석기시대의 사람들은 피자의 가장 기본적인 식재료인 밀가루 반죽을 만들기 위해 뜨겁게 달군 바위 위에 곡물을 놓고 요리했다.(보기 ③ 근거) 시간이 지남에 따라 사람들은 밀가루 반죽을 (일종의 접시 같은) 판으로 사용했고 그 밀가루 반죽 위를 다양한 종류의 음식, 약초, 향신료 등으로 뒤덮었다. 세계 최초로 피자를 만든 사람들은 바로 그들이었다.

16세기 초에 유럽의 탐험가들은 아메리카 대륙으로부터 처음 토마토를 가져왔다.(보기 ① 근거) 토마토는 오늘날 많은 피자에서 사용되는 기본적인 식재료이다. 그러나 토마토가 처음 소개되었을 때 많은 유럽 사람들은 토마토에 독이 들어 있다고 생각했다. 대략 200년 동안 극소수의 사람들만이 토마토를 먹었다. 천천히 유럽 사람들은 토마토가 맛도 있고 안전한 먹을거리라는 것을 알게 되었다. 19세기 초, 이탈리아 나폴리의 요리사들은 구운 밀가루 반죽 위에 토마토를 올려놓는 전통을 시작했다. 납작한 빵은 곧 나폴리 전역에 있는 가난한 사람들 사이에서 인기를 얻게 되었다. 1830년, 나폴리의 요리사들은 세계 최초로 피자 레스토랑을 오픈하는(보기 ④ 근거) 것을 통해 피자의 역사에서 한발 더 나아간 진전을 이루어 냈다. 오늘날 세계 전역에서 해마다 50억 판이 넘는 피자가 만들어져 서빙되고 있다.

| 보기분석 | ① Tomatoes had not existed in Europe until the early 16th century.
토마토는 16세기 초까지 유럽에 존재하지 않았다.
② In Europe, tomatoes became an ingredient in pizza in the early 19th century.
유럽에서 토마토는 19세기 초에 피자 재료가 되었다.
③ People in the Stone Age used hot rocks to make dough.
석기시대의 사람들은 반죽을 만들기 위해 뜨거운 돌을 사용했다.
④ Cooks in Naples opened the world's first pizza restaurant.
나폴리의 요리사들이 세계 최초의 피자 가게를 열었다.
⑤ The flat bread cost a lot, so only ~~rich~~ people in Naples ate it. 지문 내용과 불일치
그 평평한 빵은 값이 많이 들어서 오직 나폴리에서 부유한 사람들만 먹었다.

| 정답분석 | 지문에서 '납작한 빵은 곧 나폴리 전역에 있는 가난한 사람들 사이에서 인기를 얻게 되었다.'고 언급했으므로 ⑤는 지문과 일치하지 않는다.

6강 부분 이해 (지시어, 밑줄 추론)

Practice

01	①	02	④	03	④	04	②	05	⑤	06	①	07	③	08	④	09	③	10	⑤
11	②	12	①	13	③	14	④	15	①	16	③	17	④	18	④	19	④	20	②

01 2018 가천대 정답 ①

| 구문분석 | (At the beginning of the 1960s), Andy Warhol(S) began to produce(V) flat, commodified, curiously exact paintings of household goods(O) (everyone in America knew and handled daily).
that(관계대명사) 생략

1960년대 초, 앤디 워홀(Andy Warhol)은 미국의 모든 사람들이 알고 매일 다루는 가정용품들의 평면적이고 상품화된, 그리고 신기할 정도로 정밀한 그림들을 만들기 시작했다.

(Starting(분사구문) with a series of Coke bottles), he(S) progressed(V) rapidly (to Campbell's soup cans, food stamps and dollar bills).
병렬구조 A, B and C

그는 일련의 코카콜라 병을 시작으로 캠벨 수프 캔, 식권, 달러 지폐까지 (만드는 것을) 빠르게 진행했다.

He(S) would soon be(V) the most famous and charismatic proponent of Pop Art(C).

그는 곧 팝아트의 가장 유명하고 카리스마 있는 지지자가 될 것이었다.

One(S_1) talks(V_1) (about the shock of the new), but(등위접속사) part of the reason(S_2) (Pop Art caused such a wringing of hands among artists, gallerists and critics alike), is(V_2) that it looked on first glance like a category error(C), = a painful collapse (of the seemingly unquestionable boundary) (between high and low culture; good taste and bad).
세미콜론: and 역할

사람들은 새로운 것의 충격에 대해 이야기하지만, 팝아트가 예술가들, 갤러리 운영자들, 그리고 비평가들 모두에게 그렇게 큰 불안을 일으켰던 이유의 일부는 팝아트가 처음에는 범주의 오류처럼 보였고, 즉 고급문화와 저급문화, 그리고 좋은 취향과 나쁜 취향 간의 겉보기에 의심할 여지 없는 경계가 고통스러운 붕괴처럼 보였기 때문이었다.

Warhol(S) was painting(V) things(O) (to which(관계대명사) he was sentimentally attached, even loved; objects (whose(관계대명사) value derives not because they're rare or individual but because they are reliably the same).
세미콜론: 부연설명 / not A but B: A가 아니라 B

워홀은 그가 감정적으로 애착을 갖고 심지어 사랑했던 것들을 그림으로 그렸는데, 그 대상들은 희귀하거나 개인적인 것이기 때문이 아니라 확실히 같은 것들이기 때문에 가치가 파생되는 그런 것들이다.

One dollar bill(S) is(V) not more attractive than another(C); drinking Coke(S) puts(V) the coal miner(O) (among the company of presidents and movie stars).
세미콜론: and 역할

1달러 지폐는 다른 지폐보다 더 매력적이지 않고 콜라를 마시는 것은 탄광 노동자를 대통령들과 영화배우들과 같은 부류에 들어가게 한다.

It(S)'s(V) the same democratic inclusive impulse(C) (that(관계대명사) made Warhol want to call Pop Art Common Art).

그것은 워홀이 팝아트를 커먼아트라고 부르고 싶게 만든 것과 같은 민주적, 포괄적 충동이다.

| 어휘 |
commodify ⓥ (예술품 등을) 상품화하다
household goods 가사용품
handle ⓥ 다루다, 처리하다
proponent ⓝ 지지자
Pop Art 팝 아트(대중문화를 기반으로 1960년대에 발달한 예술형식)
on the first glance 일견하여
collapse ⓝ 붕괴
sentimentally ⓐⓓ 감상적으로

be attached to ~에 애착[애정]을 가지다 derive ⓥ 유래하다
inspired ⓐ 영감을 받은 democratic ⓐ 민주(주의)적인 inclusive ⓐ 포괄적인
impulse ⓝ 충동

| 전문해석 | 1960년대 초, 앤디 워홀(Andy Warhol)은 미국의 모든 사람들이 알고 매일 다루는 가정용품들의 평면적이고 상품화된, 그리고 신기할 정도로 정밀한 그림들을 만들기 시작했다. 그는 일련의 코카콜라 병을 시작으로 캠벨 수프 캔, 식권, 달러지폐까지 (만드는 것을) 빠르게 진행했다. 그는 곧 팝아트의 가장 유명하고 카리스마 있는 지지자가 될 것이었다.
사람들은 새로운 것의 충격에 대해 이야기하지만, 팝아트가 예술가들, 갤러리 운영자들, 그리고 비평가들 모두에게 그렇게 큰 불안을 일으켰던 이유의 일부는 팝아트가 처음에는 범주의 오류처럼 보였고, 즉 고급문화와 저급문화, 그리고 좋은 취향과 나쁜 취향 간의 겉보기에 의심할 여지 없는 경계가 고통스러운 붕괴처럼 보였기 때문이었다. 워홀은 그가 감정적으로 애착을 갖고 심지어 사랑했던 것들을 그림으로 그렸는데, 그 대상들은 희귀하거나 개인적인 것이기 때문이 아니라 확실히 같은 것들이기 때문에 가치가 파생되는 그런 것들이다. 1달러 지폐는 다른 지폐보다 더 매력적이지 않고 콜라를 마시는 것은 탄광 노동자를 대통령들과 영화배우들과 같은 부류에 들어가게 한다. 그것은 워홀이 팝아트를 커먼아트라고 부르고 싶게 만든 것과 같은 민주적, 포괄적 충동이다.

| 보기분석 | ✓ disturbance 불안, 방해, 소란 ② joy 기쁨, 성공
③ apathy 무관심 ④ applause 박수(갈채)

| 정답분석 | 동사 'wring'은 '쥐어짜다' 또는 '움켜쥐다'라는 뜻을 가지고 있다. 그래서 wring one's hands는 '걱정이나 절망 때문에 두 손을 잡고 쥐어짜거나 비비는 모습'을 표현한다. 따라서 보기 ①의 disturbance(불안)가 정답이다.

02 2018 가톨릭대

정답 ④

| 구문분석 | You(S) already know(V) that making a good first impression can go a long way(O).
당신은 좋은 첫인상을 만드는 것이 큰 도움이 될 수 있다는 것을 이미 알고 있다.

But(등위접속사) forget(V) all the advice(O) ((that) you've received about dressing) (to impress(부사적용법: ~하기 위하여)) or putting on a cheesy smile.
하지만 (좋은) 인상을 주도록 옷을 입거나 가식적인 미소를 짓는 것에 관해 당신이 받았던 모든 조언을 잊어라.

The true secret(S) (to building a lasting connection) reaches(V) much deeper than (what you wear).
지속적인 관계를 만드는 진정한 비밀은 당신이 입는 것보다 훨씬 더 깊은 곳에 있다.

(According to Dr. Turner), (who(관계대명사) has researched first impressions for more than 10 years), everyone(S) (consciously or subconsciously) asks(V) two questions(O) (when meeting someone new)(부사절: ~할 때): can I trust this person? And can I respect this person?(콜론: 동격)

10년 이상 첫인상을 연구해 온 터너(Turner) 박사에 따르면, 모든 사람은 (의식적이든 무의식적이든) 새로운 누군가를 만날 때 두 가지 질문을 한다: 내가 이 사람을 믿을 수 있을까? 그리고 내가 이 사람을 존경할 수 있을까?

Both questions(S) help(V) you(O) measure(O.C) a person's warmth and competence, respectively.
그 두 질문은 모두 당신이 어떤 사람의 따뜻함과 능력을 판단하는 데 각각 도움을 준다.

But(등위접속사), Dr. Turner(S) says(V), you should put gaining your peers' trust over winning their respect, (even in a workplace setting)(O).

그러나 터너 박사는 심지어 직장에서도 동료들의 존경을 받는 것보다 신뢰를 얻는 것을 우선시해야 한다고 말한다.

세미콜론: 부연설명

"If someone you're trying to influence doesn't trust you, you're not going to get very far; in fact, you might even elicit suspicion (because you come across as manipulative," Dr. Turner wrote (in her article).

O / 접속부사 / S V

"만약 당신이 영향력을 행사하려는 누군가가 당신을 믿지 않는다면, 당신은 그다지 잘되지 못할 것입니다; 사실, 당신은 조종하려는 것으로 보여서 심지어 의심을 불러일으킬 수도 있습니다."라고 터너 박사는 그녀의 글에 썼다.

등위접속사

"A warm, trustworthy person (who is also strong elicits admiration), but (only after you've established trust) does your strength become a gift (rather than a threat)."

only + 부사절 도치 / S / 관계대명사 / 부사절: ~한 후에 / S V C

"마음이 따뜻하고 믿을 수 있으며 또한 강한 사람은 존경을 이끌어 내지만, 신뢰를 형성한 후에야 당신의 장점은 위협이 아닌 재능이 됩니다."

| 어휘 |

first impression 첫인상　**go a long way** 크게 도움이 되다　**impress** ⓥ 깊은 인상을 주다
cheesy ⓐ 가식적인　**lasting** ⓐ 영속적인, 지속적인　**consciously** ⓐⓓ 의식적으로
subconsciously ⓐⓓ 잠재의식적으로　**measure** ⓥ 판단하다　**competence** ⓝ 능력, 자격
respectively ⓐⓓ 각각　**influence** ⓥ (사람의 행동이나 사고에) 영향을 미치다
elicit ⓥ (정보나 반응을) 이끌어 내다　**suspicion** ⓝ 의심　**come across as** ~라는 인상을 주다
manipulative ⓐ (흔히 교묘하고 부정직하게 사람이나 사물을) 조종하는　**establish** ⓥ 설립하다, 설정하다
threat ⓝ 위협

| 전문해석 | 당신은 좋은 첫인상을 만드는 것이 큰 도움이 될 수 있다는 것을 이미 알고 있다. 하지만 (좋은) 인상을 주도록 옷을 입거나 가식적인 미소를 짓는 것에 관해 당신이 받았던 모든 조언을 잊어라. 지속적인 관계를 만드는 진정한 비밀은 당신이 입는 것보다 훨씬 더 깊은 곳에 있다. 10년 이상 첫인상을 연구해 온 터너(Turner) 박사에 따르면, 모든 사람은 (의식적이든 무의식적이든) 새로운 누군가를 만날 때 두 가지 질문을 한다: 내가 이 사람을 믿을 수 있을까? 그리고 내가 이 사람을 존경할 수 있을까?

그 두 질문은 모두 당신이 어떤 사람의 따뜻함과 능력을 판단하는 데 각각 도움을 준다. 그러나 터너 박사는 심지어 직장에서도 동료들의 존경을 받는 것보다 신뢰를 얻는 것을 우선시해야 한다고 말한다. "만약 당신이 영향력을 행사하려는 누군가가 당신을 믿지 않는다면, 당신은 그다지 잘되지 못할 것입니다; 사실, 당신은 조종하려는 것으로 보여서 심지어 의심을 불러일으킬 수도 있습니다."라고 터너 박사는 그녀의 글에 썼다. "마음이 따뜻하고 믿을 수 있으며 또한 강한 사람은 존경을 이끌어 내지만, 신뢰를 형성한 후에야 당신의 장점은 위협이 아닌 재능이 됩니다."

| 보기분석 |

① you happen to meet somebody you can control easily
　당신은 당신이 쉽게 통제할 수 있는 누군가를 우연히 만나게 된다
② you're considered as a competent and creative person
　당신은 유능하고 창의적인 사람으로 여겨진다
③ you're not confident but only suggestive in your discussion
　당신은 자신감은 없지만 당신의 토론에서는 도발적이다
④ you make an impression as being influential in a negative way
　당신은 부정적인 방식으로 영향력이 있다는 인상을 준다

| 정답분석 | 밑줄 친 부분을 번역하면 '당신이 조종하려는 듯한 인상을 준다'이다. 다른 사람을 조종한다는 것은 '부정적인 방식으로 영향력을 행사하는 것'에 가까운 의미이므로 보기 중에서 ④가 밑줄 친 부분의 의미로 가장 적절하다.

03 2018 경기대

정답 ④

| 구문분석 | Nobody reveals an accurate picture (of their actual lives on social media).

S V O

아무도 소셜 미디어에 자신들의 실제 삶의 정확한 모습을 공개하지 않는다.

They omit the bickering, boring and unflattering aspects (of their lives in favor of the fabulous moments).

S V O

그들은 멋진 순간들을 선호하여 다투거나, 지루하고, 그들의 삶의 노골적인 측면들을 생략한다.

The downside (of this "success theater") is that daily exposure to Facebook leaves people feeling inadequate.
S V C
이 "성공 극장"의 단점은 매일 페이스북에 노출되는 것이 사람들로 하여금 (자신에 대한) 부족함을 느끼게 한다는 것이다.

That constant barrage (of other people's best moments) creates the illusion (that everyone else in the world is living these wonderful lives (filled with success and joy and adventure) (while you're sitting there, well, looking at Facebook).
S V O = 부사절: ~하는 동안 분사구문
다른 사람들의 최고의 순간들의 세례는 당신이 거기 앉아서 페이스북을 보는 동안 모든 사람들이 성공과 기쁨과 모험으로 가득 찬 이런 멋진 삶을 살고 있는 것처럼 착각하게 한다.

This occurs (on other sites) (like Instagram).
S V 전치사: ~와 같은
이것은 인스타그램과 같은 다른 사이트들에서도 발생한다.

| 어휘 | **reveal** ⓥ (비밀 등을) 드러내다, 밝히다 **social media** ⓝ 소셜 미디어(사회 관계망에 사용되는 웹사이트와 소프트웨어)
omit ⓥ 생략하다 **bicker** ⓥ (사소한 일로) 다투다
unflattering ⓐ 아부하지 않는, 노골적인 **fabulous** ⓐ 기막히게 좋은[멋진]
downside ⓝ 부정적인 면 **inadequate** ⓐ 불충분한, 부적당한 **exposure** ⓝ 노출
barrage ⓝ 일제 엄호사격, 세례 **illusion** ⓝ 오해, 착각, 환상

| 전문해석 | 아무도 소셜 미디어에 자신들의 실제 삶의 정확한 모습을 공개하지 않는다. 그들은 멋진 순간들을 선호하여 다투거나, 지루하고, 그들의 삶의 노골적인 측면들을 생략한다. 이 "성공 극장"의 단점은 매일 페이스북에 노출되는 것이 사람들로 하여금 (자신에 대한) 부족함을 느끼게 한다는 것이다. 다른 사람들의 최고의 순간들의 세례는 당신이 거기 앉아서 페이스북을 보는 동안 모든 사람들이 성공과 기쁨과 모험으로 가득 찬 이런 멋진 삶을 살고 있는 것처럼 착각하게 한다. 이것은 인스타그램과 같은 다른 사이트들에서도 발생한다.

| 보기분석 | ① The opposite illusion
정반대의 착각
② The boring aspect of others' lives 지루한 측면은 언급되지 않음
다른 사람들의 삶의 지루한 측면
③ The more accurate picture 비교의 근거가 언급되지 않음
더 정확한 모습
④ The same phenomenon
같은 현상

| 정답분석 | This는 보통 직전 문장의 명사나 문장 등을 다시 언급할 때 사용되는 지시사이다. 밑줄이 포함된 문장을 번역하면 '이것은 인스타그램과 같은 다른 사이트들에서도 발생한다'이다. 직전 문장까지 다른 사람들이 페이스북을 통해 멋진 삶을 공개하며 이 모습을 보는 사람들은 자신의 부족함을 느끼게 된다는 내용이 전개되었다. 따라서 같은 현상이 인스타그램과 같은 다른 사이트들의 경우에도 발생한다고 서술해야 글의 흐름상 자연스럽다. 그러므로 밑줄 친 This의 의미로는 보기 중 ④가 적절하다.

04 2018 서울여대

정답 ②

| 구문분석 | Do not wake up (to the blue hue of your smartphone) and immediately start working.
V1 등위접속사 do not 생략 V2
스마트폰이 파란색으로 바뀌면 일어나 즉시 일을 시작하지 말라.

Place it (across the room, or better yet, in an adjacent one), and force yourself (up and out of bed) to turn off your alarm each morning.
V1 O1 등위접속사 V2 O2 force A to B: A가 B하게 하다
그것을 방 맞은편에 두거나 근처 방에 두는 것이 더 좋고, 매일 아침 일어나서 침대에서 일어나 알람을 꺼라.

(When the alarm does go off), get up and prepare for your day (as you would for an office job): take a shower and get dressed.
부사절: ~할 때 V1 등위접속사 V2 부사절: ~처럼, ~하듯이 콜론: 예시
알람이 울리면, 일어나서 사무실에 일하러 가기 위해 하는 것처럼 하루를 준비하라: 샤워를 하고 옷을 입어라.

Business attire is (obviously) not required, but act (as though you will be interacting with colleagues in person).

등위접속사 / S / V_1 / V_2 / 부사절: 비록 ~일지라도

비즈니스 복장은 (분명히) 필수는 아니지만, 당신이 직접 동료들과 교류할 것처럼 행동하라.

After all, you never know when they may want to video chat, and you do not want to beg off (because you are not wearing a shirt).

명사절 / 등위접속사 / 접속부사 / S_1 / V_1 / O / S_2 / V_2 / 부사절: ~ 때문에

결국, 당신은 사람들이 언제 화상통화를 원할지는 모르고, 당신이 셔츠를 입고 있지 않다는 이유로 화상통화를 거절하고 싶지 않다.

This also sets the tempo (for the day) and discourages the sleepy notion (that, perhaps, just maybe, you can crawl back into bed for a nap around lunch), (although there is something to be said for workday naps).

등위접속사 / S / V_1 / O_1 / V_2 / O_2 / = / 부사절: 비록 ~일지라도

이것은 또한 하루의 속도를 설정하고, 아마도, 비록 일하는 시간에 낮잠을 자는 것에 대해 당신 나름의 할 말이 있더라도 점심 무렵에 침대 속으로 다시 기어 들어가서 낮잠을 잘 수도 있겠다는 나른한 생각을 단념시킨다.

| 어휘 |

hue ⓝ 색깔, 색조 **immediately** ⓐⓓ 즉시, 즉각 **adjacent** ⓐ 인접한
go off (무엇을 하러) 자리를 뜨다, (경보 등이) 울리다 **attire** ⓝ 복장
interact ⓥ 상호작용하다 **in person** 직접, 몸소
beg off (하기로 한 일을) 못하겠다고 하다 **tempo** ⓝ 박자, (활동 등의) 속도
crawl ⓥ 네발로 기다, 포복하다 **nap** ⓝ 낮잠

| 전문해석 | 스마트폰이 파란색으로 바뀌면 일어나 즉시 일을 시작하지 말라. 그것을 방 맞은편에 두거나 근처 방에 두는 것이 더 좋고, 매일 아침 일어나서 침대에서 일어나 알람을 꺼라. 알람이 울리면, 일어나서 사무실에 일하러 가기 위해 하는 것처럼 하루를 준비하라: 샤워를 하고 옷을 입어라. 비즈니스 복장은 (분명히) 필수는 아니지만, 당신이 직접 동료들과 교류할 것처럼 행동하라. 결국, 당신은 사람들이 언제 화상통화를 원할지는 모르고, 당신이 셔츠를 입고 있지 않다는 이유로 화상통화를 거절하고 싶지 않다. 이것은 또한 하루의 속도를 설정하고, 아마도, 비록 일하는 시간에 낮잠을 자는 것에 대해 당신 나름의 할 말이 있더라도 점심 무렵에 침대 속으로 다시 기어 들어가서 낮잠을 잘 수도 있겠다는 나른한 생각을 단념시킨다.

| 보기분석 |
① You need something for workday naps. 언급 안 한 정보
당신은 근무일의 낮잠을 위한 무언가가 필요하다.
② Workday naps might be good for you.
근무일 낮잠이 당신에게 좋을 수도 있다.
③ No employers will allow workday naps.
어떤 고용주도 근무일 낮잠을 허락하지 않을 것이다.
④ Workday naps are something that you can talk about. 키워드는 있지만 낮잠의 장점에 대한 언급은 없음
근무일 낮잠은 여러분이 이야기할 수 있는 것이다.

| 정답분석 | 밑줄 친 부분을 번역하면 '일하는 시간에 낮잠을 자는 것에 대해 당신은 뭔가 할 말이 있다'이다. 마지막 문장의 주절에서 '집에서 일을 할 때 낮잠을 잘 수도 있겠다는 생각을 단념시킨다'는 서술이 있고 밑줄 친 부분 이전에 'although'라는 양보의 부사절 접속사가 있으므로 주절과는 역접되는 내용이 나와야 할 것이다. 보기 중 ②가 '낮잠을 자야 하는 타당한 이유'에 해당될 수 있는 내용이다.

05 2018 인하대

정답 ⑤

| 구문분석 | Machines won't bring (about the economic robot apocalypse) — but greedy humans will, (according to physicist Stephen Hawking).

S_1 / V_1 / 등위접속사 / 대시: 부연설명 / S_2 / V_2 / 술부(bring ~ apocalypse) 생략

물리학자 스티븐 호킹(Stephen Hawking)에 따르면, 기계는 로봇에 의한 경제적 종말을 초래하지 않을 것이지만 탐욕스러운 인간이 그렇게(경제적 종말을 초래) 할 것이다.

(In a recent seminar), the scientist predicted that economic inequality will skyrocket (as more jobs become automated and the rich owners of machines refuse to share their fast-proliferating wealth).
S V 명사절 O 부사절: ~함에 따라

최근 세미나에서, 그 과학자는 더 많은 일자리가 자동화되고 부유한 기계 소유자들이 그들의 급증하는 부를 공유하기를 거부함에 따라 경제적 불평등이 치솟을 것이라고 예측했다.

부사절: 만약 ~라면
He said, "(If machines produce everything we need), the outcome will depend on how things are distributed.
S V O

그는 "기계가 우리가 필요로 하는 모든 것을 생산한다면, 그 결과는 물건들이 어떻게 분배되느냐에 달려 있을 것입니다.

Everyone can enjoy a life of luxurious leisure (if the machine-produced wealth is shared), or most people can end up poor (if the machine owners monopolize wealth).
S_1 V_1 O_1 부사절: 만약 ~라면 등위접속사 S_2 V_2 부사절: 만약 ~라면

만약 기계가 생산한 부가 공유된다면 모든 사람이 사치스러운 여가생활을 즐길 수 있고, 만약 기계를 소유한 사람들이 부를 독점한다면, 대부분의 사람들이 결국 가난해질 것입니다.

So far, the trend seems to be toward the second option, (with technology driving ever-increasing inequality)."
S V C with 분사구문

지금까지는 기술이 불평등을 더욱 심화시키면서 추세가 두 번째 선택지를 향하고 있는 것처럼 보입니다."라고 말했다.

Essentially, machine owners will become the bourgeoisie of a new era, [(in which the corporations (they own) won't provide jobs (to actual human workers)].
S V C 관계대명사 (that)

본질적으로, 기계 소유자들은 새로운 시대의 부르주아(유산계급)가 될 것이고, 그 시대에는 그들이 소유한 기업들이 실제 인간 노동자들에게 일자리를 제공하지 않을 것이다.

부사절: ~처럼
(As it is), the chasm (between the super rich and the rest) is growing.
S between A and B: A와 B 사이 V

현재로서는, 슈퍼리치(큰 부자)와 나머지의 격차가 점점 커지고 있다.

대시: 부연설명 등위접속사
Capital — such as stocks or property — accrues value (at a much faster rate than wages increase), and the working class can never even catch up.
S_1 V_1 O S_2 V_2

주식이나 부동산과 같은 자본은 임금 상승률보다 훨씬 빠른 속도로 가치를 축적하고, 노동자 계층은 (그 속도를) 결코 따라잡을 수 없다.

등위접속사
But (if Hawking is right), the problem won't be (about catching up).
부사절: 만약 ~라면 S V

그러나 만약 호킹의 말이 맞는다면, 문제는 따라잡는 것이 아닐 것이다.

가주어
It'll be a struggle to even move past the starting line.
V C 진주어

출발선을 넘어서기조차 힘들 것이다.

| 어휘 |

apocalypse ⓝ (세계의) 파멸, 종말 greedy ⓐ 탐욕스러운 physicist ⓝ 물리학자
predict ⓥ 예측[예견]하다 inequality ⓝ 불평등 skyrocket ⓥ 급등하다
automate ⓥ (일을) 자동화하다 fast-proliferating ⓐ 급속도로 확산되는
outcome ⓝ 결과 distribute ⓥ 분배하다 monopolize ⓥ 독점하다
corporation ⓝ 기업, 법인 chasm ⓝ 아주 깊은 틈, 구멍 stock ⓝ 주식, 증권
property ⓝ 재산, 자산 accrue ⓥ 누적되다, 축적되다 wage ⓝ 임금

| 전문해석 | 물리학자 스티븐 호킹(Stephen Hawking)에 따르면, 기계는 로봇에 의한 경제적 종말을 초래하지 않을 것이지만 탐욕스러운 인간이 그렇게(경제적 종말을 초래) 할 것이다. 최근 세미나에서, 그 과학자는 더 많은 일자리가 자동화되고 부유한 기계 소유자들이 그들의 급증하는 부를 공유하기를 거부함에 따라 경제적 불평등이 치솟을 것이라고 예측했다. 그는 "기계가 우리가 필요로 하는 모든 것을 생산한다면, 그 결과는 물건들이 어떻게 분배되느냐에 달려 있을 것입니다. 만약 기계가 생산한 부가 공유된다면 모든 사람이 사치스러운 여가생활을 즐길 수 있고, 만약 기계를 소유한 사람들이 부를 독점한다면,

대부분의 사람들이 결국 가난해질 것입니다. 지금까지는 기술이 불평등을 더욱 심화시키면서 추세가 두 번째 선택지를 향하고 있는 것처럼 보입니다."라고 말했다. 본질적으로, 기계 소유자들은 새로운 시대의 부르주아(유산계급)가 될 것이고, 그 시대에는 그들이 소유한 기업들이 실제 인간 노동자들에게 일자리를 제공하지 않을 것이다. 현재로서는, 슈퍼리치(큰 부자)와 나머지의 격차가 점점 커지고 있다. 주식이나 부동산과 같은 자본은 임금 상승률보다 훨씬 빠른 속도로 가치를 축적하고, 노동자 계층은 (그 속도를) 결코 따라잡을 수 없다. 그러나 만약 호킹의 말이 맞는다면, 문제는 따라잡는 것이 아닐 것이다. 출발선을 넘어서기조차 힘들 것이다.

| 보기분석 | ① It will be hard to start a business.
사업을 시작하는 것은 어려울 것이다.
② It will be hard to benefit from robot automation.
로봇 자동화의 혜택을 받기는 어려울 것이다.
③ It will be hard to tell who is rich and who is poor.
누가 부자이고 누가 가난한지 구별하기 어려울 것이다.
④ It will be hard to achieve a fast accumulation of capital.
빠른 자본 축적을 달성하기는 어려울 것이다.
(①~④: 전부 언급 안 한 정보)
⑤ It will be hard to get opportunities to overcome the inequality.
불평등을 극복할 기회를 얻기는 어려울 것이다.

| 정답분석 | 밑줄 친 문장의 직전 문장에서는 '호킹의 말이 맞는다면'이라는 조건을 걸고 있다. 본문에서 호킹은 '미래에 기계 소유자들이 탐욕으로 부를 독점한다면 대부분의 사람들이 가난해지고 부의 격차가 크게 벌어질 것'이라 예측했다. 따라서 마지막 문장이 이러한 상황을 '경주'에 비유한 것이라 생각해 보면 '출발선을 넘어서기조차 힘들 것이다'라는 것은 경제적 불평등 때문에 부를 성취하기 위해 경주에서 빠른 속도로 앞서 나가는 부자가 있는 반면에 나머지는 출발선을 넘어서지 못할 만큼 경제적 격차가 벌어진 상황을 빗댄 것으로 보인다. 따라서 보기 ⑤가 밑줄 친 문장의 의미로 가장 적절하다.

06 2016 광운대

정답 ①

| 구문분석 | "(In my view) the acquisition (S) (of the South China Morning Post) was driven (V) completely (by Jack Ma), (whose (관계대명사) hubris is his main motivating factor).

"내 생각에, 사우스 차이나 모닝 포스트의 인수는 완전히 마윈(Jack Ma)에 의해 추진되었는데 그의 지나친 자신감이 (인수의) 주된 동기를 부여한 요소이다.

One (S) (of Ma's top role models) is (V) the more cerebral Jeff Bezos (C), = founder of Amazon, (who (관계대명사) made a similar purchase of the storied Washington Post in 2013).

마윈의 최고 롤 모델 중 한 명은 아마존(Amazon)의 설립자인 더 똑똑한 제프 베이조스(Jeff Bezos)인데, 2013년에 그 유명한 워싱턴 포스트의 비슷한 인수를 했었다.

I (S) haven't heard (V) much (O) (about changes at the Washington Post) (since then).
나는 그 인수 이후에 워싱턴 포스트의 변화에 대해서 많이 듣지 못했다.

But (등위접속사) I (S) do think (V) (that) it was wise for Bezos to buy the newspaper personally rather than using Amazon funds (O), (so that (~하기 위해서) he won't be accused of burdening his company with such a problematic and also renowned asset).
하지만 나는 베이조스가 그 신문사를 인수함에 있어서 아마존의 자금을 사용하는 대신에 개인적으로 구매한 것은 현명했다고 생각한다. 그는 그렇게 문제가 많고 유명한 자산(워싱턴 포스트)을 인수해서 그의 회사(아마존)에 부담을 주었다는 비난은 피하기 위해서였다.

Ma (S) appeared (V_1) to be taking a similar approach (C), but (등위접속사) changed (V_2) course (O) and (등위접속사) decided (V_3) to make this purchase (O) (through (전치사: ~을 통해) Alibaba).
마윈도 이와 비슷한 접근법을 취하는 것처럼 보였지만, 그는 방향을 바꿔, 알리바바(Alibaba)를 통해 이 구매(사우스 차이나 모닝 포스트를 인수)를 하기로 결정했다.

(If that's the case), his motivation is probably a desire (to find a place for the newspaper) (among his small but growing stable of related media assets like the Twitter of China).
부사절: 만약 ~라면 / S / V / C

만약 그것이 사실이라면, 그의 동기는 아마도 중국의 트위터처럼 작지만 안정적으로 성장하고 있는 매체 자산에, 그 신문사(사우스 차이나 모닝 포스트)가 한 자리를 차지하고자 하는 바람이었다.

The company will need to use those resources and move (quickly to revive the paper), but will also need to be careful (of politically sensitive issues)."
S / V_1 / O / 등위접속사 / V_2 / 부사적용법: ~하기 위하여 / 등위접속사 / V_3 / O

그 회사(알리바바)는 그러한 자원들을 이용해서 그 신문을 되살리기 위해 신속히 움직여야 할 필요가 있다. 그러나 정치적으로 민감한 문제에 대해서도 주의를 기울여야 한다."

| 어휘 |

acquisition ⓝ 인수, 습득
hubris ⓝ 자만심, 거만, 교만
cerebral ⓐ 뇌의, 지적인
storied ⓐ 유명한, 잘 알려진
accuse ⓥ 고발하다, 비난하다
burden ⓥ 부담[짐]을 지우다
renowned ⓐ 유명한
stable ⓝ 마구간, 같은 장소에서 일하는 사람들, 같은 회사의 상품들
asset ⓝ 자산
resource ⓝ 자원, 자산, (공급 · 원조의) 원천
revive ⓥ 활기를 되찾다

| 전문해석 | "내 생각에, 사우스 차이나 모닝 포스트의 인수는 완전히 마윈(Jack Ma)에 의해 추진되었는데 그의 지나친 자신감이 (인수의) 주된 동기를 부여한 요소이다. 마윈의 최고 롤 모델 중 한 명은 아마존(Amazon)의 설립자인 더 똑똑한 제프 베이조스(Jeff Bezos)인데, 2013년에 그 유명한 워싱턴 포스트의 비슷한 인수를 했었다. 나는 그 인수 이후에 워싱턴 포스트의 변화에 대해서 많이 듣지 못했다. 하지만 나는 베이조스가 그 신문사를 인수함에 있어서 아마존의 자금을 사용하는 대신에 개인적으로 구매한 것은 현명했다고 생각한다. 그는 그렇게 문제가 많고 유명한 자산(워싱턴 포스트)을 인수해서 그의 회사(아마존)에 부담을 주었다는 비난은 피하기 위해서였다. 마윈도 이와 비슷한 접근법을 취하는 것처럼 보였지만, 그는 방향을 바꿔, 알리바바(Alibaba)를 통해 이 구매(사우스 차이나 모닝 포스트를 인수)를 하기로 결정했다. 만약 그것이 사실이라면, 그의 동기는 아마도 중국의 트위터처럼 작지만 안정적으로 성장하고 있는 매체 자산에, 그 신문사(사우스 차이나 모닝 포스트)가 한 자리를 차지하고자 하는 바람이었다. 그 회사(알리바바)는 그러한 자원들을 이용해서 그 신문을 되살리기 위해 신속히 움직여야 할 필요가 있다. 그러나 정치적으로 민감한 문제에 대해서도 주의를 기울여야 한다."

| 보기분석 |

① Purchase of the South China Morning Post by Jack Ma
마윈의 사우스 차이나 모닝 포스트 구매
② Purchase of the Washington Post by Jeff Bezos
제프 베이조스의 워싱턴 포스트 구매
③ Purchase of Amazon by Jeff Bezos
제프 베이조스의 아마존 인수
④ Purchase of Alibaba by Jack Ma
마윈의 알리바바 인수
⑤ Purchase of the Twitter of China by Alibaba
알리바바의 중국 트위터 구매

| 정답분석 | 밑줄 친 부분인 '거래'의 의미는 마윈이 사우스 차이나 모닝 포스트를 인수한 것을 의미하므로 보기 ①이 정답이다.

07 2016 상명대

정답 ③

| 구문분석 | (In a society) (that worships (at the altar of supermodels like Claudia, Christy and Kate), white teenagers are obsessed (with staying thin).
관계대명사 / S / V

Claudia, Christy, Kate 등과 같은 슈퍼모델들의 제단을 숭배하는 사회에서, 백인 십 대들은 날씬함을 유지하는 것에 집착한다.

But there's growing evidence (that black and white girls view their bodies in dramatically different ways).
등위접속사 / 유도부사 / V / S / =

그러나 흑인과 백인 소녀들이 그들의 몸을 상당히 다른 방식으로 본다는 증거가 증가하고 있다.

The latest findings come (in a study) (to be published in the journal *Human Organization* this spring (by a team of black and white researchers at the University of Arizona).
S V

가장 최근의 (연구)결과물은 Arizona 대학의 흑인과 백인 연구원들로 구성된 연구팀에 의해 *Human Organization* 지에 발표될 연구에서 나왔다.

(While 90 percent of the white junior-high and high-school girls studied voiced dissatisfaction with their weight), 70 percent (of African-American teens) were satisfied (with their bodies).
부사절: 반면에 / S / V

백인 중고등학교 여학생의 90%가 자신의 몸무게에 대해서 불만을 드러낸 반면, 아프리카계 미국인 십 대의 70%는 자신의 몸에 만족했다.

In fact, even significantly overweight black teens described themselves as happy.
접속부사 S V O O.C

사실, 심지어 심각할 정도로 과체중인 흑인 십 대들조차도 자신들이 행복하다고 묘사했다.

That confidence may not carry over (to other areas of black teens' lives), but the study suggests that, at least here, it's a lifelong source of pride.
S V 등위접속사 S V O

그러한 자신감은 흑인 청소년들의 삶의 다른 영역에까지는 미치지 않을 수 있지만, 적어도 여기서(연구에서)는, 그것이 평생 동안 이어지는 자존심의 원천임을 암시한다.

(Asked to describe women as they age), two thirds (of the black teens) said (that) they get more beautiful, and many cited their mothers (as examples).
분사구문 S_1 V_1 O_1 등위접속사 S_2 V_2 O_2

나이가 들어 가는 여성을 묘사하라는 요구를 받았을 때, 흑인 십 대의 3분의 2는 그들이 나이가 들어 감에 따라 더 아름다워질 것이라고 말했고, 많은 학생들이 그들 어머니를 예로 들었다.

White girls responded that their mothers may have been beautiful — (back in their youth).
S V O 대시: 부연설명

반면에 백인 소녀들은 그들 자신의 어머니가 젊었을 때 아름다웠을지도 모른다고 대답했다.

Says anthropologist Mimi Nichter, one of the study's coauthors, "(In white culture), the window of beauty is so small."
V S = O

이 연구의 공동저자 중 한 명인 인류학자 Mimi Nichter는 "백인 문화에서는 아름다움의 창이 매우 작습니다."라고 말한다.

| 어휘 |
worship ⓝ 예배, 숭배 **altar** ⓝ 제단
obsess ⓥ (어떤 생각이 사람의 마음을) 사로잡다 **dramatically** ⓐⓓ 극적으로
dissatisfaction ⓝ 불만 **significantly** ⓐⓓ (영향을 주거나 두드러질 정도로) 상당히
overweight ⓐ 과체중의, 비만인 **anthropologist** ⓝ 인류학자 **coauthor** ⓝ 공동저자

| 전문해석 | Claudia, Christy, Kate 등과 같은 슈퍼모델들의 제단을 숭배하는 사회에서, 백인 십 대들은 날씬함을 유지하는 것에 집착한다. 그러나 흑인과 백인 소녀들이 그들의 몸을 상당히 다른 방식으로 본다는 증거가 증가하고 있다. 가장 최근의 (연구)결과물은 Arizona 대학의 흑인과 백인 연구원들로 구성된 연구팀에 의해 *Human Organization* 지에 발표될 연구에서 나왔다. 백인 중고등학교 여학생의 90%가 자신의 몸무게에 대해서 불만을 드러낸 반면, 아프리카계 미국인 십 대의 70%는 자신의 몸에 만족했다.

사실, 심지어 심각할 정도로 과체중인 흑인 십 대들조차도 자신들이 행복하다고 묘사했다. 그러한 자신감은 흑인 청소년들의 삶의 다른 영역에까지는 미치지 않을 수 있지만, 적어도 여기서(연구에서)는, 그것이 평생 동안 이어지는 자존심의 원천임을 암시한다. 나이가 들어 가는 여성을 묘사하라는 요구를 받았을 때, 흑인 십 대의 3분의 2는 그들이 나이가 들어 감에 따라 더 아름다워질 것이라고 말했고, 많은 학생들이 그들 어머니를 예로 들었다. 반면에 백인 소녀들은 그들 자신의 어머니가 젊었을 때 아름다웠을지도 모른다고 대답했다. 이 연구의 공동저자 중 한 명인 인류학자 Mimi Nichter는 "백인 문화에서는 아름다움의 창이 매우 작습니다."라고 말한다.

| 보기분석 | ① In general, black girls are slimmer than the whites.
일반적으로, 흑인 소녀들은 백인 소녀들보다 날씬하다.

② The white people are less interested in their appearance than the black people.
백인들은 흑인들보다 외모에 관심이 적다.

③ White teens have more strict standards for the beauty.
백인 십 대들은 아름다움에 대한 더 엄격한 기준을 가지고 있다.

④ Most beautiful women are described as white girls.
대부분의 아름다운 여성들은 백인 소녀들로 묘사된다.

⑤ The black girls are perceived to be more beautiful than the white.
흑인 소녀들은 백인들보다 더 아름답다고 인식된다.

밑줄 친 부분 모두 본문에서 언급하지 않은 정보

| 정답분석 | 밑줄 친 문장 중 'the window of beauty'에서 'window'의 사전적 정의에는 '마음의 창이나 눈'이라는 의미도 포함되어 있다. 본문에서 소개한 연구의 결과를 참고할 때 백인 소녀들이 흑인 소녀들에 비해 나이가 들어 가는 여성의 아름다움을 보는 시선이 상대적으로 편협하다는 것을 보여 주고 있다. 따라서 '백인 문화에서 아름다움의 창이 작다'는 의미는 백인의 아름다움에 대한 기준이 더 엄격하다고 볼 수도 있으므로 보기 ③이 정답으로 적절하다.

08 2016 경기대

정답 ④

| 구문분석 | (When I (Jane) was 12), my father decided (that) the family should move to a nicer house 50 miles from his job.
부사절: ~할 때 / my father: S / decided: V / the family ... job: O
내가(Jane) 12살이었을 때, 나의 아버지는 가족이 그의 직장으로부터 50마일 떨어져 있는 더 좋은 집으로 이사해야 한다고 결심했다.

The move was an expensive one and Mom had to go to work.
The move: S_1 / was: V_1 / an expensive one: C / and: 등위접속사 / Mom: S_2 / had to go to work: V_2
그 이사는 돈이 많이 들었고 어머니는 일을 해야만 했다.

Dad bought a new car (for commuting) (while Mom walked a mile to the bus stop).
Dad: S / bought: V / a new car: O / (while ...): 부사절: 반면에
아버지는 통근을 위해 새 차를 구입했지만, 어머니는 일하러 가기 위해 1마일이나 떨어져 있는 버스 정류장까지 걸어가야만 했다.

Dad spent his weekends (at the track), (playing the horses).
Dad: S / spent: V / his weekends: O / (playing the horses): 분사구문
아버지는 주말마다 경마장에 가서 경마를 했다.

(If one of us was sick), that was Mom's responsibility.
부사절: 만약 ~라면 / that: S / was: V / Mom's responsibility: C
우리들 가운데 그 누군가가 아프기라도 하면, 그것은 엄마의 책임이 되었다.

(If the plumbing broke), it was our fault.
부사절: 만약 ~라면 / it: S / was: V / our fault: C
만약 배관이 망가졌다면, 우리의 잘못이었다.

My sister and I worked our way through college.
My sister and I: S / worked: V
내 여동생과 나는 대학을 졸업할 때까지 일했다.

Dad never gave us a dime.
Dad: S / never gave: V / us: I.O / a dime: D.O
아버지는 우리에게 단 한 푼도 주지 않았다.

Mom got cancer (a few years after Dad retired), and everything (that needed doing) fell (on me).
Mom: S_1 / got: V_1 / cancer: O / (a few years after ...): 부사절: ~한 후에 / everything: S_2 / that: 관계대명사 / fell: V_2
아버지가 퇴직하고 몇 년 후에 어머니는 암에 걸렸고 해야 할 모든 일들은 나에게 맡겨졌다.

He never lifted a finger.
He: S / never lifted: V / a finger: O
아버지는 손가락 하나 까딱하지 않았다.

병렬구조 A, B and C

(When Mom died), he found himself a girlfriend, bought a new car and had no time (for our phone calls), (the last time I called and asked, "What have you been doing lately?") He replied, "That's none of your business."

(부사절: ~할 때 / S / V_1 / O / O.C / V_2 / O_2 / V_3 / O_3 / 마지막으로 ~할 때 / S_2 / V_4 / O)

어머니가 돌아가셨을 때, 그는 여자친구를 만났고 새 차를 샀으며 우리와 전화 통화할 시간이 없었고 마지막으로 내가 전화해서 "요즘 뭐 하고 지내세요?"라고 물었을 때 아버지는 "그건 네가 상관할 바 아니다."라고 대답했다.

This Christmas we won't worry that Dad is alone (because he has a new car and a girlfriend and lots of stories to tell about how rotten his daughters are).

(S / V / O / 부사절: ~ 때문에)

이번 크리스마스에 우리는 혼자가 된 아버지에 대해서 걱정하지 않을 것인데 왜냐하면 아버지에게는 새 차와 여자친구가 있고 그의 딸들이 얼마나 못되었는지에 대한 많은 이야기들이 있기 때문이다.

| 어휘 | commute ⓥ 통근하다 play the horses 경마에 돈을 걸다 responsibility ⓝ 책임, 의무
plumbing ⓝ 배관 dime ⓝ 다임(미국 · 캐나다의 10센트짜리 동전), 푼돈
rotten ⓐ 썩은, 형편없는, 끔찍한

| 전문해석 | 내가(Jane) 12살이었을 때, 나의 아버지는 가족이 그의 직장으로부터 50마일 떨어져 있는 더 좋은 집으로 이사해야 한다고 결심했다. 그 이사는 돈이 많이 들었고 어머니는 일을 해야만 했다. 아버지는 통근을 위해 새 차를 구입했지만, 어머니는 일하러 가기 위해 1마일이나 떨어져 있는 버스 정류장까지 걸어가야만 했다. 아버지는 주말마다 경마장에 가서 경마를 했다. 우리들 가운데 그 누군가가 아프기라도 하면, 그것은 엄마의 책임이 되었다. 만약 배관이 망가졌다면, 우리의 잘못이었다. 내 여동생과 나는 대학을 졸업할 때까지 일했다. 아버지는 우리에게 단 한 푼도 주지 않았다.
아버지가 퇴직하고 몇 년 후에 어머니는 암에 걸렸고 해야 할 모든 일들은 나에게 맡겨졌다. 아버지는 손가락 하나 까딱하지 않았다. 어머니가 돌아가셨을 때, 그는 여자친구를 만났고 새 차를 샀으며 우리와 전화 통화할 시간이 없었고 마지막으로 내가 전화해서 "요즘 뭐 하고 지내세요?"라고 물었을 때 아버지는 "그건 네가 상관할 바 아니다."라고 대답했다. 이번 크리스마스에 우리는 혼자가 된 아버지에 대해서 걱정하지 않을 것인데 왜냐하면 아버지에게는 새 차와 여자친구가 있고 그의 딸들이 얼마나 못되었는지에 대한 많은 이야기들이 있기 때문이다.

| 보기분석 | ① demonstrates how chic Dad looks
아버지의 세련된 모습을 보여 준다
② shows how poor Dad's sense of humor is
아버지의 유머 감각이 얼마나 부족한지 보여 준다
③ shows Dad's deep concern for Jane's waste of time 아버지가 딸을 우려하는 내용은 본문에서 언급 안 함
제인의 시간 낭비에 대한 아버지의 깊은 우려를 보여 준다
④ indicates that Dad gives Jane the cold shoulder
아버지가 제인을 냉대했다는 것을 나타낸다

| 정답분석 | 밑줄 친 부분은 안부를 묻는 딸에게 하는 아버지의 대답이다. "그건 네가 상관할 바 아니다."라는 대답은 딸에 대한 아버지의 냉대를 표현하고 있으므로 보기 중 ④가 정답으로 적절하다.

09 2016 국민대

정답 ③

| 구문분석 | Mathematics departments (around the world) regularly receive letters (from amateur mathematicians) (who claim to have solved famous problems), and (virtually without exception) these 'solutions' are not merely wrong, but laughably so.

(S_1 / V_1 / O / 관계대명사 / not A but B: A가 아니라 B / 등위접속사 / S_2 / V_2 / C_1 / C_2)

전 세계의 수학과들은 유명한 (수학) 문제들을 풀었다고 주장하는 아마추어 수학자들로부터 정기적으로 편지를 받지만 사실상 예외 없이 이러한 해답들은 단순히 틀릴 뿐만 아니라 우습게도 그러하다.

Some, (while not exactly mistaken), are so unlike a correct proof of anything (that they are not really attempted solutions at all).
S 분사구문 V C 관계대명사

어떤 것들은, 정확하게 틀리지는 않았지만, 어떤 것에 대한 정확한 증거와는 너무 달라서 그것들은 실제로 시도된 해결책들이 전혀 아니다.

Those (that follow at least some of the normal conventions of mathematical presentation) use very elementary arguments (that would, (had they been correct), have been discovered centuries ago).
S 관계대명사 V O 관계대명사 if(부사절 접속사) 생략 도치 V S

최소한의 수학적 설명에 관한 일반적인 관습의 일부를 따르고 있는 것들은, 만일 그것들이 올바르다면, 수 세기 전에 발견되었을 매우 초보적인 수학적 주장을 사용한다.

The people (who write these letters) have no conception (of how difficult mathematical research is), (of the years of effort needed to develop enough knowledge and expertise to do significant original work), or (of the extent (to which mathematics is a collective activity).
S 관계대명사 V O 병렬구조 병렬구조 A, B, or C 관계대명사

이러한 편지들을 쓰는 사람들은 수학적 연구가 얼마나 어려운지에 대한 개념, 중요한 독창적인 연구를 하기에 충분한 지식과 전문성을 개발하는 데 필요한 수년간의 노력에 대한 개념, 또는 수학이 어느 정도까지는 집단적인 활동이라는 개념에 대해 전혀 알지 못한다.

| 어휘 | **amateur** ⓐ 아마추어의, 취미로 하는 **convention** ⓝ 관습, 관례 **elementary argument** 기초적인 주장 **conception** ⓝ (계획 등의) 구상 **expertise** ⓝ 전문지식[기술] **original** ⓐ 원래의, 독창적인

| 전문해석 | 전 세계의 수학과들은 유명한 (수학) 문제들을 풀었다고 주장하는 아마추어 수학자들로부터 정기적으로 편지를 받지만 사실상 예외 없이 이러한 해답들은 단순히 틀릴 뿐만 아니라 우습게도 그러하다. 어떤 것들은, 정확하게 틀리지는 않았지만, 어떤 것에 대한 정확한 증거와는 너무 달라서 그것들은 실제로 시도된 해결책들이 전혀 아니다. 최소한의 수학적 설명에 관한 일반적인 관습의 일부를 따르고 있는 것들은, 만일 그것들이 올바르다면, 수 세기 전에 발견되었을 매우 초보적인 수학적 주장을 사용한다. 이러한 편지들을 쓰는 사람들은 수학적 연구가 얼마나 어려운지에 대한 개념, 중요한 독창적인 연구를 하기에 충분한 지식과 전문성을 개발하는 데 필요한 수년간의 노력에 대한 개념, 또는 수학이 어느 정도까지는 집단적인 활동이라는 개념에 대해 전혀 알지 못한다.

| 보기분석 | 밑줄 친 부분 모두 수학자 개인이 아닌 집단의 노력이므로 밑줄의 의미와 일치함

① Combined efforts of mathematicians usually lead the development of mathematics.
수학자들의 결합된 노력은 항상 수학의 발전을 이끌었다.

② Many mathematicians are simultaneously engaged in tackling mathematical questions.
많은 수학자들이 동시에 수학 문제를 해결하는 데 몰두하고 있다.

③ A genius of mathematics is required to solve particularly difficult mathematical questions.
특히 어려운 수학 문제를 풀려면 수학의 천재가 필요하다.

④ A lot of mathematicians contributed to the development of mathematics over a long period of time.
많은 수학자들이 오랜 시간에 걸쳐 수학의 발전에 기여했다.

| 정답분석 | 밑줄 친 부분에서 '수학은 집단적인 활동'이라고 했다. 따라서 보기 ③처럼 개인인 한 천재가 수학 문제 풀이에 필요하다는 진술은 밑줄 친 부분의 의미와 일치하지 않는다.

10 2016 성균관대

정답 ⑤

| 구문분석 | An argument (often advanced for the encouragement of religion) is that, (to paraphrase St. Mathew's report of Jesus's words), it leads people to love their neighbors as themselves.
S V C

종교를 장려하기 위해 종종 제기되는 주장은, 예수님의 말씀에 대한 마태복음을 바꾸어 말한다면, 종교가 사람들로 하여금 그들의 이웃을 그들 자신처럼 사랑하도록 한다는 것이다.

That would be a powerful point (were 'it' true).
S V C if(부사절 접속사) 생략

만일 이것이 진실이라면 이것은 매우 강력한 주장이다.

But is it?
등위접속사
하지만 과연 그럴까?

(that)
This was the question (Jean Decety, a developmental neuroscientist at the University of Chicago, asked in a study just published in *Current Biology*).
S V C S = V

이것은 시카고 대학의 발달 신경과학자인 장 데서티(Jean Decety)가 *Current Biology*에 실린 연구논문에서 던진 질문이다.

Dr. Decety is not the first (to wonder), (in a scientific way, about the connection between religion and altruism).
S V C
between A and B: A와 B 사이

데서티 박사가, 과학적인 면에서, 종교와 이타주의의 관련성에 대해서 의문을 제기한 첫 번째 인물은 아니다.

He is, though, one of the first (to do it) (without recourse to that standard but peculiar laboratory animal (beloved by psychologists), the undergraduate student).
S V 접속부사 C
animal과 동격 =

그럼에도 불구하고, 그는 심리학자들에 의해서 사랑받는, 표준적이지만 특이한 실험용 동물인 (대학) 학부생에 의존하지 않고 처음으로 이 일을 수행한(실험한) 인물들 중 한 사람이다.

Instead, he collaborated (with researchers) (in Canada, China, Jordan, South Africa and Turkey), as well as (with fellow Americans), (to look at children aged between 5 and 12 and their families).
접속부사 S V
B as well as A: A뿐만 아니라 B

대신에, 그는 5세부터 12세 사이의 아이들과 그들의 가족들을 관찰하기 위해서 미국인 동료들뿐만 아니라 캐나다, 중국, 요르단, 남아프리카 공화국 그리고 튀르키예에 있는 연구자들과도 협력했다.

| 어휘 |
encouragement ⓝ 격려(가 되는 것) **advance** ⓥ 다가가다, (아이디어나 계획을) 제기하다
argument ⓝ 논쟁, 언쟁 **developmental neuroscientist** 발달 신경과학자
altruism ⓝ 이타주의, 이타심 **peculiar** ⓐ 이상한, 기이한 **undergraduate student** ⓝ 대학생
collaborate ⓥ 협력하다, 공동으로 작업하다

| 전문해석 | 종교를 장려하기 위해 종종 제기되는 주장은, 예수님의 말씀에 대한 마태복음을 바꾸어 말한다면, 종교가 사람들로 하여금 그들의 이웃을 그들 자신처럼 사랑하도록 한다는 것이다. 만일 이것이 진실이라면 이것은 매우 강력한 주장이다. 하지만 과연 그럴까? 이것은 시카고 대학의 발달 신경과학자인 장 데서티(Jean Decety)가 *Current Biology*에 실린 연구논문에서 던진 질문이다.

데서티 박사가, 과학적인 면에서, 종교와 이타주의의 관련성에 대해서 의문을 제기한 첫 번째 인물은 아니다. 그럼에도 불구하고, 그는 심리학자들에 의해서 사랑받는, 표준적이지만 특이한 실험용 동물인 (대학) 학부생에 의존하지 않고 처음으로 이 일을 수행한(실험한) 인물들 중 한 사람이다. 대신에, 그는 5세부터 12세 사이의 아이들과 그들의 가족들을 관찰하기 위해서 미국인 동료들뿐만 아니라 캐나다, 중국, 요르단, 남아프리카 공화국 그리고 튀르키예에 있는 연구자들과도 협력했다.

| 보기분석 |
① Most people are religious.
대부분의 사람들은 종교적이다.
② The object of belief is not important.
믿음의 대상은 중요하지 않다.
③ Jesus emphasized the love of people. 앞 문장에서 언급한 적 없음
예수님은 사람들의 사랑을 강조했다.
④ Science and religion are not different.
과학과 종교는 다르지 않다.
⑤ Religion makes people help others.
종교는 사람들이 다른 사람들을 돕도록 만든다.

| 정답분석 | 밑줄 친 지시사 'it'은 직전 문장에서 주장인 "종교가 사람들로 하여금 그들의 이웃을 그들 자신처럼 사랑하도록 한다"는 마태복음의 내용을 나타낸다. 따라서 보기 ⑤가 정답으로 적절하다.

11 2015 성균관대

정답 ②

| 구문분석 |

Much (of the ink) (spilt over drones) concerns their targets.
S V O
드론을 향해 쏟아진 많은 잉크(출판물)는 그것들의 목표물과 관계된 것들이다.

Some celebrate the ease (with which America can now vaporize its foes).
S V O 관계대명사
어떤 사람들은 미국이 이제 그들의 적들을 쉽게 증발시킬 수 있다고 축하한다.

Others fret that innocents are too often caught in the blast zone.
S V O
다른 사람들은 무고한 사람들이 폭발지역에서 너무 자주 드론의 목표물이 된다고 우려한다.

Less attention has been paid (to the men and women) (who hold the joysticks).
S V 관계대명사
조이스틱(비행기 등의 제어장치)을 쥐고 드론을 조종하는 남성과 여성들에게는 관심이 덜 쏠렸다.

등위접속사
But (now that the air force is training more drone pilots than fighter and bomber pilots combined), this is starting to change.
부사절: ~ 때문에 S V
하지만 이제 공군이 전투기와 폭격기 조종사를 합친 것보다 더 많은 드론 조종사를 훈련시키고 있기 때문에, 이것(드론 조종사에 대한 무관심)은 변하기 시작하고 있는 중이다.

"People assume these pilots have been desensitized, like they're playing a video game," says Nancy Cooke, a professor at Arizona State University.
O V S =
"사람들은 드론 조종사들이 마치 비디오 게임을 하는 것처럼 무감각해졌다고 가정합니다."라고 애리조나 주립대학의 교수인 Nancy Cooke은 말한다.

"The opposite is true."
S V C
"사실은 정반대입니다."

등위접속사
Being out of harm's way makes the job less fretful (in some respects), but more so (in others).
S V O O.C₁ O.C₂
위험한 지역에서 벗어나 있는 것은 어떤 면에서는 그 일(작전을 수행하는)을 덜 걱정하게 하지만 다른 면에서는 더 그렇게(걱정하게) 만든다.

spend 시간 ~ing: ~ing하는 데 시간을 보내다
(Whereas fighter pilots drop a bomb and fly away), drone pilots may spend weeks monitoring a village or convoy, (sussing out patterns and getting to know their enemies).
부사절: 반면에 S V O 분사구문
전투기 조종사들이 폭탄을 투하하고 날아가 버리는 반면에, 드론 조종사들은 마을이나 호송대를 감시하고 공격의 패턴을 검토하며 그들의 적들에 대해 알아 가면서 몇 주를 보낼 것이다.

This makes the act (of killing) more personal, (particularly as these pilots are forced to witness the fallout).
S V O O.C 부사절: ~ 때문에
이것은 특히 드론 조종사들이 공격의 여파를 목격하도록 강요받기 때문에 살인행위를 더 개인적인 것으로 만든다.

Afterwards, (instead of bonding with fellow servicemen at a base), drone warriors go home, (where they must keep their daily exploits a secret).
전치사: ~ 대신에 S V 관계부사
그 후(적들을 공격한 후), 드론 조종사들은 군사기지에 있는 동료 병사들과 유대를 맺는 대신, 그들이 날마다 하는 일들을 비밀로 해야 하는 집으로 돌아간다.

| 어휘 |

ease ⓝ 쉬움, 용이함 **vaporize** ⓥ 증발시키다 **fret** ⓥ 안달하다, 초조해하다
blast zone 폭발지역 **desensitize** ⓥ 둔감하게 만들다 **suss out** 파악하다, 검토[검사]하다
convoy ⓝ 호송대 **fallout** ⓝ 낙진; 좋지 못한 결과

| 전문해석 | 드론을 향해 쏟아진 많은 잉크(출판물)는 그것들의 목표물과 관계된 것들이다. 어떤 사람들은 미국이 이제 그들의 적들을 쉽게 증발시킬 수 있다고 축하한다. 다른 사람들은 무고한 사람들이 폭발지역에서 너무 자주 드론의 목표물이 된다고 우려

한다. 조이스틱(비행기 등의 제어장치)을 쥐고 드론을 조종하는 남성과 여성들에게는 관심이 덜 쏠렸다. 하지만 이제 공군이 전투기와 폭격기 조종사를 합친 것보다 더 많은 드론 조종사를 훈련시키고 있기 때문에, 이것(드론 조종사에 대한 무관심)은 변하기 시작하고 있는 중이다. "사람들은 드론 조종사들이 마치 비디오 게임을 하는 것처럼 무감각해졌다고 가정합니다."라고 애리조나 주립대학의 교수인 Nancy Cooke은 말한다. "사실은 정반대입니다." 위험한 지역에서 벗어나 있는 것은 어떤 면에서는 그 일(작전을 수행하는)을 덜 걱정하게 하지만 다른 면에서는 더 그렇게(걱정하게) 만든다. 전투기 조종사들이 폭탄을 투하하고 날아가 버리는 반면에, 드론 조종사들은 마을이나 호송대를 감시하고 공격의 패턴을 검토하며 그들의 적들에 대해 알아 가면서 몇 주를 보낼 것이다. 이것은 특히 드론 조종사들이 공격의 여파를 목격하도록 강요받기 때문에 살인행위를 더 개인적인 것으로 만든다. 그 후(적들을 공격한 후), 드론 조종사들은 군사기지에 있는 동료 병사들과 유대를 맺는 대신, 그들이 날마다 하는 일들을 비밀로 해야 하는 집으로 돌아간다.

| 보기분석 | ① are not affected by their mission not을 소거하면 정답에 가깝지만 '정신적인 영향'이 언급되어야 하므로 오답
그들의 임무에 영향을 받지 않는다
② might experience mental problems
정신적인 문제를 경험할 수도 있다
③ are among the most highly educated
가장 높은 교육을 받은 사람들 중 하나이다
④ consider their work boring and worthless 언급하지 않음
그들의 일을 지루하고 무가치하다고 생각한다
⑤ can handle stress on their own 이후 전개되는 내용에서는 드론 조종사들이 스스로 스트레스를 해결하지 못함
스트레스를 스스로 해결할 수 있다

| 정답분석 | 밑줄 친 문장에서 'the opposite'은 직전 문장을 참고해서 의미를 파악한다. 앞 문장에서 '드론 조종사들이 무감각해졌다'는 사람들의 가정과는 반대로 드론 조종사들은 공격하기 전에 피해자들을 오랫동안 관찰하기 때문에 공격 후에는 정신적인 문제를 겪을 가능성이 오히려 더 높다고 판단할 수 있다. 따라서 보기 ②가 정답으로 가장 적절하다.

12 2015 한국외대

정답 ①

| 구문분석 |

barely A without B: B 없이는 A할 수 없다(A하면 반드시 B하다)
Barely a week goes by (without a celebrity) ("opening up" about their "battle with depression.")
S: a week / V: goes by
거의 매주 유명 인사들은 그들의 "우울증과의 싸움"에 대해 있다는 사실을 "발표"한다.

This, apparently, is a brave thing (to do) (because, (despite all efforts) (to get rid of prejudice against depression), it is still seen as some kind of mental and emotional weakness).
S: This / V: is / C: a brave thing / because 부사절: ~ 때문에
우울증에 대한 편견을 없애기 위한 모든 노력에도 불구하고, 우울증이 여전히 정신적, 정서적 약점으로 여겨지기 때문에 이것(자신이 우울증 환자라고 발표하는 것)은 분명히 용감한 일이다.

What if ~?: ~면 어쩌지?
But what if it was nothing (of the sort)?
But 등위접속사 / S: it / V: was / C: nothing
그러나 만일 이것(우울증)이 그런 종류의 것이 아니라면 어떤가?

What if it was a physical illness (that just happens to make people feel pretty lousy)?
S: it / V: was / C: a physical illness / that 관계대명사
만일 우울증이 사람들을 아주 꽤 엉망인 상태로 느껴지게 만드는 신체적 질병이라면 어떤가?

Would that make it less (of a big deal) to admit to?
V: Would make / S: that / it 가목적어 / C: less / to admit to 진목적어
만일 그렇게 된다면 우울증을 인정하는 것이 덜 큰일이 될까?

(According to a growing number of scientists), this is exactly how we should be thinking (about the condition).
S: this / V: is / C: how we should be thinking
점점 더 많은 과학자들에 따르면, 이것이 바로 우리가 이 상태(우울증)에 대해서 생각해야 하는 방식이다.

spend 시간 ~ing: ~ing하는 데 시간을 보내다 / and 등위접속사
George Slavich, (a clinical psychologist), has spent years studying depression, and has come (to the conclusion) (that it has as much to do with the body as the mind).
S: George Slavich = a clinical psychologist / V_1: has spent / O: years / V_2: has come / the conclusion = that절 / as ~ as ...: …만큼 ~한
임상 심리학자인 George Slavich는 우울증을 연구하는 데 수년을 보냈고, 우울증은 정신만큼이나 신체와도 많은 관련이 있다는 결론에 도달했다.

"I don't even talk about it as a psychiatric condition anymore," he says.
O S V

그는 "나는 더 이상 우울증을 정신질환이라고 말하지 않습니다."라고 말한다.

등위접속사
"It does involve psychology, but it also involves equal parts (of biology and physical health)."
S_1 V_1 O_1 S_2 V_2 O_2

"그것(우울증)은 심리학과 연관을 맺고 있지만, 또한 동등한 정도로 생물학 및 육체적 건강과 관련된 문제입니다."

The basis (of this new view) is blindingly obvious (once it is pointed out; everyone feels miserable when they are ill).
S V C 부사절: 일단 ~하면 세미콜론: 부연설명

이 새로운 견해의 기반은, '모든 사람은 그들이 아플 때 비참함을 느낀다.'라는 점을 지적하고 나면, 아주 명백해진다.

That feeling (of being too tired, bored, and fed up) (to move off the sofa and get on with life) is known (among psychologists as sickness behavior).
S A, B, and C 병렬구조 V

너무 피곤하고, 지루하며 소파에서 벗어나 생활을 계속하기가 지겹다는 느낌은 심리학자들 사이에서 질병행동으로 알려져 있다.

It happens (for a good reason), (helping us avoid doing more damage or spreading an infection any further).
S V 분사구문

그것이 발생하는 데는 많은 이유가 있는데, 이러한 행동은 우리로 하여금 더 많은 피해를 입거나 더 이상 감염을 확산시키지 않도록 돕는다.

| 어휘 | **depression** ⓝ 우울증, 우울함 **lousy** ⓐ (아주) 안 좋은, 엉망인
have much to do with ~와 관련이 크다 **miserable** ⓐ 비참한
blindingly ⓐⓓ 아주, 극도로 **fed up** 지긋지긋한, 신물 난 **get on with** ~와 (함께) 잘 지내다

| 전문해석 | 거의 매주 유명 인사들은 그들의 "우울증과의 싸움"에 대해 있다는 사실을 "발표"한다. 우울증에 대한 편견을 없애기 위한 모든 노력에도 불구하고, 우울증이 여전히 정신적, 정서적 약점으로 여겨지기 때문에 이것(자신이 우울증 환자라고 발표하는 것)은 분명히 용감한 일이다. 그러나 만일 이것(우울증)이 그런 종류의 것이 아니라면 어떤가? 만일 우울증이 사람들을 아주 꽤 엉망인 상태로 느껴지게 만드는 신체적 질병이라면 어떤가? 만일 그렇게 된다면 우울증을 인정하는 것이 덜 큰일이 될까?
점점 더 많은 과학자들에 따르면, 이것이 바로 우리가 이 상태(우울증)에 대해서 생각해야 하는 방식이다. 임상 심리학자인 George Slavich는 우울증을 연구하는 데 수년을 보냈고, 우울증은 정신만큼이나 신체와도 많은 관련이 있다는 결론에 도달했다. 그는 "나는 더이상 우울증을 정신질환이라고 말하지 않습니다."라고 말한다. "그것(우울증)은 심리학과 연관을 맺고 있지만, 또한 동등한 정도로 생물학 및 육체적 건강과 관련된 문제입니다."라고 말한다.
이 새로운 견해의 기반은, '모든 사람은 그들이 아플 때 비참함을 느낀다.'라는 점을 지적하고 나면, 아주 명백해진다. 너무 피곤하고, 지루하며 소파에서 벗어나 생활을 계속하기가 지겹다는 느낌은 심리학자들 사이에서 질병행동으로 알려져 있다. 그것이 발생하는 데는 많은 이유가 있는데, 이러한 행동은 우리로 하여금 더 많은 피해를 입거나 더 이상 감염을 확산시키지 않도록 돕는다.

| 보기분석 | ① Depression is a social stigma.
우울증은 사회적 낙인이다.
② Depression occurs to those who are afraid.
두려움을 느끼는 사람들에게 우울증이 발생한다.
③ Depression is experienced by everybody.
우울증은 모든 사람들이 경험한다.
④ Depression is like the heart catching a cold.
우울증은 심장이 감기에 걸리는 것과 같다.

| 정답분석 | 밑줄을 포함하는 문장에서 우울증이 정신적 및 정서적 약점으로 여겨진다는 이유의 부사절을 참고한다면 우울증을 고백하는 것이 용감한 일이라는 밑줄 친 부분을 이해할 수 있다. 따라서 보기 ①이 정답으로 적절하다.

13 2015 한양대

정답 ③

| 구문분석 | I set down choice experiences (so that my own writings may inspire me), and at last I may make wholes of parts.

S1 V1 O1 ~하기 위해서 / 마침내 / 등위접속사 S2 V2 O2

나는 내가 쓴 글들이 나에게 영감을 줄 수 있도록 선택의 경험들을 적어 놓았고, 마침내 나는 (선택의 경험들의) 부분들로 한 편의 글을 썼다.

Certainly, it is a distinct profession (to rescue from oblivion) and (to fix the sentiments and thoughts) (which visit all men less generally), that the contemplation of the unfinished picture may suggest its harmonious completion.

가주어 V C 병렬구조 관계대명사 진주어 that

확실히, 미완성된 그림에 대한 사유가 조화로운 완성을 암시하는 것은 망각으로부터 구하고 덜 일반적으로 모든 사람들에게 찾아오는 감정들과 생각들을 고치기 위한 확실한 작업이다.

Associate reverently and (as much as you can) (with your loftiest thoughts).

V as much as S can: S가 할 수 있는 한

당신 자신을 경건하게 그리고 당신이 가능한 한 고귀한 생각들과 연관시켜라.

Each thought (that is welcomed and recorded) is a nest egg, (by the side) (of which more will be laid).

S 관계대명사 V C 관계대명사

당신이 기꺼이 받아들이고 기록한 각각의 생각은 귀중한 밑천이 되어 그 옆에는 더 많은 것이 놓일 것이다.

Thoughts (accidentally thrown together) become a frame (in which more may be developed and exhibited).

S V C 관계대명사

우연히 떠올라 함께 결합한 생각들은 더 많이 진전되고 더 많은 것이 개발되고 보여지는 (생각의) 틀이 될 것이다.

| 어휘 | **set down** ~을 (원칙 등으로) 정하다 **inspire** ⓥ (욕구 · 자신감을 갖도록) 고무하다
oblivion ⓝ 의식하지 못하는 상태, 망각 **sentiment** ⓝ 정서, 감정
contemplation ⓝ 사색, 명상 **reverently** ⓐⓓ 경건하게 **nest egg** 비상금, 저축, 예비금

| 전문해석 | 나는 내가 쓴 글들이 나에게 영감을 줄 수 있도록 선택의 경험들을 적어 놓았고, 마침내 나는 (선택의 경험들의) 부분들로 한 편의 글을 썼다. 확실히, 미완성된 그림에 대한 사유가 조화로운 완성을 암시하는 것은 망각으로부터 구하고 덜 일반적으로 모든 사람들에게 찾아오는 감정들과 생각들을 고치기 위한 확실한 작업이다. 당신 자신을 경건하게 그리고 당신이 가능한 한 고귀한 생각들과 연관시켜라. 당신이 기꺼이 받아들이고 기록한 각각의 생각은 귀중한 밑천이 되어 그 옆에는 더 많은 것이 놓일 것이다. 우연히 떠올라 함께 결합한 생각들은 더 많이 진전되고 더 많은 것이 개발되고 보여지는 (생각의) 틀이 될 것이다.

| 보기분석 | ① surprise heretofore not discovered
지금까지 발견되지 않은 놀라움
② journal entry to be treasured and joined with other entries 너무 지엽적
다른 항목들과 함께 보관되고 결합된 저널
③ a thought that will manifest itself as yet another thought
또 다른 사상으로 나타날 사상
④ a memory that will stimulate thought and solicit a recording in a journal 너무 지엽적
생각을 자극하고 저널에 기록을 남길 수 있는 기억

| 정답분석 | 밑줄 친 'a nest egg'의 사전적 정의는 '비상금'으로 이 글에서는 비유적 표현으로 '경험의 기록들'로 이해해야 한다. 본문 마지막 문장에서 이렇게 기록한 생각들이 결합되어 더 많은 것이 개발되고 보여지는 생각의 틀이 되므로 'nest egg'의 의미로는 보기 ③이 적절하다.

14 2015 한국외대

정답 ④

| 구문분석 | The Chinese city (of Chongqing) has created a smartphone sidewalk lane.

S V O

중국의 충칭시는 스마트폰 전용 인도를 만들었다.

It's a path (for those) (who are messaging and tweeting) (to watch where they are going).
S V C toR 의미상 주어 관계대명사
이 인도는 메시지와 트윗을 하는 사람들이 그들이 어디로 가고 있는지를 알아보도록 하는 길이다.

The property manager says it's intended to remind people that it's dangerous to message or tweet (while walking in the street).
S V O 분사구문

부동산 관리인은 이 인도가 길을 걷는 동안에 메시지와 트위터를 주고받는 것이 위험하다는 사실을 사람들에게 상기시키기 위해서 고안되었다고 말한다.

"There are a lot (of elderly people and children) (in the street), and using cellphones on the go may cause unnecessary collisions here," said Nong Cheng (who manages the area in the city's entertainment zone).
유도부사 V S 등위접속사 O V S 관계대명사
충칭시의 유흥가를 관리하는 Nong Cheng은 "거리에는 많은 노인들과 어린이들이 있고, 걸어가면서 휴대 전화를 사용하는 것은 불필요한 충돌을 일으킬 수도 있습니다."라고 말했다.

It has a 165-foot stretch (of pavement) (with two lanes); one (that prohibits cellphone use) is (next to the other) (that allows pedestrians to use their cellphones at their "own risk.")
S V O 세미콜론: 부연설명 S 관계대명사 V 관계대명사
이것(인도)은 2개의 차선이 있는 165피트의 인도를 가지고 있다; 휴대 전화 사용을 금지하는 레인은 보행자들이 충돌의 위험을 무릅쓰고 휴대 전화를 사용하는 것이 허용된 다른 레인 옆에 나란히 있다.

Nong said the idea came from a similar stretch (of pavement in Washington), (which National Geographic Television created as part of a behavior experiment).
S V O 관계대명사

Nong은 이 아이디어가 내셔널 지오그래픽 TV가 행동 실험의 일환으로 만든 워싱턴의 비슷한 길이의 인도로부터 나왔다고 말했다.

She said, however, that pedestrians were not taking the new lanes seriously.
S V 접속부사 O
그러나 그녀는 보행자들이 이 새로운 인도를 진지하게 여기지 않는다고 말했다.

Many were snapping pictures (of the signs and sidewalks).
S V O
많은 보행자들은 표지판과 인도의 사진을 찍고 있었다.

"Those (using their cellphones) have not heeded the markings on the pavement," she said.
O S V
"휴대 전화를 사용하는 사람들은 인도 위에 그려져 있는 표식에는 주의를 기울이지 않습니다."라고 그녀는 말했다.

"They don't notice them."
S V O
"그들은 표식이 있다는 것을 알아차리지 못한답니다."

| 어휘 |

lane ⓝ 도로, 길 / **property manager** (부동산) 자산관리자
entertainment zone 위락 지구 / **collision** ⓝ 충돌(사고) / **pavement** ⓝ 인도
snap a picture (스냅) 사진을 찍다 / **heed** ⓥ (~에) 주의[유의]하다

| 전문해석 | 중국의 충칭시는 스마트폰 전용 인도를 만들었다. 이 인도는 메시지와 트윗을 하는 사람들이 그들이 어디로 가고 있는지를 알아보도록 하는 길이다. 부동산 관리인은 이 인도가 길을 걷는 동안에 메시지와 트위터를 주고받는 것이 위험하다는 사실을 사람들에게 상기시키기 위해서 고안되었다고 말한다. 충칭시의 유흥가를 관리하는 Nong Cheng은 "거리에는 많은 노인들과 어린이들이 있고, 걸어가면서 휴대 전화를 사용하는 것은 불필요한 충돌을 일으킬 수도 있습니다."라고 말했다. 이것(인도)은 2개의 차선이 있는 165피트의 인도를 가지고 있다; 휴대 전화를 사용을 금지하는 레인은 보행자들이 충돌의 위험을 무릅쓰고 휴대 전화를 사용하는 것이 허용된 다른 레인 옆에 나란히 있다. Nong은 이 아이디어가 내셔널 지오그래픽 TV가 행동 실험의 일환으로 만든 워싱턴의 비슷한 길이의 인도로부터 나왔다고 말했다. 그러나 그녀는 보행자들이 이 새로운 인도를 진지하게 여기지 않는다고 말했다. 많은 보행자들은 표지판과 인도의 사진을 찍고 있었다. "휴대 전화를 사용하는 사람들은 인도 위에 그려져 있는 표식에는 주의를 기울이지 않습니다."라고 그녀는 말했다. "그들은 표식이 있다는 것을 알아차리지 못한답니다."

| 보기분석 |

① ⓐ they ─ 보기 모두 '보행자'를 가리킴 ─ ② ⓑ their
③ ⓒ their ④ ⓓ them

| 정답분석 | 보기 ④의 them은 보행자가 아닌 인도의 표식들을 가리킨다.

15 2015 가천대

정답 ①

| 구문분석 | It happens that (in England) the State went somewhat further, and was compelled to make some attempt to control the movement of labour.

(가주어 It / V happens / 진주어 that / 병렬구조: went ~ and was compelled)

영국에서 국가는 어느 정도 더 나아가 노동의 이동을 통제하기 위해 어떤 시도를 할 수밖에 없었다.

(So long as labour was provided within the manor by labourers) (who themselves had interests in the land of manor), the problem was one (for the manor alone); but hired labour became more and more the practice (as specialization developed), (in ancillary trades as well as in agriculture itself), and labourers left their manors, (with the result (that the State interfered in the interests of public order and the needs of employers).

(So long as 부사절: ~하는 한 / who 관계대명사 / the problem S_1 was V_1 one C_1 / hired labour S_2 became V_2 more and more the practice C_2 / as 부사절: ~함에 따라 / B as well as A: A뿐만 아니라 B / and 등위접속사 / labourers S_3 left V_3 their manors O)

노동이 영주의 장원에 이해관계를 가진 노동자들에 의해서 장원 내에서 제공되는 한, 그 문제는 단지 장원만의 문제였다; 하지만 고용된 노동은 농업 그 자체뿐만 아니라 부수적인 직업들에서 전문화가 진행됨에 따라 점점 더 관행이 되었고, 노동자들은 그들의 장원을 떠났다, 그 결과 국가가 공공질서와 고용주들의 필요에 개입했다.

This was especially so (after the Black Death created a dearth of labour).

(This S / was V / so C / after 부사절: ~한 후에)

이러한 현상은 흑사병이 노동력의 부족을 만든 후에 특히 그러했다.

Justices of labour were created to regulate labour, and were subsequently merged (with the justices of the peace), (who were originally concerned only with the apprehension of criminals).

(Justices of labour S / were created to V_1 / were subsequently merged V_2 / who 관계대명사)

노동 재판관들은 노동을 규제하기 위해 만들어졌고, 그 이후 원래 범죄자들의 체포에만 관련이 있었던 치안판사들과 통합되었다.

| 어휘 |

be compelled to *do* 어쩔 수 없이 ~하다
manor ⓝ 영주의 저택, 장원
ancillary ⓐ 보조적인, 부수적인
the Black Death 흑사병(중세 유럽의 유행성 감염 질환)
merge ⓥ 합병하다
apprehension ⓝ 우려, 불안, 체포

| 전문해석 | 영국에서 국가는 어느 정도 더 나아가 노동의 이동을 통제하기 위해 어떤 시도를 할 수밖에 없었다. 노동이 영주의 장원에 이해관계를 가진 노동자들에 의해서 장원 내에서 제공되는 한, 그 문제는 단지 장원만의 문제였다; 하지만 고용된 노동은 농업 그 자체뿐만 아니라 부수적인 직업들에서 전문화가 진행됨에 따라 점점 더 관행이 되었고, 노동자들은 그들의 장원을 떠났다, 그 결과 국가가 공공질서와 고용주들의 필요에 개입했다. 이러한 현상은 흑사병이 노동력의 부족을 만든 후에 특히 그러했다. 노동 재판관들은 노동을 규제하기 위해 만들어졌고, 그 이후 원래 범죄자들의 체포에만 관련이 있었던 치안 판사들과 통합되었다.

| 보기분석 |

① The intervention of the State was needed.
국가의 개입이 필요했다.
② The specialization of labour was emphasized.
노동의 전문화가 강조되었다.
③ The tradition of manor system should be kept.
장원 제도의 전통은 지켜져야 한다.
④ The movement of labour need not to be controlled.
노동의 이동은 통제될 필요가 없다.

| 정답분석 | 밑줄 친 문장에서 지시사 'This'는 직전 문장의 내용을 참고하도록 한다. '국가가 공공질서와 고용주들의 필요에 개입'한 것으로 'This'의 의미를 이해한다면 보기 ①이 정답으로 적절하다.

16 2015 서울여대 정답 ③

| 구문분석 | (In the Middle Ages) the inn was supplemented (to some extent by the monastic houses), but these, (as a rule), entertained only two classes, the very rich and the very poor.

(S1: the inn / V1: was supplemented / 어느 정도까지는: to some extent / 등위접속사: but / S2: these / V2: entertained / O: only two classes / =: the very rich and the very poor)

중세시대에 여관은 수도원에 의해서 어느 정도 보완되었지만, 이것들은 일반적으로 오직 두 부류의 계급인 매우 부유한 사람들과 매우 가난한 사람들만을 손님으로 맞이했다.

The first were received (by the monks) (because they did not dare to refuse them), but many were their complaints (regarding the excesses of their unwelcome guests).

(S1: The first / V1: were received / 부사절: ~ 때문에 / 등위접속사: but / S2: many / V2: were / C: their complaints)

첫 번째(부유한 사람들을 손님으로 맞이한 것)는 그들을 감히 거절할 수 없었기 때문이었지만 (부유한) 손님들의 지나친 행동에 대한 불만이 많았다.

The monastery door, however, was always open (to the poor man), (who was never turned empty away).

(S: The monastery door / 접속부사: however / V: was / C: open / 관계대명사: who)

그러나 수도원의 문은 가난한 사람에게는 언제나 열려 있었고, 그들이 빈손으로 돌아가는 경우는 절대 없었다.

The inns were used (by the people) (between these two extremes), (for they were too miserable for the nobility, and too expensive for the poor).

(S: The inns / V: were used / 등위접속사: 왜냐하면: for)

그 여관들은 이런 양극단 사이에 있는 사람들에 의해 이용되었는데, 그 이유는 귀족들이 사용하기에는 너무 형편없고 가난한 사람들이 이용하기에는 너무 비싼 것이었기 때문이다.

They were frequented (by the smaller gentry, merchants, packmen, and other traders).

(S: They / V: were frequented)

그 여관들은 소규모 신사(계급), 상인, 행상인, 그리고 무역업자들이 자주 방문했다.

The entertainment was poor enough; a number of beds were spread out (in one room on the floor), and each guest bought what food he required.

(S: The entertainment / V: was / C: poor / 세미콜론: 부연설명 / S1: a number of beds / V1: were spread out / S2: each guest / V2: bought / O: what food he required)

여관의 서비스는 매우 형편없었는데 수많은 침대들이 한 방의 바닥에 널려 있었고 손님들은 각자 그가 필요한 음식을 모두 사 왔다.

| 어휘 |

inn ⓝ (보통 시골 지역에 있는) 여관	**supplement** ⓥ 보충[추가]하다	**monastic** ⓐ 수도자의, 수도원의
entertain ⓥ (손님을) 접대하다	**miserable** ⓐ 비참한	**the nobility** 귀족들
frequent ⓥ 자주 다니다	**the gentry** 상류 사람들	**packman** ⓝ 행상인
spread out 몸을 뻗다, (집단에서) 떨어져 나가다, 더 널리 퍼지다		

| 전문해석 | 중세시대에 여관은 수도원에 의해서 어느 정도 보완되었지만, 이것들은 일반적으로 오직 두 부류의 계급인 매우 부유한 사람들과 매우 가난한 사람들만을 손님으로 맞이했다. 첫 번째(부유한 사람들을 손님으로 맞이한 것)는 그들을 감히 거절할 수 없었기 때문이었지만 (부유한) 손님들의 지나친 행동에 대한 불만이 많았다. 그러나 수도원의 문은 가난한 사람에게는 언제나 열려 있었고, 그들이 빈손으로 돌아가는 경우는 절대 없었다.

그 여관들은 이런 양극단 사이에 있는 사람들에 의해 이용되었는데, 그 이유는 귀족들이 사용하기에는 너무 형편없고 가난한 사람들이 이용하기에는 너무 비싼 것이었기 때문이다. 그 여관들은 소규모 신사(계급), 상인, 행상인, 그리고 무역업자들이 자주 방문했다. 여관의 서비스는 매우 형편없었는데 수많은 침대들이 한 방의 바닥에 널려 있었고 손님들은 각자 그가 필요한 음식을 모두 사 왔다.

| 보기분석 |

① the poor 가난한 사람들
② the inns 여관
③ the nobility 귀족들
④ the monastic houses 수도원의 집들

| 정답분석 | 글의 흐름상 밑줄 친 'them'은 부유한 손님에 해당하는 귀족을 가리킨다. 따라서 정답으로 보기 ③이 적절하다.

17 2015 한양대

정답 ④

| 구문분석 | (In 1966), Eddie Arnold earned induction (into the Country Music Hall of Fame).
S V O

1966년 에디 아놀드(Eddie Arnold)는 컨트리 음악 명예의 전당에 입성했다.

(Ranked among the most popular country singers in U.S. history), Arnold used his smooth voice (to escape from poverty).
분사구문 S V O

미국 역사상 가장 인기 있는 컨트리 가수 중 한 명인 아놀드는 가난에서 벗어나기 위해 그의 부드러운 목소리를 사용했다.

(When his father died), the family farm was lost (to creditors), and the Arnolds were forced to become sharecroppers.
부사절: ~할 때 S_1 V_1 등위접속사 S_2 V_2 O.C

그의 아버지가 돌아가셨을 때, 가족 농장은 채권자들에게 빼앗겼고, 아놀드 가족들은 소작농이 될 수밖에 없었다.

(Even when achieving his lifelong dream of becoming a top-selling this country) boy never lost touch (with his roots).
부사절: 심지어 ~할 때 S V O

심지어 음반을 가장 많아 판 가수가 된다는 그의 평생의 꿈을 이룰 때에도 이 시골 소년(아놀드)은 그의 근본에 대한 감각을 잃지 않았다.

(Even while gaining a rather sophisticated fan base with his succession of hits), he always referred to himself as the "Tennessee Plowboy."
부사절: 심지어 ~하는 동안에 S V O O.C

그의 연속적인 히트로 다소 세련된 팬층을 얻었지만, 그는 항상 자신을 '테네시의 시골 소년'이라고 불렀다.

(In his mind), his background (as a hard-working farm hand) prepared him (for the demanding role of a successful singer).
S V O

그의 마음속에는, 열심히 일하는 농장 일꾼으로서의 그의 배경은 그로 하여금 성공한 가수에게 요구되는 역할을 준비할 수 있게 해 주었다.

cut a ~ figure: ~한 모습을 드러내다

(From the beginning), he cut a different figure (from most of his contemporaries in the world of country singers).
S V O

처음부터, 그는 컨트리 가수들의 세계에서 동시대를 산 대부분의 컨트리 가수들과 다른 존재였다.

(Unlike most of them) (who appeared either in jeans and plaid shirts or glittering sequins and spangles), Arnold always dressed (in debonair attire).
~와는 달리 관계대명사 either A or B: A든지 B든지 S V

청바지와 격자무늬 셔츠 혹은 반짝이는 시퀸(스팽글)을 입고 나타난 대부분의 가수들과 달리, 그는 항상 남자다운 의상을 입었다.

(When he died in May 2008), the music world lost an immensely popular crooner (of romantic ballads).
부사절: ~할 때 S V O

그가 2008년 5월에 사망했을 때, 음악계는 엄청나게 인기 있는 낭만적인 발라드 남자가수를 잃었다.

| 어휘 | **induction** ⓝ 취임, 입성, 유도, 제시 **sharecropper** ⓝ 소작인
plowboy ⓝ 쟁기를 멘 소[말]를 모는 소년, 시골 젊은이 **plaid** ⓝ 격자[타탄]무늬 천
sequin ⓝ 스팽글(반짝거리도록 옷에 장식으로 붙이는 작고 동그란 금속편) **debonair** ⓐ 멋지고 당당한
attire ⓝ 의복, 복장 **crooner** ⓝ 조용한 사랑 노래를 부르는 남자 가수

| 전문해석 | 1966년 에디 아놀드(Eddie Arnold)는 컨트리 음악 명예의 전당에 입성했다. 미국 역사상 가장 인기 있는 컨트리 가수 중 한 명인 아놀드는 가난에서 벗어나기 위해 그의 부드러운 목소리를 사용했다. 그의 아버지가 돌아가셨을 때, 가족 농장은 채권자들에게 빼앗겼고, 아놀드 가족들은 소작농이 될 수밖에 없었다. 심지어 음반을 가장 많아 판 가수가 된다는 그의 평생의 꿈을 이룰 때에도 이 시골 소년(아놀드)은 그의 근본에 대한 감각을 잃지 않았다. 그의 연속적인 히트로 다소 세련된 팬층을 얻었지만, 그는 항상 자신을 '테네시의 시골 소년'이라고 불렀다. 그의 마음속에는, 열심히 일하는 농장 일꾼으로서의 그의 배경은 그로 하여금 성공한 가수에게 요구되는 역할을 준비할 수 있게 해 주었다. 처음부터, 그는 컨트리 가수들의

세계에서 동시대를 산 대부분의 컨트리 가수들과 다른 존재였다. 청바지와 격자무늬 셔츠 혹은 반짝이는 시퀸(스팽글)을 입고 나타난 대부분의 가수들과 달리, 그는 항상 남자다운 의상을 입었다. 그가 2008년 5월에 사망했을 때, 음악계는 엄청나게 인기 있는 낭만적인 발라드 남자가수를 잃었다.

| 보기분석 | ① Arnold remained connected to the family farm and continued to pursue agriculture. 아놀드는 컨트리 가수로 활동하므로 오답
아놀드는 가족 농장과 연결되어 있었고 농업을 계속 추구했다.
② Arnold eschewed his humble beginnings and indulged in a more sophisticated lifestyle.
아놀드는 자신의 초라한 시작을 피하고 좀 더 세련된 생활 방식에 탐닉했다.
③ Arnold liked to be known as a farm hand and favored jeans and cowboy boots when he performed. 언급 안 한 정보
아놀드는 농장 일꾼으로 알려지기를 좋아했고 그가 공연할 때 청바지와 카우보이 부츠를 선호했다.
④ Arnold continued to identify himself with the attitudes and values of hardworking rural Americans.
아놀드는 계속해서 열심히 일하는 시골 미국인들의 태도와 가치에 자신을 동일시했다.

| 정답분석 | 밑줄 친 부분 바로 다음 문장에서 컨트리 가수 아놀드는 자신을 '테네시의 시골 소년'이라 칭했으므로 그가 잊지 않은 것은 미국의 시골에 사는 농부들의 가치라고 볼 수 있다. 따라서 보기 ④가 정답으로 적절하다.

18 2017 국민대

정답 ④

| 구문분석 | Individual guilt (S) is triggered (V) (when we don't meet our own expectations). (부사절: ~할 때)
개인의 죄책감은 우리가 자신의 기대를 충족시키지 못할 때 발생한다.

Psychologist Heidi Wiedemann (S) describes (V) this feeling (O) as an internal struggle (O.C) (between what we presume our values to be and how we fail to live up to them). (between A and B: A, B 둘 사이)

심리학자 하이디 비데만(Heidi Wiedemann)은 이 감정을 우리가 우리의 가치를 무엇으로 생각하는지와 어떻게 그것에 부응하지 못하는지 사이의 내적 갈등이라고 설명한다.

(For many of us), she (S) says (V), especially women, the impulse can be triggered (O) (by unrealistic social norms), (whether they involve balancing family life and professional goals or maintaining fitness). (부사절: ~이든 아니든)
그녀는 우리 중 많은 사람들, 특히 여성들에게 가사와 직업적 목표 사이에서 균형을 잡는 것이든 건강을 관리하는 것이든, 비현실적인 사회규범들로 인해 그 자극이 유발될 수 있다고 말한다.

(To overcome individual guilt) (부사적용법: ~하기 위해서), Wiedemann (S) says (V) (that) we should try to be cognisant of any internalised unattainable expectations, then work on self-acceptance and letting go of judgement (O). (콤마: and 기능) (등위접속사)
개인의 죄책감을 극복하기 위해서, 비데만은 우리의 내면에 있는 실현 불가능한 기대를 인식하고, 그다음에는 자기수용과 판단의 포기에 대해 노력해야 한다고 말한다.

We (S) also need (V) to remind ourselves (of personal successes) (O).
우리는 또한 우리 자신에게 개인적인 성공들을 상기시켜 주어야 한다.

"People don't think anything of speaking to themselves negatively," (O_1) she (S) says (V), "but (when you tell them to start speaking to themselves with compassion) (부사절: ~할 때), they look at you (as though you're from another planet) (부사절: 비록 ~일지라도)." (O_2)
"사람들은 자신에게 부정적으로 말하는 것에 대해 아무렇지도 않게 생각합니다. 하지만 자신에게 동정심을 가지고 말하기 시작하면, 그들은 당신을 마치 다른 행성에서 온 것처럼 바라봅니다."라고 그녀는 말한다.

| 어휘 |

guilt ⓝ 죄책감	**trigger** ⓥ 유발하다, 일으키다	**expectation** ⓝ 기대, 예상
internal ⓐ 안의, 내부의, 정신적인	**struggle** ⓝ 갈등, 투쟁	**impulse** ⓝ 충동, 자극
norm ⓝ 규범, 기준	**involve** ⓥ 포함하다	**fitness** ⓝ 적합함
cognisant of ~을 인식하고 있는	**unattainable** ⓐ 도달하기 어려운	**self-acceptance** ⓝ 자아수용
let go of (쥐고 있던 것을) 놓다	**compassion** ⓝ 연민, 동정심	

| 전문해석 | 개인의 죄책감은 우리가 자신의 기대를 충족시키지 못할 때 발생한다. 심리학자 하이디 비데만(Heidi Wiedemann)은 이 감정을 우리가 우리의 가치를 무엇으로 생각하는지와 어떻게 그것에 부응하지 못하는지 사이의 내적 갈등이라고 설명한다. 그녀는 우리 중 많은 사람들, 특히 여성들에게 가사와 직업적 목표 사이에서 균형을 잡는 것이든 건강을 관리하는 것이든, 비현실적인 사회규범들로 인해 그 자극이 유발될 수 있다고 말한다.

개인의 죄책감을 극복하기 위해서, 비데만은 우리의 내면에 있는 실현 불가능한 기대를 인식하고, 그다음에는 자기수용과 판단의 포기에 대해 노력해야 한다고 말한다. 우리는 또한 우리 자신에게 개인적인 성공들을 상기시켜 주어야 한다. "사람들은 자신에게 부정적으로 말하는 것에 대해 아무렇지도 않게 생각합니다. 하지만 자신에게 동정심을 가지고 말하기 시작하면, 그들은 당신을 마치 다른 행성에서 온 것처럼 바라봅니다."라고 그녀는 말한다.

| 보기분석 | ① People feel at a loss in
사람들은 ~에 대해 막막함을 느낀다
② People think it abnormal
사람들은 그것을 비정상적으로 생각한다
③ People think too highly of
사람들은 ~을 너무 높이 평가한다
④ People do not care much about
사람들은 ~에 대해 별로 신경 쓰지 않는다

| 정답분석 | 밑줄 친 'People don't think anything of'의 의미는 '~에 대해 아무렇지도 않게 생각한다'이다. 따라서 비슷한 의미의 보기 ④가 정답으로 적절하다.

19 2017 단국대

정답 ④

| 구문분석 | University of Pennsylvania researchers found that spouses (who had major cardiac surgery) had better functional recovery within two years than patients (who were divorced, separated or widowed).
(S: University of Pennsylvania researchers / V: found / O: that spouses ... widowed / who: 관계대명사)

펜실베이니아 대학 연구원들은 주요 심장 수술을 받은 배우자들이 배우자가 이혼을 했거나 별거하거나 사별을 한 환자들보다 (수술 후) 2년 이내에 더 나은 심장 기능 회복을 보인다는 것을 발견했다.

That means (that) they were more able to get dressed, bathe or go to the bathroom on their own.
(S: That / V: means / O: they were ... on their own)

이것은 그들이 스스로 옷을 입거나 목욕하거나 화장실에 갈 수 있다는 것을 의미한다.

In fact, those (who were no longer married) were (about 40%) more likely to die or develop a new functional disability (in the first two years postsurgery than those with a spouse at home).
(In fact: 접속부사 / S: those / who: 관계대명사 / V: were / C: more likely to die or develop a new functional disability)

실제로, 배우자가 없는 사람들은 배우자가 있는 사람들보다 수술 후 첫 2년 안에 사망하거나 새로운 기능 장애가 발생할 확률이 약 40% 더 높았다.

(There were not enough never-married people (in the study) (to make an assessment on them).)
(There: 유도부사 / V: were / S: enough never-married people / to make: 부사적용법: ~하기 위해서)
(결혼한 적이 없는 사람들은 연구에서 그들에 대해 평가하기에 그 수가 충분하지 못했다.)

The researchers are not sure (whether the results are because less-healthy people are more likely to be unmarried or because spouses make a big difference in rehabilitation).
(S: The researchers / V: are / C: sure / whether A or B: A이든지 B든지)

연구원들은 그 결과가 덜 건강한 사람들이 미혼일 가능성이 높기 때문인지 아니면 배우자들이 재활에 있어서 큰 차이를 만들기 때문인지(배우자의 존재가 재활에 큰 도움이 되기 때문인지)를 확신하지 못한다.

Either way, they say (that) hospitals should consider marital status (when helping people plan their post-heart-attack life).
(S: they / V: say / O: hospitals should consider marital status / when helping: 분사구문)

어느 쪽이든 간에, 그들은 병원에서는 사람들이 심장마비 이후 삶을 계획하는 것을 도울 때, 결혼 상태를 고려해야만 한다고 말한다.

| 어휘 |

spouse ⓝ 배우자
cardiac surgery 심장 수술
functional ⓐ 기능의, 기능을 가진
disability ⓝ 장애
divorce ⓥ 이혼하다
separate ⓥ 분리하다, 별거하다

widowed ⓐ 미망인이 된 **post-surgery** ⓐ 수술 후의
assessment ⓝ (사람 · 사물 등의) 평가, 판단 **rehabilitation** ⓝ 사회 복귀, 재활
marital status 혼인 상태

| 전문해석 | 펜실베이니아 대학 연구원들은 주요 심장 수술을 받은 배우자들이 배우자가 이혼을 했거나 별거하거나 사별을 한 환자들보다 (수술 후) 2년 이내에 더 나은 심장 기능 회복을 보인다는 것을 발견했다. 이것은 그들이 스스로 옷을 입거나 목욕하거나 화장실에 갈 수 있다는 것을 의미한다. 실제로, 배우자가 없는 사람들은 배우자가 있는 사람들보다 수술 후 첫 2년 안에 사망하거나 새로운 기능 장애가 발생할 확률이 약 40% 더 높았다. (결혼한 적이 없는 사람들은 연구에서 그들에 대해 평가하기에 그 수가 충분하지 못했다.)

연구원들은 그 결과가 덜 건강한 사람들이 미혼일 가능성이 높기 때문인지 아니면 배우자들이 재활에 있어서 큰 차이를 만들기 때문인지(배우자의 존재가 재활에 큰 도움이 되기 때문인지)를 확신하지 못한다. 어느 쪽이든 간에, 그들은 병원에서는 사람들이 심장마비 이후 삶을 계획하는 것을 도울 때, 결혼 상태를 고려해야만 한다고 말한다.

| 보기분석 | ① To make an assessment, we need enough married people.
평가를 하기 위해서, 우리는 충분한 기혼자들이 필요하다.
② There were not enough people to marry before the surgery.
수술 전에 결혼할 사람들이 충분하지 않았다.
③ Never-married people were easy to assess. '평가 자료의 부족'에 대해 언급해야 함
결혼하지 않은 사람들은 평가하기 쉬웠다.
④ The data to assess never-married people were not enough.
결혼하지 않은 사람들을 평가하기 위한 자료는 충분하지 않았다.

| 정답분석 | 밑줄 친 부분은 '결혼한 적이 없는 사람들은 연구에서 그들에 대해 평가하기에 그 수가 충분하지 못했다.'라고 번역된다. 연구 대상이 되는 미혼자들의 수가 적은 것은 그들에 대한 연구 자료가 충분하지 않은 것을 의미하므로 보기 ④가 정답으로 적절하다.

20 2017 한국외대

정답 ②

| 구문분석 | Have(V) you(S) ever heard (of a double Irish)?

더블 아이리시에 대해 들어 보았는가?

not A but B: A가 아니라 B

It(S) is(V) not a drink(C1) but one of the controversial tax strategies(C2) (that(관계대명사) help some American companies keep profits abroad at lower rates).

그것은 음료가 아니라 일부 미국 기업들이 해외에서 더 낮은 세율로 수익을 유지하도록 돕는 논란이 많은 조세 전략들 중 하나이다.

Such strategies(S) are(V) (at the heart of the Aug. 30 ruling) (by the European Union) (demanding that Ireland claw back $14.5 billion in allegedly unpaid taxes from Apple, = the world's most valuable tech company).

그러한 전략은 아일랜드가 세계 최고의 가치 있는 기술 회사인 Apple로부터 받지 못했다고 주장되는 145억 달러의 (미납) 세금을 환수할 것을 요구하는 유럽연합의 8월 30일 판결의 핵심이다.

The European regulators' investigation(S) concluded(V) that tax arrangements Ireland offered Apple in 1991 and 2007 were illegal(O), (allowing(분사구문) the firm to pay annual tax rates of 0.005% to 1% on its European profits from 2003 to 2014).

유럽 규제 당국의 조사는 아일랜드가 1991년과 2007년에 Apple에 제공한 세금 조정(tax arrangement)은 불법이라는 결론을 내렸고, (그 세금 조정은) 2003년부터 2014년까지 Apple로 하여금 그 회사가 유럽에서의 수익에 대해 0.005%에서 1%의 연간 세율을 지불하게 했다.

Those(S) are(V) much lower(C) than Ireland's standard corporate rate, (which(관계대명사) is the second lowest in the E.U., at 12.5%).

이 세율은 유럽에서 두 번째로 낮은 아일랜드의 표준 법인세율인 12.5%보다 훨씬 더 낮은 것이다.

(In an open letter), CEO Tim Cook disputed the decision and vowed to appeal, (adding, "Apple follows the law, and we pay all the taxes we owe.")

(S: CEO Tim Cook / V_1: disputed / O: the decision / 등위접속사: and / V_2: vowed to appeal / 분사구문: adding)

공개서한을 통해, Apple의 CEO 팀 쿡(Tim Cook)은 그 결정에 이의를 제기하고 항소를 다짐했으며 "Apple은 법을 준수하고 우리가 납부해야 할 세금을 냅니다."라고 덧붙였다.

Ireland's Finance Minister said (that) the country would also fight the ruling.

(S: Ireland's Finance Minister / V: said / O: the country would also fight the ruling)

아일랜드 재무장관은 아일랜드도 그 판결에 대해 맞서 싸울 것이라고 말했다.

| 어휘 |

double Irish ⓝ 기업의 조세회피전략(아일랜드의 독특한 세법을 이용해 글로벌 기업이 아일랜드에 두 개의 법인을 세워 세금을 줄여 온 방식)
controversial ⓐ 논란이 많은
claw back (교부금 등을 세금으로) 환수하다, 되찾다
ruling ⓝ 판결
regulator ⓝ (산업 · 상업 분야의) 규제[단속] 기관
corporate rate 법인세율
dispute ⓥ 반박하다, 분쟁을 벌이다
appeal ⓝ 항소

| 전문해석 | 더블 아이리시에 대해 들어 보았는가? 그것은 음료가 아니라 일부 미국 기업들이 해외에서 더 낮은 세율로 수익을 유지하도록 돕는 논란이 많은 조세 전략들 중 하나이다. 그러한 전략은 아일랜드가 세계 최고의 가치 있는 기술 회사인 Apple로부터 받지 못했다고 주장되는 145억 달러의 (미납) 세금을 환수할 것을 요구하는 유럽연합의 8월 30일 판결의 핵심이다. 유럽 규제 당국의 조사는 아일랜드가 1991년과 2007년에 Apple에 제공한 세금 조정(tax arrangement)은 불법이라는 결론을 내렸고, (그 세금 조정은) 2003년부터 2014년까지 Apple로 하여금 그 회사가 유럽에서의 수익에 대해 0.005%에서 1%의 연간 세율을 지불하게 했다. 이 세율은 유럽에서 두 번째로 낮은 아일랜드의 표준 법인세율인 12.5%보다 훨씬 더 낮은 것이다. 공개서한을 통해, Apple의 CEO 팀 쿡(Tim Cook)은 그 결정에 이의를 제기하고 항소를 다짐했으며 "Apple은 법을 준수하고 우리가 납부해야 할 세금을 냅니다."라고 덧붙였다. 아일랜드 재무장관은 아일랜드도 그 판결에 대해 맞서 싸울 것이라고 말했다.

| 보기분석 |

① Apple's tax evasion in Ireland 'Apple'은 사례로 언급될 뿐 '조세 전략'에 관해 언급해야 정답
아일랜드에서 Apple의 탈세

② Ireland's two-tiered corporate tax rates
아일랜드의 이중 법인세율

③ Doubled tax penalty for Ireland
아일랜드에 대한 과세처벌

④ The E.U.'s different standard for Ireland
아일랜드에 대한 EU의 다른 기준

| 정답분석 | 본문의 도입부에서 작가는 '더블 아이리시' 개념을 소개하는데 그에 따르면 아일랜드는 표준 법인세율보다 훨씬 낮은 세율을 미국 기업들에 적용하여 그들의 수익을 유지하도록 도왔다. 필자는 이어서 Apple에 조정해 준 법인세율을 예를 들어 설명했다. 그러므로 '더블 아이리시'는 '아일랜드가 기업에 달리 적용하는 법인세율'을 가리킨다고 볼 수 있으므로 보기 ②가 정답으로 적절하다.

7강 연결사 / 빈칸 추론

Practice

01	③	02	①	03	③	04	⑤	05	④	06	④	07	③	08	⑤	09	①	10	④
11	②	12	②	13	④	14	②, ①	15	③	16	③	17	①	18	①	19	③	20	①, ③

01 2018 가천대

정답 ③

| 구문분석 | The theory (that skin color adapts to the level of ultraviolet radiation) makes some sense.
S = V

피부색이 자외선의 수준에 적응한다는 이론은 어느 정도 일리가 있다.

The ancestors (of modern humans) (who lived predominantly near the equator in Africa) had darker skin (because it was more efficient at reflecting heat), (helping the body cool down and preventing the skin from receiving harmful ultraviolet rays).
S 관계대명사 등위접속사 V O 부사절: ~ 때문에 분사구문 1 분사구문 2

아프리카의 적도 부근에 주로 거주했던 현생 인류의 조상들은 피부색이 더 검었는데 그 이유는 검은 피부가 열을 반사하는 데 더 효율적이었기 때문이고, 몸을 시원하게 해 주고 피부가 유해한 자외선을 받지 못하도록 해 주었기 때문이다.

However, less exposure (to ultraviolet rays) can lead (to a deficiency in Vitamin D), (also known as the "sunshine vitamin.")
S V

그러나 자외선에 덜 노출되면 '햇빛 비타민'이라고도 알려진 비타민 D의 결핍으로 이어질 수 있다.

This is the main reason (why black people are at higher risk of contracting rheumatoid arthritis) (due to vitamin D deficiency).
S V C 관계부사

이것이 흑인들이 비타민 D 결핍으로 류머티즘성 관절염에 걸릴 위험이 더 높은 주요 이유이다.

| 어휘 |

adapt ⓥ (상황에) 적응하다	**ultraviolet radiation** ⓝ 자외선	**make sense** 타당하다
ancestor ⓝ 조상	**predominantly** ⓐⓓ 주로	**equator** ⓝ (지구의) 적도
efficient ⓐ 효율적인	**reflect** ⓥ 반사하다	**deficiency** ⓝ 결핍, 부족
contract ⓥ (병에) 걸리다	**rheumatoid arthritis** 류머티즘성 관절염	

| 전문해석 | 피부색이 자외선의 수준에 적응한다는 이론은 어느 정도 일리가 있다. 아프리카의 적도 부근에 주로 거주했던 현생 인류의 조상들은 피부색이 더 검었는데 그 이유는 검은 피부가 열을 반사하는 데 더 효율적이었기 때문이고, 몸을 시원하게 해 주고 피부가 유해한 자외선을 받지 못하도록 해 주었기 때문이다. 그러나 자외선에 덜 노출되면 '햇빛 비타민'이라고도 알려진 비타민 D의 결핍으로 이어질 수 있다. 이것이 흑인들이 비타민 D 결핍으로 류머티즘성 관절염에 걸릴 위험이 더 높은 주요 이유이다.

| 보기분석 |
① For instance 순접(예시) 예를 들면
② Therefore 순접(인과관계) 그러므로
③ However 역접 그러나
④ In conclusion 순접(인과관계) 결론적으로

| 정답분석 | 빈칸에 알맞은 접속부사를 고르는 문제이므로 직전 문장과 빈칸으로 시작되는 문장과의 관계를 고려해 본다. 빈칸 직전 문장에서는 검은 피부의 장점을 설명하고 빈칸 다음부터는 검은 피부의 단점을 설명하므로 빈칸은 역접의 접속부사가 오는 것이 적절하다. 따라서 보기 ③ However가 정답이다.

02 2018 건국대

정답 ①

| 구문분석 | Many reports show that there are still very few women in high government positions.
S V O
많은 보고서들은 여전히 정부의 고위직에 여성들이 거의 없다는 것을 보여 준다.

In fact, only about 15% (of the positions in government) are held (by women).
S V
사실상, 정부 고위직의 약 15%만을 여성들이 맡고 있다.

In addition, more than half (of the people) (who can't read and write) are women.
접속부사 S 관계대명사 V C
게다가, 글을 읽고 쓸 줄 모르는 사람들의 절반 이상이 여성이다.

Being illiterate doesn't mean (that) people are not intelligent.
S V O
문맹인 것은 사람들이 똑똑하지 않다는 뜻은 아니다.

However, not being able to read and write does make it more difficult (for people) to change their lives.
접속부사 S 등위접속사 V 가목적어 O.C 의미상 주어 진목적어
하지만, 글을 읽고 쓸 수 없다는 것은 사람들이 그들의 삶을 변화시키는 것을 더 어렵게 만든다.

There are many programs (to help people improve their farming skills).
유도부사 V S
사람들이 농사 기술을 향상시키는 것을 돕는 많은 프로그램들이 있다.

However, (for years), these programs provided money and training (for men) but not (for women).
접속부사 S V 등위접속사 O 등위접속사
그러나, 수년 동안, 이 프로그램들은 남성들에게는 지원금과 교육을 제공했지만 여성들에게는 제공하지 않았다.

Now this is changing.
S V
이제 이것은 변하고 있다.

International organizations and programs are helping women, as well as men, (to) improve their agricultural productions.
등위접속사 S V B as well as A: A뿐만 아니라 B 역시 O.C

국제기구들과 프로그램들은 남성들뿐만 아니라 여성들도 그들의 농업 생산을 향상시키는 것을 돕고 있다.

| 어휘 | **illiterate** ⓐ 무식한, 문맹의, 무학의 **intelligent** ⓐ 똑똑한, 지적인 **farming** ⓝ 농업, 농사 **agricultural** ⓐ 농업의, 경작의

| 전문해석 | 많은 보고서들은 여전히 정부의 고위직에 여성들이 거의 없다는 것을 보여 준다. 사실상, 정부 고위직의 약 15%만을 여성들이 맡고 있다. 게다가, 글을 읽고 쓸 줄 모르는 사람들의 절반 이상이 여성이다. 문맹인 것은 사람들이 똑똑하지 않다는 뜻은 아니다. 하지만, 글을 읽고 쓸 수 없다는 것은 사람들이 그들의 삶을 변화시키는 것을 더 어렵게 만든다. 사람들이 농사 기술을 향상시키는 것을 돕는 많은 프로그램들이 있다. 그러나, 수년 동안, 이 프로그램들은 남성들에게는 지원금과 교육을 제공했지만 여성들에게는 제공하지 않았다. 이제 이것은 변하고 있다. 국제기구들과 프로그램들은 남성들뿐만 아니라 여성들도 그들의 농업 생산을 향상시키는 것을 돕고 있다.

| 보기분석 | ① In fact – However
사실 – 그러나
② In fact – As a result
사실 – 결과적으로
③ In other words – As a result
다른 말로 하자면 – 결과적으로
④ Therefore – However
그러므로 – 그러나
⑤ Therefore – For example
그러므로 – 예를 들면

(②③⑤) 두 번째 빈칸에는 '순접' 표현이 적절하지 않음
(④⑤) 앞뒤 내용이 '인과관계' 아니므로 오답

| 정답분석 | 빈칸 [A]의 앞 문장에서 '정부의 고위직에 여성들이 거의 없다'고 했고 빈칸 [A]의 다음으로는 '고위직의 약 15%만을 여성들이 맡고 있다'고 했으므로 순접 기능이 있는 연결표현이 적절하다. 이미 언급한 내용에 보충설명을 할 때 사용하는 In

fact가 [A]에 가장 적절하다. 빈칸 [B] 앞에서는 '사람들이 농사 기술을 향상시키는 것을 돕는 많은 프로그램들이 있다'고 했고 빈칸 [B] 뒤로는 '이 프로그램들이 수년 동안 남성들에게만 제공되었다'고 했으므로 역접 기능을 하는 접속부사 However가 가장 적절하다. 따라서 ①이 정답이다.

03 2018 가천대

정답 ③

| 구문분석 | (In the early 19th century), adventure stories(S) gave(V) Americans(I.O) a taste(D.O) (for fast-paced, exciting tales of danger and(등위접속사) heroism in distant places).

19세기 초, 모험 소설들은 미국인들에게 먼 곳에서의 위험과 영웅주의에 대한 속도감 있고 흥미로운 이야기들에 대한 취향(흥미)을 갖게 해 주었다.

At the same time, the growth(S) (of newspapers for the general public) created(V) a market(O) (for inexpensive publications) (aimed at a wide audience).

동시에, 일반 대중을 위한 신문들의 증가는 광범위한 독자를 겨냥한 저렴한 출판물 시장을 만들었다.

These two conditions(S) led(V) (to the advent of a new kind of literature): the "dime novel."(콜론: 동격)

이 두 가지 조건은 새로운 종류의 문학, "싸구려 소설"의 출현으로 이어졌다.

The dime novel(S) was(V) a short work(C) (of fiction), (cheaply printed and often crudely written, about the adventures of a hero or heroine).

싸구려 소설은 단편 소설로, 값싸게 인쇄되었고 종종 조잡하게 쓰였으며, 영웅이나 여주인공의 모험에 관한 것이었다.

(Though(부사절: 비록 ~일지라도) dime novels were usually pure fantasy), they(S) provided(V_1) readers(O) (with an escape from the boredom of humdrum life), and(등위접속사) helped(V_2) (to) create the popular image(O) (of outlaws and cowboys) (as romantic and even heroic figures).

비록 싸구려 소설이 대개 순전히 공상 소설이었지만, 그것들은 독자들을 평범한 삶의 지루함으로부터 벗어나게 해 주었으며, 무법자와 카우보이의 낭만적이고 심지어 영웅적인 인물로서의 대중적인 이미지를 만드는 데 일조했다.

| 어휘 |
adventure story 모험담
fast-paced ⓐ (이야기 등이) 빨리 진행되는
heroism ⓝ 영웅적인[대단히 용감한] 행위
advent ⓝ 도래, 출현
dime novel ⓝ 싸구려 소설, 삼류 소설
a work of fiction 소설 작품
crudely ⓐⓓ 대충, 조잡하게
escape ⓝ (힘든 일 등을 잊기 위한) 도피
boredom ⓝ 권태, 지루한 것
outlaw ⓝ 무법자, (범죄를 저지른) 도망자
cowboy ⓝ (미국 서부 지역의) 목동

| 전문해석 | 19세기 초, 모험 소설들은 미국인들에게 먼 곳에서의 위험과 영웅주의에 대한 속도감 있고 흥미로운 이야기들에 대한 취향(흥미)을 갖게 해 주었다. 동시에, 일반 대중을 위한 신문들의 증가는 광범위한 독자를 겨냥한 저렴한 출판물 시장을 만들었다. 이 두 가지 조건은 새로운 종류의 문학, "싸구려 소설"의 출현으로 이어졌다.
싸구려 소설은 단편 소설로, 값싸게 인쇄되었고 종종 조잡하게 쓰였으며, 영웅이나 여주인공의 모험에 관한 것이었다. 비록 싸구려 소설이 대개 순전히 공상 소설이었지만, 그것들은 독자들을 평범한 삶의 지루함으로부터 벗어나게 해 주었으며, 무법자와 카우보이의 낭만적이고 심지어 영웅적인 인물로서의 대중적인 이미지를 만드는 데 일조했다.

| 보기분석 |
① uncanny 신비로운
② hallowed 신성한
③ humdrum 평범한
④ otherworldly 저승의, 내세의

| 정답분석 | 빈칸 뒤의 'and'는 등위접속사이며 빈칸을 포함한 문장의 내용과 'and' 이후 내용이 순접으로 연결되어야만 한다. 빈칸 뒤

로는 싸구려 소설이 '무법자와 카우보이의 낭만적이고 심지어 영웅적인 인물로서의 대중적인 이미지를 만드는 데 도움이 된다'는 내용이 오며 이와 순접으로 연결되려면 빈칸에는 독자들의 삶이 '평범한 삶의 지루함'을 벗어나야 할 것이다. 따라서 '평범한, 단조로운'이란 의미의 보기 ③ humdrum이 정답으로 적절하다.

04 2018 인하대

정답 ⑤

| 구문분석 | The growing importance (of education) contributed (to the emergence of a separate youth culture).
(The growing importance: S / contributed: V)

교육의 중요성이 커지면서 별도의 청소년 문화가 생겨나는 데 기여했다.

The idea (of adolescence as a distinct period in the life of an individual) was (for the most part) new (to the twentieth century).
(The idea: S / was: V / new: C)

개인의 인생에서 뚜렷한 시기로서의 청소년기 개념은 대개 20세기는 대부분 새로운 것(새로운 개념)이었다.

(In some measure) it was a result (of the influence of Freudian psychology).
(it: S / was: V / a result: C)

어떤 면에서 그것은 프로이트 심리학에 영향받은 결과였다.

But it was a result, too, (of society's recognition) (that a more extended period of training and preparation was necessary (before a young person was ready to move into the workplace).
(it: S / was: V / a result: C / recognition = that절 / before: 부사절: ~ 전에)

그러나 그것은 또한 젊은 사람(청소년)이 직장생활을 시작할 준비가 되기 전에 더 긴 훈련과 준비 기간이 필요하다는 사회의 인식에서 비롯된 결과이기도 했다.

Schools and colleges provided adolescents (with a setting) (in which they could develop their own social patterns, their own hobbies, their own interests and activities).
(Schools and colleges: S / provided: V / adolescents: C / in which: 관계대명사)

학교와 대학은 청소년들에게 그들 자신의 사회적 생활 방식, 취미, 흥미, 활동을 개발할 수 있는 환경을 제공했다.

An increasing number (of students) saw school as a place (not just for academic training but for organized athletics, other extracurricular activities, clubs, and fraternities and sororities — that is, as an institution that allowed them to define themselves more in terms of their peer group).
(An increasing number: S / saw: V / school: O / as a place: O.C / not A but B: A가 아니라 B / that is: 대시: 부연설명(즉, 다시 말해서))

점점 더 많은 학생들이 학교를 단지 학업 훈련을 하기 위한 장소가 아니라, 조직화된 운동, 다른 과외 활동, 동호회, 남녀 친목회 등을 위한 장소로—즉 그들이 또래 집단의 관점에서 자신을 더 정의할 수 있도록 해 주는 기관으로 간주했다.

| 어휘 |

contribute ⓥ 기부하다, 기여[공헌]하다
emergence ⓝ 출현, 탈출, 발생
separate ⓐ 분리된, 독립된, 별개의
adolescence ⓝ 청소년기
distinct ⓐ 별개의, 뚜렷한
in some measure 다소, 약간
influence ⓝ 영향
Freudian ⓐ 프로이트의
psychology ⓝ 심리학
recognition ⓝ 인지, 승인, 인정
extend ⓥ 뻗다; 확장하다; 연장하다, 늘이다
preparation ⓝ 준비; 각오
organize ⓥ 조직하다
extracurricular ⓐ 과외의, 정규 과목 이외의
fraternity ⓝ (직종 · 이해관계 · 신념이 같은 사람들의) 협회, (미국 대학의) 남학생 사교클럽
sorority ⓝ (미국 대학의) 여학생 클럽
institution ⓝ 학회, 기관

| 전문해석 | 교육의 중요성이 커지면서 별도의 청소년 문화가 생겨나는 데 기여했다. 개인의 인생에서 뚜렷한 시기로서의 청소년기 개념은 대개 20세기는 대부분 새로운 것(새로운 개념)이었다. 어떤 면에서 그것은 프로이트 심리학에 영향받은 결과였다. 그러나 그것은 또한 젊은 사람(청소년)이 직장생활을 시작할 준비가 되기 전에 더 긴 훈련과 준비 기간이 필요하다는 사회의 인식에서 비롯된 결과이기도 했다. 학교와 대학은 청소년들에게 그들 자신의 사회적 생활 방식, 취미, 흥미, 활동을 개발할

수 있는 환경을 제공했다. 점점 더 많은 학생들이 학교를 단지 학업 훈련을 하기 위한 장소가 아니라, 조직화된 운동, 다른 과외 활동, 동호회, 남녀 친목회 등을 위한 장소로—즉 그들이 또래 집단의 관점에서 자신을 더 정의할 수 있도록 해 주는 기관으로 간주했다.

| 보기분석 | ① led young people to look for low-paying jobs
젊은이들이 저임금 일자리를 찾도록 이끄는
② specialized in teaching technical skills demanded in the modern economy
현대 경제에 요구되는 기술 능력을 가르치는 데 특화된
③ helped many men and women make more money to support their families
많은 남자들과 여자들이 그들의 가족을 부양하기 위해 더 많은 돈을 버는 것을 돕는
④ offered both instruction and services in traditional disciplines
전통적인 분야의 교육과 서비스를 모두 제공하는
⑤ allowed them to define themselves more in terms of their peer group
또래 그룹의 관점에서 자신을 더 정의할 수 있도록 허용하는

| 정답분석 | 'that is'는 '다시 말해서'라는 의미의 재진술 표현이다. 따라서 빈칸 직전에 나열된 '운동 경기, 과외 활동, 동호회, 남녀 학생 친목회 등을 위한 장소'를 빈칸에서 부연 설명하는 내용이 적절하다. 나열된 활동들은 모두 또래와 만나거나 어울리는 기회에 해당하므로 보기 ⑤가 정답으로 적절하다.

05 2015 건국대

정답 ④

| 구문분석 | The globe (S) is losing (V) valuable species (O) day by day; (세미콜론: 부연설명) 20% to 50% (S_1) (of the world's biological diversity) may be gone (V_1) (before the end of the next century) (부사절: ~ 전에), and (등위접속사) the irony (S_2) is (V_2) that human beings will have contributed overwhelmingly to that loss (C).

지구는 귀중한 생물의 종들을 매일매일 잃고 있는 중이다; 세계의 다양한 생물의 종들 20%에서 50%가 다음 세기가 끝나기 전에 사라질 수도 있고 아이러니하게도 인간들이 그(생물의 종) 손실에 압도적으로 기여할 것이다.

The human population (S) is expected (V) nearly (to double) (within the next few decades).
인구는 앞으로 다가올 수십 년 안에 거의 두 배로 증가할 것이라고 예상된다.

(For third world agrarian economies especially), the competition (S_1) (for space and resources) will grow (V_1) (during (전치사: ~ 동안) this "demographic winter,") and (등위접속사) the losers (S_2) will be (V_2) the wild animals (C).
특히 제3세계 농업 경제의 경우, 이 "인구학적 겨울" 동안 공간과 자원에 대한 경쟁이 커질 것이며, (이 경쟁에서) 패자들은 야생동물이 될 것이다.

| 어휘 | **globe** ⓝ 세계, 지구본 **irony** ⓝ 풍자, 비꼬기, 빈정댐 **contribute to** ~에 기여하다
overwhelmingly ⓐⓓ 압도적으로 **agrarian** ⓐ 농업의
demographic winter 인구통계학적인 측면에서 퇴보의 시기(출생률이 저하되고 고령화 사회가 되며 발전 없이 겨울과 같이 정체되어 있는 상황)

| 전문해석 | 지구는 귀중한 생물의 종들을 매일매일 잃고 있는 중이다; 세계의 다양한 생물의 종들 20%에서 50%가 다음 세기가 끝나기 전에 사라질 수도 있고 아이러니하게도 인간들이 그(생물의 종) 손실에 압도적으로 기여할 것이다. 인구는 앞으로 다가올 수십 년 안에 거의 두 배로 증가할 것이라고 예상된다. 특히 제3세계 농업 경제의 경우, 이 "인구학적 겨울" 동안 공간과 자원에 대한 경쟁이 커질 것이며, (이 경쟁에서) 패자들은 야생동물이 될 것이다.

| 보기분석 | ① natural resources 너무 포괄적
천연자원
② ozone layer
오존층
③ oil supply
석유 공급
④ biological diversity
생물학적 다양성
⑤ financial institutions
금융기관

| 정답분석 | 빈칸의 직전 문장과 빈칸을 포함한 문장 사이에 '세미콜론(;)'은 앞 내용을 재진술하는 기능이 있는 구두점이다. 세미콜론 직전의 내용이 '지구가 귀중한 생물의 종들을 잃어버리고 있다'는 것이므로 빈칸에도 '생물'에 관련된 표현이 어울린다. 따라서 보기 ④가 정답으로 가장 적절하다.

06 2016 단국대

정답 ④

| 구문분석 | (Although psychology was not recognized as its own field) (until the late nineteenth century), its early roots can be traced (to the ancient Greeks).
부사절: 비록 ~일지라도 / S / V

비록 심리학이 19세기 후반까지 고유한 학문 분야로 인정되지 않았지만, 그것의 초기 뿌리는 고대 그리스인들로까지 거슬러 올라갈 수 있다.

Plato and Aristotle, for instance, were philosophers (concerned with the nature of the human mind).
S / 접속부사 / V / C

예를 들어, 플라톤(Plato)과 아리스토텔레스(Aristotle)는 인간 정신의 본질에 관심이 있는 철학자들이었다.

(In the seventeenth century), René Descartes distinguished (between the mind and body) (as aspects) (that interact to create human experience, (thus paving the way for modern psychology).
S / V / between A and B: A와 B 사이 / 관계대명사 / 접속부사 / 분사구문

17세기, 르네 데카르트(René Descartes)는 상호작용하여 인간의 경험을 만들어 내는 측면으로써 정신과 육체를 구별했는데, 이를 통해 현대 심리학의 길을 열었다.

(While philosophers relied on observation and logic to draw their conclusions), psychologists began to use scientific methods (to study human thought and behavior).
부사절: ~하는 동안 / S / V / O / 부사적용법: ~하기 위해서

철학자들이 그들의 결론을 도출하기 위해서 관찰과 논리에 의존했던 데 반해, 심리학자들은 인간의 생각과 행동을 연구하기 위해 과학적인 방법을 사용하기 시작했다.

A German physiologist, Wilhelm Wundt, opened the world's first psychology laboratory (at the University of Leipzig in 1879).
S / = / V / O

독일의 생리학자인 빌헬름 분트(Wilhelm Wundt)는 1879년 라이프치히 대학에서 세계 최초의 심리학 실험실을 열었다.

He used experimental methods (to study mental processes), (such as reaction times).
S / V / O / 부사적용법: ~하기 위해서 / 전치사: ~와 같은

그는 반응시간과 같은 정신의 과정을 연구하기 실험적인 방법들을 사용했다.

This research is regarded (as marking the beginning of psychology as a separate field).
S / V

이 연구는 독립된 분야로서의 심리학의 시작을 알리는 것으로 여겨진다.

The term psychiatry was first used (by a German physician, Johann Reil, in 1808).
S / V / =

정신의학이라는 용어는 1808년 독일인 의사 요한 레일(Johann Reil)에 의해서 처음으로 사용되었다.

However, psychiatry (as a field) did not become popular (until Sigmund Freud proposed a new theory of personality) (that focused on the role of the unconscious).
접속부사 / S / V / C / 부사절: ~할 때까지 / 관계대명사

그러나 학문 분야로서의 정신의학은 지그문트 프로이트(Sigmund Freud)가 무의식의 역할에 초점을 맞춘 새로운 성격이론을 제시하기 전까지는 대중화되지 않았다.

Before that time, psychologists were concerned primarily (with the conscious aspects of the mind), (including perceptions, thoughts, memories, and fantasies (of which a person is aware).
S / V / 전치사: ~을 포함하여 / 관계대명사

그 이전에, 심리학자들은 주로 사람이 인식하고 있는 인식, 생각, 기억, 환상을 포함한 정신의 의식적인 측면에 관심이 있었다.

| 어휘 | trace ⓥ 추적하다, (기원 · 원인을) 찾아내다 aspect ⓝ 측면, 양상
interact ⓥ 소통하다, 교류하다 pave the way for ~을 위해 길을 열다, ~에 대해 준비하다
observation ⓝ 관찰, 주목 logic ⓝ 논리
physiologist ⓝ 생리학자(생물체의 생물학적 기능과 작용 또는 그 원리를 연구하는 자)
reaction ⓝ 반응, 반작용 psychiatry ⓝ 정신의학 unconscious ⓐ 무의식의적인
perception ⓝ 지각, 인식, 지각력 fantasy ⓝ 공상, 상상

| 전문해석 | 비록 심리학이 19세기 후반까지 고유한 학문 분야로 인정되지 않았지만, 그것의 초기 뿌리는 고대 그리스인들로까지 거슬러 올라갈 수 있다. 예를 들어, 플라톤(Plato)과 아리스토텔레스(Aristotle)는 인간 정신의 본질에 관심이 있는 철학자들이었다. 17세기, 르네 데카르트(René Descartes)는 상호작용하여 인간의 경험을 만들어 내는 측면으로써 정신과 육체를 구별했는데, 이를 통해 현대 심리학의 길을 열었다. 철학자들이 그들의 결론을 도출하기 위해서 관찰과 논리에 의존했던 데 반해, 심리학자들은 인간의 생각과 행동을 연구하기 위해 과학적인 방법을 사용하기 시작했다. 독일의 생리학자인 빌헬름 분트(Wilhelm Wundt)는 1879년 라이프치히 대학에서 세계 최초의 심리학 실험실을 열었다. 그는 반응시간과 같은 정신의 과정을 연구하기 실험적인 방법들을 사용했다. 이 연구는 독립된 분야로서의 심리학의 시작을 알리는 것으로 여겨진다. 정신의학이라는 용어는 1808년 독일인 의사 요한 레일(Johann Reil)에 의해서 처음으로 사용되었다. 그러나 학문 분야로서의 정신의학은 지그문트 프로이트(Sigmund Freud)가 무의식의 역할에 초점을 맞춘 새로운 성격이론을 제시하기 전까지는 대중화되지 않았다. 그 이전에, 심리학자들은 주로 사람이 인식하고 있는 인식, 생각, 기억, 환상을 포함한 정신의 의식적인 측면에 관심이 있었다.

| 보기분석 | ① For example – In the meantime 첫 번째 빈칸에서 '순접' 기능의 접속부사는 적절하지 않음
예를 들어 – 그 동안
② Otherwise – At the same time 사건의 전후 관계를 나누는 데는 적절하지 않음
그렇지 않은 경우 – 동시에
③ As a result – After that time 첫 번째 빈칸에서 '순접' 기능의 접속부사는 적절하지 않음
결과적으로 – 그 이후
④ However – Before that time
그러나 – 그 이전에

| 정답분석 | 두 빈칸의 각각 직전과 직후 내용을 참고하여 문제를 해결한다. 빈칸 [A]의 경우 빈칸 앞에서는 정신의학이라는 용어를 처음으로 사용한 독일 의사를 소개하고 빈칸 뒤에서는 정신의학을 학문 분야로서 대중화한 프로이트가 소개되므로 역접 부사가 적절하다. 빈칸 [B]는 이후 내용에서 학문 분야로서 무의식을 연구한 프로이트와 달리 정신의 의식적 측면에 관심이 있었던 심리학자들이 소개되므로 프로이트의 연구가 더 나중에 발생했을 것이라는 추론이 가능하다. 따라서 두 빈칸의 조건에 가장 적절한 보기는 ④이다.

07 2016 한양대(에리카)

정답 ③

| 구문분석 | (Looking back over a twenty year career of playing, composing, and conducting different types of orchestra music), I often feel a sense of wonder — not (at what I have accomplished), but (how someone (with my agrarian, rather workaday upbringing) should have chosen such a path at all).

분사구문 / 대시: 부연설명 / S V O / not A but B: A가 아니라 B

다양한 종류의 오케스트라 음악을 연주하고, 작곡하고, 지휘했던 지난 20년간의 경력을 뒤돌아보면서, 나는 종종 일종의 경이로움을 느낀다—내가 이룬 것에 대한 것이 아니라, 어떻게 나처럼 평범한 농부의 가정에서 자라난 사람이 그와 같은 길을 선택하게 되었는가에 대한 것이다.

It would have been easy (for me) to stay (on the family farm) (as my parents wished, eventually to become part owner), (as my brother did quite successfully).

가주어 / V C 의미상 주어 진주어 / 부사절: ~처럼 / 부사절: ~처럼

부모님이 바라시던 대로, 나의 형이 꽤 성공적으로 했듯이, 가족 농장에서 지내고 결국에는 농장의 공동소유자가 되는 것이 쉬웠을 것이다.

세미콜론: and 역할

However, (rewarding as this existence was), it was somehow unfulfilling; my youthful imagination, (much to my parents' dismay), often cast about for other, greater pursuits (to occupy it).

접속부사 / 부사절: 비록 ~일지라도 / S V C / S / V

하지만, 그런 존재는 보람이 있었지만, 그런 종류의 삶은 성취감을 주지 못했다; 나의 젊은 시절의 상상력은, 나의 부모님에게는 매우 실망스러운 일이었지만, 이와는 다른, 더 큰일을 추구했다.

Still, (growing up as I did in a household) (where the radio dispensed milk prices instead of Mozart and hog futures instead of Handel), the thought (of embarking on a career in classical music) went beyond (even my wildest imagination).

접속부사 / 부사절: ~처럼 / 관계부사 / 전치사: ~ 대신에 / S / V go beyond: ~을 넘어서다

그럼에도 불구하고, 나는 라디오에서 모차르트 대신 우윳값이 나오고 헨델 대신 돼지고기 선물을 주는 그러한 가정에서 자랐기 때문에, 내가 고전 음악 분야에서 경력을 시작한다는 생각은 아주 엉뚱한 상상이었다.

| 어휘 |

look back (과거를) 되돌아보다 / compose ⓥ 구성하다, 작곡하다 / conduct ⓥ 지휘하다
agrarian ⓝ 농업[농민]의, 토지의 / workaday ⓐ 일하는 날의, 평일의, 보통의
upbringing ⓝ (유년기의) 양육, 훈육 / part-owner ⓝ 공동 소유자
rewarding ⓐ 보람 있는, 수익이 많이 나는 / unfulfilling ⓐ 성취감을 주지 못하는
cast about 찾아다니다, 궁리하다 / dispense ⓥ 제공하다, 나누어 주다 / hog ⓝ 돼지, (식용) 수퇘지
versatile ⓐ 다재다능한, 다용도의 / wild ⓐ 야생의, 터무니없는

| 전문해석 | 다양한 종류의 오케스트라 음악을 연주하고, 작곡하고, 지휘했던 지난 20년간의 경력을 뒤돌아보면서, 나는 종종 일종의 경이로움을 느낀다—내가 이룬 것에 대한 것이 아니라, 어떻게 나처럼 평범한 농부의 가정에서 자라난 사람이 그와 같은 길을 선택하게 되었는가에 대한 것이다. 부모님이 바라시던 대로, 나의 형이 꽤 성공적으로 했듯이, 가족 농장에서 지내고 결국에는 농장의 공동소유자가 되는 것이 쉬웠을 것이다. 하지만, 그런 존재는 보람이 있었지만, 그런 종류의 삶은 성취감을 주지 못했다; 나의 젊은 시절의 상상력은, 나의 부모님에게는 매우 실망스러운 일이었지만, 이와는 다른, 더 큰일을 추구했다. 그럼에도 불구하고, 나는 라디오에서 모차르트 대신 우윳값이 나오고 헨델 대신 돼지고기 선물을 주는 그러한 가정에서 자랐기 때문에, 내가 고전 음악 분야에서 경력을 시작한다는 생각은 아주 엉뚱한 상상이었다.

| 보기분석 |

① delight 기쁨
② approval 승인
③ dismay (충격을 받은 뒤의) 실망, 경악
④ dejection 낙담, 우울 — 정답 ③과 마찬가지로 부정적 표현이긴 하지만 너무 극단적이므로 오답

| 정답분석 | 빈칸을 포함하는 문장의 앞 문장에서는 글쓴이가 가족 농장을 운영하기를 바랐던 부모님에 대한 설명이 나온다. 그러나 빈칸을 포함한 문장에서 글쓴이는 '그런 종류의 삶이 성취감을 주지 못했고 더 큰일을 추구했다'고 했으므로 빈칸에는 그런 결정에 따른 '부모님의 실망'과 관련된 표현이 적절하다. 따라서 보기 ③이 정답이다.

08 2014 건국대

정답 ⑤

| 구문분석 | The half (of the world's people) (who now live in cities) experience the most artificial environment (ever created by humans).

S / 관계대명사 / V / O

현재 도시에 사는 세계 인구의 절반은 인간이 지금까지 만든 가장 인공적인 환경을 경험한다.

Large areas (of countryside) have been destroyed (by the spread of houses, factories, roads and shopping centers) (across what were once fields, open spaces and woodland).

S / V

시골의 넓은 지역은 한때 들판이나, 공지나 숲이었던 곳을 가로질러 주택, 공장, 도로와 쇼핑센터들이 확장됨에 따라 파괴되었다.

(In the 1990s alone) over 800,000 hectares (of European land) was built on — (if this rate continued through the rest of the twenty-first century) it would result in a doubling (of the current urban area).

S: over 800,000 hectares / V: was built on / 대시: 부연설명 / 부사절: 만약 ~라면 / S: it / V: would result in

1990년대에만 유럽의 토지 80만 헥타르가 넘는 면적에 건물이 들어섰고—이 비율이 21세기의 나머지 시간에도 계속된다면 그 결과로 지금의 도시 면적은 두 배가 될 것이다.

Cities also depend (on very high energy use) (in building and sustaining them and in moving millions of people to and from work every day).

S: Cities / V: depend / and: 등위접속사

도시는 또한 건설하고 유지하는 데에, 그리고 매일 수백만 명의 사람들을 직장으로 이동시키는 데에 매우 많은 에너지 소비에 의존한다.

Cities have many benefits — they are usually centers (of cultural activity) and have a much wider range (of facilities than rural areas).

S_1: Cities / V_1: have / O: many benefits / 대시: 부연설명 / S_2: they / V_2: are / C: centers / and: 등위접속사 / V_3: have / O: a much wider range

도시는 많은 이점을 가지고 있다—도시는 보통 문화 활동의 중심지이고 시골 지역보다 훨씬 더 많은 종류의 시설들을 갖추고 있다.

However, [although (in some working-class areas) strong, but informal, systems of community support developed], (in general) the flood (of people into cities) destroyed existing social bonds and institutions (without creating new ones) (capable of helping and sustaining the inhabitants).

However: 접속부사 / although: 부사절: 비록 ~일지라도 / but: 등위접속사 / S: the flood / V: destroyed / O: existing social bonds and institutions

그러나 비록 일부 노동자 계층 지역에서는 강력하지만 비공식적인 공동체 지원체제가 개발되었지만, 일반적으로 도시로 몰려드는 사람들은 주민들을 돕고 유지시키는 새로운 유대와 제도를 만들어 내지 못한 채 기존의 사회적 유대와 제도를 파괴했다.

Cities, (as the nineteenth-century American writer Henry David Thoreau wrote), tend to be places (characterized by 'millions of people being lonely together').

S: Cities / 부사절: ~하듯이, ~처럼 / V: tend / O: to be places

19세기 미국 작가 헨리 데이비드 소로(Henry David Thoreau)가 썼듯이, 도시는 '함께 외로워하는 수백만 명의 사람들'의 특징을 가진 장소가 되는 경향이 있다.

| 어휘 |

artificial ⓐ 인공의, 인위적인 **countryside** ⓝ 시골 지역 **woodland** ⓝ 삼림(지대)
rural ⓐ 시골의, 지방의 **sustain** ⓥ 떠받치다, 유지하다 **working-class** ⓝ 노동자 계층
flood ⓝ 홍수, 쇄도, 폭주 **social bond** 사회 유대 **institution** ⓝ 학회, 기관

| 전문해석 | 현재 도시에 사는 세계 인구의 절반은 인간이 지금까지 만든 가장 인공적인 환경을 경험한다. 시골의 넓은 지역은 한때 들판이나, 공지나 숲이었던 곳을 가로질러 주택, 공장, 도로와 쇼핑센터들이 확장됨에 따라 파괴되었다. 1990년대에만 유럽의 토지 80만 헥타르가 넘는 면적에 건물이 들어섰고—이 비율이 21세기의 나머지 시간에도 계속된다면 그 결과로 지금의 도시 면적은 두 배가 될 것이다. 도시는 또한 건설하고 유지하는 데에, 그리고 매일 수백만 명의 사람들을 직장으로 이동시키는 데에 매우 많은 에너지 소비에 의존한다. 도시는 많은 이점을 가지고 있다—도시는 보통 문화 활동의 중심지이고 시골 지역보다 훨씬 더 많은 종류의 시설들을 갖추고 있다. 그러나 비록 일부 노동자 계층 지역에서는 강력하지만 비공식적인 공동체 지원체제가 개발되었지만, 일반적으로 도시로 몰려드는 사람들은 주민들을 돕고 유지시키는 새로운 유대와 제도를 만들어 내지 못한 채 기존의 사회적 유대와 제도를 파괴했다. 19세기 미국 작가 헨리 데이비드 소로(Henry David Thoreau)가 썼듯이, 도시는 '함께 외로워하는 수백만 명의 사람들'의 특징을 가진 장소가 되는 경향이 있다.

| 보기분석 |

① citizens helping and sustaining each other
서로 돕고 지탱하는 시민들

② abundant opportunities of cultural activities
문화 활동의 풍부한 기회

③ new facilities with large open spaces
넓은 공터가 있는 새로운 시설들

④ the destruction of houses and factories 부정적 의미이긴 하지만 '사회적 유대'와는 관련이 없으므로 오답
주택과 공장의 파괴

⑤ millions of people being lonely together
함께 외로워하는 수백만 명의 사람들

| 정답분석 | 빈칸 직전 문장에서 '도시로 몰려든 사람들은 새로운 유대와 제도를 만들어 내지 못한 채 기존의 사회적 유대와 제도를 파괴했다'고 설명했다. 빈칸을 포함하는 문장에 별다른 역접의 표현이 없는 이상 앞 문장과 순접으로 연결되어야 한다. 따라서 빈칸에는 도시에 생활하며 유대관계가 파괴된 사람들에 관한 내용이 와야 앞 문장과 가장 자연스럽게 연결된다. 따라서 보기 ⑤가 정답으로 가장 적절하다.

09 2014 서울여대

정답 ①

| 구문분석 |

from A to B to C: A로부터 B에서 C까지

(From Ben Franklin to Horatio Alger to Oprah Winfrey), American heroes(S) seem(V) always to be the self-made men or women(C) (who(관계대명사) strode into the world all on their own).

벤저민 프랭클린(Ben Franklin)부터 허레이쇼 앨저(Horatio Alger)에서 오프라 윈프리(Oprah Winfrey)에 이르기까지, 미국의 영웅들은 항상 스스로 세상 속으로 성큼성큼 걸어 들어온 자수성가한 남자나 여자인 것처럼 보인다.

It(가주어)'s(V) almost a source(C) (of shame) to follow in a parent's footsteps(진주어).

부모의 발자취를 따라가는 것은 거의 수치의 근원이다.

But(등위접속사), actually, it(가주어)'s(V) a great idea(C) to study the example of your ancestors(진주어), (as revealed(분사구문) in the stories of how they spent their lives).

하지만, 사실, (이 연구를 통해서) 조상들이 어떤 삶을 살아왔는가가 드러나기 때문에 조상들의 선례를 연구하는 것은 좋은 생각이다.

You(S) may find(V) clues(O) (to what to do based on shared talents, dispositions, or interests).

당신은 (당신의 조상들과) 공유하는 재능과 성향과 관심사에 근거해서 무엇을 해야 할지에 대한 단서를 찾을 수 있다.

There(유도부사) may be(V) a compelling reason(S) (beyond good connections) (why(관계부사) so many medical school students have a parent (who(관계대명사)'s a doctor) or(등위접속사) (why(관계부사) farmers or firefighters run in some families).

왜 많은 의과대학 학생들이 의사인 부모를 두고 또는 농부와 소방관들이 몇몇 가정에서 대를 이어 내려오는지에 대해서 단순한 인맥 이상의 설득력 있는 이유가 있을지도 모른다.

But(등위접속사) you(S) may find(V) signs(O) (that(관계대명사) are just as strong about what not to do).

그러나 당신은 (조상의 선례를 연구하며) 하지 말아야 할 일에 대해서도 그만큼 설득력 있는 징후를 발견할 수 있다.

(If your mother despised sitting in an office all day)(부사절: 만약 ~라면), you(S) might think(V) twice (about business school).

만일 당신의 어머니가 하루 종일 사무실에 앉아 있는 것을 싫어했다면, 당신은 경영대학원에 진학하는 것에 대해 다시 생각할지도 모른다.

On the other hand(접속부사), (if Uncle Louie wore out early as a construction worker)(부사절: 만약 ~라면), a desk job(S) might not look(V) too bad(C).

반면에, 당신의 삼촌인 루이(Louie)가 건설 노동자로 일찌감치 몸이 약해졌다면, 사무직 노동도 그리 나쁘지 않아 보일 수도 있을 것이다.

| 어휘 |

self-made ⓐ 자수성가한 **stride** ⓥ 성큼성큼 걷다 **shame** ⓝ 수치, 창피
ancestor ⓝ 조상, 선조 **disposition** ⓝ (타고난) 기질, 성격 **firefighter** ⓝ 소방관
despise ⓥ 경멸하다, 멸시하다 **construction** ⓝ (도로 · 빌딩 등의) 건설, 공사

| 전문해석 | 벤저민 프랭클린(Ben Franklin)부터 허레이쇼 앨저(Horatio Alger)에서 오프라 윈프리(Oprah Winfrey)에 이르기까지, 미국의 영웅들은 항상 스스로 세상 속으로 성큼성큼 걸어 들어온 자수성가한 남자나 여자인 것처럼 보인다. 부모의 발자취를 따라가는 것은 거의 수치의 근원이다. 하지만, 사실, (이 연구를 통해서) 조상들이 어떤 삶을 살아왔는가가 드러나기 때문에 조상들의 선례를 연구하는 것은 좋은 생각이다. 당신은 (당신의 조상들과) 공유하는 재능과 성향과 관심사에 근거해서 무엇

을 해야 할지에 대한 단서를 찾을 수 있다. 왜 많은 의과대학 학생들이 의사인 부모를 두고 또는 농부와 소방관들이 몇몇 가정에서 대를 이어 내려오는지에 대해서 단순한 인맥 이상의 설득력 있는 이유가 있을지도 모른다. 그러나 당신은 (조상의 선례를 연구하며) 하지 말아야 할 일에 대해서도 그만큼 설득력 있는 징후를 발견할 수 있다. 만일 당신의 어머니가 하루 종일 사무실에 앉아 있는 것을 싫어했다면, 당신은 경영대학원에 진학하는 것에 대해 다시 생각할지도 모른다. 반면에, 당신의 삼촌인 루이(Louie)가 건설 노동자로 일찌감치 몸이 약해졌다면, 사무직 노동도 그리 나쁘지 않아 보일 수도 있을 것이다.

| 보기분석 | ✔ what not to do 하지 말아야 할 것
② what not to share 언급 안 한 정보 공유하지 말아야 할 것
③ what you are good at 당신이 잘하는 것
④ what you want to do 당신이 하고 싶은 것

| 정답분석 | 빈칸을 포함하는 문장이 'But'으로 시작되므로 직전 문장과 역접 관계로 연결한다. 빈칸 직전 내용은 조상의 선례를 연구했을 때 '무엇을 해야 할지'에 대한 단서를 찾을 수 있고 그 예로 의과대학, 농부, 소방관들의 가문이 소개된다. 빈칸을 포함한 문장의 다음 문장부터는 어머니와 삼촌의 사례를 들어 조상의 선례를 연구하는 것이 '하지 말아야 할 일'에 대한 단서도 제공한다고 서술해야 역접의 관계로 자연스럽다.

10 2014 인하대

정답 ④

| 구문분석 | The theory (of constructivism) was developed (by Jean Piaget, the Swiss biologist and philosopher) (who became interested in the child's growing ability to think).
S / V / = / 관계대명사

구성주의 이론은 아이들의 사고력의 성장에 관심을 가졌던 스위스의 생물학자이자 철학자인 장 피아제(Jean Piaget)에 의해 개발되었다.

However, Piaget studied children (as a way) (to understand the human mind and the origins of intelligence) (independent of culture).
S / V / O

그러나 피아제는 문화와 무관하게 인간의 마음과 지능의 원천을 이해하는 방법으로 아이들을 연구했다.

Piaget believed that many concepts (that we heretofore had considered elementary, such as the concept of *hidden*), were actually extremely complicated and that we needed a new theory to explain how children younger than a year were able to learn such complicated notions.
S / V / 관계대명사 / O_1 / 등위접속사 / O_2

피아제는 '숨겨진'의 개념과 같이 우리가 이전에 초보적이라고 생각했던 많은 개념들이 실제로는 매우 복잡한 것이며, 어떻게 한 살 미만의 아이들이 그렇게 복잡한 개념들을 배울 수 있는지를 설명할 새로운 이론이 필요하다고 믿었다.

In other words, the concepts (learned at 2 years, 7 years, and 13 years) were qualitatively more complex, (necessitating a developmental theory) (that accounted for each stage of cognitive development).
S / V / C / 분사구문 / 관계대명사

다시 말해, 2살, 7살, 13살에 배운 개념들은 질적으로 더 복잡하여, 인지적 발달의 각 단계를 설명해 줄 발달이론이 필요했다.

| 어휘 |
constructivism ⓝ 구성주의
biologist ⓝ 생물학자
independent of ~와는 관계없이, ~와는 별도로
intelligence ⓝ 지성, 사고력
heretofore ⓐⓓ 지금까지는, 이전에는
elementary ⓐ 기본의, 초보의
hidden ⓐ 숨은, 숨겨진, 비밀의
complicate ⓥ (더) 복잡하게 만들다
concept ⓝ 개념, 생각
qualitative ⓐ 질적인
necessitate ⓥ 필요로 하다
account for 설명하다, 처리하다

| 전문해석 | 구성주의 이론은 아이들의 사고력의 성장에 관심을 가졌던 스위스의 생물학자이자 철학자인 장 피아제(Jean Piaget)에 의해 개발되었다. 그러나 피아제는 문화와 무관하게 인간의 마음과 지능의 원천을 이해하는 방법으로 아이들을 연구했다. 피아제는 '숨겨진'의 개념과 같이 우리가 이전에 초보적이라고 생각했던 많은 개념들이 실제로는 매우 복잡한 것이며, 어떻게

한 살 미만의 아이들이 그렇게 복잡한 개념들을 배울 수 있는지를 설명할 새로운 이론이 필요하다고 믿었다. 다시 말해, 2살, 7살, 13살에 배운 개념들은 질적으로 더 복잡하여, 인지적 발달의 각 단계를 설명해 줄 발달이론이 필요했다.

| 보기분석 | ① In fact – Nonetheless
사실 – 그럼에도 불구하고
② In fact – Likewise
사실 – 마찬가지로
('역접'의 기능을 할 때는 보통 앞뒤에 '정반대' 진술이 오기 때문에 오답)
③ However – In contrast 두 번째 빈칸에는 '역접' 표현이 적절하지 않음
그러나 – 대조적으로
④ However – In other words
그러나 – 다른 말로 하자면

| 정답분석 | 첫 번째 빈칸의 직전 문장에서는 '아이의 사고력의 성장'에 대한 관심이 언급되고 빈칸 뒤에서는 '인간의 마음과 지능의 원천'에 대한 관심이 언급되므로 둘 사이에 역접 표현을 넣어야 자연스럽다. 두 번째 빈칸의 경우에는 빈칸으로 시작되는 문장이 빈칸 직전 문장에 대한 재진술 및 예시에 해당된다. 따라서 두 빈칸의 조건을 만족시키는 보기 ④가 정답으로 가장 적절하다.

11 2013 한국외대

정답 ②

| 구문분석 | Copyright initially was conceived (as a way) (for government) (to restrict printing); the contemporary intent (of copyright) is to promote the creation of new works (by giving authors right to control and profit from them).
(Copyright: S_1, was conceived: V_1, 세미콜론: 부연설명, the contemporary intent: S_2, is: V_2, to promote the creation of new works: C, by ~ing: ~함으로써, and: 등위접속사)
저작권은 처음에 정부가 인쇄물을 제한하려는 방법으로 고안되었다; 저작권의 현대적 목적은 작가에게 새로운 작품을 통제하고 그 작품들로부터 수익을 얻을 권리를 부여함으로써 새로운 작품들의 창작을 촉진하기 위한 것이다.

Copyrights are said to be territorial, (which means that they do not extend beyond the scope of a specific state) (unless that state is a party to an international agreement).
(Copyrights: S, are said to be: V, territorial: C, which: 관계대명사(계속적용법), beyond: 전치사: ~ 너머, unless: 부사절: 만약 ~이 아니라면)
저작권은 지역에 한정된다고 일컬어지는데, 이것은 특정 국가가 국제협정의 당사자가 아니라면, 저작권은 특정 국가의 범위를 넘어가지 않는다는 것을 의미한다.

(While many aspects of national copyright laws have been standardized through international copyright agreements), copyright laws (of most countries) have their own unique features.
(While: 부사절: 반면에, copyright laws: S, have: V, their own unique features: O)
국가 저작권법의 많은 측면이 국제 저작권 협정을 통해 표준화되었지만, 대부분 국가의 저작권법은 그들만의 독특한 특징을 가지고 있다.

| 어휘 |
copyright ⓝ 저작권, 판권
conceive ⓥ (생각 · 계획 등을) 마음속으로 하다, 상상하다
restrict ⓥ 제한하다, 한정하다
contemporary ⓐ 동시대의
scope ⓝ 범위, 영역
party ⓝ 당사자
standardize ⓥ 표준화하다

| 전문해석 | 저작권은 처음에 정부가 인쇄물을 제한하려는 방법으로 고안되었다; 저작권의 현대적 목적은 작가에게 새로운 작품을 통제하고 그 작품들로부터 수익을 얻을 권리를 부여함으로써 새로운 작품들의 창작을 촉진하기 위한 것이다. 저작권은 지역에 한정된다고 일컬어지는데, 이것은 특정 국가가 국제협정의 당사자가 아니라면, 저작권은 특정 국가의 범위를 넘어가지 않는다는 것을 의미한다. 국가 저작권법의 많은 측면이 국제 저작권 협정을 통해 표준화되었지만, 대부분 국가의 저작권법은 그들만의 독특한 특징을 가지고 있다.

| 보기분석 | ① conservative
보수적인
② territorial
영토의
③ international
국제적인
④ comprehensive
포괄적인

| 정답분석 | 빈칸 뒤 관계대명사 'which'는 계속적 용법으로 앞 내용의 부연 설명이 가능하다. 빈칸 뒤에서 '저작권은 특정 국가의 범위를 넘어가지 않는다'고 했으므로 빈칸에는 '저작권이 특정 국가나 지역에 한정된다'는 내용이 와야 한다. 따라서 보기 ②가 정답으로 적절하다.

12 2015 성균관대

정답 ②

| 구문분석 |

The most common treatment (for post-traumatic stress disorder) is known (as exposure-based therapy).
S / V

외상 후 스트레스 장애를 위한 가장 흔한 치료는 노출 기반 치료법으로 알려져 있다.

This asks those (afflicted) to imagine the sights and sounds (that traumatized them), and helps them (to) confront those memories.
S / V_1 / O / O.C / 관계대명사 / V_2 / O / O.C

이것은 고통받는 사람들에게 정신적 외상을 초래한 장면과 소리를 상상할 것을 요구하고, 그들이 그 기억들을 마주할 수 있도록 도와준다.

It often works. But (it is) not always.
S / V / 등위접속사

종종 이러한 치료법은 효과가 있다. 하지만 항상 그런 것은 아니다.

And it would undoubtedly be better (if troops did not develop the condition in the first place).
등위접속사 / S / V / 부사절: 만약 ~라면

만일 군대가 애초에 그 증상을 발병시키지 않았다면 의심할 여지 없이 더 좋았을 것이다.

(With this in mind), a team (of engineers, computer scientists and psychologists) (led by Dr Skip Rizzo) propose a form (of psychological vaccination).
S / V / O

이것을 염두에 두고, Skip Rizzo 박사가 이끄는 공학자들과 컴퓨터 과학자들과 심리학자들로 이루어진 연구팀이 심리학적인 백신의 한 형태를 제안했다.

(By presenting soldiers with the horrors of war before they go to fight), Dr Rizzo hopes to inure squaddies (to anything) (that) (they might witness on the field of battle).
by ~ing: ~함으로써 / S / V / O

군인들이 전투에 나가기 전에 전쟁의 공포를 보여 줌으로써, Rizzo 박사는 전쟁터에서 목격하게 될 어떤 것에 대해 신병들을 단련시키기를 희망한다.

The idea (of doing this) developed (from Dr Rizzo's work) (using virtual reality) (to help with exposure-based therapy).
S / V / 부사적용법: ~하기 위해서

이러한 생각은 노출 기반 치료를 돕기 위해 가상현실을 사용하는 Rizzo 박사의 연구로부터 발전했다.

Such VR enables the sights, sounds, vibrations and even smells of the battlefield to be recreated (in the safety of a clinic), and trials suggest (that) (it can help those (who do not respond to standard exposure-based therapy).
S_1 / V_1 / O_1 / O.C / 등위접속사 / S_2 / V_2 / 관계대명사 / O_2

이러한 VR(가상현실)은 안전한 진료소 안에서 전쟁터의 광경, 소리, 진동 그리고 심지어는 냄새까지 재현될 수 있게 하며, (가상현실) 실험은 표준적인 노출 기반 치료에 반응하지 않는 사람들에게 도움을 줄 수 있다는 것을 시사한다.

The success (of such simulation) led Dr Rizzo to wonder if a similar regime, (experienced before actual battle), might prepare troops mentally in the way that traditional training prepares them physically.
S / V / O / O.C / 명사절: ~인지 아닌지

그러한 모의실험의 성공은 Rizzo 박사가 실제 전투 전에 전투 상황을 경험하게 하는 이와 유사한 치료법이 병사들에게 전통적인 군사 훈련이 군인들을 신체적으로 준비하게 만드는 것과 같은 방식으로 병사들을 정신적으로 준비시킬 수 있을지 의문을 가지게 만들었다.

His preliminary results suggest (that) it might.
S / V / O

그의 실험의 예비결과는 그럴 수도 있음을 시사한다.

| 어휘 |

post-traumatic stress disorder 외상 후 스트레스 장애(큰 정신적 충격 때문에 겪게 되는 의학적 증상)

exposure-based therapy 노출 치료

afflict ⓥ 괴롭히다, 피해를 입히다

traumatize ⓥ 정신적 외상을 초래하다, 엄청난 충격을 주다

confront ⓥ 닥치다, (문제 · 곤란한 상황에) 맞서다

work ⓥ 효과가 있다, 작용하다

troop ⓝ 병력, 군대

inure ⓥ 익히다, 단련하다

squaddie ⓝ 신병, 졸병

vibration ⓝ 진동　regime ⓝ 정권, 제도, 체제　simulation ⓝ 모의실험
preliminary ⓐ 예비의, 준비의

| 전문해석 | 외상 후 스트레스 장애를 위한 가장 흔한 치료는 노출 기반 치료법으로 알려져 있다. 이것은 고통받는 사람들에게 정신적 외상을 초래한 장면과 소리를 상상할 것을 요구하고, 그들이 그 기억들을 마주할 수 있도록 도와준다. 종종 이러한 치료법은 효과가 있다. 하지만 항상 그런 것은 아니다. 만일 군대가 애초에 그 증상을 발병시키지 않았다면 의심할 여지 없이 더 좋았을 것이다. 이것을 염두에 두고, Skip Rizzo 박사가 이끄는 공학자들과 컴퓨터 과학자들과 심리학자들로 이루어진 연구팀이 심리학적인 백신의 한 형태를 제안했다. 군인들이 전투에 나가기 전에 전쟁의 공포를 보여 줌으로써, Rizzo 박사는 전쟁터에서 목격하게 될 어떤 것에 대해 신병들을 단련시키기를 희망한다. 이러한 생각은 노출 기반 치료를 돕기 위해 가상현실을 사용하는 Rizzo 박사의 연구로부터 발전했다. 이러한 VR(가상현실)은 안전한 진료소 안에서 전쟁터의 광경, 소리, 진동 그리고 심지어는 냄새까지 재현될 수 있게 하며, (가상현실) 실험은 표준적인 노출 기반 치료에 반응하지 않는 사람들에게 도움을 줄 수 있다는 것을 시사한다. 그러한 모의실험의 성공은 Rizzo 박사가 실제 전투 전에 전투 상황을 경험하게 하는 이와 유사한 치료법이 병사들에게 전통적인 군사 훈련이 군인들을 신체적으로 준비하게 만드는 것과 같은 방식으로 병사들을 정신적으로 준비시킬 수 있을지 의문을 가지게 만들었다. 그의 실험의 예비결과는 그럴 수도 있음을 시사한다.

| 보기분석 | ① making soldiers relive the horrors of war as they come back
군인들이 돌아오면서 전쟁의 공포를 다시 느끼게 하는 것
② presenting soldiers with the horrors of war before they go to fight
군인들에게 그들이 싸우기 전에 전쟁의 공포를 선물하는 것
③ preparing soldiers more physically for battle '육체적' 준비가 아닌 '정신적' 준비로 봐야 함
군인들을 전투를 위해 더 육체적으로 준비시키는 것
④ using a variety of stress-reduction tactics
다양한 스트레스 해소 전략을 사용하는 것
⑤ speeding up the healing process with virtual training courses 치유가 아닌 '준비'나 '대비'에 관해 언급해야 함
가상 교육 과정을 통해 치유 과정의 속도를 높이는 것

| 정답분석 | 빈칸에 방법이나 수단을 나타내는 'By ~ing' 표현을 완성해야 한다. 따라서 빈칸 이후 내용에서 Rizzo 박사가 '전쟁터에서 목격할지도 모르는 어떤 것들을 신병들에게 단련시키기' 위해서는 가상현실 실험이 필요할 것이다. 빈칸 다음 문장에서는 이러한 생각이 가상현실을 사용하는 박사의 연구로부터 발전했다고 부연하고 있으므로 정답은 보기 ②가 적절하다.

13 2015 가천대　정답 ④

| 구문분석 | The general notion (S) is (V) that the press can form, control or at least strongly influence public opinion (C).
일반적인 통념은 언론이 여론을 형성하고 통제하거나 적어도 강력하게 영향을 미칠 수 있다는 것이다.

Can (V) it (S) really do any of these things (O)?
정말 언론이 이러한 것들을 할 수 있을까?

Hugh Cudlipp (S), (=) editorial director of *The London Daily Mirror*, and a man (who (관계대명사) should know something about the effect of newspapers on public opinion), doesn't share (V) this general notion (O) (about their power).
런던 데일리 미러의 편집장이자 신문이 여론에 미치는 영향력에 대해서 알아야 할 사람인 휴 커들립(Hugh Cudlipp)은 언론의 힘에 대한 이러한 일반적인 견해를 공유하지 않았다(견해가 달랐다).

He (S) thinks (V) (that) newspapers can echo and stimulate a wave of popular feeling (O_1), but (등위접속사) that's all (O_2).
그는 신문이 여론의 흐름을 반영하고 자극할 수는 있지만, 그것이 전부라고 생각했다.

"A newspaper (S) may successfully accelerate (V_1) but (등위접속사) never reverse (V_2) the popular attitude (O) (that (관계대명사) common sense has commended to the public)."

"신문은 상식이 대중에게 맡긴(상식을 따르는) 대중의 태도를 가속화할 수는 있지만 그것을 결코 뒤집지는 못할 것입니다."

In short, it can jump aboard the bandwagon (once the bandwagon's under way), and exhort others to jump aboard too; but it can't start the bandwagon rolling, or (it can't) change its direction (after it's started).

S_1 등위접속사 V_1 O_1 / 부사절: 일단 ~하면 / 등위접속사 V_2 O_2 O.C / 세미콜론: 부연설명 S_2 V_3 O_3 O.C 등위접속사 V_4 O_4 부사절: ~한 후에

요컨대, 신문은 시류의 흐름이 시작되면 그 시류의 흐름에 편승하고 다른 사람들에게 그 시류의 흐름에 가담할 것을 권할 수는 있다; 그러나 그 시류의 흐름을 시작하거나 이미 시작된 후에 시류의 방향을 바꿀 수는 없다.

| 어휘 |

press ⓝ 신문, 언론
echo ⓥ (소리가) 울리다, (사상이나 의견에) 반향을 보이다
commend ⓥ 칭찬하다, 권하다
jump aboard[on] the bandwagon 우세한 편에 붙다, 시류에 편승하다
exhort ⓥ 열심히 권하다, 촉구하다

| 전문해석 | 일반적인 통념은 언론이 여론을 형성하고 통제하거나 적어도 강력하게 영향을 미칠 수 있다는 것이다. 정말 언론이 이러한 것들을 할 수 있을까? 런던 데일리 미러의 편집장이자 신문이 여론에 미치는 영향력에 대해서 알아야 할 사람인 휴 커들립(Hugh Cudlipp)은 언론의 힘에 대한 이러한 일반적인 견해를 공유하지 않았다(견해가 달랐다). 그는 신문이 여론의 흐름을 반영하고 자극할 수는 있지만, 그것이 전부라고 생각했다. "신문은 상식이 대중에게 맡긴(상식을 따르는) 대중의 태도를 가속화할 수는 있지만 그것을 결코 뒤집지는 못할 것입니다." 요컨대, 신문은 시류의 흐름이 시작되면 그 시류의 흐름에 편승하고 다른 사람들에게 그 시류의 흐름에 가담할 것을 권할 수는 있다; 그러나 그 시류의 흐름을 시작하거나 이미 시작된 후에 시류의 방향을 바꿀 수는 없다.

| 보기분석 |

① Conversely 역접(정반대) 반대로
② In addition '순접'의 기능을 하지만 '요약'에는 적절하지 않음 추가로
③ Nonetheless 역접(양보) 그럼에도 불구하고
④ In short 순접(요약) 요컨대

| 정답분석 | 빈칸 직전 문장과 빈칸 다음에 오는 문장의 내용이 유사하므로 빈칸에는 순접 표현이 오는 것이 바람직하다. 빈칸 이후 내용은 글의 앞 내용 전체를 요약하고 있으므로 보기 ④가 정답으로 가장 적절하다.

14 2015 국민대

정답 ②, ①

| 구문분석 |

Sugar contributes (to premature ageing), (just as cigarettes and UV rays do).

S V 부사절: ~하듯이

설탕은 담배와 자외선이 그러하듯이 조기 노화에 기여한다.

(When collagen and elastin — components that support the skin — break down from sun or other free-radical exposure), cells try to repair themselves.

부사절: ~할 때 / 대시: 동격 / S V O

피부를 지탱하는 성분인 콜라겐과 엘라스틴이 햇빛이나 다른 유리기에 노출돼 분해될 때, 세포는 스스로를 회복하려고 노력한다.

But this process slows down (with age).

S V

하지만 이 과정은 나이가 들면서 (그 속도가) 느려진다.

And (when sugar is present in the skin), it forms cross-links (with amino acids) (that may have been damaged by free radicals).

부사절: ~할 때 / S V O / 관계대명사

그리고 피부에 당분이 존재할 때, 그것은 유리기에 의해서 손상되었을지도 모르는 아미노산과 교차결합을 형성한다.

These cross-links jam the repair mechanism and, (over time), leave you (with prematurely old-looking skin).

S V_1 O_1 등위접속사 V_2 O_2

이러한 교차 결합은 (피부의) 복구 메커니즘의 작동을 방해하고, 시간이 지남에 따라, 일찍 늙어 보이는 피부를 남긴다.

(Once cross-links form), they won't unhitch, so keep sugar intake as low as you can.

부사절: 일단 ~하면 / S V_1 등위접속사 V_2 O

일단 교차결합이 형성되면, 그것은 풀어지지 않아서 그 결과 설탕 섭취량을 가능한 한 줄여야 한다.

Avoid soft drinks and pastries, and swap sugar (for cinnamon) — it seems to slow down cross-linking, (as do cloves, ginger and garlic).

(등위접속사: and / V1: Avoid / O: soft drinks and pastries / V2: swap / O: sugar / 대시: 부연설명 / S: it / V: seems / C: to slow down cross-linking / 부사절: ~처럼: as)

탄산음료와 페이스트리(빵의 한 종류)를 피하고 설탕은 계피와 바꿔라—계피는 정향, 생강, 마늘과 마찬가지로 교차결합을 늦추는 것처럼 보인다.

| 어휘 | **contribute** ⓥ 기부하다, 기여하다 **break down** 고장 나다, 실패하다, 아주 나빠지다 **free-radical** ⓝ 유리기(짝짓지 않은 전자를 가지는 원자단) **amino acid** 아미노산 **jam** ⓥ 움직이지[작동하지] 못하게 하다 **unhitch** ⓥ 풀다, 떼어 내다 **swap** ⓥ 맞바꾸다, 물물 교환하다 **cinnamon** ⓝ 계피 **clove** ⓝ 정향(열대성 정향나무의 꽃을 말린 것)

| 전문해석 | 설탕은 담배와 자외선이 그러하듯이 조기 노화에 기여한다. 피부를 지탱하는 성분인 콜라겐과 엘라스틴이 햇빛이나 다른 유리기에 노출돼 분해될 때, 세포는 스스로를 회복하려고 노력한다. 하지만 이 과정은 나이가 들면서 (그 속도가) 느려진다. 그리고 피부에 당분이 존재할 때, 그것은 유리기에 의해서 손상되었을지도 모르는 아미노산과 교차결합을 형성한다. 이러한 교차 결합은 (피부의) 복구 메커니즘의 작동을 방해하고, 시간이 지남에 따라, 일찍 늙어 보이는 피부를 남긴다. 일단 교차결합이 형성되면, 그것은 풀어지지 않아서 그 결과 설탕 섭취량을 가능한 한 줄여야 한다. 탄산음료와 페이스트리(빵의 한 종류)를 피하고 설탕은 계피와 바꿔라—계피는 정향, 생강, 마늘과 마찬가지로 교차결합을 늦추는 것처럼 보인다.

| 보기분석 | Blank [A]

① with artificially sweetened cells
인공 감미 세포로
② with prematurely old-looking skin ✓
일찍 늙어 보이는 피부를 가진
③ with radically repaired mechanism
급진적으로 회복된 체계를 가진
④ with a nutritionally balanced body
영양적으로 균형 잡힌 몸을 가진

Blank [B]

① as low as you can ✓
가능한 한 낮게
② as soon as possible
가능한 한 빨리
③ as long as you can
가능한 한 오래
④ as much as possible
가능한 한 많이
(③, ④: 유사한 의미는 소거함)

| 정답분석 | 빈칸 [A]의 경우에는 직전 내용에서 '교차결합은 (피부의) 복구 메커니즘의 작동을 방해한다'고 했으므로 빈칸이 포함된 분사구문의 내용은 보기 ②가 적절하며 빈칸 [B]는 다음 문장에서 '탄산음료와 페이스트리를 피하고 설탕은 계피와 바꿔라'는 명령문과 순접으로 연결되어야 하므로 '설탕의 섭취를 가능한 한 줄여야 한다'는 보기 ①이 정답으로 가장 적절하다.

15 2017 인하대

정답 ③

| 구문분석 | (Between 1790 and 1861), approximately 400,000 Africans were imported (into the United States).

(S: approximately 400,000 Africans / V: were imported)

1790년에서 1861년 사이에, 약 40만 명의 아프리카인들이 미국으로 수입되었다.

Yet (by 1860), the black population had grown (to more than 4 million) — a tenfold increase (in 160 years).

(접속부사: Yet / S: the black population / V: had grown / 대시: 부연설명)

그러나 1860년까지, 흑인 인구는 400만 명 이상으로 증가했다—160년 만에 10배가 증가한 것이다.

These numbers suggest a tremendous rate (of natural increase).

(S: These numbers / V: suggest / O: a tremendous rate)

이 수치들은 엄청난 자연 증가율을 시사한다.

Some planters continued to buy slaves (brought into the country illegally after 1808).

(S: Some planters / V: continued / O: to buy slaves)

일부 농장주들은 1808년 이후에도 불법적으로 미국으로 데려온 노예들을 계속해서 사들였다.

But most (of the increase) stemmed (from births).
S V

하지만 그 증가(인구증가)의 대부분은 출생에서 비롯되었다.

The preferences (of both slave owners and slaves) account (for this development).
S V

노예 소유주들과 노예들 모두의 선호도가 이러한 인구증가의 원인이 되었다.

Southern planters encouraged black women to bear many children.
S V O O.C

남부 농장주들은 흑인 여성들에게 많은 아이를 낳도록 장려했다.

세미콜론: 부연설명

At the same time, enslaved African Americans valued the family (as a social unit); family ties provided support and solace (for a people) (deprived of fundamental human rights).
S V O S V 등위접속사 O

그와 동시에, 노예가 된 아프리카계 미국인들은 가정을 사회의 구성단위로 중요하게 여겼다; 가족 간의 유대는 기본적인 인간의 권리를 박탈당한 사람들에게 지지와 위안을 제공했다.

등위접속사

(Even under harsh conditions), black people fell in love, married, had children, and reared families.
S V_1 V_2 V_3 V_4 O

심지어 혹독한 환경 속에서도, 흑인들은 사랑에 빠지고, 결혼하고, 아이를 낳고, 가족들을 부양했다.

(Despite the lack of protection) (from local, state, and national authorities), the slave family proved a remarkably resilient institution.
전치사: ~에도 불구하고 S V C

지역, 주, 국가 당국의 보호가 부족했지만, 노예가정은 놀라울 정도로 회복력 있는 단체임이 판명되었다.

| 어휘 |

approximately ⓐⓓ 거의, 대략	**import** ⓥ 수입하다, 불러오다	**tenfold** ⓐ 10배의
tremendous ⓐ 엄청난, 굉장한	**illegally** ⓐⓓ 불법적으로	**stem** ⓥ 일어나다, 생기다, 유래하다
preference ⓝ 선호, 애호	**account for** 설명하다	**planter** ⓝ 경작자, 대농장 주인
encourage ⓥ 격려하다, 조장하다	**enslave** ⓥ 노예로 하다, 예속시키다	**solace** ⓝ 위안, 위로
deprive ⓥ (사람에게서 물건을) 빼앗다, (권리를) 박탈하다		**fundamental** ⓐ 기초의, 근본의
harsh ⓐ 가혹한, 냉혹한	**rear** ⓥ (어린아이 · 동물 등을) 기르다, 사육하다	
authority ⓝ 권위, 권력, (*pl.*) 당국	**resilient** ⓐ 회복력이 있는	**institution** ⓝ 학회, 기관, 제도

| 전문해석 | 1790년에서 1861년 사이에, 약 40만 명의 아프리카인들이 미국으로 수입되었다. 그러나 1860년까지, 흑인 인구는 400만 명 이상으로 증가했다—160년 만에 10배가 증가한 것이다. 이 수치들은 엄청난 자연 증가율을 시사한다. 일부 농장주들은 1808년 이후에도 불법적으로 미국으로 데려온 노예들을 계속해서 사들였다. 하지만 그 증가(인구증가)의 대부분은 출생에서 비롯되었다. 노예 소유주들과 노예들 모두의 선호도가 이러한 인구증가의 원인이 되었다. 남부 농장주들은 흑인 여성들에게 많은 아이를 낳도록 장려했다. 그와 동시에, 노예가 된 아프리카계 미국인들은 가정을 사회의 구성단위로 중요하게 여겼다; 가족 간의 유대는 기본적인 인간의 권리를 박탈당한 사람들에게 지지와 위안을 제공했다. 심지어 혹독한 환경 속에서도, 흑인들은 사랑에 빠지고, 결혼하고, 아이를 낳고, 가족들을 부양했다. 지역, 주, 국가 당국의 보호가 부족했지만, 노예가정은 놀라울 정도로 회복력 있는 단체임이 판명되었다.

| 보기분석 |

① Thus – For example 순접(인과관계)
따라서 – 예를 들면

② Furthermore – Instead 순접(부연)
더욱이 – 대신에

③ But – At the same time
그러나 – 그와 동시에

④ Thus – Meanwhile 순접(인과관계)
따라서 – 그동안에

⑤ But – In contrast 역접(대조), 두 번째 빈칸은 역접 표현이 적절하지 않음
그러나 – 대조적으로

| 정답분석 | 빈칸 [A]의 경우 빈칸의 앞 문장에서는 '미국의 계속된 흑인 노예의 유입'을 언급했으나 빈칸을 포함하는 문장에서는 '인구증가의 대부분이 흑인의 출생으로 인한 것임'을 언급했다. 따라서 빈칸을 전후로 글의 흐름이 역접되어 보기 중 역접 표현

인 'But'이 적절하다. 빈칸 [B]의 경우 빈칸의 앞 문장에서 '남부 농장주들이 흑인 여성들에게 많은 아이를 낳을 것을 장려한 것'과 빈칸을 포함한 문장에서 '아프리카계 미국인들은 가정을 사회의 구성단위로 소중하게 여긴 것'은 모두 흑인 인구가 증가하게 된 배경에 해당한다. 빈칸의 직전과 직후 내용이 순접으로 연결되므로 보기 ③ At the same time이 빈칸 [B]에 들어가야 한다. 따라서 정답은 두 빈칸의 조건을 만족하는 보기 ③이다.

16 2017 단국대

정답 ③

| 구문분석 | (For decades), feminists and feminism (S) were almost exclusively evoked (V) (by newspapers, magazines and punditry) (as an ideological punching bag).

수십 년 동안, 페미니스트들과 페미니즘은 거의 전적으로 신문, 잡지 그리고 전문가들에 의해 이념적인 공격의 표적으로 인식되었다.

Not so today, (when [부사절: ~할 때] those terms are breathlessly deployed by the likes of *CoverGirl*, Taylor Swift and Facebook's Sheryl Sandberg).

그러나 *CoverGirl*, 테일러 스위프트(Taylor Swift), 페이스북의 셰릴 샌드버그(Sheryl Sandberg)와 같은 사람들이 그러한 용어들을 숨 돌릴 새 없이 쓰는 오늘날은 그렇지 않다.

Feminism (S), (for better and for worse), has become (V) trendy (C).

페미니즘은 좋든 나쁘든 유행이 되었다.

This kind (S) (of marketplace feminism) is (V) welcome (C) (because [부사절: ~ 때문에] its optics are considered a media-friendly improvement) (on past feminist movements — [대시: 부연설명] more cleavage, less anger).

이러한 종류의 시장 페미니즘은 환영받고 있는데, 이러한 페미니즘의 렌즈가 과거의 페미니스트 운동에 대해 미디어 친화적으로 개선된 것—여성의 가슴골은 더 많이 보여 주고, 분노는 덜 표출하는 것—으로 간주되기 때문이다.

But [등위접속사] it (S) also pulls (V_1) focus (O_1) (from systemic issues) and [등위접속사] places (V_2) it (O_2) (on individuals and personalities).

하지만 그것은 또한 초점을 체제적 문제로부터 끌어와 개인과 성격으로 옮겨 놓았다.

It [가주어]'s (V) easy (C) to see [진주어] Sandberg, for instance, urging women to lean in, and [등위접속사] forget that leaning in puts the onus on women themselves — [대시: 부연설명] rather than on the corporate systems and values (that [관계대명사] oppress all workers regardless of gender).

예를 들어, 샌드버그가 여성들에게 적극적으로 밀고 나아갈 것을 촉구하고, 그런 적극적인 자세가 성별과 상관없이 모든 노동자들을 억압하고 있는 기업 시스템과 가치관보다는 여성 자신에게 부담을 지운다는 점은 잊는 것을 쉽게 볼 수 있다.

| 어휘 |

for decades 수십 년간
feminism ⓝ 페미니즘(여성과 남성의 권리 및 기회의 평등을 핵심으로 하는 여러 형태의 사회적, 정치적 운동과 이론)
exclusively ⓐⓓ 배타적으로, 독점적으로
evoke ⓥ (기억 · 감정을) 불러일으키다
punditry ⓝ 전문가적 의견[방법]
punching bag 샌드백, 공격의 표적
deploy ⓥ 전개하다, 배치하다
the like of ~와 같은 사람[것]
optic ⓝ 눈, (광학 기계의) 렌즈
cleavage ⓝ (옷깃 사이로 보이는) 유방 사이 오목한 부분; (집단의) 분열
personality ⓝ 개성, 성격, 인격
urge ⓥ 재촉하다
lean in (몸을) 기울이다, 적극적으로 밀고 나아가다
onus ⓝ 부담, 무거운 짐
corporate ⓐ 법인[회사]의, 단체의
oppress ⓥ 압박하다, 억압하다
gender ⓝ 성, 성별

| 전문해석 | 수십 년 동안, 페미니스트들과 페미니즘은 거의 전적으로 신문, 잡지 그리고 전문가들에 의해 이념적인 공격의 표적으로 인식되었다. 그러나 *CoverGirl*, 테일러 스위프트(Taylor Swift), 페이스북의 셰릴 샌드버그(Sheryl Sandberg)와 같은 사람

들이 그러한 용어들을 숨 돌릴 새 없이 쓰는 오늘날은 그렇지 않다. 페미니즘은 좋든 나쁘든 유행이 되었다.

이러한 종류의 시장 페미니즘은 환영받고 있는데, 이러한 페미니즘의 렌즈가 과거의 페미니스트 운동에 대해 미디어 친화적으로 개선된 것—여성의 가슴골은 더 많이 보여 주고, 분노는 덜 표출하는 것—으로 간주되기 때문이다. 하지만 그것은 또한 초점을 체제적 문제로부터 끌어와 개인과 성격으로 옮겨 놓았다. 예를 들어, 샌드버그가 여성들에게 적극적으로 밀고 나아갈 것을 촉구하고, 그런 적극적인 자세가 성별과 상관없이 모든 노동자들을 억압하고 있는 기업 시스템과 가치관보다는 여성 자신에게 부담을 지운다는 점은 잊는 것을 쉽게 볼 수 있다.

| 보기분석 | ① however 역접 그러나 ② nevertheless 역접(양보) 그럼에도 불구하고 ③ for instance 예를 들면 ④ in addition 순접 기능을 하지만 '예시'에는 적절하지 않음 게다가

| 정답분석 | 빈칸의 직전 문장에서 '오늘날의 시장 페미니즘이 관심의 초점을 체제적 문제에서 개인과 개성으로 옮겨 놓았다'는 언급과 빈칸을 포함하고 있는 문장에서 샌드버그가 '여성들에게 적극적으로 밀고 나아갈 것을 촉구'하는 것이 '여성 자신에게 부담을 지운다'는 내용은 순접으로 연결된다. 빈칸의 직전 문장에 대한 사례가 빈칸이 포함된 문장이라 볼 수 있다. 따라서 빈칸에는 '예를 들면'이란 의미의 보기 ③이 적절하다.

17 2017 건국대

정답 ①

| 구문분석 | (After simple animal skins), wool(S) is(V) probably the oldest material(C) (used for making clothing).

단순한 동물 가죽 이후에, 양모는 아마도 옷을 만드는 데 사용되는 가장 오래된 재료일지도 모른다.

We(S) do not know(V) exactly when people started to make woolen clothing(O), but(등위접속사) it(S) was(V) probably quite early(C) (in human history).

우리는 사람들이 언제부터 모직 옷을 만들기 시작했는지 정확히 알지 못하지만, 그것은 아마도 인류 역사에서 꽤 이른 시기였을 것이다.

The wool(S) was made(V) (from the hair of whatever kind of animal people had available).

양모는 사람들이 사용할 수 있었던 모든 종류의 털로 만들어졌다.

(Most of the time) these(S) were(V) sheep(C), but (in some desert areas) people(S) made(V) cloth(O) (from camel hair).

대부분 이것들은 양의 털이었지만, 일부 사막 지역에서는 사람들이 낙타의 털로 옷을 만들었다.

(In other areas), they(S_1) used(V_1) goat hair(O_1), and(등위접속사) (in the mountains of South America), they(S_2) used(V_2) the hair(O_2) (from llamas).

다른 지역에서는, 사람들은 염소 털을 사용했고, 남아메리카의 고산지대에서는 라마의 털을 사용했다.

All these kinds(S) (of wool) have(V) one thing(O) (in common): (콜론: 동격) They(S) protect(V) a person's body(O) (from outside changes in temperature).

이런 모든 종류의 양모에는 한 가지 공통점이 있다: 그것들은 외부의 온도 변화로부터 사람의 몸을 보호해 준다는 것이다.

Woolen clothing(S) keeps(V) the body(O) cool($O.C_1$) (in summer) and(등위접속사) warm($O.C_2$) (in winter).

모직 옷은 여름에는 사람의 몸을 시원하게 하고 겨울에는 따뜻하게 해 준다.

| 어휘 | **wool** ⓝ 양털, 양모 **clothing** ⓝ 옷 **woolen** ⓐ 양털의, 모직물의 **camel** ⓝ 낙타 **llama** ⓝ 라마(남미에서 털을 얻거나 짐을 운반하기 위해 가르는 가축)

| 전문해석 | 단순한 동물 가죽 이후에, 양모는 아마도 옷을 만드는 데 사용되는 가장 오래된 재료일지도 모른다. 우리는 사람들이 언제부터 모직 옷을 만들기 시작했는지 정확히 알지 못하지만, 그것은 아마도 인류 역사에서 꽤 이른 시기였을 것이다. 양모는 사람들이 사용할 수 있었던 모든 종류의 털로 만들어졌다. 대부분 이것들은 양의 털이었지만, 일부 사막 지역에서는 사람들이 낙타의 털로 옷을 만들었다. 다른 지역에서는, 사람들은 염소 털을 사용했고, 남아메리카의 고산지대에서는 라마의 털을

사용했다. 이런 모든 종류의 양모에는 한 가지 공통점이 있다: 그것들은 외부의 온도 변화로부터 사람의 몸을 보호해 준다는 것이다. 모직 옷은 여름에는 사람의 몸을 시원하게 하고 겨울에는 따뜻하게 해 준다.

| 보기분석 | ① have one thing in common
한 가지 공통점이 있다
② should be handled carefully
조심스럽게 취급되어야 한다
③ contain special chemical elements
특수 화학 원소를 함유하고 있다
④ are made from the same species of animal
같은 종의 동물로부터 만들어진다
⑤ originate from a specific region in the world
세계의 특정 지역에서 나온다

| 정답분석 | 빈칸 뒤 '콜론(:)'은 재진술의 기능이 있는 구두점이다. 따라서 빈칸 뒤의 '그것들은 외부의 온도 변화로부터 사람의 몸을 보호해 준다는 것이다'라는 내용을 앞 내용의 부연 설명으로 보고 정답을 고른다. 보기 ①을 제외한 나머지 보기들은 모두 부연 설명의 기능을 할 수 없는 의미로 소거법을 활용하여 나머지 보기들을 제거하고 보기 ①을 정답으로 한다.

18 2013 성균관대

정답 ①

| 구문분석 | (At first sight), East Coast Beach is an unlikely place (for Singapore's open-water swimmers) (to gather).
S V C
얼핏 보면 이스트 코스트 해안은 싱가포르의 바다 수영객들을 위해 있을 것 같지 않은 장소이다.

(On any given day), dozens (of ships) lie (at anchor off the shore, (from tramp freighters to oil tankers), (while others cruise the horizon).
S V from A to B: A부터 B까지 부사절: ~하는 동안

언제든, 다른 배들이 수평선을 항해하는 동안, 부정기 화물선에서 유조선에 이르는 수십 척의 배들이 해안에서 닻을 내린다.

등위접속사
But the fast-moving currents (that affect Singapore's isolated beaches) are absent there, (accounting for East Coast Beach's popularity).
S 관계대명사 V C

그러나 싱가포르의 고립된 해변들에 영향을 미치는 빠른 해류가 그곳에는 없고 그것이 이스트 코스트 해안이 인기 있는 이유이다.

대시: 부연설명
True, visibility (in the water) isn't good — the sea gets clouded (by sand) (churned up by all those sluicing hulls and whirling propellers) — but the Singaporean government, (which monitors the quality of water at all public beaches), deems these waters safe and clean (enough for swimming).
S_1 V_1 C S_2 V_2 C S_3 관계대명사 V_3 O O.C
사실, 물속의 가시성은 좋지 않다—물을 튀기고 다니는 선체와 회전하는 프로펠러에 의해 뒤집힌 모래로 바다는 혼탁해졌다—하지만 모든 공공 해변의 수질을 감시하는 싱가포르 정부는 이 물이 수영하기에 충분히 안전하고 깨끗하다고 생각한다.

"Most swimmers are afraid of the dim visibility underwater," says Dad Lim, operator of local swimming school Yellowfish, "but there's no reason to be."
O V S = 등위접속사 V S
"대부분의 수영객들은 물속의 흐릿한 가시성에 대해 걱정합니다."라고 지역 수영 학교 Yellowfish의 운영자 대드 림(Dad Lim)은 말한다. "하지만 그럴 이유가 없습니다."

가주어
And besides, it's best to keep your head above water, (where you can look out for all the waterborne traffic).
접속부사 V C 진주어 관계부사

게다가 머리는 물 밖에 내놓는 게 좋고, 그래야 물 위를 다니는 교통수단에 대해 경계할 수 있다.

| 어휘 | **open-water** ⓝ 개방구역, 바다 **anchor** ⓝ 닻 **tramp** ⓝ 부랑자, 떠돌이
freighter ⓝ 화물선, 화물 수송기 **oil tanker** 유조선[차]
cruise ⓥ 순항하다, (정처 없이) 돌아다니다 **visibility** ⓝ 가시성

churn ⓥ 마구 휘두르다, 휘젓다　　sluice ⓥ (물줄기를 흘려서) 씻다; ~에 수문을 달다
hull ⓝ 선체　　whirl ⓥ 빙빙 돌다, 회전하다　　deem ⓥ ~로 간주하다
dim ⓐ (빛이) 어둑한, 흐릿한　　waterborne ⓐ 물 위에 뜨는, 수상의

| 전문해석 | 얼핏 보면 이스트 코스트 해안은 싱가포르의 바다 수영객들을 위해 있을 것 같지 않은 장소이다. 언제든, 다른 배들이 수평선을 항해하는 동안, 부정기 화물선에서 유조선에 이르는 수십 척의 배들이 해안에서 닻을 내린다. 그러나 싱가포르의 고립된 해변들에 영향을 미치는 빠른 해류가 그곳에는 없고 그것이 이스트 코스트 해안이 인기 있는 이유이다.
사실, 물속의 가시성은 좋지 않다—물을 튀기고 다니는 선체와 회전하는 프로펠러에 의해 뒤집힌 모래로 바다는 혼탁해졌다—하지만 모든 공공 해변의 수질을 감시하는 싱가포르 정부는 이 물이 수영하기에 충분히 안전하고 깨끗하다고 생각한다. "대부분의 수영객들은 물속의 흐릿한 가시성에 대해 걱정합니다."라고 지역 수영 학교 Yellowfish의 운영자 대드 림(Dad Lim)은 말한다. "하지만 그럴 이유가 없습니다." 게다가 머리는 물 밖에 내놓는 게 좋고, 그래야 물 위를 다니는 교통수단에 대해 경계할 수 있다.

| 보기분석 | ① an unlikely place 있을 것 같지 않은 장소
② too far away 너무 멀리
③ the best place 최고의 장소
④ too crowded a place 사람이 너무 많은 장소
⑤ an exciting place 신나는 장소

| 정답분석 | 빈칸과 빈칸의 다음 문장은 순접으로 연결된다. 빈칸의 다음 문장에서 '수십 척의 배들이 해안에서 닻을 내린다'고 했으므로 빈칸을 포함한 문장에서는 이스트 코스트 해안은 언뜻 보기에는 바다 수영객들에게 적당한 해안이 아닌 것처럼 여겨져야 할 것이다. 따라서 두 문장의 흐름을 고려할 때 보기 ①이 정답으로 가장 적절하다.

19 2015 한양대(에리카)

정답 ③

| 구문분석 | Farmers(S) are shifting(V) their spending priorities(O) (from fertilizers and pesticides) (to genetically altered seeds) (that(관계대명사) do the same job).

농부들은 그들의 지출 우선순위를 비료와 살충제로부터 똑같은 일을 하는 유전자 변형 종자로 바꾸고 있다.

Eventually plants(S) could be given(V) desirable traits(D.O) (from animals).
마침내 식물은 동물로부터 바람직한 형질을 얻을 수 있다.

For example, a gene(S) (from bacteria) (that(관계대명사) kills insects) can be put into(V) a plant.
예를 들어, 곤충을 죽이는 박테리아의 유전자가 식물에 심어질 수 있다.

Insects(S) will then avoid(V) it(O).
그러면 곤충들은 그 식물을 피할 것이다.

Biotechnology researchers(S) realized(V) (early on) [that(O) (if(부사절: 만약 ~라면) the genetic instructions for the manufacture of a desirable protein are inserted in a living cell's DNA), that cell not only manufactures the protein but also passes it on to future generations]. (not only A but also B: A뿐만 아니라 B)

생명공학 연구자들은 만약 바람직한 단백질의 제조를 위한 유전적인 명령을 살아 있는 세포의 DNA에 주입하면, 그 세포는 단백질을 제조할 뿐만 아니라 미래 세대에게도 전달한다는 것을 일찍 깨달았다.

(To create(부사적용법: ~하기 위해서) an insect-repellent plant), the appropriate gene(S) needs(V) to be injected(O) only into the parent plant, (which(관계대명사(계속적용법)) subsequently hands down the characteristic to its offspring).
곤충에 강한(병충해에 강한) 식물을 만들기 위해서는, 적절한 유전자가 오직 모체 식물에만 주입될 필요가 있는데 그러면 모체 식물은 그 특성을 자손에게 물려준다.

| 어휘 | **fertilizer** ⓝ 비료 / **pesticide** ⓝ 살충제, 농약 / **protein** ⓝ 단백질 / **repellent** ⓐ 역겨운; (벌레 따위를) 쫓아 버리는 / **subsequently** ⓐⓓⓥ 그 뒤에, 나중에 / **hand down** (후세에) 물려주다 / **offspring** ⓝ 자식, 자손

| 전문해석 | 농부들은 그들의 지출 우선순위를 비료와 살충제로부터 똑같은 일을 하는 유전자 변형 종자로 바꾸고 있다. 마침내 식물은 동물로부터 바람직한 형질을 얻을 수 있다. 예를 들어, 곤충을 죽이는 박테리아의 유전자가 식물에 심어질 수 있다. 그러면 곤충들은 그 식물을 피할 것이다. 생명공학 연구자들은 만약 바람직한 단백질의 제조를 위한 유전적인 명령을 살아 있는 세포의 DNA에 주입하면, 그 세포는 단백질을 제조할 뿐만 아니라 미래 세대에게도 전달한다는 것을 일찍 깨달았다. 곤충에 강한(병충해에 강한) 식물을 만들기 위해서는, 적절한 유전자가 오직 모체 식물에만 주입될 필요가 있는데 그러면 모체 식물은 그 특성을 자손에게 물려준다.

| 보기분석 |
① Largely 순접 기능을 하지만 '예시'에는 적절하지 않음 / 대체로
② However / 그러나 — '역접' 표현이므로 오답
③ For example / 예를 들면
④ On the other hand / 반면에 — '역접' 표현이므로 오답

| 정답분석 | 빈칸의 직전 문장에서 '식물은 동물로부터 바람직한 형질을 얻을 수 있다'고 했으므로 빈칸을 포함하는 문장은 그 사례로서 '곤충을 죽이는 박테리아의 유전자가 식물에 심어질 수 있음'을 설명한 것으로 보인다. 따라서 정답은 예를 들 때 사용되는 보기 ③이 적절하다.

20 2015 이화여대

정답 ①, ③

| 구문분석 |

Originality(S) is(V) what distinguishes art from craft(C).

독창성은 예술과 공예를 구분시켜 주는 것이다.

We(S) may say(V), therefore(접속부사), that it is the yardstick of artistic greatness or importance(O, 명사절).

그러므로 우리는 그것이 예술적 위대함이나 중요성의 척도라고 말할 수 있다.

Unfortunately, it(S_1) is(V_1) also very hard(C) (to define); (세미콜론: 부연설명) the usual synonyms(S_2) — uniqueness, novelty, freshness —(대시: 동격) do not help(V_2) us(O) very much, and(등위접속사) the dictionaries(S_3) tell(V_3) us(I.O) only that an original work must not be a copy, reproduction, imitation, or translation(D.O).

불행하게도, 그것은 또한 정의하기가 어렵다; 일반적인 동의어들—독특함, 새로움, 신선함—은 우리에게 큰 도움을 주지 못하며 사전들은 우리에게 오직 독창적인 작품은 복사, 복제, 모방 또는 번역이 되어서는 안 된다고만 말해 준다.

What they fail to point out(S) is(V) that originality is always relative(C): (콜론: 동격) There(유도부사) is(V) no such thing(S) (as a completely original work of art).

그들이 지적하지 못한 것은 독창성이 항상 상대적이라는 것이다: 완벽하게 독창적인 예술작품 같은 것은 존재하지 않는다.

Thus(접속부사), (if we want to rate works of art on an "originality scale")(부사절: 만약 ~라면) our problem(S) does not lie(V) (in deciding whether or not(~인지 아닌지) a given work is original) but (lie 생략) (in establishing just exactly how original it is). (not A but B: A가 아니라 B)

그러므로, 만일 우리가 "독창성 척도"로 예술작품들을 평가하기를 원한다면, 우리의 문제는 주어진 예술작품이 독창적인지 아닌지를 결정하는 것이 아니라 그것이 정확히 얼마나 독창적인지를 확립하는 것에 있다.

| 어휘 | **originality** ⓝ 독창성 / **synonym** ⓝ 동의어, 유의어 / **novelty** ⓝ 신기함, 진기함 / **reproduction** ⓝ 생식; 복사 / **imitation** ⓝ 모방 / **scale** ⓝ 눈금, 척도 / **rate** ⓥ (특정한 수준으로) 평가하다

| 전문해석 | 독창성은 예술과 공예를 구분시켜 주는 것이다. 그러므로 우리는 그것이 예술적 위대함이나 중요성의 척도라고 말할 수 있다. 불행하게도, 그것은 또한 정의하기가 어렵다; 일반적인 동의어들—독특함, 새로움, 신선함—은 우리에게 큰 도움을 주

지 못하며 사전들은 우리에게 오직 독창적인 작품은 복사, 복제, 모방 또는 번역이 되어서는 안 된다고만 말해 준다. 그들이 지적하지 못한 것은 독창성이 항상 상대적이라는 것이다: 완벽하게 독창적인 예술작품 같은 것은 존재하지 않는다. 그러므로, 만일 우리가 "독창성 척도"로 예술작품들을 평가하기를 원한다면, 우리의 문제는 주어진 예술작품이 독창적인지 아닌지를 결정하는 것이 아니라 그것이 정확히 얼마나 독창적인지를 확립하는 것에 있다.

| 보기분석 | Blank [A]

① yardstick
잣대, 척도

② creativity
창의력

③ pitfall
함정

④ tradition
전통

⑤ craftsmanship
장인정신

Blank [B]

① achieving something original
독창적인 것을 성취하는 것

② distinguishing art from non-art
예술과 비예술을 구별하는 것

③ establishing just exactly how original it is
그것이 정확히 얼마나 독창적인지를 확립하는 것

④ assuming that there are timeless values in art
예술에 시대를 초월한 가치가 있다고 가정하는 것

⑤ representing the lowest common denominator for popular taste
대중적 취향에 대한 가장 낮은 (수준의) 공통분모를 나타내는 것

| 정답분석 | 빈칸 [A]의 경우 빈칸 앞 문장에서 '독창성은 예술과 공예를 구분시켜 준다'고 했기 때문에 인과관계를 나타내는 'therefore'가 포함된 다음 문장에서도 독창성이 '예술적 위대함이나 중요성'을 구분하는 '기준이나 척도'로 설명되어야 한다. 따라서 보기 ①이 정답으로 가장 적절하다. 빈칸 [B]의 경우에는 빈칸 앞 문장에서 '독창성이 항상 상대적이다'고 했으므로 인과관계를 나타내는 'thus'가 포함된 다음 문장에서도 '독창성의 상대적 판단'에 관련된 설명이 필요하다. 따라서 보기 ③이 정답으로 가장 적절하다.

LEVEL 3 특수유형 익히기

8강 문장 배열

Practice

01	②	02	④	03	④	04	②	05	④	06	②	07	④	08	④	09	③	10	③
11	①	12	①	13	④	14	③	15	②	16	④	17	③	18	③	19	①	20	②

01 2018 인하대

정답 ②

| 구문분석 | (For the long centuries of the Middle Ages (500–1350 AD)) the canon of scientific knowledge(S) had experienced(V) little change(O), and(등위접속사) the Catholic Church(S) had preserved(V) acceptance(O) (of a system of beliefs based on the teachings of the ancient Greeks and Romans which it had incorporated into religious doctrine).

중세(서기 500~1350년)의 오랜 세월 동안, 과학지식의 규범에는 거의 변화가 없었으며 가톨릭교회는 스스로가 종교 교리 속으로 통합해 넣었던 고대 그리스와 로마의 가르침을 바탕으로 한 신앙체계를 고수하고 있었다.

[B] (During this period) there(유도부사) was(V) little scientific inquiry(S_1) and experimentation(S_2). Rather(접속부사), students of the sciences(S) simply read(V_2) the works(O_1) of the alleged authorities and accepted(V_3) their word(O_2) (as truth).

이 기간 동안, 과학적 탐구와 실험은 거의 없었다. 오히려, 과학을 배우는 학생들은 권위자라고 전해지는 사람들이 쓴 작품을 그저 읽기만 했고 그들의 말을 진리로 받아들였다.

[A] However(접속부사), (during the Renaissance) this doctrinal passivity(S) began(V) to change(O). The quest(S) (to understand the natural world) led to(V) the revival of botany and anatomy(O) (by thinkers such as(전치사: ~와 같은) Andreas Vesalius during the later sixteenth century).

그러나 르네상스 동안에 이와 같은 교리적인 수동성이 변하기 시작했다. 자연의 세계를 이해하고자 하는 탐구는 뒤이어 16세기 후반 동안 안드레아스 베살리우스(Andreas Vesalius)와 같은 사상가들에 의해 식물학과 해부학의 부활을 유발했다.

[C] These scientific observers(S) were surprised(V) (to find that their conclusions did not always match up with the accepted truths), and(등위접속사) this finding(S) inspired(V) others(O) to delve further into the study of the world around them(O.C).

이들 과학적 관찰자들은 자신들이 내린 결론이 일반적으로 받아들여지고 있는 진리와 항상 일치하는 것은 아니라는 사실을 알고서 깜짝 놀랐으며, 이러한 발견은 다른 사람들로 하여금 그들 주위의 세상에 대한 연구를 더 깊이 파고들도록 영감을 주었다.

| 어휘 |

- canon ⓝ 법규; 규범, 표준
- preserve ⓥ 보전하다, 유지하다; 보존하다
- acceptance ⓝ 받아들임; 수락, 승인
- incorporate ⓥ 통합하다; 혼합하다
- doctrine ⓝ 교의, 교리; 신조
- passivity ⓝ 수동성; 복종
- revival ⓝ 소생, 재생, 부활
- botany ⓝ 식물학
- anatomy ⓝ 해부학
- inquiry ⓝ 조사; 연구, 탐구
- experimentation ⓝ 실험, 실험법
- alleged ⓐ (근거 없이) 주장된, 추정된
- authority ⓝ 권위; 권위자, 대가
- conclusion ⓝ 결론
- match up with ~와 일치하다, ~와 조화되다
- accepted ⓐ 인정된, 받아들여진
- delve ⓥ 탐구하다

| 전문해석 | 중세(서기 500~1350년)의 오랜 세월 동안, 과학지식의 규범에는 거의 변화가 없었으며 가톨릭교회는 스스로가 종교 교리

속으로 통합해 넣었던 고대 그리스와 로마의 가르침을 바탕으로 한 신앙체계를 고수하고 있었다. [B] 이 기간 동안, 과학적 탐구와 실험은 거의 없었다. 오히려, 과학을 배우는 학생들은 권위자라고 전해지는 사람들이 쓴 작품을 그저 읽기만 했고 그들의 말을 진리로 받아들였다. [A] 그러나 르네상스 동안에 이와 같은 교리적인 수동성이 변하기 시작했다. 자연의 세계를 이해하고자 하는 탐구는 뒤이어 16세기 후반 동안 안드레아스 베살리우스(Andreas Vesalius)와 같은 사상가들에 의해 식물학과 해부학의 부활을 유발했다. [C] 이들 과학적 관찰자들은 자신들이 내린 결론이 일반적으로 받아들여지고 있는 진리와 항상 일치하는 것은 아니라는 사실을 알고서 깜짝 놀랐으며, 이러한 발견은 다른 사람들로 하여금 그들 주위의 세상에 대한 연구를 더 깊이 파고들도록 영감을 주었다.

| 정답분석 | '중세시대에 과학지식의 규범은 거의 변화가 없었다'는 주어진 문장과 같은 맥락의 [B]가 먼저 와야 하며 반전이 일어나고 과학적 변화의 시작인 [A]가 그 뒤를 이어야 하며 [C] 문장의 내용도 과학과 관련된 이야기인데 [A] 문장이 과학적 변화의 시작이므로 [C] 문장이 마지막으로 이어지는 것이 자연스럽다.

02 2012 명지대

정답 ④

| 구문분석 | Why does Dickens, (so associated with the affairs of his own time), mean so much (to the British nearly two centuries after his birth)?
(의문문 도치 / Dickens: S / mean: V / much: O)

그가 살았던 시대의 사건들에 밀접하게 관여된 디킨스(Dickens)는 그가 태어난 지 거의 2세기가 지난 지금에도 영국인들에게 왜 그렇게도 많은 의미를 가지는 걸까?

[D] There are two reasons.
(There: 유도부사 / are: V / two reasons: S)
거기에는 두 가지 이유가 있다.

[C] The first is that Dickens never dates.
(The first: S / is: V / that Dickens never dates: C)
첫 번째는 디킨스는 결코 시대에 뒤처지지 않는다.

[A] His novel speaks (as directly to us today) (as it did to its first readers 150 years ago).
(His novel: S / speaks: V / did: 대동사: speak를 받음)
그의 소설은 150년 최초의 독자들에게 그랬던 것처럼 오늘날에도 우리에게 직접 말을 걸고 있다.

[B] The other reason is his infectious confidence (in the essential goodness of human nature).
(The other reason: S / is: V / his infectious confidence: C)
또 다른 이유는 인간 본성의 근본적 선함에 대한 그의 확신이 우리를 감화시킨다는 것이다.

| 어휘 | **affair** ⓝ 사건, 일 **infectious** ⓐ 전염되기 쉬운, 감염성의 **date** ⓥ 낡아빠지다, 시대에 뒤떨어지다

| 전문해석 | 그가 살았던 시대의 사건들에 밀접하게 관여된 디킨스(Dickens)는 그가 태어난 지 거의 2세기가 지난 지금에도 영국인들에게 왜 그렇게도 많은 의미를 가지는 걸까? [D] 거기에는 두 가지 이유가 있다. [C] 첫 번째는 디킨스는 결코 시대에 뒤처지지 않는다. [A] 그의 소설은 150년 최초의 독자들에게 그랬던 것처럼 오늘날에도 우리에게 직접 말을 걸고 있다. [B] 또 다른 이유는 인간 본성의 근본적 선함에 대한 그의 확신이 우리를 감화시킨다는 것이다.

| 정답분석 | 찰스 디킨스의 소설이 인기 있는 이유를 두 가지로 설명하고 있는 글이므로 두 가지 이유가 있다는 포괄적 진술인 [D]가 제일 먼저 오고 the first로 시작하는 문장인 [C]가 그 뒤에 오며, [C] 문장의 내용인 '시대에 뒤처지지 않는다'의 세부적인 재진술인 [A]가 이어지고 마지막으로 the other reason(다른 이유) 문장인 [B]가 이어지는 것이 자연스럽다.

03 2018 한성대

정답 ④

| 구문분석 | For the past 30 years, computer-vision technologies have struggled to perform well, (even in tasks as (mundane) as correctly recognizing faces in photographs).
(computer-vision technologies: S / have struggled: V / to perform well: O)
(as ~ as 원급 구문에서 앞의 as는 부사이며 뒤의 as는 부사절을 이끄는 접속사이다.)

지난 30년에 걸쳐, 컴퓨터 시각 기술은 사진에서 얼굴을 올바르게 인식하는 것만큼 평범한 과제에서조차도 나은 성과를 내도록 노력을 기울여 왔다.

Recently, however, breakthroughs (in deep learning) have finally enabled computers to interpret several kinds of images better (than people do).
접속부사 S V O O.C
부사 well의 비교급
하지만, 최근에 딥 러닝의 획기적인 발전으로 마침내 컴퓨터는 여러 종류의 이미지를 인간보다 더 잘 해석할 수 있게 되었다.

[D] Recent progress (in a deep-learning approach) (known as a convolutional neural network (CNN)) is essential (to the latest strides).
S V C
CNN(회선신경망)이라고 알려진 딥 러닝 접근법에서의 최근의 발전은 딥 러닝의 가장 새로운 도약에 필수적이다.

[C] For instance, consider images of dogs and cats (to understand its prowess).
접속부사 V O 부사적용법: ~하기 위하여
예를 들어, CNN의 뛰어난 능력을 이해하기 위해 개와 고양이의 이미지를 생각해 보자.

[E] (Whereas humans can easily differentiate between them), CNNs allow machines to categorize specific breeds more successfully than people can.
부사절: ~ 반면에 S V O O.C
인간은 쉽게 그 이미지들을 서로 분간할 수 있는 반면에, CNN은 기계들이 특정 품종들을 인간보다 더 잘 분류하도록 도움을 준다.

[B] It excels (because it is better able to learn, and draw inferences from subtle, revealing patterns in the images).
S V 부사절: 때문에
CNN은 이미지들에 있는 미세하고 의미 있는 패턴들을 학습하고 또 거기서 추론해 내는 일을 더 잘 해낼 수 있기 때문에 뛰어나다.

| 어휘 | **breakthrough** ⓝ 획기적인 발전 **interpret** ⓥ 이해하다, 해석하다 **subtle** ⓐ 미묘한, 포착하기 어려운
revealing ⓐ 흥미로운 사실을 드러내는 **prowess** ⓝ 용기, 역량; 뛰어난 능력 **convolutional** ⓐ 나선형의
stride ⓝ 진보, 발전, 도약 **differentiate** ⓥ 분간하다 **breed** ⓝ 품종

| 전문해석 | 지난 30년에 걸쳐, 컴퓨터 시각 기술은 사진에서 얼굴을 올바르게 인식하는 것만큼 평범한 과제에서조차도 나은 성과를 내도록 노력을 기울여 왔다. 그러나 최근에 딥 러닝의 획기적인 발전으로 마침내 컴퓨터는 여러 종류의 이미지를 인간보다 더 잘 해석할 수 있게 되었다.
[D] CNN(회선신경망)이라고 알려진 딥 러닝 접근법에서의 최근의 발전은 딥 러닝의 가장 새로운 도약에 필수적이다. [C] 예를 들어, CNN의 뛰어난 능력을 이해하기 위해 개와 고양이의 이미지를 생각해 보자. [E] 인간은 쉽게 그 이미지들을 서로 분간할 수 있는 반면에, CNN은 기계들이 특정 품종들을 인간보다 더 잘 분류하도록 도움을 준다. [B] CNN은 이미지들에 있는 미세하고 의미 있는 패턴들을 학습하고 또 거기서 추론해 내는 일을 더 잘 해낼 수 있기 때문에 뛰어나다.

| 정답분석 | 이 글의 앞부분에서 '컴퓨터는 최근 딥 러닝의 발전으로 여러 종류의 이미지를 인간보다 더 잘 해석할 수 있게 되었다'고 하였다. 여기에 이어지는 단락의 첫 문장은 딥 러닝의 획기적인 발전이 무엇인지에 대한 세부적인 내용이 이어져야 한다. 따라서 최근에 발전된 딥 러닝 접근 방식인 '회선신경망(CNN)'을 처음 언급한 [D]가 처음으로 와야 하고, 회선신경망의 예시로 개와 고양이를 다룬 [C]가 그다음에 오고, 그리고 개와 고양이를 specific breeds로 받을 수 있는 [E]가 그다음에 오며, 마지막으로 회선신경망이 왜 뛰어난지를 설명한 [B]가 와야 자연스럽다.

04 2012 인하대

정답 ②

| 구문분석 | (In recent decades), large numbers of Americans have led physically inactive lives.
S V O
최근 수십 년 동안, 많은 미국인들은 신체적으로 활동적이지 않은 생활을 해 왔다.

ⓐⓓ 집으로
[A] People shuffle out (to their cars in the morning), sit or stand (in one place most of the day), ride home, and settle (into easy chairs).
S V_1 V_2 V_3 V_4
사람들은 아침에 발을 질질 끌며 차로 걸어 나와서, 낮 시간 대부분을 한 장소에서 앉거나 서서 보내고, 집까지 차를 타고 와서, 편한 의자에 앉는다.

[D] In the process, people get little vigorous exercise.
S V O
이러한 과정에서, 사람들은 활기찬 운동을 거의 하지 않는다.

[C] Today, however, more and more people are jogging, swimming, bicycling, and engaging (in other forms of aerobic exercise).
접속부사 S V_1 V_2 V_3 V_4

하지만 오늘날, 점점 더 많은 사람들이 조깅을 하고, 수영을 하고, 자전거를 타고 기타 여러 가지의 에어로빅 운동을 한다.

[B] The exercise boom is a good example (of how general social values and expectations affect health-related behaviors).
S V C

이런 운동의 대유행은 보편적인 사회의 가치와 기대가 건강에 관련된 행동에 어떻게 영향을 끼치는지를 보여 주는 좋은 예이다.

| 어휘 | **shuffle** ⓥ 발을 질질 끌며 걷다 **settle into** 자리 잡다 **vigorous** ⓐ 정력적인, 활기찬

| 전문해석 | 최근 수십 년 동안, 많은 미국인들은 신체적으로 활동적이지 않은 생활을 해 왔다. [A] 사람들은 아침에 발을 질질 끌며 차로 걸어 나와서, 낮 시간 대부분을 한 장소에서 앉거나 서서 보내고, 집까지 차를 타고 와서, 편한 의자에 앉는다. [D] 이러한 과정에서, 사람들은 활기찬 운동을 거의 하지 않는다. [C] 하지만 오늘날, 점점 더 많은 사람들이 조깅을 하고, 수영을 하고, 자전거를 타고 기타 여러 가지의 에어로빅 운동을 한다. [B] 이런 운동의 대유행은 보편적인 사회의 가치와 기대가 건강에 관련된 행동에 어떻게 영향을 끼치는지를 보여 주는 좋은 예이다.

| 정답분석 | 최근 수십 년 동안 미국인들이 신체적으로 활동적이지 않았다는 문제를 지적하는 첫 문장에 이어서 그 문제점을 구체적으로 진술하는 내용의 [A], [D] 문장이 그 뒤에 오는 게 자연스럽다. 그리고 그 뒤에 반전과 함께 오는 오늘날 운동이 유행하고 있다는 내용의 [B], [C] 문장이 나와야 한다. [A], [B] 중에서는 [A] 문장 이후에 앞 문장의 내용을 받는 In the process가 들어 있는 [D] 문장이 와야 하며, 이어서 역접의 however가 있는 [C] 문장이 와야 자연스럽다.

05 2016 한양대(에리카) 정답 ④

| 구문분석 | [C] Social networking makes it very easy to have friends — lots and lots of friends.
가목적어
S V O.C 진목적어
소셜 네트워킹을 통해서 우리는 아주 많은 친구를 쉽게 사귈 수 있다.

[A] Hundreds of millions of people have joined Facebook, KakaoTalk, and other sites (so that they can communicate (with those friends online).
S V O 부사절: 결과 S V

수억 명의 사람들이 페이스북, 카카오톡, 그리고 그 이외의 다른 사이트에 가입했기 때문에 사람들은 친구들과 온라인상에서 대화를 나눌 수 있다.

[B] However, the meaning of the word "friend" seems (to have changed).
접속부사 S V
그러나 (온라인상에서) '친구'라는 단어의 의미는 변한 것처럼 보인다.

(In the past), a friend was someone (that) (you had a close personal relationship with).
S V C
과거에, 친구는 당신과 가까운 인간관계를 맺고 있던 사람이었다.

Now, anyone in the world can be your friend (online)!
S V C
지금은 이 세계의 누구라도 온라인상에서 당신의 친구가 될 수 있다!

Some people have thousands of friends, but what do you do (if you don't want so many friends)?
S V O 의문문 도치 부사절: 만일 ~라면
어떤 사람들은 수천 명의 친구를 가지고 있다. 그러나 만일 당신이 그처럼 많은 친구를 원하지 않는다면 어떻게 하겠는가?

Easy! You can dump an unwanted friend (with just one press of your finger).
S V O
그 문제는 쉽게 해결된다! 손가락을 한번 누르는 것을 통해서 당신은 원치 않는 친구를 버릴 수 있다.

| 어휘 | communicate ⓥ 의사소통하다 personal relationship 대인 관계 dump ⓥ 버리다, 헤어지다

| 전문해석 | [C] 소셜 네트워킹을 통해서 우리는 아주 많은 친구를 쉽게 사귈 수 있다. [A] 수억 명의 사람들이 페이스북, 카카오톡, 그리고 그 이외의 다른 사이트에 가입했기 때문에 사람들은 친구들과 온라인상에서 대화를 나눌 수 있다. [B] 그러나 (온라인상에서) '친구'라는 단어의 의미는 변한 것처럼 보인다. 과거에, 친구는 당신과 가까운 인간관계를 맺고 있던 사람이었다. 지금은 이 세계의 누구라도 온라인상에서 당신의 친구가 될 수 있다! 어떤 사람들은 수천 명의 친구를 가지고 있다. 그러나 만일 당신이 그처럼 많은 친구를 원하지 않는다면 어떻게 하겠는가? 그 문제는 쉽게 해결된다! 손가락을 한번 누르는 것을 통해서 당신은 원치 않는 친구를 버릴 수 있다.

| 정답분석 | 소셜 네트워킹을 통해 친구를 사귀기 쉬워졌다는 포괄적이고 일반적인 진술인 [C]가 첫 문장으로 적합하며 그러한 소셜 네트워킹의 구체적 진술이라 할 수 있는 페이스북, 카카오톡에 관련된 진술인 [A]가 그 뒤를 이어야 하며, 하지만 그 친구의 의미는 변한 것 같다고 진술하는 [B]가 그 뒤에 이어져야 그다음 문장부터 진술하는 과거와 현재의 친구의 의미의 변화와도 자연스럽게 연결된다.

06 2018 국민대

정답 ②

| 구문분석 | [B] A study(S) (conducted by the University of Queensland's School of Pharmacy) (involving more than 12,000 Australians) revealed(V) that the benefits of a fresh produce-rich diet extend beyond physical health(O).

퀸즐랜드(Queensland) 대학교 약학대학에서 12,000명 이상의 호주 국민들을 대상으로 실시한 한 연구에 따르면, 신선한 농산물이 풍부한 식단이 가져다주는 이점은 신체적인 건강 이상인 것으로 나타났다.

[C] (With every added daily portion of fruits or vegetables (up to eight)), the subjects' happiness levels(S) rose(V) slightly.

하루에 과일이나 채소를 먹는 횟수가 매일 늘어날 때마다 (최대 8회까지) 피실험자의 행복 수준은 약간씩 상승했다.

[D] The researchers(S) calculated(V) [that(O) (if someone were to switch from a diet free of fruit and vegetables to eight servings per day), he or she(S) would theoretically gain(V) **as** much life satisfaction(O) **as** someone who transitioned from unemployment to a job].

as ~ as 원급 구문에서 앞의 as는 부사이며 뒤의 as는 부사절을 이끄는 접속사이다.

연구원들은 누군가가 과일과 채소가 전혀 없는 식단으로부터 하루에 8번 과일과 채소를 먹는 것으로 바꾸는 경우, 이론적으로 그 사람은 실업 상태에서 일자리를 얻게 된 사람만큼의 삶의 만족도를 얻게 될 것이라고 계산했다.

[A] The exact reason(S) is(V) unclear(C), but it(S) may be related(V) (to the effect of carotenoid levels in the blood).

정확한 이유는 분명하지 않지만, 혈중 카로티노이드 수준이 미치는 영향과 관련이 있을지 모른다.

| 어휘 | **pharmacy** ⓝ 약학, 약국 **benefit** ⓝ 이익, 이득
produce-rich ⓐ 농산물[천연산물]이 풍부한 **extend** ⓥ 퍼지다, 연장되다; 미치다
portion ⓝ 일부, 부분 **slightly** ⓐⓓ 약간, 조금 **calculate** ⓥ 계산하다, 산정[추산]하다
theoretically ⓐⓓ 이론상, 이론적으로 **transition** ⓥ 이행하다, 변천하다

| 전문해석 | [B] 퀸즐랜드(Queensland) 대학교 약학대학에서 12,000명 이상의 호주 국민들을 대상으로 실시한 한 연구에 따르면, 신선한 농산물이 풍부한 식단이 가져다주는 이점은 신체적인 건강 이상인 것으로 나타났다. [C] 하루에 과일이나 채소를 먹는 횟수가 매일 늘어날 때마다 (최대 8회까지) 피실험자의 행복 수준은 약간씩 상승했다. [D] 연구원들은 누군가가 과일과 채소가 전혀 없는 식단으로부터 하루에 8번 과일과 채소를 먹는 것으로 바꾸는 경우, 이론적으로 그 사람은 실업 상태에서 일자리를 얻게 된 사람만큼의 삶의 만족도를 얻게 될 것이라고 계산했다. [A] 정확한 이유는 분명하지 않지만, 혈중 카로티노이드 수준이 미치는 영향과 관련이 있을지 모른다.

| 정답분석 | 새로운 연구의 결과를 알려 주는 포괄적 진술인 [B]가 글의 첫 부분으로 가장 적절하고, [B]의 끝에서 언급한 연구 결과의 내용인 '신체 건강상의 이득'에 대해 구체적으로 부연설명하고 있는 내용인 [C]과 [D]가 그다음에 와야 하는데, 구체적인 실험 결과인 채소 먹는 횟수가 늘어날 때마다 행복 수준이 올라갔다는 [C]가 먼저 오고 이 결과를 놓고 구체적으로 계산(추정)한 [D]가 이어져야 한다. 마지막으로 앞 문장들의 내용에 대한 이유를 언급하고 있는 [A]가 마지막에 와야 자연스럽다.

07 2018 한양대(에리카)

정답 ④

| 구문분석 | All cultures(S) have(V) collections of tales(O) (handed down from generation to generation) (that(관계대명사) are collectively known as "folklore.")

모든 문화에는 대대로 전해져 내려오는 이야기 모음들을 가지고 있는데, 이것은 다 집합해서 '민속'이라 알려져 있다.

Urban legends(S) are(V) simply contemporary examples(O) (of folklore). But what, exactly, are(V) urban legends(S)? (의문문 도치)

도시 전설은 단순히 민속의 현대적인 예이다. 그러나 정확하게 도시 전설이란 무엇인가?

For one thing, (despite their name), they(S) do not necessarily concern(V) big cities(O). A better name(S) (for them) might be(V) contemporary legends(C).

우선, 그 명칭에도 불구하고, 도시 전설은 반드시 대도시에 관한 것은 아니다. 도시 전설의 더 나은 명칭은 '현대 전설'일지도 모른다.

[C] The name urban legends(S) — which was invented by folklorist Richard Dorson in the 1960s — was first used(V) (to distinguish them from legends of an earlier time)(부사적용법: ~하기 위하여), (which(관계대명사) primarily had rural settings).

도시 전설이라는 명칭은 1960년대에 민속학자 리처드 도슨(Richard Dorson)에 의해 만들어진 것으로, 처음에는 주로 시골을 배경으로 했던 이전 시대의 전설들과 구별하기 위해 사용되었다.

[A] But (in some ways) the term urban legends(S) is(V) quite appropriate(C).

그러나 어떤 면에서는 '도시 전설'이라는 용어가 매우 적절하다.

[B] (Just as many medieval stories were set in forests, full of dangers and mysteries)(부사절: ~처럼, ~듯이), many modern legends(S) take place(V) (in big cities).

많은 중세 이야기들이 위험과 신비로 가득한 숲을 배경으로 했던 것처럼, 많은 현대 전설들은 대도시에서 발생한다.

Our cities(S) sometimes seem(V) as frightening(C) (as those dark forests did to our ancestors). (as ~ as 원급 구문에서 앞의 as는 부사이며 뒤의 as는 부사절을 이끄는 접속사이다.)

우리의 도시들은 때때로 어두운 숲들이 우리 조상들에게 무섭게 여겨졌던 것만큼 무섭게 여겨진다.

| 어휘 |
hand down 전하다, 남기다
collectively ⓐⓓ 집합적으로, 일괄하여
folklore ⓝ 민간전승, 민속; 민속학
urban legend 도시(형) 전설(확실한 근거가 없는데도 사실인 것처럼 사람들 사이에 퍼지는 놀라운 이야기)
contemporary ⓐ 동시대의; 현대의, 당대의
concern ⓥ 관계하다, 관련하다
appropriate ⓐ 적합한, 적절한
folklorist ⓝ 민속학자
distinguish ⓥ 구별[분간]하다, 식별하다
frightening ⓐ 무서운, 놀라운

| 전문해석 | 모든 문화에는 대대로 전해져 내려오는 이야기 모음들을 가지고 있는데, 이것은 다 집합해서 '민속'이라 알려져 있다. 도시 전설은 단순히 민속의 현대적인 예이다. 그러나 정확하게 도시 전설이란 무엇인가? 우선, 그 명칭에도 불구하고, 도시 전설은 반드시 대도시에 관한 것은 아니다. 도시 전설의 더 나은 명칭은 '현대 전설'일지도 모른다. [C] 도시 전설이라는 명칭은 1960년대에 민속학자 리처드 도슨(Richard Dorson)에 의해 만들어진 것으로, 처음에는 주로 시골을 배경으로 했던 이전 시대의 전설들과 구별하기 위해 사용되었다. [A] 그러나 어떤 면에서는 '도시 전설'이라는 용어가 매우 적절하다. [B] 많은 중세 이야기들이 위험과 신비로 가득한 숲을 배경으로 했던 것처럼, 많은 현대 전설들은 대도시에서 발생한다. 우리의 도시들은 때때로 어두운 숲들이 우리 조상들에게 무섭게 여겨졌던 것만큼 무섭게 여겨진다.

| 정답분석 | 앞에서 도시 건설이 반드시 대도시에 관한 것은 아니기 때문에 더 나은 명칭은 현대 전설일지도 모른다고 했으므로, 도시 전설이라는 명칭은 누구에 의해 만들어졌으며 처음에 어떻게 사용되었는지에 대해 설명하고 있는 [C]가 가장 먼저 와야 한다. 그리고 역접의 접속사 But이 온 후에 어떤 면에서는 도시 전설이라는 용어가 적절하다고 한 [A]가 그다음에 와야 하고, 많은 현대 전설들은 대도시에서 발생한다고 이에 대한 부연설명을 하고 있는 [B]가 마지막에 와야 적절하다. 그러면 '오늘날의 도시도 과거의 숲만큼이나 무섭다'고 한 마지막 문장에 잘 연결되며 자연스럽다.

08 2018 서강대

정답 ④

| 구문분석 | [C] The uncanny ability (to withstand prolonged cold) results (in part) (from an adaptation) (that thirteen-lined ground squirrels have developed in molecules they share with other mammals).
S / V / 관계대명사

미국 줄무늬 밭다람쥐들이 장기간 이어지는 추위를 버텨 낼 수 있는 불가사의한 능력은 부분적으로 그들이 다른 포유류들과 공유하는 분자들 속에 발달시킨 어떤 적응의 결과이다.

[A] Unique properties of TRPM8, a cold-sensing protein (found in their systems), shield these rodents (from harsh weather).
S / = / V / O

그들의 몸에서 발견되는 저온 감지 단백질인 TRPM8의 고유한 특성으로 인해 이 설치류들은 혹독한 날씨를 견뎌 낼 수 있다.

부사절: 때문에

[D] It's really important [because (if they're too cold), they can't hibernate].
S V / C / 부사절: 만일 ~라면

그것은 정말 중요한데, 만약 체온이 너무 떨어지면 그들은 동면할 수 없기 때문이다.

[B] This new research (about TRPM8) brings scientists (closer to understanding enigmas of hibernation).
S / V / O

TRPM8에 대한 이러한 새로운 연구는 과학자들이 동면의 수수께끼를 이해하는 데 더 가까이 가도록 해 주었다.

| 어휘 |

protein ⓝ 단백질 **rodent** ⓝ 설치류 **enigma** ⓝ 수수께끼
uncanny ⓐ 기묘한 **withstand** ⓥ 견디다, 이겨 내다 **prolonged** ⓐ 오래 계속되는, 장기적인
thirteen-lined ground squirrel ⓝ 미국 줄무늬 밭다람쥐 **mammal** ⓝ 포유류
hibernate ⓥ 동면하다

| 전문해석 | [C] 미국 줄무늬 밭다람쥐들이 장기간 이어지는 추위를 버텨 낼 수 있는 불가사의한 능력은 부분적으로 그들이 다른 포유류들과 공유하는 분자들 속에 발달시킨 어떤 적응의 결과이다. [A] 그들의 몸에서 발견되는 저온 감지 단백질인 TRPM8의 고유한 특성으로 인해 이 설치류들은 혹독한 날씨를 견뎌 낼 수 있다. [D] 그것은 정말 중요한데, 만약 체온이 너무 떨어지면 그들은 동면할 수 없기 때문이다. [B] TRPM8에 대한 이러한 새로운 연구는 과학자들이 동면의 수수께끼를 이해하는 데 더 가까이 가도록 해 주었다.

| 정답분석 | 나머지 문장들은 대명사나 지시사가 존재하기 때문에 첫 문장으로 불가능하지만 [C] 문장은 대명사나 지시사가 존재하지 않기 때문에 첫 문장으로 가장 적합하다. 그리고 [C]의 thirteen-lined ground squirrels를 their와 these rodents로 받은 [A]가 그다음에 와야 하며, [A]의 TRPM8을 It으로 받아서 중요하다고 언급한 [D]가 그다음에 와야 하며, [D]의 hibernate를 hibernation으로 받은 [B]가 마지막으로 오는 것이 자연스럽다.

09 2012 이화여대

정답 ③

| 구문분석 | [C] (With the granting of the vote to women), 'citizen' finally became a universally available identity (in Britain).
S / V / C

여성에게 참정권이 부여되면서 마침내 '시민'은 영국에서 보편적으로 얻을 수 있는 정체성이 되었다.

[E] (For the first time), every adult was promised the right (to participate fully and equally in social and economic life) and (to help shape its future forms), (together with a responsibility to contribute to building a sense of communality).

S V D.O 등위접속사

처음으로 모든 성인들이 사회적 · 경제적 삶에 있어서 완전하고 평등하게 참여할 수 있는 권리, 그리고 공동체의 연대감을 형성해 가는 데 기여하는 책임감과 더불어 미래의 형태를 형성할 권리를 약속받았다.

[A] This new social contract was underwritten (by the expectation) (that the resources (needed to support it) would be forthcoming).

S V = S V C

이러한 새로운 사회계약은 그 계약이 유지되는 데 필요한 자원들이 계속될 것이라는 기대에 의하여 승인되었다.

[D] Some of these were material (such as an adequate lifetime income, healthcare and personal safety).

S V C 전치사: ~와 같은

이러한 것의 일부는 충분한 종신 수입, 건강관리, 그리고 개인의 안전 등이다.

[B] Others were cultural resources (for citizenship): information, knowledge, representation, and participation.

S V C 콜론: 세부적 내용 재진술

또 다른 것들로는 정보, 지식, 대의, 그리고 참여와 같은 시민권에 대한 문화적 자원들이다.

| 어휘 | **social contract** 사회 계약설, 사회 계약(임금 상승률에 관한 정부 · 노동자 간의 협정)
underwrite ⓥ ~의 아래에 쓰다[기명하다] **forthcoming** ⓐ 곧 닥쳐올; 솔직한
granting ⓝ 승낙, 수여, 인정 **identity** ⓝ 정체성 **responsibility** ⓝ 의무, 책임
contribute ⓥ 기여하다, 공헌하다 **communality** ⓝ 공동체, 연대감

| 전문해석 | [C] 여성에게 참정권이 부여되면서 마침내 '시민'은 영국에서 보편적으로 얻을 수 있는 정체성이 되었다. [E] 처음으로 모든 성인들이 사회적 · 경제적 삶에 있어서 완전하고 평등하게 참여할 수 있는 권리, 그리고 공동체의 연대감을 형성해 가는 데 기여하는 책임감과 더불어 미래의 형태를 형성할 권리를 약속받았다. [A] 이러한 새로운 사회계약은 그 계약이 유지되는 데 필요한 자원들이 계속될 것이라는 기대에 의하여 승인되었다. [D] 이러한 것의 일부는 충분한 종신 수입, 건강관리, 그리고 개인의 안전 등이다. [B] 또 다른 것들로는 정보, 지식, 대의, 그리고 참여와 같은 시민권에 대한 문화적 자원들이다.

| 정답분석 | 가장 일반적인 문장 [C]가 먼저 나와야 하며 [C]의 내용에 있는 '시민'에 대한 구체적 설명이 이어지는 문장인 [E]가 그다음으로 적합하다. 그리고 [E] 문장에서 모든 성인들이 권리와 책임을 동시에 부여받고 있다고 했는데 이것은 기존과 다른 새로운 계약이므로 [A]의 This new social contract로 받을 수 있다. 그리고 [A]에 있는 자원들의 예를 Some과 others를 이용하여 예를 들고 있으므로 [D] 다음 [B]가 이어져야 자연스럽다.

10 2018 서강대

정답 ③

| 구문분석 | [C] A diet of fiber-rich foods reduces the risk (of developing diabetes, heart disease and arthritis).

S V O

섬유질이 풍부한 식단은 당뇨병, 심장병 그리고 관절염 발병의 위험을 낮춘다.

[A] Indeed, the evidence (for fiber's benefits) extends (beyond any particular ailment).

접속부사 S V

실제로는, 섬유질의 장점들에 대한 증거는 특정한 질병을 넘어선다.

[D] That's why experts are always saying how good dietary fiber is for us.

S V C

바로 그것이 전문가들은 식이 섬유가 우리에게 얼마나 좋은지를 항상 말하는 이유이다.

[B] But (while the benefits are clear), it's not so clear why fiber is so great.

부사절: ~ 반면에 가주어 C 진주어

그러나 그 이점들이 명백한 반면, 섬유질이 왜 그리 좋은지는 불분명하다.

| 어휘 | fiber ⓝ 섬유질 ailment ⓝ 질병 diabetes ⓝ 당뇨병
arthritis ⓝ 관절염 dietary ⓐ 음식물의

| 전문해석 | [C] 섬유질이 풍부한 식단은 당뇨병, 심장병 그리고 관절염 발병의 위험을 낮춘다. [A] 실제로는, 섬유질의 장점들에 대한 증거는 특정한 질병을 넘어선다. [D] 바로 그것이 전문가들은 식이 섬유가 우리에게 얼마나 좋은지를 항상 말하는 이유이다. [B] 그러나 그 이점들이 명백한 반면에, 섬유질이 왜 그리 좋은지는 불분명하다.

| 정답분석 | '섬유질이 당뇨병, 심장병, 그리고 관절염 발병의 위험을 낮춘다'는 섬유질의 특정 질병에 유리하다는 일반적 사실을 진술하는 내용인 [C]를 가장 먼저 언급해야 하며, 섬유질의 장점은 그러한 특정한 질병에만 제한되지 않고 더 큰 장점이 있다는 내용의 [A]가 이어져야 하며, 그다음 [D]에서 이러한 섬유질의 특정 질병에 대한 이점과 그것을 넘어서는 이점으로 인해 전문가들이 식이 섬유 섭취를 권장한다는 문장이 와야 하며 [B]에서 그러나 왜 섬유질이 그렇게 우리 몸에 좋은지는(구체적으로 어떤 작용을 해서 좋은지) 아직 불분명하다고 말하는 것이 자연스러운 순서이다.

11 2011 강남대

정답 ①

| 구문분석 | [D] (Many centuries ago), (in a far-off country), there(유도부사) lived(V) a king (who(관계대명사) had some rather strange ideas).
수 세기 전 아주 먼 나라에 조금 이상한 생각을 가진 한 왕이 살았다.

[A] (For one thing), this king(S) had(V) his own particular principle(O) (of carrying out justice and deciding cases of law).
우선, 이 왕은 정의를 실행하고 법률소송을 결정하는 자신만의 독특한 원칙을 가지고 있었다.

[E] (When(부사절: 때) a person was accused of some crime), he(S) was not taken(V) (before(전치사: ~ 앞에(시간× 공간○)) a judge or the usual court of law).
한 사람이 어떤 범죄혐의로 고소되었을 때, 그는 판사 앞으로, 즉 보통의 법정으로 끌려가지 않았다.

[C] Instead(접속부사), he(S) was taken(V) (to a large arena).
그 대신에, 그는 큰 경기장으로 끌려갔다.

[B] Here(유도부사) he(S) was made(V) to stand a special trial(O.C) (before the king himself).
여기에서 그는 국왕이 주재하는 특별재판에 서게 되었다.

| 어휘 | **for one thing** 우선 첫째로, 우선 한 가지 이유는 **carry out** 수행하다, 이행하다
be made to *do* (강제로) ~하게 되다 **arena** ⓝ 경기장, 무대 **far-off** ⓐ 먼
be accused of ~로 비난받다, 고소되다

| 전문해석 | [D] 수 세기 전 아주 먼 나라에 조금 이상한 생각을 가진 한 왕이 살았다. [A] 우선, 이 왕은 정의를 실행하고 법률소송을 결정하는 자신만의 독특한 원칙을 가지고 있었다. [E] 한 사람이 어떤 범죄혐의로 고소되었을 때, 그는 판사 앞으로, 즉 보통의 법정으로 끌려가지 않았다. [C] 그 대신에, 그는 큰 경기장으로 끌려갔다. [B] 여기에서 그는 국왕이 주재하는 특별재판에 서게 되었다.

| 정답분석 | '수 세기 전 어느 먼 나라에 이상한 생각을 가진 한 왕이 살았다'는 글 전체의 배경을 알려 주면서 포괄적인 진술인 (D)가 가장 앞에 나와야 한다. 그리고 구체적 진술들은 지시어와 지시 대상과의 관계를 따져 가며 정답을 찾을 수 있다. [D] 문장의 a king은 [A] 문장의 this king으로 받아야 하므로 [D] 다음 [A]가 이어져야 하며, [E] 문장에서 범죄혐의로 고소되었을 때, 법정으로 가지 않았다고 하였기 때문에 그 뒤에는 '그 대신 큰 경기장으로 끌려갔다'는 내용의 [C]가 이어져야 자연스럽다. 그리고 또한 [C] 문장의 a large arena는 [B] 문장의 here로 받을 수 있다.

12 2013 이화여대

정답 ①

| 구문분석 | [C] Languages are vanishing (in all parts of the world), and the course (of events) is similar (everywhere).
S V S V C

전 세계 모든 곳에서 언어들이 사라지고 있고, 그 전개 상황은 모든 곳에서 다 비슷하다.

[A] People stop using a local language (with few speakers) and shift (to one) (that has more speakers and is in general use over a larger area).
S_1 V_1 O V_2 관계대명사

사람들은 사용자가 적은 지역 언어 사용을 중단하고 더 많은 사용자가 있고 일반적으로 더 널리 사용되는 언어로 이동한다.

[E] The reasons are similar (everywhere).
S V C

그 이유들은 어디서나 비슷하다.

[D] School education is expanding (in almost all countries), and is usually offered (only in big languages). Business and communications also become more important, (which means a larger need for a language used by more people).
S V_1 등위접속사 V_2 S V C 관계대명사

모든 나라에서 학교 교육이 확장되고 있고 흔히 주요 언어로만 제공된다. 사업과 통신 분야 역시 더욱 중요해지고 있는데, 이것은 더 많은 사람들이 하나의 언어에 대한 필요성이 커진다는 것을 의미한다.

[B] All of these mean more contacts (with people) (who do not belong to the local environment and do not speak the local language).
S V O 관계대명사

이 모든 것은 그 지역 사회에 속하지도 않고 그 지역 언어를 사용하지 않는 사람들과 더 많이 접촉한다는 것을 의미한다.

| 어휘 | **shift** ⓥ 이동하다 **vanish** ⓥ 사라지다 **the course of events** 전개 상황

| 전문해석 | [C] 전 세계 모든 곳에서 언어들이 사라지고 있고, 그 전개 상황은 모든 곳에서 다 비슷하다. [A] 사람들은 사용자가 적은 지역 언어 사용을 중단하고 더 많은 사용자가 있고 일반적으로 더 널리 사용되는 언어로 이동한다. [E] 그 이유들은 어디서나 비슷하다. [D] 모든 나라에서 학교 교육이 확장되고 있고 흔히 주요 언어로만 제공된다. 사업과 통신 분야 역시 더욱 중요해지고 있는데, 이것은 더 많은 사람들이 하나의 언어에 대한 필요성이 커진다는 것을 의미한다. [B] 이 모든 것은 그 지역 사회에 속하지도 않고 그 지역 언어를 사용하지 않는 사람들과 더 많이 접촉한다는 것을 의미한다.

| 정답분석 | 이 글은 지역 언어들이 사라지고 있다고 말하며 그 이유에 대해 설명하고 있다. 현재 전 세계 모든 곳에서 언어가 사라지고 있다고 '문제점'을 포괄적으로 진술하고 있는 [C]가 가장 먼저 와야 하고, 그와 같은 진술이면서 조금 더 구체적 진술인 [A]가 그 뒤에 와야 하며, 이어서 지역 언어가 사라지는 '이유'들이 존재한다는 포괄적 진술인 [E]가 나와야 한다. 그리고 그 이유를 구체적으로 진술하고 있는 [D]와 [B]가 나와야 하는데, [B] 문장의 'All of these'는 앞 문장들을 요약하는 진술이며 글의 결론으로 적합하므로 마지막에 위치해야 자연스럽다.

13 2013 한양대

정답 ④

| 구문분석 | Some sports heroes have overcome daunting obstacles (to rise to the top of their sport). In 1957, for example, Jackie Robinson of the Brooklyn Dodgers became the first African-American (to play in the modern major leagues).
S V O 부사적용법: 결과 S V C

몇몇 스포츠 영웅들은 벅찬 장애를 극복하고 그들 분야 스포츠에서 최고에까지 도달하였다. 예를 들어 1957년 브루클린 다저스의 재키 로빈슨(Jackie Robinson)은 현대 메이저 리그에서 뛴 첫 흑인 선수가 되었다.

[D] Former Olympian Wilma Rudolph was born (with polio and survived pneumonia and scarlet fever as a child).
S V

올림픽 출전 선수였던 윌마 루돌프(Wilma Rudolph)는 소아마비를 가지고 태어났고, 어릴 때 폐렴과 성홍열에 걸렸었다.

[B] All these ailments left her (with a bad leg) (that some said would prevent her even from walking).
S V O (so) that절: 결과

이 모든 병 때문에 그녀의 다리 상태는 좋지 않아서 몇몇 사람들은 그녀가 심지어 걸어 다니지 못하리라고 말했다.

[A] (Although she wore a leg brace from the time) (she was 5 until she was 11), Rudolph still managed to play basketball and participate (in track) (when she was 13). (While still a high school sophomore), she competed (in the 1956 Olympic Games).
부사절: 비록 ~일지라도 S V_1 O 등위접속사 V_2 S V

그녀는 5세부터 11세까지 금속 다리 보호 기구를 착용해야 했지만, 여전히 농구를 즐겼고, 13세가 되던 해에는 육상에 참가했다. 고등학교 2학년 재학하는 동안, 그녀는 1956년 올림픽에 참가하여 경쟁했다.

[C] These days, Rudolph is remembered (for her inspirational determination to overcome her physical challenges), and (for her courage in rising above segregation and racism).
S V 등위접속사

요즘에, 루돌프는 신체적 어려움을 극복하고자 했던 용기가 넘치는 결심으로, 그리고 인종차별을 극복했던 용기 때문에 기억되고 있다.

| 어휘 |

daunting ⓐ 벅찬, 힘겨운	**leg brace** 금속 다리 보호 기구	**ailment** ⓝ 질병
inspirational ⓐ 용기를 북돋는	**segregation** ⓝ 인종차별	**polio** ⓝ 소아마비
pneumonia ⓝ 폐렴	**scarlet fever** 성홍열(발열을 동반한 세균성 발진)	

| 전문해석 | 몇몇 스포츠 영웅들은 벅찬 장애를 극복하고 그들 분야 스포츠에서 최고에까지 도달하였다. 예를 들어 1957년 브루클린 다저스의 재키 로빈슨(Jackie Robinson)은 현대 메이저 리그에서 뛴 첫 흑인 선수가 되었다. [D] 올림픽 출전 선수였던 윌마 루돌프(Wilma Rudolph)는 소아마비를 가지고 태어났고, 어릴 때 폐렴과 성홍열에 걸렸었다. [B] 이 모든 병 때문에 그녀의 다리 상태는 좋지 않아서 몇몇 사람들은 그녀가 심지어 걸어 다니지 못하리라고 말했다. [A] 그녀는 5세부터 11세까지 금속 다리 보호 기구를 착용해야 했지만, 여전히 농구를 즐겼고, 13세가 되던 해에는 육상에 참가했다. 고등학교 2학년 재학하는 동안, 그녀는 1956년 올림픽에 참가하여 경쟁했다. [C] 요즘에, 루돌프는 신체적 어려움을 극복하고자 했던 용기가 넘치는 결심으로, 그리고 인종차별을 극복했던 용기 때문에 기억되고 있다.

| 정답분석 | 글 속에서 사람의 이름을 언급할 때 이름 전체를 먼저 말해야 한다. 따라서 첫 문장으로 가장 적합한 것은 [D]라고 할 수 있다. 또한 이 글은 루돌프의 성장 과정을 시간의 흐름으로 진술하고 있는 것도 단서이다. 그리고 마지막 문장으로 루돌프에 대한 오늘날의 기억에 관한 진술이 나와야 하므로 마지막 문장으로는 [C]가 오는 것이 자연스럽다.

14 2015 중앙대

정답 ③

| 구문분석 | (Because of the demands of measuring behavioral change across different ages), developmental researchers use several unique methods.
전치사: 때문에 S V O

서로 다른 연령대를 포괄하는 행동변화를 측정하고자 하는 요구 때문에 (행동)발달 연구자들은 몇 가지 독특한 방법들을 사용한다.

The most frequently used cross-sectional research compares people (of different ages at the same point in time).
S V O

가장 흔히 사용되는 횡단면 연구는 같은 지점의 시간대에 있는 상이한 연령대의 사람들을 비교한다.

Cross-sectional studies provide information (about differences in development) (between different age groups).

횡단면 연구는 서로 다른 연령 집단들 사이에 존재하는 성장 과정의 차이들에 대한 정보를 제공한다.

[B] Suppose, (that) (for instance), we were interested (in the development of intellectual ability in adulthood). (To carry out a cross-sectional study), we might compare a sample (of 25-, 45-, and 65-year-olds) (who all take the same IQ test). We then can determine whether average IQ test scores differ in each age group.

예를 들어서, 우리가 성인 시기의 지적 능력의 성장에 관해서 흥미를 가지고 있다고 가정해 보자. 횡단면 연구를 실행하기 위해서 우리는 똑같은 IQ 테스트를 치른 25세 집단의 샘플과 45세 집단의 샘플 그리고 65세 집단의 샘플을 비교해 볼 수 있을 것이다. 그런 다음 우리는 각각의 연령 집단의 평균 IQ 점수가 다른지 여부를 결정할 수 있을 것이다.

[C] Cross-sectional research has limitations, however. For instance, we cannot be sure that the differences in IQ scores we might find in our example are due to age differences alone. Instead, the scores may reflect differences (in the educational attainment of the cohorts represented).

그러나 횡단면 연구는 한계를 가지고 있다. 가령, 우리는 우리가 제시한 예에서 발견한 IQ 점수의 차이가 오직 나이 때문이라고 확신할 수는 없다. 그 대신 IQ 점수는 대표(샘플) 집단들의 학력의 차이를 반영하고 있는 것인지도 모른다.

[A] A cohort is a group of people (who grow up at similar times and places). (In the case of IQ differences), any age differences (we find in a cross-sectional study) may reflect educational differences (among the cohorts studied): people in the older age group may belong (to a cohort) (that was less likely to attend college than were the people in the younger groups).

집단이란 유사한 시대와 장소에서 성장한 사람들의 무리이다. IQ 점수 차이의 경우, 횡단면 연구에서 우리가 발견한 연령 집단 간의 차이는 연구 대상인 집단들의 교육적 차이를 반영하는 것이다. 나이가 많은 연령대에 속하는 집단은 젊은 연령대에 속하는 집단에 비해 대학 교육을 받았을 가능성이 높지 않다.

| 어휘 | **cross-sectional** ⓐ 횡단면의; (전체를 대표하는) 단면의

cohort ⓝ (통계적으로 동일한 특색이나 행동 양식을 공유하는) 집단 **attainment** ⓝ 성과, 성취, 달성

| 전문해석 | 서로 다른 연령대를 포괄하는 행동변화를 측정하고자 하는 요구 때문에 (행동)발달 연구자들은 몇 가지 독특한 방법들을 사용한다. 가장 흔히 사용되는 횡단면 연구는 같은 지점의 시간대에 있는 상이한 연령대의 사람들을 비교한다. 횡단면 연구는 서로 다른 연령 집단들 사이에 존재하는 성장 과정의 차이들에 대한 정보를 제공한다. [B] 예를 들어서, 우리가 성인 시기의 지적 능력의 성장에 관해서 흥미를 가지고 있다고 가정해 보자. 횡단면 연구를 실행하기 위해서 우리는 똑같은 IQ 테스트를 치른 25세 집단의 샘플과 45세 집단의 샘플 그리고 65세 집단의 샘플을 비교해 볼 수 있을 것이다. 그런 다음 우리는 각각의 연령 집단의 평균 IQ 점수가 다른지 여부를 결정할 수 있을 것이다. [C] 그러나 횡단면 연구는 한계를 가지고 있다. 가령, 우리는 우리가 제시한 예에서 발견한 IQ 점수의 차이가 오직 나이 때문이라고 확신할 수는 없다. 그 대신 IQ 점수는 대표(샘플) 집단들의 학력의 차이를 반영하고 있는 것인지도 모른다. 그 대신 IQ 점수는 샘플 집단들의 학력의 차이를 반영하고 있는 것인지도 모른다. [A] 집단(cohort)이란 유사한 시대와 장소에서 성장한 사람들의 무리이다. IQ 점수 차이의 경우, 횡단면 연구에서 우리가 발견한 연령 집단 간의 차이는 연구 대상인 집단들의 교육적 차이를 반영하는 것이다. 나이가 많은 연령대에 속하는 집단은 젊은 연령대에 속하는 집단에 비해 대학 교육을 받았을 가능성이 높지 않다.

| 정답분석 | 주어진 앞부분 문장에서 횡단면 연구의 필요성을 제시했는데 그다음에는 횡단면 연구에 대한 구체적 예시가 이어져야 하므로 [B]가 먼저 나와야 한다. 그리고 반전과 함께 횡단면 연구의 한계점을 기술한 [C]가 이어져야 하며 [C] 문장의 마지막에 언급한 'cohort'(집단)가 무엇인지를 구체적으로 정의해 주며 IQ 점수 차이 경우에 적용해서 기술하는 [A]가 이어져야 자연스럽다.

15 2015 한양대

정답 ②

| 구문분석 |

[D] The development of an adult body is not the only change (adolescents are experiencing). They are also developing adult thinking skills, (which include reasoning and abstract thinking skills). By now, they are able to consider multiple variables and contemplate hypothetical situations.

성인 몸으로서 성장하는 것은 청소년들이 경험하는 유일한 변화가 아니다. 그들은 또한 추론과 추상적 사고 기술을 포함하는 성인들의 사고 기술도 발전시킨다. 이제 그들은 다양한 변수를 고려할 수 있고 가설적인 상황에 대해서 깊이 생각할 수 있다.

[C] These are important skills (when establishing identity), (which involves getting a clear sense of one's values and beliefs, and determining one's goals and ambitions for the future). (Through decision making, problem solving, and reasoning), adolescents become independent people, (who make their own decisions and forge their own relationships).

이것들은 중요한 기술들인데, 자신의 가치와 믿음을 명백히 인식하는 것과 미래를 위해 자신의 목표와 야망을 결정하는 것 등을 포함하고 있는 정체성을 확립할 때 중요하다. 의사결정, 문제 해결, 그리고 추론을 통해서 청소년은 스스로 결정을 내리고 그들 스스로의 관계를 구축해 나가는 독립적인 인간이 된다.

[B] Adolescents are now responsible (for their decisions), and they establish their own moral code (based on introspection) (as opposed to abiding by the rules prescribed to them by their parents). All of these fascinating psycho-social changes result (in additional changes in the behavior of adolescents).

청소년들은 이제 그들의 의사결정에 책임을 져야 한다. 그리고 그들은 부모들에 의해서 처방된 규칙을 따르는 것과는 반대로 내적 자기성찰을 기반으로 자기 자신만의 도덕 규칙을 만든다. 이러한 모든 놀라운 심리-사회적 변화는 청소년들의 행동에 있어서 추가적인 변화들을 초래한다.

[A] Teens typically spend less time (with their families and more with their friends). Privacy becomes very important (to some), and they may start locking their bedroom door. Some become argumentative or rebellious, but that is just part (of establishing autonomous values and principles).

십 대들은 일반적으로 가족들과 지내기보다는 친구들과 더 많은 시간을 보낸다. 몇몇 십 대에게 사생활은 매우 중요한 것이 되고 그들은 자기 방문을 굳게 걸어 잠근다. 몇몇 십 대는 논쟁적으로 되거나 반항적인 사람이 된다. 그러나 이러한 변화는 단지 자발적인 가치와 원칙들을 확립하기 위한 부분이다.

| 어휘 |

argumentative ⓐ 논쟁적인
rebellious ⓐ 반항적인, 반역하는
autonomous ⓐ 자율적인, 독립적인
adolescent ⓝ 청소년
moral code 도덕적 규칙
identity ⓝ 정체성
reasoning ⓝ 추론
forge ⓥ 구축하다; 위조하다; (금속을) 벼리다
abstract ⓐ 추상적인
variable ⓝ 변수, 변하는 것
contemplate ⓥ 숙고하다
hypothetical ⓐ 가설의, 가정된

| 전문해석 |

[D] 성인 몸으로서 성장하는 것은 청소년들이 경험하는 유일한 변화가 아니다. 그들은 또한 추론과 추상적 사고 기술을 포함하는 성인들의 사고 기술도 발전시킨다. 이제 그들은 다양한 변수를 고려할 수 있고 가설적인 상황에 대해서 깊이 생각할 수 있다. [C] 이것들은 중요한 기술들인데, 자신의 가치와 믿음을 명백히 인식하는 것과 미래를 위해 자신의 목표와 야망을 결정하는 것 등을 포함하고 있는 정체성을 확립할 때 중요하다. 의사결정, 문제 해결, 그리고 추론을 통해서 청소년은 스스로 결정을 내리고 그들 스스로의 관계를 구축해 나가는 독립적인 인간이 된다. [B] 청소년들은 이제 그들의 의사결정에 책임을 져야 한다. 그리고 그들은 부모들에 의해서 처방된 규칙을 따르는 것과는 반대로 내적 자기성찰을 기반으로 자기 자신만의 도덕 규칙을 만든다. 이러한 모든 놀라운 심리-사회적 변화는 청소년들의 행동에 있어서 추가적인 변화들을 초래한다. [A] 십 대들은 일반적으로 가족들과 지내기보다는 친구들과 더 많은 시간을 보낸다. 몇몇 십 대에게 사생활은 매우 중요한 것이 되고 그들은 자기 방문을 굳게 걸어 잠근다. 몇몇 십 대는 논쟁적으로 되거나 반항적인 사람이 된다. 그러나 이러한 변화는 단지 자발적인 가치와 원칙들을 확립하기 위한 부분이다.

| 정답분석 | 이 글은 전체적으로 청소년기의 변화에 관해 기술하는 글이다. 다양한 청소년기의 변화가 존재하겠지만, 그중에서 신체의 변화, 사고의 변화, 행동의 변화에 관해 다루는 글이다. 문장 배열 시 항상 처음으로 등장하는 말에 주의해야 하며, 또한 같은 진술이라면 포괄적 진술이 앞으로 가고 구체적 진술은 뒤로 가야 한다. [D] 문장에서 첨가 표현 also를 통해 '청소년기 사고의 변화'가 일어난다는 내용은 이 글 속에서 처음으로 등장했다는 것을 알 수 있다. [C] 문장에서 these는 [D] 문장에서 언급한 변화된 사고하는 기술을 받아야 하므로 [D] 다음으로 [C]가 이어져야 한다. 한편 [B] 문장에서도 마지막 부분에 첨가 표현인 'additional'을 통해 '청소년기 행동의 변화'가 처음으로 등장했다는 것을 알 수 있으며, [A] 내용인 '십 대들이 가족보다는 친구들과 더 많은 시간을 보내는 것'과 '방문을 걸어 잠그는 것'은 청소년 행동 변화의 구체적 진술이므로 [B] 다음 [A]가 이어져야 자연스럽다.

16 2015 국민대(오전A형)

정답 ④

| 구문분석 | That genius is unusual(S) goes(V) (without saying).

천재성이 비범한 것이라는 것은 말할 필요도 없다.

[C] But is(V) it(S) so unusual(C) [that it(S) requires(V) the brains of those(O) (that possess it) to be unusual(O.C) (in other ways), too]?

(so ~ that: 너무 ~해서 …하다)

하지만 천재성은 너무나도 비범해서, 그 결과, 천재성을 가진 사람들의 뇌 또한 다른 방식에 있어서 비범함(정상적이지 않음)을 요구하는 것일까?

[B] A link(S) (between artistic genius(A) on the one hand and(등위접속사) schizophrenia and manic-depression(B) on the other) is widely debated(V).

(between A and B: A와 B 사이의)

한편으로는 예술적 천재성, 또 다른 한편으로 정신 분열 혹은 우울증 사이의 연결에 관한 광범위한 논쟁이 있다.

[A] However(접속부사) another link(S), (between savant syndrome and autism), is well established(V).

그러나 서번트 증후군과 자폐증 사이에 존재하는 또 다른 연관성에 대한 연구도 잘 확립되어 있다.

[D] It(S) is(V), for example(접속부사), the subject(C) (of films such as "Rain Man"), (in which(관계대명사) the autistic brother shows an extraordinary talent of memorizing figures).

예를 들어서, 이런 연관성이, 자폐증에 걸린 형이 숫자를 암기하는 데에 특별한 재능을 보이는 내용인 '레인맨'과 같은 영화의 주제이다.

| 어휘 |

go without saying that ~은 말할 필요도 없다

savant syndrome 서번트 증후군(자폐증 환자가 특정 분야에서 천재적 재능을 보이는 것)

autism ⓝ 자폐증 **schizophrenia** ⓝ 정신 분열증 **manic-depression** ⓝ 조울증

extraordinary ⓐ 비범한, 특별한

| 전문해석 | 천재성이 비범한 것이라는 것은 말할 필요도 없다. [C] 하지만 천재성은 너무나도 비범해서, 그 결과, 천재성을 가진 사람들의 뇌 또한 다른 방식에 있어서 비범함(정상적이지 않음)을 요구하는 것일까? [B] 한편으로는 예술적 천재성, 또 다른 한편으로 정신 분열 혹은 우울증 사이의 연결에 관한 광범위한 논쟁이 있다. [A] 그러나 서번트 증후군과 자폐증 사이에 존재하는 또 다른 연관성에 대한 연구도 잘 확립되어 있다. [D] 예를 들어서, 이런 연관성이(천재와 자폐 사이의 연관성), 자폐증에 걸린 형이 숫자를 암기하는 데에 특별한 재능을 보이는 내용인 '레인맨'과 같은 영화의 주제이다.

| 정답분석 | 이 글은 서번트 증후군에 대해 다루는 글이다. 주어진 첫 문장에서 천재성은 일반적이지 않다는 진술 이후 [C]의 반전 뒤 물음의 문장으로 '천재성을 가지면 뇌 또한 정상적이지 못할까?'라는 이 글에서 다룰 내용을 소개하는 기술이 와야 한다. [B]와 [C]는 천재성과 각종 뇌 관련된 질병 사이의 관련성에 대해 일관된 기술을 하고 있는데, [C] 문장은 another link라고 했기 때문에 [B]보다 뒤에 위치해야 한다. 마지막으로 [C] 문장의 뒤를 이어 천재성과 자폐증에 관련된 예시인 [D]가 나오는 것이 자연스럽다.

17 2015 한양대(에리카)

정답 ③

| 구문분석 | Exercise can truly become addictive (for women).
S V C
여성들에게, 운동은 정말로 중독이 될 수도 있다.

The term "runner's high" does not simply refer (to a psychological state of mind), (because excessive running actually produces a morphine-like hormone known as beta-endorphin), (which deadens pain, creating a certain stimulation).
S V 부사절: 때문에 관계대명사 분사구문

"runner's high"라는 용어가 단순히 심리적 측면에서의 정신 상태를 언급하고 있는 것은 아닌데, 그 이유는, 격렬한 달리기가 베타 엔도르핀으로 알려진 모르핀 같은 호르몬을 실제로 분비하며, 이 호르몬이 어떤 자극을 발생시키면서 고통을 누그러뜨리기 때문이다.

[C] Fitness obsession reaches (far beyond "runner's high") (as it begins to affect other aspects of a woman's lifestyle), (such as her job or personal relationships).
S V 부사절: 때

운동에 대한 과도한 집착은 직업이나 개인적인 인간관계 등과 같은, 여성의 생활방식의 다른 측면들에 영향을 끼치기 시작하게 되면, 그것은 "runner's high"를 훨씬 넘어서 버린다.

so ~ that절: 너무 ~해서 그 결과 …하다
[B] I know two women, both lawyers, (who have become so preoccupied with their fitness) (that not only must they begin and end their days with exercise, but they feel uncomfortable or irritable if someone or something prevents them from exercising).
S V O = not only A but (also) B: A뿐만 아니라 B도

나는 변호사로 일하고 있는 두 명의 여성을 알고 있는데, 그들은 운동에 완전히 빠져서 하루를 운동으로 시작해서 운동으로 끝내야 할 뿐만 아니라 어떤 사람이나 일로 인해 운동을 못 하게 되면 불안해하거나 화를 낸다.

[A] (Just like drug addicts), they need their daily "fix" (to function normally), and they don't realize that they are abandoning former friends and interests.
S V O 부사적용법: ~하기 위하여 S V O

마약 중독자들처럼, 그들은 정상적인 생활을 하기 위해서 날마다 '운동이라는 마약 주사'를 맞아야 한다. 그리고 그들은 자신이 예전의 친구들과 흥밋거리들을 포기하고 있다는 사실을 깨닫지 못한다.

Exercise, (like alcohol), can provide a means of escape (so that a woman may never confront her fears or problems).
S V O 부사절: 결과

알코올과 마찬가지로, 운동도 도피 수단을 제공하고 여성은 운동을 통해서 두려움이나 문제에 맞서는 것을 피할 수 있다.

The victim herself may never notice the problem (unless she hits a distinct abyss).
S V O 부사절: 만일 ~이 아니라면(= if not)
운동 중독의 피해자가 된 그녀 자신은, 분명한 나락에 이르기 전까지 그 문제에 대해서 알지 못할 것이다.

| 어휘 |

addictive ⓐ 중독의
deaden ⓥ (통증 따위를) 약하게 하다
fix ⓝ 1회분의 마약, 마약 주사
abandon ⓥ (계획 · 습관 등을) 단념하다, 그만두다
preoccupy ⓥ 몰두[열중]하게 하다
fitness ⓝ 운동; 건강; 적합, 적절
irritable ⓐ 짜증을 내는; 화가 난
abyss ⓝ 심연; 나락

| 전문해석 | 여성들에게, 운동은 정말로 중독이 될 수도 있다. "runner's high"라는 용어가 단순히 심리적 측면에서의 정신 상태를 언급하고 있는 것은 아닌데, 그 이유는, 격렬한 달리기가 베타 엔도르핀으로 알려진 모르핀 같은 호르몬을 실제로 분비하며, 이 호르몬이 어떤 자극을 발생시키면서 고통을 누그러뜨리기 때문이다. [C] 운동에 대한 과도한 집착은 직업이나 개인적인 인간관계 등과 같은, 여성의 생활방식의 다른 측면들에 영향을 끼치기 시작하게 되면, 그것은 "runner's high"를 훨씬 넘어서 버린다. [B] 나는 변호사로 일하고 있는 두 명의 여성을 알고 있는데, 그들은 운동에 완전히 빠져서 하루를 운동으로 시작해서 운동으로 끝내야 할 뿐만 아니라 어떤 사람이나 일로 인해 운동을 못 하게 되면 불안해하거나 화를 낸다. [A] 마약 중독자들처럼, 그들은 정상적인 생활을 하기 위해서 날마다 '운동이라는 마약 주사'를 맞아야 한다. 그리고 그들은 자신이 예전의 친구들과 흥밋거리들을 포기하고 있다는 사실을 깨닫지 못한다. 알코올과 마찬가지로, 운동도 도피 수단을 제공하고 여

성은 운동을 통해서 두려움이나 문제에 맞서는 것을 피할 수 있다. 운동 중독의 피해자가 된 그녀 자신은, 분명한 나락에 이르기 전까지 그 문제에 대해 알지 못할 것이다.

| 정답분석 | 주어진 문장에서 다루는 "러너스 하이"에 대한 설명을 이어서 받을 수 있는 문장으로 적절한 것을 먼저 고른다. "러너스 하이"보다 증세가 더 심각한 운동 강박증에 관한 설명이 이어지는 [C]가 첫 문장으로 적절하며, [C]에서 언급한 운동 강박증의 구체적인 사례로 변호사인 두 여성의 예를 들고 있는 [B]가 그다음으로 와야 하며, 이러한 중독 증세를 마약 중독에 비유하고 있는 [A]가 마지막으로 오는 것이 자연스럽다.

18 2017 가톨릭대

정답 ③

| 구문분석 | (If we lived on a planet where nothing ever changed), there would be little to do.
부사절: 만일 ~라면 / 유도부사 / V / S
만일 우리가 아무것도 변하지 않는 행성에 살고 있다면, 할 일이 아무것도 없을 것이다.

There would be nothing (to figure out).
유도부사 / V / S
이해할 것이 아무것도 존재하지 않을 것이다.

[D] There would be no impetus (for science).
유도부사 / V / S
과학을 위한 자극제가 존재하지 않을 것이다.

[A] And (if we lived in an unpredictable world), (where things changed in random or very complex ways), we would not be able to figure things out.
부사절: 만일 ~라면 / 관계부사 / S / V / O
그리고 모든 것이 무작위로 매우 복잡한 방식으로 변화하는 예측할 수 없는 세계에서 산다면, 우리는 아무것도 이해할 수 없을 것이다.

[B] (Again), there would be no such thing (as science).
유도부사 / V / S
다시 한번 과학과 같은 것은 존재하지 않을 것이다.

[C] But we live (in an in-between universe), (where things change, but according to patterns, rules, or, as we call them, laws of nature).
S / V / 관계부사
그러나 우리는 모든 것이 변하면서도 하지만 패턴이나, 규칙이나, 소위 자연법칙에 따라 변하는 (앞의 두 세계 사이) 중간 세계에서 살아가고 있다.

(If I throw a stick up in the air), it always falls down.
부사절: ~한다면 / S / V
허공에 막대기를 집어 던지면 막대기는 반드시 땅으로 다시 떨어진다.

(If the sun sets in the west), it always rises again the next morning in the east.
부사절: ~한다면 / S / V
태양이 서쪽에서 지면, 다음 날 아침 동쪽에서 항상 다시 떠오른다.

And so it becomes possible to figure things out.
가주어 / V / C / 진주어
그래서 모든 것을 이해하는 것이 가능해진다.

We can do science, and with it we can improve our lives.
S / V / O / S / V / O
우리는 과학을 할 수 있고, 이를 통해 우리의 삶을 발전시킬 수 있다.

| 어휘 | **figure out** 생각해 내다, 이해하다 **unpredictable** ⓐ 예언[예측]할 수 없는
random ⓐ 임의의, 무작위(無作爲)의 **in-between** ⓐ 중간의
impetus ⓝ (일의 추진에 필요한) 자극(제)[추동력] **fall down** 떨어지다; 실패하다

| 전문해석 | 만일 우리가 아무것도 변하지 않는 행성에 살고 있다면, 할 일이 아무것도 없을 것이다. 이해할 것이 아무것도 존재하지 않을 것이다. [D] (그런 세계에서는) 과학을 위한 자극제가 존재하지 않을 것이다. [A] 그리고 모든 것이 무작위로 매우 복잡한 방식으로 변화하는 예측할 수 없는 세계에서 산다면, 우리는 아무것도 이해할 수 없을 것이다. [B] 다시 한번 과학과 같은

것은 존재하지 않을 것이다. [C] 그러나 우리는 모든 것이 변하면서도 하지만 패턴이나, 규칙이나, 소위 자연법칙에 따라 변하는 (앞의 두 세계 사이) 중간 세계에서 살아가고 있다. 허공에 막대기를 집어 던지면 막대기는 반드시 땅으로 다시 떨어진다. 태양이 서쪽에서 지면, 다음 날 아침 동쪽에서 항상 다시 떠오른다. 그래서 모든 것을 이해하는 것이 가능해진다. 우리는 과학을 할 수 있고, 이를 통해 우리의 삶을 발전시킬 수 있다.

| 정답분석 | 첫 문장에서 "만일 우리가 아무것도 변하지 않는 행성에 살고 있다면, 할 일이 아무것도 없을 것이다. 이해할 것이 아무것도 존재하지 않을 것이다."라고 했는데, 이는 아무런 변화가 없는 세상에 사는 것을 가정한 것이다. 생각할 필요가 없는 세상의 경우에는 어떠한 과학적 동기도 없을 것이므로 재진술이라 할 수 있는 [D]가 첫 문장으로 적절하며, 또한 두 번째 가정한 세상인 변화는 하는데 예측 불가능한 세상을 언급한 [A]가 그 뒤에 이어지며, 그 세상 또한 역시 과학이 존재하지 않을 것이므로 [B]가 그 뒤에 와야 한다. 마지막으로, 하지만 현재 우리가 살고 있는 세상은 절대불변의 첫 번째 가정한 세상도 아니고, 무작위로 예측 불가능하게 변하는 두 번째 가정한 세상도 아닌 그 중간 세상에 살고 있다고 언급한 [C]가 마지막으로 뒤 문장과 연결이 자연스럽다. 한편, [B]와 [D]는 내용은 같지만 [B]에는 Again이 들어 있으므로 [B]는 [D]보다 뒤에 있어야 한다.

19 2019 서강대(인문계)

정답 ①

| 구문분석 | [B] I happen to go (to a professional meeting) and hear papers presented, or (afterwards), people talking (in lobbies or corridors or restaurants) (— all those words, all those ideas), (spoken by men and women) (who have no doubt about their importance, their achievements, and certainly, their ability to "communicate.")

(I: S / happen to go: V_1 / hear: V_2 / papers: O_1 / presented: $O.C_1$ / people: O_2 / talking: $O.C_2$ / happen toR: 우연히 ~하다 / or: 등위접속사)

나는 전문가들의 모임에 가서 논문발표를 듣든지, 혹은 나중에 사람들이 로비나 복도나 식당에서 나누는 이야기를 듣는데, 그 모든 것은 자신들의 중요성과 업적에 대해 그리고 분명 "의사소통" 능력에 대해 전혀 의심하지 않는 사람들이 하는 말들과 생각들이다.

[D] No one is proposing that jargon-filled scholars of one sort or another overcome their "cultural disadvantage."

(No one: S / is proposing: V / that ~ disadvantage: O)

전문용어로 가득 찬 이런저런 종류의 학자들에게 그들의 "문화적 불이익"을 극복하라고 제안하는 사람은 아무도 없다.

[C] Few are examining ever so closely the rhetoric (of various business and professional people), nor the dreary, ponderous, smug, deadly words and phrases (such people use).

(Few: S / are examining: V / the rhetoric: O_1 / the dreary ~ phrases: O_2 / nor: 등위접속사: 또한 ~이 아니다)

다양한 기업인들과 전문 직업인들의 수사(修辭)나, 그런 사람들이 사용하는 따분하고, 지루하고, 독선적이고, 지독한 말과 표현들을 아주 면밀하게 조사하는 사람은 거의 없다.

[A] Relatively few are looking (at the way) (such people are taught) (in elementary school and high school and beyond).

(few: S / are looking: V)

그런 사람들이 초등학교와 고등학교 그리고 그 이상의 교육기관에서 배우는 방식에 대해 알아보는 사람은 상대적으로 거의 없다.

| 어휘 |

relatively ⓐⓓ 비교적, 상대적으로
present ⓥ 주다, 제공하다; 나타내다
corridor ⓝ 복도
rhetoric ⓝ 수사(修辭); 수사학; 웅변술
various ⓐ 여러 가지의, 가지각색의
dreary ⓐ 황량한; 따분한; 음울한
ponderous ⓐ 묵직한, 육중한; 지루한
smug ⓐ 독선적인, 점잔 빼는
deadly ⓐ 치명적인; 맹렬한, 지독한
jargon ⓝ 뜻을 알 수 없는 말; 전문용어

| 전문해석 | [B] 나는 전문가들의 모임에 가서 논문발표를 듣든지, 혹은 나중에 사람들이 로비나 복도나 식당에서 나누는 이야기를 듣는데, 그 모든 것은 자신들의 중요성과 업적에 대해 그리고 분명 "의사소통" 능력에 대해 전혀 의심하지 않는 사람들이 하는 말들과 생각들이다. [D] 전문용어로 가득 찬 이런저런 종류의 학자들에게 그들의 "문화적 불이익"을 극복하라고 제안하는 사람은 아무도 없다. [C] 다양한 기업인들과 전문 직업인들의 수사(修辭)나, 그런 사람들이 사용하는 따분하고, 지루하고, 독선적이고, 지독한 말과 표현들을 아주 면밀하게 조사하는 사람은 거의 없다. [A] 그런 사람들이 초등학교와 고등학교 그리고 그 이상의 교육기관에서 배우는 방식에 대해 알아보는 사람은 상대적으로 거의 없다.

| 정답분석 | 이 지문은 글쓴이가 경험한 소위 전문가들의 언어 사용의 문제점을 지적하고, 그들이 사용하는 말과 언어를 의심하는 사람은 거의 없다는 글이다. 이 글의 중심소재인 전문가들의 언어 사용에 대해 처음으로 소개하는 [B]가 가장 먼저 와야 하며, [A], [C], [D] 내용은 모두 그러한 전문가들에게 문제점을 지적하든지, 그들이 사용하는 언어, 표현, 그들의 교육 배경을 의심하는 사람이 없다는 내용인데, [A]의 such people은 [C]의 various business and professional people을 가리키고 있으므로 [A]는 [C]의 뒤에 위치해야 한다.

20 2019 이화여대

정답 ②

| 구문분석 | [E] "I am convinced (when I say that color has been a neglected art,)" Faber Birren declared in 1934.
S V S V
1934년, 파버 비렌(Faber Birren)은 "나는 색상은 무시된 기술이라고 확신한다."라고 선언했다.

[B] No one could make the same claim (today), (eight decades on).
S V O
그 후 80년이 지난 지금, 똑같은 주장을 할 수 있는 사람은 아무도 없을 것이다.

[D] Certain slivers of ROYGBIV (— like Tiffany blue or T-Mobile magenta —) have been copyrighted (under federal law), (while others have inspired scientific inquiry and even public policy interventions).
S V
부사절: ~ 동안, 동시에
빨주노초파남보의 어떤 조각들—티파니 블루나 T-모바일의 자홍색—은 연방법하에서 저작권의 보호를 받고 있으며, 동시에 다른 조각(색깔)들은 과학적 탐구와 심지어 공공정책의 개입들에 영감을 주었다.

[C] Take Baker-Miller pink, a shade [(some believe) has a soothing effect].
삽입구
V O = (that)
베이커-밀러 핑크색을 예로 들어 보자. 이것은 일부 사람들이 진정 효과가 있다고 믿는 색조이다. (과학적 사용)

[A] Endorsers include supermodel Kendall Jenner, (who painted her living room in the bubblegum-like hue), and prison officials (in Switzerland), (where every fifth prison or police station has at least one pink cell).
S V O_1 관계대명사
등위접속사 O_2 관계부사
이를 보증하며 선전하는 사람들로는 자신의 거실을 풍선껌 같은 빛깔로 칠한 슈퍼모델 켄달 제너(Kendall Jenner)와 스위스의 교도소 공무원들이 있는데, 스위스에는 교도소나 경찰서 다섯 곳 중 한 곳에 최소한 하나의 핑크색 감방이 있다. (공공정책에 사용)

| 어휘 |
endorser ⓝ 배서인; 지지하는 사람, 보증 선전하는 사람(유명인)
hue ⓝ 색조, 빛깔, 색상
prison ⓝ 교도소, 감옥
cell ⓝ 작은방; (교도소의) 독방; 세포
decade ⓝ 10년간
shade ⓝ 그늘; 색조, 명암
soothing ⓐ 달래는, 진정시키는
effect ⓝ 결과; 효과; 영향
sliver ⓝ 쪼개진 조각, (나무 · 재목 따위의) 길고 가느다란 조각
magenta ⓝ 마젠타색, 자홍색
copyright ⓥ ~의 판권을 얻다, (작품을) 저작권으로 보호하다
federal ⓐ 동맹의, 연합의; 연방정부의
inspire ⓥ 고무하다, 영감을 주다; (사상 · 감정 등을) 일어나게 하다
inquiry ⓝ 질문, 문의; 탐구, 연구
intervention ⓝ 조정, 중재
convince ⓥ ~에게 납득시키다, 확신시키다
neglect ⓥ 무시[경시]하다; 방치하다, 소홀히 하다
declare ⓥ 선언하다, 발표하다

| 전문해석 | [E] 1934년, 파버 비렌(Faber Birren)은 "나는 색깔은 무시된 기술이라고 확신한다."라고 선언했다. (과거에 색깔은 색이 가진 어떤 효과에 대해 생각하지 않았다는 진술) [B] 그 후 80년이 지난 지금, 똑같은 주장을 할 수 있는 사람은 아무도 없을 것이다. [D] 빨주노초파남보의 어떤 조각들—티파니 블루나 T-모바일의 자홍색—은 연방법하에서 저작권의 보호를 받고 있으며, 동시에 다른 조각(색깔)들은 과학적 탐구와 심지어 공공정책의 개입들에 영감을 주었다. [C] 베이커-밀러 핑크색을 예로 들어 보자. 이것은 일부 사람들이 진정 효과가 있다고 믿는 색조이다. [A] 이를 보증하며 선전하는 사람들로는 자신의 거실을 풍선껌 같은 빛깔로 칠한 슈퍼모델 켄달 제너(Kendall Jenner)와 스위스의 교도소 공무원들이 있는데, 스위스에는 교도소나 경찰서 다섯 곳 중 한 곳에 최소한 하나의 핑크색 감방이 있다.

| 정답분석 | 이 지문은 '과거에는 색깔에 크게 의미를 두지 않았으나, 오늘날은 색깔의 효과를 인정한다.'는 내용의 글이다. 색깔에 대한 과거 대우에 대해 언급한 [E]가 글의 첫 부분에 와야 하고, [E] 속의 인용문의 내용을 the same claim으로 받고 있는 [B]가 그 뒤에 와야 한다. 그리고 과거와 다르게 오늘날 색깔이 가진 의미와 각종 효과에 대해 언급한 [D]가 그 뒤에 와야 하며, [D]에서 이야기하고 있는 과학적 탐구와 공공정책에 사용한 내용, 즉 진정 효과와 감방의 색상을 구체적으로 이야기하고 있는 [C]와 [A]가 차례로 이어져야 자연스럽다.

9강 문장 삽입

Practice

01	②	02	②	03	④	04	④	05	④	06	③	07	②	08	③	09	②	10	③
11	③	12	①	13	①	14	③	15	③	16	③	17	②	18	③	19	②	20	③

01 2018 한양대(에리카)

정답 ②

| 구문분석 | Archaeopteryx(S), (a toothy, feathered fossil found in Germany in the 19th century), hinted(V) (at a crucial moment in the history of life) — the point(대시: 동격) (when(관계부사) dinosaurs took to the skies, and birds were thus born).

19세기 독일에서 발견된 이빨과 깃털이 있는 화석인 시조새는 생명의 역사상 매우 중요한 순간을 시사했는데, 즉 공룡이 하늘을 날고 조류가 그 결과 탄생한 순간이었다.

There(유도부사) are(V_1) not many evolutionary journeys(S_1) (that(관계대명사) can rival this), but that(S_2) (made by the descendants of some small, terrestrial mammals), (which(관계대명사) turned into the gigantic aquatic krill-eaters (called baleen whales), is(V_2) one such(C).

이에 필적할 만한 진화적 과정은 많지 않지만, 몇몇 작은 육상 포유동물의 후손들이 크릴새우를 먹는 수염고래라고 불리는 거대한 수생동물로 변한 진화 과정이 바로 그런 진화적 과정 중 하나이다.

Baleen whales(S_1) suck(V_1) (in large volumes of water) and then force(V_2) it(O) (out of their mouths) (through fibrous outgrowths) (known as baleen plates), (to filter out small animals for consumption)(부사적용법: ~하기 위해서).

수염고래는 많은 양의 물을 빨아들이고 나서 작은 동물들을 먹기 위해 고래수염 판이라고 알려진 섬유질의 돌출부를 통해 강제로 물을 입 밖으로 뱉어 낸다.

These plates(S_1) sit(V_1) (where(관계부사) other mammals have teeth, but (rather than robust dentine)(rather than: ~라기보다는), (the principal ingredient of teeth)(=), they(S_2) are composed(V_2) (of keratin), a flexible material(=) (that(관계대명사) also makes up hair and fingernails).

이 수염 판은 다른 포유동물들의 이빨이 자라는 위치에 있지만, 치아의 주요성분인 튼튼한 상아질보다는 머리카락과 손톱을 구성하는 유연한 물질인 케라틴으로 구성되어 있다.

Some researchers(S) theorize(V) that suction-filter feeding in whales began with teeth(O_1) (that(관계대명사) could be gnashed together to form a simple sieve), and(등위접속사) that only subsequently were these teeth replaced by baleen(O_2).

일부 연구자들은 고래의 흡입 · 여과 방식으로 먹이 먹기는 다 함께 갈려서 하나의 단순한 체를 형성할 수 있는 이빨로 시작되었고, 그 후에야 이 이빨들이 고래수염으로 대체되었다는 이론을 제시한다.

| 어휘 |
- **archaeopteryx** ⓝ 아르카이오프테릭스 새, 시조새(1억 5천만 년 전에 존재한 것으로 여겨지는 새)
- **toothy** ⓐ 많은[큰] 이가 있는; 뻐드렁니의, 이를 드러낸
- **feathered** ⓐ 깃털이 있는; 깃을 단
- **hint at** ~을 암시하다
- **rival** ⓥ ~에 맞서다, 경쟁하다
- **descendant** ⓝ 자손, 후손
- **terrestrial** ⓐ 육생의, 지구의
- **mammal** ⓝ 포유동물
- **gigantic** ⓐ 거대한
- **aquatic** ⓐ 수생의, 수중의
- **baleen whale** 수염 고래
- **finned** ⓐ 지느러미를 가진
- **baleen** ⓝ 고래수염 (= whalebone)
- **illuminate** ⓥ 조명하다, 밝게 하다, 비추다
- **fibrous** ⓐ 섬유(질)의
- **outgrowth** ⓝ 결과, 부산물
- **filter out** ~을 걸러 내다
- **robust** ⓐ 튼튼한, 강건한
- **dentine** ⓝ (이의) 상아질
- **ingredient** ⓝ 성분, 원료, 재료

flexible ⓐ 유연한 **theorize** ⓥ 이론을 세우다, 이론화하다 **gnash** ⓥ 이를 갈다, 이를 악물다
sieve ⓝ 체(가루 등을 거르는 데 쓰는 부엌 도구) **subsequently** ⓐⓓ 그 후, 뒤에

| 전문해석 | 19세기 독일에서 발견된 이빨과 깃털이 있는 화석인 시조새는 생명의 역사상 매우 중요한 순간을 시사했는데, 즉 공룡이 하늘을 날고 조류가 그 결과 탄생한 순간이었다. [A] 이에 필적할 만한 진화적 과정은 많지 않지만, 몇몇 작은 육상 포유동물의 후손들이 크릴새우를 먹는 수염고래라고 불리는 거대한 수생동물로 변한 진화 과정이 바로 그런 진화적 과정 중 하나이다. **[B] 〈북아메리카에서 새롭게 발견된 날카로운 이빨과 지느러미가 있는 고래수염 화석을 분석하면 이런 놀라운 진화 과정 중의 한 부분을 설명할 수 있게 될 것으로 보인다.〉** 수염고래는 많은 양의 물을 빨아들이고 나서 작은 동물들을 먹기 위해 고래수염 판이라고 알려진 섬유질의 돌출부를 통해 강제로 물을 입 밖으로 뱉어 낸다. [C] 이 수염 판은 다른 포유동물들의 이빨이 자라는 위치에 있지만, 치아의 주요성분인 튼튼한 상아질보다는 머리카락과 손톱을 구성하는 유연한 물질인 케라틴으로 구성되어 있다. [D] 일부 연구자들은 고래의 흡입 · 여과 방식으로 먹이 먹기는 다 함께 갈려서 하나의 단순한 체를 형성할 수 있는 이빨로 시작되었고, 그 후에야 이 이빨들이 고래수염으로 대체되었다는 이론을 제시한다.

| 보기분석 | Analysis (S) (of a newly discovered toothy, finned baleen fossil) (from North America) promises (V) to illuminate (O) one part (of this remarkable journey).

〈북아메리카에서 새롭게 발견된 날카로운 이빨과 지느러미가 있는 고래수염 화석을 분석하면 이런 놀라운 진화 과정 중의 한 부분을 설명할 수 있게 될 것으로 보인다.〉

| 정답분석 | 주어진 문장에 지시어 'this'가 포함되어 있으므로 이에 유의하여 삽입 가능한 위치를 고려해 보도록 한다. 'this remarkable journey'라는 표현이 나오려면 주어진 문장 앞에 '고래의 진화'와 관련된 내용이 있어야 할 것이다. 따라서 주어진 문장을 [B]에 넣는 것이 가장 적절하다.

02 2012 한양대

정답 ②

| 구문분석 | (Since [부사절: ~ 때문에] we have lived in a world in which the printed word was paramount), the chief burden (S) (of school) has been (V) to enable children to understand (C₁) and [등위접속사] produce (C₂) (with facility) the written language (of their society).

우리는 인쇄된 글이 최고인 세상에 살고 있기 때문에, 학교의 주요 과제는 아이들에게 사회의 문자 언어들을 이해하고 쉽게 생산할 수 있게 만드는 것이었다.

Much communication (S) (in our world) takes place (V) (through [전치사] graphic means) — [대시: 부연설명] both static and dynamic.

우리 세상의 많은 의사소통은 정적이거나 동적인 그래픽이라는 수단을 통하여 발생한다.

Web sites (S_1) incorporate (V_1) print (O), but they (S_2) also feature (V_2) cartoons, films, music, and the like (O_2).

웹사이트들은 물론 인쇄물을 포함하지만, 그들은 만화, 영화, 음악 등도 특징으로 한다.

Representational redescriptions (S) abound (V).

재현적인 재묘사들이 넘쳐 나고 있다.

Moreover, [접속부사] the print (S) (on computer screens) is (V) often far less linear (C) (in form and argument) (than the print in a book). [less ~ than ...: …보다 덜 ~하다]

게다가, 컴퓨터 화면의 인쇄물은 책의 인쇄물에 비해 그 형태와 주장에 있어서 흔히 훨씬 덜 선형적이다.

| 어휘 | **paramount** ⓐ 최고의, 지상의, 주요한 **chief** ⓐ 최고의, 우두머리의, 주요한 **with facility** 쉽게, 수월하게
static ⓐ 정적인, 정지 상태의 **dynamic** ⓐ 역동적인 **incorporate** ⓥ 통합하다, 포함시키다
representational ⓐ 재현적인, 묘사적인, 구상주의의 **redescription** ⓝ 재묘사, 재기술
abound ⓥ 아주 많다, 풍부하다 **linear** ⓐ 직선의, 선과 같은 **literacy** ⓝ 읽고 쓰는 능력, 교양

| 전문해석 | [A] 우리는 인쇄된 글이 최고인 세상에 살고 있기 때문에, 학교의 주요 과제는 아이들에게 사회의 문자 언어들을 이해하고 쉽게 생산할 수 있게 만드는 것이었다. **[B] 〈그러나 다른 형태의 읽고 쓰는 능력이 21세기에 들며 점점 중요해지고 있다.〉** 우리 세상의 많은 의사소통은 정적이거나 동적인 그래픽이라는 수단을 통하여 발생한다. 웹사이트들은 물론 인쇄물을 포함하지만, 그들은 만화, 영화, 음악 등도 특징으로 한다. 재현적인 재묘사들이 넘쳐 나고 있다. [C] 게다가, 컴퓨터 화면의 인쇄물은 책의 인쇄물에 비해 그 형태와 주장에 있어서 흔히 훨씬 덜 선형적이다. [D]

| 보기분석 | Yet(등위접속사) other forms(S) (of literacy) have become(V) increasingly important(C) (in the twenty-first century).

〈그러나 다른 형태의 읽고 쓰는 능력이 21세기에 들며 점점 중요해지고 있다.〉

| 정답분석 | 주어진 문장에서 'other forms of literacy'라는 표현을 참고하면 삽입할 위치를 추론할 수 있다. 다른 형태의 해독력(literary)에 대해 언급하려면 주어진 문장 앞에는 '특정한 해독력'이 먼저 소개되어야 할 것이다. 첫 번째 문장에서 이에 해당하는 '문자 해독력'에 관해 언급했고 [B] 다음으로는 '다른 형태의 해독력'의 예시에 해당하는 '정적이거나 동적인 그래픽'이 소개되고 있으므로 그 사이인 [B]에 주어진 문장을 넣는 것이 적절하다.

03 2014 건국대

정답 ④

| 구문분석 | Questions(S) (about whether snakes ever walked on legs) have long intrigued(V) scientists(O).

뱀이 다리로 걸었던 적이 있었는지는 오랫동안 과학자들의 호기심을 불러일으켜 왔다.

But (without any fossil evidence), there(유도부사) seemed(V) no possibility(S) (of an answer).

하지만 어떠한 화석 증거도 없이, 답이 나올 가능성은 없어 보였다.

That state(S) (of affairs) changed(V) dramatically, however(접속부사), (when(부사절: ~할 때) what appear to be ancient fossils were discovered in an Israeli quarry).

그러나 그런 상황은, 고대 화석들로 보이는 것들이 이스라엘의 채석장에서 발견됨에 따라 극적으로 달라졌다.

(To everyone' s surprise)(to one's surprise: 놀랍게도), the fossil evidence(S) indicates(V) that some prehistoric snakes had hind legs(O), (which(관계대명사) could have been used for walking).

모두가 놀랍게도, 이 화석 증거는 몇몇 선사시대의 뱀들이 걸을 때 사용했을 수 있는 것으로 보이는 뒷다리들을 가지고 있었다는 것을 보여 주었다.

(According to(전치사) paleontologists Michael Caldwell and Michael Lee), the specimens(S) (found in Israel) have(V) hind legs(O) (along with characteristics) (that(관계대명사) appear only in snakes).

고생물학자 Michael Caldwell과 Michael Lee에 따르면, 이스라엘에서 발견된 그 표본들은 뱀에서만 나타나는 특징들과 함께 뒷다리들을 갖고 있다.

In addition(접속부사), the jaws(S) are loosely connected(V), (allowing(분사구문) for wide-mouthed flexibility — exactly the kind snakes need to swallow large prey)(대시: 부연설명).

게다가, 턱들이 느슨하게 연결되어 있어서 입을 크게 벌릴 수 있도록 유연성을 주는데, 이것이 정확히 뱀들이 큰 먹잇감을 삼킬 때 필요한 유연성이다.

Even the number and kind of vertebrae(S) suggest(V) that the fossils are those of ancient snakes(O).

심지어 척추뼈의 수와 종류도 이 화석이 고대 뱀의 화석임을 암시한다.

Finally, there(유도부사) may be(V) just enough fossil evidence(C) (to prove that some snakes once walked on two legs).

마지막으로, 몇몇 뱀들은 한때 두 다리로 걸었음을 증명할 수 있는 충분한 화석 증거가 있을지도 모른다.

| 어휘 |

intrigue ⓥ ~의 호기심[흥미]을 유발하다; 매혹하다		dramatically ⓐⓓ 극적으로
fossil ⓝ 화석	quarry ⓝ 채석장	prehistoric ⓐ 선사시대의
hind legs ⓝ 〈동물학〉 뒷다리	paleontologist ⓝ 고생물학자	specimen ⓝ 표본, 견본, 샘플

prey ⓝ (사냥 동물의) 먹이, 사냥감　　vertebrae ⓝ (동물의) 등골뼈, 척추골

| 전문해석 | 뱀이 다리로 걸었던 적이 있었는지는 오랫동안 과학자들의 호기심을 불러일으켜 왔다. 하지만 어떠한 화석 증거도 없이, 답이 나올 가능성은 없어 보였다. [A] 그러나 그런 상황은, 고대 화석들로 보이는 것들이 이스라엘의 채석장에서 발견됨에 따라 극적으로 달라졌다. [B] 모두가 놀랍게도, 이 화석 증거는 몇몇 선사시대의 뱀들이 걸을 때 사용했을 수 있는 것으로 보이는 뒷다리들을 가지고 있었다는 것을 보여 주었다. [C] 생물학자 Michael Caldwell과 Michael Lee에 따르면, 이스라엘에서 발견된 그 표본들은 뱀에서만 나타나는 특징들과 함께 뒷다리들을 갖고 있다. **[D] 〈예를 들어 뇌 상자가 완전히 뼈로 감싸져 있다.〉** 게다가, 턱들이 느슨하게 연결되어 있어서 입을 크게 벌릴 수 있도록 유연성을 주는데, 이것이 정확히 뱀들이 큰 먹잇감을 삼킬 때 필요한 유연성이다. [E] 심지어 척추뼈의 수와 종류도 이 화석이 고대 뱀의 화석임을 암시한다. 마지막으로, 몇몇 뱀들은 한때 두 다리로 걸었음을 증명할 수 있는 충분한 화석 증거가 있을지도 모른다.

| 보기분석 | The brain case(S), for example(접속부사), is fully covered(V) (in bone).
〈예를 들어 뇌 상자가 완전히 뼈로 감싸져 있다.〉

| 정답분석 | 주어진 문장은 앞 내용에 대한 '예시'로 기능한다. 본문에서는 뒷다리를 가지고 있는 뱀의 화석에 대한 설명으로 시작되는데 [D] 앞 문장에서는 그 화석 표본이 '뱀에서만 나타나는 특징들과 함께 뒷다리들을 갖고 있다'고 했다. 따라서 [D]에 주어진 문장을 넣는다면 그 뒤 문장을 'In addition'으로 시작해서 뱀의 다른 특징들을 추가하는 것이 자연스러워 보인다. [D]가 주어진 문장을 삽입할 위치로 가장 적절하다.

04 2018 인하대

정답 ④

| 구문분석 | The Irish newcomers(S) soon realized(V) that their struggle against poverty, discrimination, and(등위접속사) religious persecution would not end in the United States(O).

아일랜드 이민자들은 가난, 차별, 그리고 종교적 박해에 대한 그들의 투쟁이 미국에서 끝나지 않을 것임을 곧 깨달았다.

The large numbers of Irish immigrants(S) (who(관계대명사) came to America in the 1830s) threatened(V) the jobs of native-born Protestants(O), (who(관계대명사) reacted with resentment and violence).

1830년대에 미국으로 온 수많은 아일랜드 이민자들은 토착 개신교도들의 일자리를 위협했는데, 그 개신교도들은 이에 대해 분노와 폭력으로 반응했다.

Employers(S) posted(V) signs(O) (outside their doors) (reading "No Irish Need Apply.")

고용주들은 "아일랜드인들은 입사 지원할 필요 없음"이라고 적힌 표지판을 문밖에다 내걸었다.

(Despised(분사구문) for their Roman Catholicism and their supposed "clannishness,") the Irish(S) competed(V) (with African Americans) (for the low-paying jobs) (at the bottom of the economic ladder).

그들이 로마 가톨릭교도라는 이유와 그들의 소문난 "배타성"을 이유로 경멸받았던 아일랜드인들은 경제적 사다리(경제적 지위)의 바닥에서 저임금 일자리를 놓고 흑인들과 경쟁했다.

They(S) filled(V_1) many high positions(O) (in the Catholic Church) and became(V_2) active(C) (in the Democratic party).

그들은 가톨릭교회의 많은 고위직을 차지했고 민주당에서 활발하게 활동했다.

| 어휘 |
newcomer ⓝ 새로 온 사람, 신입자　　realize ⓥ 깨닫다, 인식하다, (목표 등을) 실현하다
struggle ⓝ 노력, 투쟁　　discrimination ⓝ 구별, 식별, 차별　　religious ⓐ 종교(상)의, 종교적인
persecution ⓝ 박해　　immigrant ⓝ (다른 나라로 온) 이민자, 이주민
Protestant ⓝ (개)신교도, 프로테스탄트　　resentment ⓝ 분개, 원한
despise ⓥ 경멸하다, 멸시하다　　clannishness ⓝ 파벌[배타]적임　　compete ⓥ 겨루다, 경쟁하다
a measure of 어느 정도의　　influence ⓝ 영향(력), 작용

| 전문해석 | 아일랜드 이민자들은 가난, 차별, 그리고 종교적 박해에 대한 그들의 투쟁이 미국에서 끝나지 않을 것임을 곧 깨달았다. [A] 1830년대에 미국으로 온 수많은 아일랜드 이민자들은 토착 개신교도들의 일자리를 위협했는데, 그 개신교도들은 이에 대해 분노와 폭력으로 반응했다. [B] 고용주들은 "아일랜드인들은 입사 지원할 필요 없음"이라고 적힌 표지판을 문밖에다 내걸었다. [C] 그들이 로마 가톨릭교도라는 이유와 그들의 소문난 "배타성"을 이유로 경멸받았던 아일랜드인들은 경제적 사다리(경제적 지위)의 바닥에서 저임금 일자리를 놓고 흑인들과 경쟁했다. **[D] 〈그럼에도 불구하고, 1850년대까지 아일랜드인들은 미국에서 어느 정도의 영향력을 획득했다.〉** 그들은 가톨릭교회의 많은 고위직을 차지했고 민주당에서 활발하게 활동했다. [E]

| 보기분석 | Nevertheless, (by the 1850s), the Irish had gained a measure (of influence in America).
접속부사 / S / V / O
〈그럼에도 불구하고, 1850년대까지 아일랜드인들은 미국에서 어느 정도의 영향력을 획득했다.〉

| 정답분석 | 주어진 문장은 역접 표현인 'Nevertheless'로 시작되기 때문에 이 문장의 앞에는 '아일랜드인들이 영향력이 없거나 부족했던 시기'에 대해 언급해야 역접 연결이 자연스럽다. 그리고 주어진 문장의 뒤에는 아일랜드인들이 획득한 영향력의 내용을 예로 들거나 부연하는 것이 가능하다. 따라서 [D]가 주어진 문장을 삽입할 위치로 가장 적절하다.

05 2018 인하대

정답 ④

| 구문분석 | The Egyptians believed that life continued after death.
S / V / O
이집트인들은 삶이 죽은 뒤에도 계속된다고 믿었다.

The dead were taken (to the underworld) (where gods judged them by weighing their heart against the "feather of truth.")
S / V / 관계부사
죽은 사람들은 신들이 죽은 사람들의 심장과 "진실의 깃털"의 무게를 비교함으로써 그들을 심판하는 지하세계로 보내졌다.

Those (who passed the test) went (to the Field of Reeds) (to live forever), (while the heart of a person (who failed the test) was eaten by a creature (called Ammut) and the person was thus destroyed.
S / 관계대명사 / V / 부사적용법: ~해서 그 결과 / 부사절: 반면에 / 관계대명사
시험을 통과한 사람들은 갈대밭으로 가서 영원히 살았고 반면에 시험에 떨어진 사람의 심장은 암무트(Ammut)라는 생명체에게 먹혀서 그 사람은 파멸을 맞게 되었다.

(To allow people to enter the afterlife), Egyptians believed it necessary to preserve their bodies after death.
부사적용법: ~하기 위해서 / S / V / 가목적어 / O.C / 진목적어
사람들이 사후세계에 들어갈 수 있도록 하기 위해서, 이집트인들은 죽은 후에 몸을 보존하는 것이 필요하다고 믿었다.

(At first), they buried the dead (in the desert sands), (which soaked up the fluids and preserved the bodies naturally).
S / V / O / 관계대명사(계속적용법)
처음에, 그들은 죽은 사람들을 사막의 모래에 묻었는데, 시체에서 나오는 분비물들을 빨아들여 시체를 자연적으로 보존해 주었기 때문이다.

Later they developed a method (of preserving bodies) (by embalming them), (known as mummification).
S / V / O / by ~ing: ~함으로써 / 분사구문
나중에 그들은 방부처리를 함으로써 시체를 보존하는 방법을 개발했는데, 이것은 '미라화'라고 알려졌다.

Then they dried the body, coated it (in resin) and wrapped it (in layers of linen strips).
S / V_1 / O_1 / V_2 / O_2 / V_3 / O_3
그다음에 그들은 시체를 말렸고, 수지를 바르고 리넨 조각을 겹겹이 감쌌다.

Embalming was expensive and only the pharaoh and senior officials could afford the best treatment.
S_1 / V_1 / C / S_2 / V_2 / O
방부처리는 비용이 많이 들었고 그래서 파라오와 고위 관리들만이 그와 같은 가장 좋은 시체 처리를 할 수 있었다.

| 어휘 |
weigh ⓥ (저울에) 달다, (~의) 무게를 달다, (체중을) 달다
afterlife ⓝ 내세, 사후세계
preserve ⓥ 보전하다, 유지하다
soak ⓥ (액체 속에 푹) 담그다[담기다]
fluid ⓝ 유동체, 유체

mummification ⓝ 미라화　resin ⓝ 수지, 송진, 합성수지　layer ⓝ 층, 단층
linen ⓝ 리넨, 아마섬유　pharaoh ⓝ (고대 이집트의) 왕, 파라오　senior official ⓝ 고관, 고위층
embalmer ⓝ (시체를) 방부처리 하는 사람, 미라를 만드는 사람　remove ⓥ 옮기다, 제거하다
organ ⓝ (생물의) 기관

| 전문해석 | 이집트인들은 삶이 죽은 뒤에도 계속된다고 믿었다. 죽은 사람들은 신들이 죽은 사람들의 심장과 "진실의 깃털"의 무게를 비교함으로써 그들을 심판하는 지하세계로 보내졌다. 시험을 통과한 사람들은 갈대밭으로 가서 영원히 살았고 반면에 시험에 떨어진 사람의 심장은 암무트(Ammut)라는 생명체에게 먹혀서 그 사람은 파멸을 맞게 되었다. [A] 사람들이 사후세계에 들어갈 수 있도록 하기 위해서, 이집트인들은 죽은 후에 몸을 보존하는 것이 필요하다고 믿었다. [B] 처음에, 그들은 죽은 사람들을 사막의 모래에 묻었는데, 시체에서 나오는 분비물들을 빨아들여 시체를 자연적으로 보존해 주었기 때문이다. [C] 나중에 그들은 방부처리를 함으로써 시체를 보존하는 방법을 개발했는데, 이것은 '미라화'라고 알려졌다. **[D] 〈시체를 방부처리 하는 사람들은 맨 처음에 모든 내장을 제거하고, 심판을 받을 수 있도록 심장만을 그대로 남겨 두었다.〉** 그다음에 그들은 시체를 말렸고, 수지를 바르고 리넨 조각을 겹겹이 감쌌다. [E] 방부처리는 비용이 많이 들었고 그래서 파라오와 고위 관리들만이 그와 같은 가장 좋은 시체 처리를 할 수 있었다.

| 보기분석 | First the embalmers(S) removed(V) all the internal organs(O), (leaving only the heart in place)(분사구문) (so that it could be judged)(부사절: ~하기 위해서).

〈시체를 방부처리 하는 사람들은 맨 처음에 모든 내장을 제거하고, 심판을 받을 수 있도록 심장만을 그대로 남겨 두었다.〉

| 정답분석 | 주어진 문장은 시체를 방부처리 하여 '미라화'하는 절차의 시작을 설명하고 있는 것으로 보인다. 본문에서는 이집트인들이 시체를 보존하는 방법에 대해 사막의 모래에 묻는 것을 가장 먼저 소개했고 [C] 이후 방부처리 하는 방법을 개발한 것으로 설명했다. 따라서 주어진 문장은 시체를 방부처리 하는 세부적 과정을 설명하고 있으므로 [D]나 [E]에 삽입하는 것이 적절하나 [D] 이후에 'Then'으로 문장을 시작하여 방부처리 하는 과정이 이어서 설명되고 있으므로 그 앞부분인 [D]에 주어진 문장이 들어가는 것이 적절하다.

06 2016 한양대(에리카)

정답 ③

| 구문분석 | Sharks(S) are(V) no crueler(C) (than any other predator in the sea).

상어는 바다에 있는 다른 어떤 포식자와 마찬가지로 잔인하지 않다.

The marine environment(S) is(V) a harsh and(등위접속사) pitiless world(C).

해양 환경은 가혹하고 무자비한 세계이다.

(From the very start of life in the planktonic community), microscopic animal(S) attacks and devours(V) microscopic animal(O), in turn(차례로) (to be(부사적용법: ~해서 그 결과) consumed by some larger form of life (fighting the vicious and never-ending battle of survival).

플랑크톤 공동체에서 생명체가 시작되는 바로 그때부터, 미세한 동물들이 공격하고 다른 미세한 동물들을 잡아먹고, 다시 이들은 생존을 위한 사악하고 끝나지 않는 전쟁을 하는 보다 큰 동물에게 소비된다(잡아먹힌다).

And (it is) so on upward (in size) (through the cycle) (to the sharks, = the dominant predator of the oceans).

그리고 이러한 주기를 통해 바다의 주요한 포식자인 상어에 이르기까지 크기가 점점 커졌다.

But the consumption(S) (of one living thing by another form of life) is(V) the order of survival(C), (with nothing being wasted in nature)(with 분사구문).

그러나 하나의 생명체가 다른 종의 생명체에 의해 소비되는(먹히는) 것은 생존의 질서이며, 자연에서는 낭비되는 것이 없다.

Only man is the indiscriminate killer.
S V C
오직 인간만이 무차별적인 살인자다.

| 어휘 | **predator** ⓝ 포식자, 포식동물 **pitiless** ⓐ 인정사정없는, 냉혹한 **planktonic** ⓐ 부유생물의, 플랑크톤의 **microscopic** ⓐ 미세한, 현미경으로 봐야만 보이는 **indiscriminate** ⓐ 무분별한, 무차별적인

| 전문해석 | 상어는 바다에 있는 다른 어떤 포식자와 마찬가지로 잔인하지 않다. [A] 해양 환경은 가혹하고 무자비한 세계이다. [B] 플랑크톤 공동체에서 생명체가 시작되는 바로 그때부터, 미세한 동물들이 공격하고 다른 미세한 동물들을 잡아먹고, 다시 이들은 생존을 위한 사악하고 끝나지 않는 전쟁을 하는 보다 큰 동물에게 소비된다(잡아먹힌다). [C] **〈작은 물고기는 플랑크톤의 작은 생명체를 먹고 살고 그들은 차례로 큰 물고기와 다른 동물들에게 먹힌다.〉** 그리고 이러한 주기를 통해 바다의 주요한 포식자인 상어에 이르기까지 크기가 점점 커졌다. [D] 그러나 하나의 생명체가 다른 종의 생명체에 의해 소비되는(먹히는) 것은 생존의 질서이며, 자연에서는 낭비되는 것이 없다. 오직 인간만이 무차별적인 살인자다.

| 보기분석 | Small fish feed (upon the minute life forms) (in plankton), and they in turn are fed (upon by large fish and other animals).
S_1 V_1 S_2 차례로 V_2

〈작은 물고기는 플랑크톤의 작은 생명체를 먹고 살고 그들은 차례로 큰 물고기와 다른 동물들에게 먹힌다.〉

| 정답분석 | 주어진 문장에서는 '플랑크톤을 먹이로 하는 작은 물고기가 차례로 큰 물고기에게 먹힌다'는 내용이므로 '해양 생태계의 먹이사슬'에 대해 설명하는 것으로 보인다. 본문에서는 [B] 이후에 먹이사슬에 대해 처음으로 소개했고 [C] 이후로는 '이러한 주기가 상어에 이르기까지 크다'는 내용이 온다. 따라서 주어진 문장은 먹이사슬이 상어에게 도달하기 직전의 내용에 해당하는 내용이므로 [C]에 넣는 것이 흐름상 가장 적절하다.

07 2016 인하대

정답 ②

| 구문분석 | There are 140 known natural satellites, also called moons, (in orbit around the various planets in our solar system), (ranging from bodies larger than our own moon to small pieces of debris).
유도부사 V S = 분사구문

달이라고도 불리는 우리 태양계에서 여러 행성들의 궤도를 돌고 있는 140개의 자연 위성들이 있는데, 우리의 달보다 더 큰 위성에서부터 또 어떤 위성은 작은 파편에 이르기까지 다양하다.

(From 1610 to 1977), Saturn was thought (to be the only planet with rings).
from A to B: A에서 B까지 S V
1610년부터 1977년까지, 토성은 고리를 가진 유일한 행성으로 여겨졌다.

Particles (in these ring systems) range (in size from dust to boulders to house-size).
S V from A to B: A에서 B까지
이 고리 구조를 구성하는 입자들은 먼지에서부터 집 크기의 바위에 이르기까지 다양하다.

And they may be rocky and/or icy.
S V C
그리고 그것들은 암석이나 얼음, 혹은 그 두 가지 모두로 이루어져 있기도 하다.

Ancient astronomers believed that Earth was the center of the universe, and that the sun and all the other stars revolved around Earth.
S V O_1 O_2

고대 천문학자들은 지구가 우주의 중심이고, 태양과 다른 모든 별들이 지구 주위를 돈다고 믿었다.

Copernicus proved that Earth and the other planets in our solar system orbit our sun.
S V O
코페르니쿠스(Copernicus)는 지구와 우리 태양계의 다른 행성들이 태양 주위를 돈다는 것을 증명했다.

(Little by little), we are charting the universe.
S V O
조금씩, 우리는 우주의 그림을 그리고 있다.

| 어휘 | satellite ⓝ (인공) 위성, (행성의) 위성 orbit ⓝ 궤도 debris ⓝ 부스러기, 파편
particle ⓝ 미립자, 분자, 작은 조각 boulder ⓝ (물이나 비바람에 씻겨 반들반들해진) 바위
astronomer ⓝ 천문학자 revolve ⓥ (축을 중심으로) 돌다, 회전하다
chart ⓥ 도표[차트]로 만들다, 계획하다

| 전문해석 | 달이라고도 불리는 우리 태양계에서 여러 행성들의 궤도를 돌고 있는 140개의 자연 위성들이 있는데, 우리의 달보다 더 큰 위성에서부터 또 어떤 위성은 작은 파편에 이르기까지 다양하다. [A] 1610년부터 1977년까지, 토성은 고리를 가진 유일한 행성으로 여겨졌다. **[B] 〈이제 우리는 목성, 천왕성, 그리고 해왕성 역시 고리 구조를 가지고 있다는 것을 알고 있다.〉** 이 고리 구조를 구성하는 입자들은 먼지에서부터 집 크기의 바위에 이르기까지 다양하다. [C] 그리고 그것들은 암석이나 얼음, 혹은 그 두 가지 모두로 이루어져 있기도 하다. [D] 고대 천문학자들은 지구가 우주의 중심이고, 태양과 다른 모든 별들이 지구 주위를 돈다고 믿었다. [E] 코페르니쿠스(Copernicus)는 지구와 우리 태양계의 다른 행성들이 태양 주위를 돈다는 것을 증명했다. 조금씩, 우리는 우주의 그림을 그리고 있다.

| 보기분석 | We now know that Jupiter, Uranus, and Neptune also have ring systems.
S V O
〈이제 우리는 목성, 천왕성, 그리고 해왕성 역시 고리 구조를 가지고 있다는 것을 알고 있다.〉

| 정답분석 | 주어진 문장에는 'also'라는 표현이 들어 있는데 이것은 유사한 내용이 직전에 나와야 함을 의미한다. 따라서 고리 구조를 가진 유일한 행성으로 여겨졌던 '토성'을 먼저 소개한 뒤 [B]에 주어진 문장을 넣어야 현재 우리가 알고 있는 목성, 천왕성, 해왕성이 고리 구조를 가진 행성으로 추가로 언급되는 것이 흐름상 가장 자연스럽다.

08 2012 인천대

정답 ③

| 구문분석 | Generosity is also defined as the habit (of giving freely) (without expecting anything) (in return).
S V O.C
관대함은 또한 보답으로 아무것도 기대하지 않고 자유롭게 베푸는 습관으로 정의된다.

It can involve offering time, assets or talents (to aid someone in need).
S V O 부사적용법: ~하기 위해서
그것은 도움이 필요한 누군가를 돕기 위해 시간, 재산 또는 재능을 제공하는 것을 포함할 수 있다.

(Often equated with charity as a virtue), generosity is widely accepted (in society as a desirable trait).
분사구문 S V
종종 미덕으로 자선과 동일시되는 관대함은 바람직한 특성으로 사회에서 널리 받아들여진다.

Generosity is a guiding principle (for many registered charities, foundations and non-profit organizations).
S V C
관대함은 많은 등록된 자선단체, 재단 및 비영리 단체들에 대한 지침 원칙이다.

Rather, it includes the individual's pure intentions (of looking out for society's common good and giving from the heart).
접속부사 S V O 등위접속사

오히려, 그것은 사회의 공동선을 바라보고 마음으로부터 베풀려는 개인의 순수한 의도를 포함한다.

Generosity should reflect the individual's passion (to help others); (in Buddhism), generosity is the antidote (to the self-chosen poison) (called greed).
S_1 V_1 O 세미콜론: 부연설명 S_2 V_2 C

관대함은 다른 사람들을 도우려는 개인의 열정을 반영해야 한다; 불교에서, 관대함은 탐욕이라 불리는 스스로 선택한 독에 대한 해독제이다.

| 어휘 | generosity ⓝ 관대함 asset ⓝ 자산, 재산
equate ⓥ 서로 같음을 나타내다, 동일시하다 charity ⓝ 자비, 동정
virtue ⓝ 미덕, 선행 trait ⓝ 특색, 특징 non-profit ⓐ 이익이 없는, 비영리의

common good ⓝ 공익, 공유재산 status ⓝ 상태, 지위 reflect ⓥ 반영하다, 반사하다
Buddhism ⓝ 불교 antidote ⓝ 해독제, 대책 greed ⓝ 탐욕

| 전문해석 | 관대함은 또한 보답으로 아무것도 기대하지 않고 자유롭게 베푸는 습관으로 정의된다. 그것은 도움이 필요한 누군가를 돕기 위해 시간, 재산 또는 재능을 제공하는 것을 포함할 수 있다. [A] 종종 미덕으로 자선과 동일시되는 관대함은 바람직한 특성으로 사회에서 널리 받아들여진다. [B] 관대함은 많은 등록된 자선단체, 재단 및 비영리 단체들에 대한 지침 원칙이다. **[C] 〈관대함은 오직 개인의 경제적인 상태에 의존하는 것은 아니다.〉** 오히려, 그것은 사회의 공동선을 바라보고 마음으로부터 베풀려는 개인의 순수한 의도를 포함한다. [D] 관대함은 다른 사람들을 도우려는 개인의 열정을 반영해야 한다; 불교에서, 관대함은 탐욕이라 불리는 스스로 선택한 독에 대한 해독제이다.

| 보기분석 | Generosity is not solely based (on one's economic status).
S V
〈관대함은 오직 개인의 경제적인 상태에 의존하는 것은 아니다.〉

| 정답분석 | 주어진 문장에서 '관대함은 개인의 경제적 상태에만 의존하는 것이 아니다'라고 했으므로 '경제적 상태'와는 다른 관대함의 특징이 다음에 언급되어야 할 것이다. [C] 이후 문장에서는 역접의 기능이 있는 'Rather'를 활용하여 '사회의 공동선을 바라보는 개인의 의도'가 설명되고 있다. 따라서 주어진 문장을 [C]에 넣는 것이 가장 자연스럽다.

09 2018 한양대

정답 ②

| 구문분석 | Theory is built (upon an underlying assumption) (that specific events are not unique and do not have unique causes).
S V =

이론은 특정한 사건들이 고유하지 않고 특유한 원인이 없다는 기본 가정에 기초한다.

Rather, we assume that most important events are single instances (of broader patterns).
접속부사 S V O
오히려, 우리는 가장 중요한 사건들은 더 넓은 패턴들의 단일 사례들이라고 가정한다.

(If we want to prevent wars), we must have some notion (of what causes them).
부사절: 만약 ~라면 S V O
만약 우리가 전쟁을 예방하길 원한다면, 우리는 전쟁의 원인에 대한 개념을 가져야만 한다.

This requires a supposition (that different wars have something in common).
S V O =
이것은 서로 다른 전쟁들이 공통점을 가지고 있다는 가정을 필요로 한다.

가주어
For example, it might seem dubious to equate the causes (of World War I) with the causes (of World War II).
접속부사 V C 진주어
예를 들어, 제1차 세계 대전의 원인들을 제2차 세계 대전의 원인들과 동일시하는 것은 의심스러워 보일 수 있다.

However, (if the lessons of the past are to be applied to the problems of today), we must assume that events (in the future) are somehow related (to those) (in the past).
접속부사 부사절: 만약 ~라면 S V O

하지만, 만약 과거의 교훈들이 현재의 문제에 적용되려면, 미래의 사건들이 과거의 사건들과 어느 정도는 관련이 있다고 가정해야만 한다.

There is a big difference (between assuming that similar events have something (in common) and assuming that they are identical).
유도부사 V S between A and B: A와 B 사이

유사한 사건들 사이에 공통점이 있다고 가정하는 것과 그 사건들이 동일하다고 가정하는 것은 큰 차이가 있다.

(To develop a theory of wars), we only need assume that there are some causes in common.
부사적용법: ~하기 위해서 S V O
전쟁에 관한 하나의 이론을 발전시키기 위해서, 우리는 오직 몇 가지 공통적인 원인이 있다고 가정할 필요가 있다.

| 어휘 | underlying ⓐ (겉으로 잘 드러나지는 않지만) 근본적인[근원적인] supposition ⓝ 상상, 추측, 가정
dubious ⓐ 의심하는, 미심쩍어하는 equate A with B A와 B를 동일시하다

starkly ⓐⓓ 전혀, 완전히 problematical ⓐ 문제의, 의문의, 의심스러운

| 전문해석 | 이론은 특정한 사건들이 고유하지 않고 특유한 원인이 없다는 기본 가정에 기초한다. 오히려, 우리는 가장 중요한 사건들은 더 넓은 패턴들의 단일 사례들이라고 가정한다. [A] 만약 우리가 전쟁을 예방하길 원한다면, 우리는 전쟁의 원인에 대한 개념을 가져야만 한다. 이것은 서로 다른 전쟁들이 공통점을 가지고 있다는 가정을 필요로 한다. **[B] 〈그렇게 노골적으로 말할 때, 이 생각은 많은 사람들에게 문제가 있는 것처럼 보인다.〉** 예를 들어, 제1차 세계 대전의 원인들을 제2차 세계 대전의 원인들과 동일시하는 것은 의심스러워 보일 수 있다. [C] 하지만, 만약 과거의 교훈들이 현재의 문제에 적용되려면, 미래의 사건들이 과거의 사건들과 어느 정도는 관련이 있다고 가정해야만 한다. 유사한 사건들 사이에 공통점이 있다고 가정하는 것과 그 사건들이 동일하다고 가정하는 것은 큰 차이가 있다. [D] 전쟁에 관한 하나의 이론을 발전시키기 위해서, 우리는 오직 몇 가지 공통적인 원인이 있다고 가정할 필요가 있다.

| 보기분석 | (When stated so starkly), this idea will appear problematical (to many).
부사절: ~할 때 / this idea: S / will appear: V / problematical: C
〈그렇게 노골적으로 말할 때, 이 생각은 많은 사람들에게 문제가 있는 것처럼 보인다.〉

| 정답분석 | 주어진 문장에 'this idea'라는 표현이 있으므로 직전 내용에 '특정한 사상이나 가정'이 먼저 소개되어야 할 것이다. 또한 [B]의 앞 문장과 [B] 이후 문장이 'For example'로 연결되기에는 흐름상 자연스럽지 않다. 따라서 주어진 문장을 [B]에 삽입하면 주어진 문장의 'this idea'가 직전 문장에 언급된 'supposition'을 지시하며 '문제가 있는 것처럼 보이는' 예시가 [B] 이후 내용으로 연결되어 가장 자연스럽다.

10 2012 국민대

정답 ③

| 구문분석 | (Just before Christmas 1887), a young Dutch doctor M. E. Dubois arrived (in Sumatra), (in the Dutch East Indies), (with the intention of finding the earliest human remains on Earth).
before: 전치사 / a young Dutch doctor M. E. Dubois: S / arrived: V

1887년 크리스마스 직전에, 젊은 네덜란드 의사 뒤부아(M. E. Dubois)가 지구상에서 가장 초기의 인간 유적을 발견할 의도로 네덜란드 동인도 수마트라에 도착했다.

Several things were extraordinary (about this).
Several things: S / were: V / extraordinary: C
이것에 대해 몇 가지 특별한 점이 있었다.

(To begin with), no one had gone looking (for ancient human bones before).
no one: S / had gone looking: V
우선, 이전에는 아무도 고대인의 뼈를 찾아간 적이 없었다.

Everything (that had been found to this point) had been found accidentally, and nothing (in Dubois's background) suggested that he was the ideal candidate to make the process intentional.
Everything: S_1 / that: 관계대명사 / had been found: V_1 / nothing: S_2 / suggested: V_2 / that he was the ideal candidate to make the process intentional: O
이 시점까지 발견된 모든 것은 우연히 발견되었고, 뒤부아의 배경에는 그 어떤 것도 그가 의도적으로 이 과정을 수행하기에 이상적인 후보임을 암시하지 않았다.

He was an anatomist (by training), (with no background in paleontology).
He: S / was: V / an anatomist: C
그는 훈련을 받은 해부학자이고, 고생물학에 대한 경력은 없었다.

Nor was there any special reason (to suppose that Sumatra would hold early human remains).
Nor: 접속사: 또한 아니다 / was: V / any special reason: S
또한 수마트라가 초기 인간의 유해를 보유하고 있을 것이라고 추측할 특별한 이유도 없었다.

Dubois was driven (to Sumatra) (on nothing) (stronger than a hunch and the knowledge) (that Sumatra was full of caves, the environment (in which most of the important hominid fossils had so far been found).
Dubois: S / was driven: V / the knowledge = that Sumatra was ~ / full of caves = the environment / in which: 관계대명사
뒤부아는 오로지 직감과 수마트라가 지금까지 대부분의 중요한 유인원 화석이 발견된 환경인 동굴로 가득 차 있다는 지식으로 수마트라로 이끌렸다.

What is most extraordinary (in all this) is that he found what he was looking for.
S V C
이 모든 것 중에서 가장 놀라운 것은 그가 자신이 찾던 것을 발견했다는 것이다.

| 어휘 | remains ⓝ 유적, 유물, 유해 intentional ⓐ 의도적인, 고의로 한 extraordinary ⓐ 기이한, 놀라운
anatomist ⓝ 해부학자 paleontology ⓝ 고생물학 hunch ⓝ 예감, 직감
hominid ⓝ 인류, 인류의 조상(진화 인류의 모체가 된 사람이나 동물)
fastness ⓝ 요새, (접근하기 어려운) 피난처, 은둔처 archipelago ⓝ 군도, 다도해

| 전문해석 | 1887년 크리스마스 직전에, 젊은 네덜란드 의사 뒤부아(M. E. Dubois)가 지구상에서 가장 초기의 인간 유적을 발견할 의도로 네덜란드 동인도 수마트라에 도착했다. [A] 이것에 대해 몇 가지 특별한 점이 있었다. [B] 우선, 이전에는 아무도 고대인의 뼈를 찾아간 적이 없었다. 이 시점까지 발견된 모든 것은 우연히 발견되었고, 뒤부아의 배경에는 그 어떤 것도 그가 의도적으로 이 과정을 수행하기에 이상적인 후보임을 암시하지 않았다. 그는 훈련을 받은 해부학자이고, 고생물학에 대한 경력은 없었다. 또한 수마트라가 초기 인간의 유해를 보유하고 있을 것이라고 추측할 특별한 이유도 없었다. **[C] 〈논리학은 만약 고대인의 유해가 발견된다면, 그곳은 군도의 요새(같은 곳)가 아니라 크고 오랫동안 인간이 거주해 온 땅일 것이라고 지시한다.〉** [D] 뒤부아는 오로지 직감과 수마트라가 지금까지 대부분의 중요한 유인원 화석이 발견된 환경인 동굴로 가득 차 있다는 지식으로 수마트라로 이끌렸다. 이 모든 것 중에서 가장 놀라운 것은 그가 자신이 찾던 것을 발견했다는 것이다.

| 보기분석 | Logic dictated that (if ancient people were to be found at all), it would be on a large and long-populated landmass, (not in the comparative fastness of an archipelago).
S V O 부사절: 만약 ~라면 B, not A: A가 아니라 B

〈논리학은 만약 고대인의 유해가 발견된다면, 그곳은 군도의 요새(같은 곳)가 아니라 크고 오랫동안 인간이 거주해 온 땅일 것이라고 지시한다.〉

| 정답분석 | 주어진 문장에서는 '고대인의 유해는 군도의 요새가 아니라 크고 오랫동안 인간이 거주해 온 곳에서 발견될 것'이라는 논리학의 지시를 언급하고 있다. 이는 수마트라섬이 고대인의 유해를 발견하기에 부적절한 곳이었다는 학문적 내용이라 볼 수 있다. 본문에서는 뒤부아가 수마트라에서 초기 인간의 화석을 발견함에 있어서 몇 가지 특별한 점이 소개되고 있는데 그중 수마트라섬에 관한 언급은 [C] 직전에 나온다. 따라서 '수마트라가 초기 인간의 유해를 보유하고 있을 것을 추측할 특별한 이유도 없었다'는 내용과 [C] 이후에 '뒤부아는 오직 직감에 이끌려 수마트라에 갔다'는 내용 사이에 주어진 문장을 넣는 것이 가장 적절하다.

11 2011 가톨릭대

정답 ③

| 구문분석 | There has never been a period (in medicine) (when the future has looked so bright).
유도부사 V S 관계부사
의학에 있어 미래가 이렇게 밝아 보이는 시기는 전혀 없었다.

The scientists (who do research on the cardiovascular system) are entirely confident (that they will soon be working close to the center of things), and they no longer regard the mechanisms of heart disease as impenetrable mysteries.
S_1 관계대명사 V_1 C S_2 더 이상 ~ 않다 V_2 O O.C
심혈관계를 연구하는 과학자들은 그들이 곧 이 연구의 핵심에 다다를 것으로 전적으로 확신하고 있으며, 더 이상 심장병의 체계를 불가해한 미스터리로 여기지 않는다.

The cancer scientists, (for all their public disagreements) (about how best to organize their research), are in possession (of insights) (into the intimate functioning) (of normal and neoplastic cells) (that were unimaginable a few years back).
S V C 관계대명사

암 전문가들은 그들의 연구를 가장 잘 구성하는 방법에 대한 여론 분열(대중들의 의견 차이)에도 불구하고 몇 년 전에는 상상할 수 없었던 정상 세포와 종양 세포의 세부적 기능에 대한 통찰력을 가지고 있다.

The neurobiologists can do all sorts (of things) (in their investigation), and the brain is an organ (different from what it seemed 25 years ago).
S1 V1 O S2 V2 C

신경 생물학자들은 그들의 연구에 있어서 모든 종류의 일을 할 수 있고, 뇌는 25년 전에 보였던 것과는 다른 (신체)기관이다.

In short, I believe that the major diseases (of human beings) have become approachable biological puzzles, (ultimately solvable).
접속부사 S V O

간단히 말해서, 나는 인간이 가지는 주요 질병들이 접근 가능한 생물학적 퍼즐이 되었고, 궁극적으로는 해결 가능한 퍼즐이라고 믿는다.

가주어
It follows (from this) that it is now possible to begin thinking (about a human society) (relatively free of disease).
V 진주어 that

이 때문에 상대적으로 질병이 없는 인간사회에 대해 생각하기 시작하는 것이 이제는 가능하다고 하다.

This would surely have been an unthinkable notion a half century ago.
S V C
이는 확실하게 반세기 전에는 생각할 수 없는 개념이었다.

What will we do (about dying, and about all that population), (if such things were to come about)?
의문사 V S 부사절: 만약 ~라면
만일 그런 일들이 일어난다면, 우리는 죽음에 대해, 그리고 그 모든 인구에 대해 무엇을 할 것인가?

What can we die of, (if not disease)?
의문사 V S 부사절: 만약 ~라면
질병이 아니라면, 우리는 무엇에 의해 죽게 될 것인가?

| 어휘 | **cardiovascular** ⓐ 심혈관의 **no longer** 더 이상 ~ 아닌[하지 않는] **mechanism** ⓝ 기계(장치), 구조, 구성
impenetrable ⓐ 불가해한, 이해할 수 없는 **organize** ⓥ 조직하다, 구성하다
in possession of ~을 소유하여 **insight** ⓝ 통찰력, 이해 **intimate** ⓐ 친밀한, 깊은, 정통한
functioning ⓝ 기능, 작용 **neoplastic cell** 종양 세포, 신생 세포
unimaginable ⓐ 상상할[생각할] 수 없는 **neurobiologist** ⓝ 신경생리학자
approachable ⓐ 가까이하기 쉬운, 접근할 수 있는, 이해하기 쉬운 **ultimately** ⓐⓓ 궁극적으로, 결국
free of ~이 없는 **unthinkable** ⓐ 생각할[상상할] 수 없는
apocalyptic ⓐ 종말론적, 세계의 종말을 예언하는

| 전문해석 | 의학에 있어 미래가 이렇게 밝아 보이는 시기는 전혀 없었다. 심혈관계를 연구하는 과학자들은 그들이 곧 이 연구의 핵심에 다다를 것으로 전적으로 확신하고 있으며, 더 이상 심장병의 체계를 불가해한 미스터리로 여기지 않는다. 암 전문가들은 그들의 연구를 가장 잘 구성하는 방법에 대한 여론 분열(대중들의 의견 차이)에도 불구하고 몇 년 전에는 상상할 수 없었던 정상 세포와 종양 세포의 세부적 기능에 대한 통찰력을 가지고 있다. 신경 생물학자들은 그들의 연구에 있어서 모든 종류의 일을 할 수 있고, 뇌는 25년 전에 보였던 것과는 다른 (신체)기관이다.
간단히 말해서, 나는 인간이 가지는 주요 질병들이 접근 가능한 생물학적 퍼즐이 되었고, 궁극적으로는 해결 가능한 퍼즐이라고 믿는다. [A] 이 때문에 상대적으로 질병이 없는 인간사회에 대해 생각하기 시작하는 것이 이제는 가능하다고 하다. [B] 이는 확실하게 반세기 전에는 생각할 수 없는 개념이었다. **[C] 〈이상하게도, 이러한 생각은 종말론적인 뉘앙스를 가진다.〉** 만일 그런 일들이 일어난다면, 우리는 죽음에 대해, 그리고 그 모든 인구에 대해 무엇을 할 것인가? [D] 질병이 아니라면, 우리는 무엇에 의해 죽게 될 것인가?

| 보기분석 | (Oddly enough), it has an apocalyptic sound today.
S V O
〈이상하게도, 이러한 생각은 종말론적인 뉘앙스를 가진다.〉

| 정답분석 | 주어진 문장의 지시사 'it'에 유의하자. 주어진 문장에서는 의미상 역접 표현에 해당하는 'Oddly enough' 표현을 사용하여 무언가가 '종말론적인 뉘앙스'를 가진다는 부정적인 내용이 서술되었다. 본문의 시작은 질병이 없는 인간사회에 대한 긍정적일 내용이 소개되지만 [C] 이후에는 '죽음'과 '죽지 않는 사람들로 인한 인구의 증가'와 같은 부정적인 뉘앙스로 글이 전개

된다. 따라서 주어진 문장은 긍정적인 내용과 부정적인 내용 사이인 [C]에 넣는 것이 흐름상 가장 적절하다.

12 2011 동덕여대

정답 ①

| 구문분석 | (In the United States), the top-status occupations are the professions — physicians, lawyers, professors, and clergy — (requiring many years of education and training).
S: the top-status occupations / V: are / C: the professions / 대시: 부연설명

미국에서, 최고 지위의 직업은 의사, 변호사, 교수 그리고 성직자와 같은 수년간의 교육과 훈련을 필요로 하는 직업이다.

(At the other end of the hierarchy), the lowest prestige is associated (with occupations) (requiring little formal education) — for example, bus drivers, sanitation workers, and janitors.
S: the lowest prestige / V: is associated / 대시: 부연설명 / for example: 접속부사

계층의 반대쪽 끝에서, 가장 낮은 명성은 버스 운전사, 환경미화원 그리고 (아파트, 사무소) 관리인과 같은 정규 교육을 거의 필요로 하지 않은 직업들과 관련이 있다.

Prestige is linked (to income), but there are exceptions, (such as college professors, (who have high prestige but relatively low salaries compared to physicians and lawyers).
S: Prestige / V: is linked / there: 유도부사 / V: are / S: exceptions / such as: 전치사 / who: 관계대명사

명성은 소득과 연계돼 있지만, 대학교수들의 경우는 예외도 있는데 이들은 위신은 높지만 의사와 변호사에 비해 상대적으로 낮은 급여를 받는다.

Conversely, some low-prestige workers receive high union wages and benefits.
Conversely: 접속부사 / S: some low-prestige workers / V: receive / O: high union wages and benefits

반대로, 일부 하위직 근로자들은 높은 노조 임금과 혜택을 받는다.

Criminals are often well rewarded (with income and respect) (in their communities), (while politicians — many of whom are wealthy — are frequently less respected than occupations) (such as secretary and bank teller).
S: Criminals / V: are often well rewarded / while: 부사절: 반면에 / 대시: 부연설명 / such as: 전치사

범죄자들은 종종 그들의 지역 사회에서 (금전적) 수입과 존경으로 보상을 잘 받는 반면에 정치인들은—그들 중 많은 수가 부자이다—비서와 은행 창구 직원 같은 직업들보다 종종 덜 존중을 받는다.

| 어휘 |

status ⓝ 지위, 신분	**physician** ⓝ 의사	**clergy** ⓝ 목사
hierarchy ⓝ (사회나 조직 내의) 계급(계층)		**prestige** ⓝ 위신, 명망
be associated with ~와 관련되다	**sanitation** ⓝ 공중위생	**janitor** ⓝ 잡역부
exception ⓝ 예외	**relatively** ⓐⓓ 상대적으로	**compared to** ~와 비교하여
conversely ⓐⓓ 거꾸로, 반대로	**wage** ⓝ 임금	**bank teller** 은행 창구 직원
postindustrial ⓐ 탈공업화의, 탈공업화 시대의		

| 전문해석 | **[A] 〈탈공업화 사회에서 소득 또한 중요하지만, 명성은 직업적 지위와 연관되어 있다.〉** 미국에서, 최고 지위의 직업은 의사, 변호사, 교수 그리고 성직자와 같은 수년간의 교육과 훈련을 필요로 하는 직업이다. [B] 계층의 반대쪽 끝에서, 가장 낮은 명성은 버스 운전사, 환경미화원 그리고 (아파트, 사무소) 관리인과 같은 정규 교육을 거의 필요로 하지 않은 직업들과 관련이 있다. 명성은 소득과 연계돼 있지만, 대학교수들의 경우는 예외도 있는데 이들은 위신은 높지만 의사와 변호사에 비해 상대적으로 낮은 급여를 받는다. [C] 반대로, 일부 하위직 근로자들은 높은 노조 임금과 혜택을 받는다. [D] 범죄자들은 종종 그들의 지역 사회에서 (금전적) 수입과 존경으로 보상을 잘 받는 반면에 정치인들은—그들 중 많은 수가 부자이다—비서와 은행 창구 직원 같은 직업들보다 종종 덜 존중을 받는다.

| 보기분석 | (In postindustrial societies), prestige is linked (to occupational status), (although income is also important).
S: prestige / V: is linked / although: 부사절: 비록 ~일지라도

〈탈공업화 사회에서 소득 또한 중요하지만, 명성은 직업적 지위와 연관되어 있다.〉

| 정답분석 | 글의 전개가 보통 일반화된 내용에서 구체적인 내용으로 이어진다는 점을 참고하여 삽입할 위치를 추론해 본다. 주어진 문장을 번역하면 "탈공업화 사회에서 소득 또한 중요하지만, 명성은 직업적 지위와 연관되어 있다."이다. 따라서 주어진 문장을 명성과 직업의 관련성을 소개하기 위한 일반화된 내용으로 본다면 [A] 이후에 나오는 미국의 구체적 사례가 자연스럽게 연결된다. [A]가 주어진 문장을 넣기에 가장 적절하다.

13 2013 경희대

정답 ①

| 구문분석 | that(명사절 접속사) 생략

Globalization(O), argues(V) *New York Times* columnist Tom Friedman(S), is "making it possible for corporations to reach farther, faster, cheaper, and deeper around the world" and is fostering "a flowering of both wealth and technological innovation the likes of which the world has never before seen."

both A and B: A, B 둘 다

'뉴욕타임스' 칼럼니스트 톰 프리드먼(Tom Friedman)은 세계화가 "기업이 더 멀리, 더 빨리, 더 싸게, 더 깊숙이 세계 곳곳에 도달하는 것을 가능하게 한다"며 "세계가 이전에 본 적이 없었던 부와 기술 혁신의 번영을 가져온다"고 주장한다.

(To David Korten, a former Ford Foundation official and now a prominent globalization critic), it(S) is(V) "market tyranny(C) (extending its reach) (across the planet) (like a cancer), (destroying livelihoods), and(등위접속사) (feeding on life) (in an insatiable quest for money)."

포드 재단의 전 관료이자 현재 저명한 세계화 비평가인 데이비드 코튼(David Korten)에게 그것(세계화)은 "암처럼 지구 전역으로 범위를 확장하고 생계를 파괴하며 돈에 대한 탐욕스러운 추구를 위해 인간의 삶에 기생하고 있는 시장 횡포"이다.

The careful listener(S) (to this by-now-familiar debate) can actually discern(V) a striking point(O) (of agreement).

이제는 익숙한 이 논쟁을 주의 깊게 듣는 사람은 실제로 합의점을 식별할 수 있다.

Yet(등위접속사) there(유도부사)'s(V) mounting evidence(S) (that multinational firms may be less capable of delivering competitive products than national or local firms).

그러나 다국적 기업이 국내 또는 현지 기업보다 경쟁력 있는 제품을 생산할 능력이 부족할 수도 있다는 증거가 늘어나고 있다.

Any first-year economics student(S) learns(V) that firms can lower average costs(O) (by expanding), but(등위접속사) (only up to a point).

경제학과 1학년 학생이라면 누구나 기업이 확장함으로써 평균 비용을 낮출 수 있지만, 어느 정도까지만 절감할 수 있다는 것을 배운다.

(Beyond(전치사) that point) ((according to(전치사) the law of diminishing returns to scale)), complexities, breakdowns, and inefficiencies(S) begin to drive(V) average costs back up.

그 정도를 넘어가면 (수확체감법칙(규모에 대한 수익률 감소의 법칙)에 따라) 복잡성, 고장, 그리고 비효율성이 평균 비용을 다시 증가시키기 시작한다.

The collapse(S_1) (of massive state-owned enterprises) (in the old Soviet Union) and the bankruptcies(S_2) (of Chrysler and New York City) are(V) notable reminders(C) (of a lesson) (that) (we should have absorbed from the dinosaur: Bigger is not always better). 콜론: 동격

구소련의 거대한 국영 기업들의 붕괴와 크라이슬러와 뉴욕시의 파산은 우리가 거대 기업들에서 얻을 수 있는 교훈을 상기시켜 준다: 큰 것이 항상 좋은 것은 아니다.

| 어휘 |

globalization ⓝ 세계화 **foster** ⓥ 조성하다, 발전시키다 **flower** ⓥ 번영하다, 전성기에 이르다
innovation ⓝ 혁신 **prominent** ⓐ 현저한, 뛰어난 **tyranny** ⓝ 압제, 독재
insatiable ⓐ 탐욕스러운, 채울 수 없는 **quest** ⓝ 탐구, 추구 **discern** ⓥ 식별하다, 분간하다
mount ⓥ 오르다, 증가하다 **up to a point** 어느 정도(는)
the law of diminishing returns to scale 수확 체감의 법칙(일정한 농지에서 작업하는 노동자 수가 증가할수록 1인당 수확량은 점차 적어진다는 경제법칙) **notable** ⓐ 주목할 만한 **euphoria** ⓝ (극도의) 행복감, 희열

| 전문해석 | '뉴욕타임즈' 칼럼니스트 톰 프리드먼(Tom Friedman)은 세계화가 "기업이 더 멀리, 더 빨리, 더 싸게, 더 깊숙이 세계 곳곳에 도달하는 것을 가능하게 한다"며 "세계가 이전에 본 적이 없었던 부와 기술 혁신의 번영을 가져온다"고 주장한다. 포드 재단의 전 관료이자 현재 저명한 세계화 비평가인 데이비드 코튼(David Korten)에게 그것(세계화)은 "암처럼 지구 전역으

로 범위를 확장하고 생계를 파괴하며 돈에 대한 탐욕스러운 추구를 위해 인간의 삶에 기생하고 있는 시장 횡포"이다. 이제는 익숙한 이 논쟁을 주의 깊게 듣는 사람은 실제로 합의점을 식별할 수 있다. **[A] 〈간단히 말해서, 양측은 한쪽은 행복감을 가지고 다른 한쪽은 두려움을 가지고 세계적 규모의 사업이 미래의 흐름이라고 가정한다.〉** 그러나 다국적 기업이 국내 또는 현지 기업보다 경쟁력 있는 제품을 생산할 능력이 부족할 수도 있다는 증거가 늘어나고 있다. [B] 경제학과 1학년 학생이라면 누구나 기업이 확장함으로써 평균 비용을 낮출 수 있지만, 어느 정도까지만 절감할 수 있다는 것을 배운다. 그 정도를 넘어가면 (수확체감법칙(규모에 대한 수익률 감소의 법칙)에 따라) 복잡성, 고장, 그리고 비효율성이 평균 비용을 다시 증가시키기 시작한다. [C] 구소련의 거대한 국영 기업들의 붕괴와 크라이슬러와 뉴욕시의 파산은 우리가 거대 기업들에서 얻을 수 있는 교훈을 상기시켜 준다: 큰 것이 항상 좋은 것은 아니다. [D]

| 보기분석 | In short(접속부사), both sides(S) assume(V), one with euphoria and the other with fear(=), that global-scale business is the wave of the future(O).

〈간단히 말해서, 양측은 한쪽은 행복감을 가지고 다른 한쪽은 두려움을 가지고 세계적 규모의 사업이 미래의 흐름이라고 가정한다.〉

| 정답분석 | 본문의 도입부에서는 세계화에 대한 양쪽의 의견 차이가 소개되고 세 번째 문장부터 양쪽의 '합의점'이 언급되었다. 주어진 문장에서는 논쟁의 양측이 모두 '세계적 규모의 사업이 미래의 흐름'이라고 가정하고 있으므로 최초로 '합의점'을 언급한 뒤에 그 구체적 내용인 주어진 문장을 삽입하는 것이 자연스러울 것이다. 따라서 [A]가 정답으로 가장 적절하다.

14 2015 중앙대

정답 ③

| 구문분석 | Animals(S) rely on(V) many kinds (of chemical signals) (to regulate their body activities)(부사적용법: ~하기 위해서).

동물들은 그들의 신체 활동을 조절하기 위해 많은 종류의 화학적 신호에 의존한다.

The estrogens(S) are(V) one kind(C) (of signal), a hormone(=).

에스트로겐은 신호의 한 종류인 호르몬이다.

An animal hormone(S) is(V) a chemical signal(C) (that(관계대명사 1) is carried by the circulatory system (usually in the blood) and(등위접속사) (that(관계대명사 2) communicates regulatory messages throughout the body).

동물 호르몬은 일반적으로 혈액 속의 순환계에 의해 운반되고 몸 전체에 조절 메시지를 전달하는 화학적 신호이다.

Hormones(S) are made and secreted(V) mainly (by organs) (called endocrine glands).

호르몬은 주로 내분비샘이라고 불리는 기관에 의해 만들어지고 분비된다.

Collectively, all(S) (of an animal's hormone-secreting cells) constitute(V) its endocrine system(O), one (of two bodily systems) (for communication and chemical regulation)(=).

집합적으로 동물의 호르몬을 분비하는 모든 세포들은 의사소통과 화학적 조절을 위한 두 가지 신체 시스템 중 하나인 내분비계를 구성한다.

The other system(S) (of internal communication and regulation) is(V) the nervous system(C).

내부 의사소통과 조절의 또 다른 체계는 신경계이다.

The flick(S_1) (of a frog's tongue) (catching a fly) and the jerk(S_2) (of your hand away from a flame) result(V) (from high-speed nerve signals).

개구리의 혀가 파리를 잡는 소리와 불꽃에서 손을 튕기는 소리는 고속 신경 신호에서 비롯된다.

The endocrine system(S) coordinates(V) slower but longer-lasting responses(O).

내분비계는 더 느리지만 더 오래 지속되는 반응들을 조절한다.

(In some cases), the endocrine system takes hours or even days (to act), (partly because of the time) (that) (it takes for hormones to be made and transported to all their target organs) and (partly because the cellular response may take time).

S: the endocrine system / V: takes / O: hours or even days / 전치사: because of / 등위접속사: and / 부사절: ~ 때문에: because

어떤 경우에는, 내분비계가 작용하는 데 몇 시간 또는 심지어 며칠이 걸리는데, 부분적으로는 호르몬이 만들어지고 타깃이 되는 모든 신체기관에 전달되는 데 시간이 걸리기 때문이고 또 다른 한편으로는 세포 반응에 시간이 걸리기 때문이다.

| 어휘 |

regulation ⓥ 조절하다	**secrete** ⓥ 분비하다	**endocrine gland** ⓝ 내분비샘
endocrine system ⓝ 내분비계	**flick** ⓝ 휙 치는 소리, 경쾌한 움직임	**jerk** ⓝ (갑자기 날카롭게) 홱 움직임
coordinate ⓥ 조정하다	**cellular** ⓐ 세포의, 세포상의	**split-second** ⓐ 순식간의, 순간적인

| 전문해석 | 동물들은 그들의 신체 활동을 조절하기 위해 많은 종류의 화학적 신호에 의존한다. 에스트로겐은 신호의 한 종류인 호르몬이다. [A] 동물 호르몬은 일반적으로 혈액 속의 순환계에 의해 운반되고 몸 전체에 조절 메시지를 전달하는 화학적 신호이다. [B] 호르몬은 주로 내분비샘이라고 불리는 기관에 의해 만들어지고 분비된다. 집합적으로 동물의 호르몬을 분비하는 모든 세포들은 의사소통과 화학적 조절을 위한 두 가지 신체 시스템 중 하나인 내분비계를 구성한다. 내부 의사소통과 조절의 또 다른 체계는 신경계이다. [C] **〈혈관을 통해서 화학적 신호를 전달하는 내분비계와 달리, 신경계는 신경세포를 통해서 전기적 신호를 즉시 전달한다. 이러한 빠른 메시지가 빠른 반응을 제어한다.〉** 개구리의 혀가 파리를 잡는 소리와 불꽃에서 손을 튕기는 소리는 고속 신경 신호에서 비롯된다. 내분비계는 더 느리지만 더 오래 지속되는 반응들을 조절한다. [D] 어떤 경우에는, 내분비계가 작용하는 데 몇 시간 또는 심지어 며칠이 걸리는데, 부분적으로는 호르몬이 만들어지고 타깃이 되는 모든 신체기관에 전달되는 데 시간이 걸리기 때문이고 또 다른 한편으로는 세포 반응에 시간이 걸리기 때문이다.

| 보기분석 | (Unlike the endocrine system), (which sends chemical signals) (through the bloodstream), the nervous system promptly transmits electrical signals (via nerve cells). These rapid messages control split-second responses.

전치사: Unlike / 관계대명사: which / 전치사: through / S: the nervous system / V: transmits / O: electrical signals / 전치사: via / S: These rapid messages / V: control / O: split-second responses

〈혈관을 통해서 화학적 신호를 전달하는 내분비계와 달리, 신경계는 신경세포를 통해서 전기적 신호를 즉시 전달한다. 이러한 빠른 메시지가 빠른 반응을 제어한다.〉

| 정답분석 | 주어진 문장에서는 'Unlike'라는 표현을 통해 내분기계와 신경계의 기능 차이를 설명했다. 본문의 [C] 직전 문장에서 신경계를 최초로 언급했으므로 주어진 문장을 [C]에 넣게 되면 그 뒤로 개구리의 사례는 주어진 문장에서 언급한 '신경세포를 통한 전기적 신호 전달'의 사례가 될 수 있다. [C]가 정답으로 가장 적절하다.

15 2013 한양대

정답 ③

| 구문분석 | (In 1993), about 7 percent (of America's high schools) had eliminated ranking their students (by grade point average (GPA)); thus, the schools also did away with honoring a valedictorian — the individual with the highest GPA — at graduation.

S_1: about 7 percent / V_1: had eliminated / O: ranking their students / 세미콜론: and 역할 / 접속부사: thus / S_2: the schools / V_2: did away with / 대시: 부연설명

1993년에, 미국 고등학교의 약 7%가 성적 평균(GPA)으로 학생들의 등수를 매기는 것을 없앴다. 따라서 이 학교들은 졸업식에서 가장 평점(GPA)이 높은 학생에게 고별사를 하는 명예를 주는 것도 폐지하였다.

(Since then), scrapping the valedictorian tradition has become a national trend.

전치사: Since / S: scrapping the valedictorian tradition / V: has become / C: a national trend

그 이후로, 고별사 전통을 폐지하는 것이 전국적인 추세가 되었다.

Those (who support the elimination of class rankings and valedictorians) claim that ranking students makes the lower-performing students feel inadequate.

S: Those / 관계대명사: who / V: claim / O: that ranking students makes the lower-performing students feel inadequate

학급의 성적 순위와 고별사 폐지를 지지하는 사람들은 학생들의 등수를 매기는 일이 성적이 낮은 학생들에게 부족함을 느끼게 한다고 주장한다.

강조구문
It's the desire (to be the best) that makes achievement a reality.
V 강조구문의 that
성취를 현실로 만드는 것은 최고가 되고 싶은 욕망이다.

세미콜론: 부연설명
Maintaining the valedictorian tradition spurs student achievement; (without it), our students have no incentive (to excel).
S_1 V_1 O_1 S_2 V_2 O_2
고별사 전통을 유지하는 것이 학생들의 성취를 자극한다; 그것이 없다면, 우리 학생들은 (다른 학생보다) 우수하려는 어떤 동기도 가지지 못하게 될 것이다.

| 어휘 | GPA ⓝ (미국 교육 제도에서 일정 기간 동안의) 평균 평점 do away with ~을 버리다[폐지하다]
honor ⓥ ~에게 명예를 주다 valedictorian ⓝ 졸업생 대표(졸업식에서 고별사를 하는 수석 졸업생)
scrap ⓥ 폐기하다, 버리다 spur ⓥ 자극하다, 원동력이 되다 incentive ⓝ 유인, 동기

| 전문해석 | 1993년에, 미국 고등학교의 약 7%가 성적 평균(GPA)으로 학생들의 등수를 매기는 것을 없앴다. 따라서 이 학교들은 졸업식에서 가장 평점(GPA)이 높은 학생에게 고별사를 하는 명예를 주는 것도 폐지하였다. [A] 그 이후로, 고별사 전통을 폐지하는 것이 전국적인 추세가 되었다. [B] 학급의 성적 순위과 고별사 폐지를 지지하는 사람들은 학생들의 등수를 매기는 일이 성적이 낮은 학생들에게 부족함을 느끼게 한다고 주장한다. **[C] 〈이런 비평가들은 경쟁이 미국 사회의 일부라는 사실을 직면하기를 거부한다.〉** 성취를 현실로 만드는 것은 최고가 되고 싶은 욕망이다. [D] 고별사 전통을 유지하는 것이 학생들의 성취를 자극한다; 그것이 없다면, 우리 학생들은 (다른 학생보다) 우수하려는 어떤 동기도 가지지 못하게 될 것이다.

| 보기분석 | These critics refuse to face the fact (that competition is part of American society).
S V O =
〈이런 비평가들은 경쟁이 미국 사회의 일부라는 사실을 직면하기를 거부한다.〉

| 정답분석 | 주어진 문장이 지시사를 포함한 표현인 'These critics'로 시작되므로 직전 내용에는 무엇에 대한 비판적인 내용이 나와야 한다. 또한 주어진 문장에서는 '경쟁이 미국 사회의 일부라는 것'을 사실로 여기고 있다. 본문의 시작에서 성적 순위와 성적이 높은 학생에게 주어지는 고별사 전통을 없애는 추세에 대한 이유를 설명한 뒤 [C] 이후에는 '최고가 되려는 욕망 때문에 성취가 현실이 된다'며 고별사의 전통을 지지하는 내용이 오기 때문에 주어진 문장은 [C]에 삽입하는 것이 흐름상 자연스럽다.

16 2015 한양대

정답 ③

| 구문분석 | A best-selling book offers "Seven Ways to Become a Better Person."
S V O
베스트셀러는 "더 나은 사람이 되는 일곱 가지 방법"을 제공한다.

(that)
A radio ad promises you will feel great (in 30 days or less) (just by taking some pills).
S V by ~ing: ~함으로써
라디오 광고는 당신이 약을 먹는 것만으로도 30일 이내에 기분이 최고가 될 것이라고 약속한다.

(that)
(If you buy our exercise equipment), a TV ad guarantees you will have the body (you have always wanted).
부사절: 만약 ~라면 S V O (that)
TV 광고는, 당신이 만일 우리의 운동기구를 산다면, 당신은 당신이 항상 원하던 몸을 가지게 될 것이라고 보장한다.

(In today's society), we are continually bombarded (with the latest techniques) (of how to better ourselves, = a focus (which some feel) is unhealthy.
S V 관계대명사
오늘날 사회에서, 우리는 우리 자신을 향상시키는 방법에 대한 최신 기술들로 계속해서 폭격을 받고 있는데, 요점은 일부 사람들이 건강하지 않다고 느낀다는 것이다.

A better approach would be to help people grow (in character).
S V C
더 좋은 접근법은 사람들의 인격을 성장시키는 데 도움을 주는 것이다.

Building character involves taking a person's strengths and building on them.
S V O
인격을 형성하는 것은 한 사람의 장점들을 취하고 그 장점들을 바탕으로 하는 것을 포함한다.

Such strengths (as unselfishness) can be developed (into a lifelong habit of generosity), (a positive spirit) (into an unfailing compassion for others).
S V =

이기심이 없는 것과 같은 장점은 평생을 가는 관대함의 습관으로 발전될 수 있는데, 긍정적인 정신은 다른 사람들에 대한 변함없는 연민으로 발전될 수 있다.

Everyone has strength (in character) and the ability (to build on these strengths through self-improvement).
S V O_1 O_2
모든 사람은 성격상의 강점을 가지고 있고 자기 계발을 통해 이러한 강점들을 바탕으로 (인격을) 형성하는 능력을 가지고 있다.

For example, impatience can be turned (into determination) (to accomplish goals).
접속부사 S V
예를 들어, 성급함은 목표를 달성하기 위한 결단력으로 전환될 수 있다.

Strong will turns (into perseverance).
S V
강한 의지는 인내로 전환될 수 있다.

(If a person can just find a way to capitalize on a weakness), it can be turned (into a strength).
부사절: 만약 ~라면 S V
만약 어떤 사람이 자신의 약점을 활용할 수 있는 방법을 찾을 수 있다면, 그것은 강점으로 전환될 수 있을 것이다.

Self improvement is the best way (to do this).
S V C
자기 향상은 이를 위한 최선의 방법이다.

| 어휘 | **take a pill** 약을 복용하다 **bombard with** (질문 등을) 퍼붓다 **determination** ⓝ 투지, 결심
perseverance ⓝ 인내(심) **capitalize on** ~을 이용하다, ~을 활용하다

| 전문해석 | 베스트셀러는 "더 나은 사람이 되는 일곱 가지 방법"을 제공한다. 라디오 광고는 당신이 약을 먹는 것만으로도 30일 이내에 기분이 최고가 될 것이라고 약속한다. TV 광고는, 당신이 만일 우리의 운동기구를 산다면, 당신은 당신이 항상 원하던 몸을 가지게 될 것이라고 보장한다. 오늘날 사회에서, 우리는 우리 자신을 향상시키는 방법에 대한 최신 기술들로 계속해서 폭격을 받고 있는데, 요점은 일부 사람들이 건강하지 않다고 느낀다는 것이다. [A] 더 좋은 접근법은 사람들의 인격을 성장시키는 데 도움을 주는 것이다. [B] 인격을 형성하는 것은 한 사람의 장점들을 취하고 그 장점들을 바탕으로 하는 것을 포함한다. 이기심이 없는 것과 같은 장점은 평생을 가는 관대함의 습관으로 발전될 수 있는데, 긍정적인 정신은 다른 사람들에 대한 변함없는 연민으로 발전될 수 있다. 모든 사람은 성격상의 강점을 가지고 있고 자기 계발을 통해 이러한 강점들을 바탕으로 (인격을) 형성하는 능력을 가지고 있다. **[C] 〈약점들은 결점이 아니고, 자기 향상을 통해, 더욱 긍정적인 특성들로 발전할 수 있는 부정적인 특성들일 뿐이다.〉** 예를 들어, 성급함은 목표를 달성하기 위한 결단력으로 전환될 수 있다. 강한 의지는 인내로 전환될 수 있다. [D] 만약 어떤 사람이 자신의 약점을 활용할 수 있는 방법을 찾을 수 있다면, 그것은 강점으로 전환될 수 있을 것이다. 자기 향상은 이를 위한 최선의 방법이다.

not A but B: A가 아니라 B 전치사
| 보기분석 | Weaknesses are not flaws, but rather negative traits (that, (through self-improvement), can be developed into more positive traits).
S V C 관계대명사

〈약점들은 결점이 아니고, 자기 향상을 통해, 더욱 긍정적인 특성들로 발전할 수 있는 부정적인 특성들일 뿐이다.〉

| 정답분석 | 주어진 문장에서는 약점을 결점으로 보지 않고 '긍정적으로 발전시킬 수 있는 특성'으로 소개했다. 따라서 주어진 문장의 예시가 [C]에 'For example' 뒤로 소개된다고 보면 주어진 문장의 일반화된 내용이 그 뒤에 구체적 사례로 연결되어 흐름상 자연스럽다. [C]가 정답으로 적절하다.

17 2015 중앙대(오후) 정답 ②

| 구문분석 | Cities are where almost all remaining population growth will occur, demographers say.
O S V

인구통계학자들은 도시들이 거의 모든 남아 있는 인구 증가가 발생하는 곳이라고 말한다.

from A to B: A에서 B까지

The roster (of megacities), those (with populations exceeding 10 million), is widely expected to climb, (from 20 today to 36 by 2015).
S = V O.C

인구 천만 명을 초과하는 거대도시들의 수는 현재 20개에서 2015년까지 36개로 증가할 것으로 널리 예상된다.

These vast metropolises have been widely characterized (as a nightmarish element) (of the new century), (sprawling and chaotic and spawning waste and illness).
S V

이 거대도시들은 넓게 퍼져 있고 무질서하며 쓰레기와 질병을 퍼뜨리는 새로운 세계의 악몽 같은 요소로 널리 특징지어져 왔다.

(Most significantly), they say, (that) family size drops sharply in urban areas.
S V O

가장 중요한 것은 도시지역에서 가족의 규모가 작아지는 것이라고 그들은 말한다.

(For the poor), access (to health care), schools and other basic services is generally greater (in the city than in the countryside).
S V O

가난한 사람들의 경우, 의료서비스, 학교 및 기타 기본 서비스에 대한 접근성이 시골보다 도시에서 일반적으로 더 높다.

Energy is used more efficiently, and drinking and wastewater systems, (although lacking now), can be built relatively easily.
S_1 V_1 S_2 분사구문 V_2

에너지는 더 효율적으로 사용되고, 비록 지금은 부족하지만 식수 체계나 폐수 체계도 (시골 지역에 비해) 비교적 쉽게 건설될 수 있다.

And (for every person) (who moves to a city), that is one person (fewer chopping firewood or poaching game).
관계대명사 S V C

그리고 도시로 이주하는 모든 사람들에게, 그것은 한 사람이 장작을 위해 나무를 자르고 밀렵게임을 덜 하는 것이다.

Still, many cities face decisions now (that may permanently alter the quality of human lives and the environment).
S V O (decisions = that절)

여전히, 많은 도시들은 인간의 삶과 환경의 질을 영구적으로 바꿀 수 있는 결정들에 직면해 있다.

The pivotal nature (of these times) is perfectly illustrated (by Mexico City), (which is just behind Tokyo atop the list of megacities).
S V 관계대명사

이 시대의 핵심적인 본질은 거대도시의 리스트에서 도쿄 바로 뒤에 있는 멕시코시티에 의해서 완벽하게 설명된다.

be about toR: 막 ~하려 하다

The sprawling megalopolis, (where traffic is paralyzed), is about to choose (in a referendum) (between double-decking its downtown highways or expanding its subway system).
S 관계부사 V between A or B: A 혹은 B 사이

교통이 마비되는 거대도시들은 도심고속도로를 이중으로 건설할지 혹은 지하철 시스템을 확장할지를 국민투표를 통해서 선택해야 한다.

세미콜론: and 역할

One course could encourage sprawl and pollution; the other would conserve energy, experts say.
O S V

전문가들은 전자(도심고속도로의 이중 건설)는 도심 난개발과 오염을 촉진할 것이고, 후자(지하철 시스템 확장)의 경우는 에너지를 절약할 수 있을 것이라고 말한다.

| 어휘 |

megacity ⓝ 메가시티(인구 1,000만 명이 넘는 거대도시)
roster ⓝ 근무자 명부, 명단
nightmarish ⓐ 악몽 같은, 무서운
sprawling ⓐ 제멋대로 뻗어 나가는
spawn ⓥ 알을 낳다; 생기게 하다
poaching ⓝ (밀렵 따위를 하기 위해 남의 땅에 몰래 들어가는) 불법 침입
pivotal ⓐ 중심축이 되는
referendum ⓝ 국민 투표
double-deck ⓥ (다리 · 도로 따위에) 이단을 놓다

| 전문해석 | 인구통계학자들은 도시들이 거의 모든 남아 있는 인구 증가가 발생하는 곳이라고 말한다. 인구 천만 명을 초과하는 거대도시들의 수는 현재 20개에서 2015년까지 36개로 증가할 것으로 널리 예상된다. [A] 이 거대도시들은 넓게 퍼져 있고 무질서하며 쓰레기와 질병을 퍼뜨리는 새로운 세계의 악몽 같은 요소로 널리 특징지어져 왔다. **[B] 〈하지만 점점 더 많은 인구 통계학자들과 다른 전문가들은, 도시가 실제로 환경파괴를 제한하는 중요한 수단이 될 수 있다고 말한다.〉** 가장 중요한 것은 도시지역에서 가족의 규모가 작아지는 것이라고 그들은 말한다. 가난한 사람들의 경우, 의료서비스, 학교 및 기타 기본 서비스에 대한 접근성이 시골보다 도시에서 일반적으로 더 높다. 에너지는 더 효율적으로 사용되고, 비록 지금은 부족하지만 식수 체계나 폐수 체계도 (시골 지역에 비해) 비교적 쉽게 건설될 수 있다. 그리고 도시로 이주하는 모든 사람들에게, 그것은 한 사람이 장작을 위해 나무를 자르고 밀렵게임을 덜 하는 것이다. [C] 여전히, 많은 도시들은 인간의 삶과 환경의 질을 영구적으로 바꿀 수 있는 결정들에 직면해 있다. 이 시대의 핵심적인 본질은 거대도시의 리스트에서 도쿄 바로 뒤에 있는 멕시코시티에 의해서 완벽하게 설명된다. 교통이 마비되는 거대도시들은 도심고속도로를 이중으로 건설할지 혹은 지하철 시스템을 확장할지를 국민투표를 통해서 선택해야 한다. [D] 전문가들은 전자(도심고속도로의 이중 건설)는 도심 난개발과 오염을 촉진할 것이고, 후자(지하철 시스템 확장)의 경우는 에너지를 절약할 수 있을 것이라고 말한다.

| 보기분석 | But increasingly, demographers and other experts (S) say (V) that cities may actually be a critical means (O) (of limiting environmental damage).

〈하지만 점점 더 많은 인구 통계학자들과 다른 전문가들은, 도시가 실제로 환경파괴를 제한하는 중요한 수단이 될 수 있다고 말한다.〉

| 정답분석 | 주어진 문장은 역접 표현인 'But'으로 시작해서 도시가 환경파괴를 제한하는 긍정적인 기능을 한다는 전문가적 의견이 소개된다. 본문에서는 [B] 이후로 거대도시의 긍정적인 면이 나열되고 있으므로 주어진 문장은 [B]에 삽입하는 것이 가장 적절하다.

18 2015 가톨릭대

정답 ③

| 구문분석 | All human beings (S), (in their understanding of themselves), build (V) sets (O) (of defenses) (to protect the ego).

모든 인간은, 자신에 대한 이해 속에서, 자아를 보호하기 위한 일련의 방어기제를 구축한다.

The newborn baby (S) has (V) no concept (O) (of its own self); (세미콜론: but 역할) gradually it (S) learns (V) to identify a self (O) (that (관계대명사) is distinct from others).

신생아는 자아에 대한 개념을 가지고 있지 않다; (그러나) 신생아는 점차 다른 사람들과 구별되는 자아를 식별하는 것을 배운다.

(In childhood), the growing degrees (S) (of awareness, responding, and valuing) begin (V) to create a system (O) (of affective traits) (that (관계대명사) individuals identify with themselves).

유년기에, 인식, 반응, 그리고 가치관의 증가는 개인이 자신과 동일시하는 정서적 특성의 체계를 만들기 시작한다.

(In adolescence), the physical, emotional, and cognitive changes (S) (of the pre-teenager and teenager) bring (V) (on mounting defensive inhibitions) (to protect a fragile ego), (to ward off ideas, experiences, and (등위접속사) feelings) (that (관계대명사) threaten to dismantle the organization (of values and beliefs) (on which (관계대명사) appraisals of self-esteem have been founded).

청소년기에, 십 대 이전과 십 대의 신체적, 정서적, 인지적 변화들은 취약한 자아를 보호하고, 자존감 평가의 기초가 된 가치와 믿음의 조직을 해체할 위협이 되는 생각, 경험, 감정을 피하기 위해 방어적 억제를 증가시킨다.

Some persons (S_1) — those with higher self-esteem and ego strength (대시: 부연설명) — are more able to withstand (V_1) threats (O) (to their existence), and thus (접속부사) their defenses (S_2) are (V_2) lower (C).

어떤 사람들은—더 높은 자존감과 강한 자아를 가진 사람들—그들의 존재에 대한 위협을 더 잘 견딜 수 있고, 따라서 그들의 방어기제는 낮아진다.

Those (with weaker self-esteem) maintain walls (of inhibition) (to protect what is self-perceived to be a weak or fragile ego, or a lack of self-confidence (in a situation or task).
S / V / O / 부사적용법: ~하기 위해서

자존감이 더 약한 사람들은 약하거나 연약한 자아라고 스스로 여기거나 혹은 어떤 상황이나 과제에 대한 자신감의 부족을 보호하기 위해서 억제의 벽(방어기제)을 유지한다.

| 어휘 |

defense ⓝ 방어, 수비	**distinct** ⓐ 뚜렷한, 구별되는	**affective** ⓐ 감정적인, 정서적인
adolescence ⓝ 청소년기, 사춘기	**bring on** ~을 초래하다[야기하다]	**inhibition** ⓝ (생각 · 감정 표현의) 억제
fragile ⓐ 부서지기[손상되기] 쉬운	**ward off** ~을 피하다[물리치다]	
dismantle ⓥ (기계 · 구조물을) 분해[해체]하다		
appraisal ⓝ (가치 · 업적 · 본질에 대한) 평가		

| 전문해석 | 모든 인간은, 자신에 대한 이해 속에서, 자아를 보호하기 위한 일련의 방어기제를 구축한다. 신생아는 자아에 대한 개념을 가지고 있지 않다; (그러나) 신생아는 점차 다른 사람들과 구별되는 자아를 식별하는 것을 배운다. [A] 유년기에, 인식, 반응, 그리고 가치관의 증가는 개인이 자신과 동일시하는 정서적 특성의 체계를 만들기 시작한다. [B] 청소년기에, 십 대 이전과 십 대의 신체적, 정서적, 인지적 변화들은 취약한 자아를 보호하고, 자존감 평가의 기초가 된 가치와 믿음의 조직을 해체할 위협이 되는 생각, 경험, 감정을 피하기 위해 방어적 억제를 증가시킨다. **[C] 〈방어기제를 세우는 과정은 다음 단계로 이어지며 계속된다.〉** 어떤 사람들은—더 높은 자존감과 강한 자아를 가진 사람들—그들의 존재에 대한 위협을 더 잘 견딜 수 있고, 따라서 그들의 방어기제는 낮아진다. [D] 자존감이 더 약한 사람들은 약하거나 연약한 자아라고 스스로 여기거나 혹은 어떤 상황이나 과제에 대한 자신감의 부족을 보호하기 위해서 억제의 벽(방어기제)을 유지한다.

| 보기분석 | The process (of building defenses) continues (into the next phase).
S / V

〈방어기제를 세우는 과정은 다음 단계로 이어지며 계속된다.〉

| 정답분석 | 주어진 문장에서는 방어기제를 세우는 과정이 'the next phase'로 이어진다고 설명한다. 본문에서 청소년기에 증가하는 '방어적 억제'에 대한 설명이 끝나고 그다음 단계로 [C] 이후 방어기제의 강함과 약함이 사람마다 다름을 설명하는 내용이 나온다. 따라서 주어진 문장은 [C]에 들어가야 할 것이다.

19 2019 건국대

정답 ②

| 구문분석 | Mark Twain observed, "We are all ignorant, but about different things."
S / V / O

마크 트웨인(Mark Twain)은 "우리는 모두 무지하지만, 다만 서로 다른 것들에 대해서 무지하다."라고 말했다.

One mistake (technical professionals mark) (when writing for non-technical readers) is assuming (that) their readers are as knowledgeable as they are about the subject.
S / as ~ as: …만큼 ~한 / 부사절: ~할 때 / V / O

기술 전문가들(작가들)이 비전문적인 독자들을 위해 글을 쓸 때 나타나는 한 가지 실수는 그들의 독자들이 그 주제에 대해 그들이 아는 만큼 지식이 있다고 생각하는 것이다.

(Just because it's clear to you) does not make it clear (of your reader).
make clear: 분명하게 하다 / 부사절: ~ 때문에 / V / O / O.C

그것이 당신에게 분명하다고 해서 당신의 독자들에게도 분명한 것은 아니다.

(If you are an engineer or accountant writing to others in your field), then perhaps there will be less need (to explain all aspects of your message).
부사절: 만약 ~라면 / 유도부사 / V / S

만약 당신이 당신 분야의 다른 사람들에게 글을 쓰는 기술자나 회계사라면, 아마도 당신의 메시지의 모든 측면을 설명할 필요가 줄어들 것이다.

(If you're writing to the senior vice president of marketing), (who is not familiar with software applications), then you will need to "walk" that reader (through your message).
부사절: 만약 ~라면 / 관계대명사 / S V O

만약 당신이 소프트웨어 응용프로그램에 익숙하지 않은 마케팅 담당 상무에게 글을 쓴다면, 당신은 당신의 메시지를 읽는 사람에게 '걸음마를 가르치듯 차근차근 설명할' 필요가 있을 것이다.

명령문 / when it comes to: ~에 관한 한

Remember that (when it comes to technical knowledge), writers and readers are hardly equal.
(You) V O

전문적인 지식에 관한 한, 글을 쓰는 사람과 읽는 사람은 전혀 동등하지 않다는 것을 기억하라.

| 어휘 | **ignorant** ⓐ 무지한, 무식한 **clear** ⓐ (의심할 여지 없이) 확실한 **mark** ⓥ 나타내다, 눈에 띄게 하다
senior vice president (회사의) 상무 **fatal** ⓐ 치명적인, 돌이킬 수 없는 **assumption** ⓝ 가정

| 전문해석 | 마크 트웨인(Mark Twain)은 "우리는 모두 무지하지만, 다만 서로 다른 것들에 대해서 무지하다."라고 말했다. [A] 기술 전문가들(작가들)이 비전문적인 독자들을 위해 글을 쓸 때 나타나는 한 가지 실수는 그들의 독자들이 그 주제에 대해 그들이 아는 만큼 지식이 있다고 생각하는 것이다. **[B] 〈이것은 당신의 독자에게 혼란과 좌절을 가져다줄 뿐인 잘못된 가정이다.〉** 그것이 당신에게 분명하다고 해서 당신의 독자들에게도 분명한 것은 아니다. [C] 만약 당신이 당신 분야의 다른 사람들에게 글을 쓰는 기술자나 회계사라면, 아마도 당신의 메시지의 모든 측면을 설명할 필요가 줄어들 것이다. [D] 만약 당신이 소프트웨어 응용프로그램에 익숙하지 않은 마케팅 담당 상무에게 글을 쓴다면, 당신은 당신의 메시지를 읽는 사람에게 '걸음마를 가르치듯 차근차근 설명할' 필요가 있을 것이다. [E] 전문적인 지식에 관한 한, 글을 쓰는 사람과 읽는 사람은 전혀 동등하지 않다는 것을 기억하라.

| 보기분석 | This is a fatal assumption (that will only result in confusion and frustration for your reader).
S V C 관계대명사

〈이것은 당신의 독자에게 혼란과 좌절을 가져다줄 뿐인 잘못된 가정이다.〉

| 정답분석 | 주어진 문장은 지시사 'This'로 시작되며 '이것이 독자에게 혼란과 좌절을 가져다줄 뿐인 잘못된 가정'이라 했다. 따라서 그 직전 문장으로 본문 [A] 이후의 내용 '작가가 독자를 위해 글을 쓸 때 나타나는 실수'가 자연스럽다. 따라서 주어진 문장은 [B]에 삽입하는 것이 자연스럽다.

20 2017 한양대

정답 ③

| 구문분석 | (In 1916), Swedish geologist Lennart von Post showed that (by identifying and counting pollen) (preserved at different depths in Swedish peat bogs) he could infer changes (in forest composition through time).
S V by ~ing: ~함으로써 O

1916년, 스웨덴 지질학자인 렌나르트 폰 포스트(Lennart von Post)는 스웨덴의 토탄 늪지대에 다른 깊이로 보존된 꽃가루를 확인하고 그 수를 헤아림으로써 시간(경과)에 따른 숲 구성의 변화를 추론할 수 있음을 보여 주었다.

(Following his pioneering work), pollen analysis quickly became established (as a key tool) (for understanding past vegetation, climate, and ecosystems).
분사구문 S V 등위접속사

그의 선구적인 연구에 이어, 꽃가루 분석은 과거의 식물, 기후, 그리고 생태계를 이해하기 위한 핵심 도구로 빠르게 확립되었다.

Today, it is used widely (to reconstruct past ecosystems and (to) test hypotheses about drivers of ecosystem change).
S V 부사적용법: ~하기 위해서 등위접속사

오늘날, 그것은 과거 생태계를 재구성하고 생태계 변화의 원동력에 대한 가설을 검증하기 위해 널리 사용된다.

(Using pollen analysis), von Post explored the temporal changes (in postglacial forest composition) (at many sites in southern Sweden).
분사구문 S V O

꽃가루 분석을 사용하여, 폰 포스트는 스웨덴 남부의 많은 지역에서 빙하기 이후 숲 구성의 시간적 변화를 탐구했다.

He then demonstrated the spatial patterns (of change) (by mapping his pollen data at selected times).
S V O by ~ing: ~함으로써

그러고 나서 그는 선택된 여러 시기의 꽃가루 자료를 지도로 만듦으로써 변화의 공간적 패턴을 보여 주었다.

He also developed pollen analysis (as a relative-dating technique) (for resolving postglacial sea-level changes).
S V O

그는 또한 빙하기 이후 해수면 변화를 설명하기 위한 상대적 연대측정 기법으로 꽃가루 분석을 발전시켰다.

(In the 1930s to 1950s), pollen-analytical studies (around the world) were performed (to establish vegetation history, (to) estimate pollen-accumulation rates, (to) elucidate the relationship of modern pollen spectra to vegetation, and (to) map pollen data through time).
S V 부사적용법: ~하기 위해서

1930년대와 50년대 사이에, 전 세계적인 꽃가루 분석 연구는 식물의 역사를 확립하고, 꽃가루 축적률을 추정하고, 현대 꽃가루 스펙트럼과 식물과의 관계를 밝히고, 시간에 따른 꽃가루 자료의 지도를 만들기 위해 실행되었다.

| 어휘 | **geologist** ⓝ 지질학자 **count** ⓥ (올바른 순서로 수를) 세다 **pollen** ⓝ 꽃가루, 화분
peat bog 토탄 늪지 **hypothesis** ⓝ 가설 **temporal** ⓐ 시간의, 일시적인
postglacial ⓐ 빙하기 후의 **spatial** ⓐ 공간의, 장소의
relative-dating technique 상대적 연대측정 기법(지층을 다른 지층과 비교하여 상대적인 순서를 결정하는 방법)
accumulation ⓝ 축적, 누적 **elucidate** ⓥ (문제 등을) 밝히다, 명료하게 하다
formulate ⓥ 공식화하다, 설명하다, 표현하다 **parallelism** ⓝ 평행, 유사

| 전문해석 | 1916년, 스웨덴 지질학자인 렌나르트 폰 포스트(Lennart von Post)는 스웨덴의 토탄 늪지대에 다른 깊이로 보존된 꽃가루를 확인하고 그 수를 헤아림으로써 시간(경과)에 따른 숲 구성의 변화를 추론할 수 있음을 보여 주었다. 그의 선구적인 연구에 이어, 꽃가루 분석은 과거의 식물, 기후, 그리고 생태계를 이해하기 위한 핵심 도구로 빠르게 확립되었다. [A] 오늘날, 그것은 과거 생태계를 재구성하고 생태계 변화의 원동력에 대한 가설을 검증하기 위해 널리 사용된다. 꽃가루 분석을 사용하여, 폰 포스트는 스웨덴 남부의 많은 지역에서 빙하기 이후 숲 구성의 시간적 변화를 탐구했다. **[B] 〈그는 지역적 평행성의 개념을 공식화했는데, 그에 따르면 기후 변화에 대한 식물의 반응들은 전 세계의 다른 지역에서 평행했다.〉** 그러고 나서 그는 선택된 여러 시기의 꽃가루 자료를 지도로 만듦으로써 변화의 공간적 패턴을 보여 주었다. [C] 그는 또한 빙하기 이후 해수면 변화를 설명하기 위한 상대적 연대측정 기법으로 꽃가루 분석을 발전시켰다. [D] 1930년대와 50년대 사이에, 전 세계적인 꽃가루 분석 연구는 식물의 역사를 확립하고, 꽃가루 축적률을 추정하고, 현대 꽃가루 스펙트럼과 식물과의 관계를 밝히고, 시간에 따른 꽃가루 자료의 지도를 만들기 위해 실행되었다.

| 보기분석 | He formulated the concept (of regional parallelism), (according to which vegetation responses to climate change were parallel in different parts of the world).
S V O 관계대명사(계속적용법)

〈그는 지역적 평행성의 개념을 공식화했는데, 그에 따르면 기후 변화에 대한 식물의 반응들은 전 세계의 다른 지역에서 평행했다.〉

| 정답분석 | 주어진 문장에서 연구자는 '기후 변화에 대한 식물의 반응들이 전 세계의 다른 지역에서 유사했음'을 공식화했다. 본문에서 폰 포스트는 꽃가루 분석을 사용하여 [B] 이후에 '변화의 공간적 패턴'을 보여 주었으므로 주어진 문장은 그다음인 [C]에 오는 것이 가장 적절하다.

10강 무관한 문장 / 단어 고르기

Practice

01	④	02	④	03	④	04	②	05	②	06	③	07	④	08	⑤	09	④	10	④
11	③	12	②	13	③	14	②	15	⑤	16	③	17	①	18	④	19	④	20	④

01 2018 인하대

정답 ④

| 구문분석 |

(Soon after an infant is born), many mothers hold their infants (in such a way) (that they are face-to-face and gaze at them).
부사절: ~ 직후에 / S: many mothers / V: hold / O: their infants

아기가 태어난 직후에, 많은 엄마들은 얼굴을 마주하여 바라보는 식으로 아기를 안는다.

Mothers have been observed (to address their infants, vocalize to them, ask questions, and greet them).
S: Mothers / V: have been observed

엄마가 아기에게 말을 걸고, 아기에게 소리를 들려주고, 질문을 하고 아기에게 인사를 하는 것을 우리는 관찰해 왔다.

In other words, (from birth on), the infant is treated (as a social being and as an addressee in social interaction).
접속부사: In other words / S: the infant / V: is treated

다시 말해 태어나면서부터, 아기는 사회적 존재로 그리고 사회적 상호작용에 있어서 말을 거는 대상으로서 다루어진다.

The infant's vocalizations, and physical movements and states are often interpreted (as meaningful) and are responded (to verbally) (by the mother or other care-giver).
S: The infant's vocalizations, and physical movements and states / V_1: are often interpreted / V_2: are responded

아기의 음성, 그리고 신체의 움직임과 상태는 종종 의미 있는 것으로 해석되고, 엄마나 다른 보호자는 그에 대해 말로써 응답한다.

The cultural dispreference (for saying what another might be thinking or feeling) has important consequences (for the organization of exchanges between care-giver and child).
S: The cultural dispreference / V: has / O: important consequences

다른 사람이 생각하거나 느끼고 있는 것을 말하는 것에 대한 문화적인 비선호는 보호자와 아이 사이에 이뤄지는 대화의 구조에 중대한 영향을 미친다.

(In this way), protoconversations are established and sustained (along a two-party, turn-taking model).
S: protoconversations / V: are established and sustained

이러한 방식으로, (아이와 엄마 사이의) 최초의 대화가 확립되고 이것은 양자가 의사소통을 주고받는 형태로 유지된다.

(Throughout this period and the subsequent language-acquiring years), care-givers treat very young children (as communicative partners).
S: care-givers / V: treat / O: very young children

이 시기와 뒤이은 언어 습득 시기에, 보호자는 매우 어린 아이들을 의사소통의 상대로 대우한다.

| 어휘 |

infant ⓝ 유아
address ⓥ ~에게 말을 걸다
vocalize ⓥ 목소리를 내다, 말하다
addressee ⓝ (우편물이나 메시지의) 수신인
interaction ⓝ 상호작용
interpret ⓥ 해석하다, 설명하다, 판단하다
respond to ~에 대답[응답]하다
verbally ⓐⓓ 말로, 구두로
dispreference ⓝ 선호하지 않음, 비선호
protoconversation ⓝ 원시 대화(엄마와 아기 사이에서의 음성적 상호작용)
establish ⓥ 확립하다, 제정하다
sustain ⓥ 유지하다, 부양하다; (손해 따위를) 입다
subsequent ⓐ 차후의, 다음의; 결과로서 일어나는
communicative ⓐ 말하기 좋아하는; 의사 전달의

| 전문해석 | 아기가 태어난 직후에, 많은 엄마들은 얼굴을 마주하여 바라보는 식으로 아기를 안는다. [A] 엄마가 아기에게 말을 걸고, 아기에게 소리를 들려주고, 질문을 하고 아기에게 인사를 하는 것을 우리는 관찰해 왔다. [B] 다시 말해 태어나면서부터, 아기는 사회적 존재로 그리고 사회적 상호작용에 있어서 말을 거는 대상으로서 다루어진다. [C] 아기의 음성, 그리고 신체의 움직임과 상태는 종종 의미 있는 것으로 해석되고, 엄마나 다른 보호자는 그에 대해 말로써 응답한다. **[D] 〈다른 사람이 생각하거나 느끼고 있는 것을 말하는 것에 대한 문화적인 비선호는 보호자와 아이 사이에 이뤄지는 대화의 구조에 중대한 영향을 미친다.〉** [E] 이러한 방식으로, (아이와 엄마 사이의) 최초의 대화가 확립되고 이것은 양자가 의사소통을 주고받는 형태로 유지된다. 이 시기와 뒤이은 언어 습득 시기에, 보호자는 매우 어린 아이들을 의사소통의 상대로 대우한다.

| 정답분석 | 본문은 '아기가 태어났을 때부터 부모는 말로 아기에게 의사를 전달하고, 아기도 발성과 신체의 움직임과 상태로 부모에게 의사를 전달하여 부모의 반응(말)을 유발하여 쌍방 간의 교환적인 대화가 진행됨'을 이야기하고 있는 내용인데, [D]는 '문화가 개인의 대화에 영향을 줄 수 있음'에 대한 내용이므로 글의 흐름상 적절하지 않다. 참고로 [A], [B], [C], [E]는 전부 엄마와 아이의 의사소통에 해당하므로 글의 흐름상 적절하다.

02 2020 국민대

정답 ④

| 구문분석 | The current academic system(S) has fudged(V) the distinctions(O) (between training and education).
between A and B: A와 B 사이
현재의 대학교육제도는 훈련과 교육 사이의 차이를 회피해 왔다.

Administrations(S) (of most colleges and universities) have responded(V) (to the economic and cultural uncertainties) (provoked by budget constraints and a volatile job market) (by constructing their institutions on the model of the modern corporation).

대부분의 대학들의 행정당국은 예산의 제약과 불안정한 고용시장으로 촉발된 경제적, 문화적 불확실성을 그들의 기관인 대학을 현대 기업을 표방하여 구축함으로써 응답해 왔다.

Consequently(접속부사), many(S) have thrust(V_1) training(O) (to the fore) and called(V_2) it(O) education(O.C).
그 결과, 많은 대학들은 훈련을 전면에 내세우고, 그것을 교육이라고 불러 왔다.

(Lacking(분사구문 1) a unified national culture into which to socialize students and in any case lacking(분사구문 2) an educational philosophy capable of steering an independent course), the academic system(S) as a whole is caught(V) (in a market logic) (that(관계대명사) demands students be job-ready upon graduation).
학생들을 사회화시킬 일관된 국가 문화가 부족하고 그리고 어쨌든, 독립적인 과정을 운영할 수 있는 교육 철학도 부족해서, 전반적인 대학교육제도는 학생들에게 졸업하자마자 취업준비가 되어 있기를 요구하는 시장 논리에 사로잡혀 있다.

be unable toR: ~할 능력이 없다
(Under these imperatives) colleges and universities(S) are unable to implement(V) an educational program(O) (that(관계대명사) prepares students for the competitive job market).

이러한 명령들하에서는, 대학들은 학생들을 경쟁적인 취업시장에 대비시키는 교육 프로그램을 시행할 수 없다.

Instead(접속부사), academic leaders(S) chant(V) the mantra(O) (of "excellence,") (which(관계대명사) means that all of the parts of the university "perform" and are judged) (according to how(according to의 목적어 1) well they deliver knowledge and qualified labor to the corporate economy and how(according to의 목적어 2) well the administration fulfills the recruitment and funding goals needed to maintain the institution).

그 대신, 대학교육의 지도자들은 대학의 모든 부분이 '잘 작동하고 있다'는 것을 의미하는 '우수함'이라는 진언만을 반복해서 말하고 있으며, 그리고 (대학 지도자들은) 지식과 자격을 갖춘 노동력을 기업경제에 얼마나 잘 전달하는가와, 대학 행정당국이 대학을 유지 관리하는 데 필요한 신입생 모집과 대학기금 조달이라는 목표를 얼마나 잘 달성하는가에 맞춰 판단되고 있다.

| 어휘 | fudge ⓥ (문제 따위에) 대한 정면 대처를 회피하다; 날조하다, 얼버무리다 distinction ⓝ 차이, 대조
administration ⓝ 관리, 경영 volatile ⓐ 불안정한 thrust ⓥ 밀다, 밀치다
to the fore 전면에, (문제 따위가) 표면화하여 steer ⓥ 조종하다, 움직이다
imperative ⓝ 필요(성), 의무, 명령 chant ⓥ 단조로운 말투로 계속하다 mantra ⓝ (불교 · 힌두교의) 기도, 진언
excellence ⓝ 우수, 탁월(성) judge ⓥ 판단하다 deliver ⓥ 전달하다
qualified ⓐ 자격이 있는 fulfill ⓥ 이행하다, 다하다

| 전문해석 | 현재의 대학교육제도는 훈련과 교육 사이의 차이를 회피해 왔다. 대부분의 대학들의 행정당국은 예산의 제약과 불안정한 고용시장으로 촉발된 경제적, 문화적 불확실성을 그들의 기관인 대학을 현대 기업을 표방하여 구축함으로써 응답해 왔다. 그 결과, 많은 대학들은 훈련을 전면에 내세우고, 그것을 교육이라고 불러 왔다. 학생들을 사회화시킬 일관된 국가 문화가 부족하고 그리고 어쨌든, 독립적인 과정을 운영할 수 있는 교육 철학도 부족해서, 전반적인 대학교육제도는 학생들에게 졸업하자마자 취업준비가 되어 있기를 요구하는 시장 논리에 사로잡혀 있다. 이러한 명령들하에서는, 대학들은 학생들을 **〈경쟁적인 취업시장에〉** 대비시키는 교육 프로그램을 시행할 수 없다. 그 대신, 대학교육의 지도자들은 대학의 모든 부분이 '잘 작동하고 있다'는 것을 의미하는 '우수함'이라는 진언만을 반복해서 말하고 있으며, 그리고 (대학 지도자들은) 지식과 자격을 갖춘 노동력을 기업경제에 얼마나 잘 전달하는가와, 대학 행정당국이 대학을 유지 관리하는 데 필요한 신입생 모집과 대학기금 조달이라는 목표를 얼마나 잘 달성하는가에 맞춰 판단되고 있다.

| 정답분석 | 이 글은 현재의 대학들이 진정한 교육은 하지 못하고 취업에만 초점을 두고 운영되고 있다는 문제를 제기하는 글이다. 이러한 현재의 상황에서 대학들은 학생들을 취업이 아닌 진정한 교육에 맞는 프로그램을 시행할 수 없을 것이다. 따라서 [D]의 '경쟁적인 취업시장'은 문맥상 진정한 교육을 나타내는 어휘로 고쳐야 한다. 참고로 원문을 보면 [D] 부분은 'a world of great complexity'이다.

03 2016 인하대 정답 ④

| 구문분석 | Teotihuacan(S) was(V) one of the first true urban centers(C) (in the Western Hemisphere), (covering(분사구문) nearly eight square miles at its heyday).

테오티우아칸(Teotihuacan)은 서반구에 존재한 진정한 최초의 도시들 중 하나였고, 전성기 시절에는 거의 8평방마일에 이르렀다.

Precious artifacts(S) (recovered from the Pyramid of the Moon and other structures) reveal(V) that this was a wealthy trade metropolis with far-reaching connections(O).

달의 피라미드(Pyramid of the Moon)와 다른 구조물들에서 발견된 귀중한 유물들은 이곳이 멀리 떨어져 있는 지역들과도 연결되어 있는 대도시로서 부유한 무역의 중심지였음을 보여 주고 있다.

Inexplicably, the city(S) suffered(V) sudden and violent collapse(O) (in about A.D. 600) and many people(S) fled(V).

불가해하게도, 테오티우아칸은 서기 600년경에 갑작스럽게 급속히 몰락했고 많은 사람들은 달아났다.

(Assuming that(분사구문) some of the buildings were tombs), they(S) called(V) the boulevard(O) Street of the Dead(O.C).

그들은 몇몇 건물들을 무덤이라고 가정하면서 그 대로를 죽음의 거리로 불렀다.

They(S) left(V) few written records(O_1), just the ruins of their city(O_2) and intriguing clues(O_3) (about a once powerful culture).

그들은 문서기록들을 거의 남기지 않았고, 남아 있는 것은 그들이 살았던 도시의 잔해와 한때 강력했던 문화에 대한 흥미로운 단서들뿐이다.

| 어휘 | heyday ⓝ 전성기 artifact ⓝ 인공물, 가공품, 유물
far-reaching ⓐ 멀리까지 미치는; 광범위한 inexplicably ⓐⓓ 불가해하게
collapse ⓝ 붕괴, 와해 assume ⓥ 가정하다; 추정하다 boulevard ⓝ 큰길, 대로
intriguing ⓐ 흥미를 자아내는

| 전문해석 | [A] 테오티우아칸(Teotihuacan)은 서반구에 존재한 진정한 최초의 도시들 중 하나였고, 전성기 시절에는 거의 8평방마일에 이르렀다. [B] 달의 피라미드(Pyramid of the Moon)와 다른 구조물들에서 발견된 귀중한 유물들은 이곳이 멀리 떨어져 있는 지역들과도 연결되어 있는 대도시로서 부유한 무역의 중심지였음을 보여 주고 있다. [C] 불가해하게도, 테오티우아칸은 서기 600년경에 갑작스럽게 급속히 몰락했고 많은 사람들은 달아났다. **[D] 〈그들은 몇몇 건물들을 무덤이라고 가정하면서 그 대로를 죽음의 거리로 불렀다.〉** [E] 그들은 문서기록들을 거의 남기지 않았고, 남아 있는 것은 그들이 살았던 도시의 잔해와 한때 강력했던 문화에 대한 흥미로운 단서들뿐이다.

| 정답분석 | 이 글은 테오티우아칸 지역과 관련된 설명문이다. [A], [B]는 그 도시와 관련된 정보를 기술해 주고 있어서 문맥의 흐름상 자연스러우며, [C]부터 테오티우아칸 지역의 몰락과 달아난 사람과 관련된 정보를 기술하고 있다. [D]와 [E]에서 언급하는 '그들'은 테오티우아칸 지역을 달아난 사람을 가리키는 것인데, [E]의 내용은 달아난 사람들과 관련된 내용이 맞지만, [D]는 달아난 사람들과 관련이 없으므로 문맥 흐름상 부적절하다.

04 2012 명지대

정답 ②

| 구문분석 | The bright lights of the big city(S) are getting(V) a little bit duller(C).

대도시의 밝은 불빛이 조금씩 희미해지고 있다.

Conservationism, rising energy costs and stricter building codes(S) have conspired(V) (to transform Manhattan's nightscape into one with a gentler glow)(부사적용법: 결과).

보호주의와, 에너지 비용의 상승, 엄격한 건축법들이 결합하여 맨해튼의 야경을 좀 더 부드러운 불빛들로 바꾸어 놓고 있다.

Manhattan(S) currently boasts(V) one of the best nightscapes(O) (in the world).

맨해튼은 현재 전 세계 최고의 야경을 자랑하고 있다.

(Instead of(전치사: ~ 대신에) tower after tower shining at all hours), the skyline(S) is becoming(V) a patchwork(C) (of sparsely sparkling buildings) (decorated with lighted tops).

언제나 빛나고 있는 줄줄이 늘어선 고층 건물들 대신, 불 켜진 옥상으로 장식된 드문드문 불 밝혀진 건물들이 여기저기 볼 수 있는 스카이라인이 되고 있다.

The tall towers(S) (with the illuminated floors on all night) have become(V) a thing of the past(C).

밤새 불 밝히는 높은 건물들은 이제는 과거의 것이 되어 버렸다.

| 어휘 |

dull ⓐ 흐릿한, 둔탁한	**conservationism** ⓝ 자원보호론	**conspire** ⓥ 서로 겹치다
nightscape ⓝ 야경	**patchwork** ⓝ 조각	**sparsely** ⓐⓓ 드물게, 희박하게

| 전문해석 | 대도시의 밝은 불빛이 조금씩 희미해지고 있다. [A] 보호주의와, 에너지 비용의 상승, 엄격한 건축법들이 결합하여 맨해튼의 야경을 좀 더 부드러운 불빛들로 바꾸어 놓고 있다. **[B] 〈맨해튼은 현재 전 세계 최고의 야경을 자랑하고 있다.〉** [C] 언제나 빛나고 있는 줄줄이 늘어선 고층 건물들 대신, 불 켜진 옥상으로 장식된 드문드문 불 밝혀진 건물들이 여기저기 볼 수 있는 스카이라인이 되고 있다. [D] 밤새 불 밝히는 높은 건물들은 이제는 과거의 것이 되어 버렸다.

| 정답분석 | 이 글은 여러 가지 사정으로 인해 맨해튼의 야경이 어두워지고 있다는 내용인데, [A], [C], [D]는 그 내용과 맞는 일관된 기술이지만 [B]는 아름다운 야경에 대해 기술하고 있으므로 [B]는 문맥상 적절하지 않다.

05 2014 건국대

정답 ②

| 구문분석 | Darwin(S) was(V) quite familiar(C) (with the concept of selective breeding).

다윈은 선택적 교배라는 개념에 매우 친숙하였다.

(From his experience with livestock), he knew that over generations a breeder could eventually maintain the appearance of an animal or plant.
S V O

그는 가축과의 경험을 통해서, 교배자는, 여러 세대 후에는 결국 동물이나 식물의 외형을 유지할 수 있다는 것을 알았다.

For example, the common rock pigeon is a relatively plain-looking bird.
접속부사 S V C
예를 들어, 흔한 바위 비둘기는 비교적 평범해 보이는 새이다.

(Being)
(Native to southern Europe and northern Africa), it is now common (in parks and cities throughout the world).
분사구문 S V C
남부 유럽과 북부 아프리카에 토종인 이 새는 전 세계를 걸쳐 공원과 도시에서 흔히 볼 수 있다.

Humans first began keeping pigeons several thousand years ago.
S V O
사람들은 수천 년 전부터 비둘기들을 집에서 기르기 시작하였다.

Breeders chose male and female birds (with interesting variations of feathers, colors, neck, beak shape, or flying behaviors and allowed them to breed).
S V O

교배자들은 깃털, 색깔, 목, 부리 모양, 비행습관 등의 흥미로운 변이를 가진 수컷과 암컷 새를 선택하였다.

Over several generations, these traits became more pronounced (in their offspring) (until the features were well established in the birds).
S V C 부사절: ~까지

여러 세대에 걸쳐 이러한 특징들은 후손들에 있어서 더욱 뚜렷하게 되어서 결국 이 모습들이 새들에게 잘 안정화되었다.

Thus, we now have different varieties (of pigeons), (such as the fan tail, archangel, and tumbler), each (with its own distinct features).
접속부사 S V O 대명사: fan tail, archangel, and tumbler 각각을 받음

이렇게 하여 우리는 부채꼬리 비둘기, 천사 비둘기, 공중제비 비둘기 등과 같이 제각각 특별한 특징을 갖춘 여러 종류의 비둘기들을 갖게 되었다.

| 어휘 | **breeding** ⓝ 번식, 부화, 양육, 사육 **generation** ⓝ 세대, 대, 발생
maintain ⓥ 지속하다, 유지하다, 속행하다, 계속하다, 옹호하다, 지지하다 **appearance** ⓝ 외관; 출현; 발표; 징조
beak ⓝ (새의) 부리 **pronounced** ⓐ 명백한, 뚜렷한, 발음되는
offspring ⓝ 자식, 새끼, 자손 **establish** ⓥ 설립하다, 입증하다 **distinct** ⓐ 별개의, 독특한, 뚜렷한
feature ⓝ 얼굴의 생김새, 특징 ⓥ ~의 특징을 이루다

| 전문해석 | 다윈은 선택적 교배라는 개념에 매우 친숙하였다. 그는 가축과의 경험을 통해서, 교배자는, 여러 세대 후에는 결국 동물이나 식물의 외형을 **〈유지할〉** 수 있다는 것을 알았다. 예를 들어, 흔한 바위 비둘기는 비교적 평범해 보이는 새이다. 남부 유럽과 북부 아프리카에 토종인 이 새는 전 세계를 걸쳐 공원과 도시에서 흔히 볼 수 있다. 사람들은 수천 년 전부터 비둘기들을 집에서 기르기 시작하였다. 교배자들은 깃털, 색깔, 목, 부리 모양, 비행습관 등의 흥미로운 변이를 가진 수컷과 암컷 새를 선택하였다. 여러 세대에 걸쳐 이러한 특징들은 후손들에 있어서 더욱 뚜렷하게 되어서 결국 이 모습들이 새들에게 잘 안정화되었다. 이렇게 하여 우리는 부채꼬리 비둘기, 천사 비둘기, 공중제비 비둘기 등과 같이 제각각 특별한 특징을 갖춘 여러 종류의 비둘기들을 갖게 되었다.

| 정답분석 | [B] 뒤 문장 예시 이하를 보면 비둘기들이 교배를 통해 특정한 외형을 가진 비둘기로 여러 세대에 걸쳐 바뀌고 변이된다고 언급하고 있다. 따라서 [B]의 'maintain'은 반의어인 'change'(변화하다)로 고쳐야 한다.

06 2018 인하대

정답 ③

| 구문분석 | (Before the Industrial Revolution), most goods were produced (by hand in rural homes or urban workshops).
S V
산업혁명 이전에는 대부분의 상품이 시골의 가정이나 도시의 작업장에서 수작업으로 생산됐다.

Merchants, (known as entrepreneurs), distributed the raw materials (to workers), collected the finished products, paid for the work, then sold them.
S / V_1 / O / V_2 / V_3 / V_4

기업가로 알려져 있던 상인들은 원자재를 노동자들에게 배급하고, 완제품을 모은 다음, 그 일에 대해 돈을 지불한 후에 그 완제품들을 내다 팔았다.

Growing demand (for consumer products), (together with a shortage of labour), placed pressure (on entrepreneurs) (to find new, more efficient methods of production).
S / V / O

소비재에 대한 증가하는 수요는, 노동력의 부족과 더불어, 새롭고 보다 효율적인 생산방법을 찾아야 한다는 기업가들에게 압력을 가했다.

The great era (of European exploration) (that began in the 15th century) arose primarily (out of a desire) (to seek out new trade routes and partners).
S / V

15세기에 시작된 유럽의 위대한 탐험 시대는 주로 새로운 교역로와 파트너를 찾고자 하는 욕구에서 비롯되었다.

(With the development of power-driven machines), it made economic sense to bring workers, materials and machines together in one place, (giving rise to the first factories).
가주어 / 진주어 / 분사구문

동력 기계가 개발됨에 따라, 노동자, 자재, 기계를 한곳에 모으는 것이 경제적으로 타당하게 되었고, 최초의 공장이 생겨나게 되었다.

(For added efficiency), the production process was broken down (into basic individual tasks) (that a worker could specialize in), a system (known as the division of labour).
S / V / = 앞 문장 전체를 나타내는 동격명사

효율성을 더 높이기 위해, 생산과정은 노동자가 전문적으로 할 수 있었던 기본적인 개별 작업들로 나뉘었는데, 이것은 분업으로 알려져 있는 시스템이다.

| 어휘 |

Industrial Revolution 산업혁명
goods ⓝ 물건, 물품, 상품
rural ⓐ 시골의, 지방의
workshop ⓝ 일터, 작업장, 직장
merchant ⓝ 상인
entrepreneur ⓝ 실업가, 기업가
distribute ⓥ 분배하다, 배급하다
raw material 원료
finished product 완제품
consumer product 소비재
efficient ⓐ 능률적인, 효과적인
era ⓝ 시대, 시기
exploration ⓝ 답사, 탐험; (문제 등의) 탐구
specialize in ~을 전문으로 하다, ~을 전공하다
division of labor 분업

| 전문해석 | 산업혁명 이전에는 대부분의 상품이 시골의 가정이나 도시의 작업장에서 수작업으로 생산됐다. [A] 기업가로 알려져 있던 상인들은 원자재를 노동자들에게 배급하고, 완제품을 모은 다음, 그 일에 대해 돈을 지불한 후에 그 완제품들을 내다 팔았다. [B] 소비재에 대한 증가하는 수요는, 노동력의 부족과 더불어, 새롭고 보다 효율적인 생산방법을 찾아야 한다는 기업가들에게 압력을 가했다. **[C] 〈15세기에 시작된 유럽의 위대한 탐험 시대는 주로 새로운 교역로와 파트너를 찾고자 하는 욕구에서 비롯되었다.〉** [D] 동력 기계가 개발됨에 따라, 노동자, 자재, 기계를 한곳에 모으는 것이 경제적으로 타당하게 되었고, 최초의 공장이 생겨나게 되었다. [E] 효율성을 더 높이기 위해, 생산과정은 노동자가 전문적으로 할 수 있었던 기본적인 개별 작업들로 나뉘었는데, 이것은 분업으로 알려져 있는 시스템이다.

| 정답분석 | 이 글은 '수공업으로 생산되던 상품이 산업혁명으로 인해 공장에서 분업을 통해 대량으로 생산이 이뤄지게 된 상황과 배경'에 관한 내용이다. [A], [B], [D], [E]는 모두 그 내용과 통일되고 일관되지만 [C]는 '15세기에 시작된 지리상의 발견의 배경'에 관한 내용이므로 글의 흐름상 적절하지 않다.

07 2018 건국대

정답 ④

| 구문분석 | Why don't we "think something different" more often? There are several main reasons.
의문문 도치 S / V / O / 유도부사 V / S

우리는 왜 "다른 생각"을 좀 더 자주 하지 않는가? 여기에는 몇 가지 중요한 이유들이 있다.

The first is that we don't need to be creative (for most of what we do).
S V C

첫째, 우리가 하는 대부분의 일은 창의적일 필요가 없기 때문이다.

For example, we don't need to be creative (when we're driving on the freeway, or riding in an elevator, or waiting in line at a grocery store).
S V O 부사절: 때

예를 들어, 고속도로에서 운전하고 있거나, 엘리베이터를 타거나, 식료품점에서 줄을 서서 기다리는 경우, 우리는 창의적일 필요가 없다.

We are creatures (of habit) (when it comes to the business of living) (— from doing paperwork to tying our shoes).
S V C when it comes to: ~에 관한 한

서류 작업에서부터 신발 끈을 매는 것에 이르기까지 일상적인 일에 있어서는 우리는 습관의 산물이다.

(For most of our activities), these routines are indispensable.
S V C

대부분의 활동에서 이러한 판에 박힌 행동들은 없어서는 안 되는 것이다.

(Without them), our lives would be (in chaos), and we wouldn't get much accomplished.
S V S V C

그것들이 없다면, 우리의 삶은 혼란스러워질 것이고, 우리는 많은 것을 이루어 낼 수 없을 것이다.

(If you got up this morning and started contemplating the bristles on your toothbrush or questioning the meaning of toast), you probably wouldn't make it (to work).
부사절: 만일 ~라면 make it: 성공하다, 해내다
S V O

만약 아침에 일어나서 칫솔모에 대해 생각하거나 토스트의 의미에 대해 의문을 갖기 시작한다면, 당신은 아마도 회사에 출근하지 못할 것이다.

get in the way: 방해하다

These attitudes are necessary (for most of what we do), but they can get (in the way) (when we're trying to be creative).
S V C S V 부사절: 때

이러한 태도는 우리가 하는 대부분의 일에서 반드시 필요하지만, 우리가 창의적인 사람이 되고자 노력할 때 방해가 될 수 있다.

Staying on routine thought paths enables us to do the many things (we need to do) (without having to think about them).
S V O O.C

판에 박힌 사고 과정을 유지하는 것은 우리가 사고하지 않고 필요한 많은 일을 할 수 있도록 해 준다.

| 어휘 |

creative ⓐ 창조적인, 창의적인 **freeway** ⓝ 고속도로 **grocery store** ⓝ 식료품점
routine ⓝ 판에 박힌 일, 일상의 일[과정] ⓐ 판에 박힌 **indispensable** ⓐ 없어서는 안 될
chaos ⓝ 혼돈, 혼란 **contemplate** ⓥ 고려하다, 심사숙고하다
bristle ⓝ 빳빳한 털, 강모 **attitude** ⓝ 태도[자세], 사고방식 **get in the way** 방해되다

| 전문해석 | 우리는 왜 "다른 생각"을 좀 더 자주 하지 않는가? 여기에는 몇 가지 중요한 이유들이 있다. 첫째, 우리가 하는 대부분의 일은 창의적일 필요가 없기 때문이다. [A] 예를 들어, 고속도로에서 운전하고 있거나, 엘리베이터를 타거나, 식료품점에서 줄을 서서 기다리는 경우, 우리는 창의적일 필요가 없다. [B] 서류 작업에서부터 신발 끈을 매는 것에 이르기까지 일상적인 일에 있어서는 우리는 습관의 산물이다. 대부분의 활동에서 이러한 판에 박힌 행동들은 없어서는 안 되는 것이다. 그것들이 없다면, 우리의 삶은 혼란스러워질 것이고, 우리는 많은 것을 이루어 낼 수 없을 것이다. [C] 만약 아침에 일어나서 칫솔모에 대해 생각하거나 토스트의 의미에 대해 의문을 갖기 시작한다면, 당신은 아마도 회사에 출근하지 못할 것이다. **[D] 〈이러한 태도는 우리가 하는 대부분의 일에서 반드시 필요하지만, 우리가 창의적인 사람이 되고자 노력할 때 방해가 될 수 있다.〉** [E] 판에 박힌 사고 과정을 유지하는 것은 우리가 사고하지 않고 필요한 많은 일을 할 수 있도록 해 준다.

| 정답분석 | 이 글은 우리가 창의적인 생각을 할 필요가 없는 경우와 습관적으로 하는 것들에 관해 설명하는 글이다. [D]의 these attitudes는 앞 문장의 "아침에 일어나서 칫솔모에 대해 생각하거나 토스트의 의미에 대해 의문을 갖기 시작하는 것"이라는 창의적인 생각을 가리키는데, [D] "이러한 태도가 대부분의 일에서 반드시 필요하지만 창의적인 사람이 되려 할 때 방해가 될 수 있다"는 것은 글의 전체 주제에서 벗어난 내용이므로 글의 흐름상 적절하지 않다.

08 2020 건국대

정답 ⑤

| 구문분석 | Abraham Lincoln's election (to the presidency in 1860) brought (to a climax) the long festering debate (about the relative powers of the federal and the state government).
(Abraham Lincoln's election: S, brought: V, the long festering debate: O)

1860년에 에이브러햄 링컨(Abraham Lincoln)의 대통령 당선은 연방 정부와 주 정부의 상대적인 권력에 대한 오래되고 지겨운 논쟁을 절정에 이르게 했다.

(By the time of his inauguration), six Southern states had seceded (from the Union) and formed the Confederate States (of America), (soon to be followed by five more).
(six Southern states: S, had seceded: V_1, formed: V_2, the Confederate States: O)

그가 취임했을 때쯤, 이미 남부의 여섯 개 주들이 미합중국에서 탈퇴하여 남부 연방을 만들었고 뒤이어 다섯 개의 주가 더 합류했다.

The war (that followed between North and South) put constitutional government (to its severest test).
(The war: S, that: 관계대명사, put: V, constitutional government: O)

뒤이은 북부와 남부 사이의 전쟁은 입헌 정부를 가장 가혹한 시험대에 올렸다.

(After four bloody years of war), the Union was preserved, four million African American slaves were freed, and an entire nation was released (from the oppressive weight of slavery).
(the Union: S_1, was preserved: V_1, four million African American slaves: S_2, were freed: V_2, an entire nation: S_3, was released: V_3)

4년에 걸친 피 흘리는 전쟁 후에 미합중국은 유지되었고, 400만 명의 미국 흑인 노예가 해방되었으며, 국가 전체가 노예제도의 억압적인 중압에서 벗어나게 되었다.

The war can be viewed (in several different ways): as the final, violent phase in a conflict of two regional subcultures; as the breakdown of a democratic political system; as the climax of several decades of social reform; or as a pivotal chapter in American racial history.
(The war: S, can be viewed: V, 콜론: 세부적인 사항 재진술, 세미콜론: 등위접속사 역할)

이 전쟁은 다양한 면으로 바라볼(해석할) 수 있는데, 두 지역 하위문화의 충돌의 폭력적인 최종 국면으로나, 민주적인 정치 체제의 몰락으로나, 수십 년 동안 이어진 사회 개혁의 절정으로나, 혹은 미국 인종 역사의 핵심적 부분으로 볼 수 있다.

as ~ as 원급 구문에서 앞의 as는 부사이며 뒤의 as는 부사절을 이끄는 접속사이다.
(As) important (as the war itself) was the tangled problem (of how to reconstruct the defeated South).
(important: C, was: V, the tangled problem: S)

전쟁 자체만큼이나 중요한 것은 패배한 남부를 어떻게 재건할 것인가에 대한 뒤얽힌 문제였다.

(However interpreted), the Civil War stands (as a story of great heroism, sacrifice, triumph, and tragedy).
(However interpreted: 부사절: 아무리 ~한다 해도, the Civil War: S, stands: V)

해석이 어떻든지 간에, 남북전쟁은 위대한 영웅주의, 희생, 승리, 그리고 비극의 이야기이다.

| 어휘 |
festering ⓐ 지겨운, 싫증이 나는 **inauguration** ⓝ (대통령·교수 등의) 취임(식)
secede from ~에서 탈퇴[분리]하다 **the Union** 미합중국, (남북전쟁 때 연방정부를 지지한) 북부의 여러 주, 북부 연합
Confederate States (of America) (the ~) 남부 연방 (= the Confederacy) **bloody** ⓐ 피비린내 나는
preserve ⓥ 보전하다, 유지하다 **oppressive** ⓐ 압제적인, 압박하는 **subculture** ⓝ 하위문화
pivotal ⓐ 중심(축)이 되는 **tangled** ⓐ 헝클어진; 복잡한; 뒤얽힌 **reconstruct** ⓥ 재건[복원]하다
interpret ⓥ 설명[해석]하다, 이해하다

| 전문해석 | 1860년에 에이브러햄 링컨(Abraham Lincoln)의 대통령 당선은 연방 정부와 주 정부의 상대적인 권력에 대한 오래되고 지겨운 논쟁을 절정에 이르게 했다. [A] 그가 취임했을 때쯤, 이미 남부의 여섯 개 주들이 미합중국에서 탈퇴하여 남부 연방을 만들었고 뒤이어 다섯 개의 주가 더 합류했다. [B] 뒤이은 북부와 남부 사이의 전쟁은 입헌 정부를 가장 가혹한 시험대에 올렸다. [C] 4년에 걸친 피 흘리는 전쟁 후에 미합중국은 유지되었고, 400만 명의 미국 흑인 노예가 해방되었으며, 국가 전체가 노예제도의 억압적인 중압에서 벗어나게 되었다. [D] 이 전쟁은 다양한 면으로 바라볼(해석할) 수 있는데, 두 지역 하위문화의 충돌의 폭력적인 최종 국면으로나, 민주적인 정치 체제의 몰락으로나, 수십 년 동안 이어진 사회 개혁의 절정으로나, 혹은 미국 인종 역사의 핵심적 부분으로 볼 수 있다. **[E] 〈전쟁 자체만큼이나 중요한 것은 패배한 남부를 어떻게 재건할 것인가에 대한 뒤얽힌 문제였다.〉** 해석이 어떻든지 간에, 남북전쟁은 위대한 영웅주의, 희생, 승리, 그리고 비극의 이야기이다.

| 정답분석 | 이 글은 남북전쟁의 과정과 결과, 그리고 그것의 역사적 의미에 대해 기술하는 글인데 [D] 문장의 마지막에서 남북전쟁의 역사적 해석을 기술했고, 이 글의 마지막 문장도 남북전쟁의 역사적 해석에 대해 기술하고 있다. 그런데 [E] 문장은 앞뒤와는 다른 패배한 남부 연합을 어떻게 재건할 것인지에 대한 내용이므로 [E] 문장을 삭제해야 글의 흐름이 자연스럽다.

09 2018 건국대

정답 ④

| 구문분석 | Everyone knows what sharks look like. We also know that sharks can be dangerous.
S V O S V O
모든 사람들은 상어가 어떻게 생겼는지 알고 있다. 우리는 또한 상어가 위험할 수도 있다는 것을 알고 있다.

However, many people may not realize [that sharks are one of the oldest species of animals on earth, as well as one of the most interesting].
접속부사 S V O B A
B as well as A: A뿐만 아니라 B도
그러나 많은 사람들이 상어가 가장 흥미로운 동물일 뿐만 아니라 지구상에서 가장 오래된 동물 중 하나라는 사실은 잘 모를 수도 있다.

Sharks share some things (in common with other fish), but they are somewhat different.
S V O S V C
상어는 다른 어류와 몇 가지 면에서 공통점이 있기는 하지만, 다소 다른 점도 있다.

First of all, almost all sharks are carnivores, or meat eaters. They eat dolphins, seals, other sharks, and other fish.
S V C S V O
우선, 거의 모든 상어들은 고기를 먹는 육식동물이다. 상어는 돌고래, 바다표범, 다른 상어들과 그 외의 물고기를 먹고 산다.

(Like all fish), though, sharks are cold-blooded animals (— their bodies change temperature as the water temperature changes).
접속부사 S V C
하지만, 모든 어류들처럼 상어 또한 냉혈 동물이다. 그래서 상어의 체온은 수온의 변화에 따라 변한다.

Also, like other fish, the shark's body has gill slits, or openings (that help the shark breathe in the water).
S V O = 관계대명사
또한 다른 어류처럼 상어의 몸은 아가미구멍, 즉 물속에서 상어가 숨을 쉴 수 있도록 도와주는 개구부가 있다.

However, a shark's skeleton is unusual (for a fish). Its bones are tough and inflexible.
접속부사 S V C S V C
그러나 상어의 골격은 물고기치고는 특이하다. 그 상어의 뼈는 강하고 잘 구부러지지 않는다.

In fact, shark bones feel (like a human ear). In addition, a shark's skin is unusual (for a fish). Its skin is (like armor).
S V S V C S V
실제로 상어의 뼈는 인간의 귀와 비슷하다. 게다가, 상어의 피부는 물고기치고는 특이하다. 상어의 피부는 갑옷과 같다.

It has many sharp spikes or nails (to protect it).
S V C
피부를 보호하기 위한 날카로운 많은 돌기가 달려 있다.

Consequently, you can hurt yourself (by just touching a shark's skin).
접속부사 S V O
결과적으로, 상어의 피부를 건드리기만 해도 상처를 입을 수 있다.

| 어휘 |

carnivore ⓝ 육식동물	**dolphin** ⓝ 돌고래	**seal** ⓝ 바다표범; 물개
cold-blooded animal ⓝ 냉혈 동물	**gill slit** 아가미구멍	**skeleton** ⓝ 뼈대, 골격
armor ⓝ 갑옷; 철갑	**spike** ⓝ 못, 뾰족한 것	**nail** ⓝ 못; 손톱, 발톱

| 전문해석 | 모든 사람들은 상어가 어떻게 생겼는지 알고 있다. 우리는 또한 상어가 위험할 수도 있다는 것을 알고 있다. 그러나 많은 사람들이 상어가 가장 흥미로운 동물일 뿐만 아니라 지구상에서 가장 오래된 동물 중 하나라는 사실은 잘 모를 수도 있다. 상어는 다른 어류와 몇 가지 면에서 공통점이 있기는 하지만, 다소 다른 점도 있다. 우선, 거의 모든 상어들은 고기를 먹는 육

식동물이다. 상어는 돌고래, 바다표범, 다른 상어들과 그 외의 물고기를 먹고 산다. 하지만, 모든 어류들처럼 상어 또한 냉혈 동물이다. 그래서 상어의 체온은 수온의 변화에 따라 변한다. 또한 다른 어류처럼 상어의 몸은 아가미구멍, 즉 물속에서 상어가 숨을 쉴 수 있도록 도와주는 개구부가 있다. 그러나 상어의 골격은 물고기치고는 특이하다. 상어의 뼈는 강하고 **〈잘 구부러지지 않는다〉**. 실제로 상어의 뼈는 인간의 귀와 비슷하다. 게다가, 상어의 피부는 물고기치고는 특이하다. 상어의 피부는 갑옷과 같다. 피부를 보호하기 위한 날카로운 많은 돌기가 달려 있다. 결과적으로, 상어의 피부를 건드리기만 해도 상처를 입을 수 있다.

| 정답분석 | [D]의 뒤 문장에서 실제로 상어의 뼈는 인간의 귀와 비슷하다고 했다. 따라서 상어의 뼈는 인간의 귀처럼 잘 구부러져야 하므로 [D]의 inflexible을 flexible로 고쳐야 한다. 참고로 냉혈 동물은 '외부의 온도 변화에 따라 체온이 변화하는 동물[배경지식이 필요했음]'이기 때문에 [B]의 cold-blooded(냉혈 동물)는 바로 뒤에 나온 설명과 부합하므로 문맥상 적절하다.

10 2016 국민대

정답 ④

| 구문분석 | Humans(S) are hardwired(V) (to hate uncertainty); we(S)'re constantly trying(V) to find "sure things"(O) (to help us succeed).

인간은 불확실성을 미워하도록 굳어져 있다. 그리고 우리는, 우리가 성공하는 것에 도움을 주는 확실한 것을 발견하기 위해 지속적으로 노력한다.

But ironically, Jamie Holmes(S) argues(V) (in his new book), this aversion(S) (to ambiguity) often hinders(V) our ability(O) (to make the best decisions).

그러나 아이러니하게도, 제이미 홈스(Jamie Holmes)는 그의 새 책에서 이러한 불확실함에 대한 혐오가 종종 최선의 선택을 하는 우리의 능력을 방해한다고 주장했다.

In medicine, for instance(접속부사), one study(S) found(V) [that(O) doctors(S) (who acknowledged that their patient had unclear symptoms) would(V) nevertheless(부사: 그럼에도 불구하고) order a definitive test or prescription(O) (77% of the time) — often without asking follow-up questions].

예를 들어, 의학의 경우, 한 연구는, 의사들이 그들의 환자가 불확실한 증상을 가지고 있다는 것을 인정함에도 불구하고 종종 추가적인 질문을 던지지도 않은 채 77%의 경우 확정적인 테스트나 처방을 명령한다는 사실을 발견했다.

How can(의문문 도치) we(S) combat(V) this impulsive desire(O) (for resolution)? (For starters), Holmes(S) writes(V), we should be open (to second-guessing ourselves)(O).

우리는 어떻게 결정을 내리고자 하는 이러한 충동적인 욕망과 싸울 수 있을까? 초심자들에게, 홈스가 글로 쓰길, 우리는 반드시 두 번째 추론을 향해 우리 자신을 열어 두어야 한다고 했다.

This(S) is(V) especially true(C) (in schools), (where(관계부사) teachers should encourage students to take the unfamiliar side of an argument or ignore a problem riddled with errors) (—(대시: 부연설명) all in an attempt to hone their critical-thinking skills).

학생들에게 비판적 사고의 기술을 연마시키려는 시도로써 교사들이 학생들로 하여금 논쟁의 익숙하지 않은 측면을 포착하게 하고 에러들로 가득 찬 문제들을 무시하라고 권장해야만 하는 학교에서 특히나 사실이다.

After all(접속부사), Holmes(S) writes(V), "sometimes the illusion of knowing is more dangerous (than not knowing at all)."(O)

결국, 홈스는 "때로는 알고 있다는 환상이 전혀 모르는 것보다 더 위험하다"라고 글로 썼다.

| 어휘 |

hardwire ⓥ (보고 듣는 것에서) (행동 양식을) 고정화시키다, 굳어 버리게 하다		**aversion** ⓝ 혐오
ambiguity ⓝ 애매모호함	**hinder** ⓥ 방해하다, 막다	**definitive** ⓐ 최종적인, 확정적인
follow-up ⓐ 잇따른, 후속의	**combat** ⓥ 싸우다	**hone** ⓥ 연마하다, 갈다

| 전문해석 | 인간은 불확실성을 미워하도록 굳어져 있다. 그리고 우리는, 우리가 성공하는 것에 도움을 주는 확실한 것을 발견하기 위해

지속적으로 노력한다. 그러나 아이러니하게도, 제이미 홈스(Jamie Holmes)는 그의 새 책에서 이러한 불확실함에 대한 혐오가 종종 최선의 선택을 하는 우리의 능력을 방해한다고 주장했다. 예를 들어, 의학의 경우, 한 연구는, 의사들이 그들의 환자가 불확실한 증상을 가지고 있다는 것을 인정함에도 불구하고 종종 추가적인 질문을 던지지도 않은 채 77%의 경우 확정적인 테스트나 처방을 명령한다는 사실을 발견했다. 우리는 어떻게 결정을 내리고자 하는 이러한 충동적인 욕망과 싸울 수 있을까? 우리는 어떻게 결정을 내리고자 하는 이러한 충동적인 욕망과 싸울 수 있을까? 초심자들에게, 홈스가 글로 쓰길, 우리는 반드시 두 번째 추론을 향해 우리 자신을 열어 두어야 한다고 한다. 학생들에게 비판적 사고의 기술을 연마시키려는 시도로써 교사들이 학생들로 하여금 논쟁의 익숙하지 않은 측면을 포착하게 하고 에러들로 가득 찬 문제들을 **<무시하라고>** 권장해야만 하는 학교에서 특히나 사실이다. 결국, 홈스는 "때로는 알고 있다는 환상이 전혀 모르는 것보다 더 위험하다"라고 글로 썼다.

| 정답분석 | 이 글은 제이미 홈스(Jamie Holmes)의 책 내용과 관련한 글이다. 이 글에 기술된 홈스의 책 내용에 비추어 보았을 때, 교사들이 학교에서 학생들에게 비판적 사고를 습득시키려면 각종 에러들로 가득 찬 문제들을 '무시'하는 것이 아니라 '다루고, 대처하고, 해결해야' 할 것이다. 따라서 [D]의 ignore는 문맥상 적절하지 않다.

11 2011 인하대

정답 ③

| 구문분석 | The most depressing response (that) (I encounter) (when I'm chatting someone up and I ask them if they ever go to the theatre) is this: "I should go but I don't."

S / 부사절: ~할 때 / V / C / 콜론: 동격

누군가와 대화를 하다가 그에게 극장에 가느냐고 물었을 때 내가 마주치는 가장 우울한 반응은 이것이다: "가야 하는데 그러질 못해요."

That emphatic "should" tells you all (that) (you need to know).

S / V / O / O.C

"가야 하는데"라는 그 단호한 표현은 당신에게 당신이 알 필요가 있는 모든 것을 말해 준다.

(You) Imagine it (in other contexts): "I should play Grand Theft Auto"; "I should watch Strictly Come Dancing."

V / O / 콜론: 예시 / 세미콜론: and 역할

그것을 다른 맥락에서 한번 상상해 보라: "Grand Theft Auto 게임을 해야 하는데"; "Strictly Come Dancing 프로그램을 봐야 하는데".

Many critics still believe (that) theatre has a quasi-educational/political role; that a play posits an argument (that the playwright then proves or disproves).

S / V / O_1 / 세미콜론: and 역할 / O_2 / 관계대명사

많은 비평가들이 여전히 연극이 준 교육적, 정치적 역할을 하고 연극은 극작가가 증명하거나 반증하는 주장을 제기한다는 것을 믿는다.

That "should" tells you that people see theatre-going not as entertainment but as self-improvement, and the critical/academic establishment have to take some blame (for that).

not A but B: A가 아니라 B / S_1 / V_1 / I.O / D.O / S_2 / V_2 / O_2

그 "가야 하는데"라는 표현은 사람들이 극장에 가는 것을 오락이 아니라 자기 계발로 보고 있다는 것을 말해 주고, 비판적/학문적 기득권층은 그것에 대해 어느 정도 책임을 져야만 한다.

| 어휘 |

depressing ⓐ 우울하게 만드는, 우울한
chat ⓥ ~와 잡담하다, 이야기하다
emphatic ⓐ (진술 · 대답 등이) 강한, 단호한
context ⓝ (글의) 전후 관계, 맥락, 배경
Grand Theft Auto 그랜드 테프트 오토(컴퓨터 게임의 일종)
Strictly Come Dancing (영국 BBC가 방송해 큰 인기를 끈 댄싱 프로그램)
quasi-educational ⓐ 유사 교육적인, 사회교육 기능을 수행하는
playwright ⓝ 각본가, 극작가
disprove ⓥ 반증하다, 논박하다
entertainment ⓝ 오락(물)
self-improvement ⓝ 자기 개선
establishment ⓝ (사회)기득권층, 시설
take the blame (잘못의) 책임을 지다

| 전문해석 | 누군가와 대화를 하다가 그에게 극장에 가느냐고 물었을 때 내가 마주치는 가장 우울한 반응은 이것이다: "가야 하는데 그러질 못해요." [A] "가야 하는데"라는 그 단호한 표현은 당신에게 당신이 알 필요가 있는 모든 것을 말해 준다. [B] 그것을 다른 맥락에서 한번 상상해 보라: "Grand Theft Auto 게임을 해야 하는데"; "Strictly Come Dancing 프로그램을 봐야

하는데". [C] **〈많은 비평가들이 여전히 연극이 준 교육적, 정치적 역할을 하고 연극은 극작가가 증명하거나 반증하는 주장을 제기한다는 것을 믿는다.〉** [D] 그 "가야 하는데"라는 표현은 사람들이 극장에 가는 것을 오락이 아니라 자기 계발로 보고 있다는 것을 말해 주고, 비판적/학문적 기득권층은 그것에 대해 어느 정도 책임을 져야만 한다.

| 정답분석 | 무관한 문장을 고를 때는 '지시사'를 참고하여 앞 내용과의 연결성을 따져 본다. 본문에서는 사람들이 연극을 보러 극장에 가는 것을 오락이 아닌 자기 계발로 여기는 것을 비판하고 있다. 첫 문장에서 "I should go but I don't." 부분이 [A]의 That emphatic "should"와 자연스럽게 연결되고 [B]의 'Imagine it'도 앞에 지시한 'should'를 다른 맥락에서 상상해 보는 뜻이므로 흐름상 무리가 없다. 그러나 [C]의 경우에는 연극을 교육적이거나 정치적인 역할을 하는 것으로 믿는 비평가의 의견이 나오므로 앞 내용과 자연스럽게 연결되지 못한다. [D] 또한 'That "should"'라는 표현과 관련해서 연극에 대한 사람들의 태도를 이어 설명하고 있으므로 [C]만 삭제하면 자연스러운 글이 완성된다.

12 2019 단국대

정답 ②

| 구문분석 | Sports facilities(S) (built in the late 1970s, 80s, and early 90s) were routinely designed(V_1) (to enhance in-facility experiences) [부사적용법: ~하기 위해서] but[등위접속사] routinely ignored(V_2) the potential(O) (for harnessing associated economic activity) (that[관계대명사] could take place on adjacent real estate).

1970년대 후반, 1980년대, 1990년대 초반에 건설된 스포츠 시설들은 시설 내부에서의 경험을 향상시킬 목적으로 판에 박힌 듯 설계되었으나, 시설 인근의 부동산에서 발생할 수 있는 (시설에) 관련된 경제활동의 잠재력은 일상적으로 무시했다.

Facilities(S) (built) (during[전치사] this time period) were constructed(V) (with substantial public investments).

이 시기에 건설된 시설들은 상당한 공공투자로 지어졌다.

The failure(S) (to diminish property values and[등위접속사] (to) capitalize on the economic activity) (taking place within the venue) generated(V) substantial levels(O) (of discontent) (with the decision) (to support a team's effort to secure a new venue).

부동산 가치를 내리지 못하고 경기장 시설 내에서 발생하는 경제활동을 활용하지 못한 것은 새로운 경기장 시설을 확보하려는 구단의 노력을 지원하기로 한 결정에 상당한 수준의 불만을 야기했다.

As a result[접속부사], all(S) (of the benefits from the building of venues) accrued(V) (to team owners and others) (linked to the sports industry).

그 결과 경기장 건설로 인한 모든 편익은 구단주들과 다른 스포츠업계 관계자들에게 돌아갔다.

There[유도부사] was(V) little(S) (if any financial return to the public sector partners)[부사절: 비록 ~일지라도].

공공부문 협력사에 돌아가는 금전적인 수익은 설령 있다 해도 거의 없는 수준이었다.

The situation(S) was made(V) worse(O.C) (when team owners were allowed to retain most)[부사절: ~할 때], (if not all)[부사절: 비록 ~일지라도], (of the revenue streams) (that[관계대명사] were created in these new state-of-the-art facilities).

그 상황은 새로운 최첨단 시설들에서 발생하는 수입원의 대부분을, 전부는 아니지만, 구단주들이 가질 수 있도록 허용되었을 때, 더욱 악화되었다.

| 어휘 |

routinely ⓐⓓ 일상적으로, 판에 박힌 듯
harness ⓥ (동력원 등으로) 이용하다
take place 일어나다, 발생하다
adjacent ⓐ 인접한, 가까운
real estate 부동산
diminish ⓥ 약화시키다, 줄어들다
property value 부동산 가치
capitalize on ~을 이용하다
discontent ⓝ 불평, 불만
accrue ⓥ 생기다, 축적되다
return ⓝ 귀환, 회복, 보답, 수익
retain ⓥ 보류하다, 보유하다
revenue stream (기업의) 수입원, 매출원
state-of-the-art ⓐ 최신의, 최신 기술의

| 전문해석 | 1970년대 후반, 1980년대, 1990년대 초반에 건설된 스포츠 시설들은 시설 내부에서의 경험을 향상시킬 목적으로 판에 박힌 듯 설계되었으나, 시설 인근의 부동산에서 발생할 수 있는 (시설에) 관련된 경제활동을 활용할 잠재력은 일상적으로 무시했다. 이 시기에 건설된 시설들은 상당한 공공투자로 지어졌다. 부동산 가치를 **〈내리지〉** 못하고 경기장 시설 내에서 발생하는 경제활동을 활용하지 못한 것은 새로운 경기장 시설을 확보하려는 구단의 노력을 지원하기로 한 결정에 상당한 수준의 불만을 야기했다. 그 결과 경기장 건설로 인한 모든 편익은 구단주들과 다른 스포츠업계 관계자들에게 돌아갔다. 공공부문 협력사에 돌아가는 금전적인 수익은 설령 있다 해도 거의 없는 수준이었다. 그 상황은 새로운 최첨단 시설들에서 발생하는 수입원의 대부분을, 전부는 아니지만, 구단주들이 가질 수 있도록 허용되었을 때, 더욱 악화되었다.

| 정답분석 | 글의 흐름을 고려하여 어색한 표현을 고를 때는 밑줄 친 부분을 그대로 해석해 보고 어색할 경우 그 자리에 '반의어'를 넣거나 밑줄 친 부분 앞에 'not'을 넣어 해석해 본다. 본문에서는 1970년대 후반부터 1990년대 초반에 지어진 스포츠 시설들은 시설 인근의 부동산에서 일어날 수 있는 시설에 관련된 경제활동을 활용해 볼 가능성을 무시했다고 했다. [B]에서 스포츠 시설들이 인근 부동산 가치를 '내리지' 못한 것이 아니라, 부동산 가치를 '올리지' 못한 것이 되어야 문맥상 적절하다. 따라서 [B]의 'diminish'를 반의어인 'elevate(높이다, 증가시키다)'로 고쳐야 한다.

13 2015 인하대

정답 ③

| 구문분석 | (According to study experts), one tip (for exam success) is regular daily and weekly study.
전치사 / S / V / C
학습 전문가들에 따르면, 시험에 성공하기 위한 한 가지 팁은 매일 그리고 매주 규칙적으로 공부하는 것이다.

Another tip is to focus (on, (in your study sessions), ideas) (that the instructor has emphasized in class).
S / V / C / 관계대명사
또 다른 팁은 수업 시간에 교사가 강조한 개념들에 집중하는 것이다.

In addition, (you) use the night (before an exam) (for a careful review) (rather than a stressful cramming).
접속부사 / V / O / rather than: ~라기보다는
게다가, 스트레스가 많은 벼락치기보다는 신중한 복습을 위해 시험 전날 밤을 이용하라.

Then (you) get up a bit early the next morning and review your notes one more time.
V_1 / 등위접속사 / V_2 / O
그러고 나서 다음 날 아침에 조금 일찍 일어나서 노트를 한 번 더 복습하는 것이다.

Study skills are tools and strategies (used to make learning more efficient, organized, and successful).
S / V / C
학습 기술은 학습을 더 효율적이고, 체계적이며, 성공적으로 만드는 데 사용되는 도구와 전략이다.

Last, (once the test begins), the advice (of experts) is to answer the easiest question first; then go back and tackle the hard ones.
부사절: 일단 ~하면 / S / V / C / 세미콜론: and 역할

마지막으로, 일단 시험이 시작되면, 전문가의 조언은 가장 쉬운 문제에 먼저 답을 하고 나서 다시 처음으로 돌아가 어려운 문제를 해결하는 것이다.

| 어휘 |

session ⓝ 학기	**cram** ⓥ 억지로 밀어 넣다; 벼락치기 공부를 하다
strategy ⓝ 전략	**tackle** ⓥ (힘든 일과) 씨름하다, (다른 사람과) 대결하다

| 전문해석 | 학습 전문가들에 따르면, 시험에 성공하기 위한 한 가지 팁은 매일 그리고 매주 규칙적으로 공부하는 것이다. 또 다른 팁은 수업 시간에 교사가 강조한 개념들에 집중하는 것이다. [A] 게다가, 스트레스가 많은 벼락치기보다는 신중한 복습을 위해 시험 전날 밤을 이용하라. [B] 그러고 나서 다음 날 아침에 조금 일찍 일어나서 노트를 한 번 더 복습하는 것이다. **[C] 〈학습 기술은 학습을 더 효율적이고, 체계적이며, 성공적으로 만드는 데 사용되는 도구와 전략이다.〉** [D] 마지막으로, 일단 시험이 시작되면, 전문가의 조언은 가장 쉬운 문제에 먼저 답을 하고 나서 다시 처음으로 돌아가 어려운 문제를 해결하는 것이다.

| 정답분석 | 본문에서는 시험에서 성공하기 위한 구체적인 전략들을 나열하고 있다. [A]에서는 'In addition' 표현을 이용하여 앞에 소개한 전략에 이어 추가적 전략을 소개하고 있다. [B] 역시 'Then'을 사용하여 그 이후 전략을 연결하고 있지만 [C]는 시험에 성공하기 위한 구체적인 전략이라기보다는 학습 기술에 대한 일반적 기능에 대한 언급을 하고 있으므로 앞 문장과 자연스럽게 연결되지 못한다. 참고로 [D] 또한 'Last'라는 표현과 함께 마지막 전략을 제시하고 있으므로 맥락상 자연스럽다. 따라서 [C]를 삭제해야 한다.

14 2017 가톨릭대

정답 ②

| 구문분석 | The natural surveillance (provided by passers-by or by windows and balconies) (overlooking streets) is enough to deter most crime and vandalism.
S / V / C

행인이나 거리가 내려다보이는 창문과 발코니에 의해 제공되는 자연스러운 감시는 대부분의 범죄와 공공기물 파손을 막기에 충분하다.

Well-designed neighborhoods promote this casual policing, (which can work alongside more formal schemes for watching over one another's homes).
S / V / O / 관계대명사(계속적용법)

잘 계획된 거주 지역은 이러한 일상적인 치안 유지를 촉진하며, 이는 서로의 집을 감시하기 위한 보다 공식적인 계획들과 함께 효과를 거둘 수 있다.

Homes should be flexible (to adapt to a household's changing needs over time).
S / V / C / 부사적용법: ~하기 위해서

가정은 시간이 지남에 따라 변화하는 가정의 필요에 적응할 수 있도록 유연해야만 한다.

Thoughtfully sited car parking and bicycle storage, (as well as well-integrated recycling bins), contribute not only (to a sense of order) but also (to reducing litter, vandalism and theft).
S / B as well as A: A뿐만 아니라 B / V / not only A but also B: A뿐만 아니라 B / 등위접속사

잘 통합된 재활용 쓰레기통들뿐만 아니라 주차장과 자전거 보관소도 잘 배치되어 있어, 질서의식에 기여할 뿐 아니라 쓰레기 버리기, 기물 파손, 절도 행위를 줄이는 데에도 기여한다.

부사적용법: ~하기 위해서
(To encourage these changes), police services award Secured by Design certificates (to homes and developments) (whose design deters crime).
S / V / O / 관계대명사

이러한 변화들을 장려하기 위해, 경찰 서비스는 범죄를 방지하도록 설계된 주택과 발전에 '방범 환경 설계(SBD: Secured By Design)' 인증을 수여한다.

It considers the materials and design (of entry points) (such as doors and windows, the deployment of burglar alarms and video entry systems, and the natural surveillance) (offered by windows to open spaces).
S / V / O / 전치사

그것(인증 제도)은 문과 창문과 같은 입구의 재료와 설계, 도난 경보 및 비디오 출입 시스템의 배치 그리고 개방된 공간으로 나 있는 창문에 의해 제공되는 자연스러운 감시 등을 고려한다.

| 어휘 |
surveillance ⓝ 감시
passer-by ⓝ 행인(특히 예상 밖의 일이 일어나던 순간에 지나던 사람)
overlook ⓥ 내려다보다; 간과하다
policing ⓝ (경찰의) 치안 유지 활동
deter ⓥ 단념시키다, 그만두게 하다
vandalism ⓝ 반달리즘, 공공기물 파손죄
litter ⓝ 쓰레기
deployment ⓝ 전개, 배치
burglar ⓝ 절도범, 빈집털이범

| 전문해석 | 행인이나 거리가 내려다보이는 창문과 발코니에 의해 제공되는 자연스러운 감시는 대부분의 범죄와 공공기물 파손을 막기에 충분하다. [A] 잘 계획된 거주 지역은 이러한 일상적인 치안 유지를 촉진하며, 이는 서로의 집을 감시하기 위한 보다 공식적인 계획들과 함께 효과를 거둘 수 있다. **[B] 〈가정은 시간이 지남에 따라 변화하는 가정의 필요에 적응할 수 있도록 유연해야만 한다.〉** [C] 잘 통합된 재활용 쓰레기통들뿐만 아니라 주차장과 자전거 보관소도 잘 배치되어 있어, 질서의식에 기여할 뿐 아니라 쓰레기 버리기, 기물 파손, 절도행위를 줄이는 데에도 기여한다. [D] 이러한 변화들을 장려하기 위해, 경찰 서비스는 범죄를 방지하도록 설계된 주택과 발전에 '방범 환경 설계(SBD: Secured By Design)' 인증을 수여한다. 그것(인증 제도)은 문과 창문과 같은 입구의 재료와 설계, 도난 경보 및 비디오 출입 시스템의 배치 그리고 개방된 공간으로 나 있는 창문에 의해 제공되는 자연스러운 감시 등을 고려한다.

| 정답분석 | 본문은 범죄와 공공기물 파손을 막기 위한 환경 조성에 관한 세부사항들을 소개하고 있다. [A]의 경우 'Well-designed neighborhoods'가 제공하는 치안 유지 기능을, [C]는 'Thoughtfully sited car parking and bicycle storage'의 기능을 각각 제시하고 있으므로 흐름이 자연스럽다. [D] 역시 'To encourage these changes'라는 표현을 사용하여 앞 문장에서 언급한 '변화'에 대해 이어서 설명하고 있으므로 정답에서는 제외된다. 하지만 [B]의 "가정은 시간이 지남에 따라 변화하는 가정의 필요에 적응할 수 있도록 유연해야만 한다."라는 내용은 문맥과는 관계가 없으므로 삭제해야 한다.

15 2017 인하대

정답 ⑤

| 구문분석 |

(Although scattered local airline companies began offering flights to passengers as early as 1913), scheduled domestic flights did not become widely available (in the United States) (until the 1920s).

부사절: 비록 ~일지라도 / S / V / C

비록 흩어진 지역 항공사들이 1913년부터 승객들에게 항공편을 제공하기 시작했지만, 예정된 국내선들은 1920년까지 미국에서 널리 이용할 수 없었다.

(During the early years of commercial aviation), U.S. airline travel was limited (to a small population) (of business travelers and wealthy individuals) (who could afford the high ticket prices).

전치사 / S / V / 관계대명사

상업 비행이 이뤄지던 초창기 동안, 미국 항공 여행은 높은 항공요금을 지불할 여유가 있던 소수의 비즈니스 여행객과 부유한 개인들에게만 제한되었다.

The majority (of travelers) relied (instead) (on more affordable train services) (for their intercity transportation needs).

S / V / 부사: 그 대신

대부분의 여행객들은 그들의 도시 간 교통의 필요를 위해 비행기 대신에 보다 적당한 (가격의) 기차 서비스에 의존하고 있었다.

(Over ninety-five years later), the airlines have grown (to be one of the most important and heavily used transportation options) (for American business and leisure travelers).

S / V / 부사적용법: ~해서 그 결과

95년 이상의 세월이 흐른 뒤, 항공편은 미국의 비즈니스와 레저 여행객들에게 가장 중요하고 많이 이용되는 운송 수단 중 하나로 성장해 왔다.

(Following deregulation of the airline industry by the U.S. government in 1978), airline routes increased, ticket fares decreased, and discount carriers prospered, thus (making airline travel accessible to a much broader segment of the U.S. population).

분사구문 / S_1 / V_1 / S_2 / V_2 / 등위접속사 / S_3 / V_3 / 접속부사 / 분사구문

1978년에 미국 정부에 의한 항공 산업의 규제 완화에 따라, 항공 노선이 증가하고, 항공요금은 내려갔으며, 할인 항공사들이 번영하였고, 결과적으로 이것이 항공 여행을 더 광범위한 계층의 미국인들이 접근할 수 있게 만들었다.

Plane tickets were generally prepared (by hand) (using carbon paper) and were given (to passengers) (upon their arrival) (at the airports).

S / V_1 / 등위접속사 / V_2

비행기표는 일반적으로 탄소 종이(먹지)를 사용해서 손으로 써서 준비되었고 공항에 도착하면 승객들에게 곧바로 주어졌다.

(In 2008 alone), 649.9 million passengers traveled (on domestic flights) (on U.S. airlines).

S / V

2008년에만, 6억 4,990만 명의 승객들이 미국 항공사의 국내선으로 여행했다.

| 어휘 |

scatter ⓥ (흩)뿌리다, 흩어지다
passenger ⓝ 승객, 여객
domestic ⓐ 가정의, 국내의, 자국의
commercial ⓐ 상업의, 상업적인
aviation ⓝ 비행, 항공
afford ⓥ ~할 여유가 있다, 제공하다
affordable ⓐ 감당할 수 있는
majority ⓝ 대부분, 대다수
transportation ⓝ 운송, 수송
deregulation ⓝ 규제[제한] 철폐
fare ⓝ 운임, 통행료
prosper ⓥ 번영하다, 번영시키다
accessible ⓐ 접근[입장]하기 쉬운, 이용할 수 있는, 이해하기 쉬운
segment ⓝ 단편, 조각, 부분
carbon paper ⓝ 카본지, (복사용의) 먹지

| 전문해석 |

비록 흩어진 지역 항공사들이 1913년부터 승객들에게 항공편을 제공하기 시작했지만, 예정된 국내선들은 1920년까지 미국에서 널리 이용할 수 없었다. [A] 상업 비행이 이뤄지던 초창의 동안, 미국 항공 여행은 높은 항공요금을 지불할 여유가 있던 소수의 비즈니스 여행객과 부유한 개인들에게만 제한되었다. [B] 대부분의 여행객들은 그들의 도시 간 교통의 필요를 위해 비행기 대신에 보다 적당한 (가격의) 기차 서비스에 의존하고 있었다. [C] 95년 이상의 세월이 흐른 뒤, 항공편은 미국의 비즈니스와 레저 여행객들에게 가장 중요하고 많이 이용되는 운송 수단 중 하나로 성장해 왔다. [D] 1978년에 미국 정부에 의한 항공 산업의 규제 완화에 따라, 항공 노선이 증가하고, 항공요금은 내려갔으며, 할인 항공사들이 번영하였고, 결

과적으로 이것이 항공 여행을 더 광범위한 계층의 미국인들이 접근할 수 있게 만들었다. **[E] 〈비행기표는 일반적으로 탄소 종이(먹지)를 사용해서 손으로 써서 준비되었고 공항에 도착하면 승객들에게 곧바로 주어졌다.〉** 2008년에만, 6억 4,990만 명의 승객들이 미국 항공사의 국내선으로 여행했다.

| 정답분석 | 본문의 1913년부터 2008년까지 미국의 항공 산업의 발달 과정을 시간순으로 설명하고 있다. [A]부터 [D]까지의 설명은 시간의 흐름을 잘 반영하여 전개되고 있지만 [E]는 비행기표의 준비와 발권 방식에 대해 설명하고 있으므로 글의 흐름상 적절하지 않다. 따라서 [E]를 삭제해야 한다.

16 2017 인하대

정답 ③

| 구문분석 | Vigorous activity is usually a healthful pursuit but it can become maladaptive (when carried to extremes).
S_1 V_1 C_1 S_2 V_2 C_2 분사구문

활발한 활동은 보통 건강에 좋지만, 극단적으로 흐르면 부적응 상태가 될 수도 있다.

There are runners and body builders, for instance, (who use their obsessive workouts to avoid taking responsibility for other aspects of their lives), (allowing little time for family, friends, or additional interests).
유도부사 V S 접속부사 관계대명사 분사구문 등위접속사

예를 들어, 가족, 친구 혹은 추가적인 관심사에는 시간을 거의 허용하지 않으면서, 그들의 삶의 다른 측면들에 대한 책임을 회피하기 위해 강박적인 운동을 하는 달리기 선수와 보디빌딩 선수들이 있다.

(Rather than enjoying their fitness endeavors), they feel powerless (to make any adjustments in their routines) (except to try to do more).
~라기보다는 S V C 전치사

몸을 단련시키는 노력들을 즐기는 대신, 그들은 오직 더 많은 운동을 하려고 노력하는 것 외에는, 자신들의 정해진 일상에 다른 조정을 하는 데에는 무기력함을 느낀다.

Pursuing pleasurable fitness endeavors can be a great coping strategy (for lessening daily pressures).
S V C

즐겁게 신체 단련을 하는 노력을 추구하는 것은 일상에서 겪는 압박감들을 완화시키기 위한 훌륭한 대처 전략이 될 수 있다.

Unfortunately, the exercise patterns (of some adolescents and adults) reflect deep-seated psychological problems.
S V O

불행하게도, 일부 청소년들과 성인들이 운동을 하는 방식은 뿌리 깊은 심리적 문제들을 나타낸다.

They become dangerously fixated (on trying to change their bodies) (by a combination of exhausting exercise and dieting), (increasing their risk of serious health problems) (including substance abuse and eating disorders).
S V 분사구문

그들은 약물 남용과 섭식 장애를 비롯한 심각한 건강상의 문제를 겪게 될 위험을 증가시키면서, 지치게 만드는 운동과 다이어트의 조합으로 그들의 몸을 변화시키려고 노력하는 것에 위험하게 집착하게 된다.

| 어휘 |
vigorous ⓐ 활발한, 건강한 **pursuit** ⓝ 추적, 추구
maladaptive ⓐ 순응성이 없는, 부적응의 **extreme** ⓝ 극단, 극도, 극단적인 행위
obsessive ⓐ 강박적인, 사로잡혀 있는 **workout** ⓝ (건강 · 몸매 유지를 위해서 하는) 운동
responsibility ⓝ 책임, 의무 **fitness** ⓝ 신체 단련, (신체적인) 건강 **endeavor** ⓝ 노력, 시도
adjustment ⓝ 조정, 정리, 조절 **routine** ⓝ (일상의) 틀, (판에 박힌) 일상; 정해진 순서
cope ⓥ 대처하다, 극복하다 **strategy** ⓝ 전략 **lessen** ⓥ 적게 하다, 줄이다
adolescent ⓝ 청소년, 젊은이 **fixate** ⓥ 정착[고정]시키다, 응시하다
exhausting ⓐ 진을 빼는, 기진맥진하게 만드는 **substance abuse** 약물[물질] 남용
eating disorder 섭식 장애

| 전문해석 | 활발한 활동은 보통 건강에 좋지만, 극단적으로 흐르면 부적응 상태가 될 수도 있다. [A] 예를 들어, 가족, 친구 혹은 추가적인 관심사에는 시간을 거의 허용하지 않으면서, 그들의 삶의 다른 측면들에 대한 책임을 회피하기 위해 강박적인 운동을 하는 달리기 선수와 보디빌딩 선수들이 있다. [B] 몸을 단련시키는 노력들을 즐기는 대신, 그들은 오직 더 많은 운동을 하려고 노력하는 것 외에는, 자신들의 정해진 일상에 다른 조정을 하는 데에는 무기력함을 느낀다. **[C] 〈즐겁게 신체 단련을 하는 노력을 추구하는 것은 일상에서 겪는 압박감들을 완화시키기 위한 훌륭한 대처 전략이 될 수 있다.〉** [D] 불행하게도, 일부 청소년들과 성인들이 운동을 하는 방식은 뿌리 깊은 심리적 문제들을 나타낸다. [E] 그들은 약물 남용과 섭식 장애를 비롯한 심각한 건강상의 문제를 겪게 될 위험을 증가시키면서, 지치게 만드는 운동과 다이어트의 조합으로 그들의 몸을 변화시키려고 노력하는 것에 위험하게 집착하게 된다.

| 정답분석 | 본문의 첫 문장에서는 과도하게 활발한 활동(운동)이 부적응 상태를 야기할 수 있다고 설명한다. [A]에서는 그 예로 달리기 선수와 보디빌더들을 소개하고 [B]의 주절 'they'부터는 그들의 부적응 상태에 대해 부연 설명한다. [D]와 [E] 역시 과도한 운동으로 인한 부적응 상태에 관련된 서술이다. 그러나 [C]는 신체 단련의 장점에 관한 내용이므로 글의 흐름상 적절하지 않다. 따라서 [C]를 삭제해야 한다.

17 2017 중앙대

정답 ①

| 구문분석 | One phase (of the business cycle) is the expansion phase.
S V C
경기주기의 한 국면은 확장 단계이다.

This phase is a twofold one, (including recovery and prosperity).
S V C 전치사
이 단계는 회복과 번영을 포함한 두 측면을 갖고 있다.

강조구문
It is not prosperity itself but expectation of prosperity that triggers the expansion phase.
not A but B: A 아니라 B 강조구문의 that
번영 그 자체가 아니라 번영에 대한 기대가 확장 국면을 촉발한다.

(During the recovery period) there is ever-growing expansion (of existing facilities), and new facilities (for production) are created.
전치사 유도부사 V_1 S_1 S_2 V_2
회복기에는 기존설비가 계속 확장되고 생산을 위한 새로운 설비들이 생겨난다.

More businesses are created and older ones expanded.
S_1 V_1 S_2 V_2
더 많은 사업체들이 생겨나며 기존의 사업체들은 확장된다.

Improvements (of various kinds) are made.
S V
다양한 종류의 개선이 이루어진다.

There is an ever-increasing optimism (about the future of economic growth).
유도부사 V S
경제성장의 미래에 대한 낙관론이 점점 증가한다.

Much capital is invested (in machinery or heavy industry).
S V
많은 자본이 기계나 중공업에 투자된다.

More labor is employed.
S V
더 많은 노동력이 고용된다.

More materials are required.
S V
더 많은 원자재가 필요하게 된다.

(As one part of the economy develops), other parts are affected.
부사절: ~함에 따라 S V
경제의 한 부분이 발전함에 따라 다른 부분들도 영향을 받는다.

For example, a great expansion (in automobiles) results (in an expansion of the steel, glass, and rubber industries).
접속부사 S V

예를 들어, 자동차 산업에서의 대규모 확장은 철강, 유리 고무산업의 확장을 가져온다.

세미콜론: and 역할
Roads are required; thus the cement and machinery industries are stimulated.
S V 접속부사 S V
도로도 필요하게 된다; 따라서 시멘트와 기계 산업이 활성화된다.

Demand (for labor and materials) results (in greater prosperity) (for workers and suppliers) (of raw materials), (including farmers).
S V
전치사
노동력과 원자재에 대한 수요는 농부들을 포함하는 원자재를 공급하는 측과 노동자들의 더 큰 번영을 가져온다.

This increases purchasing power and the volume (of goods) (bought and sold).
S V O_1 O_2
이는 다시 구매력과 사고 팔리는 상품의 양을 증가시킨다.

Thus, prosperity is diffused (among the various segments of the population).
접속부사 S V
따라서 번영이 전체 인구의 다양한 부분들에 걸쳐 확산된다.

This prosperity period may continue to rise and rise (without an apparent end).
S V O
이 번영은 뚜렷한 종말 없이 계속 상승과 상승을 거듭할 수 있다.

However, a time comes (when this phase reaches a peak and stops spiraling upwards).
접속부사 S V 관계부사
그러나 이 시기가 정점에 달하고 나선형의 상승을 멈추는 시기가 찾아온다.

This is the end (of the expansion phase).
S V C
이때가 바로 확장국면의 끝이다.

| 어휘 |

phase ⓝ 단계, 국면
twofold ⓐ 두 부분[요소]으로 된, 이중적인; 2배의
optimism ⓝ 낙관주의
heavy industry ⓝ 중공업
raw material ⓝ 원료, 원자재
volume ⓝ 용량, 부피, 크기
diffuse ⓥ 확산하다, 분산되다
segment ⓝ 단편, 구획, 부분
apparent ⓐ 뚜렷한, 명백한
peak ⓝ 정점, 정상
spiraling ⓐ 상승하는

| 전문해석 | 경기주기의 한 국면은 확장 단계이다. 이 단계는 회복과 번영을 포함한 두 측면을 갖고 있다. **[A] 〈번영 그 자체가 아니라 번영에 대한 기대가 확장 국면을 촉발한다.〉** 회복기에는 기존설비가 계속 확장되고 생산을 위한 새로운 설비들이 생겨난다. 더 많은 사업체들이 생겨나며 기존의 사업체들은 확장된다. 다양한 종류의 개선이 이루어진다. 경제성장의 미래에 대한 낙관론이 점점 증가한다. 많은 자본이 기계나 중공업에 투자된다. 더 많은 노동력이 고용된다. 더 많은 원자재가 필요하게 된다. 경제의 한 부분이 발전함에 따라 다른 부분들도 영향을 받는다. [B] 예를 들어, 자동차 산업에서의 대규모 확장은 철강, 유리 고무산업의 확장을 가져온다. 도로도 필요하게 된다; 따라서 시멘트와 기계 산업이 활성화된다. [C] 노동력과 원자재에 대한 수요는 농부들을 포함하는 원자재를 공급하는 측과 노동자들의 더 큰 번영을 가져온다. 이는 다시 구매력과 사고 팔리는 상품의 양을 증가시킨다. 따라서 번영이 전체 인구의 다양한 부분들에 걸쳐 확산된다. [D] 이 번영은 뚜렷한 종말 없이 계속 상승과 상승을 거듭할 수 있다. 그러나 이 시기가 정점에 달하고 나선형의 상승을 멈추는 시기가 찾아온다. 이때가 바로 확장국면의 끝이다.

| 정답분석 | 본문은 경기주기 중 확장 국면의 두 측면에 대해 설명하고 있다. [B]는 'for example' 표현을 사용해 앞 문장의 사례를 들고 있고 [C]도 경제의 한 부분의 발전이 다른 부분에 긍정적인 영향을 주는 것과 관련된 사례를 언급한다. [D] 역시 'This prosperity'는 직전 문장의 'prosperity'를 뜻하므로 글의 맥락상 자연스럽다. 하지만 [A]의 경우에는 앞 문장에서 설명한

측면인 '번영'이 아닌 '번영에 대한 기대가 확장 국면을 촉진한다'고 했기 때문에 이후에는 이에 대한 구체적 설명이 나와야 하는데 바로 다음 문장에서는 '회복'에 대한 설명이 나오기 때문에 맥락상 어색하다. 따라서 [A]를 삭제해야 한다.

18 2019 건국대 정답 ④

| 구문분석 | Why do people choose to home educate their child?
의문사 V S
왜 사람들은 그들의 아이를 가정에서 교육하기로 선택할까?

Some families make a carefully considered decision (to home educate) (long before their child reaches "school age.")
S V O 부사절: ~하기 오래전에
어떤 가족들은 그들의 아이가 '학령기'에 도달하기 훨씬 전에 가정에서 교육하기로 주의 깊게 고려한 결정을 내린다.

There may be philosophical, religious or various other reasons (for their choice) and ultimately they feel that (in some way) they can offer a more suitable education (for their child at home).
유도부사 V_1 S_1 등위접속사 S_2 V_2 O
그들의 선택에는 철학적, 종교적 또는 다양한 다른 이유들이 있고, 궁극적으로 그들은 어떤 방식으로든 집에서 그들의 자녀들에게 더 적절한 교육을 제공할 수 있다고 생각한다.

It is also a natural choice (for parents) (who have enjoyed participating in their child's early learning and (who) see no reason (to give up this responsibility) (when the child reaches the age of five).
S V C 관계대명사 등위접속사 부사절: ~할 때
그것은 또한 자녀의 조기학습에 참여하는 것을 즐겼고 아이가 5세가 되었을 때 이 책임을 포기할 이유를 찾지 못하는 부모들에게는 당연한 선택이다.

Other parents send their child (into the school system), but later find that school does not work (for their child).
S V_1 O_1 등위접속사 V_2 O_2
다른 부모들은 그들의 아이를 학교에 보내지만, 나중에 학교가 그들의 아이에게 효과가 없다는 것을 알게 된다.

(In schools), students can get comparatively high marks (by remembering what teachers have said).
S V O by ~ing: ~함으로써
학교에서, 학생들은 선생님들이 말한 것을 기억함으로써 비교적 높은 점수를 받을 수 있다.

School does not suit everyone.
S V O
학교가 모든 사람에게 적합한 것은 아니다.

Sometimes children may find it hard to "fit in" so their parents may also decide to home educate.
가목적어 등위접속사
S_1 V_1 O.C 진목적어 S_2 V_2 O
때때로 아이들은 '어울리는 것'이 어렵다고 생각해서 그 결과 그들의 부모들이 또한 가정에서 교육시키기로 결정할 수도 있다.

| 어휘 | **considered** ⓐ 깊이 생각한 **school age** 취학 연령 **comparatively** ⓐⓓ 비교적(으로)
fit in (자연스럽게 ~와) 어울리다

| 전문해석 | 왜 사람들은 그들의 아이를 가정에서 교육하기로 선택할까? 어떤 가족들은 그들의 아이가 '학령기'에 도달하기 훨씬 전에 가정에서 교육하기로 주의 깊게 고려한 결정을 내린다. [A] 그들의 선택에는 철학적, 종교적 또는 다양한 다른 이유들이 있고, 궁극적으로 그들은 어떤 방식으로든 집에서 그들의 자녀들에게 더 적절한 교육을 제공할 수 있다고 생각한다.
[B] 그것은 또한 자녀의 조기학습에 참여하는 것을 즐겼고 아이가 5세가 되었을 때 이 책임을 포기할 이유를 찾지 못하는 부모들에게는 당연한 선택이다. [C] 다른 부모들은 그들의 아이를 학교에 보내지만, 나중에 학교가 그들의 아이에게 효과가 없다는 것을 알게 된다. **[D] 〈학교에서, 학생들은 선생님들이 말한 것을 기억함으로써 비교적 높은 점수를 받을 수 있다.〉**
[E] 학교가 모든 사람에게 적합한 것은 아니다. 때때로 아이들은 '어울리는 것'이 어렵다고 생각해서 그 결과 그들의 부모들이 또한 가정에서 교육시키기로 결정할 수도 있다.

| 정답분석 | 본문은 부모들이 자녀들을 가정에서 교육하기로 선택하는 이유에 대한 질문을 던지고 그 답을 설명하고 있다. [A]는 '철학

적, 종교적 또는 다양한 이유'가 언급되고 [B]와 [C] 역시 부모들이 어떤 이유로 자녀를 가정에서 교육시키는지에 관한 설명이 이어진다. 하지만 [D]에서는 가정에서의 교육과 관련이 없는 '학교에서 학생들이 점수를 잘 받는 방법'을 언급하고 있으므로, 문맥상 적절하지 않은 문장이다. 따라서 [D]를 삭제해야 한다.

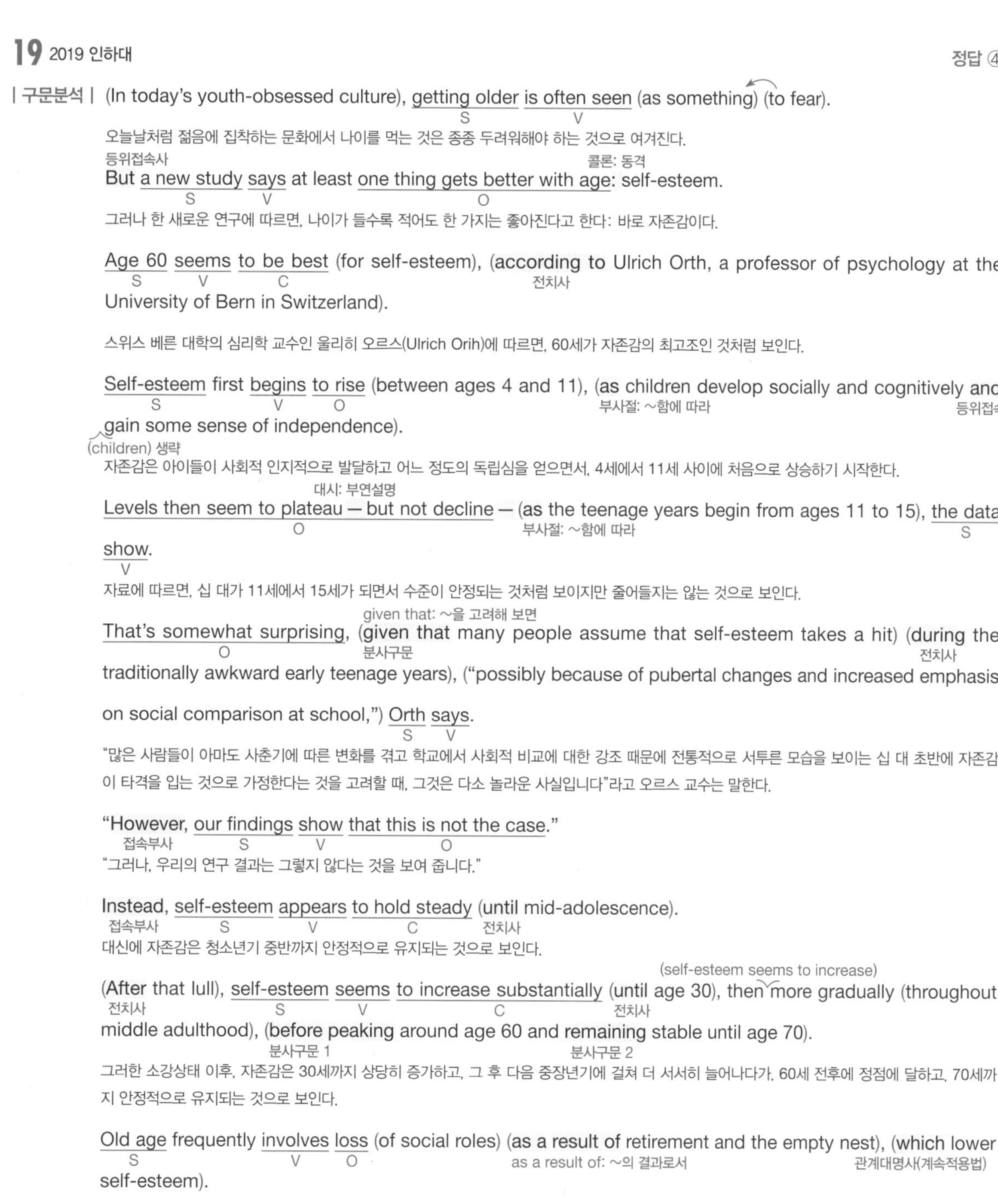

19 2019 인하대

정답 ④

| 구문분석 | (In today's youth-obsessed culture), getting older is often seen (as something) (to fear).

오늘날처럼 젊음에 집착하는 문화에서 나이를 먹는 것은 종종 두려워해야 하는 것으로 여겨진다.

등위접속사 / 콜론: 동격

But a new study says at least one thing gets better with age: self-esteem.

그러나 한 새로운 연구에 따르면, 나이가 들수록 적어도 한 가지는 좋아진다고 한다: 바로 자존감이다.

Age 60 seems to be best (for self-esteem), (according to Ulrich Orth, a professor of psychology at the University of Bern in Switzerland).

전치사

스위스 베른 대학의 심리학 교수인 울리히 오르스(Ulrich Orih)에 따르면, 60세가 자존감의 최고조인 것처럼 보인다.

Self-esteem first begins to rise (between ages 4 and 11), (as children develop socially and cognitively and gain some sense of independence).

부사절: ~함에 따라 / 등위접속사 / (children) 생략

자존감은 아이들이 사회적 인지적으로 발달하고 어느 정도의 독립심을 얻으면서, 4세에서 11세 사이에 처음으로 상승하기 시작한다.

대시: 부연설명

Levels then seem to plateau — but not decline — (as the teenage years begin from ages 11 to 15), the data show.

부사절: ~함에 따라

자료에 따르면, 십 대가 11세에서 15세가 되면서 수준이 안정되는 것처럼 보이지만 줄어들지는 않는 것으로 보인다.

given that: ~을 고려해 보면

That's somewhat surprising, (given that many people assume that self-esteem takes a hit) (during the traditionally awkward early teenage years), ("possibly because of pubertal changes and increased emphasis on social comparison at school,") Orth says.

분사구문 / 전치사

"많은 사람들이 아마도 사춘기에 따른 변화를 겪고 학교에서 사회적 비교에 대한 강조 때문에 전통적으로 서투른 모습을 보이는 십 대 초반에 자존감이 타격을 입는 것으로 가정한다는 것을 고려할 때, 그것은 다소 놀라운 사실입니다"라고 오르스 교수는 말한다.

"However, our findings show that this is not the case."

접속부사

"그러나, 우리의 연구 결과는 그렇지 않다는 것을 보여 줍니다."

Instead, self-esteem appears to hold steady (until mid-adolescence).

접속부사 / 전치사

대신에 자존감은 청소년기 중반까지 안정적으로 유지되는 것으로 보인다.

(self-esteem seems to increase)

(After that lull), self-esteem seems to increase substantially (until age 30), then more gradually (throughout middle adulthood), (before peaking around age 60 and remaining stable until age 70).

전치사 / 전치사 / 분사구문 1 / 분사구문 2

그러한 소강상태 이후, 자존감은 30세까지 상당히 증가하고, 그 후 다음 중장년기에 걸쳐 더 서서히 늘어나다가, 60세 전후에 정점에 달하고, 70세까지 안정적으로 유지되는 것으로 보인다.

Old age frequently involves loss (of social roles) (as a result of retirement and the empty nest), (which lower self-esteem).

as a result of: ~의 결과로서 / 관계대명사(계속적용법)

노년에는 종종 은퇴와 빈 둥지(자식들의 분가)로 인한 사회적인 역할의 상실을 포함하고 그것은 자존감을 낮추게 된다.

(that)
"Many people," Orth says, "are able to maintain a relatively high level of self-esteem (even during old age)."
O S V 전치사
오르스는 "많은 사람들이 노년에도 상대적으로 높은 수준의 자존감을 유지할 수 있습니다'"라고 말한다.

| 어휘 | youth-obsessed ⓐ 젊음에 집착하는 self-esteem ⓝ 자존감 cognitively ⓐⓓ 인식적으로
plateau ⓥ 안정[정체] 상태를 유지하다 steady ⓐ 꾸준한, 고정적인 adolescence ⓝ 사춘기
lull ⓝ 잠잠한 시기, 소강상태 substantially ⓐⓓ 상당히, 많이, 대체로 gradually ⓐⓓ 차츰, 서서히
adulthood ⓝ 성인기 peak ⓥ 절정[최고조]에 달하다 stable ⓐ 안정된
retirement ⓝ 은퇴 empty nest 빈 둥지(자녀가 장성하여 집을 떠나고 부모만 남은 상황)
maintain ⓥ 지속하다, 유지하다 relatively ⓐⓓ 상대적으로

| 전문해석 | 오늘날처럼 젊음에 집착하는 문화에서 나이를 먹는 것은 종종 두려워해야 하는 것으로 여겨진다. [A] 그러나 한 새로운 연구에 따르면, 나이가 들수록 적어도 한 가지는 좋아진다고 한다: 바로 자존감이다. 스위스 베른 대학의 심리학 교수인 울리히 오르스(Ulrich Orih)에 따르면, 60세가 자존감의 최고조인 것처럼 보인다. 자존감은 아이들이 사회적 인지적으로 발달하고 어느 정도의 독립심을 얻으면서, 4세에서 11세 사이에 처음으로 상승하기 시작한다. [B] 자료에 따르면, 십 대가 11세에서 15세가 되면서 수준이 안정되는 것처럼 보이지만 줄어들지는 않는 것으로 보인다. "많은 사람들이 아마도 사춘기에 따른 변화를 겪고 학교에서 사회적 비교에 대한 강조 때문에 전통적으로 서투른 모습을 보이는 십 대 초반에 자존감이 타격을 입는 것으로 가정한다는 것을 고려할 때, 그것은 다소 놀라운 사실입니다"라고 오르스 교수는 말한다. "그러나, 우리의 연구 결과는 그렇지 않다는 것을 보여 줍니다." [C] 대신에 자존감은 청소년기 중반까지 안정적으로 유지되는 것으로 보인다. 그러한 소강상태 이후, 자존감은 30세까지 상당히 증가하고, 그 후 다음 중장년기에 걸쳐 더 서서히 늘어나다가, 60세 전후에 정점에 달하고, 70세까지 안정적으로 유지되는 것으로 보인다. **[D] 〈노년에는 종종 은퇴와 빈 둥지(자식들의 분가)로 인한 사회적인 역할의 상실을 포함하고 그것은 자존감을 낮추게 된다.〉** [E] 오르스는 "많은 사람들이 노년에도 상대적으로 높은 수준의 자존감을 유지할 수 있습니다'"라고 말한다.

| 정답분석 | 본문은 '노년에 자존감이 최고조에 달한다'는 새로운 연구를 소개하고 있다. [D] 직전 문장에서 '60세 전후에 자존감이 정점'이라고 했고 [E] 또한 '노년에도 상대적으로 높은 수준의 자존감을 유지'한다고 했으므로 그 중간 [D]에 노년에 자존감이 줄어든다는 내용이 오는 것은 문맥상 자연스럽지 않다. 따라서 [D]를 삭제해야 한다.

20 2019 인하대

정답 ④

| 구문분석 | The close relationship (between language and religious belief) pervades cultural history.
S between A and B: A와 B 사이 V O
언어와 종교적 믿음 사이의 밀접한 관계는 문화사에 널리 퍼져 있다.

(to have)
Often, a divine being is said (to have invented speech, or writing, and given it (as a gift to mankind).
S V 등위접속사
종종, 신적인 존재가 말이나 글을 발명했고, 그것을 인류에게 선물로 주었다고 한다.

One (of the first things (Adam has to do), (according to the Book of Genesis), is to name the acts of creation.
S (that) 전치사 V C
창세기에 따르면, 아담이 가장 먼저 해야 할 일 중 하나는 창조의 행위들에 이름을 붙이는 것이었다.

Many other cultures have a similar story.
S V O
많은 다른 문화들도 비슷한 이야기를 가지고 있다.

(In Egyptian mythology), the god Thoth is the creator (of speech and writing).
S V C
이집트 신화에서, 토트 신은 말과 글의 창조자이다.

It is Brahma who gives the knowledge (of writing) (to the Hindu people).
강조구문 강조구문의 who
힌두교 사람들에게 글에 대한 지식을 주는 사람은 브라마다.

Odin is the inventor (of runic script), (according to the Icelandic sagas).
S V C 전치사
아이슬란드 전설에 따르면, 오딘은 룬 문자의 발명가다.

Literacy is often introduced (into a community) (by the spread of a religion).
S V
읽고 쓰는 능력은 종종 종교의 확산에 의해 공동체에 도입된다.

A heaven-sent water turtle, (with marks on its back), brings writing (to the Chinese).
S V O
하늘에서 보낸 등에 표시가 있는 물거북은 중국인들에게 글을 가져다준다.

(All over the world), the supernatural provides a powerful set (of beliefs) (about the origins of language).
S V O
전 세계적으로, 초자연적인 것들이 언어의 기원에 대한 일련의 강한 믿음을 제공한다.

| 어휘 |

pervade ⓥ 만연하다, (구석구석) 스며들다
mankind ⓝ 인류, (모든) 인간
the Book of Genesis 창세기(성경의 첫 번째 책, 성경 속 모든 이야기의 시작)
mythology ⓝ 신화; 근거 없는 믿음
Thoth ⓝ 토트(고대 이집트 신화에 나오는 지혜와 정의의 신)
Brahma ⓝ 브라마(힌두교 최고의 신)
Odin ⓝ 오딘(지식, 문화, 군사를 맡아 보는 최고신)
supernatural ⓐ 초자연적인

| 전문해석 | 언어와 종교적 믿음 사이의 밀접한 관계는 문화사에 널리 퍼져 있다. 종종 신적인 존재가 말이나 글을 발명했고, 그것을 인류에게 선물로 주었다고 한다. 창세기에 따르면, 아담이 가장 먼저 해야 할 일 중 하나는 창조의 행위들에 이름을 붙이는 것이었다. 많은 다른 문화들도 비슷한 이야기를 가지고 있다. [A] 이집트 신화에서, 토트 신은 말과 글의 창조자이다. [B] 힌두교 사람들에게 글에 대한 지식을 주는 사람은 브라마다. [C] 아이슬란드 전설에 따르면, 오딘은 룬 문자의 발명가다. **[D] 〈읽고 쓰는 능력은 종종 종교의 확산에 의해 공동체에 도입된다.〉** [E] 하늘에서 보낸 등에 표시가 있는 물거북은 중국인들에게 글을 가져다준다. 전 세계적으로, 초자연적인 것들이 언어의 기원에 대한 일련의 강한 믿음을 제공한다.

| 정답분석 | 본문에서는 언어의 발명과 종교 사이의 관련성에 대해 설명하고 있다. 세 번째 문장부터는 그 예로 창세기의 내용이 설명되고 그다음 문장에서는 '많은 다른 문화들도 비슷한 이야기를 가지고 있다'고 한 뒤 [A]에서는 이집트 신화, [B]는 힌두교, [C]는 아이슬란드 그리고 [E]의 중국문화에 이르기까지 언어의 발명과 종교적 믿음이 어떻게 관련되는지를 각각 서술했다. 하지만 [D]에서는 읽고 쓰는 능력의 공동체 확산에 있어서 종교의 역할을 언급했으므로 직전 직후 문장과 흐름이 연결되지 않는다. 따라서 [D]를 삭제해야 한다.

여러분의 작은 소리
에듀윌은 크게 듣겠습니다.

본 교재에 대한 여러분의 목소리를 들려주세요.
공부하시면서 어려웠던 점, 궁금한 점,
칭찬하고 싶은 점, 개선할 점, 어떤 것이라도 좋습니다.

에듀윌은 여러분께서 나누어 주신 의견을
통해 끊임없이 발전하고 있습니다.

에듀윌 도서몰 book.eduwill.net
- 부가학습자료 및 정오표: 에듀윌 도서몰 → 도서자료실
- 교재 문의: 에듀윌 도서몰 → 문의하기 → 교재(내용, 출간) / 주문 및 배송

에듀윌 편입 솔루션 독해 Basic

발 행 일 2023년 7월 12일 초판
편 저 자 에듀윌 편입 LAB
펴 낸 이 김재환
펴 낸 곳 (주)에듀윌
등록번호 제25100-2002-000052호
주 소 08378 서울특별시 구로구 디지털로34길 55
코오롱싸이언스밸리 2차 3층

www.eduwill.net
대표전화 1600-6700

독해
BASIC

에듀윌은 합격이다!

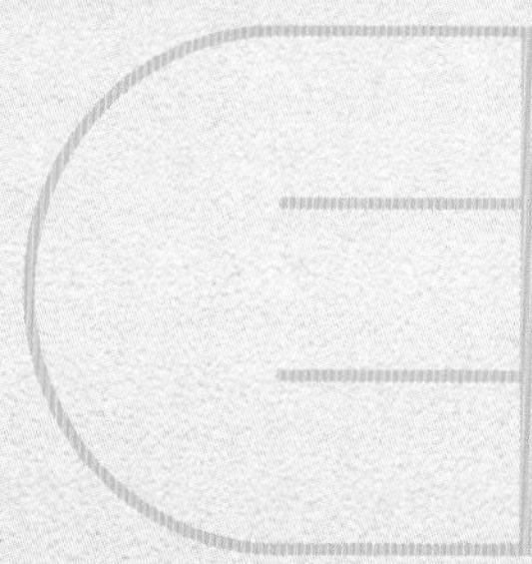
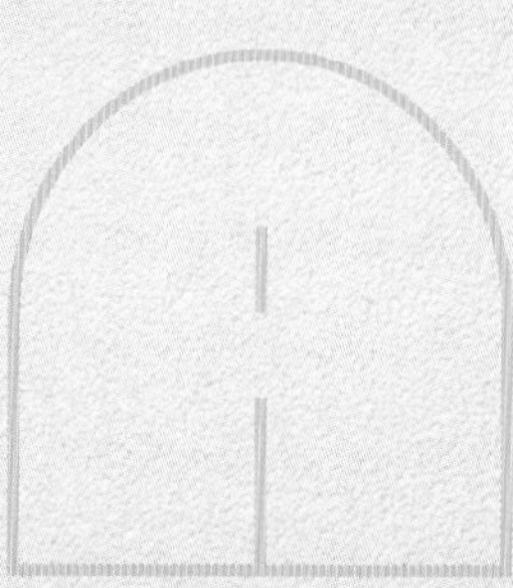
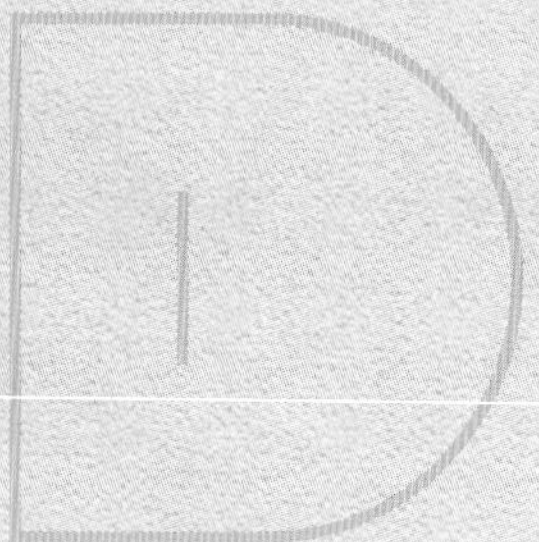

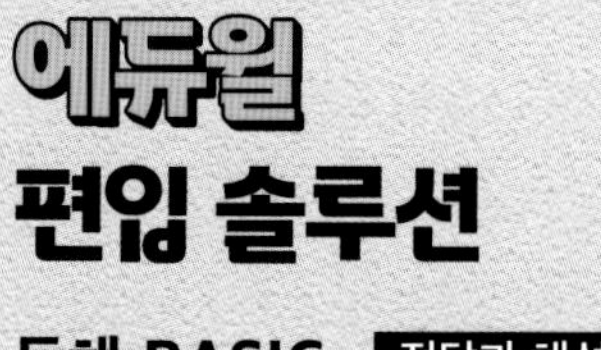

편입 솔루션

독해 BASIC 정답과 해설

펴낸곳 (주)에듀윌 **펴낸이** 김재환 **출판총괄** 오용철
개발책임 김진우, 김기임, 윤대권 **개발** 허은지 **디자인** 디자인본부
주소 서울시 구로구 디지털로34길 55 코오롱싸이언스밸리 2차 3층
대표번호 1600-6700 **등록번호** 제25100-2002-000052호

에듀윌 도서몰 book.eduwill.net
• 부가학습자료 및 정오표: 에듀윌 도서몰 → 도서자료실
• 교재 문의: 에듀윌 도서몰 → 문의하기 → 교재(내용, 출간) / 주문 및 배송

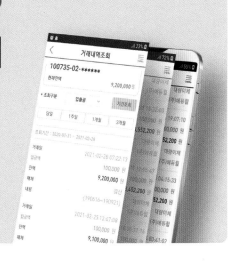